STAND, COLUMBIA

STAND, COLUMBIA

A History of Columbia University in the
City of New York, 1754–2004

Robert A. McCaughey

 COLUMBIA UNIVERSITY PRESS | NEW YORK

COLUMBIA UNIVERSITY PRESS

Publishers Since 1893

New York   Chichester, West Sussex

Copyright © 2003 Columbia University Press

All rights reserved

Library of Congress Cataloging-in-Publication Data

McCaughey, Robert A.

Stand, Columbia : a history of Columbia University

in the city of New York, 1754–2004

Robert McCaughey.

p. cm.

Includes bibliographical references and index.

ISBN 0–231–13008–2 (cloth : alk. paper)

1. Columbia University—History. I. Title

LD1248.M33   2003

378.747'1—dc21   2003051557

Columbia University Press books are printed on permanent
and durable acid-free paper.

Printed in the United States of America

Designed by Linda Secondari

c 10 9 8 7 6 5 4 3 2 1

I have seen many a comer to Columbia a little lost because he has not yet found anything to worship. . . . We are an extraordinary insinuation. We are inextricably mixed up with what is going on in the world. It is a spirit that does not look inward at itself, but outward on a city and a world.

—Frederick J. E. Woodbridge, 1929

CONTENTS

THE idea for this book, a one-volume interpretive history of Columbia University, was mine. So are the judgments made and opinions expressed in it. This said, many people have provided crucial help at every point along the way.

Beginning at the beginning, I wish to acknowledge the support and encouragement provided by the members of the Publications Committee of the Columbia 250th Anniversary Celebration, especially its chairman Ashbel Green (CC 1948) and also committee members William T. de Bary, Fritz Stern, Rosalind Rosenberg, Michael Rosenthal, and Jerry Kisslinger. Their quiet confidence in my ability to complete the book has been both a comfort and a spur. Also, from the outset, the cochairs of the 250th Committee, Trustee Emeritus Henry King (CC 1948) and Professor of History Kenneth T. Jackson, have provided every assistance in seeing the project through. So, too, the executive director of the committee, Roger Lehecka (CC 1967), and his predecessor, Claudia Bushman.

I wish also to acknowledge the help of Presidents Emeriti Michael I. Sovern and George Rupp, who enthusiastically endorsed the idea of my writing an interpretive—as opposed to an "official"—history of the university over which they presided for a combined twenty-three years. It was on their authority that I secured access to all the materials I requested relating to their presidencies. In addition, Mike Sovern generously shared with me his experiences as a Columbian stretching back over six decades.

The research process was much facilitated by the assistance of several of Columbia's highly skilled librarians and archivists. These included Jean Ashton and Bernard Crystal of the Rare Book and Manuscript Library, Marilyn Pettit and Jocelyn Wilk of the Columbia University Archives–Columbiana Library, Ronald Griele and Mary Marshall Clark of the Oral History Research Office, Stephen E. Novak of Health Sciences Archives and Special Collections, Whitney Bagnall of Special Collections in the Law School Library, Donald Glassman of the Barnard College Archives, and David Ment and Bette Winick of the Teachers College Special Collections.

As the manuscript evolved, it benefited from critical readings by several participant-observers of the Columbia scene. First among these have been my Barnard departmental colleagues Rosalind Rosenberg, Herb Sloan, and Nancy Woloch and also Barnard's president, Judith Shapiro (CU Ph.D. 1968), who rather liked the idea of a Barnard faculty member writing Columbia's history. Thanks, too, to Elizabeth Boylan, my successor as Barnard's dean of the faculty, and Lew Wyman, vice president for planning.

Parts of the manuscript also benefited from readings by several Columbia history department colleagues, among them, Jack Garraty, Henry Graff, Fritz Stern, and Isser Woloch. Other members of the Columbia faculty who reviewed parts of the manuscript included David J. Helfand, Carl Hovde, and Michael Rosenthal. Among Columbia faculty, administrators, and staff whom I interviewed and who are listed in the bibliographic note, I wish especially to acknowledge the extraordinary forthcomingness of the late Eli Ginzberg, George Fraenkel, and Marion Jemmott. Two other longtime Columbians who took an active interest in the book and its author were Roger Hackett and Chauncey Olinger. Among non-Columbians who did likewise, Roger L. Geiger and Bill Whelan.

Columbia and Barnard undergraduates, past and present, played a role in seeing this project through. As interns in the Barnard Electronic and Teaching Laboratory (BEATL), which I direct, as students in my long-running seminar "The Higher Learning in America" or in my lecture course "The Social History of Columbia," they have performed much of the statistical and biographical research that has gone into the database on which the book rests. They have also been generous in offering their own perspective on substantive matters. While the numbers in this category are in the dozens, I mention here only few by name (and some because I promised I would): Perry Creeden (BC 1999), Rachel Furst (BC 2001), Elissa Harel (BC 2001), Michael Foss (CC 2003), Brian Hamilton (CC 2004), and Peter Carlson-Bancroft (GS 2004).

Nor should another category of enablers go unnoted, even if the listing here is incomplete. They include graduates of Columbia and Barnard who have read parts of the manuscript that sought to describe events in 1968 in which they played a direct part or were close observers. Among them are Frank da Cruz, Gerald Sherwin, Michael Rothfeld, and Bill White.

I also wish to acknowledge the friendly professionalism with which Columbia University Press handled its responsibilities throughout. Special thanks here to John Moore and William B. Strachan, its past directors, Anne McCoy and Suzanne Ryan, who guided the book through production, and to Sarah St. Onge, my valiant and vigilant copy editor.

My last acknowledgments are by another ordering my first. They are of my daughter, Hannah, and son, John, who maintained a lively interest in my work even when it intruded on times together. And, finally, I wish to acknowledge my wife, Ann, who has lived with this project for six years and has served as first editor throughout, even as she pursued her own career and took the lead in matters familial. This book's for you.

STAND, COLUMBIA

CHAPTER 1

Tory Preamble: The Short History of King's College

Providence has not called us alone to found a University in New York, nor to urge the slow, cold councils of that city.

William Samuel Johnson (son) to Samuel Johnson (father), 1753

The clamour I raised against [the College] . . . when it was first founded on its present narrow principles, has yet and probably never will totally silence.

William Livingston to William Livingston Jr., 1768

Prologue

COLUMBIA's has been a disputatious history. Even the designation of its pre-founder has two opposing candidates. The one far more often cited for this distinction has been Colonel Lewis Morris (1671–1746), a considerable presence in the public life of both New York and New Jersey in the early eighteenth century. The claims of his being the prefounder of Columbia turn on a letter said by at least two historians of Columbia to date from 1702 to the Society for the Propagation of the Gospel in Foreign Parts (SPGFP), the missionary arm of the Anglican Church established in 1701 in London. There, he writes: "New York is the centre of English America and a fit place for a Colledge."[1]

Lewis Morris, the first lord of Morrisania Manor (now much of the Bronx), makes for the relatively more attractive prefounder. This is in part because of his reputation as the early leader of New York's Country Party and a doughty champion of the popular cause in the colonial assemblies of New York and New Jersey against the Court Party centered in the governor's council and aligned with a string of supposedly corrupt and power-grabbing governors. His being the grandfather of the King's College graduate (1766) and revolutionary states-man Gouverneur Morris (1752–1816) and ancestor of numerous other Morrises and Ogdens who figure in Columbia's subsequent history further strenghthens his case. Mid-nineteenth-century Columbia trustees Lewis M. Rutherford and Gouverneur M. Ogden were direct descendants.

Morris's recommendation of New York City as "a fit place for a Colledge" occurred in the middle of delicate negotiations involving Queen's Farm on Manhattan's West Side, thirty-two acres running east to west from Broadway to the Hudson River and north to south from modern-day Fulton Street to approximately Christopher Street. Reference to the "Colledge" is immediately followed, without so much as a sentence break, by: "and that farme in A little time will be of considerable Vallue and its pitty such a thing should be lost for want of asking for wch. at another time wont be so Easily Obteined." Named the King's Farm—for King William—when it was laid out in 1693 and renamed Queen's Farm on Anne's accession to the throne in 1702, the farm was assumed to be in the gift of the Royal Governor of New York. It became a source of political conflict in 1697 when Governor John Fletcher (1692–98) leased it to Trinity Church, New York's first Anglican parish, for seven years. The city's non-Anglicans, who constituted a substantial majority, thought the royal authorities had already been more than generous to Trinity Church in providing its rector, through the Ministry Act of 1693, with a salary derived from general tax revenues and, in 1796, with a royal charter for the church itself. Meanwhile, the city's Dissenting majority were expected to make do without either public support for their ministers or the security of a royal charter for their churches.[2]

New Yorkers opposed to the lease had looked to Fletcher's successor, Governor Richard Coote (1698–1701), the earl of Bellomont, a Whig and "no friend of the Church," to take back the land when the lease expired. But before Bellomont could do so, he died, in 1701. His successor was Edward Hyde (1702–8), the earl of Cornbury, a "stalwart Churchman" and cousin of Queen Anne. Shortly after his arrival in New York in May 1702, Governor Cornbury took up the matter of the farm.[3]

The rector of Trinity Church, the Reverend William Vesey (1696–1742), and most of the church's vestrymen hoped the new governor would simply deed the farm permanently to the church for whatever uses it deemed fit. Although himself a vestryman, Morris seems to have wanted it to go to the SPGFP and made his point about New York being "a fit place for a Colledge" as an argument for the society's acquiring the farm. Indeed, his letter may have been intended to thwart Cornbury's already announced plan, which was to cede the farm permanently to Trinity Church.

Evidence of Cornbury's intentions is contained in the records of Trinity Church for February 19, 1703: "It being moved which way the King's farme which is now vested in Trinity Church should be let to Farm. It was unanimously agreed that the Rector and Church wardens should wait upon my Lord Cornbury, the Govr to know what part thereof his Lordship did design towards the Colledge which his Lordship designs to have built."[4]

While Morris's letter has been described as having been written in 1702, a few months before the Trinity Church entry, it now seems clear that it was not written until June 1704, more than a year later. But even assuming the earlier date, the letter was written after Cornbury's assumption of his governorship and almost certainly after he had revealed his own plans for the farm. More-over, Morris only mentioned a possible use for a portion of a piece of property over which he had no control—only designs—whereas Cornbury had it in his gift to dispose of the property as he saw fit. The Trinity Church entry makes clear that his "design for the Colledge" was already well known and that the church recognized the need to be responsive to it. Thus Cornbury's claim to being the prefounder of New York's first college seems at least as strong as that of Morris. Why, then, is he so seldom mentioned in this regard?

There is first of all the matter of wardrobe. Soon after Cornbury arrived in New York, rumors began circulating about the colonies and back at court that he was a cross-dresser and very possibly a transvestite. The most charitable form these rumors took was to repeat the explanation Cornbury supposedly offered members of the New York Assembly: that, as the representative of the queen, he thought it appropriate to approximate her attire as well, hence the gowns and ladies' wigs. Other reports had him not only taking regularly morn-ing walks attired in a manner "so unaccountable that if hundred[s] of specula-tors did not dayly see him it would be incredible" but also "dresst in Women's Cloaths" on the occasion of his wife's death, "and this not privately but in the face of the Sun and sight of the Town." And then there is the portrait now hang-ing in prominence at the New-York Historical Society, long said to be that of Edward Hyde, Viscount Cornbury. Plain facial features and body shape make the subject's sex indeterminate, but the dress and coiffure are unquestionably those of a woman.[5]

There is also the serious matter of corruption. Cornbury came under local attack from both his New York and New Jersey subjects for squandering public funds and tax revenues for private purposes. Attempted bribery of assembly members was another frequently leveled charge. In 1708, after six years in New York and with his reputation in England savaged by reports of his misdeeds, Cornbury was recalled and shortly thereafter replaced by the decidedly less controversial Robert Hunter (1710–19). In all the annals of English colonial rule, hardly a litany of selfless public service, few governors have fared worse than Cornbury.

Who was the chief source of the reputation-ravaging charges against Corn-bury? A recent book by Columbia-trained historian Patricia Bonomi, *The Lord Cornbury Scandal: The Politics of Reputation in British America*, suggests the principal source, other than Dissenters angered by Cornbury's aggressive Anglicanization efforts, was none other than Colonel Lewis Morris. Bonomi also argues that charges of cross-dressing and corruption were likely false and certainly politically motivated. The portrait is dismissed as a misattribution. Cornbury was only trying to do his job as the crown's representative in two colonies already adept at bringing governors around to their live-and-let-live style of governance. Whereas Bonomi's Morris was an opportunistic provincial on the make, economically and politically, Cornbury was a competent imperial administrator done in by the scurrilous Morris. Whom do we believe? And as to the preferred prefounder of Columbia, take your pick.[6]

Before proceeding to the actual founding of New York's "Colledge," three points of a more general nature might be made about Morris's endorsement of the idea. The first is the stress he put on geographical location. With the "centre of English America," Morris was reminding his London correspondents of New York's advantageous location between the crown's New England colonies and those to the south around Chesapeake Bay, in the Carolinas, and in the West Indies. Should someone in England wish to underwrite a college for all of English America, or establish permanent military presence there, or install a bishop, where better than New York?

The second is the fact already alluded to that the idea for a college was linked to a New York City real estate transaction. New York City real estate and the political economy of New York City play a central role throughout all of Columbia's history, although this was somewhat diminished after 1985 with the sale by the university of the land on which Rockefeller Center stands.

The third point is that Morris's endorsement occurred more than four decades before another New Yorker is again heard on the subject of a college— and a full half-century before the colony acquired its own college. Morris did not exactly start a rush to college building among his fellow New Yorkers. Then again, he had more than one purpose in mind. New Yorkers usually do.

Welcome to New York

The first reported European sighting of what became New York City was by the Florentine Giovanni da Verrazzano (1485–1528) as he was coasting up the Atlantic strand in the employ of France. Sailing his three-masted caravelle *La Dauphine* through the opening in the Lower Bay now spanned by the bridge named for him (but with one less "z"), Verrazzano entered the inner New York Harbor sometime around the first of May 1524. His afternoon's reconnoitering, cut short by a thunderstorm, likely brought him just off Lower Manhattan's West Side and within view of the future site of King's College. Upon returning to *La Dauphine*, he declared the region surrounding the harbor "not without some properties of value."[7]

A more permanent encounter occurred in 1609, when the Englishman Henry Hudson sailed his *Half Moon* into New York Harbor. He proceeded some ninety miles up the river now bearing his name that flows by the western side of the island of Manhattan. Before departing the region, he claimed it for his employer, the Dutch West India Company. Two years later, the Dutch explorer Adrian Block sailed up the east side of Manhattan, paused at an intersection he called "Hell's Gate," noted the left-hand turn into the Harlem River, which twists westward to rejoin the Hudson (and makes Manhattan an island), and followed the right-hand turn flowing eastward into Long Island Sound. New York was on the map.[8]

Hudson's claims on behalf of the Dutch West India Company were followed in 1623 by the arrival of the first European settlers in "New Netherland." They were directed up the Hudson, where Fort Orange (later Albany) was settled that year as the interior site for trading for furs with the Indians. A year later, "New Amsterdam" was established at the bottom of Manhattan Island to serve as the transfer point where furs sent down the Hudson were put on oceangoing ships for the trip across the Atlantic to Holland. New Netherland's governor general, Peter Minuit (1580–1638), then promptly confirmed the Europeans' intention of staying on Manhattan by purchasing it from the resident Lanapes Indians for the reported sixty guilders, or twenty-four dollars.[9]

The Dutch settlement of New York occurred between the English settlements of Plymouth (1620) and Boston (1630), which mark the European beginnings of New England, and within a year of so of the 1624 destruction by Indian reprisals of the first English settlement in the Chesapeake Bay area, at Jamestown, Virginia (settled in 1607). The arrival in New Amsterdam in 1647 of Peter Stuyvesant, with his municipal reforms—among them, incorporation—brought an added measure of permanence to the European presence, if not, as it turned out, to Dutch suzerainty. By the 1650s, the population of New Netherland topped three thousand, including a fair number of Africans, half of whom were ensconced within a mile of the Battery at the southern tip of Manhattan.

In 1664 the Dutch colony of New Netherland passed into English hands, specifically those of the Duke of York, on whom proprietorship was conferred by his brother, King Charles II. New Netherland became "New York" and, in a lapse of English literary imagination, so did New Amsterdam. But then something strange happened. Rather than packing up and leaving—or being ordered to do so by the new management—many of the Dutch stayed on. Following some provisional toing-and-froing, including a temporary take-back of the colony by the Dutch for a few months in 1673, the old-line Dutch and the newly arriving English, joined in the 1680s by French Huguenots following the revocation of the Edict of Nantes, proceeded to effect the first instance of a workable European pluralism in America.[10]

Two traits shared by the original Dutch, the usurping English, and the émigré Huguenots made this novel social arrangement work. All saw themselves as being in New York to do business, to make money. Few were disposed to let differences in religion, much less nationality, get between them and mutually profitable relationships. And insofar as these worldly priorities were shared by virtually all the royal governors dispatched from England to New York after 1665, New York early on became known throughout the Atlantic world as first and foremost a place of business, with little time or energy left for ethnic squeamishness, religious squabbling, or cultural uplift. There was little of the puritanical about it.

One manifestation of these go-along-get-along ways was the unparalleled proliferation of religious sects existing cheek by jowl in colonial New York City. "New York has first a Chaplain belonging to the Fort of the Church of England," Governor Thomas Dongan (1683–88)—himself a closet Roman Catholic—reported back to London authorities in 1687, "secondly, a Dutch Calvinist; thirdly, a French Calvinist; fourthly, a Dutch Lutheran—Here be not many of the Church of England; few Roman Catholics." The outer fringes of Christendom, however, were well represented: "Quaker's preachers, men and women especially, Singing Quakers, ranting Quakers; Sabbatarians; Anti-Sabbatarians; Some Anabaptist; some Independents; some Jews."[11]

Jews first arrived in New Amsterdam in the 1650s, and by the 1690s they enjoyed many benefits of citizenship. The Mill Street synagogue opened in 1728. Catholics, though legally proscribed from practicing their faith in colonial New York, did so privately with only occasional harassment. "In short," said Dongan, concluding his religious survey, "of all sorts of opinions there are some, and for the most part none at all." And so it remains.

However accommodating of diverse religious persuasions, colonial New Yorkers were a politically contentious lot. Beginning with the Leisler Rebellion in 1689, a challenge to Stuart royal authority led by the Dutch merchant Jacob Leisler (1640–91), and continuing up to the Revolution, provincial politics regularly divided along ethnic, religious, and even class lines, prompting some historians to define these groupings as rudimentary parties. But such contentiousness was susceptible to negotiated deals that left whole the principals at the table. Indeed, what distinguishes colonial New York's politics was just how few New Yorkers had a place at the table. Between the families of large landowners and leading urban merchants at the top and rural tenants, unpropertied urban laborers, and enslaved blacks at the bottom, New York possessed the smallest and least politically empowered "middling classes" of all the colonies.[12]

Compared to Pennsylvania and the Carolinas, with their more generous and immigrant-friendly land policies, colonial New York as a whole was not an especially attractive destination for Europeans in search of economic opportunity. As Richard Hofstadter and others have noted, it remained as late as 1750 a medium-sized colony, little larger in population than New Jersey. By then New York City had narrowed its earlier population gap with Boston, only to see that with the more rapidly growing Philadelphia widen. It was still a good half-century away from becoming America's largest and most economically active city.[13]

"College Enthusiasm"

New York's focus on the commercial main chance, its religious pluralism, and its demographic character all likely contributed to the nine-decade lag between its establishment as an English colony and the emergence of any sustained interest in a college. The Puritans of Massachusetts Bay had allowed only six years to lapse between settlement in Boston and the 1636 founding of Harvard College. They did so, as they stated in the first fund-raising document produced by an American college, *New Englands First Fruits*, both "to advance Learning and perpetuate it to Posterity" and so as not "to leave an illiterate Ministry to the Churches, when our present Ministers shall lie in the Dust." Not trusting Anglican Oxford or even the more Puritan-leaning Cambridge to train their Congregational clergy and magistrates, they invented the local means to do so.[14]

A similar impulse prompted the establishment in Virginia of the College of William and Mary in 1693, by which time Virginian Anglicans had tired of their reliance on the dregs of the English episcopacy to fill their pulpits and sought (unsuccessfully, as it turned out) to provide themselves with a learned homegrown clergy. And so it was again, in 1701, when an increasingly Arminian-leaning Harvard no longer met the religious standards of Connecticut's unreconstructed Calvinists, many of them Harvard graduates, that the "Collegiate School" that would become Yale College came into being. Its opening ended the first wave of college making in prerevolutionary America.[15]

More than four decades passed between the founding of the first three American colleges and the next six, which together constituted the nine colleges chartered before the Revolution. For much of that intervening time, three seemed enough. Even with William and Mary's early slide into a grammar school, Harvard and Yale seemed fully capable of absorbing the limited demand for college going that existed throughout the northern colonies, while the occasional southerner resorted to Oxford, Cambridge, or the Inns of Court for his advanced instruction.

What restarted colonial college making in the 1740s—what Yale's worried Ezra Stiles called "college enthusiasm"—was the Great Awakening, a religious

upheaval within American Protestantism that divided older churches, their settled clergy, and their often formulaic liturgical ways from the dissident
founders of upstart churches, their itinerant clergy, and their evangelical
enthusiasms. The first collegiate issue of the Great Awakening was the College
of New Jersey (later, Princeton), which was founded in 1746 by "New Light"
Presbyterians of New Jersey and New York. They did so in protest against "Old
Light" Yale's hostility to the preaching of the English itinerant George Whitefield and his even more flamboyant ministerial emulators, among them, Gilbert
Tennent (1703–64) and his brother, William (1705–77), founders of Pennsylvania's "Log College," from which Princeton traces its prehistory. The subsequent
foundings of the College of Rhode Island (later Brown) by Baptists in 1764, of
Queens College (later Rutgers) by a revivalist wing of the Dutch Reformed
Church in 1766, and of Dartmouth by "New Side" Congregationalists in 1769 are
all the products of the midcentury religious ferment that seized the dissenting
branches of American Protestantism.[16]

Two other colleges founded in this second wave of colonial college making
reflect more secular, civic considerations. There is some merit to the case made
by University of Pennsylvania historians in claiming Benjamin Franklin as
founder, if less for a founding date of 1740. The latter claim—which would have
Penn jump from sixth to fourth in the precedence list of American colleges—
requires dating its founding to the Presbyterian-backed Charity School built in
Philadelphia in 1740. It is this soon-moribund institution that Franklin transformed in 1749 into the municipally funded Philadelphia Academy, which was
chartered in the spring of 1755 under joint "Old Light" Presbyterian and Anglican auspices as the College of Philadelphia. By then, however, New Yorkers had
sufficiently bestirred themselves to have anticipated their Philadelphia rivals
by some months in the chartering of yet another college, to whose history we
now turn.[17]

The founding of Harvard in 1636 and Yale in 1701 had set no competitive
juices flowing in New York's merchants. But the announcement in the summer
of 1745 that New Jersey—which had only seven years before secured a government separate from New York's and was still considered by New Yorkers to be
within their cultural catch basin—was about to have its own college demanded
an immediate response.

On March 13, 1745, James Alexander (1691–1756), a leading New York City
attorney and pew holder of Trinity Church, altered his will to offset his earlier
50-pound contribution to the construction fund for the proposed college in New
Jersey, where he had extensive land holdings and a growing legal practice, with
a commitment of 100 pounds to support a similar college in New York. The following October, on the very day that the New Jersey Assembly approved a char-

ter for the College of New Jersey, the New York Assembly took up discussion of a college of its own. In December the assembly, with the backing of Governor George Clinton (1741–53), authorized a provincial lottery to raise 2,250 pounds "for the encouragement of learning, and towards the founding a college."[18]

The assembly's actions in support of a new college left unaddressed the matters of its site and denominational auspices. The first prompted three separate proposals in the months following the establishment of the lottery. The first came from the scientist and provincial officeholder Cadwallader Colden, who recommended as a site for the college his adopted Newburgh, forty miles up the Hudson. The Reverend James Wetmore weighed in shortly thereafter in favor of establishing the college in the Westchester village of Rye, adjacent to the Boston Post Road. The Reverend Samuel Seabury then called for its establishment in the Long Island village of Hempstead.[19]

Although all three were Anglicans, Wetmore and Seabury being Anglican clergy, none seems to have been as interested in pressing specifically Anglican auspices for the college (although they may have assumed them) as in assuring it a rural setting well removed from New York City. With the last of these proposals, Seabury's in 1748, public discussion of the college all but ceased. Momentarily embarrassed three years earlier by the New Jersey initiative and still more recently by Franklin's efforts at college making in Philadelphia, most New Yorkers seemed once again preoccupied with their various commercial enterprises to the exclusion of any culturally uplifting projects. Not so William Livingston (1723–90).

William Livingston: Antifounder

Columbia's story often departs from the typical collegiate saga. The same goes for its founding. Mostly, these are recounted in terms of the determined and ultimately successful efforts of a founder, founders, or benefactors. So it is with John Harvard's timely benefaction of eight hundred pounds in 1638 to the Massachusetts General Court to support its fledgling college in Cambridge. So it was with those ten Connecticut clergymen and the benefactor Elihu Yale who were instrumental in the founding of Yale, and with Benjamin Franklin and the University of Pennsylvania, and with the Reverend Eleazar Wheelock (1711–79), the founder of Dartmouth. By contrast, The story of Columbia's founding is less about the successful efforts of its founders than about the ultimately unsuccessful efforts of a band of gentlemen determined to prevent its establishment. Pride of place among Columbia's antifounders belongs to William Livingston.[20]

Livingston was an odd duck: a tall, hawk-faced, dark-complexioned cultural uplifter and moral scold in a city full of roly-poly, flushed-faced, live-and-let-live moneymakers. The Loyalist historian Thomas Jones described him as having an "ill-natured, morose, sullen disposition." Born in Albany in 1723, he was the grandson of Robert Livingston (1673–1728), the first lord of Livingston Manor, whose 160,000 acres on the east bank of the Hudson above Poughkeepsie made him New York's second-largest landowner. Family ties extended back to the earliest Dutch settlers (among them the Van Rensselaers, who owned the largest of the New York patroonships) and forward to the subsequent English mercantile elite centered in Albany and New York City.[21]

William followed three brothers to Yale, graduating in 1741. He then settled in New York City, where he turned to law, his brothers having already gained status there as leading merchants. In 1745 he entered into an apprenticeship with the city's leading attorney, James Alexander, whose defense a decade earlier of the newspaperman Peter Zenger against charges brought by Governor William Cosby (1690–1736) and his attorney general, James DeLancey, had made him a leader of New York's Country Party and enemy of the DeLancey-led Court Party. Livingston's early professional association with Alexander likely reinforced in him a personal commitment to civil libertarianism. His family's position in colonial New York politics, however, identified him with the popular cause of the elected assembly, which rural landowners controlled and which was perpetually at odds with the Governor's Council, dominated by urban merchants.[22]

Livingston demonstrated throughout his life a streak of perverse independence. Early in his legal apprenticeship he took it upon himself to reprove publicly the socially pretentious wife of his mentor, James Alexander. Afterward, he shifted his legal apprenticeship to William Smith Sr. (1697–1769), whose politics, like Alexander's, aligned him with the popular or anti-Court cause. That William's branch of the Livingstons consisted of thoroughgoing Calvinists of either the Dutch Reformed or, as in his case, the Presbyterian persuasion further fueled his antipathy to the Anglican elite of the city. Indeed, Livingston's lifelong anti-Anglicanism was exceeded only by his rabid anti-Catholicism, and he readily accommodated both within an even more comprehensive anticlericalism.[23]

Livingston initially looked on Alexander's 1745 proposal to construct a college as socially uplifting. It was of a piece with his own efforts three years later to interest New York's young professionals in forming a "Society for the Promotion of Useful Knowledge" as an alternative to their degenerating into tavern-frequenting "bumper men." In 1749, hoping to revive a flagging project, he anonymously published *Some Serious Thoughts on the Design of Erecting a College in the Province of New York*. In it, he listed among the many benefits to be derived from a college its potential to deflect the city's unruly young from "the practice of breaking windows and wresting off knockers."[24]

In the fall of 1751 the New York Assembly appointed a ten-member Lottery Commission to manage the lottery funds already accrued to the College— some 3,443 pounds 18 shillings—and to decide on an appropriate site. Livingston was named one of the ten commissioners, in recognition of his ongoing interest in the project and his family's standing in the assembly. He was the only Presbyterian in the group, with two others Dutch Reformed and the remaining seven Anglicans (including five members of Trinity Church). This lopsided arrangement (Anglicans represented barely 10 percent of the province's population) would subsequently be cited as evidence of the prior existence of a secret plot by Anglicans to use public funds to create a "College of Trinity Church." It is noteworthy, however, that Livingston, suspicious by nature, quietly took up his commission and turned to the task of bringing a college of the New York Assembly's conceiving into being.[25]

In March 1752 the vestrymen of Trinity Church offered the Lottery Commission the six northernmost acres of its Queen's Farm property as the site for the new college. No conditions then being set on the offer, Livingston joined the other commissioners in accepting it. This settled the matter of the college's location, with all ten commissioners concurring that it would be in New York City on the site provided, which was seven blocks north of Trinity Church and just above the moving edge of commercial development.[26]

Still undecided was the matter of under whose auspices the college would be established. Livingston assumed that the College, as the creation of the popularly elected assembly, would be publicly directed and nonsectarian. In contrast, the Anglican commissioners assumed that that it would be established under religious auspices and that in New York, where Anglicanism enjoyed a legally privileged and semiestablished position, this would mean Anglican auspices. Neither faction could have imagined that the sorting out of this local matter would provide the first airing for arguments that would shape both sides of the subsequent ideological debate over the American Revolution.[27]

On October 24, 1752, another William Smith (1721–1803), this one an Anglican Scot and newcomer to New York employed as a tutor by the DeLanceys, published *Some Thoughts on Education: With Reasons for Erecting a College in This Province*. The college he proposed would be under Anglican control and incorporated with a royal charter. When these suggestions were repeated two weeks later in a letter to the *New-York Mercury*, Smith added the recommendation that the Reverend Samuel Johnson (1696–1772), a prominent Anglican minister from Stratford, Connecticut, be appointed head of the college. As to the source of a salary sufficient to attract Johnson to New York, Smith helpfully proposed that Johnson might be given a joint appointment at Trinity Church. The cat was out of the bag.[28]

Samuel Johnson and the Anglican Project

William Livingston was second to no man in divining conspiracies where none existed. In the case of a college for New York, however, paranoia was warranted. For several years before 1752, a quiet plan had existed among New York Anglicans to use the assembly's funds to found a specifically "Episcopal College." William Smith likely happened upon the plan during his job hunt in New York City and either wrote *Thoughts on Education* to ingratiate himself with the Anglicans privy to the plan or was recruited by these same folks to write it.[29]

There is no question that Samuel Johnson was in on the plan. As early as 1749 he was regularly and proprietarily discussing the establishment of a college with his stepson, Benjamin Nicoll (1720–60), a Trinity vestryman and later a lottery commissioner, and the Reverend Henry Barclay (1715–64), the rector of Trinity Church and Johnson's sometime ministerial student in Connecticut. These discussions extended across the Atlantic to England and included both the bishop of London, Joseph Secker, who oversaw the religious welfare of the American colonies, and the eminent philosopher and Church of Ireland prelate, George Berkeley, whom Johnson had befriended during his stay in Newport in the 1730s and who pronounced Johnson singularly suited to preside over "a proper Anglican college" in America.[30]

Berkeley's estimate of Johnson's standing was widely shared by American Anglicans. He was the best-known Anglican minister in the colonies by virtue of seniority, his role as mentor for many of the next generation of ministers, his activities as senior missionary in the Society for the Promotion of the Gospel, and his apologetical writings in defense of the Church of England. Along with Benjamin Franklin and Jonathan Edwards, Johnson was one of only three mid-eighteenth-century Americans whose writings received any serious attention in England. He was moreover the best credentialed, if least original, of the three.

Unlike Edwards, a Dissenter and a religious "enthusiast," or Franklin, a free-thinking autodidact who in the early 1750s had yet to win his way into English intellectual circles, Johnson was an ordained minister of the Church of England and the recipient of an M.A. from Oxford in 1722 and of a doctorate from Oxford, awarded in absentia in 1748 after the appearance in England of his philosophical treatise *Elementa Philosophica*. (Franklin published the American edition of Johnson's book, which lost money.) Johnson had the further distinction of being the first American to have a nonscientific article appear in an

English learned journal. Johnson in turn was an all-out Anglophile. Despite his family's three generations in Connecticut, the first two as Puritans, he regularly referred in his ecclesiastical correspondence to America as "these uncultivated parts" and to England as "home."[31]

Johnson's life before his involvement with King's College was marked by a single act of religious rebellion, though, as befit the man, even this was in the cause of a higher orthodoxy. He was born in 1696 in Guilford, Connecticut, the son of a prosperous farmer and deacon of the local Congregational church. At fifteen he proceeded to Yale College, from which he was graduated in 1715. For the next three years, until he was called to be the settled minister of the Congregational church of West Haven, he served as a tutor at the College, studied for the Congregational ministry, and acted as a substitute preacher. During this period, he and several other Yale friends, influenced by their exposure to Locke, Newton, and Anglican apologists by way of a 1718 gift of books to the Yale Library, found themselves questioning all manner of locally accepted doctrine. In particular, Johnson became concerned about the legitimacy of his own recent ordination by the members of his congregation. Further discussions with a missionary from the Anglican-sponsored Society for the Propagation of the Gospel convinced him that only ordination by an Anglican bishop would do. When Johnson and five other Yaleys, including the just-installed president, Timothy Cutler, voiced these views at Yale's 1722 commencement, their apostasy became a matter of public record and local scandal.[32]

Johnson resigned his West Haven pulpit, bade his congregation farewell, and proceeded to England to secure a proper ordination. On his return to Connecticut in 1723, he established the colony's first Anglican church, at Stratford. Over the next three decades he was a vigorous advocate for the Anglican cause, meanwhile providing instruction and encouragement for some dozen young men who followed him out of the Calvinist ranks into the Anglican fold. (By 1750 Johnson-trained ministers were rectors of many of the Anglican churches in New England, New York, and New Jersey.) First and last a denominational polemicist, Johnson was as opposed to the Calvinistic Puritanism of his New England ancestors as he was to the newer "enthusiasms" of the English revivalist George Whitefield and such native-born Great Awakeners as Jonathan Edwards and Gilbert Tennent. His Anglicanism represented a middle way, marked by respect for authority, good order, and edifying ritual, without the emotional excess and egalitarian leanings of evangelical revivalism. Others called it a gentleman's way to salvation.

Thus, when New York's Anglicans determined to provide denominational auspices for the college, Johnson was a natural choice to head it. Why Johnson might wish to do so was another matter. At first, he expressed reluctance to exchange the comforts of his Stratford parsonage for the stress of a new job in New York City. His older son, William Samuel Johnson, gave voice to familial reservations when he reminded his father that "Providence has not called us alone to found a University in New York. Nor to urge the slow, cold councils of that city." Johnson assured his son that he would not resign his Stratford pulpit until installed as president.[33]

Johnson's interest was almost certainly linked to the impact a successfully established Anglican college in New York might have on a campaign he had been waging throughout his ministerial career to convince the ecclesiastical and political authorities in England that the colonists needed an American bishop. Understandably, this was a minority view among American colonists, most of whom, dissenters from the Church of England, felt themselves well rid of the ecclesiastical authority vested in bishops. That it had been English Dissenters who had effectively blocked Parliament from sending a bishop to the colonies in the early 1740s made the need for such a bishop all the more palpable in Johnson's view. Once installed, he could ordain young men, avoiding the costs and dangers of a sea voyage to England. One of Johnson's favorite arguments with English ecclesiastical authorities was that five of the eleven colonists sent to England for ordination between 1720 and 1750 had been killed in transit or by disease in England. This was to be the fate of his younger son, Samuel William, in 1756.[34]

Johnson further argued that a resident bishop could settle the jurisdictional questions that inevitably arose among the scattered American Anglican clergy, represent the Anglican cause in colonies where Dissenters held political sway, and everywhere insist on the Anglicans' right to religious practice, all tasks that by default regularly fell to him. And, finally, the presence of a locally installed bishop would provide the occasions for the ritual pomp and sartorial elegance that American Anglicans otherwise missed in the "uncultivated wilderness." Only "the awe of a bishop," Johnson wrote in 1750, "would abate enthusiasms."[35]

Where such a bishop would reside was not as contentious as one might think. It was generally agreed that he should take up residence where Anglicanism enjoyed a legally protected and socially privileged position. This eliminated all of New England, especially Boston, where Dissenters exercised local authority, and also Pennsylvania, particularly Philadelphia, where William Penn's charter enshrined the principles of full religious toleration. The Anglican Church was officially established in the southern colonies, but practice had rendered the local Anglican practices barely distinguishable from those of the Dissenters. And anyway the southern colonies lacked a city of sufficient size to provide the entourage appropriate to a bishop of the Church of England, and they were at too great a remove from the rest of American Anglicandom.

This left New York City, as Lewis Morris had it, "in the centre of English America," where Anglicans enjoyed local status as the established church. (The Ministry Act of 1693 so provided for the five lower counties of New York, with the rest of the province operating on a "local option" arrangement.) Trinity Church was the largest and grandest church in the colonies and the only one possessed of an organ, as well as a separate chapel, St. George's, with another (St. Paul's) on the drawing board. The city's leading families were nearly all either Anglican or Dutch-Reformed-on-the-way-to-becoming-Anglican. New York was already the seat of royal government for the colony and headquarters for his majesty's army in North America. The establishment of an Anglican college in the city would, rather like the completion of a skating rink or bobsled run in a competition to become the next Olympics site, sew up New York's case as British America's first Anglican see.[36]

Who the first American bishop should be was also a question about which there was not much controversy, especially should he be an American. Apparently, Johnson never mentioned the possibility of his own appointment when pressing the case in his frequent communications with the bishop of London and the archbishop of Canterbury, who would make the appointment. But other American Anglicans were less circumspect, and Samuel Johnson was their odds-on favorite. His acceptance of the presidency of the proposed college for New York would not only help the cause of the college and advance the case for an American episcopacy but also confirm his position as bishop presumptive.[37]

"A Hideous Clamour"

The privately hatched plans for "an Episcopal College" were already well advanced when, in the fall of 1752, William Livingston divined it. For his part, the timing was fortuitous. For some three years Livingston had been discussing with two fellow attorneys, John Morrin Scott (1730–84) and William Smith Jr.(1728–93) (the latter was the son of the lawyer William Smith Sr. and no relation to the Reverend William Smith)—like him, Yale graduates and Presbyterians—the possibility of publishing a weekly newspaper in New York along the lines of the *Independent Whig*, a London weekly published in the 1720s by the Whig essayists Thomas Gordon and John Trenchard. Like Livingston, Scott and Smith wished to turn their spare time to cultural and political purposes, and the idea of a weekly brought the three into such protracted and noteworthy company that they were long thereafter referred to as "the Triumvirate."[38]

The *Independent Reflector* was launched in November 1752. By then, Livingston and his comrades-in-ink had already settled on its first major editorial cause. "If it falls into the hands of Churchmen," Livingston wrote privately to a Dissenting friend on the eve of publishing his first assault on the College, "it will either ruin the College or the Country, and in fifty years, no Dissenter, however deserving, will be able to get into any office."[39]

The *Independent Reflector* had been in print for three months before in its seventeenth number, published March 22, 1753, offered "Remarks on our Intended COLLEGE." It had already attracted a considerable readership and some notoriety for its editorial support for the Moravian minority in New York and for jibes at the office-mongering proclivities of the DeLanceys. When it turned to the College, in numbers 17 through 22, the essayist (assumed to be Livingston) began civilly enough. He supported the idea of a college and agreed that it should be located in or near New York City. He called for an expansive curriculum, to render its graduates "better members of society, and useful to the public in proportion to its expense." Otherwise, "we had better be without it." He went on to castigate both Harvard and Yale for inculcating in their impressionable students "the Arts of maintaining the Religion of the College" and made similar animadversions against the English universities when they justified the polygamies of Henry VIII and the "jesuitically artful" projects of the popish James II. By contrast, he concluded with respect to New York's proposed college, "it is of the last importance, that ours be so constituted, that the Fountain being pure, the Streams (to use the language of Scripture) may make glad the City of our GOD."[40]

In the next issue, "A Continuation of the Same Subject," Livingston went to the heart of his objection to a college in the control of a single religious denomination. By listing English and Dutch Calvinists, Anabaptists, Lutherans, Quakers, and his recently championed Moravians along with the Anglicans, he implied that each of New York's religious sects had an equal claim—and thus no sustainable claim—to the sole governance of the College. And should such solitary rights of governance be conferred on any one of these sects, he warned, the College would instantly become "a Nursery of Animosity, Dissention and Disorder." Moreover, no one would attend but the children of the governing sect, limiting both the College's enrollment and its potential for advancing the public good. New Yorkers not of that sect, he prophesied, would repair elsewhere for college, never to return.[41]

The result would be a "Party-College" made all the more unacceptable to those not of that party by the public funds that went into its creation and maintenance. Surely, Livingston asked rhetorically, the legislature could never have intended its proposed college "as an Engine to be exercised for the purposes of a party"? What it must have intended was "a mere civil institution [that] cannot with any tolerable propriety be monopolized by any religious sect." Such a college, in contrast to a "party-college," would attract students from the neighboring colonies, among them New Englanders averse to the region's prevailing Calvinists and Pennsylvanians of all denominations but one ("I should always, for political reasons, exclude Papists"). Such a vast "importation of religious refugees" to flow from the establishment of a nonsectarian college in New York could not be other than "commendable, advantageous, and politic."[42]

In a third essay, "The Same Subject Continued," Livingston argued against positing the governance of the College in a corporation created by a royal charter. To do so would remove the College from legislative scrutiny, and public oversight would be lost. Instead, he proposed in his fourth essay, "A Farther Prosecution of the Same Subject," that the College be incorporated by an act of the assembly. The logic for doing so Livingston presented succinctly: "If the Colony must bear the expense of the College, surely the Legislature will claim the superintendency of it." To the argument that superintending an educational institution was not the proper business of the legislature, he responded by asking: "Are the rise of Arts, the Improvement of Husbandry, the Increase of Trade, the Advancement of Knowledge in Law, Physic, Morality, Policy, and the Rules of Justice and civil Government, Subjects beneath the Attention of our Legislature?"[43]

In his fifth essay, Livingston stipulated eleven terms of incorporation, chief among them: the trustees to be elected by the legislature; the president's election by the trustees to be subject to legislative veto; the faculty to be elected by the trustees and president; students to "be at perfect liberty to attend any Protestant Church at their pleasure"; divinity not to be taught as a science.[44]

The sixth and last essay appeared on April 26, 1753. In it, Livingston made direct appeals to the respective "Gentlemen of the CHURCH of ENGLAND," "Gentlemen of the DUTCH CHURCH," "Gentlemen of the English PRESBYTERIAN Church," "my FRIENDS, in Derision called QUAKERS," as well a collective appeal to "Gentlemen of the FRENCH, of the MORAVIAN, of the LUTHERAN, and the ANABAPTIST Congregations," attempting in each to show that their best interest would be served by all having "an *equal* share in the Government of what *equally* belongs to all." But he could not let off the "Gentlemen of the CHURCH of ENGLAND ... the most numerous and richest Congregation in the City," without noting that, unlike those of the other persuasions, they had the singular backing of "the Mother Church of the Nation" and were "at the least risk of being denied your just Proportion in the Management of the College." This is as close as Livingston ever came to identifying the Anglicans as those intent on creating "an Academy founded in Bigotry, and reared by Party-Spirit," but it left no doubt as to which "Gentlemen" he had in mind.[45]

Supporters of an Anglican-controlled College grumbled in private during the six-week assault on them and their eminently reasonable plans for the College. What Livingston had proposed, Johnson reported to his ecclesiastical superiors in London, was nothing short of "a latitudinarian academy" that would exclude religion from its curriculum and churchmen from its governance. Public responses were few and scattered, mostly in the form of anonymous letters in the *New-York Mercury* written by the Reverends Thomas Bradbury Chandler, James Wetmore, Samuel Seabury, and Henry Barclay. All subscribed to the view that all proper colleges possessed a religious character and that, given the favored place of the Anglican church in New York, not to mention its established status in the mother country, New York's college should be Anglican. All also demonstrated a profound discomfort at having to confront their polemically more effective critics in print. Johnson said he left the "writing in the Church's defense" to his New York promoters, who were, he assured the archbishop of Canterbury, "endeavoring not without some success to defeat their pernicious scheme."[46]

The prolific William Smith came forth with *A General Idea of the College of Mirana* in April 1753, just as the *Independent Reflector* series wound down. But he did not directly engage Livingston's arguments so much as describe a model two-track curriculum for a very different kind of college from the one Livingston had in mind. The first track was designed for those students destined for the learned professions, "divinity, law, physic, and the chief officers of the state," and would include instruction in dancing and fencing. The second track, for those aspiring to the mechanical professions "and all the remaining people of the country," would have less Latin and dispensed with instruction in dancing and fencing. Before setting sail for England to take holy orders, the still unemployed Smith commended to his readers the Anglican liturgy for all College services. Samuel Johnson was sufficiently impressed with Smith's good sense to suggest to his New York coconspirators that "he would make an excellent tutor." Too late. By then Smith had already been approached by Benjamin Franklin about a professorship at the Philadelphia Academy, and it was to Philadelphia that he went upon his return, to become the provost of the College of Philadelphia.[47]

Rather than mount a full-scale counterattack against the radical ideas advanced by Livingston, the self-described "Anti-*Reflectors*" put their energies into behind-the-scenes campaigns to get the *Independent Reflector* shut down. Help came in the form of a suicide. Five days after taking his post as governor of New York on October 7, 1753, Sir Danvers Osborne took his own life. This brought to power the acting governor, James DeLancey, the "natural leader of the Episcopal party" and the *bête noire* of the Livingston-led Popular or Country Party. DeLancey promptly withdrew all provincial business from the printer of the *Independent Reflector*, which soon thereafter ceased publication. Although Livingston and William Smith Jr. persisted through 1753 in their attacks on "the College of Trinity Church," using several public outlets, including a periodical of their own with the catchy title *The Occasional Reverberator*, the backers of the College pressed on through the fall of 1753.[48]

As the war of words continued, the center of action shifted to the Lottery Commission. There, Livingston's position as the lone commissioner favoring a legislatively directed college put him at a disadvantage. With neither an alternative site to propose nor a presidential candidate of his own, he proceeded with uncharacteristic caution. On November 22, 1753, he moved that the Lottery Commissioners elect Samuel Johnson as their unanimous choice to preside over the new college. He then proposed that Chauncey Whittelsey be elected as the College's "second tutor." Both motions were adopted, and Livingston was assigned the responsibility of informing the president- and first tutor–elect. Lacking a credible nominee to bring forward, Livingston conceded the number one spot to assure getting his own man in as number two.[49]

And who was Chauncey Whittelsey? First, he was not an Anglican clergyman but an "Old Light" Congregationalist merchant residing in New Haven. Second, he had been Livingston's tutor at Yale and an occasional correspondent since. There might also have been a third credential, though allowing so requires extending to Livingston a sense of humor not evidenced in the historical record or suggested by his grim visage. As Livingston and others, including Johnson, who followed Yale affairs well knew, Whittelsey had played a small but memorable part in Yale's encounter with the Great Awakening. In 1740, in the immediate wake of George Whitefield's visit to New Haven, during which he warned against "the dangers of an unconverted ministry," David Brainerd, a particularly exercised undergraduate (and nephew of Jonathan Edwards) felt moved to conduct a survey on the state of the souls of his teachers. Most passed muster, but tutor Chauncey Whittelsey, he sadly reported to Yale's indignant president, Thomas Clap, did not have "any more grace than the chair I then lean'd on." Just the man for New York's intended college.[50]

As it turned out, Livingston's efforts to plant Whittelsey came to naught when Johnson, in the politest letter imaginable, frightened him off with a description of his expected duties. By then, that is, the spring of 1754, Johnson had pretty much completed haggling with the Lottery Commissioners over the terms of his appointment. Too far committed to back off now, especially when his salary demands were met, he nonetheless extracted two further concessions from the commissioners upon his acceptance of the presidency: the right to take a year's leave of absence from his Stratford parish rather than resign immediately and explicit authorization to leave New York whenever smallpox threatened the city. Both bespoke serious reservations about his new home, which would only increase with time.[51]

On May 14, 1754, shaken by the "hideous clamour" produced by Livingston's attacks on the College, the vestrymen of Trinity Church informed the Lottery Commission that their earlier gift of land for the intended college was now subject to two conditions: (1) the president of the College must always be a member of the Church of England; (2) religious services at the College must be conducted in accord with Anglican liturgical forms. Should College authorities ever fail to meet either of these conditions, the vestrymen made it clear that the land on which the College sat would revert to Trinity Church.[52]

In that half of its members were also Trinity vestrymen, the Lottery Commission could not have been taken by surprise by the new conditions. A majority promptly voted to accept both, with only Livingston arguing against them as effectively creating "a College of Trinity Church." Taking no public notice of Livingston's "Twenty Unanswerable Questions," the commissioners incorporated both conditions into the draft charter for the College being prepared by attorneys and Trinity churchmen John Chambers and Joseph Murray, in consultation with president-elect Johnson and the favorably disposed acting governor, James DeLancey.[53]

Although Livingston was still far from beaten, the momentum behind the College was now such that he could not stop its opening. On May 31, an "Advertisement for the College of New York," signed by Samuel Johnson, appeared in the *New York Gazette*. After setting out the admission requirements and proposed curriculum "for the intended Seminary or College of New York," Johnson proceeded directly to assure non-Anglican parents of prospective students that "there is no intention to impose on the scholars, the peculiar tenets of any particular sect of Christians." Instead, the College would seek "to inculcate upon their tender minds, the great principles of Christianity and morality in which true Christians of each denomination are generally agreed."[54]

Johnson sought to soften the new stipulation as to the use of Anglican prayers in College services by assuring that College prayers would be drawn directly from Holy Scriptures, thereby minimizing denominational offense. And then a final ecumenical reassurance: "The chief thing that is aimed at in this college is to teach and engage the children to know God in Jesus Christ, and to love and serve Him in all sobriety, godliness, and righteousness of life, with a perfect heart, and a willing mind; and to train them up in all virtuous habits and all such useful knowledge as may render them creditable to their families and friends, ornaments to their country, and useful to the public weal in their generations."[55]

The advertisement stated that classes were to commence on July 1, held in the vestry room of the new schoolhouse adjoining Trinity Church "till a convenient place may be built." A half-century after Lewis Morris declared "New York a fit place for a Colledge," New York would finally have one.

"To Make a Flourish"

Classes got under way on July 17, 1754, the delay stemming from problems securing faculty. With Whittelsey frightened off and William Smith slated for the College of Philadelphia, Johnson looked closer to home. In a piece of nepotism that might have surprised even New Yorkers, he announced his intention to install his two Yale-educated sons as tutors. The elder, William Samuel, begged off in favor of pursuing the law in Connecticut (his Columbia duties lay a generation in the future), but the twenty-two-year-old Samuel William, or "Billy," assisted his father in providing instruction, agreeing to do so for only the few months before he was to sail to England for Anglican ordination.[56]

Still, the instructional burden on Johnson *père et fils* could not have been all that heavy, with only eight recorded students, all freshmen. Even that count may have been high. Livingston reported to Whittelsey in August that the school "consists of seven students, the Majority of whom were admitted tho' utterly unqualified in order to make a Flourish."[57]

Now under way, the College was still not out of the political woods. The draft charter presented to the Anglican-dominated Governor's Council on June 14 had passed but with two dissents, from James Alexander and William Smith Sr. Their opposition suggested the charter could expect difficult going when, and if, it went before the assembly, where dissenters were in a majority and where Livingston's arguments against creating an "Episcopal College" with public funds carried force.[58]

On October 31, 1754 ("Charter Day"), Acting Governor DeLancey submitted a final version of the charter for a "College in the Province of New York . . . in the City of New York in America . . . named King's College" to the Governor's Council. The council approved, this time with only William Smith Sr. dissenting. Two days later DeLancey signed the charter in the name of King George II. He had simply bypassed the assembly rather than risk its disapproval. In the face of such executive high-handedness, the assembly, at Livingston's urging, promptly impounded the proceeds of the three provincial lotteries (upwards of seven thousand pounds) and suspended payment of the first of five annual grants of five hundred pounds. The College now had a royal charter and a forty-one-member board of governors charged with the welfare of the new college but none of the anticipated financial wherewithal.

It would be two years before the assembly accepted the fact of the College's existence and made good on its original assurances of financial support. What made even this modest rapprochement possible was a war and a new governor. The war was between England and France, locally called the French and Indian War, and it commenced in the fall of 1756; the governor was Sir Charles Hardy, who had arrived a year earlier and used the intervening months to impress the contending political forces in the province with his evenhandedness. Under the threat of invasion by the French and their Native American allies along the province's exposed northern and western borders, but also flush with wartime profits, New Yorkers in the assembly accepted Hardy's proposed compromise for ending the College controversy. The lottery proceeds were to be divided between the College and New York City, the city to use its share to build a municipal pest house. William Smith Sr., second only to William Livingston as a critic of the College, could not resist characterizing (with a borrowed barb) the accord as splitting the lottery money between New York's "two pest houses."[59]

With this compromise, which provided the College with a one-time grant of thirty-six hundred pounds in provincial funds (the earlier agreed-upon annual support of five hundred pounds was quietly dropped), the College's financial survival was assured. Even Livingston conceded as much. "Relative to the affair of the College," he wrote resignedly to an ally in 1757, "we stood as long as our legs would support us, and, I may add, even fought for some time on our stumps." A decade later, Livingston could still work up a sweat about his old nemesis, as in a letter to his son at Princeton: "You are very severe on our famous New York College, but I believe not more sarcastical than it deserves. It makes indeed a most contemptible figure. . . . The partial bigotted and iniquitous plan upon which it was constructed deserved the opposition of every friend of civil and religious liberty; and the clamour I raised against it . . . when it was first founded on its present narrow principles, it has yet and probably never will totally silence."[60]

Of all colonial colleges, none more fully exhausted its prospects for subsequent legislative support and popular approbation by "the clamour" protesting its founding than did King's College. Moreover, twenty years later, some of the arguments first used against establishing King's College on "its present narrow principles" would be extended to the crown itself.[61]

Who Governs?

The royal charter signed by Lieutenant Governor James DeLancey transferred responsibility for the College from the Lottery Commission to a forty-one-member board of governors. This included seventeen ex officio members, three of whom were crown officials (the Archbishop of Canterbury, the Secretary for

Plantations, and the governor), the senior member of the Governor's Council, the speaker of the Assembly, the five justices of the Supreme Court, and the Mayor of New York. The president of the College also served as a member ex officio. A further twenty-four individuals were named in the charter, serving without term, their successors selected by the continuing governors.[62]

While not explicitly excluded from being elected to a vacant position, the College faculty were not provided seats ex officio on the governing board. This was in keeping with the evolved practice of other colonial colleges, where external boards had become the rule. It was, however, at variance with the contemporary practice at Oxford and Cambridge, where the faculty were directly engaged in the governance of their respective colleges.

In theory, the King's College board of governors encompassed a broad spectrum of New York religious life. The charter permitted Protestants of all persuasions to serve as governors, though it excluded Roman Catholics by an oath provision and Jews as non-Christians. Only three members—the Archbishop of Canterbury, the rector of Trinity Church, and the president of the College—would necessarily be Anglicans, and they were offset by four other ex-officio ministers (those of the city's Dutch Reformed, French, Lutheran, and Presbyterian churches).

In practice, however, the King's College board of governors was from the start dominated by Anglicans and even more narrowly by Trinity churchmen. When its named members were announced, Henry Barclay, the rector of Trinity Church and ex officio College governor, could triumphantly report to ecclesiastical officials in London, "we have a majority." This would only increase with time. Of the fifty-nine men who eventually served as King's College governors, only the three ex officio members representing the French, Lutheran, and Dutch Reformed churches were neither Anglican nor Dutch Reformed. The city's Presbyterian minister declined his right to membership, as did William Livingston when he became eligible to serve ex officio as speaker of the assembly in 1759. All replacements chosen by the board were either Anglicans or members of the Dutch Reformed Church.[63]

The half-dozen Dutch Reformed governors were a special case. They generally followed the lead of Joannes Ritzema, minister of the Dutch Reformed Church, who regarded himself and his followers as both theologically and socially closer to his Anglican brethren than to either the Presbyterian dissenters or the Dutch-speaking "enthusiasts" in his own denominational ranks. Moreover, the Anglicans on the board cultivated Ritzema, as when at the very first meeting of the governors in 1755 it was moved that the charter be revised to allow a theology professorship to be filled by someone of the Dutch Reformed governors' choosing.

Nothing came of the offer of a Dutch theology chair, and Ritzema was ultimately unsuccessful in keeping his sectarian rival, Theodore Frelinghuysen, from drawing some Dutch support away from King's College when Queen's College was founded in 1766 in New Jersey. Throughout Ritzema's twenty-two years as a governor (1754–76), he and the other Dutch Reformed governors never constituted a separate voting bloc on the board. The fact that many of them, along with their families, were well along in the transfer of their religious allegiance from the Dutch Reformed Church to the Anglican communion only made any such division increasingly remote. As in matters of commerce, so in the governance of King's College: the Dutch and the Anglicans found ways of getting on with each other, if only to the exclusion of others.[64]

The control of the College by the board of governors was facilitated by its increasing homogeneity. The initial presence enjoyed by Trinity Church ministers and vestrymen on the board increased over time, as Anglicans assumed places freed when non-Anglican governors named in the charter died or resigned. Meanwhile, the board's ex officio members played a smaller and smaller part. Lieutenant Governor DeLancey, for example, almost never attended board meetings, his involvement in the founding of the College having already cost him whatever political reputation he had to spare.

The governors of King's College met 102 times in twenty-two years, or about five times a year. Most meetings were attended by scarcely more than the quorum of fifteen governors. A quarter of the governors attended fewer than ten meetings, and another half were absent more often than present. That left a core of just sixteen governors, who, by virtue of their extended tenure and faithful attendance, ran the College. Of these, seven were members of the clergy, five in the employ of Trinity Church. At least five of the remaining nine were Trinity communicants.[65]

The Reverend Samuel Auchmuty epitomizes the governor-as-ministerial-insider. A Bostonian by birth and a 1742 Harvard graduate, he was Barclay's assistant minister at Trinity when he became the first governor to be elected to the board in 1759. Five years later, he succeeded Barclay as Trinity's rector. In his sixteen years as a governor, Auchmuty appears not to have missed a meeting. A forceful personality, he had little patience for Barclay's live-and-let-live ways either as rector or as governor. It was Auchmuty who pressed the board in 1760, during one of the president's frequent absences, to look to England for Johnson's successor and who, on Myles Cooper's arrival in New York in 1762, proceeded to ease Johnson out of the presidency.[66]

During Cooper's incumbency, Auchmuty could always count on at least two votes besides his own: those of the compliant president (who also acted as proxy for the Archbishop of Canterbury) and, after 1770, Auchmuty's assistant minister at Trinity, the Reverend Charles Inglis. That it was Inglis who was placed "in effective charge of the College" during Cooper's leave in 1771 and that yet another Trinity assistant minister, Benjamin Moore (KC 1766) was installed as acting president after Cooper's hasty departure in 1775 speak both to Auchmuty's authority within the board and his partiality to men of the cloth.

Ever the militant churchman, Auchmuty complained to the Bishop of London whenever resident royal officials made the slightest gesture toward the non-Anglican majority within the province. The rumor that Governor Sir Charles Moore was thinking about appointing a Presbyterian—William Smith Sr.—to the Governor's Council in 1767 was enough to prompt visions of imperial apocalypse: "My dear sir, if no opposition is made to such impolitic proceedings, and if these people are upon all occasions to be indulged, while the Clergy and professors of the Established Church meet with little countenance, or promotion, the event must be the final ruin of the Church on the Continent. If this once takes place, farewell Loyalty, Obedience, and Dependance."[67]

The only governor who attended more meetings than Auchmuty was Leonard Lispenard, who served throughout the board's twenty-one-year history, sixteen of them as College treasurer. One of New York City's leading merchants, Lispenard was head of one of the city's oldest Dutch families, members of which by the 1750s had quietly left behind their inherited Dutch Reformed affiliations (and their Dutch language) for membership in the city's Anglican and English-speaking commercial elite. Like most of the laymen on the board, Lispenard had not gone to college and willingly left such academic matters as faculty appointments, the curriculum, and admission requirements to his degree-bearing ministerial colleagues. On financial matters, however, such as the construction of College Hall, the rentals on the College's water lots, or the salary of the College steward, Lispenard and the other half-dozen most active governors drawn from the mercantile and legal ranks of the city exacted a reciprocal acquiescence.

This informal division of the educational and financial responsibilities of the College's governing board, which was present almost from the start, proved long-lived. It survived the reorganization of King's College as Columbia College in 1784 and persisted into the twentieth century. Indeed, on the testimony of two recent Columbia presidents, it continued to be fully operational, if by then anachronistic and dysfunctional, through the 1960s.[68]

The First President Johnson, 1754–1763

The expected working relationship of the governors and President Johnson was not laid out in the charter. There were reasons to believe that the president would be in charge of the College, with the governors leaving to him the day-to-day responsibilities. Johnson's personal prestige as a churchman, scholar, and intercolonial personage, as well as his gravitas, were grounds for deference. The fact that he had been recruited by the commissioners and then had to be persuaded to take the presidency further implies an initial willingness on the part of the governors to follow his lead on collegiate matters. This seems to have been Johnson's expectation as well. But that is not how it worked out.

However compelling as president-elect, Johnson turned out to be an indifferent administrator. Fifty-eight when he assumed his duties, he was not invigorated by them. He soon handed over most of his teaching responsibilities. The loss of his younger son, Billy—who died of smallpox while he was being ordained in England in 1756—the death of his wife in 1759, and that of his New Yorker stepson, Benjamin Nicoll, in 1760 cast a pall over much of his presidency. Midway through his third year as president, he began scouting around for a successor.[69]

The fact is that this third-generation son of Connecticut never fully unpacked, much less made an effort to become a New Yorker. The city unsettled him. His remarriage in 1761—to his son's mother-in-law—restored a measure of happiness to his life but only increased his desire to return to his native Connecticut and the lighter responsibilities of ministering to a settled church in a familiar town.

President Johnson's absences from the College, ostensibly to reduce the risk of contracting smallpox, left it in the hands of two faculty members, often only one. Some governors began in 1761 to look to England for a successor. That this happened even as Johnson was cultivating the American-born, Harvard-trained rector of the Anglican Church in Cambridge, Massachusetts, Reverend East Apthorpe while also privately trying to interest his son William Samuel in the job, suggests that the idea of an English successor neither was his idea nor had his blessing. When Myles Cooper (1735–85) appeared on the scene in the fall of 1762, officially as professor of moral philosophy but clearly expecting to assume the presidency upon the incumbent's imminent departure, Johnson may well have wondered if he was being handed his hat. The transfer the following spring was attended by some wounded feelings and indecorous haggling about a pension but no public recriminations.[70]

Samuel Johnson gave good service to King's College for seven years in seeing it through a respectable beginning. He died amid family and loving parishioners in Stratford in 1772, just as they were confronted with hard decisions about the looming political crisis. Regarding the choice between loyalty to the crown and American independence, however, they could have harbored no doubts as to the side their pastor took.

Myles Cooper: Ecclesiastical Placeman

It is possible that, had President Johnson not absented himself from New York as frequently as he did or not so obviously lost interest in the job, governors would not have assumed the dominant role in the direction of the College as early as they did. Their decision to bring over Johnson's successor sight unseen before Johnson was ready to leave marked a decisive shift in the power relations between president and board.

Myles Cooper was from the beginning of his presidency under the sway of the governors. His youth, appearance, inexperience, and nonassertive personality all likely contributed to his diffidence in dealing with the governors. Twenty-seven at his election to the presidency, Oxford-trained, and only recently employed as chaplain of his own Queen's College, Oxford, he had been ordained in 1761. By then, he had attracted the interest of several clerics in high positions, not least the Archbishop of Canterbury and his Oxford teachers, who recommended him for the American post.[71]

Cooper was short, of ruddy complexion and roly-poly shape, if one accepts as a true likeness his self-commissioned 1768 portrait by the then young and relatively unknown Boston painter John Singleton Copley. Cooper brought to New York a reputation as a minor poet but a poor public speaker, which led to his not being offered Johnson's place in the Trinity Sunday lineup of homilists. He did, however, insist on receiving the position's stipend, which suggests Cooper had more interest in the perquisites of the presidency than its powers and more concern with what offices would follow rather than in leaving an authoritative mark on the current one. He was first and last that stock character of eighteenth-century English public life, a placeman.

King's College's bachelor president did prove to be much more social than his early-to-bed predecessor, entertaining regularly in College rooms and just as regularly dining out. His wine cellar was said to be the best in the colonies, a compliment not paid to his library. Friends who enjoyed his company were perhaps a little too quick to deny implications that he was "in the least bit dissipated." "As for public transactions in this great city," Auchmuty wrote in 1771, "I must refer you to our friend Cooper, who knows everybody, and everything that passes here."[72]

For all his gregariousness, Cooper, like Johnson before him, never took to New York. He frequently absented himself with "rambles" into the southern colonies, where, in 1768 and again in 1774, he floated the prospect of resettling. One idea he tried out among his ecclesiastical sponsors in England was that, should two episcopal sees be created in the American colonies, he be assigned as bishop of the southern one. During a yearlong leave in England in 1771–72, he looked closely into upcoming livings nearer home.[73]

On that visit, Cooper tried to interest ecclesiastical and political authorities in a plan he and several governors had devised, by which King's College would be given university status and preside over the other colonial colleges, as Oxford and Cambridge did over their respective residential colleges. The plan, which Cooper and some governors referred to as the "American University" and which the College continued to press right up until the Revolution, had no more chance in Parliament (much less at Harvard or Yale) than did the call for an American bishop. But it did suggest that Cooper, for all his bachelor fussiness, was given to the most grandiose of imperial pipe dreams.[74]

Not that there was any likelihood of Cooper's "going native." His loyalties remained with the crown and the Church of England. As colonial resistance to British rule intensified in the early 1770s, he joined with several New York–area Anglican ministers in the anonymous publication of a series of pamphlets that declared all forms of resistance to be treason. These sentiments, once attributed to him, made him a marked man among resistance leaders and led to his hasty departure from New York City with a mob at his heels in the spring of 1775. In May he set sail for England.

In England, Cooper seems to have given neither King's College nor New York further thought, other than to publish a poem about his flight and to press claims for a continuation of his salary until the official closing of the College in 1776. After serving in several comfortable and undemanding livings, in 1787 he died at his last, in Edinburgh, at the age of fifty. Buried at his request in a graveyard reserved for Anglican clerics, Cooper lies beneath a tombstone engraved with an epitaph of his own composition:

> *Here lies a priest of English blood*
> *Who living liked whate'er was good*
> *Good company, good wine, good name,*
> *Yet never hunted after fame*
> *But as the first he still preferred,*
> *So here he chose to be interred*
> *And, unobserved, from crowds withdrew*
> *To rest among the chosen few*
> *In humble hopes, that divine love*
> *Will raise him to the bles't above.*

"It may deserve mention," his obituary in the *Gentleman's Magazine* reported, "that Cooper's estate included his library, valued at 5 pounds sterling, his wine cellar, valued at 150."[75]

Who Taught What?

Inasmuch as the governors took little interest in what was taught, it was in the curriculum that the personal stamp of the two presidents was most sharply etched upon King's College. Each drew on his own experiences. Johnson, a student and tutor at Yale four decades earlier, devised the first course of study for King's College, while Cooper took as his model the academic arrangements of mid-eighteenth-century Oxford.

President Johnson's advertisement announcing the College's imminent opening promised instruction in the generally expected ancient languages, writing, and speaking. On top of this classical base, however, would be additional instruction

in the arts of numbering and measuring, of surveying and navigation, of geography and history, of husbandry, commerce and government, and in the knowledge of all nature in the heavens above us, and in the air, water and earth around us, and the various kinds of meteors, stones, mines, and minerals, plants and animals, and of everything useful for the comfort, the convenience and elegance of life, in the chief manufactures relating to any of these things; and finally, to lead them from the study of nature to the knowledge of themselves, and of the God of nature, and their duty to Him, themselves, and one another, and everything that can contribute to their true happiness, both here and hereafter.

Such curricular overreach perhaps deserved the derisive remarks it prompted from contemporary critics of the College such as Livingston and might raise brows even from a modern educational consumer. This said, the most impressive aspect of the first Johnson presidency is the extent to which he made good on his early curricular promises.[76]

Heavy emphasis on Greek and Latin in the first years and on mathematics and rhetoric later on is entirely predictable. With the engagement in 1755 of tutor Leonard Cutting, a twenty-one-year-old Cambridge-trained classicist, as replacement for his son Billy, Johnson was able to exempt himself from language instruction. His teaching thereafter was limited to two yearlong courses: one in metaphysics, for juniors, and the other, for seniors, in moral philosophy. (Other colonial colleges had capping courses for seniors taught by their presidents, but these tended to be more theological and even doctrinal than broadly philosophical.) That Johnson drew heavily on his *Elementa Philosophica* made him the first in a long line of Columbia teachers about whom their students could say "he/she wrote the book."[77]

A more noteworthy contribution derived from Johnson's early interest in science, acquired through private study of Newton, Locke, and Bacon, which assured that subject a more prominent place at King's College than it then enjoyed at either Yale or Princeton. Accordingly, it was not to his more immediate collegiate neighbors but to Harvard's professor of natural philosophy, John Winthrop, that Johnson turned in 1756 for advice in filling the College's first professorship in mathematics and natural science. Winthrop recommended twenty-seven-year-old Daniel Treadwell, and Johnson promptly hired him in 1757. The College's first professor of mathematics and natural philosophy, in addition to teaching Greek and Latin to freshmen and sophomores, taught courses in mathematics and experimental and natural philosophy to juniors and seniors. Unfortunately for the cause of science at King's College, Treadwell died of consumption three years after his appointment.[78]

Offerings often turned on the availability of faculty. Yet Johnson's hiring of Robert Harpur, a twenty-three-year-old Glasgow-trained mathematician, within three days of his arrival in New York in 1762, to fill the place of Treadwell as professor of mathematics and natural philosophy, speaks to Johnson's commitment to science in the curriculum. So does his willingness to overlook Harpur's religion and his politics. "He is indeed a Presbyterian," Johnson wrote to his son upon Harpur's appointment, "but I think from what has yet appeared, he will do very well." As it turned out, Harpur would be the only Presbyterian ever appointed to the King's College faculty and, come 1775, its only faculty patriot.[79]

During the presidency of Myles Cooper, the curriculum reverted largely to elementary instruction in classical languages, "belles lettres," and moral philosophy, this last almost certainly taught less rigorously by Cooper than it had been by Johnson. Harpur, the faculty's only scientist and, for two years after Cutting's resignation in 1763, the only other faculty member, first had his professorship halved by Cooper to encompass only mathematics; then, in 1767, he was relegated to the status of private tutor. By that point students were regularly defying his authority.[80]

Not even the appearance of a six-member medical faculty in 1767 (about which more below) restored the attention paid to science in the College's first years. Cooper had little to do with the medical faculty nor they with him. The only member of the King's College regular faculty to provide instruction in science after Harpur's demotions was the Trinity College, Dublin–trained Irishman Samuel Clossy, who was appointed in 1764 and thereafter divided his energies among regular undergraduates, his medical students, and a thriving private practice. Cooper had no knowledge of or personal interest in the sciences and no professional reason to see them flourish at King's College. To have done so would have required venturing outside the tight circle of Oxford-trained Anglican clerics and King's College–trained clerics-in-the-making with whom he was most comfortable.[81]

It is to Cooper's presidency that the later practice of Columbia's hiring its own can be traced. The first instance of a graduate's being hired occurred in 1773, when John Vardill, class of 1766, was appointed professor of natural law and promptly dispatched to England for ordination and further study. The second was Benjamin Moore, class of 1768, who filled in as a tutor in the College before his trip to England for ordination in 1774 and later served as acting president after Cooper's departure in 1775. After the reorganization of King's College as Columbia College in 1784, he served briefly as professor of rhetoric and still later as the fifth president of Columbia College (1801–10).[82]

King's two presidents also differed in their views about the College's space issues. At the second meeting of the board of governors, in May 1755, it was decided not to wait for the assembly's release of lottery funds to the College but to press forward with the construction of College Hall. Shortly thereafter, the architect Robert Crommelin, who had designed the recently completed St. George's Chapel, was commissioned to draw up the plans. The cornerstone was laid on August 23, 1756, and the building was completed in the spring of 1760.[83]

An impressive edifice it was. Three stories, 180 feet by 30 feet, situated on the north side of the campus triangle (with its back to Murray Street), topped with a cupola. Before the building's opening in 1760, the English traveler Andrew Burnaby passed through New York and later provided a description of College Hall:

The college, when finished, will be exceedingly handsome: it is to be built on three sides of a quadrangle, fronting Hudson's or North River, and will be the most beautifully situated of any college, I believe, in the world. At present only one wing is finished, which is of stone, and consists of twenty-four sets of apartments, each having a large sitting room, with a study, and bed chamber. They are obliged to make use of some of these apartments for a master's lodge, library, chapel, hall &c, but as soon as the whole shall be completed, there will be proper apartments for each of these offices. The name of it is King's College.[84]

President Johnson envisioned the building serving three purposes: as a setting for instruction, as a library, and as lodgings for the president and faculty. And so it operated after opening, with the College vacating the rectory room of the Trinity Church School in the fall of 1760, only weeks after the president and his family moved into College Hall. Harpur and Cutting soon followed. Johnson assumed that most students would live at home or, in special circumstances, be taken into his or a faculty member's lodgings. For a while at least, with its open and approachable campus, a view of (and from) the Hudson, and residential and commercial development on all sides, the College physically presented itself not as a cloistered place removed from the city but as a multi-functional part of it.

Once president, Cooper set about reversing this presentational statement. Just as his assertion of the primacy of classics and humanities "Oxfordized" the curriculum, two moves affecting the physical plant "Oxfordized" campus life. The first was to require all matriculating students to reside in College Hall, even when doing so imposed financial hardships on their families and deprived faculty of College lodgings. The second was to fence in the campus, which Cooper did in 1765, a decision perhaps prompted by the College's location alongside on "one of the streets where the most noted prostitutes live [and are] a temptation to the youth that have occasion to pass often that way," as a Scottish visitor described its circumstances a decade later. This largely symbolic attempt to close the College off from the city—and vice versa—would not be the last.[85]

Under Cooper, the College became more residential than it had been under Johnson—or would be again until well into the twentieth century. He imposed rules requiring students to remain within the College on school nights, when the gates were locked at 10 P.M. Violators were to be fined and repeat offenders suspended. Cooper's "Black Book of Student Offenses," wherein is recorded for posterity such capital student offenses as the unlawful removal of teacups from one student's rooms by another, suggests how far Cooper went in attempting to make King's College into the spitting image of his own Queen's College, Oxford. This extended to its males-only character: after Cooper's installation, the governors resolved "that no women on any pretence whatever (Except a cook) be allowed to reside within the College for the future, and that those who are now there be removed as soon as conveniently may be."[86]

Where Johnson and Cooper were alike was in thinking of themselves not primarily as teachers or academics but as ministers. And their Anglicanism set them apart from most other American ministers, not least in their recognition that they would be professionally better off in England than in "these uncultivated parts." Both saw themselves as missionaries, the American-born Johnson ready to devote his life to bringing sacredotal order and respect for the crown to these unruly and scruffy parts, the younger and English-reared Cooper paying his dues in the provinces before being called home to a more suitable living. Neither saw any advantage to the open-ended, opportunistic, freewheeling aspects of life in the colonies and especially in New York City as against the established ways and comfortable livings of rural England. In this they differed even from the most Anglophilic of the city's leading merchants, all of whom were well aware of the very real advantages of doing business in New York. But for even the most Americanized Anglican cleric, New York City was a long way from the archbishop's Canterbury or, for that matter, Trollope's Barchester.

Small World

"The universal fact of collegiate life," a careful scholar of early American academic history, Paul H. Mattingly, has pointed out, "was competition for a modest pool of basically trained youth that required solicitation and constant cultivation." If so, the eight students with whom President Johnson began in July 1754 represented an impressive start, especially considering that five managed to stay on to graduate four years later.[87]

But then something happened or, rather, did not happen. Johnson's second class, in 1755, consisted of six students, only one of whom graduated. The 1756 entering class numbered a dozen (Johnson's largest), but half of these were gone by their third year. Even after 1757, the first year the College had students in all four years of the curriculum, total annual enrollments under Johnson never exceeded twenty-five students. By 1758, the year of the first graduating class, a pattern had been set that would persist throughout the remaining nineteen years of King's College's existence: entering classes would consist of fewer than ten students, only five or six of whom would eventually graduate. In all, 226 young men became students at King's College, exactly half of whom, 113, graduated.[88]

That the considerably older Harvard and Yale had larger entering classes, greater overall enrollments, and higher graduation rates than King's College might have been expected. But so did the rurally situated College of New Jersey, which opened only a decade before King's. And so, once under way, would the subsequently founded Rhode Island (Brown), Queens (Rutgers), and Dartmouth. Of the so-called Colonial Nine, only the virtually moribund William and Mary and the College of Philadelphia posted comparably anemic numbers.[89]

At a meeting of the board of governors in late 1761, during discussion of Cooper's possible appointment as professor of moral philosophy, the seldom-attending Oliver DeLancey asked of the other governors: "What need [have we] of so many tutors for so few scholars?" President Johnson took the question to be personally directed, evidence that some governors wanted him to resign before Cooper was appointed. The minutes of the meeting do not contain a reply. Nor is there any indication that the question was ever asked again, certainly not by DeLancey, who thereafter reverted to his earlier absentee ways.[90]

But one might ask the question. Fifteen individuals taught at King's College during its twenty-two-year history. This includes the six-member medical faculty and both presidents. There were almost never more than three King's College faculty in residence at one time, counting the president. For long stretches, the College made do with two. During President Johnson's absences in 1756–57, before Treadwell's arrival, and again in 1759–60, with Treadwell terminally ill, tutor Cutting soldiered on alone. Similarly, when Cooper was in England in 1771–72, teaching was pretty much left to Clossy and Harpur. After Cooper's hasty departure in 1775, all instruction again devolved on Clossy, with some help from acting president and sometime tutor Benjamin Moore. Thus the charge of faculty overstaffing lacks backing.

The second half of DeLancey's accusatory question—why so few scholars?—did not go unnoted. When Harvard alumnus John Adams passed through New York City on his way to the First Continental Congress in 1774, he was shown around King's College, now entering its third decade of existence. He later recorded his principal impressions: "There is but one building at this Colledge, and that is very far from full of Scholars. They never had 40 scholars at a time."[91]

Adams had not happened on King's College in an off year. In 1774 it enrolled more students—36—and conferred the highest number of baccalaureate degrees—10—in its history. Harvard in the early 1770s annually graduated five times that many, its class of 1771 numbering 63 graduates. Similarly, where Adams pegged the total enrollment at King's at under 40, enrollments at Harvard often topped 200, eight times those of King's. Yale's enrollment and graduation numbers were slightly below Harvard's but four times those of King's.[92]

Part of the College's putative enrollment problem was geographical. With Yale fifty miles to the east, Princeton (after its move from Newark) fifty miles to the southwest, and the College of Philadelphia ninety miles to the southwest, King's College was in the center of a two-hundred-mile corridor already saturated with colleges. New York above and west of Albany was still primeval forest populated by Indians. King's College lacked a hinterland of its own. There was, of course, New York City, but in the third quarter of the eighteenth century, its population between fifteen and eighteen thousand, it was smaller than both Boston and Philadelphia and growing more slowly than Philadelphia.

Finally, the addition of Queen's College (Rutgers) in 1766 added to the collegiate clutter of the Middle Colonies, and that school competed directly with King's for the sons of New York's Dutch families. The half-dozen New Englanders King's College attracted all came from southwestern Connecticut, while Long Islanders, though long part of New York Province, continued to send their college-bound sons across the Sound to Yale. King's admitted more students from the West Indies—on the order of a dozen—than from all twelve of the other American colonies.[93]

While King's College gained as many transfers as it lost, particularly with the opening of its Medical School in 1767, its dropout rate was the highest among colonial colleges. Many, as the College registry recorded, "Left to business" or "Went to Merchandize." Still others dropped out during the French and Indian War to sign on as privateers or to enlist in the army. (The participation rate of King's College students in the College's first war likely exceeded that of Columbia students in all if its subsequent nine wars!) Still other students left King's after a couple years to enter legal apprenticeships or "to study physic." And, finally, the College had perhaps more than its share of students who "after three years went to nothing" or "left in his third year and was not much regretted."[94]

The College's identification with the Anglican Church, as Livingston had warned, also imposed a low ceiling on the number of potential applicants. The few Anglican families in New England clustered around Boston, along the Connecticut River, and in southwestern Connecticut begrudgingly but dependably sent their college-going sons to Harvard or Yale. The opening of King's did not alter this pattern. Anglicans were more numerous in the south, but few sent their sons off to college, and fewer still sent them as far away as New York. For sons of southern Anglicans venturing north, the Virginian James Madison a case in point, Princeton was the college of choice. The exception-proving-the-rule case is George Washington, who did send his stepson, John Parke Custis, to King's College in 1773, accompanied by his black slave "Joe." Custis lasted three months before exhausting his year's allowance and plotting an elopement with a girl back home.[95]

All colonial colleges drew most of their students from nearby, but none from as nearby as King's did. Fully 90 percent of its students came from within thirty miles of the College, most from within easy walking distance. Of the five thousand or so families residing within the three miles that constituted settled Lower Manhattan in the two decades before the Revolutionary War, four-fifths of these families had neither the financial wherewithal nor the inclination to send an employable son to college, leaving one thousand or so families, less than a quarter of whom were likely to be Anglican, not all of these with college-age sons. This reduced the number of eligible families to perhaps one hundred fifty, or about the number attending Sunday services at Trinity Church. In calling King's College "the College of Trinity Church," William Livingston and other anti-Anglican critics sought to score a political point. They also captured a persistent demographic reality.

Considering its shallow recruitment pool, that King's managed every year to have some new students could be deemed an accomplishment. It did so by drawing nearly all of them from the same three dozen or so New York City families, Anglican, Dutch Reformed, or Dutch-becoming-Anglican. Of King's College's 226 students, I have been able to identify the family religion of 168; of these, 163 (97 percent) were Anglican, Dutch Reformed, or somewhere in between. The five identified non-Anglicans were Presbyterian (3), Moravian (1), or Jewish (1). No other colonial college student body even approached the denominational homogeneity of King's College.[96]

The almost equally endogamous character of King's College manifests itself in several ways. Half its students shared their family name with at least one other student, with just fifteen family names accounting for nearly a quarter (53 of 226) of all students. More than a quarter are identifiable as the sons, grandsons, or nephews of governors, while a substantial majority of governors (thirty-five of fifty-nine) are identifiable as blood relatives of King's College students. The twenty sons of just eight governors account for nearly 10 percent of all King's College students. If one could as easily trace the more elusive ties by marriage and maternal lines, the result would surely approximate inbreeding of Snopesian proportions. One way the faculty coped with the extended cousinage that was the King's College student body was to identify interfamilial miscreants in the "Black Book of Misdemeanors" as "Nicoll1," "Auchmuty2," "Cruger3."[97]

One instance of the College's pervasive consanguinity must suffice. The New York merchant Andrew DePeyster, ex officio governor by virtue of his position as provincial treasurer, sent his second son, Abraham, to King's College. Abraham (KC 1763) was followed by two grandsons, David and James. DePeyster's first son, James, married the daughter of Joseph Reade, another King's College governor, while one of Andrew DePeyster's daughters married into a branch of the Livingston family that sent six boys to King's. In addition, through his wife, a Van Cortlandt, Andrew DePeyster was the uncle of at least two other King's College students, Philip (KC 1758) and William Van Cortlandt (1757–59), who were in turn the cousins of Henry (KC 1766), Anthony (1757–60), and Harmin Rutgers (1770–72), James Van Horne (1760–61), and Samuel Provoost (KC 1758). Small world, indeed.[98]

Students admitted to King's College were substantially younger than elsewhere. Whereas the average entry age at Princeton was seventeen, it was fifteen at King's. Moreover, Princeton and the other colonial colleges regularly admitted students well into their twenties and financially on their own, whereas I can find only seven instances of King's admitting someone older than nineteen. Alexander Hamilton's matriculation in 1774 at seventeen places him among the oldest, while that of Gouverneur Morris (class of 1763), who began his career at the College two month shy of thirteen, was by no means the youngest.[99]

A final characteristic of King's College students is worth noting: they paid substantially higher tuition and fees. Throughout Johnson's presidency, tuition was pegged at five pounds a year, with fees adding another four pounds. Both went up under Cooper, when the total annual costs of sending a son to King's could exceed twenty-five pounds, or three times the going annual wage in New York for sailors and bookkeepers. No amount of urban indexing can wholly account for the costs of going to King's College being twice those of Princeton and half again those of Harvard. Moreover, unlike other colonial colleges, King's offered no financial aid. When the merchant Edward Antill, on giving the equivalent of twelve hundred pounds in New York currency to the College in 1757, suggested that some portion of the money might be used for the education of talented poor boys, President Johnson and the governors declined to take up the suggestion.[100]

The question remains: If all other colonial colleges charged less, discounted more deeply, recruited more aggressively, and tried all manner of other strategies to make themselves attractive to an ever-growing number of young men beyond their region and denomination who might come and remain with them through graduation, why didn't King's College? A simple two-part answer suggests itself: It did not want to, and it did not need to.

King's College Is Rich

Two imperatives prompted other colleges to increase enrollments. The first was financial necessity, which could most readily be relieved by increases in tuition income. The second was evangelical aspirations, which would best be met by aggressively recruiting students of other religious persuasions. Most colonial colleges were motivated less by belief in religious tolerance than by financial necessity and the hope of religious conversions.

The financial imperative simply did not apply at King's College: the College was rich. In 1775 it was by far the richest college in colonial America, richer even than the older and larger Harvard and Yale but also richer than the aggressively fund-raising colleges of New Jersey and Philadelphia. The accumulated endowment of all nine colonial colleges on the eve of the Revolution amounted to twenty-four thousand pounds sterling, of which debt-free King's share was ten thousand pounds sterling, three times that of its nearest competitors, Harvard and Princeton, both of which carried substantial capital debt.[101]

The College's wealth came from many sources. The four separate lotteries approved by the New York Assembly between 1748 and 1753, however diminished in the subsequent political haggling, yielded the College nearly thirty-eight hundred pounds in public funding. Together, they exceeded the public support received by any of the other colonial colleges. In addition, two private benefactions early on from two childless Trinity communicants and College governors, Paul Richard and Joseph Murray, helped pay for the building and kept the College debt-free. Murray's bequest in 1758 of eight thousand pounds was the largest single philanthropic gift made in colonial America. The land grant from Trinity Church, with an assessed value of ten thousand pounds, provided the site for the College and adjoining properties that the College leased out. Water lots acquired from New York City in the mid-1760s provided another dependable revenue stream.[102]

Fund-raising in England and the West Indies, the former orchestrated by John Jay's rather shady older brother, Sir James Jay, though fraught with recriminations and threatened litigation, yielded another six thousand pounds, including a private benefaction of five hundred pounds from King George III. And, finally, two huge grants of land east and north of Albany to the College from Governor Moore in 1768 and Governor Tryon in 1772 held out the prospect of future revenues. King's could easily afford to pay its presidents (five hundred pounds a year) and faculty (two hundred a year) more generously than their counterparts elsewhere—and still have College funds to loan out at 5 percent interest.[103]

Allowing that King's College was not under financial pressure to enroll more students, would not its leaders have done so on evangelical grounds? Anglicans in the King's College era were willing to accept converts, but they were not disposed to go far in pursuit of them. They saw no need to apologize for special privileges being conferred on them. Such privileges properly came with membership in the established church, not with membership in a numerical majority. Furthermore, such privileges, along with their aesthetically pleasing sacramental liturgy and a non-Calvinist theology, were thought to be enough to assure a steady expansion of the Anglican ranks, without resort to the extraordinary exertions Dissenters made to swell theirs. Something of the difference between Anglicans and Dissenters here calls to mind the difference imputed (by Federalists) between Federalists and Republicans a generation later: the former were willing to "stand for office," whereas the later were ready "to run for office."[104]

This difference between Dissenters and Anglicans also revealed itself in a 1772 exchange of pamphlets between Princeton's president, the Reverend Dr. John Witherspoon, and the King's College professor-elect of natural law, John Vardill. As part of a fund-raising and recruiting tour of the British West Indies, Witherspoon, a Scot recently come to America after his Republicanism made him suspect in some British quarters, had printed his *Address to the Inhabitants of Jamaica*. He began with several swipes at Oxford and Cambridge for their various shortcomings, chief among them their opulence and hostility to Dissenters. He then went on, in the way of commending Princeton, to warn his audience against sending their sons to colleges in "principal Cities." In addition to the moral temptations and pestilence, there was also the added cost of everything, including college going.[105]

It is not immediately clear why the twenty-three-year-old Vardill decided that Witherspoon's *Address* required a response. He may have been put up to it by President Cooper, who was sponsoring Vardill's pending visit to England for Anglican ordination. He may also have been hoping to ingratiate himself with his Oxford hosts by defending the English universities against charges leveled by a Scot heading a Dissenting college in the provinces. Then again, Vardill might have been unwilling to let the "peculiar complacency" of views so alien to a native New Yorker and King's College graduate go unchallenged.[106]

Vardill's *Candid Remarks on Dr. Witherspoon's Address to the Inhabitants of Jamaica* is a remarkable piece of pamphleteering. It took up each of Witherspoon's arguments in turn, to show that "the advocate of the College of Princeton has elevated it to an eminence which is far from being its due." The animadversions with respect to Oxford and Cambridge he quickly dismisses as unfair and ill advised coming from a British subject. But it is in satirizing Witherspoon's descriptions of Princeton as "the last happy asylum of virtue" that Vardill achieves a distinctly cosmopolitan voice. It is simply not true, he wrote, that the setting for King's College is any less healthy than that of Princeton. As for the cultural resources of the two locales, New York wins hands down over Princeton, which Vardill dismisses as "remote from the sea, in the middle of a country abounding in woods and swamps uncleared." Whereas in New York students could expect to mix with "the most celebrated men in law and physics, learned men in medicine and law," Princeton offered only local farmers "of no remarkable importance." [107]

Vardill took even more offense to Witherspoon's unseemly appeal to the economic self-interest of his audience. He readily conceded that Princeton was cheaper than King's College—and that it had more students. "The expenses being inconsiderable," he explained, "the Farmers around are induced to collect from their earning a pittance for the instruction of their sons at college." Whereas Witherspoon—the good country Whig that he was—argued that a college should keep its costs down to increase enrollments, Vardill—the urbane Tory—disagreed. For him, increasing enrollments should no more be a college's primary desideratum than should cost containment that locked students away in the wilderness without the cultural amenities available in urban centers like New York. What King's offered, William Smith Jr. had said on the eve of its founding, was precisely what Vardill held out for his readers eighteen years later: "the Education of all who can afford such Education."[108]

The ideological persuasion of King's College was not majoritarian or inclusive but elitist and exclusive. The governors had no plans and little incentive to open the College's doors so wide as to accommodate more than their own sons, their own kind. But more than social exclusiveness and elitist ideology were operating here. An examination of the occupational outcomes of King's College students suggests that the families who constituted King's College also had reasons of economic self-interest to restrict access to the benefits of *their* college.

"Ladder to the Top of the Profession"

More than half the fifty-nine New Yorkers who served as governors of King's College made their livings as merchants or landowner-merchants. Many were of the second or third generations in their families to do so. The next most common occupation among the governors was the law (20 percent). Ministers were next (16 percent), a considerable presence but smaller than clergymen enjoyed on most other college governing boards, where they were typically in the majority. Still, ministers easily outnumbered doctors, of whom there was only one.[109]

The occupational distribution of King's College students differs from the governors, except that about the same proportion took up the ministry (11 percent). They were less than a third as likely to enter business (13 percent) as their elders and more than twice as likely to go into the law (28 percent) or medicine (20 percent). In effect, King's College became the means by which many of the families sending their sons there shifted their economic fortunes from a reliance on the lucrative but risky and nonexclusive arena of New York commerce and trade into what they hoped would be the equally lucrative, socially more redeeming, and access-controlled New York professions.[110]

A case in point is provided by the family of the Revolutionary statesman John Jay (KC 1764). Jay's grandfather Augustus Jay, who came from Huguenot-hostile France to New York as a boy in the 1670s, and his father, Peter Jay, were both successful merchants. Marriage into the Van Cortlandt family by Augustus and into the Bayard family by Peter extended their commercial connections and confirmed their high social standing. But when it came time for Peter's sons to take up careers, their options extended beyond the family countinghouse. James Jay, Peter's first son to live into adolescence, decided to study medicine and went with his father's blessings to Edinburgh. As for John, his father approvingly reported to President Johnson at the beginning of his son's second year at King's College, he "is bent upon a learned profession. I believe it will be the law."[111]

Becoming a lawyer in New York in the 1760s required more than the appro-

priate bent. In 1730, scarcely three decades after the New York bar took rudimentary form, a half-dozen of its leading members introduced a seven-year
apprenticeship requirement to limit the number of lawyers who could practice
before the provincial supreme court. The time and expense of apprenticeship
(apprentices paid for the privilege of becoming a practicing lawyer's copy clerk)
were but the first means devised by the New York bar to limit access.

In 1756, two years after King's College opened, the New York bar, now com-
prising some forty members, proposed more restrictive measures. Henceforth,
only college graduates would be accepted for legal apprenticeships, for six years,
and members of the bar would be limited to one apprentice at a time. The bar
also agreed to support a moratorium on all apprenticeships for twelve years.

While the New York bar in the 1750s had its college graduates, about equally
divided between Cambridge (England) and Yale, most of its members had
secured their own places in the profession without benefit of a college degree.
Requiring a college degree for all future lawyers was an instance of those aboard
pulling up the ladder. For the newly underway King's College, however, the 1756
provisions added a new responsibility as gatekeeper to the New York legal profession, a responsibility both the College and the bar understood would be met
by limiting enrollments.[112]

By Jay's senior year, the twelve-year moratorium on accepting apprentices
had been lifted but not the limitation on law offices employing one apprentice
at a time. All the Jay family's social connections were needed—and a four-hun-
dred-pound fee—to secure John a place in Benjamin Kissam's law office a week
after his graduation in 1764. Similar outlays would be required of the families
of Jay's senior classmate, Richard Harison (KC 1764), as well as those of juniors
Robert R. Livingston (KC 1765) and Egbert Benson (KC 1765), sophomore Peter
Van Schaack (KC 1767), and thirteen-year-old freshman Gouverneur Morris
(KC 1768), all of whom, in the fullness of time and by calling on the necessary
connections, would join Jay at the New York bar.

Once admitted to practice, these King's College graduates came together with
a select few of their seniors at the bar and on the bench in 1771 to organize "The
Moot," a quasi-professional, quasi-social club considered the crème de la crème
of the New York legal fraternity. While a King's College degree was not a condition for membership, none of the younger members lacked for one. By the eve of
the Revolution, King's College graduates had achieved a numerically commanding position within the New York bar. Who among these favored few would have
urged their alma mater to open its doors more widely? More likely they were one
with Myles Cooper, who, following the 1764 King's College commencement ceremonies, at which there were only two graduates (both later lawyers), informed
the local newspapers: "It would be injurious to the Reputation of the College, not

to observe, that ample Amends were made for the number of candidates, by the Display of their proficiency and in the Elegance of their Performances."[113]

Another manifestation of the professional and social exclusiveness that animated the upper reaches of the New York legal community and King's College can be found in the early biography of John Jay, as related by the Columbia historian Richard Morris. In 1772 Jay rejected an application to the Dancing Assembly from one Robert Randall, who thereupon challenged Jay to a duel. Rather than take up Randall's challenge, Jay coolly explained the reasons for the rejection: "You did not appear to me to be connected with the People who frequent the Assembly and as such a connection was in my opinion necessary to entitle one to admission."[114]

The professional enclosure of medicine in late colonial New York lagged behind the law, but not so much that its leading representatives were not seeking ways to restrict practice to a learned few. In 1760, at the urging of New York's leading doctors, the New York Assembly passed a licensing requirement that obligated all future physicians within the province to pass a qualifying examination. This was the first such legislation in the American colonies.[115]

Within a decade of the founding of King's College, the idea of linking the professional aspirations of New York doctors to the progress of New York's own college took hold. The first to propose such a connection was John Jay's older brother, the Edinburgh-educated Dr. James Jay. While raising funds in the British Isles, Jay volunteered to recruit some Edinburgh physicians to come to New York and attach themselves to the College as its medical faculty. But Jay's medical colleagues in New York were leery of his motives and suspected him of "building a ladder by which he might climb to the top of the profession." Nothing ever came of Jay's proposal for King's College, though a variant of it led directly to the establishment of the first colonial medical school at the College of Philadelphia, in 1765. It did, however, bespeak the existence of the same interest in raising access requirements among New York physicians as among New York attorneys.[116]

Meanwhile, a group of forty or so New York doctors organized themselves into an informal medical society and began developing their own plans for a medical school. Chief among them was Dr. Samuel Bard, son of the city's leading physician and a student at King's College for two years before he took up medical studies in London and Edinburgh. Others included Dr. Peter Middleton, trained at St. Andrews; Dr. John Jones, a surgeon with a medical degree from the University of Rheims; and the previously mentioned Irishman, Dr. Samuel Clossy. On November 2, 1767, the governors of King's College voted to permit Bard, Middleton, and Clossy to use College Hall to deliver medical lectures to paying audiences. In all, a total of six physicians (the two others were

Drs. James Smith and John V. Tennent) were appointed to the King's College faculty, a move facilitated by the fact that all went without salaries and relied on direct student payments for compensation. Theirs was the first comprehensive course in medical studies offered in the British colonies.[117]

The relationship between King's College and the New York medical community was even tighter than the one between the College and the legal community. Intended to credential a limited number of premedical students as it did prelaw students, the College also provided medical instruction. Legal instruction was not offered at King's College. The Faculty of Medicine devised two degrees in medicine, both of which, as mandated by the 1760 licensing legislation, constituted a license to practice without recourse to the examination required of those without degrees. The first degree, an M.B., would be awarded to those who attended King's College for two years after completing a three-year apprenticeship. The M.D. was reserved for those who returned to King's College after completing their apprenticeship for a third year of lectures and a formal examination.[118]

Initial interest in the medical curriculum ran high. In the first year, 1767, three of the College's nine entering students registered as medical students; in 1768 six of thirteen; in 1769 six of twelve. Of these fifteen students, nine graduated with an M.B. degree. In the next six years, however, five more students signed up for the full program of medical lectures but only one stayed on for his M.B. degree. Of the ten M.B.s, two—Robert Tucker and Samuel Kissam—completed the requirements for the M.D.[119]

Several reasons suggest why the Medical School's early promise went unfulfilled. Like everything else at King's College, the medical program was lengthy and expensive. Nor could it assure that those who stuck it out would find their way professionally. Some of the medical faculty may have lost interest in the school once they were caught up in the planning of New York Hospital, the cornerstone for which was laid in 1770. Neither President Cooper nor the leading governors took an active interest in the Medical School. No governors directed their sons to it. Cooper may have been as much disturbed by the presence of two Presbyterians among the medical faculty as by their insistent rationalist ethic. In treating his own case of gout, the president relied on unlicensed quacks.[120]

The Medical School of King's College failed to transform the practice of medicine in New York City and was, on the eve of the Revolution, a dwindling presence at the College. But it was not without its instructive benefits, particularly if we keep in mind Columbia's subsequent involvement in professional education. Students received the best formal training then available to domestically trained American physicians; in turn, they provided much of the professional leadership for American medicine into the nineteenth century.

Equally important, the Medical School espoused an inclusive ideology otherwise absent in the College. While President Johnson had assured non-Anglicans that they would be welcome at King's College and President Cooper limited his Anglican triumphalism to his English correspondents, Professors Bard and Clossy actively recruited students from the region's Presbyterian and Quaker families. Clossy was virtually alone among faculty and governors in openly worrying about declining enrollments and urging lower fees as a means of attracting more ambitious students.[121]

It is not surprising that among the two dozen medical students and half-dozen medical faculty is to be found what passes for social diversity at King's College. Less than half the medical students were identified as Anglicans, while five of the College's seven identifiable non-Anglican students were medical students. King's College's only identifiable Jewish student, Isaac Abrahams (KC 1774), the son of a merchant-turned-rabbi, while not formally a medical student, was one of ten or so regular students who sat in on medical lectures and went on to become doctors. Presbyterian Alexander Hamilton nearly did the same but for intervening political events. But such leanings toward nondenominationalism, ethnic diversity, and the creation of a professional meritocracy to be discerned in its Medical School did not offset the overall reality of King's College as a bastion of Anglican orthodoxy, Tory self-satisfaction, and social ascription. They did, however, hold out the prospect of a more diverse college in another time.[122]

Farewell Aristocracy

Of all the ways King's College differed from its colonial peers, none stands in such sharp relief as its corporate attitude toward the struggle between the colonies and Great Britain that led to the American Revolution. Whereas other colonial colleges publicly supported the break with England when it came, with greater or lesser enthusiasm, King's College opposed it and remained loyal to the crown. The governors of the College of Philadelphia, to be sure, were not exactly rabid in their patriotic militancy, and Harvard had a few Loyalists in the faculty, on its governing boards, and among the alumni, but overall, and especially at Yale, Brown, Dartmouth, and Princeton, active support of the Revolution was the norm. As one of Yale's few Tories lamented, his college was "a nursery of sedition, of faction, and republicanism."[123]

Despite inventive efforts by Columbia chroniclers such as John Henry Van Amringe and Frederick Keppel retroactively to enlist King's College in the revolutionary cause, it was Loyalist throughout. In May 1775, in the wake of clashes at Lexington-Concord, President Cooper, who two weeks earlier had exchanged his College lodgings for the HMS *Kingfisher*, then anchored in the harbor, departed New York City. He did so just ahead of a mob bent on doing him serious harm for his Tory sentiments and alleged pamphleteering efforts on behalf of the crown. Cooper's politics were the antithesis of Princeton president John Witherspoon's, praised by John Adams in 1774 for being "as high a son of liberty as any man in America."[124]

But Cooper was far from alone in his Loyalism. Of the College's nine faculty (including the medical faculty) alive in 1775, seven aligned themselves with England. Only tutor Robert Harpur, the butt of frequent student escapades, became a vigorous patriot. Among the governors, the ratio of identifiable Loyalists (twenty-six) to Patriots (three) was more than eight to one. Whereas at Harvard an estimated 16 percent, at Yale 10 percent, and at Princeton only 2 percent of living graduates in 1776 sided with the crown, among the 148 King's College students whose revolutionary politics have been identified, 72 percent (107) were Loyalists, and 20 percent (29) were Patriots. It has been estimated that nearly half the 170 students at Princeton between 1769 and 1775 fought in the Revolution on the side of independence. Of the 226 students attending King's College during this period, 25 are known to have taken up arms, 21 on the side of the crown. These are striking numbers, even among New Yorkers, whose political leadership was far less committed to the revolutionary cause than those of Massachusetts and Virginia. With the possible exception of Trinity Church itself, it would be difficult to identify another American institution that exceeded King's College in the comprehensiveness of its continued fealty to the crown.[125]

The reason for this is clear enough. When push came to shove in 1775, virtually no one identified with King's College (or Trinity Church) could have imagined his or her life being improved by New York's withdrawal from the empire. That is not to say that they did not have individual grievances with English colonial policies. Even the most conservative governors of King's College shared with their more militant fellow New Yorkers the view that taxing colonial commercial activities was a bad idea. They so expressed themselves at the time of the Stamp Act in 1765 and upon subsequent efforts of Parliament to extract revenue from the colonies. But other issues that took on empire-breaking magnitude elsewhere, such as the imposition of troops and perceived threats to dissenting religious denominations that held political sway in several colonies, the Anglican elite of New York took in stride. Unlike Boston, for example, New York City had long accommodated a substantial military presence, and British army officers enjoyed a favored place in the city's social activities. Some sent sons to King's College, and several married into King's College families.

The leading New York merchants fully recognized the benefits they derived from membership in the empire—and the risks of going along with the demands of their less connected and more scrambling competitors. The Cruger family—with their four King's College governors and three King's College students—are a case in point. Trading links carefully developed by the patriarch, Henry Cruger, with the British West Indies, where son Teleman Cruger maintained the family countinghouse, and with Bristol, England, where son Henry Cruger Jr. represented the city (along with Edmund Burke) in Parliament, were not about to be jeopardized to satisfy the demands of New York's lesser merchants for unregulated trade. Business is business.[126]

Other King's College families, like that headed by Governor Frederick Philipse, with immense landholdings (Philipse owned one-quarter of Westchester County), title to which had come from and been confirmed by the crown, saw no economic purpose in aligning with troublemakers, especially should they seek popular support by clamoring for tenants' rights. So, too, the family of Governor William Kempe—who had such a lock on the post of provincial attorney general that upon his retirement he passed it to his son, John Tabor Kempe—had long enjoyed mutually beneficial relationships with crown officials, and claims to crown offices had become too much a way of life to be put at risk.[127]

For the New York merchants, landholders, and crown appointees who headed many King's College families, the tensions between the colonies and England were viewed as the unfortunate result of untimely parliamentary legislation and an overreaction on the part of colonial troublemakers. But for families professionally identified with the Anglican Church, the tensions were exacerbated by Parliament's unwillingness to place bishops in the colonies and to secure for the Anglican communion in America the full rights and privileges of the established church. For Trinity Church rector Henry Barclay, the terms "Presbyterian" and "Republican" were interchangeable, as they were for the Reverends Samuel Johnson and Myles Cooper. Not surprisingly, then, of all the King's College families, it was the clerics for whom the decision to remain loyal to the crown seems to have been the most foregone. Thus the son and two nephews of governor Reverend Henry Barclay—Thomas (KC 1772), James (KC 1766), and Thomas (1763–65)—all sided with the crown, as did governor Reverend Samuel Auchmuty's three sons—Samuel (KC 1775), Robert (KC 1774), and Richard (KC 1775). Richard Auchmuty was captured and died as a prisoner of the Continental Army, while his brother Samuel, though intended for the ministry, continued on in the British Army after Yorktown, eventually becoming commander-in-chief of all British forces in Ireland. All eleven King's College graduates who had been ordained as Anglican ministers sided with the crown, some as chaplains in the British Army, while another, John Vardill, exploited his college ties with the unwitting John Jay and Gouverneur Morris and other American revolutionaries (including Silas Deane) in serving as an English secret agent.[128]

What then of the famous King's Men Revolutionaries? Two points: first, there weren't many of them; and, second, for most of them, the decision to side with the Revolution was a very near thing. Perhaps least so for Alexander Hamilton (1774–75), whose links with the Anglican establishment were only as solid as a bright and ambitious young man just up from the Caribbean and raised as a Presbyterian could make them. He possessed neither wealth nor family to ease his way, and John Adams's characterization of him as "the bastard brat of a Scotch peddler," if unkind, was genealogically precise. He had little to lose in siding with the Revolution or to gain by lining up with the crown. Even so, if there is any truth to the story that it was Hamilton—"That divine boy"—who awakened Cooper in time to escape from a mob bent on his capture, it suggests Hamilton was not entirely committed to the revolutionary cause. His subsequent place in New York society was a result of his exemplary revolutionary efforts at Washington's side and then confirmed by marriage to a Schuyler. Even so, as Hamilton's postrevolutionary politics made clear, he was hardly an enthusiastic republican and favored governance by "the right sort."[129]

John Jay (KC 1764) also sided with the Revolution but as one of the more reluctant of generally reluctant New Yorkers to do so. Marriage in 1774 to the daughter of William Livingston, of *Independent Reflector* fame and subsequently the revolutionary governor of New Jersey, may had made the difference between him and, say, Peter Van Schaack (KC 1766), a college friend and law colleague. Van Schaack refused to disavow the sovereignty of the crown in 1776, and his wartime activities, while punctiliously neutral, were nonetheless deemed sufficiently conspiratorial by Jay in his official capacities as a member of the New York provisional government to confiscate Van Schaack's properties. Jay liked being sent by his friends and neighbors to represent them in various deliberative bodies, among them successive Continental Congresses, New York's provincial government, and the New York Constitutional Convention. Once at these gatherings, he managed to do as little glad-handing as possible and no more than befit his standing in both the old and new orders. After all, as this King's College revolutionary was later given to remind his correspondents, "those who own the country ought to govern it."[130]

Of the handful of King's College's notable revolutionaries, Gouverneur Morris (KC 1766) was the most consciously self-denying in siding with the future against the past. His mother, three sisters, and their husbands all remained loyal to the crown, hoping thereby to protect their estates and crown offices. Morris understood that to throw in with the Revolution was to align with a movement wherein "a herd of mechanicks are preferred before the first families in the colony." But throw in he did, perhaps under the influence of his oldest brother, Lewis Morris, a delegate to the Second Continental Congress and a signer of the Declaration of Independence. Unlike Hamilton and Jay, or even Robert R. Livingston (KC 1766), whose revolutionary activities were rewarded with the chancellorship of New York and several diplomatic posts, Morris gained little for siding with the new order. After a string of wartime jobs, a move to Pennsylvania, and participation in the 1787 Constitutional Convention, he spent a decade in Europe, where he carried out several important diplomatic assignments for President Washington. He then returned to New York in late 1799.[131]

A year later Morris was chosen by the state legislature as United States Senator from New York and served in that post for two years. Thereafter he served in a number of civic capacities that did not require popular election. His last political activities (he died in 1816) involved the 1814–15 Hartford convention, whose like-minded participants, if not openly secessionist, at least countenanced the breakup of the Republic. Such an outcome would not have surprised Morris. Thirty-eight years earlier, in 1774, the twenty-three-year-old Morris saw clearly "at a grand division of the city" what the future held:

My fellow citizens fairly contended about the future forms of our government, whether it should be founded upon aristocratic or democratic principles. . . . On my right hand were ranged all the people of property . . . and on the other all the tradesmen. . . . The spirit of the English Constitution has yet a little influence left, and but a little. The remains of it, however, will give the wealthy people a superiority this time, but the mob begin to think and reason. . . . The gentry begin to fear this. Their committees will be appointed, they will deceive the people, and again forfeit a share of their confidence. And if these instances of what with one side is policy, with the other perfidy, shall continue to increase, and become more frequent, farewell aristocracy.[132]

Farewell aristocracy—but also farewell to King's College and what William Livingston called "its present narrow principles." Monarchist and establishmentarian in its politics, elitist and exclusive in its social arrangements, the College bid fair to number among the first casualties of the American Revolution. But even should it survive into the early days of the new republic, what then? Almost certain marginality, should the College persist in its original mission of consolidating and perpetuating privilege. At least in prerevolutionary and Anglican New York, it had enjoyed the short-lived benefits of like-minded friends in high places.

FIGURE 1.1 Putative portrait of Edward Hyde, Viscount Cornbury, governor of New York and New Jersey, 1702–8. Early proponent of a college in New York.

FIGURE 1.2 Lewis Morris (1671–1748), prominent landowner and officeholder. Early proponent of a college in New York.

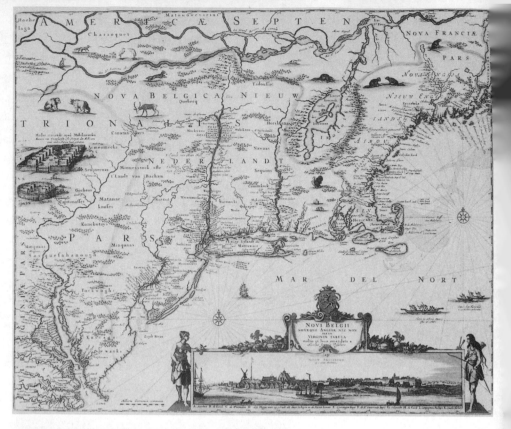

FIGURE 1.3 Novi Belgi map of New York, New Jersey, and Pennsylvania (1685).

Source: Paul E. Cohen and Robert T. Augustyn, *Manhattan in Maps: 1527–1995* (New York: Rizzoli, 1997), 33.

FIGURE 1.4 Ratzer map of Lower Manhattan (1757). Depicts original locale of King's College in upper-right corner of middle-left pane.

Source: Paul E. Cohen and Robert T. Augustyn, *Manhattan in Maps: 1527–1995* (New York: Rizzoli, 1995), 74.

FIGURE 1.5 William Livingston (1723–90), New York attorney and leading critic of the establishment of King's College. The painting is by Albert Rosenthal after Charles Wilson Peale.

Source: Columbia University Archives-—Columbiana Collection.

FIGURE 1.6 Samuel Johnson (1696-1772), leading Anglican minister in America and first president of King's College (1754–63). Painting by unknown artist hangs in the King's College Room, Columbia University.

Source: Columbia University Archives—Columbiana Collection.

FIGURE 1.7 Myles Cooper (1737–85), Oxford graduate, Anglican minister, and second president of King's College (1763–75). Portrait by John Singleton Copley hangs in King's College Room, Columbia University.

Source: Columbia University Archives—Columbiana Collection.

FIGURE 1.8 William Samuel Johnson (1727–1819), lawyer, signer of the Federal Constitution, and third president of Columbia College (1787–1800). The painting is by S. L. Waldo after Gilbert Stuart.

Source: Columbia University Archives—Columbiana Collection.

FIGURE 1.9 Palm tree detail of Columbia College. The print appeared in *Scenographia Americana; or, A Collection of Views of North America and the West Indies . . .* , published in London in 1768.

Source: Columbia University Archives—Columbiana Collection.

FIGURE 1.10 DeWitt Clinton (1769–1828), member of the first graduating class of Columbia College (1786), later governor of New York, mayor of New York City, and a leading proponent of the the construction of the Erie Canal.

Source: Columbia University Archives—Columbiana Collection.

CHAPTER 2

Flirting with Republicanism

Columbia College might suit in a worn-out aristocracy, but not in a republic like ours.

New York Courier and Enquirer, January 21, 1830

Wartime Downtime

T HE Revolutionary War disrupted operations at most American colleges. Harvard and Yale canceled their commencements in the wake of the clashes at Lexington and Concord in April 1775. During the subsequent siege of Boston, Harvard Yard was occupied by Washington's forces, and the College was relocated to Concord until the British forces evacuated Boston in March 1776. The College of Philadelphia was occupied first by revolutionary forces in the fall of 1775 and later by the British; it did not reopen until the fall of 1779. The College of Rhode Island was similarly occupied by revolutionary troops and then used to garrison French forces. Yale came under direct assault from a British expeditionary force in 1778 and again in 1779. Princeton suffered the occupation of British forces for a month in early 1777 and periodically there-after lodged revolutionary forces until resuming operations in the fall of 1778. William and Mary kept largely out of harm's way, save for a fright from Corn-wallis's forces in 1781 on the eve of the Battle of Yorktown. Dartmouth got away clean, as did Rutgers.[1]

King's College experienced the longest and most nearly fatal shutdown. It occurred in stages. Cooper's departure from the College and New York just ahead of a revolutionary mob on May 25, 1775, prompted the governors to cancel the scheduled June commencement "for want of our absent president." They then appointed as acting president the Reverend Benjamin Moore, a twenty-seven-year-old graduate of the College, assistant minister of Trinity Church, and erstwhile tutor of rhetoric. Instruction of sorts resumed in the fall for a half-dozen students and persisted into the spring until, on April 6, 1776, College Hall was commandeered by the Revolutionary Committee of Safety for use as a military hospital. The college's library and scientific apparatus (aside from the two telescopes later appropriated by General George Washington) were scattered throughout the city. The 1776 commencement was canceled, though six students were designated as graduates.[2]

With New York City in the hands of Revolutionaries in the spring of 1776, several King's College governors known for their Loyalist sympathies decamped for safer ground, including Nova Scotia and the West Indies. Others left in the wake of the belated endorsement by the New York Provincial Congress, on July 9, 1776, of the Declaration of Independence. (New York's delegates to the Second Continental Congress, including John Jay, abstained from voting on the final version, which was signed on August 2.) By then, the announced British strategy of dividing the rebellious colonies made the occupation of New York by British forces only a matter of time and tide. A week earlier, an advanced force of ten thousand men under the command of General Sir William Howe landed on Long Island.

New York City fell to the British Army on September 15, 1776, with Washington and his troops barely escaping encirclement. The following day, in the Battle of Harlem Heights (on the present site of Columbia University), Washington himself was nearly captured before crossing over the Hudson to New Jersey. College Hall now became a British army hospital, but only after almost being burned to the ground when a fire set in the wake of the departure of the Continental army, which did destroy Trinity Church and much of the city's West Side, stopped at the southern fence of College Yard.[3]

A handful of King's College governors who remained in the city met in December 1776 in Hull's Tavern and again in the home of Governor Leonard Lispenard in March 1777 to discuss the possibility of opening the College under British protection. Lispenard offered his residence on Wall Street as a temporary site—for an annual rent of sixty pounds—and Governor William Walton offered his two sons as students. Acting president Moore was by then chaplain to the British forces, while Lispenard, who survived the war without declaring his politics (his wife was an arch Tory), attended to his various businesses as circumstances allowed. Ever the conscientious college treasurer, he seems to have thought that a reopened college might facilitate the collection of unpaid rents on college property. With the city now an armed camp and only a third of its prewar population in residence, nothing came of these discussions.[4]

College Hall remained a British army hospital for another six years, until, fully two years after the decisive American victory over Cornwallis at Yorktown in October 1781 (during which Colonel Alexander Hamilton distinguished himself in an assault on the British lines) and following the signing of the Treaty of Paris on September 3, 1783, the British after seven years finally departed New York City on November 25, 1783. Among the detritus left behind was the empty shell of a college so closely identified with the losing British cause as to make its prospects for revival highly problematic.

Resurrection in Two Acts: The 1784 Charter

In the spring of 1783, Trinity Church rector, ex–King's College governor, acting president (1771–72), and unreconstructed Loyalist Charles Inglis sought "the candour and judgment" of Trinity communicant, King's College governor, and active participant in the revolutionary cause James Duane. Inglis asked if staying on in New York after the departure of the British would be advisable. Duane almost certainly counseled against it, and Inglis, his personal properties already marked for confiscation, resigned the Trinity rectorship and left New York just ahead of the departing British.[5]

Before leaving New York, Inglis petitioned British authorities in England to establish a college in Nova Scotia, his destination, that would "diffuse religious literature, loyalty and good morals among His Majesty's subjects." In 1787, on being consecrated by the archbishop of Canterbury as the first colonial bishop of the Church of England, with ecclesiastical jurisdiction over all British North America, he established his episcopal see in Halifax. Three years later, in 1790, King's College of Nova Scotia opened under the protection of its royal charter and with the requisite Anglican cleric at its head. Thus transpired seven hundred miles to the northeast, in the city of Halifax, Nova Scotia, British Canada, what New York Anglicans had such high hopes of achieving thirty years earlier in their city: the union of church, state, and college.[6]

To New York's wartime governor, George Clinton, and even more so to New York City's first postwar mayor, James Duane, go the credit for retrieving New York's King's College from the dustbin of history to which Tory loyalties and eight years out of operation had nearly consigned it. It was Clinton, a Presbyterian, prewar political ally of William Livingston, revolutionary hero and since 1777 New York's first elected governor, who opened the state legislative session in January 1784 with a call for "a revival and encouragement of seminaries of learning." And it was Duane, Clinton's appointee as mayor, member of the state senate, and one of a handful of King's College governors and Trinity Church communicants whose vigorous wartime service commended him to a favorable postwar public hearing, who initiated discussion in the New York Senate for the creation of a "state university" that would assume the property of King's College under a new name and new charter.[7]

On March 24, 1784, the senate received a "Petition of Governors of King's College" urging adoption of Duane's proposal. Of the six signatories, only Leonard Lispenard had served as a governor of King's College; the others presumed to the title by holding positions that would have rated ex officio membership on the King's College board under the 1754 charter. Three of these petitioners—John Rodgers, minister of the First Presbyterian Church; John Morrin Scott, one of William Livingston's collaborators on the *Independent Reflector*; and George Clinton—were Presbyterians and warm supporters of the revolutionary cause. One may safely assume that it was not their intention to return the College to its antebellum status quo but to use its endowment for republican purposes.[8]

On May 1, 1784, the New York Legislature passed "an act for granting certain privileges to the College heretofore called King's College, for altering the charter thereof, and erecting a University in this state." The college's new name was hereafter to be Columbia College, so as to stress its new world, non-British character. The 1784 charter was modeled after the proposed "American University" charter that Duane had helped draft as a governor of King's College back in 1774. Whereas the 1774 charter draft had tried to put King's College at the head of the other colonial colleges, rather as Oxford and Cambridge presided over their respective colleges, the 1784 charter set forth Columbia "as the mother of colleges" by giving its governing board of regents supervisory powers over all institutions of learning in New York. That there were then no other institutions of higher learning in the state was beside the point.[9]

In the 1784 charter, Columbia College would be a much more public and statewide institution than King's College had been. The 1754 charter's stipulations about the president being an Anglican and college religious services following Anglican liturgical practice were dropped. To assure an ongoing state role, the charter called for eight of the seats on the Board of Regents to be held by ranking state officials ex officio, with the remaining twenty-four regents to be appointed, two each, from the state's twelve counties. Only three places were reserved for residents of New York City. The responsibility entrusted to the regents was not only to look after Columbia College but to set about "erecting a University in this state."[10]

It is not clear whether Duane wholeheartedly supported the terms of the 1784 charter or merely saw it as a step in a process by which an institution that had so recently epitomized loyalty to the crown and Anglican Church became acceptable to Republican and Dissenting legislators. That he was of the politically expedient school, however, is suggested by a similar role he played in saving the equally suspect Trinity Church from postwar confiscations. As one of the church's few supporters of the Revolution, he and a handful of other "Whig Episcopalians," among them John Jay, took it upon themselves to rewrite the governing statutes of Trinity Church and to displace its duly elected Loyalist rector, Benjamin Moore, with a certified Patriot, Samuel Prevoost, thereby establishing the church's hearty, if belated, embrace of Republicanism. If Paris was worth a mass, how much more prime New York real estate?[11]

Welcome Back: The 1787 Charter

The first scheduled meeting of the regents of the University of the State of New York on May 4, 1784, in New York City, adjourned for lack of a quorum. The next day the requisite number appeared and promptly proceeded to elect Governor George Clinton as chancellor of the university and appoint the Reverend John Peter Tétard, a Huguenot minister who had served as a wartime aide to Robert Livingston (KC 1765), as professor of French. The regents then dispatched Regent Colonel Matthew Clarkson to France and Holland to raise funds for the college, authorized the leasing of College properties, appointed the recently disembarked Scottish schoolteacher William Cochran instructor of Greek and Latin, and called it a day.[12]

The difficulty securing a quorum pointed to a serious problem with the 1784 charter: it assumed a lively statewide interest in the affairs of Columbia College, whereas little existed outside New York City. Accordingly, on November 26, 1784, to increase quorum prospects and to capitalize on local interest, the state legislature increased the number of regents by thirty-three, including twenty residents of New York City identified by name. These included three Episcopalians with direct links to King's College: John Jay, Samuel Prevoost, and Leonard Lispenard. Most of the other locally appointed regents, however, were non-Episcopalians and unconnected with King's College. Five city clergymen, including Gershon Seixas, the rabbi of the city's synagogue, and two other non-Episcopalian clergymen who would shortly thereafter be appointed to faculty positions, the Reverend John Daniel Gross of the German Reformed Church and the Lutheran reverend Johann Christoff Kunze, were named. The reconstituted board of regents included several physicians, suggestive of the renewed interest of the New York medical community in reconnecting with the College.[13]

At the same meeting, the state legislature authorized the expenditure of 2552 pounds in local currency on the College. This infusion of state support proved especially timely as earlier hopes of securing help from America's wartime allies France and Holland had been dashed. Princeton and Dartmouth fundraisers had beaten Columbia to Paris and Amsterdam, only to come up dry themselves. Indeed, his countrymen's solicitations of America's wartime allies so embarrassed Benjamin Franklin, then minister to France, that he called on them to cease immediately. In November 1785, the regents called Colonel Clarkson home, without his having collected a sou for New York's republicanized college.[14]

This fund-raising setback did not dissuade the regents from thinking big. State money was in hand, and there was more where that came from. Two weeks after Clarkson's recall, the board recommended the creation of seven "regular" (i.e., salaried) professorships, plus eight medical professorships, two law professorships, and ten unsalaried "extra professorships." They then proceeded to fill a goodly proportion of these, appointing William Cochran professor of Latin and Greek, the Reverend Benjamin Moore professor of rhetoric, the Reverend John Daniel Gross professor of geography, the Reverend John Christopher Kunze professor of oriental languages and Dr. Samuel Bard professor of natural philosophy. Even with Tétard's removal from the faculty on medical grounds in February 1786, and still without a president, Columbia College possessed in 1786 a teaching staff substantially larger than that of King's College at any time in its history. *Vive la Révolution!*[15]

Possessed of a new name, a new charter, an enthusiastic and locally based governing board, state funding, and a substantial faculty, the College now lacked only students. This deficiency was at least symbolically addressed on May 15, 1784, when Governor Clinton persuaded his fifteen-year-old nephew, DeWitt Clinton, passing through New York City on his return to his third year of studies at Princeton, to transfer instead to Columbia. A quickly arranged entrance examination placed him as a junior. The young Clinton, along with seven others admitted that same summer, were assigned to William Cochran for interim instruction.

On April 11, 1786, the young Clinton and his seven classmates constituted the first graduating class of Columbia College. The graduation services, held in St. Paul's Chapel, were attended by members of the Confederation Congress and both houses of the New York State Legislature and, of course, Governor Clinton. As the class orator, the seventeen-year-old gave the principal speech, its title *De utilitate et necessitate studorum artium liberalum*. What else?[16]

Aggressive recruiting of students became the order of the day. In an explicit break with the policy of the governors of King's College, the regents announced in newspaper advertisements throughout New York that Columbia College tuition would be "as cheap as in any other college." In pegging it at the rate then charged by Princeton—fifteen dollars a year—the regents served notice that they had no intention of being priced out of the competitive market for the young men of the new republic. A decade after its reopening, the College regularly enrolled in excess of 100 students. In 1795 enrollments reached 140, a high that would not be surpassed for the next forty-four years.[17]

At the same 1787 New York legislative session that dispatched Robert Yates and Alexander Hamilton to the Philadelphia constitutional convention, the senate committee on education chaired by the ubiquitous James Duane took upon itself the task of reviewing the 1784 charter under which Columbia College operated. It then proceeded to recommend a radically different charter, one that would give Columbia its own self-perpetuating governing board of trustees distinct from the regents and concerned exclusively with the College's well-being. Assemblyman Alexander Hamilton urged adoption of Duane's handiwork and helped overcome resistance, particularly from non–New York City legislators who favored the retention of a state-appointed board. Since non–New York City regents seldom attended board meetings, a return to governance arrangements similar to those of King's College under the 1754 royal charter seemed only to be a formalization of recent practice. The new charter did not mark a re-Episcopalianizing of Columbia's governance (that would come later) so much as reaffirm Columbia's origins and essential character as an urban institution.[18]

On April 13, 1787 (Columbia's *other* Charter Day), the New York Legislature approved a new charter by which the College was relieved of its 1784 charge to serve a statewide public capacity and allowed to revert to its earlier status as a privately governed college serving New York City. In point of fact, the 1787 charter made the College substantially more private than either King's College under the 1754 charter or Columbia College under the 1784 charter. None of its twenty-four trustees were to be state officeholders serving as ex officio members, and all replacements for future trustees were to be elected by incumbents. The board was henceforth to be wholly self-perpetuating, as it would remain until 1908, when provisions were first made for alumni nominations to the board. No less important in terms of the institution's future identity, the charter explicitly linked for the first time governance and locale by its prepositional designation of "the Trustees of Columbia College in the City of New York."[19]

Political Reprieve

As Columbia asserted its newly acquired republicanism on several fronts, New Yorkers and Americans found themselves entering a new political era. Old Tory versus Whig pre–Revolutionary War alignments were replaced by newer and more enduring polarities that were the product of postwar circumstances. These alignments first appeared in the early 1780s with calls from critics of the revolutionary state governments for a more substantial national government than envisioned by the Declaration of Independence, the first state constitutions, or by the Articles of Confederation. On this, New Yorkers sharply divided, with a substantial and at least initial majority sentiment identified with Governor Clinton and radical upstaters such as Robert Yates who opposed any diminution of state sovereignty. Opposed to these anti-Federalists and favoring a stronger national government that could, among other things, be expected to honor both the national and state debt accumulated during the war were the self-described Federalists. Their ranks included three alumni of King's College (John Jay, Gouverneur Morris, Alexander Hamilton), a King's College governor (James Duane), a future Columbia trustee (Rufus King), and the son of a King's College first president who was himself the future first president of Columbia College (William Samuel Johnson).[20]

Hamilton, Morris, King, and William Samuel Johnson all attended the Philadelphia convention that produced the Federal Constitution in the summer of 1787. One of New York's three delegates, Hamilton came across as an unabashed nationalist and likely frightened some delegates into supporting more moderate measures being pressed by James Madison and company. Hamilton left before the late summer push that produced the final document, although he returned in time to sign it. By contrast, Gouverneur Morris, a delegate from Pennsylvania (where he had moved during the war), Rufus King, from Massachusetts, and especially William Samuel Johnson, from Connecticut and member of the convention's committee on style, all played more constructive roles in the debates and properly number among the founding fathers.[21]

Hamilton proved more effective as an advocate of the Constitution throughout the ratification process that followed Philadelphia. This he did with his pen as the principal author, along with John Jay and James Madison, of *The Federalist*, a series of essays that appeared serially in the winter of 1787–88 and were intended among other things to influence the deliberations in the swing states of Virginia and New York. Hamilton also took a leading role at the New York ratifying convention in Poughkeepsie during the summer of 1788, where he and James Duane helped New York become the eleventh state to ratify the Constitution. Without accepting the view of Columbia historian Charles A. Beard that the adoption of the Constitution marked the undoing of the Revolution, it did give New York City's mercantile and professional elite and their heretofore suspect educational institution a second chance.[22]

The Second President Johnson

On May 21, 1787, at the first meeting of the newly (re)constituted Columbia trustees, William Samuel Johnson was elected the first president of Columbia College. The elder son of the first King's College president, Samuel Johnson, and a closet Loyalist in Connecticut early in the war, he had recouped his political reputation among Connecticut's revolutionaries by providing effective legal services in its border dispute with Massachusetts. At the time of his election to the presidency, he was on his way to Philadelphia as one of Connecticut's delegates to the Constitutional Convention. Johnson waited until the end of business in Philadelphia before accepting the offer but assured the trustees he would take up his new responsibilities in time for the 1788 commencement.[23]

Johnson's acceptability as president indicates how far the rehabilitation of wartime Loyalists had gone. As compared with two others mentioned as presidential possibilities for Columbia in 1784—the English chemist Joseph Priestley and the English political essayist Richard Price—he was much the more politically conservative choice. Whereas they were Dissenters, with ties to England's dissenting academies, Johnson was an Episcopalian layman with familial links to King's College. This met the presidential stipulation required by Trinity Church when it ceded the College lands, a stipulation no longer incorporated in the charter of the College but still considered enforceable by the church. At the same time, his not being a minister likely eased concerns among the board's non-Anglicans determined to stress Columbia's republicanism and religious inclusivity. In choosing a layman as president, Columbia anticipated all the original colonial colleges but Dartmouth. Harvard followed forty-two years later, with the appointment of Josiah Quincy in 1829. By the time Princeton and Yale had their first lay presidents, Columbia had had four.[24]

William Samuel Johnson was not a controversial presidential choice. Although not a New Yorker, he was known to several of the trustees and a good friend of James Duane. He easily passed the Hamilton test later explicitly applied to Johnson's successor: that his politics be "of the right sort." The fact that he was a lawyer likely commended him to the several lawyers on the board. Indeed, as his presidency amply demonstrated, the second President Johnson was a conciliatory and nonconfrontational type who gave no cause for would-be critics of the College to take partisan or sectarian offense.[25]

Such an approach helped in dealing with the state legislature. Those urging the adoption of the 1787 charter effectively freeing Columbia College from state control and statewide responsibilities did not mean to end state subsidies. That Columbia could be both a private college in terms of its governance and public in terms of the source of at least some of its support was not only a happy thought but for the early years of the new republic a politically sustainable one. In 1790 the New York State Legislature made one-time grants totaling 8,000 pounds to Columbia to renovate College Hall, acquire books, and purchase laboratory equipment. In 1792 it also authorized an annual grant of 750 pounds to help cover faculty salaries. The annual subsidy was initially authorized to run for four years and was later extended for two more. By the mid-1790s nearly half the College's operating budget came from the state of New York.[26]

President Johnson understood that continued state support depended on operating the College in a manner that avoided offending political or religious sensibilities. Most Columbia trustees in the 1790s were Federalists, but so were consistent majorities of New York City voters throughout the decade. Episcopalians became somewhat more numerous on the board as the decade went along but remained a minority through 1817. Unlike the New York Presbyterians of the 1750s, who refused ex officio places on the King's College board of governors, both Presbyterian laymen and clergy accepted active membership on the Columbia board. But for his removal to New Jersey and death in 1791, William Livingston might have fit right in. One makes do with the fact Livingston's son, Brockholst Livingston, served as board treasurer from 1787 to 1823.[27]

On other scores, Johnson was less successful than his supporters had reason to hope. Some of this may have had to do with initial distractions, among them his service as one of Connecticut's two United States senators at the first federal Congress. He resigned when the capital moved to Philadelphia. And some of this had to do with age: He entered into his duties as the first president of the reorganized Columbia College at sixty. He was seventy-three at the time of his resignation in 1800, when he was assumed to be at death's door. Yet the fact that he lived on in retirement in Stratford—with restored health and a new wife— for another nineteen years suggests that some of the difficulties of his presidency had as much to do with the job as the man.[28]

Johnson had never taught before taking up the presidency, yet the trustees expected him to take a regular turn in the classroom. Accordingly, he taught rhetoric without enthusiasm and with growing resentment until in 1797 he announced that he would no longer do so. Aside from this singular instance of assertiveness, which may have been his way of saying he wanted out, Johnson did not challenge the trustees or the faculty on matters of collegiate policy. During flush times he went along with the hirings orchestrated by the trustees and in lean with the firings they mandated. He had no original curricular or disciplinary ideas, relying instead on his experience at Yale a half-century earlier. Nor was he was particularly effective at advancing the College's cause with the state legislature, a task made more onerous when the legislature moved from New York City to Albany in 1797. The third trustee-mandated downsizing of the faculty in 1799, on the heels of the termination of the state's annual salary subsidy, became the occasion for Johnson to announce his intention to resign in 1800.[29]

"Act as if Three": A Republican Faculty

Faculty appointments from the reopening of the College in 1784 to 1815 were both numerous and unevenly spaced. Of the seventeen arts (i.e., nonmedical) appointments, seven were made when the the College was reopened in 1784–85; another five occurred in 1792–95, following receipt of what looked to be an open-ended annual state subsidy. In 1797 the Arts Faculty had eight full-time members on the payroll, a number not to be seen again at Columbia College until the 1870s.[30]

High turnover was another characteristic, much of it involuntary. When the initial wave of appointments in 1784–86 could not be sustained by the funding available, several faculty resigned without replacements, while those staying on assumed multiple professorships. Of the eight faculty hired in the 1780s, four were gone by 1790, and two more by 1800. Of the six hired in the 1790s (one a rehire), one resigned in 1798, four were downsized in 1799, and the fifth left a year later. By 1801 the Arts Faculty was down to just two members, John Kemp, professor of mathematics and natural philosophy, and Peter Wilson, professor of Greek and Latin. When Kemp and Wilson pointed out that college statutes required a third faculty member when certain decisions were made, the trustees told the two "to act as if three."[31]

With the appointments of John Bowden as professor of moral philosophy in 1801 and James Stringham as professor of chemistry in 1802, the Arts Faculty stabilized at four members, where it would remain for the next half-century. Between 1802 and 1817 only two more appointments were made, both substitutional, that of Robert Adrain in mathematics, who replaced John Kemp, and John Griscom in chemistry, for the departing Stringham. Of the seventeen men appointed to the Columbia Arts Faculty between 1784 and 1817, only the mathematician John Kemp stayed to retirement or died in service. In Kemp's case, it was the latter, in 1812; the College paid for his funeral after twenty-six years of service. The average tenure of Columbia faculty during this period was seven years.[32]

The first generation of Columbia College faculty (1784 to 1815) was far more cosmopolitan than the King's College faculty had been or the generation of Columbia College faculty that came after it and perhaps every generation of Columbia faculty since. Only three of the seventeen appointments were King's College alumni (two of these—Benjamin Moore and Samuel Bard—were only briefly on the faculty.) Fourteen had been trained elsewhere, half of these in Europe. Several faculty were practicing Episcopalians, but most were not. Seven had been ministers, only three Episcopalian. The other ten were laymen, several with European training in the sciences, medicine, or the humanities.[33]

The first wave of appointments made in 1784 provides insight into the curricular priorities of the day. While instruction in Latin, Greek, rhetoric, and mathematics remained available through thick and thin, what distinguished Columbia's curriculum in its republican moment was the emphasis on modern languages and the physical sciences. Among the first faculty appointments in 1784 were one in French (Tétard) and another in German (Gross). Provision for instruction in non-European languages was similarly made that year by the regents with the appointment of John Christopher Kunze as professor of oriental languages, inaugurating Columbia's subsequent history as an American center for foreign area studies. None of these appointees had a prior connection to King's College or Columbia and none was Episcopalian.[34]

The best known of the first generation of Columbia faculty were both scientists, professor of natural history, chemistry, and agriculture Samuel Latham Mitchill and professor of mathematics and astronomy Robert Adrain. Neither had familial or educational ties to Columbia. Mitchill, a Quaker turned Presbyterian, was raised on Long Island and pursued medical training in Edinburgh before coming to New York City in 1787, where he began a medical practice. With the renewal of state funding in 1792, Mitchill was appointed professor of chemistry, but over the next decade he collected additional chairs, including those of natural history and agriculture. These multiple responsibilities matched his interests in both the physical and biological sciences. His principal biographer describes him as "perhaps the most versatile man of science in his time," while less kindly disposed contemporaries thought Mitchill, whose résumé identified him as a member of forty-nine scientific societies, spread himself a bit thin.[35]

While teaching at Columbia in 1797, the ever-energetic Mitchill founded the *Medical Repository*, the first medical journal to be published in the United States. His editorial labors thus initiated what later became, when renewed in the 1880s, a distinctive tradition of Columbia-based scholarly journals edited by Columbia faculty. Mitchill stayed on as editor of the *Repository* until 1824, though by then he was long gone from Columbia. A glad-handing fellow in an era that valued the citizen-scientist and a Jeffersonian by political persuasion, Mitchill inevitably found his way into politics. His first elective office came in 1797 as a member of the New York Assembly, where he sought every opportunity, he informed the trustees, "to draw something further from the Public Purse for the benefit of the College." This was not always easy, he allowed, as "it is surprising how little is known about Columbia College among the citizens of this state!" His election to Congress in 1800 prompted his resignation from the Columbia faculty the following year.[36]

Mitchill went on to serve three terms in Congress and an intervening four-year stint in the Senate. An effective representative of New York's economic interests in Washington, he regularly cited his scientific credentials in pressing for the development of steamboats and canals. Mitchill's brief career as a Columbia faculty member foreshadows a future pattern: the Columbia academic as scientific statesman and policy adviser.

Robert Adrain was a different matter—on two scores. Where Mitchill had a flair for self-promotion and an eye on public office, which for him made the Columbia faculty a temporary way station, the self-taught and self-effacing Adrain was first and last a teacher. Before transplanting to America in the late 1790s, he had been a politically active schoolmaster in his native Ireland. Immediately before the Columbia appointment in 1810, he had been professor of mathematics at Rutgers; after leaving Columbia in 1823, he returned briefly to Rutgers and then became vice provost at the University of Pennsylvania. After seven years of administrative responsibilities at Penn, where he unsuccessfully tried to impose order on its unruly students and restore comity to its no less fractious professors, he was ousted in a faculty coup. He returned to New York and, finding no place on the Columbia faculty, spent the last decade of his life teaching at the Columbia Grammar School.[37]

Another difference between the polymath Mitchill and Adrain was that Adrain was a world-class mathematician. While at Columbia he successfully produced proofs for Gauss's exponential law of errors, which earned him notice among leading European mathematicians and has since allowed him to be viewed as "the most outstanding mathematician in America in his time."[38]

Adrain's achievements are more impressive in light of the fact that his teaching was entirely given over to drilling restless fifteen-year-olds on the solution of quadratic equations and Euclid's Elements. Occasionally his enthusiasm for the job faltered, as when he informed one math-phobic Columbia sophomore in his thick Irish brogue, "If you cannot understand Euclid, Dearie, I cannot explain it to you." But more often his efforts won him the respect and affection of his students, which he returned in kind. "He seemed to love us all," recalled one of his students fifty years later, "calling us 'Tommy dear,' 'Jimmy dear,' or 'Johnnie dear.'" On the occasion of Adrain's leaving Columbia in 1823, his students commissioned a portrait as "a testimony of veneration for his learning and talents, of gratitude for his exertions in their Favor and of the most unfeigned respect for that Body under whose auspices that have passed so long, so happy and so Important a period in their lives." Perhaps those who have spent their working lives teaching Columbia undergraduates can best appreciate such testimony.[39]

Early Columbia College and the Professions: Medicine

If not on the original regents' immediate list of priorities in 1784, the need to get a degree program in medicine up and running again was certainly on the minds of several members of the New York City medical community who were named to the augmented board. With the newly renamed University of Penn-sylvania's medical school back in business and with Harvard opening a med-ical school of its own the year before, a sense of competitive urgency infused their lobbying.

Of the four King's College Medical School faculty at its closing in 1775, only Samuel Bard was around at the opening of Columbia College nine years later. The Loyalist Samuel Clossy had returned to Ireland; John Jones had moved to Philadelphia after distinguished service as a military surgeon in the Continen-tal Army; Peter Middleton, a Loyalist, died in New York City in 1781. Bard, also a Loyalist, sat out the war in Poughkeepsie, returning to the city in early 1784 under the protection of his friend James Duane. Duane also helped Bard secure appointment as Columbia College's first postwar professor of natural philoso-phy. With the regents' decision the following year to authorize a Faculty of Medicine, Bard became its first dean.[40]

Four of the city's leading physicians joined Bard in 1785, although none remained at Columbia beyond 1792. Included were Drs. Ebenezer Crosby, pro-fessor of midwifery; Benjamin Kissam (KC 1775), professor of the institutes of medicine; Charles McKnight, professor of surgery; and Nicholas Romayne, professor of the practice of medicine. Like Bard, they numbered among the original board of trustees in 1787, McKnight and Romayne having been two of the New York City residents added to the regents in November 1784. Of these, Romayne, who had attended King's College Medical School in 1774 before transferring to the University of Edinburgh, where he received his M.D., unquestionably had the greatest impact on the Medical School's subsequent history. It was wholly negative.[41]

In 1791 Romayne instigated a defection of thirty-seven of the College's med-ical students in a protest against the trustees' plan to restructure the Medical School. When the plan was approved by the state legislature and enacted by the trustees in 1792, Romayne resigned his professorship and his place on the board of trustees. He spent the next decade in Europe and then returned to New York City, where in 1806, with the active support of the newly reorganized Medical Society of New York, he secured legislative authorization and financial backing for a second medical school that would be in direct competition with Colum-bia's. The College of Physicians & Surgeons opened in 1807 on Robinson Street, with fifty students enrolled. By 1810 P & S had substantially larger enrollments than Columbia and a graduating class of eight, the total number of Columbia's medical graduates of the previous six years.[42]

Romayne's depredations were not limited to stealing students. In 1808 he wooed David Hosack away from Columbia to join the upstart P & S. A year later he secured twenty thousand dollars for P & S from the New York legislature as part of a statewide series of educational grants that grew out of legislation designed to help Union College. Columbia received nothing. In 1813 Columbia's professional program in medical education in the city of New York came to an end. The Faculty of Medicine was abolished, and the five remaining faculty members terminated. Most went over to P & S. Not until 1891, when Columbia University assumed control of the nearly bankrupt College of Physicians & Surgeons, would it again be a presence in American medical education.[43]

Political ineptitude on the part of the trustees in dealing with the state legislature, faculty infighting, professional jealousies within the New York medical community, and sheer mendacity can all be cited as the reasons for Columbia Medical School was closed. But larger factors were involved. The first was the incapacity of Columbia's medical educators to demonstrate the clear superiority of the training they provided over that acquired by on-the-job training and medical apprenticeships. The training early-nineteenth-century medical students received in the basic sciences simply did not yield therapeutically beneficial outcomes sufficient to distinguish its graduates from untrained "empirics." Even after the opening of New York Hospital in 1791, Columbia offered its students no meaningful clinical experience.[44]

Second, in the absence of a clear edge provided by formal training, would-be doctors in the early republic were understandably reluctant to put in the three years necessary to complete the degree program or bear the expense of such training. Insofar as the medical faculty were not salaried but paid directly out of student fees, they were disinclined to lower their stipends without an offsetting growth in the number of students.

Even before P & S went into direct competition in 1807, the Columbia Medical School had been losing students. The initially promising enrollments in the early 1790s, much as had been the case back in the later 1760s at King's College, could not be sustained. Still more dispiriting, only a few of those in attendance stayed on to complete the program and receive degrees. In all, the Columbia College Faculty of Medicine produced only twenty-four graduates in its twenty-eight-year history.[45]

A third factor in the demise of the Columbia Medical School in 1813 was the inability of either its medical faculty or the New York medical community to limit access to the profession by making a medical degree an essential condition of entry. Columbia medical graduates were exempted from taking a state-administered licensing exam, but this privilege in itself hardly justified the time and expense acquiring a degree involved, particularly when the licensing laws at the time were virtually unenforceable. In point of fact, there was less reason to go to medical school in the early 1800s than there had been back in the early 1770s, when there was at least the prospect of access to the profession being lim-

ited to formally trained practitioners. In the early 1800s public opinion and legislative practice were running in the other direction. By the 1820s the licensing
laws that had survived the Revolution or been enacted in its immediate wake
were repealed in state after state. In New York by the 1830s the only legal difference between a licensed and unlicensed doctor was that the latter could not sue
for his fees. Otherwise he was free to practice under the Jacksonian injunction
of "caveat emptor."[46]

Early Columbia College and the Professions: The Law

The experiment of republican Columbia College to provide a degree program
in medical education was not its only foray into professional education. There
was also a concerted effort in the mid-1790s to provide a level of formal legal
training not found elsewhere. As with the medical education experiment, inaugurating legal training also proved a failure. But unlike the medicine venture,
which lasted for twenty-eight years and involved some fifteen appointments, it
was over in three years and involved a single faculty member: James Kent.

In 1793 James Kent, a graduate of Yale and legal scholar, was appointed professor of law and asked to prepare a series of lectures on American law. The following winter he delivered twenty-six lectures on the assigned subject, attracting forty students and assorted visitors. In 1795–96 he repeated the lectures, but
to an audience of two students. In 1796–97, nobody attended. On May 5, 1797,
Kent resigned his professorship and advised the trustees to abandon the experiment in legal education until it could do so "under abler professors and in
more auspicious times."[47]

Certainly, Kent's self-deprecating resignation provides part of the answer to
the question why Columbia's first foray into legal education proved an immediate disaster. By all accounts, Kent was neither a mesmerizing nor even a
mildly interesting lecturer. What he had to say was best read, and the substance
of his lectures eventually appeared in print as *Commentaries on American Law*
(1826–28, 1830), one of the most important pieces of American legal literature
published before the Civil War. His impact on American law of his day was perhaps second only to John Marshall and Harvard's Joseph Story.

However intellectually elegant and knowledgeable Kent's lectures were, it is
doubtful they made getting on in the law any easier than an apprenticeship in a
reasonably active law office would have done. Nor did faithful attendance assure
any breaks getting a job in the law. As with medicine, many of the licensing
requirements and other restrictive practices controlling admission to the bar
enacted in colonial New York in the 1760s fell increasingly out of favor in the

two generations following the Revolution. In the 1830s the right to practice at the bar in New York State was open to all white males who paid a licensing fee. The "more propitious times" that Kent's resignation statement referred to did arrive in his long lifetime—he died at age eighty-five in 1847—although by then several law schools were under way, including one at Hamilton College, where Theodore Dwight taught for a decade before coming to New York City to reinitiate legal training at Columbia in 1858.[48]

Verging Toward Dissolution

When President Johnson resigned in April 1800, there was no rush of local candidates to succeed him. The trustees began an extensive national canvas, in which Alexander Hamilton took part, that produced the name of the Reverend Charles Henry Wharton, a native of Maryland and an Episcopalian rector in Burlington, New Jersey. Wharton, raised as a Roman Catholic and ordained as a Jesuit priest following seminary training at St. Omers, in Belgium, converted to Anglicanism while serving as a chaplain in England during the Revolutionary War. Back in America, Wharton served in a series of Episcopal churches in Maryland and New Jersey, all the while engaging in a running dispute with Catholic prelate and fellow St. Omers graduate John Carroll. Having received assurances from his Federalist contacts in Maryland that Wharton met his criteria—"he must be a gentleman as well as a sound scholar, and that his politics must be of the right sort"—Hamilton recommended Wharton's appointment.[49]

On May 25, 1801, the trustees elected the fifty-three-year-old Wharton the second president of Columbia College (the fourth when we count the two King's College presidents). Five weeks later, on July 1, the trustees received his acceptance and assurances that he would be present at the August commencement. Then something happened. Wharton apparently did not appear at the commencement ceremonies and that fall submitted his resignation, which was accepted by the board on December 11, 1801, thereby making his the shortest tenure of any of Columbia's nineteen presidents to date. To add insult to injury, upon resigning the Columbia presidency, Wharton became a trustee of Princeton.[50]

In frustration, the trustees turned to one of their own, Rev. Benjamin Moore, who had only months before become the sixth rector of Trinity Church, the same position from which he had been ousted back in 1784 because of his politically incorrect Loyalist sympathies, and also the second bishop of New York. In some ways, Moore seemed an attractive presidential possibility. He was a graduate of King's College (1765), had taught as a tutor in the early 1770s, had been acting president during the war, and had taught rhetoric from 1785 to 1788. Best of all, after receiving assurances that he would be responsible for only the ceremonial aspects of the office and would not be expected to teach, the fifty-three-year-old Moore was willing to take the job. On December 31, 1801, he became Columbia's fifth president.[51]

Moore's presidency was a disaster waiting to happen. He entered into it already overextended in ways that assured his presidential responsibilities would be the first to be neglected. His arrangement with the Columbia trustees, in the absence of any other administrator or an experienced cadre of faculty, meant that the day-to-day responsibility for the management of the College devolved on the board, which was more than occupied trying to cope with the College's deteriorating finances. This meant that some matters, such as the refurbishing of College Hall or enforcing the rule that students should not be admitted under the age of fourteen, were overlooked. Matters were not helped when, with the election in 1801 of the assistant minister of Trinity Church, the Reverend John Henry Hobart, the board took on a more partisan character. Hobart assumed head of the church party, while the Reverend John Mitchell Mason, who had succeeded his father both as minister of the Second Presbyterian Church and as a Columbia trustee, headed up the Dissenting side.[52]

Added to the structural problems besetting Moore's presidency were some personal liabilities. Early in his presidency, he began to experience immobilizing blackouts, which persisted with increasing severity and frequency. Even in the best of health, Moore lacked the personal forcefulness to make the Columbia presidency anything more than an honorific position. For evidence of his diffidence, one needs only to hear the personal assessment of Moore by a latter-day rector and historian of Trinity Church, Morgan Dix: "Not a learned man, nor a profound scholar, nor gifted with the diversity of attainments possessed by his predecessor, he was nevertheless a man of refinement and of scholarly tastes, who won affection by his gentleness, kindness and unaffected simplicity. The best commentary on his character is his life. 'Blessed are the meek; for they shall inherit the earth. . . . Blessed are the peacemakers: for they shall be called the children of God.' " "Of such was our Bishop," concluded Dix, a Columbia trustee for thirty-odd years—and of such the College's fifth president.[53]

In 1809, sensing that something was seriously wrong with Columbia's management, the trustees charged Rufus King with conducting an "Inquiry into the State of the College." The resultant report, in concluding that the "College is not what it *ought* to be, what it was *intended* to be, and what, with proper management, it *might be*," was nothing if not self-critical. Much of it was given over to decrying a decade- long slide in admission standards that resulted in admitted students who were incapable of meeting even the minimal classroom expectations. This led to disciplinary problems and the faculty's energies being diverted to remedial work. "The College is fast becoming, if it has not become already, a mere grammar school." Acknowledging that to do so would generate parental dissatisfaction and risk a diminution in students and a decline in revenues, King called on his fellow trustees to "raise the terms of admission so high as to put the subsequent course within the student's reach."[54]

King also took direct aim at the College's management. Of the president, he asserted, "his immediate and active superintendence is indispensable to the prosperity of the institution." Insofar as Moore had never actively seen to the College's superintendence, King's comment constituted a call for his resignation. This Moore was glad to give, and he did so in May 1811.

Who could be found to succeed Moore? By now the sectarian strains within the board of trustees threatened to produce a deadlock. The Hobart-led faction insisted on an Episcopalian, arguing that Trinity Church could reclaim the land conditionally deeded to the College in 1754 if not. Among Episcopalians under consideration was the Reverend William T. Harris, a Harvard graduate and the rector of St. Mark's in the Bowery. His candidacy was not enthusiastically received by Mason or the other non-Episcopalians on the board, who believed Mason to be the best man for the job.

It then fell to Hobart, whose moral earnestness was said to verge on Methodism, to propose a compromise. Harris would be made president, thereby satisfying the Trinity agreement, but he would not resign his rectorship. The actual superintendence of the College would go to the leader of the Dissenting faction on the board, John Mitchell Mason, in the newly created position of provost. This not only satisfied the non-Episcopalians on the board, it gave hope that the College might at last have a knowledgeable (Mason had been a trustee for fifteen years), young (forty-three), and forceful leader at its head. On this last characteristic, there seems to have been universal agreement. "If ever a mortal possessed decision of character," an Episcopal admirer said of the provost-elect, "that mortal was John Mitchell Mason." On June 19, 1811, Harris was appointed the College's seventh president and Mason its first provost. Mason's salary was to be thirty-four hundred dollars, Harris's five hundred.[55]

Less than two months after this odd coupling was arranged, thereby containing the disruptive potential in the board's politics, Columbia was obliged to confront disruptions on two other fronts. The first was the so-called Riotous Commencement of 1811, which took place on August 6 in Trinity Church, with the newly appointed Revs. Harris and Mason presiding. A senior scheduled to graduate, one John B. Stevenson, had been chosen by his classmates to deliver an oration, which when reviewed by Professors Wilson and Kemp was judged to be in need of toning down. Whereas Stevenson had planned to assert the Republican truism as to the absolute obligation of representatives to submit to the majority wishes of their constituencies, the faculty insisted that he at least allow "that many intelligent men thought differently." Assuming he agreed to this insertion, the College allowed Stevenson to remain on the program. When he proceeded to the altar and delivered the oration in its unexpurgated version, Harris and Mason decided to withhold his degree and had Kemp direct him to remain seated when his classmates paraded to the altar. Stevenson was apparently ready to accept this rebuff as the price of his political principles, but others in the audience proceeded to disrupt the ceremony in, according to a subsequent court record, "a tumult lasting an hour" that was halted only by the repeated calling of the constables. Among the leading agitators were two alumni, Gulian C. Verplanck (class of 1801), a recent convert from Federalism to Jeffersonianism, and Hugh Maxwell (class of 1808), who urged Stevenson to insist on receiving his diploma. Verplanck later justified his actions by arguing that "the conduct of the professors was oppressive, and he would always resist oppression."[56]

The next day the College formally charged Verplanck, Maxwell, Stevenson, and four others at the commencement with inciting to riot. The case was tried in the municipal court, presided over by yet another Columbian with a political agenda, DeWitt Clinton (CC 1786), then serving as the appointive mayor of New York but already preparing to make a run for governor. To do so, it was generally thought he would need the support of precisely the sort of Federalists prominent among the Columbians calling for Verplanck's and Maxwell's respective heads. Not surprisingly, Mayor Clinton took the charges of inciting a riot very seriously, determined that a riot had occurred—whereas the defendants' attorneys called it "an affray only"—and fined Verplanck and Maxwell two hundred dollars. Stevenson was let off with a ten-dollars fine, after testimony was heard from Professor Kemp that he was "the best behaved young man in the College—he must have been prompted by others."[57]

The disturbance attending the "Riotous Commencement of 1811" was small beer compared with the full-scale student-led disruptions at Princeton, the University of Virginia, Harvard, and dozens of other campuses, where classes were disrupted, property damaged, and lives threatened. Nor should it be viewed as a forerunner of the disturbances at Columbia in 1968, which were of an altogether different magnitude and consequence. The major participants in 1811 all went on with their lives. Five years after the riot, Stevenson was awarded an M.A. from Columbia before going on to a respectable career in medicine. A decade later Verplanck was sufficiently back in the good graces of Columbia to be elected to the board of trustees, and in 1824 he was elected to Congress, where he served four terms. Clinton, though denied the Democratic-Republican nomination for lieutenant governor in 1815 for consorting with Federalists, became governor of New York two years later when the incumbent Daniel T. Tompkins (CC 1792) became vice president under James Monroe.[58]

On another level, however, the 1811 riot offered an important lesson to those charged with Columbia's care: the College could not look to politics or politicians to secure its survival, much less to advance its prosperity. A time would come when all of American higher education, and Columbia in particular, would be the favored object of the largesse at the disposal of popularly elected public officials, but that time was beyond the horizon of Columbia trustees living in the opening decades of the nineteenth century. And because public assistance was not on its way, they needed to look to themselves for the wherewithal to survive.[59]

Bottoming Out, 1815–17

Some critical moments in the life of an institution are so dramatic and publicly played out as thereafter to remain obvious and incontrovertible; others occur so quietly and with so little contemporary public notice (or even awareness) that later on they risk being overlooked altogether. The outbreak of the American Revolution in 1775 was an instance in the early history of Columbia University of the first kind; so, too, the student-led disruptions in 1968 in its more recent history. An early instance of the second kind—the unremarked-on turning point—occurred between 1815 and 1817. During those two years, in a series of discrete actions, no single one in itself startling or unprecedented, the trustees quietly made a basic determination: without knowing how the College could be sustained and with reasons to believe that it could not be, they decided against folding. It was a close call.

Declining graduation numbers only told half the story. The class graduating at the "Riotous Commencement of 1811," for example, consisted of twenty-four seniors. But only sixteen were recommended by the faculty to the trustees for diplomas. Of the eight not recommended, the faculty stated that four "are by no means as deficient" as the other four, who were presumably without any redeeming qualities. The trustees, citing "Considerations of some delicacy," ignored the faculty recommendations and approved all twenty-four for graduation. Three years later, the class of 1814 was down to eleven seniors, only three of whom were qualified to graduate under the existing regulations, three under earlier regulations. The other five were judged the faculty to be "unqual-ified, except for their good behavior (special gratia)." All eleven were awarded diplomas.[60]

The crisis the trustees faced in 1815 was in the first instance financial. Simply put, Columbia's income had for several years failed to match its expenditures. Of the College's four principal sources of income, rents on commercial prop-erty adjacent to the College remained the most dependable and accounted for about one-third of the total income. But this income stream could be increased only by further encroachments on the College Green, which was already hemmed in by warehouses and shops.[61]

The second source, income derived from mortgages and bonds, which had earlier provided a substantial chunk of the budget, had dropped sharply with the economic dislocations attendant on the imposition of the embargo in 1809 and the War of 1812. Moreover, as more of the College's available cash was used to cover annual deficits, less was available for putting out at interest.

The third source of income, tuition, was largely dependent on the uncer-tainties of enrollments, which varied from one year to the next by as much as 20 percent, with declines occurring somewhat more often than increases. In the early 1800s Columbia abandoned its pledge "to be as cheap as any" by hiking the annual tuition to one hundred dollars. This returned Columbia to the top of the tuition list. When enrollments dropped, the trustees in 1811 again put tuition at fifty dollars. But four years later, when this discount rate failed to stimulate enrollments, while sharply cutting income, the trustees bumped it back up to eighty dollars, where it would remain for a decade. In 1817 total enrollments reached a two-decade low of seventy-seven students, and the trustees had about run out of ways to play the tuition/enrollments game.[62]

Another problem with tuition as a source of College income was that most of it went directly to the president and individual faculty without ever appear-ing on the income side of the College's ledgers. It is not clear when this practice began (it did not exist in King's College), but it seems to have been accepted by the trustees with the end of state funding in 1799. That year a trustee report set the annual fee that each student would pay the president and his individual pro-fessors at eight dollars. When the trustee committee chaired by Rufus King revisited the practice in 1809, it concluded that if these fees were to be paid directly to the College and the faculty's total income was kept whole, the salaries the College paid faculty would have to double. It also believed this cap-itation policy was responsible for the faculty's admitting students who were academically unprepared, too young, or both. Still, some form or another of this arrangement persisted in the College into the 1850s (and in the Law School into the 1880s).[63]

For their part, faculty frequently remonstrated, as they did in 1814, after the obligatory praise of the trustees' "liberalism and paternal feelings," about their "need [of] additional temporary provision necessary to enable them to maintain themselves and families in a manner decent and suitable to their station." One faculty member was so short of cash that he petitioned the trustees to allow him to sublet his College rooms, while he and his family moved to cheaper quarters. The trustees demurred.[64]

As it turned out, King and like-minded trustees failed to halt the payment of student fees to faculty. Later—necessity being the mother of sophistry—they rationalized the practice as a means by which the faculty were given a personal stake in sustaining enrollments. In 1843 a trustee resolution specified that the salaries of the president (fourteen hundred dollars) and those of the four principal professors (twelve hundred dollars) also include, "for every student who actually pays his fees, the sum of ten dollars each."[65]

If, as compared with the other, larger colleges in the early republic, early Columbia College generated little tuition income, it produced even less in the way of private benefactions. The substantial bequests of Paul Richard and Joseph Murray to King's College in the 1750s proved to be not only the largest the College would receive over the next century but among the only gifts of cash. Instead, benefactors typically favored the College with portraits or collections of books. True, Governor De Witt Clinton's son donated a chair in his father's name in 1828, but it was the one on which the governor was seated at his death. Not only was there no custom of trustee giving in the early days of Columbia College, but the trustees, unlike their counterparts at Harvard and Yale, declined to mount the kinds of subscription drives for College improvements that were already a commonplace in Boston and New Haven. The idea, common enough among New Yorkers generally, that Columbia College was somehow rich enough not to have to engage in fund-raising, seems to have enjoyed some currency even among trustees who surely knew better.[66]

That left public grants, which, in the absence of any federal involvement in higher education, meant state grants. Just as it is doubtful that King's College would have gotten under way in the 1750s without the assurance of provincial funding, it is unlikely that Columbia College would have started up again in 1784 without at least the prospect of state funding. And again New York proved to be a generous early backer of the College.

On four separate occasions between 1785 and 1796, the New York legislature made grants to Columbia, the first of 2,552 pounds in 1785. This was followed two years later by a second for 1000 pounds. In 1792 the state, in its most comprehensive action, made a one-time grant of 7000 pounds to Columbia for the expanding of the library, chemical apparatus, and buildings. It also authorized the appropriation of 500 pounds annually for five years (extended in 1796 to seven) to help with faculty salaries. In all, New York's contributions to Columbia College during its first fifteen years amounted to something in excess of forty thousand dollars, or about one-third of the College's operating budgets in those years. Not until the Bundy grants of the 1970s would state support ever again become as significant—even crucial—a factor in Columbia's finances as it was in the 1790s.[67] After 1799, however, the state legislature, now relocated in Albany, redirected its educational largesse upstate, with the principal beneficiaries being Union College, in nearby Schenectady, and, to a lesser degree, Hamilton College, off to the west in Clinton.

Columbia did receive state support on three more occasions, but in the first two instances the circumstances and amounts received made it clear that the state legislators in Albany were far more concerned with underwriting Union College than helping Columbia, which even rural Federalist legislators were prepared to dismiss as "too expensive for the accommodation of youth from the country." In 1802 Columbia was informed that lands ceded to it in 1790, which included tracts around Lake George, Ticonderoga, and Crown Point, as well as Governor's Island in New York Harbor, could now be sold but that Union College would share evenly in the proceeds. (The College eventually received nine thousand dollars as its share.)[68]

The second instance where a state grant represented a consolation prize—and where the real money went elsewhere in the state—occurred in 1814. Having persuaded his trustees that Union College should move out of Schenectady to a commanding site outside of town, and that the state should underwrite the two-hundred-thousand-dollar cost, the College's entrepreneurial president, Eliphalet Nott, introduced into the New York Assembly what came to be called "The Union College Bill." Nott assured the legislators that its passage would enable Union to become what Columbia had been expected to become when it was issued its charter in 1784: the keystone of a state-supported university system.[69]

Other educational institutions promptly attached themselves to Union's efforts, including the just-chartered Hamilton College, in Clinton, which had as one of its sponsors in Albany the governor, Daniel D. Tompkins (CC 1796). The newly founded competitor to the Columbia Medical School, the College of Physicians & Surgeons, also joined in the scramble. Rather than do likewise, the Columbia trustees reacted to what had come to be called the Literature Lottery Act by trying to kill it. When it passed, Union got its two hundred thousand, with interest, Hamilton got forty thousand, P & S got thirty thousand, and Columbia got nothing.[70]

In a separate act, the legislature did give Columbia a plot of overgrown land situated in the Ninth Ward of the city of New York, earlier the property of Dr. David Hosack, who had sold it to the state in 1811 for twenty-five thousand dollars. Those who can take the long view—or who know how the respective stories turned out—might well believe that the Hosack property, where Rockefeller Center now stands (and which Columbia sold in 1985 for four hundred million), was the more valuable grant. But such was not the view taken by the College trustees. Instead, they saw Union walk away with state money that propelled it within a decade to becoming the largest college in the country, while Columbia ended up with an overgrown botanical garden in need of costly draining.

As if to add insult to injury, the state legislature further conditioned the grant of the Hosack Garden to its being used as the future site of the College. That meant the trustees could not develop it for commercial purposes, much less consider selling it for ready cash. Although this restriction was lifted by the legislature in 1819, it was to be another thirty years before the Hosack Garden property became for Columbia anything more than a "source of expense and not of revenue." Accompanying this concession was a state grant of ten thousand. There would be no more for another century.[71]

Home Is Where They Have to Take You In

During the six decades since the gift of the land on which College Hall was built, Trinity Church made no other substantial contributions to the College. For some of this period, Trinity had had its own financial problems, with the burning to the ground of the original church in 1776 and sundry legal challenges to its property stemming from both prerevolutionary claims and postrevolutionary reprisals for its persistent Loyalism during the war. Only the earlier mentioned takeover of the Trinity vestry by such "Whig Episcopalians" as James Duane, James Prevoost, and John Jay in the immediate wake of the evacuation of British forces from New York City in late 1783 kept the church's extensive real estate holdings from being seized by the state as enemy property. These same vestrymen then set about the rebuilding of Trinity Church, a project happily concluded in 1790.[72]

By the century's turn, Trinity was again the largest property owner and richest private institution in New York. But by then its philanthropic activities focused less on higher education than on the support of aged and infirm clergymen, as well as helping to build other Episcopal churches throughout the region, including St. Mark's (1795) and Grace Church (1804–13) in the city. The opening of General Theological Seminary in 1817, for the training of Episcopal clergy, was another reason Trinity was not as likely a source of support for the College as it had once been. But it was still the best bet in town, as the Columbia trustees well knew.

There is little direct evidence to prove that sometime in 1816 the trustees of Columbia College and the vestrymen of Trinity Church agreed that the church would become a guarantor of the College's financial well-being and that, in return, the members of Trinity Church could consider Columbia College as their own "church college," with all the insider privileges that entailed. The best direct evidence that something like this *might have happened* comes with the resignation of Richard Varick as chair of the board of trustees on March 3, 1816. A communicant of the Dutch Reformed Church, Varick explained his decision as intended to "give an opportunity to the Corporation of Trinity Church to evince their further munificences to Columbia College."[73]

During the same meeting when the trustees accepted the resignation of Varick as chairman, Provost Mason announced his resignation, and the board abolished his position. This made the Episcopalian William Harris president in fact as well as name. He remained on as Columbia's full-time president until his death in 1829. His presidential successor, William A. Duer (1829–42), and the five presidents who followed him over the next 106 years (to 1948), whatever their differences, were all Episcopalians.[74]

The months on either side of the Varick-Mason resignations occurred saw the resignation of eleven other trustees, occasioning the largest turnover in the history of the board. Among those leaving were the board's only Jewish member, Gershon Seixas, and Jacob Radcliffe, one of its Dutch Reformed members. In their place came Beverley Robinson, David Bayard Ogden, Thomas L. Ogden, and Nicholas Fish, all pillars of Trinity Church. Not only would these trustees go on to serve unusually long terms, but each succeeded in perpetuating his membership another generation by seeing to the election of a family member. In Fish's case, it was his son, Hamilton Fish; in Robinson's, his son-in-law, William Betts; and in the Ogdens', their son and nephew, Gouverneur M. Ogden. Collectively, the Ogden/Robinson/Betts/Fish presence on the board would extend across nine decades and encompass 254 man-years of trustee service. The re-Episcopalianization of Columbia College was now a done deal.[75]

If such a deal was in fact made, it follows that subsequent Columbians have Trinity Church largely to thank for keeping the College "in the City of New-York," or at least out of the boroughs. In the spring of 1817 Governor Daniel D. Tompkins (CC 1797) made a proposal to the trustees that Columbia merge its resources with those of Washington College, a proposed institution of higher learning to be located on still largely rural Staten Island, where Tompkins owned considerable property. As chancellor of the State Board of Regents,

Tompkins had secured a conditional charter for the College and promises of state support. On March 3, 1817, the Columbia board met and referred Tompkins's proposal to a committee. Three weeks later, the committee urged rejection of the proposal and the "injurious suggestion" that a more rural setting would better serve Columbia's educational and moral purposes: "Your committee see no grounds upon which to conclude that during the long period of time referred to [back to 1754], the students of Columbia College have been less distinguished for literary attainments, or less pure in their morals, than those who have been educated at other places."[76]

In voting to reject the move to Staten Island, the trustees publicly committed the College to an indefinite if uncertain future in the city of its birth. Perhaps this act of faith was made a bit easier by the knowledge that, for its near future at least, the College might look to Trinity Church as more than just another downtown neighbor, if less than its underwriter of last resort. Thus protected against the uncertainties of republicanism, the College could now safely enter into a nearly four-decade hibernation that would bring it to the eve of the Civil War before again rousing.

Coda: Columbia College and the Jeffersonian Payback

On May 6, 1789, a week after his inauguration as president of the United States, George Washington attended the annual commencement of Columbia College. Joining him were members of Congress and the Supreme Court, Governor George Clinton, and other principal New York officeholders. Part of the explanation for their appearance was convenience. With both the federal and state capitals located in New York City, Columbia constituted for federal and state political leaders one of the local cultural institutions deserving of their moral support and, on celebratory occasions, their ceremonial presence. With the subsequent removal of the national capital in 1790, first back to Philadelphia and then to the banks of the Potomac, and that of the state capital to Albany in 1797, Columbia would have to make do with rather less distinguished guest lists at commencement. It was nice while it lasted.[77]

But more partisan considerations also brought public officials to Columbia in 1789. From the ratification struggles of 1787–88, culminating in New York State's adoption of the Federal Constitution on July 26, 1788, down to the election of 1800, Columbians played a role all out of proportion to their numbers in the public affairs of their country—and a larger role than they have played ever since. But, as earlier indicated, they did so almost entirely as Federalists. Fortunately for the College, throughout the decade after ratification, and especially during the quasi-war with France, New York City remained a Federalist stronghold.[78]

Whereas Madison would have second thoughts in the 1790s about his 1787 handiwork and align himself politically with his fellow Virginian Thomas Jefferson and such anti-Federalists as George Clinton to create the nation's first opposition political party, the Democratic Republicans, Hamilton and Jay remained indelibly marked as Federalists. Both were rewarded with important positions in the new federal government. Jay became the first chief justice of the Supreme Court (1789–95) and Hamilton Washington's first secretary of the treasury (1789–95). Hamilton's exertions effectively established the nation's fiscal and banking system, even as it made him a target for those, aligned with Thomas Jefferson, who favored a smaller and less assertive national government. Jay's successful if unpopular efforts to secure a commercial treaty with England in 1794, an agreement that bears his name, similarly made him an object of vilification among insurgent Jeffersonian Democratic-Republicans.[79]

Jay resigned his position on the Supreme Court in 1795 to become governor of New York, thereby breaking for at least a while George Clinton's hammerlock hold on the office. In 1798, in a Federalist sweep of state offices, he was elected to a second term. It was only in the wake of the presidential election of 1800 and the replacement of the Federalist John Adams with the Democratic-Republican Thomas Jefferson that Columbia's identification with the Federalist cause became a political liability. By then, Jay had withdrawn from the political wars, refusing a request from Hamilton in 1800 to use his position as governor to see to the election of Federalist electors as "a measure for party purposes which I think it would not become me to adopt." He then retired to his homestead in Bedford, where he lived another twenty-nine years. Hamilton did not so quietly depart the political arena, though by the time of his fateful encounter with Aaron Burr at Weehawken in 1804, he, too, likely knew that the Federalist moment had passed.[80]

Although a statue of Thomas Jefferson given to Columbia University by Joseph Pulitzer occupies a prominent place on the western side of Columbia's South Field and serves as a pendant to the statue of Hamilton on the eastern side, there is no evidence that in his day the sage of Monticello ever visited Columbia. Nor that he was ever invited. Yet, at a fairly high level of political abstraction, Jefferson could be said to have become during his lifetime and remained since, much as William Livingston in the 1750s, a nemesis of Columbia. Three ideas identified with him and by him successfully impressed on a substantial portion of the American body politic made—make—him so.

The first was his lifelong distrust and disparagement of cities, which he elaborated on in his *Notes on the State of Virginia*, written in the early 1780s. "The mobs of great cities," he wrote, "add just so much to the support of pure government, as sores do to the strength of the human body." Nor did he ever seriously modify these views. In 1823 he described New York as "a Cloacina of all the depravities of human nature." When Jefferson set about creating a university to his own specifications, he located it in Charlottesville, well removed from what in the Virginia of his later years passed for its principal cities. He was one with Princeton's President Witherspoon in believing, as John Vardill caricatured this rustic persuasion, that a proper education was to be had "not an inch too near, nor an inch too far from the ungracious cities of New York and Philadelphia."[81]

The second Jeffersonian idea was that affairs of government are best conducted away from the temptations and corruptions endemic to large, cosmopolitan cities. This idea first took concrete form in a proposal, advanced by Madison in 1790, that the nation's capital be removed from New York City, where it had been located by congressional action in 1785, and relocated to the banks of the Potomac River in the Virginia countryside. But it was Jefferson who, over dinner—with none other than Alexander Hamilton—brokered the deal. In exchange for Madison's assurances that he would not oppose the secretary of the treasury's plan for the assumption of state debts by the federal government, the linchpin of his financial policies, Hamilton agreed to support the settlement of the capital on the Potomac, with Philadelphia as the interim capital.[82]

In fall 1790 the national government decamped from New York for Philadelphia and from there, in 1800, to Washington, a place the Boston Federalist congressman Josiah Quincy called "that cemetery of all comfort." "What can we know, in this wilderness," he complained, "of the effects of our measures upon civilized and commercial life?" But it was Hamilton himself who, two years before his fateful bargain, in *Federalist No. 27* best described the negative consequence of "a government continually at a distance and out of sight": it could "hardly be expected to interest the sensations of the people." In the two centuries since, the separation of the political capital in Washington from the commercial and more latterly the cultural capital of the country in New York has had an unfortunate parochializing effect on both cities, while perpetuating the Jeffersonian notion in the rest of the country that cities are inimical to democratic institutions.[83]

The purchase of Louisiana represents the third Jeffersonian initiative to have an unfortunate impact on New York and, by extension, Columbia. As late as 1800 most Americans—and virtually all New Yorkers—conceived of the United States much as Lewis Morris had conceptualized the English colonies a century earlier: a long, narrow concave arc of settled land along the Atlantic coast, extending from the northern boundary of Massachusetts (later Maine) to the southern border of Georgia. It included several sizable towns, each situated so as to provide the hinterlands access to Atlantic trade routes. One oriented oneself by facing eastward toward the Atlantic, with north the left and south the right.

With Jefferson's purchase of Louisiana from Bonaparte in 1803, this orientation changed. Americans now pivoted 180 degrees from east to west, literally turning their backs to the Atlantic and Europe. The future of the United States would now turn more on the settlement of the West than on the further development of its eastern cities or its maritime trade with the rest of the world. It was as if with the Louisiana Purchase Jefferson provided Americans with a way out of what in the 1790s seemed to be the inexorable concentration of populations in established cities by providing them with vast amounts of underpopulated land in the West that would take a century to settle. In point of fact, the deurbanization that occurred between 1800 and 1810 proved temporary, and the eastern cities, most spectacularly New York City, continued to be magnets for both foreign and internal migrations. Nonetheless, with the expansion of the nation west, it became possible for Americans to view New York City as less at the center/heart of America than on its eastern fringes, in closer contact with Europe than Middle America. Thus New Yorkers seemed to justify the judgment, as Americans (often critically) and Europeans (more positively) would have it, that, as the English tourist and novelist Ford Maddox Ford titled his 1927 book, *New York Is Not America*. Then, by extension, neither is Columbia.[84]

CHAPTER 3

Knickerbocker Days: The Limits of Academic Reform

And yet after so long, one thinks
In those days everything was better.

> *Randall Jarrell, "In Those Days"*

Marched to the tune of "Hail, Columbia" which was the first thing to put any feeling of life into me.

> *George Templeton Strong, October 2, 1838*

The "Great Retrogression" Revisited

IN 1955 Columbia historians Richard Hofstadter and Walter Metzger published an influential history of American higher education under the misleading title *The Development of Academic Freedom in the United States.* Hofstadter wrote the first part of the study, "The Age of the College," which began with the European antecedents of the colonial colleges and concluded with American colleges on the eve of the Civil War. His analysis evoked a historical trajectory marked by modest beginnings and upward movement, especially during the years of the American Revolution and the founding of the new republic, when colleges achieved "a notable degree of freedom, vitality and public usefulness" and when their graduates played important roles in the nation's political culture. There then followed a period of decline in the intellectual reach and public regard of American colleges, even as they multiplied in numbers. Hofstadter provocatively characterized this second period in the history of American higher education, running from 1800 or so through the 1850s, as the "Great Retrogression." It was then, he argued, that the legacy of the colonial colleges as outward-looking centers of enlightened thought and political liberty gave way to sectarian squabbling, intellectual repression, needless duplication, and wide-scale institutional failure. For Hofstadter, the era of the "Old-Time College" was an obstacle to the coming "Age of the University" and best passed beyond as quickly as possible. So much for Columbia nostalgia.[1]

While some academic historians quickly applied Hofstadter's retrogression thesis to specific institutional histories, others found the evidence on which it was based too selective and questionable. Colin Burke effectively demonstrated, for example, that the failure of early-nineteenth-century colleges was not nearly as widespread a phenomenon as Hofstadter (and his sources) indicated. Others, among them Hofstadter's own students, who were more favorably disposed toward denominational colleges and less enamored of the secular university than he have offered full-throated apologias for the antebellum evangelical college. Still others have questioned Hofstadter's view that what was missing from these colleges was the implementation of a view expressed by President Paul Chadbourne of Williams College in 1873, with which Hofstadter concluded his part of the book: "Professors are sometimes spoken of as working for the college. They are the college."[2]

To be sure, Hofstadter overstated the extent of retrogression and overlooked much that was positive about American colleges in the early nineteenth century. Yet no amount of revisionism can overcome the fact that several colleges chartered before the Revolution did find surviving the opening decades of the nineteenth century a near thing. Princeton, on the history of which Hofstadter drew extensively, and the University of Pennsylvania are cases in point. And so is Columbia College, which he only touched on. It, too, had seemed to matter, both intellectually and politically, in revolutionary times, when as King's College it was at the center of the imperial and professional establishment of colonial New York, and again in the 1790s, when its graduates formed a disproportionately large national presence during the age of Federalism.[3]

Hofstadter identified two principal sources of this lamentable retrogression: the national reaction against the Enlightenment in the wake of the French Revolution and the needless "multiplying and scattering of colleges" that resulted from denominational sponsorship and sectarian competition. Together, these produced an era in which denominational colleges set the pattern, one that allowed no room for a primitive appreciation of academic freedom, Hofstadter's ostensible theme, and no hearing for the would-be sponsors of universities, his heroes. And yet, whether one decries the "Old-Time College" as a stubborn obstacle to the wished-for appearance of the secular university or, with Hofstadter's revisionist critics, defends the college and at least inferentially casts a cool eye on the secular university that succeeded it, two questions remain: why did the college resist as long as it did reforms that we now know led to the university, and why, when this resistance ceased, reform occurred at Columbia with such a rush? This chapter takes up the first question.

What Is To Be Done?

The retrospective failings of early Columbia College come easily to hand. First, in a city that by the beginning of the nineteenth century was already the largest and for the next half-century would be the fastest growing in the nation, was the College's failure to grow. Between 1800 and 1850, while New York City's population doubled every twelve years, Columbia College enrollments experienced no overall growth but operated within a narrow band ranging from a high of 125 to a low of 75 students. Graduating classes varied from a high of 35 to a low of 19, with a median of 23.[4]

Second, in the most demographically diverse city in the nation, early Columbia College failed to diversify. Instead, it continued to draw nearly all its students, faculty, presidents, and trustees from one of the city's smaller and insulated communities. If anything, the proportion of Columbians drawn from the city's Episcopalian ranks increased during the antebellum era. Allowing for the presence of a few members of the allied Dutch Reformed communion, the occasional Presbyterian, and the infrequent Baptist, Methodist, or Unitarian, the religious spectrum represented at Columbia was almost certainly the narrowest of any antebellum college. The presence of a Jewish student in the 1830s was sufficiently rare to be noted by his classmates; that of a Catholic student equally so.[5]

Third, in the "era of the common man" and in a city overwhelmingly composed of common laborers and artisans, renters and debtors, early Columbia College failed to democratize. Instead, it remained a bastion of class privilege catering to the city's tiny reservoir of property holders and professionals, capitalists and creditors. Its ninety dollar tuition, by the 1820s again the highest in the country, both reflected and reinforced its economic exclusivity. Rather than a vehicle for individual upward social mobility, early Columbia College served as an emblem of achieved familial social status.[6]

Finally, early Columbia College failed to make a place for either young women or blacks (there were some fifteen thousand of the latter in the city in 1830). To be sure, not many contemporary colleges followed the example of Oberlin, which from its opening in 1836 admitted women and actively recruited free blacks, but the case of Oberlin at least suggests the theoretical (if anachronistic) possibility of Columbia's having done so.[7]

There is an inference embedded in any such litany of early Columbia's failures that had Columbia opened its doors to a wider segment of New Yorkers—to non-Episcopalians, to the sons of middling sorts and of the working classes, to women and African Americans—they would have come. And in their coming, another inference: that Columbia College would have achieved a size that would have done justice to its location in the midst of hundreds of thousands of people. But is either inference reasonable? Was early Columbia's failure to grow a local story, susceptible to local remedy, or was it more national in character and in need of a macroeconomic explanation? It was both, but more the second than the first.[8]

The macroeconomic answer to the question "Why didn't early Columbia

College grow?" is "Because it operated within a no-growth sector of the national economy, a sector characterized by insufficient demand—for a college education—exacerbated by excess supply—in the form of competition from other colleges." In short, there were too few takers for too many providers.

Why so few takers? The macroeconomic answer is that little social and even less economic utility attached itself to college going in Jacksonian America. A college degree was not required to practice law or medicine, and all attempts to make it a requirement in the years around the Revolution were by the age of Jackson politically discredited as elitist, exclusionary, and monopolistic. As for the ministry, the absence of a college degree seems to have enhanced the prospects of some would-be ministers, if one accepts the career counselings of one of the era's most influential ministers, Charles Grandison Finney. College was deemed of no value in the world of commerce, as the success of the non-college-going John Jacob Astor, Commodore Vanderbilt, Andrew Carnegie, and John D. Rockefeller proved. Horace Greeley, Herman Melville, Walt Whitman, and Samuel Clemens all made their way as writers without benefit of college, as did Abraham Lincoln in politics, the inventor Samuel Morse, the shipbuilder Donald McKay, Thomas A. Edison, and on and on.[9]

In 1800 one man of college-going age for every two hundred or so went to college; in 1850, by even the generous estimates of Hofstadter's sharpest critics, the ratio had improved only marginally, whereas Hofstadter and others (including Columbia's tenth president, Frederick A. P. Barnard) had the ratio dropping significantly. Massive immigration swelled the denominator—and persistent skepticism as to the value of college kept down the numerator. So much for demand.[10]

On the supply side, why so many providers? Colin Burke and others have revised the numbers of colleges operating in the first half of the nineteenth century downward from the six hundred or so cited by Hofstadter, but the fact remains that the numbers were in the hundreds. It was very easy to start up a college. Little more was required for a private college than a religious or civic sponsor with the political wherewithal to put together a board of trustees and apply for a charter from the state legislature. The legislature, once having issued charters for some colleges, would be reluctant to withhold charters for others, lest it show favoritism. Established colleges were unsuccessful in efforts to block the chartering of new colleges, as Harvard's attempt to block Amherst and Yale's to block Wesleyan attest. In addition, private academies could become colleges simply by informing the legislature of their intention to offer collegiate-level instruction. No evidence of the financial wherewithal for these ventures was required. Public colleges had an even easier time securing a legislative green light.[11]

Charter in hand, the sponsors only needed a building, president, teachers, and students. A vacant building in town, the availability of a would-be president or teachers in the persons of unchurched ministers or unemployed college graduates, and a momentary surge in college-age boys about to graduate from the local academy were often all it took. And if the sponsors could not sustain the early local interest in the college, then it folded, which also happened all the time.

While such a college might never manage to attract enough students to survive, its recruiting exertions often prevented the growth of established colleges in the region beyond the point where their primary consideration was survival. The operative and conscious strategy among Jacksonian colleges was "Beggar thy neighbor." Thus it was a commonplace to hear, for example, from Union College's competitors that it actively recruited students they had just expelled. Nor was it unusual for a college to locate close to an existing one, intending thereby to lure away students, with the resulting competition killing them both off.

A few colleges prospered in this Darwinian environment. Union was a case in point, at least as long as its redoubtable president, Eliphalet Nott, kept his wits about him. And Yale did well, so well, in fact, that it was for most of the first half of the nineteenth century the largest, most financially solvent, and best-known college in the country. Even so, total annual enrollments in New Haven throughout the period never exceeded 600, the largest graduating class being 125. But most other colleges struggled mightily to stay afloat. This was even true of Harvard, where enrollments dropped to 150 in the late 1820s and showed little growth through the 1830s. It was not until the late 1840s that Harvard got safely beyond its enrollment crunch. For Penn and Princeton, the crunch hit earlier in the century and did not let up until after the Civil War. So, too, with Brown and Dartmouth, Rutgers and Colgate. For these institutions, surviving the age of Jackson was a close call.[12]

Nor did it help matters that many of the era's illustrious college graduates, among them the philosopher-poet Ralph Waldo Emerson (Harvard College 1821), the historian-politician George Bancroft (Harvard College 1817) and the essayist Henry David Thoreau (Harvard College 1837), were much given to bad-mouthing college going. For Emerson, in his 1837 "Phi Beta Kappa Address," colleges were part of the burdensome past where "meek young men grow up in libraries, believing it their duty to accept the views which Cicero, which Locke, which Bacon, have given: forgetful that Cicero, Locke and Bacon were only young men in libraries when they wrote these books." For Bancroft, the nation's well-being should not be entrusted to college graduates; better to the likes of Andrew Jackson, "the unlettered man of the West, the nursling of the wilds, the farmer of the Hermitage, little versed in books, unconnected by science with the tradition of the past." For Thoreau, college was the ultimate "in doors" activity, when what was needed was "life out of doors." Not exactly the satisfied customers Jacksonian colleges needed at the moment.[13]

Even allowing for the slow national market, could Columbia College not have increased local enrollments? Or were low enrollments intended, as with King's College, which did not grow because the College did not want them to grow? This latter was no longer the case. There is no evidence to suggest that the College turned away applicants. Admissions policies did not discriminate on the basis of religion. Jews and Catholics were not excluded from admission, as both continued to be at mid-nineteenth-century Oxford. Non-Episcopalian Protestants were not thin on the ground because they were excluded as much as because they did not seek admission.

Nor did admissions requirements set the bar particularly high. A boy seeking admission was obliged to know some Latin and Greek, as well as some mathematics beyond what would be available in a grammar school. But learning enough of each to pass the oral exams was a matter of a summer's help from a private tutor. Twenty lines of the *Aeneid*, one page of Xenophon, and a page of Plato's *Phaedo*: so much for the ancients. The mathematics portion of the admission exam consisted of manipulating simple equations and reciting some geometric theorems. Columbia's requirements were not higher than elsewhere; they were likely lower.

Given the financial arrangements under which Columbia's faculty operated throughout the antebellum period, they had every reason to facilitate admissions. Some trustees suspected as much when faculty regularly admitted students at twelve, even after the trustees in 1809 set the minimum at fourteen. To this charge the faculty predictably replied that their thirteen-year-olds were "among the best scholars."[14]

But if there was no conscious policy to limit enrollments, was enough done to increase them? The College did not advertise. But neither did its competition, other than to announce the dates of admissions exams, commencements, and special events. Some colleges, however, did get news of on-campus revivals and successful recruitment efforts for foreign missions in the religious press. These in turn encouraged the American Educational Society, organized in 1815 to prepare for careers in the ministry "every young man of proper character who may not be otherwise provided for," to provide these colleges with scholarships. For some small colleges, such as Williams and Hamilton, but also for the largest—Yale—AES scholarship students represented a sizable proportion of their enrollment and AES funds a substantial part of their income. Colleges lacking revivalist activity on campus, notably Harvard, Penn, and Columbia, shared in none of the society's largesse.[15]

In Columbia's case, the failure to recruit the sons of non-Episcopal families throughout the first half of the nineteenth century was not for want of trying. In 1830 the Columbia trustees announced that, for a onetime gift of twenty thousand dollars, any New York City Protestant church could thereafter send up to four sons of church members to the College annually without further payment of tuition or fees. A similar offer was made with respect to establishing a professorial chair: for twenty thousand dollars, a church or civic organization could name the subject and nominate the professor. Neither the Presbyterians nor any other Protestant denomination took up the trustees on either of these offers.[16]

What about altering the curriculum? Critics at the time and historians since have argued that the College's offerings could have been made more attractive, more stimulating, and more utilitarian by reducing the heavy emphasis on Greek and Latin and increasing instruction in modern foreign languages, offering practical courses in science and mathematics, and allowing students more choice in their subjects. It is certainly true that early Columbia College was innocent of the charge of promoting curricular change for the sake of change. The curriculum in place in 1809, at the time of the Rufus King–led trustee review and that in place five decades and four presidents later, in 1857, are virtually identical. Both consisted of the equivalent of thirty-two required semester units (each representing five class hours per week in a fourteen-week semester), of which fourteen were given over to Greek and Latin, eight to mathematics and science, and eight to the humanities. Greek and Latin remained part of the required course work for all four years. Mathematics was studied in three of a student's four years, beginning with algebra and culminating in differential equations. Instruction in the sciences (natural philosophy) came in the second and third years and was limited to the physical sciences, specifically to physics and chemistry, with an occasional gesture in the direction of geology. The study of rhetoric and English literature figured prominently in the second and third years, while moral philosophy, jurisprudence, and/or political economy (an early Columbia novelty first taught by John McVickar), depending on whether the president taught (Duer did; Moore and King did not), were offered to juniors and seniors.[17]

Largely missing was study of languages other than Greek and Latin. Hebrew was advertised at King's College and offered by the professor of oriental languages, Christophe Kunze, as part of his regular teaching program in the 1780s. In the early 1800s Hebrew was regarded in the same way as modern European foreign languages were viewed, that is, as an after-hours option for which a separate fee was collected. French, too, had figured prominently in the initial curricular plans of the reorganized Columbia College but by the early 1800s had become available only by special arrangement and with an additional fee. So, too, with Spanish and Italian. In the case of Italian, Lorenzo Da Ponte offered instruction in the late 1820s to Columbia students who were prepared to stay on after the regular schoolday and pay. Few were. Two decades later, when the possibility of again offering Italian as part of the regular curriculum came up at a trustee meeting in 1855, it was discovered that the College already had a professor of Italian on the books. After Da Ponte's death in 1838, one Felix Foresti had been appointed, but it turned out he had moved to Chicago in the early 1840s. The matter was dropped.[18]

The closest Columbia (or almost any other antebellum college) came to offering something even remotely classifiable as the social sciences was not until the 1830s, when Professor of Moral Philosophy John McVickar offered juniors a course in political economy. History (other than ancient history taught by the classicists) would not enter the curriculum until the late 1850s, well after Harvard and Yale introduced it.[19]

President Duer's course in international law, taught to seniors in the 1830s, could by a stretch be described as a preprofessional course, but it was the only one to be found in the curriculum after James Kent's departure in 1796 and brief return in 1826–28. And with the closing of the Medical School in 1813, Columbia students would go without instruction in the biological sciences for six decades. This helps account for the sharp drop in Columbians going into medicine during this period. Columbia also offered less to students interested in the ministry than did Yale, Princeton, Brown, and Williams, all of which were headed up by practicing ministers who taught prescribed courses in Christian apologetics. Only Penn and Harvard graduates (and Harvard had a divinity school) were as unlikely to enter the ministry as Columbia's.[20]

Finally, despite the presence of Mozart's sometime librettist Lorenzo Da Ponte, Columbia offered no instruction in the arts—musical, visual, whatever. Private music and drawing lessons were available in the city.

In 1939 a Barnard instructor of English (and later author of *The Columbia Historical Portrait of New York*), John A. Kouwenhoven, offered a spirited defense of the humanities offerings in the early Columbia College curriculum. He was particularly impressed by the presence of contemporary English authors such as Wordsworth and Shelley among the assigned readings. "It was not such a culturally barren world," he concluded, "as has been imagined." More recently, Columbia-trained historian Wilson Smith made a vigorous argument for a required curriculum of the early Columbia sort, seeing it as a noble attempt to instill coherence and community.[21]

Still, one familiar with the hundreds of undergraduate courses offered at Columbia today comes away from a review of the early Columbia College cur-

riculum with a feeling akin to that of Henry James in 1876 after he had cata-
loged what was left out of mid-nineteenth-century American culture as compared with English culture: "Everything." And yet showing that a narrow curriculum—with "everything" left out—and a small student body coexisted is
not enough to make the case that the former was responsible for the latter. It is
as logically sound to view the causal relationship as working the other way.
That is, it was because Columbia was small that its curriculum was so limited,
and expanding the curriculum would not necessarily have expanded enrollments. It would, however, have greatly increased the cost of instruction, a consideration that the trustees, given the precariousness of the College's finances,
were obliged to take seriously.[22]

The same consideration likely prevented the trustees from having the College
become residential. Doing so would have required the eviction of the president
and faculty from College Hall and probably the construction of a separate dormitory. Building on College property out on lease or acquiring new property to
accommodate a dormitory was an expensive gamble that the trustees were not
willing to take. Had they taken it, and had residential students arrived in numbers, Columbia would then have been confronted with the disruptive disciplinary problems that existed at other residential colleges. Best to hold tight.

Enter NYU

The history of early Columbia College provides an opportunity to observe the
relationship between various proposed academic reforms and enrollments. In
1831, as if things weren't bad enough, Columbia faced direct local competition
in the form of the University of the City of New York (later New York University), which opened its doors in October. That the new college first located itself
on the corner of Beekman and Nassau Streets, directly opposite City Hall Park
from Columbia College, was one indication that it intended to challenge the
older college for the sons of what its founders called "the rising mercantile
classes."[23]

The new university plan was to offer a more utilitarian curriculum than
Columbia's, more business-related courses, and no Greek or Latin, all of which
would "correspond with the practical spirit of the age." It would also appeal to
a range of religious groups on the basis of its nondenominationalism. And it
would be cheaper in the bargain. A year after opening, the University of the City
of New York announced plans to construct a building on Washington Square;
two years later, the impressive Collegiate Gothic structure opened. Its presence
spoke to the seriousness of the challenge the university posed to Columbia. By

its second year of operation, it had 158 students (half of them full-time), whereas Columbia College, eighty years after its founding, had only 120.[24]

In 1946 President-Emeritus Nicholas Murray Butler grandly observed that "nothing that NYU did ever affected Columbia in the least. . . . The institutions might just as well have been a thousand miles apart." Evidence from 1830 suggests otherwise. Even before NYU opened, Columbia Trustee John Henry Hobart oversaw the printing of *An Address to the Citizens of New York on the Claims of Columbia College and the New University to Their Patronage.* Hobart's purpose was to block the opening of the planned university altogether, but, failing that, to have the Corporation of the City of New York (to which NYU's founders had appealed for support) agree not to patronize it. Hobart offered three arguments as to why NYU was a bad idea. The first was demographic: "There are no reasonable data which warrant the conclusion that two colleges can at present flourish in the City." The second was economic: that Columbia was already carrying a debt of twenty thousand dollars and competition would only increase it. The third was sectarian: that while Columbia "has never been made to promote Episcopal views," in the face of direct competition, it "will have to become an Episcopal College."[25]

Clearly on the defensive, Hobart assured his readers that Columbia, while already cheap, open to the public, and "*not* a sectarian institution," would now become cheaper, more open, and still less sectarian. It would also, he announced with fanfare, introduce a new scientific and literary curriculum as a complement to its traditional classical curriculum.[26]

As it turned out, the trustees' concern with competition from the new university and its scientific and literary curriculum were coterminous. Lacking the support of the faculty, many of whom saw it as an added burden and quietly subverted it, the scientific and literary curriculum (which substituted a few courses in mathematics and rhetoric for junior and senior courses in Greek and Latin) was discontinued in 1843. By the mid-1830s it had ceased to attract more than a handful of students and gave no signs of helping on the admissions front. By then, however, NYU had its own problems.[27]

The huge cost of the Washington Square building ($140,000) immediately put NYU into financial straits from which it did not emerge until after the Civil War. Its financial difficulties were compounded by the fact that its first chancellor, the Reverend James Matthews (1831–38), got caught exaggerating enrollments and not paying faculty for months at a time. His immediate successors were no more successful in realizing NYU's early promise, either as the city's premier university or as a vehicle for class and social mobility.[28]

The argument here is that there was little Columbia College could have done to alter its situation—that of a small, traditional day college in the middle of the world's fastest-growing city—until larger numbers of New York's young men could be persuaded that going to Columbia was worth the candle. Meanwhile, just about every reform being proposed or implemented elsewhere carried problems and risks. Not until the early 1870s did Henry Adams report, with surprise, a student's acknowledging that "the degree of Harvard College is worth money to me in Chicago." Until a Columbia degree became similarly valuable, each of the early College's four constituent estates—presidents, faculty, trustees, and students (perhaps most of all the students)—extracted some comfort from the protracted status quo.[29]

"Excellent Persons in Want of a Situation"

From the founding of King's College in 1754 through the early history of Columbia College and down to the Civil War, nine men served as president. Six have already been mentioned: Samuel Johnson (1754–63), Myles Cooper (1763–75), William Samuel Johnson (1787–1800), Charles Henry Wharton (1801), Benjamin Moore (1801–10), and William Harris (1811–29). The next three were William Duer (1829–42), Nathaniel Fish Moore (1842–49), and Charles King (1849–63). While each brought to the office his own personality and previous experience, all nine shared characteristics that help account for the absence of any presidential challenge to the academic status quo in its first century.[30]

What is likely to be viewed as a critical collective biography should be prefaced by enumerating a few virtues of omission. None of Columbia's early presidents was terminated by scandal, unless Wharton's no-show can be so characterized, and most remained in office for reasonable terms. None was undone by student disturbances or charges of financial malfeasance; none was the subject of personal scandal or, as far as I can tell, even the rumor of one. All but President Harris survived their presidencies, with three (William Samuel Johnson, Duer, and Nathaniel Moore) experiencing protracted remissions from presidentially contracted maladies. Finally, as far as the evidentiary record allows, none produced progeny who brought shame to their fathers or the College they served. How many other colleges can say as much?

The most significant fact about all nine of these gentleman is that none saw the Columbia presidency as an instrument to bring about necessary and fundamental change. Some, like the two President Johnsons, came to the position after active and conspicuous careers elsewhere, while Myles Cooper took on the presidency at the outset of his professional career. Wharton, Benjamin Moore, and William Harris all accepted the job in midcareer, but with some expectation of important responsibilities after the Columbia presidency. Not one saw his role as being to shake up the College or challenge the standing arrangements by which it operated. Cooper might be thought to be an exception, but his reforms were essentially conservative, designed to bring the College into conformity with the approved Oxford College model. Benjamin Moore informed the trustees, in taking the job while holding down two other, more demanding ones, not to expect much in the way of change during his presidency. The circumstances by which William Harris came to the position—coupled with Provost John Mitchell Mason and told to retain his pulpit at St. Mark's—were not conducive to an activist presidency.

Indeed, of Columbia's early administrators, Mason was, at age forty-one and by temperament and professional situation, the most likely to view his responsibilities as including pressing for fundamental changes in the College's operations. "If ever mortal possessed decision of character," a contemporary allowed, "that mortal was John M. Mason." The others readily accepted their role as essentially custodial, even curatorial, in character. It is revealing that Mason's career as an administrator at Columbia was terminated after five years, ostensibly at his request but under circumstances that allow the possibility that his resignation was exacted. It is clear from his next job choice, president of Dickinson College, in Pennsylvania, that he did not leave Columbia because he was sick of college administration.[31]

The custodial presidency norm seems not to have been so much a mandate of the trustees as the consequence of cumulative precedents: of Samuel Johnson's giving away power to the King's College governors; of Myles Cooper's being too young and distracted to recoup it; of William Samuel Johnson's being too old to take control; of Benjamin Moore's being otherwise preoccupied. By 1816 it seemed natural that the forceful Provost Mason went and the compliant Harris stayed.

College presidents elsewhere were more aggressive. During his six-plus decades in office, President Eliphalet Nott at Union College left no question as to who was in charge there. Jeremiah Day (1817–47) was an only slightly less commanding presence at Yale, where in 1828 he secured faculty and trustee endorsement of the famously defensive "Yale Faculty Report" in the face of legislative and alumni calls for reform. When the Harvard Corporation in 1829 elected the ex-congressman and five-term mayor of Boston Josiah Quincy president, they knew they had themselves a force to be reckoned with. His presidency (1829–45), marked at the outset by a full-scale student rebellion and at its close by Harvard's taking its first steps to becoming a university, did not disappoint on this score. Even NYU's chancellor, James Matthews (1831–38), was clearly a man with a mission, not easily deflected by criticisms from his trustees, unpaid faculty, or disgruntled students.[32]

Of the three presidents who came after Harris, Columbia's seventh president, William A. Duer (1829–42), came to the job at forty-nine, a seasoned political figure and state supreme court judge recently put off the bench by a change in the governing party. He actively campaigned for the job, the fact that he had no relevant academic experience other than attending a public school in England being of no moment to him or his trustee backers. Duer made no bones about needing the position, its salary (twenty-six hundred dollars), the comfortable lodgings in College Hall, the free tuition for his soon-to-be college-age son, the social prestige, and the duties reliably reported to be not overly arduous. And he was ready to call on trustee friends to get it.[33]

On December 8, 1829, twenty-two trustees cast several ballots but failed to come up with the required thirteen votes for any of the three leading candidates. When Trustee Rev. Jonathan Wainwright (1824–30), the thirty-eight-year-old rector of Grace Church, with four votes, withdrew, that left Duer and Professor of Moral Philosophy John McVickar with nine votes each. The next morning all of Wainwright's votes went to Duer, and he was elected. Some of McVickar's supporters were disappointed enough that they, along with McVickar, soon thereafter engaged in laying the groundwork for NYU. Even some of Duer's backers had second thoughts. "To Duer the presidency was but one prize of many," Trustee Philip Hone (1824–51) recorded in his diary; "to M [McVickar] it was the only prize which was or could be offered in life."[34]

Duer's thirteen years as president went smoothly. He knew most of his students by name (no great feat when there were seldom more than 120) and regularly offered the junior class a course in international law, the student reviews of which were mixed. He made an effort to get a law school going and to revive medical instruction, but nothing came of either plan. In 1842, assumed to have only weeks to live, he retired on a lifetime annuity at age sixty-two but lived another sixteen years, dying in 1858. Throughout his presidency, he neither challenged the trustees nor terrorized the students, this last quality earning him the following diary entry by one of his more observant charges: "The president is not to be accused of tyranny. He has very little of the tyrant." But Duer was also the first of three successive presidents to earn the same student's collective judgment: "excellent persons in want of a situation."[35]

The second "in want of a situation" was Nathaniel Fish Moore, the apotheosis of the custodial president. Except for Cooper, who anticipated his presidency with a year as professor of moral philosophy, and Benjamin Moore, who taught on a part-time basis several years before becoming president, Nathaniel Fish Moore, the latter's nephew, was the first president to have had extensive teaching experience. From 1817, at thirty-five, when he abandoned a law practice that in twelve years had attracted no clients to become an adjunct professor upon John Bowden's death and in anticipation of Peter Wilson's retirement, until his resignation in 1833, Moore taught Greek and Latin and lived in College lodgings. His leaving was occasioned by his coming into family money (the Moores inherited Chelsea), which enabled him to spend the next several years in Europe compiling an impressive personal library. After his return to New York in 1838, he sold his books to Columbia and became the College librarian. A year later, he resigned this position as well to indulge in more traveling. He was then fifty-six, of an age when he could retire without causing notice.[36]

In 1842, when Duer retired, McVickar was again the leading inside candidate and actively seeking the position. But a sufficient number of trustees opposed his election to block it until they could come up with an alternative, even if this was someone uninterested in the position. The name of Nathaniel Fish Moore was thus put forward by the clerk of the trustees, Clement Clark Moore, Nathaniel's cousin. Besides being the putative author of "A Visit from St. Nicholas" (perhaps better known by its opening words, "'Twas the night before Christmas"), C. C. Moore was both Columbia's longest-serving and one of its more influential trustees. And so, at age sixty-two, having later reminded his cousin that "he never sought this situation" and only because "judicious friends should think me qualified for it," Nathaniel Fish Moore became the eighth president of Columbia College (1842–49).[37]

However effective as a means of thwarting McVickar's presidential aspirations, Moore was a distinct failure, even among early Columbia presidents. His discontent became sufficiently known three years into the job that the trustees received an application to succeed him four years before he actually resigned. The only thing he liked about the job was the president's "pleasant residence," which, as a bachelor, he shared with his brother and his sister-in-law. On June 4, 1849, he wrote to the trustees that "I feel I possess no longer, if I ever did, the energy and zeal which the proper discharge of my Presidential office calls for, and I shall gladly see it given into younger and more able hands." To his cousin, he described the job as a "fruitless struggle in which I am forever engaged with perverse youths, amidst the temptations and corrupting influence of this great city, at their most rampant and ungovernable age." There was also, he went on, "the daily necessity imposed on me of expostulating, remonstrating, admonishing; of complaining and appealing to parents; of making vain endeavors to reform the incorrigibly idle; to keep within some bounds of duty headstrong boys who look upon themselves as men, who spurn at obedience, have no respect for age or station, and regard their insolent contempt of authority as proof of manly independence." In sum, he told his cousin, "all these things so embitter my life that I am sometimes fairly sick of it."[38]

Even so, he admitted, the job had not been especially arduous and left him plenty of free time. And in resigning he expected to be treated generously by the trustees. Upon his resignation, they offered and, despite his independent wealth, he accepted a College annuity of five hundred dollars. He lived for another twenty-three years, became a photographer and occasionally attended College functions, before dying in 1872 at age ninety.

The third "excellent gentleman in want of a situation" was Charles King (1849–63), who, like his predecessor, had some hereditary claim to the presidency. He was the son of Rufus King, a delegate to the 1787 Constitutional Convention and Columbia trustee (1806–24). The younger King had succeeded to his father's seat on the board, serving from 1825 to 1838, when he removed himself to New Jersey. Like Duer, King never attended college, but, more than Duer and perhaps any other early Columbia president, he was a man of the world. He lived abroad as a youth. His first gainful occupation was as a merchant, which he became upon marrying Eliza Gracie in 1821 and going to work for her father, Archibald Gracie (the owner of Gracie Mansion). In 1823 King's father-in-law went bankrupt, and his wife died, leaving him with eight children and no job. Three years later, he married Henrietta Low, the daughter of the merchant Nicholas Low, and had another six children with her. During the late 1820s and 1830s he entered the newspaper business as editor of the *New York American*, a leading Whig newspaper. When in the early 1840s the paper ceased to provide the income to which he had become accustomed, he turned his attention to the Columbia presidency. "He wants that place" is how the then-young trustee, Hamilton Fish, put it in 1845. "He is making direct application to those of the trustees with whom he has the right, from old acquaintances, to speak frankly to."[39]

When Moore finally resigned four years later, there were two other candidates, both more insiders than King: the perennial John McVickar and Trustee William Betts (1842–84). McVickar, now sixty-one, was no longer the serious contender he had been in 1829 and 1842, as he and his supporters knew, and Betts's name was put into nomination as a courtesy to Trustee Beverley Robinson, who, over time, nominated his son-in-law for various Columbia jobs. (A year later, Betts was elected to succeed Clement C. Moore as clerk of the board.) The door was open for King, whose supporters on the board recommended him for the presidency in part because of his experience as the head of a large family and thus supposedly possessed of the disciplinarian skills his bachelor predecessor lacked.

If Moore left at sixty-seven because of advancing age, and if McVickar was considered too old at sixty-one, the election of the sixty-year-old Charles King as the ninth president of Columbia College might seem odd. Attribute it to his being yet another "excellent gentlemen in want of a situation," in King's case, a condition compounded by a large family and no immediate source of income until his wife's inheritance came through. (It did so in 1857, and all the Kings relaxed.) As with his predecessor, the prospect of taking up lodgings at 1 College Place was a big incentive, and, as with his predecessor's predecessor, so was the four-thousand-dollar salary that came with the job. When Columbia moved to Forty-ninth Street in 1857, the first building erected was a twenty-five-room president's house, into which the Kings reluctantly moved. During his presidency, King added another perk to his job—and struck an early blow for affirmative action—by hiring his two unmarried daughters as College registrar and clerk, at salaries of five hundred dollars each.

As the next chapter will argue, the College began to stir in all sorts of ways during King's presidency. But little evidence points to King as the prime stirrer. He did interest himself in promoting athletics, especially the manly sports of boxing and billiards, and, with the coming of the Civil War, closely identified himself and the College with the Unionist cause. His son Augustus F. King (CC 1860) was among the first Columbians to heed Lincoln's call for volunteers in 1861 by accepting a commission and attending a College service in uniform. He died in combat a year later.

It fell to Hamilton Fish in early 1864 to urge King to resign the presidency. Suffering from the gout (as had Myles Cooper and William Samuel Johnson before him) and physically exhausted, King did so. He died three years later, among members of his considerable family then residing in Frascati, Italy. Among subsequent Columbia presidents, none would be in a position to take the office so lightly. He was the last president to agree with Nathaniel Fish Moore's characterization that "the duties of my office are, in one sense, not laborious, for they leave me much spare time." Again, one thinks of Trollope, this time of his Septimus Harding, the warden of Hiram's Hospital in *The Warden*, for whom securing the position was the active part of the effort, the job being the easy part.[40]

The trouble with being president of early Columbia College was that its responsibilities were too small to take up the full energies of an ambitious and capable man. A century after Samuel Johnson became the first president, the eighth, Charles King, presided over a student body of fewer than 120 students, a five-man faculty, and a curriculum consisting of thirty-two courses. He had no administrative staff to oversee (aside from his daughters), a single janitor, and no fund-raising responsibilities. He was kept out of faculty hiring though obliged to be involved in the day-to-day disciplinary process. Nor was he expected to confer with other college presidents, government and foundation leaders, or the press. It was as close to a sinecure as a well-paying and reasonably prestigious job could be in antebellum America. No wonder someone like Charles King, who was worldly enough to spot a sinecure, set his sights on it and, once he had it, relaxed.

A word on John McVickar, the perennial presidential also-ran. The fact that he was viewed early on as a protégé of the controversial Trustee John Henry Hobart and became Hobart's first biographer may have permanently damaged him in the eyes of others on the board. So, too, his involvement in the founding of NYU might have raised questions about his loyalties. That he was an ordained Episcopal minister likely lost him non-Episcopalian votes. The fact that he so obviously wanted the job probably also harmed him, even if it did not King, and that fact that he came from the faculty might have hurt his chances as well, even if it did not Moore.[41]

Moore had retired from the faculty seven years before his election to the presidency in 1842, whereas McVickar would have come directly from it in 1829, in 1842, and even in 1849. This immediate identification with the faculty may have done him in. Trustees in McVickar's day could hardly imagine Columbia faculty except as being always around Columbia students, whose constant company, as President Moore intimated in his resignation letter, somehow unsuited them for even the modest responsibilities that went with the early Columbia presidency. It was not a Columbia faculty member but an erstwhile Harvard one, the twenty-six-year-old Edward Everett, who confessed to a female acquaintance in 1820 that he found the responsibilities of teaching at Harvard were "not respectable enough in the estimation they bring with them" and that they led him "too much into contact with some little men and many little things." Whether by "little men" Everett was referring to his students or his faculty colleagues, the point is much the same, whether made in Cambridge or New York City: extended teaching unsuited a man for executive responsibilities and left him in the end the sum of his acquired eccentricities. And so with McVickar in his last years on the Columbia faculty as viewed by a trustee (and former student): "Mac in his glazed cap, giving everybody a semi-military, semi-clerical salute, is too ridiculous a subject to be gravely treated. A sort of nineteenth-century Knight Templar."[42]

The early Columbia College trustees got the presidents they deserved. That is, they regularly appointed men much like themselves, if not actually themselves. They came to the office with little experience with academic life beyond their own college days (and not even this in the cases of Duer and King). Experience as a professor was viewed as a liability rather than an asset. Ambition was equally suspect, so they tended to favor burned-out cases unlikely to become meddlesome. That a candidate needed the job to shore up his sagging financial situation was not considered a disqualification but evidence that he would be beholden to whomever gave him the job.

Presidents enjoyed no special consideration from trustees; to the contrary, their views were more regularly ignored the longer they held office, as if extended time among the faculty and students deprived them of the mature judgment that presumably secured them the job in the first place. Not one of Columbia's first nine presidents—except the no-show Wharton—left before the trustees were ready to have him go.

"Safe Harbours of Life"

By 1810 the early Columbia College faculty had stabilized at five full-time members: one each to teach Greek, Latin, moral philosophy, mathematics and natural philosophy, and experimental science. It would remain at five for the next half-century. Short-lived enrollment surges that brought class sizes much above twenty-five or so were met with temporary hirings of part-time adjunct professors or an occasional tutor. Unlike Yale, Princeton, and many other antebellum colleges, however, where recent graduates hired as tutors had responsibility for most of the freshmen and sophomores, Columbia made do without tutors. Occasionally, too, a president might take a hand, as President Harris did in teaching rhetoric to freshmen and President Duer in teaching jurisprudence to seniors. Otherwise, early-nineteenth-century Columbia students passed each academic day of their four years in daily contact with four of the College's five-man faculty.

The turnover that characterized the first generation of Columbia College faculty (1784–1816) was such that only two of its seventeen members stayed on until death or retirement. The death of Professor of Rhetoric John Bowden in 1817, along with the advanced "infirmities of age" besetting the sixty-six-year-old Professor of Greek and Latin Peter Wilson (1789–1820), which would result in his retirement three years later, prompted the trustees to make two appointments: John McVickar (1817–64) to take Bowden's place and Nathaniel Fish Moore (1817–35) in anticipation of Wilson's retirement.

Hard on these appointments were three more: in 1820 Charles Anthon (1820–57), as adjunct professor of Latin; later that same year, James Renwick (1820–53), as professor of chemistry and experimental philosophy; and in 1825 Henry James Anderson (1825–43), as professor of mathematics and astronomy. These five appointments, made over eight years, constituted the second generation of early Columbia College faculty, which remained in place for eighteen years.[43]

The similarities among these five men and their differences with those they replaced are equally striking. All were raised in New York City, all attended and graduated from Columbia College, and all were at least nominal Episcopalians. All owed their Columbia appointments to the presence of personal sponsors on the board of trustees, and all remained within the Columbia family for the rest of their lives. McVickar was to teach at Columbia for 47 years (1817–64), Anthon for 37 (1820–57), and Renwick for 33 (1820–53). Anderson resigned his professorship after 18 years (1825–43) but returned to serve as a Columbia trustee for 24 more (1851–75). Moore's briefer tenure, of 15 years (1820–35), was followed by three years as College librarian (1838–41) and seven as president (1842–49). Together, these five were involved in Columbia as student, faculty member, trustee, or president for a total of 204 years, or half their collective lives.

Spending most of their adult lives as Columbia faculty members was no part of their original plans upon leaving college. John McVickar aspired to a career as an Episcopalian minister, was ordained in 1812 by his spiritual mentor Bishop John H. Hobart, and later that year became minister of Hyde Park's Episcopal Church. His marriage to the daughter of Hyde Park's leading citizen and one-time dean of the Columbia Medical Faculty and Columbia trustee (1787–1804), Dr. Samuel Bard, both eased his pastoral way there and assured him a second sponsor when, on the occasion of Dr. Bowen's death in 1817, McVickar expressed interest in the professorship of rhetoric.

With his maternal cousin Clement Moore newly appointed as clerk of the board and his uncle William Moore a trustee of long standing, McVickar was not likely to be overlooked. Indeed, it is probably fair to assume that, given his Trinity Church childhood, his Columbia College adolescence, and his acquaintanceship with the New York clerical fraternity, he was known to most of the Columbia trustees.

Nathaniel Fish Moore and Charles Anthon started out to become lawyers, though in neither was it a driving ambition. Moore's apprenticeship under Columbia Trustee Beverley Robinson led to his admission to the bar in 1806, which in turn led to several years during which he vied with his Columbia classmate Gulian C. Verplanck (class of 1801), with whom he shared offices, as the member of the New York bar with the least business. When Verplanck went into politics in 1809, Moore's lock on the dubious honor seemed permanent. After twelve years ostensibly practicing law, Moore allowed cousin Clement Moore to nominate him as adjunct professor of Greek and Latin.

Moore's qualifications were minimally more than any other reasonably bookish Columbia graduate. A thirty-five-year-old bachelor of independent means, Moore accepted the position less as a seriously considered career change than as the swap of one occupational cover for another, taken at the urging of well-placed relatives. He maintained this one into his early fifties, when it could be exchanged for the even less demanding avocation of world-traveling bibliophile. His later acceptance of the Columbia presidency was a personal misstep induced by family pressure and almost instantly regretted.

Anthon's stint as a lawyer was shorter than Moore's but equally half-hearted.

Four years after graduating from Columbia College in 1815, he was admitted to the New York bar. A year later, he jumped at the chance to take Moore's position as adjunct professor of Greek and Latin when Moore succeeded to Wilson's professorship. His way among the trustees was undoubtedly eased by the brilliance of his undergraduate record—still reasonably fresh in their minds—and by the fact that his father had been for nineteen years a trustee.

Unlike Moore, Anthon always wanted to be a professor. His studiousness as an undergraduate won him so many gold medals as a sophomore and junior that he was prohibited from competing as a senior. Only the lack of an academic opening prompted his resorting to the law. He relished the responsibilities that fell to the old-time college professor, not least the parietal ones. "Apart from his college work," his student protégé and later Columbia professor Henry Drisler wrote of him in 1868, "he had no hopes, no desires, no ambitions in life." He was a lifelong bachelor like Moore, but, unlike Moore, who barely tolerated adolescents, Anthon made them his life's companions.[44]

As head of the Columbia Grammar School for twenty-five years, Anthon oversaw the daily preparation of hundreds of young boys, most of whom proceeded on to Columbia College. There, he eventually taught the sons and even grandsons of his first students. For many of them, the most memorable experiences as students at Columbia College occurred in "Bull" Anthon's classes. To draw his wrath once was to be marked for life; the same went for his hard-won praise. Indeed, Anthon's tenure as a Columbia faculty member is the first of a half-dozen or so charismatic teaching careers that, when stitched together, allow those who would trace the frequently disrupted and often impersonal history of Columbia to impose on it a measure of continuity, predictability, and intimacy.

Unlike Moore or McVickar, Anthon steadfastly stuck to his knitting. Again, Drisler on his mentor and role model, after his 1820 appointment: "The only changes in his future course were the alterations in the title of his professorship, his connection with the Grammar School, and the subsequent division of the subjects of his chair."[45]

Anthon resided in 7 College Hall throughout his thirty-seven years on the Columbia faculty, only vacating in 1857 when the hall was razed and he retired. For much of this time, his mother and sisters lived with him. He seldom left the city and only infrequently attended public festivities unrelated to the College. A public welcoming to New York of the Hungarian patriot Louis Kossuth in 1852, for example, drew the entire Columbia faculty, save Professor Anthon. Politics may have played a part in his absence, but more likely College or Grammar School chores kept him to his rooms.

Beyond these responsibilities, there were galleys and proofs of the dozen or so school editions of Latin and Greek texts, classical dictionaries and grammars that he was continually revising and Harper Brothers was forever bringing out in new editions. His editions of Cicero's *Orations*, Caesar's *Commentaries*, and *The Aeneid*—to name but a few—remained for decades thereafter standard fare at American colleges. These texts also made him antebellum Columbia's best-known faculty member. The special relationship that has long existed between New York publishers of school and college texts and the Columbia faculty began with the working evenings Anthon passed in 7 College Hall.

Henry James Anderson graduated from Columbia College in 1818 with an interest in science and an occupational inclination toward medicine. In 1823, a medical degree from the College of Physicians & Surgeons in hand, he tried private practice but abandoned it two years later when the professorship of mathematics and astronomy, recently vacated by Adrian, came available. In the absence of better connected candidates, the job was his.[46]

A competent teacher by most accounts, who enjoyed scandalizing his students by professing to be an agnostic and, worse, a Democrat, Anderson stayed on as member of the faculty for eighteen years, to 1843. By then, the investments he had been making and managing in New York real estate since the mid-1820s freed him of his need for a regular salary. He then resigned, gathered up his family (he was married to the daughter of Lorenzo da Ponte), and embarked on extended travels in Europe and the Middle East. In 1849, during a visit to Rome and as if to confirm his reputation among his students as something of an eccentric, he converted to Catholicism. Two years later, after his return to New York, Anderson was elected to the Columbia board of trustees (1851–75). One would like to conclude that the election of the board's first Catholic, at a time when the city of New York had several times as many Catholics as Episcopalians, was a conscious act in the spirit of religious inclusion, but the more likely scenario is that his fellow trustees tolerated Anderson's Catholicism as being at least not of the Irish sort.[47]

Like Samuel L. Mitchill before him or his colleague Nathaniel Fish Moore, Anderson could look back on his time on the Columbia faculty as a small part of a varied life, with other, quite different parts to follow. Their stints on the faculty were not part of a preconceived career strategy, as more recent generations of mobile faculty might regard them. But neither were their stays at Columbia the sum and substance of their lives, as they were for McVickar, even more so for Anthon, and perhaps most of all for Professor of Chemistry and Experimental Philosophy James Renwick.

Renwick, born in England in 1792, acquired his New York connections on the fly. After graduation from Columbia College in 1807, he became the personal secretary of the New York writer Washington Irving. During the War of 1812 he served as a major in the United States Army and in 1817 accepted a commission as engineer in the New York State Militia. Two years earlier, he had married the daughter of Henry Brevoort (and Washington Irving's niece) and shortly thereafter joined his father-in-law's then thriving mercantile business in New York City. In 1817, just ten years after graduating from Columbia College, he was elected to its board of trustees (1817–20).[48]

The collapse of his father-in-law's firm in 1820 brought an abrupt end to Renwick's string of successes. At thirty, he was without a job or financial resources and the head of a young family. His skill with machinery of all sorts was widely acknowledged but not easily translatable into reputable employment. Irving likely laid Renwick's case before the trustees, who were already disposed to help one of their own, and it was certainly Irving who breathed a sigh of relief when the resignation of John Griscom (1813–20) as professor of chemistry provided an opening. "I am heartily glad that James Renwick is snugly nestled in the old college," Irving wrote to the professor-elect's equally relieved father-in-law. Of his ex-secretary's new position, Irving added: "[it] is a safe harbour of life and a very comfortable and honorable one."[49]

Renwick made good use of his "safe harbour." He and his family moved into 2 College Hall, and three of his sons, Henry (CC 1833), James (CC 1836), and Edward (CC 1839), eventually enrolled in the College. Then as now tuition was waived for faculty children. Renwick set up a laboratory adjoining his family quarters, which he used for his own experiments with steam combustion and hydrodynamics but also made available to his students.

He gave good service as teacher and scholar. "Jemmy" Renwick's courses in chemistry, geology, and physics (which included a section on steam engines) were the only exposure four decades of Columbia undergraduates had to science other than astronomy. Certainly not a scientist on the order of Yale's Benjamin Silliman or Harvard's Asa Gray, Renwick at least partially compensated for his lack of depth in any one part of science by his lively interest in many. He published several school texts in both chemistry and geology, performing in the sciences for the publishing Harper Brothers Anthon's role in the classics. But he also wrote books on engineering projects of his day, principally canal building and railroad construction. His publication of *Elements of Mechanics* (1832), which ran to 502 pages, and his shorter *Treatise on Steam Engines* (1830) led state agencies and corporations to retain his services. In 1840 the State Department utilized Renwick's expertise as a cartographer in determining the border between the United States and Canada as established by the Webster-Ashburton Treaty. He was the first to assume what became the frequently played role of Columbia professor as consultant.[50]

Toward the end of his teaching career, Renwick turned to writing scientific biographies for Jared Sparks' Library of American Biography. Volumes on

David Rittenhouse, Robert Fulton, and Count Rumford appeared in regular succession throughout the 1840s. Even in his last major publication, *Life of DeWitt Clinton* (1859), which focused on Clinton's role in the construction of the Erie Canal, Renwick remained what he had been to hundreds of Columbia students and thousands of fellow New Yorkers: a scientific enthusiast and popularizer. By then, each of his three sons, Henry, an engineer; James Jr., who became one of the country's leading architects; and Edward, who became an engineer of note, had begun to make his mark on the physical life of New York City. Upon his retirement in 1853, after thirty-three years on the faculty, James Renwick became Columbia's first designated professor emeritus and thus came to be anchored permanently in that "safe harbour."

Between Anderson's appointment in 1825 and his resignation in 1843, there was not a single full-time appointment to the Columbia College faculty. A few nonsalaried language teachers came and went, but otherwise the teaching lineup remained the same for eighteen years. And then, between 1843 and 1847, four appointments were made that, without radically transforming the prevailing character of the Columbia faculty, inevitably modified it. The first of these was Charles Wm. Hackley (1845–57), a West Point–trained (1829) engineer turned Episcopal minister who succeeded Anderson as professor of mathematics and astronomy. Known from the outset as an ineffectual teacher, Hackley was eased out of his position in 1857 after it was discovered that his mathematics students could not compute simple interest.[51]

The second appointment, that of Henry Drisler, in 1843, was more in keeping with earlier ones and lasted fifty-four years. Drisler was a New York–reared Columbia College graduate (1839) who broke in as an assistant teaching classics for his mentor and sponsor Charles Anthon at Columbia Grammar School. Like Anthon, Drisler was a bachelor, a prolific editor of school texts, a "deeply religious" Episcopalian, who loved Columbia inordinately. During his half-century at Columbia, he served in virtually every rank available to a faculty member: tutor (1843–45), adjunct professor of Greek and Latin (1845–57), professor of Latin (1857–67), John Jay Professor of Latin (1867–94), acting president (1867, 1888–89), dean (1889–94), and president of the Alumni Association (1872–79). He also provided the only biographical bridge between early Columbia College of the 1840s and the Columbia University of the 1890s that permanently displaced it.[52]

Drisler availed himself of an opportunity in the mid-1840s, between the tutorship and being made adjunct professor, to pursue a few months of classical studies at the University of Berlin. He was the first native-born member of the Columbia faculty to do so. Hard upon his appointment, however, was an even clearer glimpse of the future in the appointment of Johann Ludwig

Tellkampf (1843–47). After completing his Ph.D. studies in law and political science at the University of Göttingen in 1836, Tellkampf came to the United States two years later to teach Latin and modern languages at Union College. When the German-American merchant Frederick Gebhard took up the Columbia trustees' standing offer to create a professorship of the donor's choosing in exchange for a a twenty thousand dollar gift to the College and endowed the Gebhard Professorship of German Literature, it was also Gebhard's right to name the first incumbent. He chose Tellkampf, who readily left behind his appointment at Union and its eight-hundred-dollar salary for the Gebhard professorship and a salary of two thousand dollars.[53]

Tellkampf had a rough time at Columbia, not least when his efforts to discipline the freshman William Astor (CC 1849) put him at odds with his wealthy father, William B. Astor. He quickly acquired the reputation among the trustees as "a flippant little fellow" and among his colleagues as more aware of his own superior academic credentials than was deemed appropriate. Students openly defied him. There was also the problem that German was not part of the regular curriculum, but since Tellkampf was expected to carry a full share of the teaching load, he also taught Latin to freshmen and sophomores. At the first opportunity to secure a German post more in keeping with his credentials—he wanted a professorship in Berlin but settled for a lesser one in 1847 in Breslau—he was gone.[54]

Tellkampf's successor as Gebhard Professor of German, Henry Schmidt (1848–82), was more of a throwback to the early 1800s. American-born, he was a Lutheran minister, whose German carried a distinct American accent. But he seems to have been entirely without pretense, willingly teaching what he was asked and making whatever compromises necessary with his students not to become known as either a martinet or a pushover.[55]

From today's perspective, what is most striking about the early Columbia College faculty was their lack of autonomy and independent agency. All decisions were subject to trustees' approval. This included even the most mundane decisions, such as those regarding student discipline and grading. Their power was almost wholly limited to thwarting reforms initiated by trustees. A case in point was the introduction in 1830, in response to the threat posed by NYU, of the "Scientific and Literary" course. Aside from Renwick, who supported it, all the other faculty quietly set about to subvert it. An elective system at Columbia made no headway because it made no financial sense to the trustees as long as enrollments remained low. But it made no sense to the Columbia faculty either, or at least until they saw themselves as something more than teachers of undergraduates who happened to have been assigned a particular subject area and who, once that subject was gotten up, were not anxious to get up another or, worse, compete with new faculty with new subjects to offer.[56]

They were, in short, personally invested in perpetuating the curricular status quo. Had the trustees' 1830 "Scientific and Literary" curriculum been successfully implemented, as a similar faculty-initiated innovation was at Harvard later in the same decade, Columbia would have led the coming curricular revolution. Instead, adherence to a prescribed curriculum persisted at Columbia into the 1880s, by which time Harvard's curriculum had become almost wholly elective and even Yale and Princeton allowed students more choices earlier on.[57]

Early Columbia College faculty lacked non-Columbia professional colleagues with whom they could share scholarly interests. There were no conferences to attend, no learned journals to read, edit, or publish. Nearly all faculty writing was directed at students, in the form of texts or translations, or at a general reading public. Thus, by default, their lives were far more campus-centered than were those of the teachers who came only a generation later, and spent far more in the company of students.

The Rise of the Student Estate

Early Columbia College students operated in a buyer's market. Accordingly, they were not easily intimidated by faculty whose ultimate power was to expel them. Only a studious few actively sought the approbation of their teachers or the academic honors that came with diligent and faithful work. Most students supported the idea of doing away with individual evaluations altogether, a proposal that enjoyed support among some trustees (particularly those with academically slow sons) and at least one faculty member (McVickar). Most students were more intent on winning the approbation of their classmates, which came quickest through defying their teachers.

A case in point: In the spring of 1826, the faculty moved to quell rowdiness among the seniors by calling for the expulsion of the class ringleader, one Thomas R. Minturn. His twenty-four classmates responded by entering into "a bond of association" to seek "admission in a body" to either Rutgers or Union. Confronted with the loss of an entire class, the trustees overruled the faculty and restored Minturn to his class, with which he graduated some weeks later.[58]

Yet for all the latent tension in the relationship between students and faculty, more surprising from today's perspective are the quite conscious compromises each made with respect to the other, which produced a remarkably amiable and mutually accommodating state of faculty-student relations. This came all the easier when both sides understood that, as often as not, it was the students who were in charge.[59]

Going to Columbia College any time from the 1780s to the Civil War constituted a strikingly uniform experience. A student in the 1850s would have had little need to describe his schooldays to his father, an 1820s Columbia graduate, or even to his grandfather, a 1790s graduate: nothing much had changed. That such institutional continuity could exist within a city that over the same eight decades had transformed itself from some twenty thousand inhabitants to the world's third largest city, of some million, and during a period when the number of American colleges grew from under twenty to over two hundred, attests to early Columbia College's capacity to resist change. It also suggests that the experiences of one undergraduate may in many ways be descriptive of the experiences of the twelve hundred students who attended Columbia from the end of the War of 1812 to the eve of the Civil War.

One factor contributing to the interchangeability of early Columbia undergraduate life was its physical continuity. The setting remained the same for more than a century. Columbia's Park Place campus consisted of three acres, 140,000 square feet at its most expansive, before the bisection of the campus by the laying out of Robinson Street made it smaller. If still just above the moving edge of Manhattan's northward development in the 1790s, the campus soon found itself in the midst of a bustling commercial metropolis. Murray Street to the north and Barclay to the south were a mix of residential and commercial buildings, closely packed together. West Broadway to the east was made up of warehouses, as was the land area to the west that extended three blocks beyond the original bank of the Hudson. The sycamores planted in the 1790s around the outer edge of the campus came down in the 1840s when the city expanded Park Place westward. Only the University of Pennsylvania, among early colleges, had anywhere near as distinctly an urban setting as early Columbia College. Even NYU, after its move in 1835 to Washington Square, situated itself in what was then an upscale residential area.

The original College Hall, opened in 1760, went through two major renovations. The first occurred in the 1790s, but the job of adding a west wing was so badly botched that it had to be done again in 1817–20, when two three-and-a-half–story wings were added, along with a fourth story to the main hall. The resultant space was still under thirty thousand square feet, with most of it given over to presidential and faculty lodgings. By the 1850s, College Hall, after ten decades, had become one of the city's oldest buildings, its inner spaces familiar to four generations of Columbia families.[60]

Another factor conveying continuity to the early Columbia College undergraduate experience was scale. In the seventy-five years between its reorganization in 1784 and its removal from Park Place in 1857, Columbia College enrolled under 2,400 students, slightly less than Columbia College has enrolled in any single year since the 1950s. Of these early Columbia College matriculants, about

1,600 (or two-thirds) graduated. In any given year, the College enrolled somewhere between 80 and 130 students, with a slight bulge in the entering class, with 30 plus students, and the seniors more apt to be in the low twenties. The average size of a Columbia graduating class was 21 students; the largest, in 1827, had 36 graduates; the smallest, in 1844, only 14. These numbers describe a consistent enrollment pattern, with little discernible upward or downward gradient and a small standard deviation from year to year. Thus, despite the fixed curriculum that kept students sitting next to the same people for four years and despite the absence of a dormitory life, a Columbia student likely knew every other Columbia student, not only in his own class but in all four classes.[61]

Some of this familiarity, of course, antedates Columbia. Of the 174 graduates of the seven classes (1835–41) that overlapped with Strong's years at Columbia, 135 (78 percent) shared last names with other Columbians. Of these, 72 (41 percent) were both preceded and followed by contemporaries with the same last name. Add to this the fact that several students in every class were related to trustees, faculty, and the president, and one understands that this was a moment in Columbia's history when virtually everyone was a legacy.[62]

But the commonalities do not stop there. By entering age, family background, birthplace, and residence, early Columbia College students in the 1790s were not only strikingly like early Columbia students in the 1850s, but they were also different from students elsewhere. As with King's College students, they were still on average younger than collegians elsewhere, the average entering age being fifteen, and still with proportionally fewer "adult" students. They were still more likely to be Episcopalians than Harvard students were Unitarians or Yale students Congregationalists or Wesleyan students Methodists. And they were still both more likely to come from professional and commercial families and even more likely to have been born within ten miles of their alma mater than students elsewhere.[63]

The continuing absence of a residential experience was also a common characteristic of the early Columbia College experience. While this in one sense deprived Columbia students of what was, and is still, considered an essential component of going away to college, in another it gave them a common alternative experience. For all Columbia College students before the Civil War, as for most since, going to college did not mean leaving home or becoming disconnected from one's family; it meant shuttling between campus and home, but a campus and a home in the midst of a metropolis. College did not so much provide a "psychosocial moratorium" as it offered a steady point of reference in a chaotic but exciting metropolis. When a fire raged on Wall Street or a ship was lost at sea, early Columbians did not need to wait for mail from home to learn the details.[64]

In small matters, too, antebellum Columbia College remained much the same. The academic calendar provided for two semesters of approximately fifteen weeks in duration, the first running from early October to January, the second from February to June. Public examinations took up the better part of the last three weeks of the semester. To be sure, the end of the second semester and the start of the first did get moved around somewhat during these years, largely with the intent of having students out of class during the height of the cholera season. Commencement day was similarly moved around, from mid-July at the close of the second semester in the early part of the nineteenth century to the beginning of the first semester on the first Tuesday in October by the 1830s. But the principal holidays in the 1790s remained pretty much those observed in the 1850s: Evacuation Day in November, a break at Christmas, an extended break at Easter, and the Fourth of July, if the College was still in session. Thanksgiving seems to have been an annually negotiated holiday, observed some years but not others.[65]

There was also a predictability about the school week. It ran from Monday to Friday, the day beginning with a half-hour chapel service at 9:00 A.M. (more or less required, depending on the president's and trustees' policing), followed by four one-hour class periods. Classes were over by 1:30 P.M., and students were expected to return home by 2:00 P.M. for dinner. Extracurricular activities brought them back some evenings. Appearances on Saturday mornings were limited to practice sessions in public speaking (in preparation for commencement) and to disciplinary meetings with the faculty. During the thirty weeks the College was in session, Columbia students were on campus little more than twenty-four hours a week, whereas students at residential colleges were on campus all the time.[66]

While at school, early Columbia students were busy with classes. There were no free periods, no study periods, not least because there was no place to put students not in class. Each student's schedule consisted of four classes, one immediately after the other, which met in a part of the building assigned to one of the regular faculty members or the president. As students had no choice in subjects, and all students of a given year took the same subjects at the same time with the same teacher, scheduling was a breeze.

Once in their assigned location, students encountered one of two familiar teaching styles. Some teachers, particularly with juniors and seniors, lectured and expected students to take notes. More often, in the lower classes, teachers called on individual students to recite, respond, or declaim and then generally made some mark in their attendance book on the quality of the effort. It was judged a very good day if a student did not get called on more than once in more than half his classes. It was expected that students arrived in class with some preparation but not much. Daily classroom performance was not graded, but the question-answer format followed was that used at the end-of-semester public exams, when performance did count and where students, unless trustees with slow sons prevailed over faculty wishes, were publicly ranked. Anyone who bothered could easily distinguish his bright and conscientious students from his dim and/or lazy ones. Few did. For the most part, it was enough to pass or at least avoid failing, which virtually everyone did.[67]

What of such basic issues as how much was learned, how hard did students work, and how much satisfaction did they derive from their effort? The received view, supported by the autobiographies of university men such as Cornell's Andrew Dickson White (about Hobart) and Columbia's Nicholas Murray Butler and accepted by historians such as Hofstadter, is: "not much." Such a sour view is impossible to gainsay, perhaps especially at early Columbia College, where the official archival record as regards students is particularly thin. There is, however, in the student diary of George Templeton Strong (CC 1839), surely the most revealing of all American student diaries, enough at least to suggest a more positive assessment.[68]

"He Was Always Good To Me"

On Monday, October 5, 1835, sophomore George Templeton Strong began his diary. But for a two-month lapse the following spring when an explosion in Renwick's laboratory rendered his writing hand useless, Strong made entries virtually every day of his undergraduate life from then until his graduation in October 1838—and every day after that for the next thirty-five years, during the last twenty-one of which he served as a Columbia trustee (1854–75). Known only to his immediate family, Strong's diary, which ran some 2,250 pages of minutely written script, was only discovered by historians in the late 1930s and more generally when it was given over in 1941 to be edited by Columbia historian Allan Nevins and Columbia archivist-historian Milton Halsey Thomas. Much of it was published in four handsome volumes in 1952.[69]

The Strongs were really not Old New York. George's father, George Washington Strong (1783–1855), came to New York shortly after graduating from Yale (1803) to practice law. The Strongs were New Englanders and more latterly Long Islanders, as was George's mother, a Lloyd from Setauket. (The William Sydney Mount painting *Eel Fishing Expedition* hanging in the New-York Historical Society could well have used young Strong as his model for the boy fishing off the stern.) The Strongs first took up residence at 108 Greenwich Street, which ran north-south two blocks east of the Hudson River, and attended Trinity Church. Young Strong prepared for college at Columbia Grammar School and at the age of fourteen easily passed the entrance exam for Columbia

College as a member of the class of 1838. Like virtually all his classmates, he walked to Columbia and lived at home.

In several other respects, however, he differed from not only his Columbia classmates but antebellum college students generally. The biggest difference was that he took his studies seriously, even too seriously by his own admission. He did so in part because his scholarly father took his only son's studies just as seriously, rarely missing one of the twice-yearly public exams during George's four years at Columbia. Always anxious at exam time, he was especially so when, as he noted tremulously in his diary, "My father will be there." Sometimes he chastised himself for working so hard. "I believe those students are on the whole happier, who make no pretensions to any standing in the class," he once allowed. "If they never feel the triumph of success—they never have to suffer the irritating, bothering feeling which I feel now—nor the horrible mortification of failing—which I expect to feel in a few hours." The night before being examined by Anderson in spherical trigonometry, he concluded: "I'm a gone case." In other instances, as in Latin and chemistry, he got by having "cheated most scandalously."[70]

Some of Strong's exam anxieties reflected a deep streak of academic competitiveness. He studied long and hard, during the term and at exam time, and nobody kept as close an eye on the competition as he or more enjoyed recording the miscues of his classmates, especially those with familial links to College officials. When one of President Duer's sons flunked a science examination by failing to come up with the right answer to "What is the peculiar property of a magnet?" Strong's day was made. "Points to the north," he could not resist entering into his diary. So, too, the gods were about when "Frederick Anthon was the last up, and flunked sublimely." Other Columbia students occasionally went to the public examinations of classes other than their own, but Strong regularly did. It bothered him mightily when the faculty seemed to pay insufficient attention at the exams: "Prex writing a letter. Anthon reading the *Herald*, Renwick drawing picture; Anderson gaping—evidently half asleep." To be fair, Strong noted when he got the benefit of the doubt, as when Anderson awarded him a medal for his work in descriptive astronomy when he had "no more right to it than to the throne of England." Six weeks into integral calculus, he admitted that "I have not succeeded yet in comprehending what a differentiation means."[71]

In Strong, then, we have someone performing at or very close to maximum effort—a bright overachiever, someone who could easily have passed as a premed in a later day. Given his lock on prizes, only one classmate possibly winning more in four years, we can safely locate his classmates at lower levels of effort, even, if Strong's assessment of the amount of studying done by his classmates is right, very much lower.

Columbia's grading system readily accommodated students who made little effort to achieve academic distinction but instead passed their four years in unpublicized indolence. Besides the financial disincentives, professors were reluctant to fail students when doing so sometimes was viewed by parents as a reflection on their teaching skills. The one year when class rank was made public at graduation, the presence of the two sons of a trustee at the bottom of the list was thought the reason the experiment with such public rankings was discontinued. Individual course grades, as we understand them, were simply not assigned. Everything was, to use a phrase and even a dispensation usually attributed to the late 1960s, pass-fail.

Strong was also atypical of his classmates in that he was less physically robust than most. He often quietly sided with the authorities in their ongoing disputes with rowdy, and occasionally bullying, classmates. When a particularly obnoxious senior miscreant was suspended, Strong harumphed, "he can now play billiards to his heart's content." His efforts to improve his physique were not successful, as when practicing with dumbbells before breakfast resulted in two broken front teeth. When he became ill in his senior year, the attending physician diagnosed his problem as "eats too much and exercises too little." But there was the glorious occasion when he had an encounter in chapel with one George W. Quakenbos (CC 1839), the "little Hibernian, . . . whereupon I knocked him down." And the time after chemistry lab when classmates took to sniffing nitrous oxide: "I would have liked dearly to have tried it myself, but . . ."[72]

Strong likely exceeded his classmates as a close observer of his teachers, but only in degree. What is striking about his observations of faculty is how utterly lacking in awe they are, and how personal. Often critical, as in his personal assessment of Anthon—"Charley's a goose"—elsewhere Strong raised doubts about Anthon's scholarship: "He is as fit to lecture on anything above ancient geography as a deaf and dumb man on the genius of Beethoven." He noted when McVickar fell to "blarneying [about the] history of literature, composition, and I suppose all the other humbugs that pertain to his most humbuggical department." He was also alert to mood shifts, as in "Anthon and Anderson are of late getting extremely ferocious—what can be the matter?" Another occasion when Anderson was "most horribly savage," Strong wrote off to his Democrat professor's disgust with Pennsylvania's having gone Whig.[73]

Of all his professors, it was "Harry" Anderson's inner life that most intrigued him: "Upright, steady, stiff, cool, cautious, rational, moneymaking, real estate buying . . . that incarnation of the right angle. . . . In Religion no one knows his sentiments. . . . They are not far from Deism." But such nosiness extended to the president's personal affairs, as when Duer's daughter, Ellen, announced plans to marry, Strong memorialized the moment with "Prex's progeny can't do anything in the ordinary and commonplace way."[74]

For all that, Strong frequently empathized with his teachers. This was certainly so in the case of Renwick, who had a "voice like the wheezing of a broken bellows" but who also gave Strong the run of his laboratory. "Poor Jemmy!" Strong wrote, imagining how Renwick would fare with a particularly unruly upcoming class of sophomores. "They'll tease him out of his senses." And even in the case of the "blarneying" McVickar, when rumors went about that he had had a breakdown, Strong could not certify his good mental health but did acknowledge that "he was always good to me." Thirty years later, on hearing of his teacher's death, Strong acknowledged that "old McVickar's lecture-room 1835–1838 did more to influence me and mould my way of thinking than any other feature of my college life."[75]

Faculty-student relations in early Columbia College were far less top-down and hierarchically determined than might be imagined. There is no evidence of corporal punishment by faculty and little indication of students attempting physical intimidation of individual faculty, which was commonplace on some residential campuses. In contemplating a harsh penalty for a student miscue, faculty were aware of the possibility of being overruled by the trustees, who numbered among them parents of many of the more waywardly inclined undergraduates. Student petitions urging clemency toward one of their own could not be disregarded. There was also the possibility that a disciplined student might simply leave. The faculty needed students, and students knew it. Thus something of a Copenhagen Syndrome came into play; so much in each other's company, a certain parity in power was recognized by both sides. Theirs was a negotiated relationship in which faculty were disinclined to press their formal powers and students possessed considerable agency of their own. Inside College Hall existed something akin to a bilateral alliance, if not a joint conspiracy, that allowed faculty and students alike to go about their lives relatively free from the anxieties and pressures (except, as with Strong, self-imposed ones) of life outside on Barclay Street and beyond. Those were the days.

"Our Second Alma Mater"

Like many smarty-pants before and since, Strong was not a natural leader outside of class; nor was he a gifted public speaker. Upon hearing a senior's oration applauded, the sophomore Strong confessed that "I would give ten thousand dollars (if I had it) to be able to equal it." Instead, he set about making himself everybody's choice as secretary-treasurer and then vice president of every extracurricular activity around. It was in these activities, which Strong called "our second alma mater," where the real action was.[76]

Early Columbia College's extracurriculum, as compared with that at residential colleges located in towns where the college was the dominant institution, was pretty thin. Elsewhere the dormitories provided a base for a vital campus life at some remove from faculty, just as they were the natural staging ground for the numerous rebellions. Absent dormitories, Columbia had relatively little in the way of an extracurriculum—or organized rebelliousness.

This said, Columbia's two student-run societies, the Philolexian Society (1802) and the Peithologian Society (1809) could fill many nights with literary activities and political scheming. In fact, the existence of two such societies in a student body the size of Columbia assured a degree of competitiveness. Membership in each was by election and ostensibly limited to students who demonstrated an interest in debating. Elections occurred in the fall of a student's freshman year. In the 1830s, about half of every class belonged to one or the other society. Thus, at any time, the two societies might have a combined membership of some forty students, or about a third of the entire student body.[77]

The inflexibility of the curriculum and the less-than-inspired quality of daily instruction undoubtedly encouraged the development of college-centered activities that were student initiated, but no less educational and experientially valuable for being so. Whereas the classical and scientific curriculum offered few opportunities to consider contemporary social issues or recent literature, the subject matter of the weekly society meetings was nothing if not au courant. Among the issues debated by the Philolexian Society during Strong's membership:

"Are literary reviews favorable to literature?"

"Ought this country to aid Texas?"

"Ought the Europeans to have settled in this country against the will of the Natives?"

"Should universal suffrage be allowed?"

"Whether trade unions are beneficial?" ("Everyone took the negative.")

"Was Washington or Columbus the greater man?"

"Whether a monarchy or republic is best for literature?"

"Whether lawyers are beneficial?"

"Whether another slaveholding state should be admitted to the Union?"[78]

Upon election to the Philolexian midway through his freshman year, Strong made its activities the principal focus of his extracurricular life. It also became the source of his closest friendships, many of which he maintained throughout his life. The room assigned to the Philolexian and its substantial library in the basement of Main Hall served as his campus hangout several evenings a week.

Formal presentations made to his fellow Philolexians were at least as anxiety inducing as his semester exams—and as likely to bring his father to campus.

In addition to providing opportunities for students to become informed about issues of the day and sharpen their debating skills, the literary societies were arenas for political maneuvering. Upperclassmen served in the top elective positions, but subordinate posts were open to underclassmen. The political machinations and coalition forming that attended the annual elections in the Philolexian in Strong's day were worthy of comparison with the goings on at Tammany. Surely one of Strong's banner days at Columbia was when he was elected vice president of the Philolexian in his junior year: "we carried our whole ticket by large majorities."[79]

The beginnings of a fraternity system were also discernible at Columbia in the 1830s, with the incorporation of the Alpha Delta Phi chapter in 1832. Strong was elected in the fall of his sophomore year but seems to have been less engaged in it than in the Philolexian. Lacking houses, Columbia's early fraternities limited their activities to organizing songfests and tavern hopping.[80]

In Strong's junior year, he and his classmates took upon themselves the planning for a College semicentennial celebration, to commemorate the issuance of the charter of 1787 and the installation of the current governing arrangements. When alumni threatened to take over the event, the student committee threatened to "get up an opposition anniversary [and] serve up the whole concern in the *Herald*." In the end, a compromise was reached, the planning proceeded jointly, and the public celebration on April 13, 1837, which involved a five-block procession from the College to St. John's Church, even by Strong's estimate, "went off so well."[81]

Organized intercollegiate athletics were still two decades away, which was just as well for the diminutive Strong, whose halfhearted attempts at gymnastics resulted in pulled muscles or bruised toes. There was, however, a contingent among his classmates who favored billiards, drinking, and the pursuit of prostitutes, though the occasionally imbibing Strong stayed clear of such activities.[82]

To What Ends?

As compared with students since, early Columbia College students enjoyed an extraordinary autonomy over their collegiate lives. To be sure, presidents and faculty sometimes dealt with them as the wayward adolescents they often were, but at other times they acknowledged their rights to be involved in institutional decision making.

A case in point occurred during Strong's sophomore year, when the faculty unilaterally altered the Christmas holiday schedule. A student petition was gotten up, President Duer was apprised of the feelings among the students, the faculty was consulted, and the old calendar was restored. Those who look to early Columbia College for antecedents of the student-led disturbances at Columbia in 1968 will look in vain.[83]

Similarly, neither trustees nor faculty were quick to give up on a student, particularly if he had family ties to the College and paid his tuition. There were simply too few students out there to be overly demanding of them once admitted. No one was expelled for lack of work or poor academic performance, unless it was accompanied by an insolent challenge to the authority of the faculty or president. Accordingly, students could choose to study or not, without major consequences either way.

The acceptable limits of collective rabble-rousing, while never approaching those of the era's larger residential colleges, extended to classwide eruptions in class, often provoked by a single student hell-raiser. Eruptions that evoked the support of the rest of the class or other classes often went unpunished, while the refusal of other classes to condone a disruption strengthened the disciplinary hand of the faculty. In short, students helped discipline themselves. With the possible exception of Charles "Bull" Anthon, who imposed discipline by his physical presence, early Columbia faculty got along with their students by going along whenever they could. Their authority was by no means unquestioned, and neither was it safe from appeal to higher authority, as both faculty and students well knew. So, unless directly challenged by a student determined to bring on a confrontation, faculty were seldom inclined to test the limits of their police powers and preferred instead to overlook most instances of student dereliction. Students, in turn, did not push their advantage.[84]

In sum, early Columbia College was one long negotiated experience, where no one estate—not the trustees, not the faculty, not the students, and not the alumni—was in charge or even had veto power over the claims of all the others. Students learned to know when to press their advantage and when to compromise. No wonder so few of Strong's contemporaries became radicals and almost half (48 percent)—including Strong—became lawyers![85]

As for the others, about a fifth went into the ministry and another fifth into business, with only a handful going into medicine and a scattering of engineers, architects, and teachers. Yet for all these quietly successful careers, it needs to be acknowledged that, as compared with Harvard, Yale, or even Union College graduates of Strong's day and throughout the antebellum era, Columbia College's alumni numbered among them few national figures. Or so it seemed at the time, as when the Boston-based and Unitarian-directed *Christian Examiner* offered this summary description of Columbia in 1854: "Good in classics; weak in sciences; very few distinguished graduates. Other than De Witt Clinton, who else ever went to Columbia College?"[86]

The best-known Columbia graduate between 1800 and 1860 was probably Hamilton Fish (CC 1827), a New York congressman, governor, United States senator, and, throughout the Grant administration, secretary of state (1869–77). But even his admiring biographer, Columbia historian Allan Nevins, modestly ranked him as "the least known important man of his day." To be sure, several of Strong's contemporaries who went into the law distinguished themselves there, while one, Samuel Blatchford (CC 1837), in the class immediately ahead of Strong, eventually became an associate justice of the United States Supreme Court (1882–93). Among the era's military leaders, Philip Kearney (CC 1833) bears noting. Charles Anthon's nephew—Charles E. Anthon (CC 1839)—went on to become a classical scholar at CCNY, as did Henry Drisler (CC 1839) at Columbia. Oliver Wolcott Gibbs (CC 1841), about whom more in the next chapter, became a distinguished scientist at Harvard.[87]

In other areas of American life, early Columbia College alums were thin on the ground. In letters, there were the publisher and editor Evert Duyckinck (CC 1835) and the travel writer John Lloyd Stephens (CC 1822), and that was about it. The only political reformers of any note were the journalist and editor of the *Democratic Review* (in which he coined the phrase "manifest destiny"), John L. O'Sullivan (CC 1831) and the abolitionist John Jay (CC 1836). In architecture, the picture was brighter, with both Benjamin I. Haight (CC 1828) and James Renwick Jr. (CC 1836) carving out distinguished careers in church and public architecture. And there was a sprinkling of Episcopal bishops and other ecclesiastical officeholders. But perhaps most surprising of all, given the era in which Strong's contemporaries passed their adult lives, very few became fabulously or even famously rich. Even the well-to-do among them seem to have proceeded cautiously along the financial path Strong laid out for himself: "a holder of mortgages and a receiver of a fixed income."[88]

Without attempting to generalize, Strong's own life after graduation suggests why relatively few of his college contemporaries made it big. It began with a premonition just two days after commencement: "At present everything is in confusion, and the law looks like an infinite wilderness, and not a very interesting one." But interesting or not, Strong had determined during his junior year to enter his father's law office after graduation, and enter it he did. There, for a while, he enjoyed a measure of professional success, married the daughter of a friend of his father's and Columbia trustee, Samuel Ruggles (1836–81), and followed his father-in-law uptown to Twenty-first Street. About then, he tired of law and increasingly involved himself in the Trinity vestry, amateur musicale societies, and, after 1854, the Columbia board of trustees, where he always followed his father-in-law's lead. Come the Civil War, Strong was more than ready to throw his energies into the work of the United States Sanitary Commission, the forerunner of the American Red Cross, for which he earned a commendation from President Lincoln. Although he lived another ten years after the war, he did not take up his law practice again and even allowed his involvement as a trustee to fall off. He died in 1875.[89]

As boy and man, Strong was of his time and class, with all the baggage that entailed. He was a snob. Although not a founder of the Century Association in 1847, he joined a few months later only to find that the club had been "spoiled by bringing into it a herd of new people, some of whom I don't know and who may be very nice but look rather seedy and very slow—and others who I do know—so well that I don't want to know them any better." Shades of John Jay and the Dancing Assembly![90]

Strong detested the Irish and was regularly given to berating them in the safety of his diary. The comment "It is as natural for a Hibernian to tipple as for a pig to snout" and a description of Irish laborers "with prehensile paws supplied them by nature with evident reference to the handling of the spade . . . carrying a hod" will suffice as examples. Still, with his High Church theological leanings and passion for liturgical music, Strong confessed on a couple of occasions that, but for the fact that Catholicism was the faith of the Irish, he might consider converting.[91]

Although he opposed slavery and supported Lincoln's emancipation efforts, he believed blacks innately inferior. Back in 1850 he seems to have settled the question to his satisfaction: "My creed: That slave-holding is no sin . . . the slaves of the South are happier and better off than the niggers of the North." Having evinced some positive curiosity as a college junior about the religious practices of a Jewish freshman, he grew increasingly anti-Semitic with age. One of his last efforts as a Columbia trustee occurred the year before his death in 1874, when he tried to make knowledge of Latin an entrance requirement for the Law School. Why? "This will keep out the little scrubs (German Jew boys mostly) whom the School now promotes from grocery counters in Avenue B to be 'gentlemen of the bar.' "[92]

To complete Strong's violation of every principle of political correctness, this father of three sons was also very much a male chauvinist. When the Columbia trustees took under consideration the application of three women to attend the Law School in 1867, Strong wrote of "these possible Portias": "No woman shall degrade herself by practicing law, in New York especially, if I can save her."[93]

The point of all this is not to prove Strong's venality or to argue that Harvard or Yale or Union graduates of Strong's day were less given to racial, ethnic, and gender prejudice than Strong and his Columbia contemporaries. It is to suggest that four years at early Columbia College did little to challenge or undermine such prejudices, while it might well have, and that attendance at the College, by extending the homogeneous circumstances of home another four years, made such prejudices still less susceptible to later challenge. Early Columbia College did not encourage risk taking, intellectual, economic, or social, so much as it reinforced the innate and insular cautiousness of those born to privilege, even the precarious privilege of Knickerbocker New York.

For all that, Strong remained after college a serious student of the classics, as his Yale father had been, took an amateur's interest in science, as did his Yale father-in-law, and became largely of his own doing a patron of the arts, especially music. He loved his wife and paid his debts. He was an involved churchman and active alumnus. A year after graduation, Strong tried to capture his feelings about his relationship with Columbia with a literary allusion: "Alma Mater reminds me of the 'long-armed baboon' to which (vide Hood's *Zoological Report*) the young kangaroos were put to dry nurse; she is about as hopeful a parent." Thirty years later, he compared his relationship to the College to "unboiled peas in my shoes . . . a continual irritant." "Hopeful parent" or "continual irritant," early Columbia College could do worse for offsetting epitaphs.[94]

FIGURE 2.1 Early Columbia College presidents: a. Charles Henry Wharton (1748–1833), fourth president of Columbia College (1801); b. Benjamin Moore (1748–1816), King's College graduate (1768), fifth president of Columbia College (1801–11), rector of Trinity Church, and bishop of New York; c. William Harris (1765–1829), sixth president of Columbia College (1811–29); d. William Alexander Duer, seventh president of Columbia College (1829–42); e. Nathaniel Fish Moore (1782-1872), graduate of Columbia College (1802), eighth president of Columbia College (1842–49); f. Charles King (1779–1867), ninth president of Columbia College (1849–63).

Source: Columbia University Archives—Columbiana Collection.

FIGURE 2.2   Charles Anthon (1797–1867), graduate of Columbia College (1815), professor of Greek and Lat
(1820–57).

Source: Columbia University Archives—Columbiana Collection.

FIGURE 2.3   George Templeton Strong (1820–75), graduate of Columbia College (1838), trustee (1853–1875
diarist, and attorney. Original watercolor.

Source: Allen Nevins and Milton Halsey Thomas, eds., *The Diary of George Templeton Strong* (New York, Macmillan, 1952), vol.
opp. 10.

FIGURE 2.4   Oliver Wolcott Gibbs (1822–1908), graduate of Columbia College (1841), unsuccessful candidate for Columbia professorship in 1854, professor of chemistry at Harvard (1863–1887).

Source: Allen Nevins and Milton Halsey Thomas, eds., *The Diary of George Templeton Strong* (New York, Macmillan, 1952), vol. 2, opp. 275.

FIGURE 2.5   Columbia College at Park Place in 1853, viewed from the southwest. Photograph by Victor Prevost.

Source: Columbia University Archives—Columbiana Collection.

FIGURE 2.6 Samuel B. Ruggles (1800–1881), Columbia College trustee (1836–81), vigorous advocate of university reforms. 1863 photograph.

Source: Columbia University Archives—Columbiana Collection.

FIGURE 2.7 Park Place campus being demolished in 1857.

Source: Columbia University Archives—Columbiana Collection.

CHAPTER 4

Midcentury Stirrings

If poverty be our excuse, it can avail us no longer.
> Trustee Samuel Ruggles, *The Duty of Columbia to the Community* (1854)

They Also Serve Who Stand and Wait

FOLLOWING the quiet revolution of 1816, when Columbia abandoned its experiment with republicanism and returned to its denominational origins, the College's trustees became increasingly drawn from the ranks of the New York Episcopalian community. Whereas in 1811 only seven of the twenty-four trustees (29 percent) were Episcopalians, by 1854 nineteen of twenty-four (79 percent) were. Most of the non-Episcopalians were ministers of the Collegiate Dutch Reformed Church or the Brick Presbyterian Church that had since the 1780s provided Columbia with trustees from their pulpits and continued to do so in an unspoken hereditary succession.[1]

But theirs were by no means the only inherited seats on the board. In 1854, when six trustees filled seats held by occupational predecessors, fourteen had familial ties to previous or current trustees. Ten trustees were the sons of trustees and four were the sons-in-law or fathers-in-law of trustees. Of the twenty-four trustees, only four had neither direct familial or occupational links to current or past board members. Earlier in the nineteenth century, it was not unusual for a son to be elected at the point of his father's retirement or death, as with Rufus King père and Charles King fils; by midcentury, it had become common for members to see their sons-in-law elected and for them to stay on themselves. This was the case with Samuel Ruggles, who secured a place for his son-in-law, George Templeton Strong, and Beverly Robinson, who got one for his son-in-law, William Betts.[2]

One consequence of this nepotism was that trustees tended to get elected at a relatively young age and stayed on and on. Of the twenty-four trustees in 1811, fourteen (58 percent) departed the board by resignation, and ten (42 percent) by death. Four decades later, the situation had been reversed: in 1854 eight of the twenty-four trustees (33 percent) eventually departed by resigning, and sixteen (67 percent) by death. Of the thirty-three longest-serving trustees (thirty-plus years on the board) in the history of the university, twenty served during the mid-1800s.[3]

A distinctive feature of the Columbia board in the Republican era was its openness to non-Columbians. To be sure, very early on there were not many alumni from whom to choose. Nevertheless, the collegiate ecumenism of the early boards was not entirely attributable to the scarcity of Columbia graduates. The 1811 board had three graduates from Princeton, two from Harvard, and one each from Yale and Penn; the ten Columbia/King's graduates (42 percent) were in a minority. This changed with the board's re-Episcopalization. In 1854 seventeen of the twenty-four trustees (71 percent) were Columbia graduates, and only four (17 percent) of the other trustees graduated from some other American college. For more and more trustees, Columbia was the only frame of reference. Little wonder that the Yale-educated Samuel Ruggles regularly berated his trustee colleagues—to his Columbia-trained son-in-law—for their indifference to goings-on at other campuses. But little wonder, too, that Ruggles was viewed by his colleagues to be short on institutional loyalty.[4]

One characteristic of the early Columbia College board of trustees that did not change was its predilection for lawyers. In 1811 the board had eleven lawyers in its ranks and the same number in 1854. At no point during the intervening years did the representation of lawyers drop below 40 percent. Ministers continued throughout the period to constitute about a quarter of the occupational makeup of the board (half Episcopalian, half not), with physicians enjoying a smaller and less constant presence. Surprisingly, these early Columbia College boards had relatively few bankers or merchants on them. Thus, by default, the financial management of the College fell principally to its lawyers.[5]

And it was financial management that took up most of the board's energies. The eighty-thousand-dollar renovations of College Hall in 1817–20, even after a ten-thousand-dollar grant from New York, left the College with a fifteen thousand dollar debt, the first in its history. The interest on this debt thereafter represented a sizable charge against income through the 1820s, and, after enrollments (and income) slumped in the early 1830s, thanks to competition from NYU, the debt had increased by 1835 to thirty-five thousand dollars. At this point, the trustees approached the city of New York with a proposal whereby the city would be given half the seats on the board in exchange for the city's vacated almshouse. They also imposed a cut in faculty salaries, only partially offset by expanding the per capitum payment system as a way of "imparting to the members of the Faculty a direct interest in augmenting the number of students." Nor were they above tuition discounting, as in offering the city's private tutors a deal whereby every fourth student of the tutor's admitted to Columbia would come tuition-free. And, finally, they announced that a one-thousand-dollar gift to the College would permanently endow a four-year scholarship for a student of the donor's choosing.[6]

And still the debt grew. In 1839 it exceeded fifty thousand dollars; in 1845 sixty-three thousand; and by 1851 the debt stood at seventy-six thousand dollars, or three times the College's annual budget. The interest payments alone (7 percent, to James Lenox) in the late 1840s represented one-fifth of the College's annual expenditures.[7]

In light of the serious financial bind in which the trustees found themselves, it might be useful also to consider what they did not do. First, they did not close the College, although some trustees must have given thought to doing so. Nor did they move out of New York City, already a predictable suggestion in hard times. Instead, they decided to hold tight, carry the debt, make the interest payments, and wait for the city's march northward.[8]

By the late 1840s even the most bearish trustee realized that the College's financial situation was due for help. After three decades of carrying the Hosack Garden property north of the city's developed area on its books as an expenditure (to pay someone to oversee it), these twenty-one acres were about to be overtaken by the upward thrust of the city's commercial development and its unquenchable need for more developable property. Having considered selling the garden in the 1830s, the board was now faced with the challenge of how best to proceed with its capitalization.[9]

There were several options. The first was to move the College to the Hosack Garden site and sell the Park Place campus, which had long been surrounded by commercial establishments and would bring a good price. A second was to sell the Hosack Garden property to someone who would then bear the costs of grading, installing sewers, laying out streets, and so on. A third was for the trustees to take on themselves the development of the Hosack Garden for commercial purposes, which they would then lease, leaving the question of the locale of the College for another day. A fourth, always an attractive one, was to do nothing for another decade or so.

By 1852 there existed within the board an outline of a strategy for proceeding that proved very like the way things worked out four years later. It involved selling off the Park Place campus, either along with the College's adjoining properties on its own, or retaining the other properties for leasing. (The United States government had already offered seven hundred thousand dollars for the entire package.) The College would then be moved to an as-yet-undetermined new site (one out of the city in Westchester was mentioned) that would cost less than the sale of the Park Place campus fetched. The money saved in the campus swap would then be used to develop the Hosack Garden site for leasing. Any money left over might be used to expand the College curriculum and introduce postgraduate and professional studies at the new campus.[10]

To be sure, not all the trustees agreed on all points of this plan. Some, led by the treasurer, Gouverneur Morris Ogden, aggressively pressed the real estate aspects of the plan but were leery of expanding the curriculum, while others, including Trustees Samuel Ruggles and George Templeton Strong, the latter of whom joined the board in late 1853, favored expanding the curriculum but holding off on developing the Hosack Garden property for several years. But before this dollars-and-cents internal debate could be resolved, the trustees found themselves in the midst of a public donnybrook over, of all things, a faculty appointment.

The Gibbs Affair

The Gibbs affair was about many things; one thing it was not was an internal jurisdictional dispute about who got to appoint faculty. The trustees (and before them, the governors and regents) had always exercised the exclusive right to select and appoint Columbia faculty. A president might have a particular person in mind or a favorite among those under consideration, but he involved himself in the process as one of twenty-four trustees, not as president. Faculty were kept out of the process. Their explicit exclusion from the board by the 1810 charter was meant to assure their noninvolvement in the selection of their colleagues. (Back in the 1780s, when faculty did serve on the board, there had been some pretty egregious logrolling.) Needless to add, students and alumni had no say in faculty appointments.

By the early 1850s the Columbia faculty was showing its collective age. Three of its six members—McVickar, Anthon, and Renwick—were well into their fourth decade of teaching. Although McVickar was the oldest (sixty-seven) and Anthon the most senior (having taught for thirty-seven years), it was Renwick's pending retirement in 1854 that led directly to one of the most famous cases of a faculty appointment—really, nonappointment—in the history of American higher education.

It was likely not coincidental that the trustee-provocateur in the Gibbs case—Samuel Ruggles—was as a Yale graduate or that his most active ally, his son-in-law, George Templeton Strong, was the son of a Yaley. Although he would eventually become one of the longest-serving members in the history of the board (forty-eight years) and in retrospect be viewed as one of its most progressive members, Ruggles remained to his fellow trustees something of an outsider and parvenu. An active lawyer and real estate investor (he developed Gramercy Park in the 1840s), Ruggles enjoyed social and scholarly acquaintanceships up and down the Atlantic seaboard. But it was from friends among the emergent scientific community in Boston-Cambridge, New Haven, and Washington that he came by ideas about what to do with Columbia. These he in turn shared with son-in-law Strong, who could be counted on to assist with at least the nonverbal aspects of Ruggles's insurgency.[11]

The most novel idea that Ruggles and Strong brought to the Columbia board came from Benjamin Peirce (1809–80), Harvard professor of mathematics, prime faculty mover behind the first steps in Harvard's transformation into a university, and cofounder of the American Association for the Advancement of Science (1847). "Peirce holds," Strong recorded in 1852, repeating his father-in-law's rendering, "that professors may be prevented from degenerating into drones, like Renwick, by requiring of them to accomplish something every year or every six months, making it a condition of holding office that at certain periods they produce some essay, memoir, or investigation in their respective departments."[12]

The idea that Harvard professorships ought to be used to advance scientific and literary learning had been in the Cambridge air since the early 1800s (a research professorship in natural history was established in 1805), but it was only with Peirce's emergence in the 1840s as a leader of the Harvard faculty, the appointment of Asa Gray in 1842, and the arrival of Louis Agassiz in 1851 that the idea took tangible—and permanent—form. Similar views had simultaneously begun to be expressed in New Haven by a few Yale faculty, especially those identified with the chemists Benjamin Silliman and his son, Benjamin Jr., at the Sheffield Scientific School and by the physicist Joseph Henry, first at Princeton and later at the Smithsonian Institution.[13]

By this view, faculty should be encouraged, even expected, as part of their job to pursue scientific or literary studies beyond the levels they could expect to teach their undergraduates. (Not surprisingly, Peirce was a proponent of elective studies.) Those charged with appointing faculty should accordingly insist that candidates either already be engaged in or demonstrate potential for such advanced studies. But this presented two problems. First, evaluating such studies or determining potential for pursuing them was not a matter that could be left wholly to trustees. And, second, by this criterion the best candidates were not likely to be found by limiting the search to a local pool of applicants. On the contrary, making the best appointment necessarily became a national undertaking in which those with already established reputations in the field where the vacancy existed would play a crucial if not determinative role. Thus, in a stroke, faculty appointments at a college adopting this new dispensation become less a responsibility of its governing board than a responsibility of the scholarly and scientific community.[14]

Were Columbia's trustees ready for this? Ruggles was sufficiently determined to find out that as early as 1850 he settled on Oliver Wolcott Gibbs, a newly appointed professor of chemistry at the just opened Free Academy (later CCNY), as the means by which he would revive Columbia College. Gibbs was a good choice on at least two counts. First, his credentials as a Columbian were in good order. A prizewinning graduate of the College in 1841, he was the nephew of Oliver Wolcott, who had served briefly as a Columbia trustee earlier in the century. He numbered among his personal friends Ruggles's son-in-law, George Templeton Strong, whom Ruggles was about to put forward as a candidate for the next opening on the Columbia board of trustees. And, finally, Gibbs, having pursued advanced studies in Germany, was the best-trained young chemist in the country.[15]

There was the complicating fact that Gibbs was not Episcopalian but Unitarian, although, as Ruggles would later say of this blemish, his being so was more a matter of his widowed mother's doing than any personal inclination of his own toward, even by New York standards, religious eccentricity. Anyway, Gibbs could count on the endorsement of virtually every leading member of the American scientific community, many of them card-carrying Episcopalians.[16]

Now that he had his candidate, Ruggles needed an opening on the faculty. Renwick had been known for some time to complain about the burden of covering the entire expanse of the physical sciences singlehandedly. (Whereas Yale, Harvard, and Princeton had by the early 1850s separate faculty teaching physics, chemistry, and geology—and, in the case of Harvard, botany—at Columbia Renwick was responsible for all three subjects.) He also contended that the equipment provided was not adequate to his and his students' needs. In 1851 Ruggles volunteered to chair a committee to look into Renwick's complaints. He then took it upon himself to persuade Renwick to retire, simultaneously holding out the carrot of the novel appointment of professor emeritus and the stick of increased teaching responsibilities. On November 14, 1853, Renwick informed the trustees of his intention to retire the following year. Three weeks later, Ruggles's son-in-law, on his third try, was elected to the board. The battle was on.[17]

Most of what is known of the Gibbs affair, one of the classic set-tos in American academic history, comes from the account provided in George Templeton Strong's diary. The minutes of the trustees are characteristically circumspect, only occasionally recording the fact that a vote was taken, almost never noting who voted for whom. Accordingly, historians have generally given Strong's testimony credence, not least because he faulted his fellow trustees for taking positions that have since been discredited (e.g., that the religious views of a faculty member are relevant and outside evaluations by academic peers are not). Strong's often acerbic evaluations of the opposition also help enliven the story.[18]

Yet it must be remembered that Strong was very much an interested party in the Gibbs affair. Where he records in delicious detail every reactionary move on the part of the "fogy and fossil party" opposed to Gibbs, one is left to use the same source to infer the aggressive high-handedness that characterized his side.

Fortunately, Strong's diary is equal to the task. While not as publicly outspoken as Ruggles, Strong was at least as personally committed to Gibbs as his father-in-law was—and equally determined to use whatever means at hand to secure his election. This included undermining the traditional authority of the board, as when, four weeks after having been named to the board, he lobbied his old teacher Charles Anthon to declare himself publicly for Gibbs. Anthon refused. Nor was he above asking the two sons of Trustee Rev. John Knox (1836–58), an early opponent of Gibbs, to lean on their father. Finally, when "all is lost save our honor" with the trustees, Strong would attempt to get the Columbia alumni to force them to reconsider their rejection of "one of our own."[19]

Gibbs's external sponsors were so quick with their letters of recommendation that they arrived in early January 1854, before the trustees were ready to take up the matter of Renwick's successor. They included the leading names and letterheads of the embryonic scientific community in Washington: Alexander Dallas Bache, Benjamin Gould, and Edmund Blunt of the U.S. Coastal Survey; Joseph Henry of the Smithsonian Institution; J. S. Hubbard of the Washington Observatory. Local endorsements came from Horace Webster, the president of the Free Academy; from Professor John W. Draper of NYU; and from Professor John Torrey of the College of Physicians & Surgeons. From Yale came the endorsements of Benjamin Silliman and James Dana; from Harvard, those of Louis Agassiz and Benjamin Peirce. Virtually everyone who wrote was a member of the American Association for the Advancement of Science, a fact that some emphasized by so identifying themselves.[20]

A couple of Gibbs's backers were sensitive to how this barrage might be received by Columbia's trustees. "I trust," Peirce began his letter, "that that you will not consider it an impertinence," while Benjamin Gould went even further: "I will not, I trust, be deemed intrusive if those whose lives are employed in scientific studies, express their earnest interest in a step so important for the science of the country, as the election to fill the present vacancy." But it was still considered an impertinence and damned intrusive. The fact that these unsolicited endorsements came accompanied by the petition calling for Gibbs's election signed by two hundred Columbia College alumni only made some trustees more incensed.[21]

If this early barrage of outside endorsements did not put the trustees on their guard, Ruggles's attempt to preempt the issue of Gibbs's Unitarianism surely did. At the trustees meeting of January 9, 1854, he moved for a unanimous motion deploring the use of a religious test for candidates. His reminder to the trustees that the charter expressly forbade such a test and that the use of one could bring the state down upon the College only reinforced the impression of his bullying. The resolution was "indefinitely postponed."[22]

"I do not like the means which have been used to secure everything that has been shaped," Trustee Edward Jones (1849–1869) wrote the next day to the absent Hamilton Fish, "so as to put him [Gibbs] in, and keep all others out." He went on: "This is the sort of dragooning which many of us are not willing to stand, and I am prepared to vote against him on account of the indiscreet zeal of his friend." But as Jones, who eventually would vote for Gibbs, pointed out, those wanting to vote against him lacked a candidate of their own. Only then could they "administer a rebuke to the Committee which I think they richly merit, and show the community what they will not otherwise believe, that mere personal influence shall not be allowed to control the selection of candidates for any future vacant professorships, which may occur in the College."[23]

Other undecided trustees were angered the following week when the *New York Post*, edited by William Cullen Bryant, a Unitarian, urged Gibbs's appointment and decried possible opposition among trustees on religious grounds. The *Post*'s unwelcome admonition was followed by an even stronger assault on the motives of the Columbia trustees by Horace Greeley in the *New York Tribune*. Not to be left out, the Boston-based, Unitarian-sponsored *Christian Register* urged the trustees to do right by one of its coreligionists.[24]

The need for an alternative candidate to Gibbs became painfully clear to trustees feeling "dragooned" by Ruggles's campaign when a list of six candidates was presented to the board at its January 17 meeting. Of these, Dr. George C. Schaeffer, a one-time Columbia librarian (1839–47), and Robert Doremus, a teacher at the Free Academy, had some scattered support, but far short of that committed to Gibbs. A vote was deferred.[25]

That the tensions within the board reached a boiling point after this deferral is suggested by President King's letter to Board Chairman Hamilton Fish in Washington, asking him to absent himself from his senatorial duties there to attend the February 6 board meeting. King favored the appointment of Gibbs as "in the interest of the College and in deference to the voice of the men of science in this country" and assumed Fish thought likewise. Not so. Fish numbered himself among "the dragooned." And faced with the choice of staying in Washington or returning to New York to become entangled in a trustee donnybrook, the ever-cautious Fish begged off with the excuse that his vote was needed against the pending Kansas-Nebraska bill. Nor did he reconsider a week later, when Ruggles threatened that failure to appoint Gibbs could lead directly to state takeover of the College.[26]

The February 6 board meeting began with Trustee Gouverneur M. Ogden complaining about what a later generation would call leaks to the press. It was his all-but-stated opinion that Ruggles and Strong had done the leaking. Nor could Ogden have been pleased with a February 2 letter to the board from twenty parents of current College students urging the trustees to appoint Gibbs. The letter had been instigated by Strong and carried out by his classmate George C. Anthon, a colleague and friend of Gibbs's at the Free Academy. So pressed were Ogden and the other anti-Gibbs trustees that, after securing a three-day deferral on voting, they resorted to what for them was an unthinkable and subversive innovation: they placed an advertisement in several national newspapers announcing the vacancy and seeking applications.[27]

Nineteen of the twenty-two serving trustees attended the February 9 meeting. As the voting revealed, the anti-Gibbs members had effectively used the time since the January 17 meeting to coalesce around the Schaeffer candidacy, securing for it eight votes. The Gibbs candidacy had nine votes; Doremus, two. Two subsequent ballots failed to produce a majority, and another meeting was scheduled for five days later.

Two days before what would be the fifth trustee meeting devoted to filling Renwick's professorship and with no end in sight, a compromise proposal was circulated among the trustees. It called for the professorship to be divided, allowing the simultaneous appointments of Gibbs and Schaeffer. There is no evidence that the proposal emerged from the Gibbs camp, though the fact that Ruggles, disinclined to accept other peoples' compromises, declared it acceptable, suggests it might have. Ogden and Co. vetoed it. They may have done so for financial reasons or because they had become so determined to block Gibbs—and repudiate his backers—that having him on the faculty on any terms was now unacceptable. There was also a third possibility: those Strong called the "fogy party" now had the votes to block Gibbs, and the Ruggles camp knew it.[28]

The February 14 meeting produced four more ballots and no majority for any of the three candidates. At this point, the name of a fourth candidate was quietly added to the list, Richard McCulloch, a student of Joseph Henry and for the past five years professor of natural philosophy at Princeton. The next meeting was scheduled for March 6.[29]

By now, the time between meetings became the occasion for outside pressure to be brought to bear on the trustees. On March 4 Gibbs's widowed mother, Laura Walcott Gibbs, availed herself of a social acquaintanceship with Senator Hamilton Fish to write to him in Washington commending her son's candidacy. Gibbs himself was the model of professional circumspection. When asked by the Reverend John Knox, minister of the Dutch Collegiate Church and longtime trustee, to describe his religious views, he did so without taking apparent offense. Indeed, Henry James Anderson, a Gibbs supporter not in league with Ruggles and the only Catholic on the board, which allowed him to view the squabble among Protestants with a unique disinterest, tried to win

Fish over during this same interlude by assuring him that "Gibbs has no sympathy with an aggressive or anti-church party."[30]

By then, however, as all the trustees to be heard on the question agree, the Gibbs appointment had ceased to be primarily about Gibbs: it was about who would govern Columbia College. Strong admitted back in January that Gibbs's "election is unimportant compared with the question whether new life can or cannot be infused into that somnolent body [the board]. I would sacrifice him for the sake of eliminating some half dozen obstructive members of the Board." Anderson made the same point by describing Gibbs's backers "as well meaning friends of a larger liberty than is allowed to Alma mater as long as she administers the rents of College Green." From the other side, Gouverneur Ogden inferred the Gibbs supporters to have "a settled purpose—to control the action of the Board by intimidation and whatever of outside influence can be brought upon it."[31]

The March 6 trustees' meeting produced four more ballots and still no majority. The balloting did indicate, however, that the anti-Gibbs trustees had found themselves in McCulloch their dark horse. Evidence that Ruggles and Co. sensed as much was their decision to use the time before the next meeting, at which McCulloch was almost certain to win a majority, to pull out all the stops. On March 31 Ruggles published a pamphlet over which Strong had labored for weeks, entitled *The Duty of Columbia College to the Community*. While urging the superior qualifications of Gibbs, the pamphlet was primarily an indictment of the motives of those trustees who opposed him and were about to secure the appointment of a less qualified candidate. Ruggles could not have been more explicit in explaining the reason for their opposition: Gibbs was a Unitarian. Having lost his struggle to secure the two or three votes he needed among the twenty-two trustees beyond the nine core supporters he had had from the beginning, Ruggles decided to appeal his case to the court of popular opinion.[32]

If the anti-Gibbs trustees had any lingering hopes that Ruggles would in the end be a good loser, *The Duty of Columbia College to the Community* dashed them. The pamphlet opened with a comparison of Columbia College and the University of Göttingen, founded in the 1730s. By the time of Göttingen's centenary, Ruggles pointed out, it had eighty-nine faculty and enrolled 1,545 students. As Columbia entered its centennial year in 1854, it had six professors and 140 students. How to account for the difference? Not by pointing to differences in financial support, Ruggles insisted, for "if poverty be our excuse, it can avail us no longer. The difficulty lies deeper than the want of money." And then he identified the problem: "We have wanted trustees—more truly and zealously to carry out the purposes defined in our charter." Lest he spoil his indictment with a gesture of reconciliation toward his less zealous fellow trustees, especially those of the cloth, he closed with the categorical pronouncement that Columbia was "in no sense an ecclesiastical body. . . . The College is a public, not a private institution." Some outside backers of Gibbs, among them Harvard's Louis Agassiz and the New York Unitarian minister Henry Bellows, thought Ruggles's pamphlet heavy-handed. Even his son-in-law had second thoughts.[33]

The April 3 trustee meeting—the seventh given over to this single faculty appointment—attracted twenty-one trustees, including Senator Hamilton Fish. McCulloch received eleven votes, nine were for Gibbs, and one went to Alexander Dallas Bache, a noncandidate whose nomination by Fish gave him a too-clever-by-half way to secure a majority for McCulloch without voting for him. Fish belonged in Washington. As for the losers, some measure of their collective distress can be estimated by George Templeton Strong's diary entry the night of the decisive vote against Gibbs. After noting that none of the board's three Episcopal clergy voted for Gibbs, he comments: "This Columbia College business half tempts me to turn Roman Catholic."[34]

As expected, the decision of the trustees came under immediate criticism from two parties whose interest in the outcome Ruggles and Co. had cultivated throughout the protracted deliberations. Five days after the deciding vote, 40 Columbia alumni gathered at the urging of Strong and George Anthon to organize a protest of the trustees' rejection of their fellow alumnus. This was followed by a well-advertised alumni meeting on April 22, which drew 125 alumni from thirty-four classes and produced three resolutions: one condemned the rejection of Gibbs; another declared it the alumni's intention to boycott any planned centennial anniversary celebrations that fall; and the third challenged the simultaneous membership of the anti-Gibbs William Betts on the board of trustees and the nonfunctioning Law School faculty. Strong had provided the relevant details for the last resolution, with the hope that Betts's expulsion from the board could lead to a recount. The alumni concluded the meeting by overwhelmingly adopting a resolution that henceforth the College should elect a graduate to any faculty opening, "if possessing qualifications equal to those of any other candidate." So much for a national scientific meritocracy.[35]

Three weeks later, these same views were elaborated in a pamphlet that appeared with the unwieldy title *Report of the General Committee of the Alumni of Columbia College, on the Qualifications of Trustees of the College*. Its publication marks the beginning of the alumni of Columbia College as an organized constituency. A formal constitution for an association of alumni of Columbia College was adopted by the trustees in 1856. That the Columbia alumni date their origins from the Gibbs affair and that their first action was to register, in Strong's words, "a very emphatic rebuke" of the trustees, is proof that the affair, while viewed at the time as a reaffirmation of the trustees' authority, actually marked the point where their authority began to be dispersed among Columbia's several heretofore quiescent constituencies. The embattled trustees now had two publications to which a response was required.[36]

The thankless task fell to the redoubtable Gouverneur Ogden. His *Response to Samuel Ruggles' Duty of Columbia and the Alumni's Proceedings* appeared in May. Rather than duck the charge that some trustees had been influenced by the fact that Gibbs was a Unitarian, he defended their doing so, describing Gibbs's non-Trinitarian views "as radically at variance with the general sense of the religious portion of the country." He went on to insist that the charter's prohibition of a religious test was for faculty in place, while the religious views of a faculty candidate were "a legitimate issue on hiring—but not subsequently." Gibbs's amiable personal demeanor was neither here nor there. Indeed, in terms of his potential to subvert Trinitarians, "the more learned and amiable such a man, the greater the danger." Not to be all aggressive bluster, Ogden closed by calling his fellow trustee and the source of all his troubles, Samuel Ruggles, "an ingenious, plausible, and beautiful writer."[37]

Meanwhile, the trustees effected a measure of reconciliation, as evidenced by their reaction to the alumni charge that the membership of William Betts was in violation of the charter. At its June 5 meeting, the board allowed Betts to resign both his position in the Columbia law faculty, which was honorary and nonsalaried, and his seat on the trustees, only to reelect him to the board. The vote was unanimous and came on the motion of Samuel Ruggles.[38]

Tempers seem also to have cooled among the alumni, who at their July 27 meeting, which drew less than half the attendance of recent ones, advanced the then-novel idea of having Columbia alumni elect a portion of the trustees. They did not insist on this reform, or so the fact that it would not be implemented for another half-century allows us to infer.[39]

The other remaining and more threatening party at interest was the state legislature, which Ruggles had all but called upon to override the trustees' decision on Gibbs. Back in February, Strong noted mischievously that the "fogy and fossil party hates the suggestion of a committee from the legislature." And sure enough, ten days after the decisive trustee vote, the New York Senate voted seventeen to nine to investigate Columbia for possible violations of the charter's provisions against a religious test for its faculty. So eager was George James Cornell (CC 1839) to press the investigation that Strong, who was a College contemporary of Cornell, began to have second thoughts about having invited the state's scrutiny. For three days in early June, a senate committee conducted hearings in New York City, at which Columbia's trustees were asked to testify. Ruggles did so, both as to the reasoning behind his vote for Gibbs and to his previously stated belief that a majority of his colleagues had voted their religious opinions. But twelve other trustees, including at least two who voted for Gibbs, refused to provide testimony, standing by the board's stated position that it "had not at any time rejected a candidate for any professorship in the College, on account of his peculiar tenets in matters of religion." They defended their refusal to testify on the grounds that trustee deliberations were confidential.[40]

Had the backers of McCulloch, as Ruggles charged, voted on religious grounds? Some undoubtedly held Gibbs's Unitarianism against him, but the charge has about it the odor of a red herring. Not even Strong was fully convinced of it, as evidenced by his decision to absent himself from the senate hearings. It is the case that all six clerics on the board voted against Gibbs. Yet as likely an explanation for their votes as their submerging of their own interdenominational differences by lining up against a Unitarian was resentment of their authority being challenged by outsiders whose own claims to authority were based on scientific achievement. Gibbs did not represent a threat because he was a Unitarian so much as because his backers demanded consideration on the basis of criteria that, should they become the determinative ones, would leave the trustees no longer deciding appointments directly and for local reasons. Instead, they would be forced to choose from among those preselected by what King approvingly called "the men of science in this country." They might well have paused before buying in to this new, and irreversible, arrangement.[41]

Although it took the senate committee four months to finish its investigation and another nine months to file its report, when it did so, in March 1855, it concluded that it had no basis for finding the College in violation of its charter. If the Gibbs affair was the occasion when the alumni decided for the first time to butt in to the governance of Columbia College, it was also the occasion when the state of New York pretty much decided to butt out.[42]

With regard to the winning and losing candidates, McCulloch quickly accepted the trustees' offer and took up his duties as professor of chemistry and physics in the fall of 1854. On December 2 he delivered his inaugural address, which provided the occasion for Trustee Strong, of the William Livingston school of bad losers, to declare him "a feeble-looking, washed-out kind of man." Midway through his second year at Columbia, as if to confirm Strong's low opinion of his energies, McCulloch asked to have his professorship divided, with him remaining professor of physics and the trustees appointing someone else to teach chemistry. Thus the spurned compromise that might have brought Gibbs to Columbia in 1854 and saved the trustees all the troubles that followed on their rejection of him was quietly adopted three years later with the appointment of Charles A. Joy as professor of chemistry.[43]

Gibbs stayed on at City College until 1863, when his standing as the country's leading chemist led to his appointment at Harvard as Rumford Professor of Chemistry and director of the Lawrence Scientific School. Among the disappointed inside candidates he beat out for the position was the twenty-nine-year-old assistant professor Charles William Eliot, who, despite his Harvard degree, local teaching experience, and relatives on each of Harvard's two governing boards could not match Gibbs's credentials. Gibbs stayed on at Harvard, as an active scientist and promoter of university studies, until his retirement in 1887.[44]

Fourteen years earlier, in 1873, exactly two decades after his failed nomination, Wolcott Gibbs was awarded an honorary L.L.D. from Columbia. The idea to do so was likely President Barnard's but required majority approval of the board. Still on the board were ten members who had voted on the Gibbs appointment, among them the leaders of the anti-Gibbs forces, Gouverneur Ogden and William Betts, plus the 1854 fence-sitter and now secretary of state, Hamilton Fish. In the absence of a recorded tally, one is allowed to believe the trustee vote to award the degree was unanimous. Credulity is too far stretched, however, to think that Hamilton Fish cast his vote before the outcome was known.[45]

There would still be occasions after 1854 when individual trustees sought to secure the faculty appointment of a son-in-law, nephew, or out-of-work college chum. Nor were these efforts limited to the "fogy" party. Arguments would be made in favor of such candidates that now read as breathtaking in their anti-intellectualism and special pleading. Still, the vote on the Gibbs appointment viewed in light of the subsequent history of Columbia, its immediate outcome notwithstanding, was the beginning of the end of the era of trustee hegemony in matters relating to the curriculum and faculty appointments. Both areas of powers were thereafter increasingly ceded to the faculty, who within a few decades assumed an autonomy over each that one might now think God-given. This was surely no guarantee against violations of what a later generation called academic freedom, but for such violations to occur at Columbia (as they would on the eve of America's entry into World War I), the complicity of faculty was required. It also increased the likelihood that the trustees would henceforth concentrate their collective energies where their capacities and talents could be put to best use.

Columbia is Rich!

Just below the surface of the Gibbs affair roiled another struggle within the board. It was about money, and, as usual, Samuel Ruggles showed the least hesitancy in raising it. In a letter to board chair Hamilton Fish, he warned that, should Gibbs be rejected, the state might intervene and disrupt the prospect of the College's soon enjoying "income of $100,000 with a steady growth to $150,000."[46]

Meanwhile, Ruggles's son-in-law communicated to his diary his excitement over the financial implications of the Gibbs affair for the College: "It reminds me of the exciting plots and counterplots and resolutions and protests of the old Philolexian days. Only here, the stake is really great and the prize is worth fighting for." And what was the prize? "The way in which near an hundred thousand dollars per annum and perhaps more, shall be used for purpose of education, twenty years hence. Deus salvuum fac Collegium!" What both the pro-Gibbs and anti-Gibbs trustees found themselves having to contemplate was nothing less than the novel and imminent reality that Columbia was about to become rich.[47]

Money made possible the transformation of the sleepy Columbia College of the first half of the nineteenth century into the dynamic Columbia University of the end of the century. And the money that allowed this came mostly from rising returns from two parcels of College-owned Manhattan real estate. This link between education and property was not new. The College's involvement in real estate coincides with its founding in the 1750s. Even before the construction of College Hall was completed in 1760, several lots surrounding the planned College Green and part of the six-acre Trinity Church grant were put out to rent. When in 1762 the city of New York conveyed the land—water lots—between the western edge of the grant and one hundred feet beyond the waterline of the Hudson River to the College governors, they promptly leased it out. This income, along with the interest generated from individual gifts, made King's College the most financially viable—and certainly the least tuition-dependent—of the nine colonial colleges.[48]

To be sure, the Revolutionary War disrupted the income stream from these properties, and the Tory allegiance of the prewar College authorities put in doubt the College's claims to postwar ownership. Among the most important aspects of the 1784 and 1787 charters were their confirmation of the ownership of these properties. With the end of direct state grants in the late 1790s and the withdrawal of virtually all state support after 1819, their income became absolutely essential to the College's survival. In 1850 well over half the College's total operating budget of forty thousand dollars was covered by income from property rentals, while tuition income covered only about half of the remainder.

New money after 1850 came not just from bigger returns from the Park Place properties (hereinafter called the Lower Estate) but from land owned by the College for four decades that was only now acquiring commercial value. This land, first referred to as David Hosack's (or Elgin) Garden, then in the 1850s as the Upper Estate, and after 1929 as the Rockefeller Center site, was deeded to the College in 1814 by the state of New York. The state had bought it from David Hosack three years earlier, for twenty-five thousand dollars. One of the great ironies of Columbia's history is that the trustees regarded the state's actions at the time as niggardly, it having just made direct grants to upstate Union and Hamilton College far in excess of the market value of Hosack's property, which was located then three miles above the northernmost line of commercial development. Moreover, the legislature's actions initially stipulated that the land was to be used as the future site of the College and was not to be rented out. Three years of lobbying were required to have both those stipulations lifted in 1819, but even then it would be another three decades before the northward march of commercial development on Manhattan Island made the property other than a liability.[49]

Throughout these decades, the property continued to be thought of as the likely future site for the College. This assumption grew even stronger as the area around the original campus became increasingly congested with warehouses and other commercial establishments. The unbidden thought must have more than once crossed the minds of some of the more main-chance trustees that the property had become too valuable to be kept to present uses. Developers in the 1840s regularly approached the trustees with schemes for leasing parts of the College Green, schemes that, depending on the previous year's balance sheet, were summarily dismissed or seriously entertained. In 1852 a trustee committee looking into the removal of the College had plans drawn up for transferring it to the Upper Estate.[50]

There was an idea among the trustees on the committee that moving the College to a part of the property the College already owned would not only be cheaper than acquiring a new site but also raise the commercial value of the rest of the Upper Estate. The heated and contentious discussions within the board in the early 1850s as to the wisdom of borrowing money to make the Upper Estate suitable for leasing—as opposed to waiting another decade or so for the development line to move farther north—did not suggest abandonment of the earlier plan for the College eventually to move there. And when the decision was made in 1856 to borrow money to excavate, grade, and lay the property out into blocks and lots, the trustees showed considerable nerve—or faith in the upward return potential of Manhattan real estate. Ruggles and Strong opposed doing so, preferring to wait another decade.[51]

Deliberations accelerated in June 1856 when the board learned that the four-block site of the recently abandoned New York Institution for the Instruction of the Deaf and Dumb, between the then-undeveloped Forty-ninth and Fiftieth

Streets (southeast of the Upper Estate), was for sale. The initial asking price of one hundred thousand dollars was only about a sixth of what the trustees could expect to get for selling the Park Place campus. That it came with a building of eleven thousand square feet of floor space and some usable secondary sheds made it still more attractive as "a convenient substitute, at least temporarily," for a permanent College site.[52]

A board that could take decades to effect a change in the College's academic program proved in matters of real estate to be able to turn on a dime. The trustees immediately entered into negotiations with the asylum's board, got the price down to $63,000, and closed the deal on October 6, 1856. It then proceeded to put up for auction the thirteen lots that constituted the Park Place campus. These were sold on February 2, 1857, for $596,350. The trustees now had money to pay off the loans taken for the development of the Upper Estate parcel and for sprucing up the asylum, with funds to spare for curricular development.[53]

The Upper Estate proved to be very profitable. Most of its 216 lots were quickly leased for lengths up to twenty-one years. Ruggles's estimate of rents running between $100,000 and even $150,000 proved conservative; by 1875 annual income from the College's real estate holdings exceeded $200,000, the equivalent to an endowment of $4 million. Within two decades Columbia had been financially transformed from one of a dozen budgetarily strapped New York colleges into the country's richest academic institution. It would remain so into the second decade of the twentieth century.[54]

It bears noting that the late-nineteenth century transformation of Columbia's financial fortunes occurred without the federal assistance that helped Cornell and midwestern state universities such as Illinois and Wisconsin under the provisions of the Morrill Act of 1862 and the Hatch Act of 1887. Nor did it receive any support from the state of New York, the last direct subsidy from Albany (until the 1970s) coming in 1819. Nor did Columbia receive a single founder benefaction such as the ones that got Johns Hopkins ($3.5 million), Stanford ($24 million), and the University of Chicago ($34 million) under way. Nor was it the recipient of surges in organized alumni giving such as those that stimulated growth at Harvard, Yale, and Princeton. On this last point, the contrast with Harvard is especially telling. Between 1800 and 1860 Harvard received gifts from twenty-eight donors in excess of $5,000; during that same period, Columbia received just one, of $20,000, and that from a nonalumnus. Columbia's first gift from an alumnus in excess of $5,000 would not be forthcoming until the 1880s.[55]

It also bears noting that Columbia's financial turnaround was unrelated to efforts to develop a curriculum that attracted students—and their tuitions—to the College. It was the derived consequence of the rising property values of New

York City, plain and simple. And it was this financial turnaround that made possible Columbia's subsequent academic development, not the other way round.

The Move to Forty-ninth Street

In May 1857, a century almost to the month after construction of the main hall of King's College had begun in 1757, its demolition was well under way. The event was marked by at least two diary-keeping Columbians. On April 27, the Reverend Dr. Morgan Dix wrote, "Dined at the College. The place in great confusion as they are preparing to move." A week later he recorded having "took tea at Prof. McVickar's. . . . This was the last evening in which we assembled within the old walls; as the work of demolition has already commenced and the few remaining occupants move out during the week." George Templeton Strong similarly noted the occasion, though he chose to do so on May 10 by displaying both his command of Latin and his anti-Irish prejudice: "The demolition of Col: Coll: has begun, inspected yesterday the progress already made by the invading forces. Hibernia rampant and destructive in its very penetralia. 'Sic transit'—'Eheu fugaces,' as McVickar used to observe with considerable research and singular power of observation."[56]

The *New York Evening Post* reported on that same day that, following a ceremony at the College on May 5, "the cornerstone of the College building was disinterred. It is a solid block of red sand stone, measuring three feet in length, one foot in depth and one foot in thickness. The letters are as fresh and sharp as the day they were cut." (So they remain, with the cornerstone now on display in the Trustees' Room of Low Library.) A final notice, appearing in the May 17 edition of the *Post*, notes: "The old college building in Park Place is now deserted and this morning a strong force of workmen were employed in tearing off the roofing and undermining the walls." Nearly one hundred and fifty years later, one is struck by how little nostalgia attended the passing of the old college. Columbians are like that. " 'Sic transit,' . . . as McVickar used to observe."[57]

Academic Fits and Starts

The swapping of the Park Place campus for the Institution for the Deaf and Dumb on Forty-ninth Street, however much a financial bargain, was not without its attendant costs. Several trustees worried that the new campus was too far north of the residential areas of Lower Manhattan from which Columbia's students tended to come and that moving there would result in a sharp drop in enrollments. The trustees sought to offset this anticipated drop by announcing a reduction in tuition from ninety to seventy-five dollars.[58]

There was also the personal inconvenience to the trustees themselves, several of whom found the trek uptown so arduous that they persuaded the board to meet off campus. Neither President King nor the faculty who had enjoyed spacious digs in the old College Hall welcomed the move, although King persuaded the trustees of the need to construct a president's house across the street from the old asylum building. McVickar's and Anthon's retirements shortly after the move were likely precipitated by it. The trustees did little for the next fifteen years to improve the property, insisting well into the 1870s that the Forty-ninth Street campus was a temporary arrangement and that a more permanent site would soon turn up.[59]

As their reluctance to invest in improvements to the Forty-ninth Street site suggests, the rather sudden arrival of wealth did not transform the trustees into big spenders. A traditional preference for accumulating—rather than expending—was especially marked in the person of treasurer Gouverneur Ogden but not limited to him. As Strong put it, several of his colleagues manifested "a weakness for the inviolability of all endowments in real estate." Still, the income derived from the sale of the Park Place campus and the anticipated income from the Upper Estate, as well as the sale to the Dutch Reformed Church in April 1857 of sixteen lots fronting on Fifth Avenue for eighty thousand dollars, did make the trustees somewhat more venturesome in thinking about the College's future. There may even have been an understanding between the real estate empire builders on the board, led by Ogden, and the proponents of curricular reform and program expansion, led by Ruggles, that each faction would go along with the initiatives of the other.[60]

Thus it was in 1857, for the first time in forty years, the board decided to expand the faculty. It did so first by making six appointments, three of them incremental. Francis Lieber (1857–72) was appointed professor of history and political science and Charles M. Nairne (1857–81) professor of philosophy, both in anticipation of McVickar's retirement. Charles Davies (1857–65) was appointed professor of mathematics, succeeding Hackley, who had been forced out the year before. William G. Peck (1857–93), Davies's son-in-law, was hired as adjunct professor of mathematics. A new faculty position was created when the trustees quietly acceded to McCulloch's complaint that he could not teach both physics and chemistry by appointing Charles A. Joy (1857–1902) professor of chemistry. In 1860, after his graduation from the College, John H. Van Amringe (1860–1910) was appointed a tutor in mathematics. Thus, where five years ago there had been Hackley, now there were Davies, Peck, and Van Amringe; and where there had been Renwick, now there were McCulloch and Joy; where McVickar, now Lieber and Nairne.[61]

Some of these appointments worked out better than others. Lieber, a German who had immigrated to the United States in 1827, brought to Columbia an international reputation as a political theorist. After more than two decades of teaching at the University of South Carolina, where his antislavery views kept him an unwelcome outsider, he had let acquaintances in the North, including the ubiquitous Ruggles, know that he could be lured away. He also, in the wake of the Gibbs affair, helpfully mentioned that he was a practicing Episcopalian. Once installed at Columbia, he proved to be an indifferent teacher and a disappointment to his sponsors. He abandoned undergraduate teaching altogether in the early 1860s in exchange for what proved to be a sinecure in the Law School, though he remained a faculty member until he died in 1872.[62]

Charles Davies (1857–65) was a disappointment from his arrival, when Strong declared him a "Uriah Heepish personage in manner" and "a mere fifth wheel to an academic coach." Partially offsetting these deficiencies, Strong allowed that "he is rich and independent of his salary, and that is not a full salary." Davies retired after eight years, in 1865, staying on at the end as a placeholder for his son-in-law William Peck, who succeeded him in 1865 and went on to a more successful career at Columbia in mathematics. A variation on Davies, Charles Nairne was a Scot who married a southern woman of wealth and set up a fashionable house on Thirty-fourth Street. There he and his wife regularly entertained collections of town and gown. Unlike Lieber and Davies, Nairne had the misfortune of still being on the faculty when John W. Burgess joined it in 1875. More than a half century later, Burgess recalled Nairne as "the freak of the faculty [who] talked more about the good things of the table than about Plato, Aristotle, Leibniz, or Kant, or even Dugald Stewart or Hume. As a teacher he was a joke." And, more damning coming from the nothing-if-not-grownup Burgess, Nairne was in "practical matters as helpless as a child."[63]

Charles A. Joy was a serious chemist, if not quite in Gibbs's league, certainly an improvement over Renwick and McCulloch. He both shocked and impressed the trustees by asking upon his arrival for fifteen thousand dollars in start-up funds to furnish a research lab. "Only three years ago," Trustee Strong admitted, such a request "would have made our corporate hair stand on end." John H. Van Amringe, never much of a mathematician, in 1863 asked to be shifted to classics, where there was a professorial opening. Nicholas Murray Butler (CC 1882), second only to Burgess in deprecating predecessors, remembered Van Amringe as "the towering personality for freshmen and sophomores. . . . With his drooping gray mustache and square military shoulders, he loved to assume an air of terrifying fierceness, but as a matter of fact he was the kindest and most tenderhearted of men."[64]

A general observation about these six appointments. Only Van Amringe was a Columbia graduate and owed his appointment to local considerations. Lieber, Joy, and Peck had all received European postgraduate training and all enjoyed professional standing in their fields. So did Nairne. As such, these appointments were akin to Gibbs, or earlier to Tellkampf, rather than to Anderson, McVickar, or Renwick. It was still possible to find trustees willing to speak up for a local candidate, the Reverend John Knox (1836–58) recommending his son in 1857 for the position that went to Nairne being a case in point. Another example occurred eight years later, when the Reverend Benjamin Haight (1843–1879) supported an appointment in geology on the grounds that "a man without scientific name and standing was preferable to one of the highest reputation . . . because the nameless professor would work harder to secure reputation than the professor who had already secured it." These efforts noted, the day of the inside amateur as professor, or of the trustees as appointers of faculty, was drawing to an end.[65]

One of the reasons for so many new hires in 1857 was the expectation that they would be needed to accommodate the increased volume of students drawn to Columbia by its recently announced postgraduate curriculum. It consisted of a three-year program leading to a master's degree in one of three fields: letters, science, and jurisprudence. The intention was to attract students who had graduated from college elsewhere or were prepared to transfer in their fourth year. Columbia undergraduates could enroll in the program in their senior year. Along with the new full-time hires, three part-time appointments were announced, the diplomat and literary scholar George P. Marsh, the Swiss-born geographer Arnold H. Guyot and the botanist John Torrey.[66]

The driving force on the board behind this plan was (who else?) Samuel Ruggles, though this time he was unable to convince even his son-in-law of the program's viability. "I anticipate no results," Strong informed his diary in early 1858. "We have to create the demand for higher education as well as the supply. . . . This people is not yet ripe for higher education." To give Ruggles his due, he had coupled the postgraduate plan with the creation of a fellowship fund that would attract graduates from other colleges and persuade Columbia College seniors to stay on for another two years. Ogden and others on the board, already worried about the outlays for new faculty that occurred in the midst of the Panic of 1858, refused to approve these fellowships. Nonetheless, the establishment of the graduate program allowed President King to declare at the 1858 commencement that Columbia "was now a University."[67]

The postgraduate curriculum found few takers, and in April 1861 it was abandoned, the immediate victim of a retrenchment program declared by the trustees at the outset of the Civil War. It would be another fifteen years, first in the School of Mines in the mid-1870s and later, in 1881, with the establishment of the School of Political Science, again at the urging of Ruggles, before Columbia would once more venture into graduate studies. By then, its initiatives in the late 1850s were properly forgotten, while subsequent, more perdurable initiatives at Yale, Harvard, Johns Hopkins, and Cornell can be given credit for founding graduate studies in the United States. There is, however, the mitigating rarity here of attributing to Columbia the novel sin of being ahead of its time.[68]

Dwight's Law School

Something lasting did come out of Columbia's otherwise abortive effort to introduce graduate studies to New York and the nation in 1857. That one of the three proposed fields of study had been jurisprudence reflected some latent sentiment among the board for the reintroduction of legal studies, last seen at Columbia in 1826. Here, the initiative seems to have come from George Templeton Strong, who, in the same diary entry that declared his father-in-law's plans for graduate studies were premature as the country "is not yet ripe for higher education," came forward with the idea of establishing at Columbia a law school and a school of applied science. "Exhibit a seductive bait of tangible material advantage," Strong appealed to his more practical-minded trustee colleagues in the spring of 1858, "and you will catch students."[69]

To have a successful law school, whoever ran it had to be adept at catching—and holding—students. In Theodore W. Dwight (1822–92), Columbia found its man, a veritable pied piper of New York legal studies. Before coming to New York, he taught at Hamilton College, from which he graduated in 1840 and went on to attend the Yale Law School in 1841–42. He did not graduate before returning to his alma mater as a tutor and then professor of law in 1846. In 1845 he was admitted to the New York bar, having met the three-year apprenticeship requirement while teaching at Hamilton. For the early part of Dwight's twelve years as professor of law, Hamilton was the only law school operating in the state of New York. In 1859 Albany Law School opened. That same year Dwight extracted from the state legislature the provision that graduates of the Hamilton and Albany law programs would be automatically admitted to the bar in New York.[70]

Securing an identical "diploma privilege" for Columbia law graduates was one of Dwight's first orders of business in the fall of 1858 as professor of municipal law and warden of the Law School. This he did in 1860. Instead of setting up the Law School on or adjacent to the new Forty-ninth Street campus, he rented quarters downtown at 37 Lafayette Place so as to be near the law offices and courts. In 1873 he moved the school to 8 Great Jones Street, where it remained until being forced onto the Forty-ninth Street campus in 1884. This made it possible for young men working as clerks in law offices or in the courts to attend legal classes while still holding full-time jobs. He made their doing so still easier by arranging the Law School curriculum so that a full program could be taken by attending either in the mornings or in the afternoons. One recalls the postmeridian "Turkey," in the offices of Herman Melville's "Bartleby the Scrivener," slipping off to an afternoon class.[71]

These accommodations to the needs of students were facilitated by two factors. The first was that for its first sixteen years, the Law School faculty for all practical purposes consisted of only one man: Dwight. Other Columbia faculty members, such as Lieber, Nairne, and later Burgess, were assigned places on the law faculty, but insofar as their courses were not part of the required law curriculum, there was little incentive for students to enroll in them. When Lieber tried to make his courses required of law students, Dwight resisted the move and had the backing of the trustees. "We cannot yet, in the infancy of the school," Strong agreed, "require young attorneys and lawyer's clerks to sacrifice a couple of hours daily to political science and legal philosophy." He was not prepared to put at risk what Dwight had accomplished in his first year: "persuading so many (upwards of sixty) [to] consent to come in to be taught the practicalities of their profession."[72]

Another listed member of Dwight's law faculty, John Ordronaux, professor of medical jurisprudence, similarly seems to have had few if any students. Presumably he did at the Dartmouth, where he held a concurrent appointment in the medical school. It was not until the appointment in 1874 of one of Dwight's own students, George Chase (CU Law, 1873), as adjunct professor of municipal law, that law students were expected to take classes with someone other than Dwight.[73]

The second factor that made this arrangement work was Dwight's financial arrangements with the trustees. He started out with a guaranteed salary of two thousand dollars and an equal share (to be split with the other law faculty) of all the school's net profits above that. His salary was later increased to six thousand dollars, with some part of the splitting-of-profits arrangement still intact. Despite repeated efforts by trustees to put Dwight on straight salary, he maintained this profitable proprietary arrangement until his retirement in 1891.[74]

Not surprisingly, Dwight favored large enrollments. His opening class in 1858 consisted of 38 paying students; two years later, there were 135. By 1864, 171 students were enrolled in his two-year program, as against 150 in the College. That year, the Law School graduated 66 students to the College's 38. In 1877 Law School graduates had grown to 267, while those of the College had dropped to 21. In Dwight's Law School, Columbia had its first cash cow.[75]

A Note on Columbia and the Civil War

Academic historians, like economic historians before them, are much given to analyzing the impact of the Civil War on American higher education generally and on the development of individual institutions. Did the war accelerate or retard development? Were its long-term effects positive or negative? Or did it have no discernible effect, as if the war had not even occurred? While such questions are worth confronting, one might first, at the risk of seeming solipsistic, reverse the question and ask what impact Columbia had on the Civil War.

The Civil War was the sixth American war to occur in Columbia's history, counting the quasi-war with France in the late 1790s. King's College got under way on the eve of the French and Indian War and was shuttered by the Revolutionary War. There followed the quasi-war with France, in which Columbia's future president, William A. Duer, served as a naval officer and which most New Yorkers supported, and the War of 1812, which most Columbians, as anti-Jeffersonians who opposed the restraints it placed on maritime commerce, sat out. Unlike their New England counterparts and excepting Gouverneur Morris, Columbians did not actively support secession. The War of 1848 saw the active engagement of Columbia graduate Philip Kearney (CC 1833), by then a colonel, but otherwise few Columbians took part.

In 1898, in the immediate aftermath of the triumphal Spanish-American War, Columbia published a *Supplement to the General Catalogue*, in which the participation of Columbians in the Civil War was proudly detailed. Including classes as far back as 1824, the *Supplement* identified some 395 graduates or students who had participated in the war.

The classes of 1862, 1863, and 1864 consisted of sixty-three, fifty, and thirty-eight graduates, which puts their Civil War participation rates at 78, 76, and 95 percent, respectively! The inclusion of nongraduates in the count reduces the rate somewhat, but not nearly as much as does the inclusion of medical students attending the College of Physicians & Surgeons. This is reaching. Before 1861, Columbia College had no connection with P & S, while the intercorporate agreement reached that year did little to change their mutual independence. One can only conclude that the inclusion of P & S graduates, who served in great numbers during the war in Union hospitals near the front and to the rear, was meant retrospectively to improve Columbia's otherwise decidedly unimpressive war record.[76]

Columbia College alumni casualties in this bloodiest of all American wars number fewer than a dozen, none of whom was from any of the five wartime classes, which in all likelihood failed to produce fifty enlistments. In the forty-four-man class of 1862, six are listed in the 1900 *Catalogue of Columbia College* as having served in the war. At Harvard, with an enrollment of 2,400 students in 1861, including those studying medicine and law, 500 volunteered for service at the outbreak of the war. At Bowdoin, twenty-two of the forty-eight members of the class of 1861 enlisted upon graduation. At Oberlin, 147 students enlisted in 1861 and 1862. At Grinnell, where a freshman class of 12 students was enrolled at the time of Lincoln's call to arms, all but two answered the call. And so it went throughout New England and the Midwest. The enlistment rates of collegians at southern colleges were even higher. To be sure, the early enthusiasm for the war cooled on these campuses as its duration and brutality became clear in the days after the opening skirmishes. Yet many of these collegiate recruits remained in uniform for the duration—or until they became casualties. By 1865 ninety-three Harvard alumni had died in combat.[77]

Another indicator of Columbia's relative uninvolvement in the Civil War was that whereas wartime enrollments dropped sharply elsewhere, at Columbia College (and even more at the Law School) they increased. Similarly, whereas postwar enrollments increased sharply on other campuses, at Columbia College they dropped.[78]

How does one account for a Columbia record in the Civil War that prompted a historian reviewing it in the midst of World War II to conclude that he "best leave that chapter be"? Part of the answer has to do with the prewar national politics of New York City, which Lincoln lost in both 1860 (by thirty thousand votes) and 1864 (by thirty-seven thousand votes), while carrying New York State both times. But part also has to do with the politics of the families who constituted early Columbia College, which was more likely to be Whig—and Cotton Whig, at that—than Free Soil or Republican. Commercial links with the South made it difficult for many New Yorkers, including some Columbia trustees, not to feel sympathy for the southern cause. The trustees Gouverneur Ogden and his son-in-law, William Betts, were regularly characterized in Strong's diary as "doughfaces" and "Copperheads," while the diarist's own pro-Unionism derived more from conservative sentiments having to do with stiffening the moral resolve of the North and punishing the errant South than with freeing slaves. "Slavery is not a wrong per se," he had satisfied himself in 1856. But even if it were, he went on, "we are not called to interfere with it . . . any more than we are bound to attack the serfdom of Russia or the iniquities of

Naples." Aside from the abolitionist John C. Jay (CC 1827), Columbians were conspicuous by their absence from the ranks of the antislavery movement or of the organizers of the Free Soil and Republican parties. It is a fair bet that most of them voted in 1860 for the proslavery Whig John Bell or the Democrat Stephen A. Douglas rather than for the Republican Lincoln.[79]

Columbia College became a target of the New York City Draft Riots in July 1863, though this likely had more to do with class antagonisms between Irish-American immigrants and Knickerbockers than any suspicion among the antiblack rioters that Columbians favored the recently announced Emancipation Proclamation. It may also have been a reaction on the part of these rioters to the knowledge that numbers of Columbians avoided the draft by buying substitutes, who came largely from the families of those rioting.[80]

Columbia did have its individual war heroes. The College's most conspicuous Unionist in 1861 was President Charles King, who appeared at a flag-raising ceremony on April 23, in honor of Major Robert Anderson of Fort Sumter fame, with his uniformed son, Lieutenant Cornelius L. King (CC 1848), at his side. The young King went on to serve with distinction in several battles and rose to the rank of lieutenant colonel by war's end. The military exploits of Philip Kearney (CC 1833) also deserve citing. A professional soldier, Kearney entered the war as a brigadier general, was then promoted to major general, fought in a dozen engagements in the Virginia campaigns under the command of General George McClellan, and was killed on the eve of the Battle of Antietam in 1862. Lieutenant Colonel W. Carey Massett (CC 1857) died at the Battle of Whitehall in 1862; Captain Stephen Richard Reynolds (CC 1859) was mortally wounded in the Battle of the Wilderness; Captain Thomas Colden Cooper (CC 1838) died in the same campaign. "Tom fell in the Wilderness," his classmate George Templeton Strong had reason to recall in 1870, "doubtless fighting hard, for he had plenty of pluck."[81]

The lone trustee to have served in uniform during the Civil War was Colonel John Jacob Astor Jr. Hamilton Fish served as chairman of the Union Defense Committee and the Commission to Visit Union Soldiers in Confederate Prisons. Also impressive were the labors of George Templeton Strong on behalf of the United States Sanitary Commission, the forerunner of the American Red Cross, for which he received a personal commendation from President Lincoln.[82]

Among the survivors of combat were future members of the Columbia faculty such as the Union soldiers Francis L. Vinton and John W. Burgess. Among current members, Francis Lieber was a frequent adviser to President Lincoln on constitutional matters and, as author of the *Code for the Government of Armies* (1863), lent his scholarly skills to the military effort.[83]

But surely the most spectacular instance of faculty involvement in the Civil War was that of Professor of Physics Richard McCulloch (1854–63). Unfortunately for Columbia's subsequent efforts to rehabilitate its wartime record, McCulloch's involvement was on the Confederate side. Although suspected of secessionist sympathies at the time of the breakup of the Union in the spring of 1861, the Baltimore-borne McCulloch stayed at Columbia for another two years until, in the summer of 1863, he slipped out of New York, returned to Virginia behind rebel lines, and openly sided with the Confederacy. His two wartime years at Columbia may have been spent as a paid spy for the Confederacy. McCulloch served out the war in a Confederate uniform, rising to the rank of brigadier general, making him one of the only two Columbia-connected men to achieve flag rank in the Civil War. With the peace, he took up teaching positions first at Washington and Lee and then at Louisiana State University. He died in 1894.[84]

But this story has a silver lining. Upon receipt of McCulloch's letter of resignation, postmarked Richmond, Virginia, the Columbia trustees expunged his name from the list of Columbia faculty. It was the ensuing search for McCulloch's successor, though it resulted in the appointment of Ogden Rood, that first brought to the notice of the Columbia trustees a recent New England–born defector from the Confederacy (he and McCulloch may have crossed paths at the Virginia line!) and out-of-work physicist, Frederick A. P. Barnard. Missing out on the faculty appointment, despite a fulsome show of support from the country's leading scientists but likely in part because of his widely published *Letter to the President of the United States, by a Refugee*, Barnard immediately came under consideration for another job opening at Columbia. But that's another chapter.[85]

CHAPTER 5

Takeoff

We may assume it therefore as certain that Columbia College is to be the great university of this principal state in the Union, and this principal city of the western continent.

President F. A. P. Barnard, 1879

I was especially glad, also, that you traced the seed of the new life to its planting by President Barnard. I always feel that, in the largest sense, I am only watering, in most cases, the seed which he had the sagacity to plant.

President Seth Low to Nicholas Murray Butler, 1896

Presidential Synthesis Revisited

THE histories of American universities in the late nineteenth century have traditionally been written around the several outsized presidents who seemingly dominated the era. If now suspect among political historians and repudiated by the crusty economic historian Thomas Cochran, the "presidential synthesis" remains alive and well among historians of American academe.[1]

There are good reasons for this continued focus on academic presidents. Unlike political presidents of the late nineteenth century, who typically held office for only four-year terms (only Grant served eight consecutive years), academic presidents were impressively long serving. Charles William Eliot's forty-one-year term at Harvard (1869–1909) was the longest, but the twenty-five-year presidency of Daniel Coit Gilman at Johns Hopkins (1876–1901), James B. Angell's twenty-four years at Michigan (1877–1901), David Starr Jordan's twenty-two years at Stanford (1891–1913), and even Andrew Dickson White's eighteen years at Cornell (1868–86) provided the time to effect fundamental changes on their respective campuses. Conversely, at Yale and Princeton, where the presidential turnover was more frequent, less change occurred, and it met with more resistance.[2]

Of these academic giants—the iconoclastic economist Thorstein Veblen called them, after their corporate counterparts, "captains of erudition"—Harvard's Charles William Eliot has generally been acceded pride of place. Again, with good reason. Although not originating the idea of the elective system or even being the first president to introduce it at Harvard, Eliot became its consistent champion, in the face of conservative criticism from the presidents of Yale, Princeton, and denominational colleges generally, which accounts for his personal identification with one of the era's most transformative innovations. In extending the principle of student election of courses to all four years of Harvard's undergraduate program, a condition reached in 1890, Eliot went further than any of his contemporary presidents in giving students freedom to choose their academic programs—and even further than subsequent Harvard faculties have been willing to go.[3]

Eliot also understood that the spread of the elective system throughout Harvard's undergraduate curriculum meant that Harvard faculty would be able to teach students in subjects in which they specialized. More than merely accepting the reciprocal character of the elective system, Eliot openly embraced it as a means by which his faculty could meet their teaching responsibilities without disengaging from their research pursuits. Under Eliot, Harvard faculty in the 1870s increasingly came to teach what they did, and by the 1880s it became a condition of continued employment, as teachers were expected to produce publishable results of their specialized research. Here was a further difference between the old-time college and the new: the expectation that faculty would not only be members of their local collegiate communities but also members of an international scholarly community of scholars and researchers.[4]

Innovative credit also should be given Daniel Coit Gilman, who, after failing to win over his alma mater Yale to the idea of an externally oriented faculty, immediately implemented this project when he became president of the Johns Hopkins University at its opening in 1876. More than anything else, it was the prospect of losing several of Harvard's best scholars to Baltimore, among them William James, that brought Eliot around to the need to acknowledge and reward his faculty who attracted outside attention. (It also made necessary terminating heretofore serviceable Harvard faculty whose talents were limited to classroom teaching.)[5] Insofar as Gilman privileged the scholar-researcher at Hopkins, he was doing so at a new university where the training of scholars was to be its main business and the undergraduate College only an afterthought. The application of this reform to institutions with substantial undergraduate populations could expect to encounter opposition. It did. But when Eliot in 1886, presiding over the oldest and largest undergraduate college in the country, declared that "the great need of the University is to make the career of the University teacher more attractive to men of capacity and ambition," his conversion was complete. By then, the principal criterion of permanent faculty selection at Harvard had become the candidate's standing among his scholarly peers throughout the world.[6]

Eliot's assigned preeminence among his peers can be traced to other factors.

He has been fortunate in his biographers. The two-volume 1930 biography by Henry James (son of William and nephew of the novelist) is as comprehensive an account of a university president as we have. More recently, the institutional biography of Eliot by Hugh Hawkins, *Between Harvard and America* (1972), provides still more reasons for early-twenty-first-century Americans to admire him. He was, as compared with contemporaries of his class and ancestry, relatively free of many of the social prejudices common in his day and unacceptable in ours. He remained, for example, during an era that became increasingly restrictionist in its views on immigration, especially among the Boston intellectual elite, a persistent advocate of open immigration. He was also openly admiring of the accomplishments of Jews in America. To be sure, he had his doubts about the patriotism of American Catholics, opposed the movement to enfranchise women (or provide them access to Harvard), and decried the influence of labor unions. Still, and this is another instance of his posthumous luck, as compared with his successor A. Lawrence Lowell (1910–31), the Eliot who struck his contemporaries as a cold fish survives in history as a mensch.[7]

Staking a claim for Columbia's tenth president, Frederick A. P. Barnard, as one of America's truly transformative academic presidents, is not simply justified because of his difference from his nine Columbia predecessors but also in light of how he compares to the leading academic titan of his era. The case in sum: Eliot inherited the largest, wealthiest, and most nationally recognized of American colleges, including law, divinity, medical, and scientific schools, and forty-one years later turned over to his successor all that he had begun with and one of America's two or three world-class universities to boot; Barnard inherited a small, potentially wealthy, and nationally negligible college (and law school) and twenty-five years later turned over to his successor an institution within a decade of being one of America's two or three world-class universities. University presidents mattered in the late nineteenth century, and none mattered more than Columbia's—to Columbia and to American higher education.

"Admirable Frederick"

An Alabama friend later recalled Columbia's tenth president thus: "Admirable Frederick—the best at whatever he attempted to do; he could turn the best sonnet, write the best love story, take the best daguerreotype picture, charm the most women, catch the most trout, and calculate the most undoubted almanac." For Columbia's purposes, it also helped that he was one of those non-natives who made both Columbia and New York his home.[8]

Barnard was born in Sheffield, Massachusetts, in 1809, the son of Robert

Foster Barnard, an attorney, and Augusta Porter. He attended Saratoga Academy, across the state border in New York, and then Stockbridge Academy, where he was the classmate and friendly rival of Mark Hopkins, later president of Williams College (1836–72). In 1824, at age fifteen, Barnard entered Yale College, where uncles and cousins on his mother's side had traditionally gone. He was the youngest member of the class of 1828 and its best mathematician. In later life, like most of his generation of university builders, he had little good to say about his own collegiate education. Rampant alcoholism, inaccessible professors, and "students as distressing moral wrecks" figure prominently among his retrospective complaints. What training in mathematics he acquired in New Haven was through "almost literal self-education." That this was the same Yale that its president and faculty stoutly defended in their *Yale Faculty Report* in 1828 speaks to the divergence in views between faculty and students and to Barnard's later souring on his undergraduate experience.[9]

Barnard turned to teaching upon graduation. He began at the Hartford Grammar School, which served as a training ground for Yale tutors and where for two years he taught ten- to thirteen-year-olds mathematics and celestial navigation. While in Hartford he began building an extensive network of friends that he sedulously maintained with correspondence throughout his lifetime. There, he first experienced a partial loss of hearing, a hereditary condition perhaps brought on by respiratory problems, which effectively ended any thoughts he had of becoming a lawyer. In 1830 he accepted a one-year appointment as a tutor at Yale.

The traditional Yale system when Barnard began his tutorship was for a single tutor to provide all instruction for the same section of the freshman class through its first three years. Barnard had a different idea. He proposed to his fellow tutors that he take on the instruction in mathematics for the entire freshman class and that they similarly identify themselves by teaching one of the other subjects in which they were especially conversant. By this seemingly commonsensical reform, Barnard quietly effected a significant change in the Yale academic culture. His novel arrangement quickly became the norm. No longer was a disciplinary specialization something that one acquired with the bestowal of a professorial chair but rather something one pursued as a novice tutor. And no longer would a Yale tutor be so intimately involved with the same group of twenty or so boys for the bulk of their Yale days. In narrowing the gap between tutors and professors, while widening it between tutors and students, Barnard had pointed Yale, and the rest of American higher education, to the future.[10]

For all his early success as an educational innovator, Barnard was obliged by his deteriorating hearing to give up his Yale tutorship after a year. He returned to Hartford, this time as a teacher of deaf children at the Connecticut Asylum for Education of the Deaf and Dumb. In 1832 he moved to the Institution for the Deaf and Dumb (on the very New York City site that would become Columbia's second home in 1857), where his reputation as a skillful teacher of the deaf had preceded him. That Barnard himself suffered from deafness gave him an insider's understanding of the handicaps under which his students labored, while a natural facility with languages (he reportedly spoke eleven) undoubtedly contributed to his effectiveness. An 1834 article in the *North American Review* describing his instructional methods brought him national recognition in this new field.[11]

Barnard continued to think of himself principally as a scientist. His 1837 article in Benjamin Silliman's *American Journal of Science*, "On the Aurora Borealis," advertised his availability for a respectable scientific appointment. None was available at Yale, particularly in light of his recent switch from his family's (and Yale's) Congregationalism to the Episcopalianism of his New York friends. Yale's president, Jeremiah Day, however, did recommend Barnard for a professorship in mathematics and natural philosophy at the newly opened University of Alabama in Tuscaloosa. Barnard accepted the appointment and set sail from New York for the old Southwest in the summer of 1837.[12]

Barnard was slow to adapt to the rustic circumstances in Tuscaloosa. His deafness presented a persistent problem, both in class and outside. So did his occasional public drinking to excess, a tendency that persisted until his marriage to a twenty-three-year-old visitor to Alabama from Ohio, Margaret McMurray. Although local lore had him proposing while drunk, he thereafter became a conspicuous teetotaler. The ensuing forty-two-year marriage, which seems to have been a happy one, produced no children.[13]

During his eighteen years in Alabama, Barnard worked hard through public lectures and demonstrations to interest the citizens of his adopted region in supporting mathematical and astronomical studies. He specifically urged the construction of an observatory in Tuscaloosa. His efforts culminated in 1846 with the opening of the Alabama State Observatory. Barnard attracted attention in 1845 when he commandeered the recently vacated state capitol in Tuscaloosa and suspended a pendulum from its two-hundred-foot-high rotunda to replicate Foucault's experiment demonstrating the earth's orbital rotation. Such efforts at popular education endeared him to scientific colleagues in New Haven, Cambridge, and Washington, the self-styled "Scientific Lazzaroni" who sought in the 1840s and 1850s to gain public support for science. Barnard joined these colleagues as a charter member of the American Association for the Advancement of Science at its founding in 1847 and became its president in 1860 when the AAAS membership hoped electing someone from the South would speak to its national character. When not teaching and proselytizing for science throughout the South, Barnard filled in as Tuscaloosa's photographer and de facto newspaper editor.[14]

Barnard's relations with the University of Alabama's president, Basil Manly, were never cordial. Neither Manly's religion, Baptist, nor his politics, southern nationalist, attracted him to the hard-of-hearing Episcopalian Whig from the North. In 1854 they had a public falling out, first over student discipline and almost immediately thereafter over curricular reform. Earlier that year, in response to public pressure, Manly reversed the university's policy requiring student bystanders at disruptions to identify the ringleaders or be expelled along with the disrupters. It would now be sufficient for the bystanders merely to swear to their noninvolvement. Barnard publicly opposed this change as depriving the faculty of the only coercive power they had in their losing battle with rebellious undergraduates.[15]

Manly then came out in favor of an elective system in which student performance would be numerically graded. The notion of an elective system had been introduced by President Josiah Quincy at Harvard in the 1830s, and numerical grading had been advocated by President Francis Wayland at Brown in his *Thoughts on the Present Collegiate System* (1842), though Manly was politically astute enough to identify both reforms with the University of Virginia and his fellow southerner Thomas Jefferson. Barnard opposed both in a series entitled *Letters on College Government*, in which he defended the nonranked performance evaluations and required curriculum of his alma mater, Yale. Manly prevailed on both issues, and Barnard avoided being fired only by securing an appointment as professor of physics, astronomy, and civil engineering at the University of Mississippi. The precariousness of his professional situation, at age forty-seven, can be inferred from his decision, upon arriving in Oxford in 1856, to be ordained as an Episcopal priest. Just in case.[16]

Barnard remained at the University of Mississippi for seven years, the last three as university chancellor. At his appointment, questions were raised about his being "unsound on the slavery question," but his testimony to the trustees (and the fact that he owned household slaves) gave his critics few grounds to challenge his regional loyalties. Only with the university's closing in January 1861, after the state's secession from the Union and the commencement of the Civil War four months later, did Barnard make known to scientific contacts in the North his Unionist sentiments. Visiting with his wife in Norfolk, Virginia, in 1862, when Union troops overran the town, Barnard used the occasion to pass through Union lines and proceed north to Washington, where his younger brother, John, was in charge of Union forces protecting the capital. Once safely out of the South, Barnard declared both his allegiance to the Union—

fulsomely, in his *Letter to the President of the United States by a Refugee*—and his availability for more regular employment than that provided by a temporary position secured for him by friends at the U.S. Coastal Survey.[17]

Barnard's name first came to the attention of the Columbia trustees in the fall of 1863, when they were looking for a replacement for the defected McCulloch. Nominated too late to receive serious consideration for that position, which went to West Point–trained Ogden Rood, Barnard was someone at least known to the trustees on paper when eight months later they began scouting around for a presidential successor to the eighty-year-old Charles King. Many of Barnard's friends who had written on his behalf for the faculty job simply resubmitted their letters in support of his presidential candidacy.[18]

Barnard seemed a long shot. Few if any of the trustees had laid eyes on him, and his backers came from the same scientific crowd that nine years earlier had unsuccessfully pushed for Wolcott Gibbs. Still, in the absence of a viable local candidate (George Templeton Strong fancied himself as draftable) and perhaps still sensitive to criticism for harboring a Confederate spy in their midst, trustees seized on this outsider as meeting their immediate needs. Accordingly, on May 18, 1864, sight unseen, the trustees elected Frederick A. P. Barnard as the tenth president of Columbia College. The vote was fourteen to five with the sixty-six-year-old Professor of Classics Charles Anthon receiving the votes of Strong, William Betts, and Anthon's old faculty colleague, James Anderson. Ruggles, perhaps warned off Barnard by Lieber, who questioned the sincerity of Barnard's belated Unionism, voted for William T. Eliot, the founder of Washington University in St. Louis. As a case of how far off base a contemporary assessment can be, we have the disappointed Strong's initial view of Barnard: "Another instance of our electing men who want the place, instead of looking for men whom the place wants."[19]

Barnard's was the single most pivotal presidential election in the history of Columbia University. It broke with past tradition and helped establish a new pattern in Columbia presidents. Barnard was the first Columbia president to be both an outsider—that is, not from the New York City Knickerbocker community identified with Columbia and not educated there—and a career academic. Before him, only Myles Cooper and Charles Wharton could be construed as outsiders, and only Nathaniel Fish Moore had extensive prior experience as an academic. Several outsiders have since presided over Columbia—Dwight Eisenhower, Grayson Kirk, Andrew Cordier, William McGill, George Rupp, and Lee Bollinger among them—with Kirk, Cordier, and McGill having taught at Columbia and Bollinger having attended the Law School thirty-two years before becoming president. So have several career academics—Nicholas Murray Butler, Grayson Kirk, William McGill, George Rupp and Lee Bollinger among them—but only George Rupp came to the presidency in the Barnard mold as both outsider and professional academic. For insiders since Barnard, there are Seth Low, Butler, and, in education and employment but not ancestry, Michael Sovern.[20]

These two features—Barnard's standing as an outsider and his professionalism—were more than biographical curiosities during his extended presidency. When combined with two other factors, they set him on an inevitable path of conflict with the trustees, the outcome of which, while not a clear victory for either Barnard or the board, both marked and precipitated a decisive break in the governance of the university. From his presidency onward, presidents could and did exercise real power, as distinct from simply being the agents of the trustees.[21]

The first of those other factors was Barnard's feeling upon accepting the presidency that it had come to him, as he told his brother, "without any effort of my own." Nearly all his predecessors had either actively sought the Columbia presidency by lobbying individual trustees or had trustees do so on their behalf. Several had relatives and friends among the trustees choosing the president, and two had previously served on the board. Moreover, several had been elected only after the candidacy of someone equally well known to the trustees had been beaten back. Thus the beholdenness of presidential incumbents to the trustees was established from the outset—and seldom if ever challenged thereafter. Disagreement with the trustees was typically resolved by the president resigning or by the trustees requesting same.[22]

A second factor that the trustees, and certainly Strong's initial view of Barnard, overlooked, to their subsequent peril, was their new president's boundless ambition. Fifty-five at his election, with most of his professional career passed in the provinces of the old Southwest trying to stay connected with the scientific community in the Northeast, he was not about to waste the opportunity that coming to New York City and Columbia represented. As he reported during his first months in the new job to an old friend, "The President's pretty much Lord Paramount," and he intended to act accordingly.[23]

Other factors made the relationship between President Barnard and his trustees contentious. There was the matter of his deafness, which he was not above exploiting by simply ignoring their stated views. "Strange to say," George Templeton Strong noted after observing Barnard at board meetings for four years, "his inpenetrable deafness strengthens him in his leadership [he can't hear objections] so we commonly acquiesce, unless the matter be grave." There was also Barnard's general sociability. He made many important acquaintances outside the circle of the trustees. Until well into the 1880s, when age (and incipient blindness) finally slowed him down, Barnard was very much a presence on the New York City scientific-cultural-club scene, where he was more than willing to air his disagreements with his trustees while seeking support for pet projects among friends.[24]

The trustees in turn vented their frustration with the president over large matters by denying him support on small ones. Barnard's requests for even the most minor conveniences, whether the heating of the vestibule in his residence or a second clerk to handle his correspondence, regularly met with opposition. After a board meeting on April 21, 1882, Trustee Morgan Dix reported to his diary that "we accomplished nothing except to snub President Barnard on two measures which he had proposed, and to agree to report adversely on both."[25]

The relationship between Barnard and the trustees never did warm into anything approaching mutual cordiality. From early on in his presidency, individual trustees directed their negative views of Barnard to board chair Hamilton Fish, who in 1873 allowed that "the College needs a thorough shaking up" and was "unfortunate in the head of the academic staff." Eleven years later, Fish reported that fellow trustee "[William A.] Schermerhorn thinks that our President, whatever his value as such, would make a rather reckless financier." Several trustees openly urged Barnard's retirement in the mid-1880s only to find the president resolute in his determination not to cede his office "until he can see his successor." The irony, of course, is that this most combative of all presidential-trustee relationships in the history of the university may also have effected the most good for Columbia.[26]

A School of Mines for New York and the Nation

The Columbia College that Barnard inherited consisted of the undergraduate college, located in a single building on Forty-ninth Street, off Madison, at the upper edge of the city's development, and a law school, in rented quarters downtown on Lafayette Place. An intercorporate agreement had been reached with the College of Physicians & Surgeons in 1861, but for all practical purposes the Medical School operated independently of Columbia (and would do so until 1891). The board had agreed, however, eight months before Barnard became president, to authorize the creation of a School of Mines. Its establishment was the first major undertaking of his presidency and symptomatic of much that followed.[27]

Some kind of practical instruction in engineering and mining had been advocated by individual faculty and trustees at Columbia for several years before any action was taken in 1863. West Point had offered instruction in engineering since its opening in 1802. The founding of Rensselaer Polytechnic Institute in 1824 provided the country with a second school of engineering. In 1847

Harvard (in the instance of its Lawrence Scientific School, 1847) and Yale (with its Sheffield Scientific School, 1847) established schools of technology, distinct from their undergraduate colleges, that offered instruction in engineering. So did the just-opened Massachusetts Institute of Technology (1861). But the discoveries of gold in California in 1849 and the extension of the railroads westward in the 1850s, as well as the technological demands placed on the nation by the Civil War, all pointed to the likely growing demand for more such training.[28]

The immediate impetus for the Columbia School of Mines was provided by Thomas Egleston Jr. (1832–1900), an independently wealthy New Yorker and Yale graduate (1855), who had spent five years after college studying in Paris at the Ecole des Mines. After his return to New York in 1861, he set about interesting men of his social acquaintance, including George Templeton Strong and other Columbia trustees, in establishing the equivalent of the Ecole des Mines in New York City. In March 1863 he presented to the Columbia board of trustees "A Proposed Plan for a School of Mines in New York City." After assuring themselves that the authorization for such a school put them at no financial risk, Egleston would come up with the initial financing, and the school was to be established on a proprietary basis similar to that of the Law School, the trustees approved the plan. The school took up temporary quarters in some derelict sheds on the northeast corner of the Forty-ninth Street campus.[29]

Although the idea originated with Egleston, the driving force behind the growth of the School of Mines was Charles Frederick Chandler (1836–1925). Immediately upon his appointment as professor of analytical chemistry in 1864, Chandler joined Theodore Dwight (these two were later joined by John W. Burgess) as one of Columbia's three great late-nineteenth-century academic entrepreneurs. He was Samuel L. Mitchill redux, but with real scientific credentials, and he had come to stay.

Like Barnard, Chandler was a New York and Columbia outsider, and, like Barnard, he embraced them both. Born in 1836 in Lawrence, Massachusetts, he attended Harvard's Lawrence Scientific School before setting off for Germany to study chemistry. A Göttingen Ph.D. (1856) in hand, he returned to the United States to a junior teaching post at Union College under Professor of Chemistry Charles Joy. When the following year Joy moved on to Columbia, Chandler assumed his professorship. He was then twenty-one years old. Seven years later, Joy recommended him for the first faculty opening in the School of Mines, and to New York he came.[30]

Chandler became the first dean of the School of Mines in 1865, a position he held until 1897. During those three-plus decades, he oversaw virtually every one of the forty or so faculty appointments made in mining, engineering, and applied science. Chandler himself eventually held appointments in the College, in the subsequently affiliated School of Pharmacy and College of Physicians & Surgeons, and, after its organization in 1892, the Faculty of Pure Science. At one point in the 1890s, he drew four separate Columbia salaries, totaling twenty thousand dollars, while maintaining a thriving consulting business. Along the way, he helped found the American Chemical Society (1876), one of the first of the modern American scientific societies, and edited, with his brother, William, a chemist at Lehigh University, the *American Chemist*. He sometimes missed his office hours.[31]

Like the Law School, the School of Mines immediately attracted to its three-year program substantial numbers of students who willingly paid its $160 annual tuition. By its third year, it had enrolled some one hundred students. By the mid-1870s it was annually graduating twice as many students as the College.[32]

One reason for its popularity was that its graduates had no difficulty finding rewarding work. A dozen early graduates stayed on at the school as faculty, among the first Henry S. Munroe, John K. Rees, Frederick R. Hutton, Francis Crocker, Alfred J. Moses, Robert Peel, and Michael I. Pupin. Other graduates went west to work for mining companies or the railroads. But an extraordinary number remained in the metropolitan New York region, where they invented careers as consulting engineers and publicly employed technocrats in public health, urban design, sanitation, and so on. Here, too, Chandler's involvement at every level of New York's public life (he served on the Metropolitan Board of Health for seventeen years, from 1866 to 1883, ten as its chairman) served as a model of civic engagement, even as his personal contacts facilitated placing his students. What Benjamin Franklin was to mid-eighteenth-century Philadelphia, Charles Frederick Chandler bid fair to be to late-nineteenth-century New York.[33]

In other ways, Chandler's School of Mines differed markedly from Dwight's operation downtown. For one thing, it proved to be much more expensive. In addition to requiring the exclusive teaching services of Egleston, Chandler, and the French-trained Civil War veteran Francis L. Vinton (1835–79), who was appointed professor of mining in 1865, College professors Joy, Rood, and the newly appointed mathematician John Van Amringe also taught in the school. The cost of equipment and instructional supplies proved to be substantial. By 1867 the School of Mines had generated a debt of forty thousand dollars. Although the original understanding with the trustees was that the school would not draw on the College's resources, it was soon clear to its supporters, President Barnard conspicuously among them, that without College assistance the school might not survive.[34]

By then, some trustees and College faculty had begun to question the wisdom of sustaining such an avowedly professional school alongside an undergraduate college. For one thing, the Mines students were so much more serious

about their studies than those in the College. Often older and with some working experience, they made the College students look even younger and more
feckless. It was also thought by some trustees that the School of Mines attracted
students who might otherwise have gone to the College, a belief given support
by the steady flow of transfers from the College to the school. Whereas the College continued to operate on the traditional four-hour daily schedule, the academic day in the School of Mines extended from 9:00 A.M. to 5:00 P.M., with any
hours not given over to lectures devoted to laboratory work or drawing. Such
industriousness was setting a bad example.[35]

It was Barnard who took it upon himself in 1868 to defend the School of
Mines in the face of trustee second thoughts and faculty grumbling. He did so
by urging that the school become the financial responsibility of the trustees,
with the salaries of its faculty paid directly by the College, which would in turn
receive its tuition revenues. Thus, while the Law School continued on throughout Barnard's presidency as a semiautonomous enterprise, the School of Mines,
early on in Barnard's tenure, became a professional school wholly integrated
within what Barnard had been calling since 1865 "the University."[36]

Barnard's championing of the School of Mines early in his presidency revealed
several programmatic dispositions. The first of these was a willingness to spend
the College's money to advance academic objectives. Another was a willingness
to support entrepreneurial-minded faculty like Chandler who were ready to bet
the endowment on the future of their enterprises. And a third was a willingness
to promote the rapid growth of the university, which Barnard as early as 1865
described as best achieved by focusing his energies not on the College and its
undergraduates but on the university's professional schools and their students.
Each of these dispositions brought him into direct conflict with the trustees.

Taking On the Trustees

Barnard was the first Columbia president since Samuel Johnson who saw himself as more than an extension of the trustees. All the others pretty much
accepted that their job was to implement trustee views on the faculty, students,
and curriculum while staying out of financial matters and dealings with the
public. Barnard saw himself possessed of considerable agency, which could be
used to move the College in directions he saw appropriate, either by persuading
the trustees to adopt his vision or by challenging them to articulate theirs.
Barnard had his defenders among the trustees, but they tended to be issue-spe-
cific supporters rather than comprehensive admirers. And none appreciated his
tendency to go over them in promoting his vision of what Columbia could be.

Barnard's principal instrument in pressing his agenda was a new departure at Columbia: the president's annual report to the trustees. Before his presidency, no such report had been provided to the Trustees, much less published for public scrutiny. During his presidency, Barnard used his twenty-four annual reports both to argue in public for policies he privately pressed the trustees to adopt and to inform the higher-educational community of the issues engaging Columbia. Not since William Livingston's essays in the *Independent Reflector* more than a century earlier had something written about Columbia been thought to be of such moment to that community.[37]

Barnard's first use of his annual reports was to offer a critique of the curriculum and disciplinary arrangements of American colleges, including Columbia College. The problem he found with the curriculum was its fixedness, which ill accommodated the inclusion of new areas of knowledge, especially in the sciences. He also favored providing students with some choice in what they studied. His proposed solution, for Columbia and American colleges generally: the adoption of an elective system of the kind introduced at Harvard in the 1840s that allowed more subjects to be taught and more student choice in selecting what to study. It was also the system that Manly had pushed back in Alabama and a younger Barnard had resisted. By 1868, however, Barnard was calling for "a frank confession that the American college system has been attempting for at least a quarter century, to accomplish what it cannot perform."[38]

The problem with the prevailing disciplinary arrangements as Barnard saw it was that too much valuable faculty time was consumed by them. His proposed solution: encourage students to be self-disciplining by extending to them a greater role in maintaining order and by instilling a positive spirit of academic competition. College students had to stop being treated as unruly and undirected adolescents and start being regarded as serious and purposeful young men. In his enthusiasm to see these reforms succeed, he was given to premature announcements of victory, as in 1869: "A spirit of manliness pervades the student body, which has not been before by any means so distinctly marked."[39]

Failure of colleges to adopt these reforms, Barnard argued, would result in the continued decline in the place of colleges in American society. The statistical evidence that such a decline was already well under way he provided in his 1865–66 report and more fully in his 1870 report. Whereas in 1826, 1 New Englander in 1,513 attended college, in 1869 the ratio had dropped to 1 in 1,927. In New York State, while the population grew more than 50 percent between 1848 and 1870, the number of undergraduates was up by less than 10 percent. Although it is unclear that these findings had much effect on Barnard's ostensible audience, the Columbia trustees, the frequency with which they were cited by academic reformers over the next decade suggests they provided a wake-up call elsewhere.[40]

Barnard was aware that neither of these reforms, requiring more student selectivity and larger faculties, could be adopted by most colleges without putting them at greater financial peril than they already were. That was the very point he was trying to make with his own trustees. Only those few colleges with the recruitment potential of a highly populated locale like New York City and possessed of Columbia's financial wherewithal would be able to implement the reforms and thereby separate themselves from the pack of institutions lacking the resources to do so. Because Columbia could implement both, Barnard declared in only his second annual report, lifting a phrase made famous by the Columbia graduate John L. O'Sullivan (1833) two decades earlier, it was its "manifest destiny" to do so.[41]

Barnard was only partially successful in implementing either of these specific reforms at Columbia. A rise in the average entering age of freshmen, from fifteen in the 1850s to seventeen in the 1870s, did reduce adolescent high jinks, although, judging from how Nicholas Murray Butler recalled his undergraduate days in the late 1870s, turning over dray carts on Madison Avenue remained very much part of the undergraduate repertoire. Nor did the introduction of an examination system intended to stimulate academic achievement by rewarding performance, even in Barnard's view, succeed in doing so. A few students in each class so monopolized the prize winning that most of the others settled for their gentlemanly passes. Barnard did not so much solve the disciplinary problems of the College, which at commuting Columbia were less serious than at residential colleges, as direct his energies and those of his faculty elsewhere.[42]

The introduction of an elective system at Columbia also proved to be more difficult than elsewhere. A major obstacle was the College's limited academic schedule, which provided too few class hours—fifteen—in any given week to permit the expansion of the curriculum. Besides, when students were not in class, there was nothing else for them to do and nowhere for them to do it. Another restraint on implementing an elective system for Columbia, common elsewhere as well, was the opposition mounted by faculty who taught the required courses and worried that student choice would deprive them of their enrollments (and livelihoods). And, finally, most Columbia trustees refused to accept Barnard's argument that Harvard's was the way of the future.[43]

Upon Barnard's arrival in 1864, the only elective course available to College students was a semester of calculus in the senior year in place of an eighth semester of Greek. This represented 2 hours of elective work in a 120-hour curriculum. As late as 1875, a decade after Barnard praised Harvard for a curriculum that made all courses in the junior and senior years electives, only Columbia seniors had some choice for about half their courses. In 1884 all fifteen hours of senior course work consisted of electives, as did eleven hours of junior course work. The following year, however, the faculty cut back the junior electives from 11 to 5 hours, despite Barnard's arguing against doing so. By then, even Yale offered its students more choice than Columbia did. It is surely one of the curiosities in the history of American higher education that Columbia's move from college to university occurred without the wholehearted adoption of an undergraduate elective system, which played a crucial role elsewhere. Here, again, the explanation can be found in part in the outsized role the professional schools played in Columbia's transformation.[44]

Outside readers of Barnard's reports occasionally took public exception to statements they contained, as did Yale's president, Noah Porter, in 1872 after Barnard had criticized his alma mater for not keeping up with the times. "The tribunal consists, first of all," Porter responded in his *American Colleges and the American Public*, "of a limited class of lecturers and writers known as *educational reformers*, whose stock in trade consists of a scanty outfit of a few facts imperfectly conceived and incorrectly recited. . . . Some of these are men of whom we had a right to expect better things." Closer to home, Barnard's reports so irritated some of his trustees that it prompted them to attempt to limit their circulation, if not to stop publication altogether. At one point, the board withheld the funds used to cover circulation costs until Barnard threatened to use his own money to do so.[45]

Such sentiments ran strongest when Barnard used the 1873 report to air an ongoing argument with his trustees over moving the College from its temporary site to a locale more conducive to the expansion Barnard deemed necessary to assure Columbia its place among what he estimated to be the country's five or six would-be universities. His disappointment over the failure of a plan to move the College to a site in Washington Heights and then over the trustee umbrage taken with Barnard's public pique over their reluctance to undertake serious building on the current site brought them into open conflict. In a letter to Trustee Benjamin Haight, who had earlier defended him when other trustees had complained of presidential high-handedness, Barnard allowed his frustrations with what he regarded as trustee foot-dragging free play. "I shall take care that that report shall not perish; and when the day arrives in which, in the light of *faits accomplis*, men shall not merely believe, but know what the trustees of Columbia College ought to have done in the year 1873, those who came after me shall point to the fact that I knew it before."[46]

For their part, the trustees regarded Barnard as something of a loose cannon. As Hamilton Fish later said of him, "Our president when he wishes anything—and he is always wishing something—wishes it at once and would like a new law for each action." Two years before the 1873 confrontation, Fish darkly noted that "[Treasurer Gouverneur M.] Ogden thinks the internal administration of the College is very unsatisfactory. It occasions great uneasiness." (It did not help matters that sons of both Fish and Ogden were for various breaches regularly before the College's disciplinary board, administered by Barnard.)[47]

Yet in the matter of whether to build on the temporary Forty-ninth Street site, Barnard would have his way. He won in part because his arguments against waiting were persuasive but also because the trustees by the early 1870s simply had more money than they knew what to do with. In 1875 the Upper Estate properties between Forty-seventh and Fifty-first Streets brought in rents in excess of one hundred thousand dollars, while the Lower Estate, site of the first campus, earned in excess of two hundred thousand dollars. Some trustees, most conspicuously Treasurer Ogden, preferred piling up the annual surpluses in the College's Accumulation Fund, which had been begun in 1867 with the salting away of ten thousand dollars. By 1873 the fund stood at two hundred thousand dollars. (Columbia was likely the only private college in America at the time totally free of debt, whereas Harvard regularly ran deficits in the late 1870s.) But others took the point of public comments about the disparity between the extent of the College's wealth and the modesty of its academic program. Henry Adams has a character in his 1881 novel *Democracy* ask: "Do you know that we have in New York already the richest University in America, and that its only problem has always been that it can get no scholars even by paying for them?" Such comments must have served to help loosen the purse strings.[48]

In 1875 new quarters for the School of Mines opened on the northeast corner of the Forty-ninth Street site, at a cost of $130,000. This was followed in the early 1880s by the construction of a library, which also became home for the Law School, and Hamilton Hall, which for the first time since the early 1790s allowed Columbia to provide some student housing. By the late 1880s Columbia possessed an impressive urban campus, albeit one that would be left behind in yet another move northward a decade later.[49]

The outcomes of Barnard's struggles with the trustees often turned on which side could secure the backing of the faculty. More often, Barnard proved the more adept at forging such alliances. The great advantage he had over the trustees in this area was his intimate knowledge of faculty folkways. He understood, for example, the stultifying effect of teaching the same elementary subject year in and year out and sympathized with the wearisome burden of policing adolescents, particularly when some of the most disruptive were the sons of trustees. He also shared with his faculty a protectiveness toward those arrangements that, while not authorized by College statutes and subject to trustee action, provided the faculty with a modicum of autonomy.

Two such arrangements were the exemption of Columbia faculty from daily chapel services and acquiescence in their holding down outside jobs. Both came under critical trustee scrutiny early in Barnard's presidency, and both were stoutly defended by him. Insofar as neither compulsory chapel attendance nor the prohibition against moonlighting were part of the statutes applied to faculty of the Law School or the School of Mines, Barnard was able to argue that enforcement of either on the School of Arts (i.e., College) faculty would be discriminatory. Compromises were worked out in both instances that were more or less satisfactory to the faculty (though the chapel compromise failed to satisfy Ogden Rood's principled atheism) and acceptable to all but a few trustees.[50]

Even those trustees who supported these compromises came away from the discussions more fully aware that exercising their legal authority over the faculty was no longer as simple as it had been in the good old days of compliant presidents. It would henceforth have to be negotiated. Yet as Barnard was to learn in later disputes with the trustees, two could play at the three-party game of securing faculty support. As for the faculty, their relative standing benefited from being viewed by both president and trustees as desirable, even essential, allies. No one better understood this basic political fact of university life than the man who joined the Columbia faculty midway through Barnard's presidency and who thereafter, for better and worse, impressed his stamp on the university in the making.

John W. Burgess and the School of Political Science

If not as pivotal as his autobiography claims, the appointment in 1876 of the thirty-two-year-old John W. Burgess as Francis Lieber's successor as professor of history and political science represents one of the key appointments in the history of Columbia University. Burgess came to New York from Amherst College, from which he graduated in 1869 after wartime service as a teenager in the Tennessee Volunteers. He taught there for four years (1871–75), in between two years teaching at Knox College in Illinois and two studying in Germany and France. Having failed to convince its trustees to undertake the transformation of Amherst College into a German-style university, he accepted a guest lectureship at Columbia in 1875. Here, he came to the attention of that inveterate talent scout, Trustee Samuel Ruggles. The following fall Burgess decided to accept the offer of a professorship and bring his vision to New York, a city in which he was never to feel fully at home.[51]

Within the first year of his arrival, Burgess engineered the appointment of a like-minded refugee from Amherst, the statistician Richmond Mayo-Smith

(1877–1901). They were soon joined by others from Amherst, who could thereafter be counted on as loyal members of Burgess's "university party" in faculty politics. Until his retirement in 1912, Burgess was undoubtedly the most influential member of the Columbia faculty and one of the most nationally visible prototypes of the American professor as influential.[52]

Not surprisingly, then, Burgess first sought to locate his (and Mayo-Smith's) activities not in the College among undergraduates but in the Law School, where he hoped to introduce a compulsory third year of study in which Dwight's workaday lawyers would be exposed to the higher subtleties of political science and public law. When thwarted in this attempt to transform the Law School into a graduate school in jurisprudence, he remained determined not to occupy himself with Columbia undergraduates, about whom he commented, "I had never met so indifferent, ill prepared a set of students as those composing the class of 1877 in the School of Arts of Columbia College." He decided instead, with the urging of Ruggles, to create, after the model of the Ecole des Sciences Politiques in Paris, a School (and Faculty) of Political Science. The active support of Ruggles and President Barnard made it happen. On June 1, 1880, with Burgess and Mayo-Smith in Paris, Ruggles telegraphed the outcome of the trustee vote: "Thank God, the University is born. Go Ahead." Ruggles promptly hired two more Amherst products then studying in Germany, Clifford Bateman (1881–83) and E. Monroe Smith (1881–1901), thereby constituting his core faculty.[53]

As Burgess imagined it, the program of the School of Political Science would be a three-year postgraduate program, successful completion of which would result in the receipt of a Ph.D. In practice, most of the school's early Ph.D.s combined a year or so of study with Burgess and his colleagues in the Faculty of Political Science with two years in Dwight's Law School. Some were graduates of Columbia College, but, as with the students at the School of Mines and unlike graduate students at Yale or Harvard or Cornell, most of them came from other colleges. Equally unusual, most of the twenty-four Ph.D.s the Faculty of Political Science awarded through 1890 went to graduates who entered the legal profession or public service. The majority did not become professors.[54]

For Burgess and his Amherst recruits, university teaching (as opposed to college teaching) was an adult activity, performed in the company of other trained professionals and directed at serious, professionally motivated students. But it was by no means the only career option for graduates of the School of Political Science. Burgess's initial plan on coming to Columbia was not to produce professors but to "prepare young men for the duties of public life." The subsequent academicization of the school in the 1890s was neither his intention nor to his mind a wholly happy outcome.[55]

If the careers of his students changed over the years, Burgess's dismissal of most of the Columbia faculty who taught undergraduates, especially those who enjoyed doing so, never did. His assessment of seven colleagues who made up the Faculty of Arts on his arrival in 1876, as he described them six decades later, is one of the more devastating renderings of college faculty in print. First there was Henry Drisler, "the father of the company," a competent enough Greek scholar, but one whose "whole life had been spent as student, instructor, tutor, and professor in Columbia College, and the institution loomed so large in his perspective that it shut out everything else." Then there was Charles Short, "a repetition of Drisler on an even more pedantic pattern. . . . Mr. Casaubon in the teacher's chair." And then there was John Van Amringe, "the jolly-good-fellow of the group. . . . A great smoker and a great frequenter of clubs." In the case of Professor Schmidt, "a queer old Lutheran preacher," Burgess faulted his American-accented German. The only Columbia College faculty member about whom he had much good to say was Ogden Rood, "the genius of the faculty," who on meeting him promptly informed Burgess of his policy vis-à-vis undergraduates: "I do as little as I can for these dunderheads and save my time for research."[56]

Thanks to Burgess's autobiography and that of his protégé, Nicholas Murray Butler, as well as the happenstance of Columbia's bicentennial historiography, in which the founding of the Faculty of Political Science received more consideration in a volume edited by Burgess biographer R. Gordon Hoxie than did the early history of the School of Mines, its founding in 1880 has generally been used to mark the effective beginnings of Columbia University. The first Ph.D.s of the university have also been widely thought to have been those conferred by the Faculty of Political Science, beginning in 1883. In point of fact, the faculty of the School of Mines first proposed awarding the Ph.D. for advanced work as early as 1871 (when only Yale among American universities had begun to do so) and first did so in 1875 (right behind Cornell and Harvard). By 1883, the year in which the School of Political Science awarded its first, the School of Mines had already conveyed twenty-two Ph.D.s.[57]

Yet once the School of Political Science began awarding Ph.D.s, it soon outstripped the School of Mines. In 1890 more than half the sixteen Ph.D.s awarded that year were in the School of Political Science. It is also the case that the emergence of the Ph.D. at Columbia as the signature of serious, sustained academic study owes more to Burgess and his faculty than to Chandler and his colleagues in the School of Mines. More than they, Burgess insisted that what he and his best students were about deserved the professional recognition the degree soon commanded within and beyond the academy. Unlike other emergent universities, even Eliot's Harvard, where William James later admitted to second thoughts about "the Ph.D. Octopus," Burgess and his political science faculty had only praise for the degree and its wholly beneficent influence on American higher education.[58]

Columbia and the "Woman Question," Part 1

Throughout his labors in building up the School of Political Science in the early 1880s, Burgess enjoyed the support of President Barnard. Similarly, when opposition coalesced among some College faculty and a few trustees in the mid-1880s against the accelerating drive to transform Columbia into a world-class university with the professional and graduate schools at its center, Barnard never wavered in his backing of Burgess as the faculty leader of the university party. All the more reason that Burgess's all-out and ultimately successful opposition to a campaign that engaged much of Barnard's energies during his last decade as president—the admission of women to Columbia College—merits careful consideration.[59]

Both Barnard and Burgess were unabashedly university men, both were determined to push Columbia to the forefront of the ranks of American universities, and both envisioned Columbia's playing an important role in civic and national affairs. Where they differed fundamentally was on who should be considered part of the university. Whereas Barnard's vision of Columbia became increasingly inclusive and expansive as his presidency progressed, Burgess's remained exclusionary throughout. Whereas Barnard came increasingly to ask why heretofore unrepresented groups should be excluded from a Columbia education or appointment, Burgess held fast to the idea of the university as a place reserved for "the best men," which is to say well-familied, white, Anglo-Saxon, Protestant males.[60]

Not only did Burgess oppose the entry of women into the university, at any level, he saw no reason to open its doors to African Americans or "new" immigrants or to be welcoming to Jews. His vision was as comprehensively as exclusionary and elitist as Barnard's was inclusive and democratic. The conflict between them over the question of admitting women was at bottom the classic ideological one of institutional inclusiveness versus exclusiveness, dating back to King's College and forward to our own times. Whereas Barnard reveled in the growth of his university, Burgess was of the view that universities for the benefit of the greatest number were "not universities at all."[61]

Both Burgess, whose family owned slaves in his native Tennessee, and Barnard, who owned household slaves in Mississippi, experienced slavery first-hand. Both had supported the institution. Yet, in the decades after emancipation, Barnard allowed his flights of rhetorical inclusiveness to cover all "seekers after knowledge, of whatever age, sex, race, or previous condition," which at least allowed the possibility of freedmen (and thus all blacks) being considered suitable candidates for admission to Columbia College. (The School of Mines enrolled a black student in 1873.) If there is little else to suggest that he was prepared to seek out blacks to attend Columbia, there is equally little to suggest that these flourishes were hypocritical and that he opposed admitting blacks.[62]

Burgess, on the other hand, remained, as revealed in his writings on Reconstruction and as Columbia historian Eric Foner and others have amply documented, a confirmed white supremacist. The only detectable change in his views with respect to blacks was the growing assurance with which he articulated his belief in their inherent incapacity to govern themselves. The idea of blacks enrolling in his school was at least as unacceptable to him as women doing so. As long as he had a determining voice in the school, which would be well after other Columbia graduate and professional programs admitted women, neither blacks nor women were welcome.[63]

There was also about Burgess the scent of the anti-Semite, which like his negrophobia seemed to increase with age. Not coincidentally, so did his dislike of New York City. In 1910, after characterizing Jews in New York and Berlin as "members so to speak of an international brotherhood," Burgess felt obliged to assure his sympathetic correspondent, one Nicholas Murray Butler, "you know that personally I have no prejudices, at least no pronounced prejudices, against the Jews." Yet he presented evidence to the contrary during his struggle with Barnard over coeducation. His autobiography gives no precise date for his coup de grâce to Barnard's argument on behalf of admitting women to the College, but that he chose to repeat the remark five decades later suggests he used it more than once: To admit women, he contended, would be to "make the college a female seminary, and a Hebrew female seminary, in the character of the student body, at that."[64]

Burgess's opposition to women at Columbia also reflected anxieties common among professionals in the making. The goal of making an academic career more prestigious than careers in the ministry or school teaching was one that Burgess and his generation of academics very much identified as—rather than assumed to be, as the next generation would—a given. Accordingly, the presence of women among them, as peers or students, threatened to undercut claims to parity with the learned professions and with the equally all-male upper reaches of business and political life. Burgess and his like-minded colleagues in the all-male School of Political Science must have derived some satisfaction from the case of Wellesley graduate Winifred Edgerton. Her request in 1884 to undertake graduate studies in astronomy under the direction of John Krom Rees was allowed by the trustees as long as her instruction was conducted off campus and thus "established no precedent for others." No sooner had she received her Ph.D. in astronomy in 1886, the first awarded to a woman by an American university, than she announced she would not be accepting an offered appointment to Smith College but instead would be marrying Professor James Merrill of the School of Mines. "This life that opens for me," she told the Reverend Morgan Dix, who could not have been more pleased by her decision, "is brighter than the stars."[65]

In playing either the Jewish or the professional card in a controversy ostensibly about the educability of women, Burgess ran little risk of offending those opposed to the admission of women on other grounds. In the spring of 1882, when the board finally agreed to take up the president's recommendation, the Reverend Morgan Dix was made chair of the trustee committee charged with considering the matter. He saw the recommendation as part of a larger sectarian plot. The campaign "favoring higher education for girls," he noted in his diary, "was engineered from the beginning by a little knot of persevering women, most of whom are Unitarians of the Boston type or free-thinkers." The following spring he devoted his Lenten lectures at Trinity Church to the socially subversive consequences of women assuming public or professional roles. College senior Nicholas Murray Butler took it upon himself (or was it at his mentor's urging?) to draft a senior resolution against admitting women to Columbia: "It is the fixed opinion and firm conviction of the senior class that the coeducation of the sexes is undesirable from an educational as well as from a social and moral point of view, and that its introduction here would be a fatal blow to the future welfare and prosperity of the institution."[66]

Burgess, Dix, and Butler all agreed that the introduction of women into the classroom, quite aside from the deleterious effects it would have on the fair sex, would undermine College spirit and bring into question the manhood of Columbians. Professor John H. Van Amringe gave voice to a variation of the last concern in opposing coeducation on the grounds that "you can't teach a man mathematics if there's a girl in the room—and if you can, he isn't worth teaching."[67]

More than ideology was involved in Barnard's decision in 1879 to take up the cause of a group of New York women, following the lead of Lillie Devereux Blake, who had begun in 1873 to call for the admission of women to both the College of Physicians & Surgeons and Columbia College. There was also the practical matter of increasing undergraduate enrollments. By 1879 seven colleges in New York City were competing for its college-age young men: Columbia, NYU, CCNY, Cooper Union, plus two Catholic colleges (Fordham and St. John's). All had lower tuitions than Columbia, with CCNY and Cooper Union tuition free. Meanwhile, many young New York men with the financial wherewithal and cultural aspirations to attend Columbia were now regularly going off to college in New Haven, Middletown, Princeton, and Cambridge. The result was that Columbia enrolled less than one-quarter of the New Yorkers going to college in the 1870s. Barnard had realized for some time that for qualitative as well as quantitative reasons Columbia College had to begin to look farther afield than New York to attract undergraduates (as its professional schools were already doing). In his 1879 annual report he proposed that the pool should be extended to include women.[68]

Again, Barnard's practice of closely observing the operations of the competition had helped bring him to this conclusion. By 1879 women's and coeducational colleges were an established fact. Vassar, founded in 1861 with the backing of Matthew Vassar, Wellesley, founded in 1870 with the underwriting of Henry Durant, and Smith, founded in 1875 with the backing of Sophia Smith, were all up and running by the time Barnard first came forward with his proposal that Columbia begin to instruct young women. The rechartering of Mount Holyoke Seminary as Mount Holyoke College in 1882 and the founding of Bryn Mawr in 1884 soon followed.[69]

Directly relevant to Barnard's proposal was the fact that the regionally proximate Syracuse, Boston University, and Cornell were all reporting success in providing instruction to men and women. If these examples were not enough, Barnard was able to draw on his own experience with coeducation at the University of Alabama, where women from a Tuscaloosa seminary attended his classes, with consequences he judged to be uniformly positive (to which Burgess rejoined that his experience with coeducation at Knox College was "almost an abomination").[70]

There was about Barnard something of the protofeminist. He seems to have gotten along well with bright, forceful women, among them Catherine Beecher, Lillie Devereux Blake, and his own wife. One of his biographers cites his early family circumstances and education, in which women played a dominant role, as crucial in shaping his positive views about the intellectual capacities of women. His own deafness may also have made him sensitive to discriminatory prejudice directed elsewhere. In any event, there is no reason to question the sincerity of his statement in 1879 that "Columbia College is destined in the coming centuries to become as comprehensive in the scope of her teaching as to be able to furnish to inquirers after truth the instruction they may desire in whatever branch of human knowledge . . . without distinction either of class or sex."[71]

When his 1879 remarks on the "Expediency of Receiving Young Women as Students," as he put it, "failed to attract the serious attention of the Trustees," Barnard returned to the issue in 1880. This time he added Cambridge University to his list of institutions where the education of women was already under way (with the opening of the all-women Girton College). He also noted that the faculty of the Harvard Medical School had that year voted to admit women. He then cited Harvard's half-hearted gesture of providing women with higher education in 1879—it created a separate annex where Harvard faculty could teach women in segregated circumstances—perhaps hoping to stir the trustees to support a coeducational plan far more ambitious than President Eliot's. With still no reaction from the trustees, Barnard returned to the matter of the admission of women to Columbia College for a third time in his 1881 report, this time assuring the trustees that "the members of our Faculty without exception favor it."[72]

That was not the case, and the trustees knew it. Although seldom bothering himself with matters relating to the College proper, Burgess for one was very much opposed to enrolling women in any part of the university and would not have hesitated to so inform the trustees. Nor would he have held back from informing Barnard, even at the price of effectively ending their friendship and political collaboration.[73]

On March 5, 1883, the trustee committee chaired by Morgan Dix responded negatively to Barnard's recommendation that Columbia College enroll women. All members of the board save Barnard voted against the president's recommendation. Only after substantial editorial criticism of the decision, which convinced Dix that it was obvious "from the tenor of the articles pouring from the press" that "the public mind had been debauched by the women and President Barnard on the subject," did the board come forward with a compromise plan. The so-called Collegiate Course for Women, a watered-down version of Harvard's annex plan, was adopted on July 9, 1883. It allowed the enrollment of women in classes held off campus and taught by moonlighting Columbia instructors. The exams were to be comparable to those taken by the boys but administered off campus. During its six years of existence, the Collegiate Course enrolled a total of ninety-nine women, twenty-four in its last year. In all, four women completed the program and received Columbia degrees. "The opportunities offered in this course, under the conditions imposed," Barnard had concluded as early as 1885, "have failed to prove particularly attractive."[74]

Although Barnard disavowed this arrangement, insisting on full coeducation and nothing less, those of a more conciliatory sort among the New York advocates of women's higher education continued to press the Columbia trustees for a better arrangement short of full coeducation. Chief among these advocates was Annie Nathan Meyer, a New Yorker of Sephardic Jewish extraction (she was the great-granddaughter of Abraham Seixas, the first and for more than eleven decades thereafter Columbia's only Jewish trustee), who had dropped out of the Collegiate Program after a year to marry Dr. Alfred Meyer. Mrs. Meyer and others, including such respected New York names as Mrs. Joseph Choate and the Reverend Arthur Brooks, Episcopal minister of the

Church of the Incarnation, sought to persuade individual trustees to accept a plan that went beyond the Collegiate Course for Women but left Columbia College's male identity inviolate. Meyer's article in the *Nation* in January 1888 laid out the case for an "affiliated college" in a way that avoided putting the trustees on the defensive.[75]

Efforts to secure Barnard's support for this plan were initially unsuccessful, although his opposition may have reassured trustees as to its reasonableness. Dix did not take to "the lady who came to see me [in February 1888] about a plan for setting up an Annex to Columbia College" but, once persuaded that there would be outside financial backing for an affiliated women's college, came around to support it. In January 1889 the backers of the plan were advised by the Columbia trustees of their approval "in its general features." A month later, a memorial establishing Barnard College, with its own board of trustees, consti- tution, and regulations, was presented to the Columbia trustees. On April 1, 1889, the trustees approved by resolution the establishment of Barnard College. That October it opened for classes in a rented brownstone at 343 Madison Avenue, five blocks south of Columbia College.[76]

The establishment of Barnard College effectively deferred full coeducation at Columbia College for nearly a century. As such, score one for Professor Burgess and his allies. But it can also be viewed as the beginning of a substan- tial and increasing presence of women students and later women faculty and administrative staff within the larger Columbia community. As such, score one for President Barnard. In fact, both are true. What the establishment of Barnard in 1889 did unequivocally accomplish, however, was to make Colum- bia University in many ways less a male bastion than most other major private American universities in the making.

President Barnard was terminally ill in the months leading up to the reso- lution creating the college named after him and was absent at its adoption on April 1, 1889. He died three weeks later. While still preferring his own plan for full coeducation, he had been persuaded (likely by his wife) to allow his name to be attached to the new school. Insofar as Barnard College at its founding was not at all what its namesake had in mind a decade earlier in making the case for the higher education of women, it is a historical misnomer. But on another level it is an apt memorial to one of the most progressive participants in the heroic age of American higher education. If Columbia's first try at resolving the "Woman Question" resulted in an institutional compromise short of Barnard's vision of his university without sexual barriers, the opening of Barnard College in October 1889 brought Columbia one step closer to what he saw as its destiny as "the great university of this principal state of the Union, and this principal city of the western continent."[77]

Barnard succeeded as a president because he took on his trustees whenever they turned fusty or parsimonious, and he showed remarkable physical stamina in doing so. His had been the longest presidency to date, twenty-five years, and remains the second longest since. His deafness notwithstanding, he was at the top of his game well into his seventies. He was the first Columbia president who demonstrated a facility for advancing his academic views in print and must be numbered among the first of Columbia's many statistical sophisticates. He also demonstrated a willingness to share power with enterprising faculty, even some, like Burgess, who did not always play right by him. He understood that a university's income should be spent. He was a builder.

He also had his deficiencies. He was not given much to organizational and bureaucratic niceties. As Trustee William C. Schermerhorn said, he "was no businessman." He sometimes let his sarcasm get the better of him, though less with the faculty or students than with trustees. And he perhaps stayed on too long.[78]

Barnard's place in the history of American higher education is less than it should be, and for several reasons. There is no comprehensive biography of him, just as there has been no comprehensive history of the university to do him justice since Van Amringe's appeared in 1904. The classic account by Laurence R. Veysey, *The Emergence of the American University* (1965), devotes only one paragraph (if a positive and insightful one) to Barnard. Minor factors have also diminished his historical presence. The most widely reprinted image of Barnard, a late portrait of him in red robe and belt-length white beard, makes him seem a figure more out of the Old Testament than the modernizing president he was. Then there is the confusion generated by the fact that, while Barnard College is named after him, relatively little of Columbia bears his name. This local neglect is not be blamed on his immediate successor, President Seth Low, who readily acknowledged "that, in the largest sense, I am only watering, in most cases, the seed which he had the sagacity to plant." Nor does it fall on Low's successor, Nicholas Murray Butler, who was known to sing Barnard's praises if only to diminish Low's standing.[79]

In the end, Barnard owes his relatively modest place in the history of American higher education and in the history of Columbia to the fact that he was ahead of his time. Of the university's historians, one of its least recognized, the university librarian, Roger Howson, writing in 1946, may have come closest to capturing the essential meaning of the Barnard presidency when he ventured onto the treacherous ground of comparing him with his two successors (and predecessor): "Barnard was concerned more deeply about the Columbia that would be when he had passed on than about the Columbia of his time. Low was concerned about the Columbia over which he had control. Butler really went back to the days of the Columbia of Charles King and his billiard table and his dinners and his guests. It was all background. King enjoyed his time with a full sense of temporary limitations. Butler had intentions instead of visions and in the end they failed him. The call to Washington never came." Perhaps too hard on Butler, whom Howson detested and about whom he was writing, about right if a bit stingy on Low, but dead on with regard to our "Admirable Frederick."[80]

The Relegation of the College

It would be fair to characterize the view conveyed here of President Barnard as one in which even his most irritating personal characteristics—stubbornness, extravagance, and occasional fits of self-importance—take on an institution-enhancing light. My defense is that to overcome the historical neglect that has been Barnard's unmerited fate, both as a Columbia figure and a national educator, a certain amount of unabashed boostering is required. Yet one aspect of Barnard's career as president, while understandable in the context of his time and situation, represents a problematic legacy with which Columbia has had to contend ever since.

Barnard was the first of Columbia's "College Agnostics." By this, I mean Columbians who have conceived of the professional, graduate, and research functions of the university as not only distinct from its undergraduate teaching functions but as taking precedence over them. They are to be contrasted with "College Believers," those who see the College at the center of the university. In their purest form, College Agnostics have been quite prepared to countenance the disappearance of the College altogether.

Such views as to the dispensability of the undergraduate program on a university campus were not peculiar to Barnard or to Columbia. They were becoming a commonplace among younger faculty in the last quarter of the nineteenth century, when the research university came into being. In 1888 the Harvard historian Edward Channing advised President Eliot that "the College ought to be suppressed or moved out into the country where it would not interfere with the proper work of the University." Similarly, faculty at Johns Hopkins and Clark University resisted attempts by trustees to expand their undergraduate programs. But among faculty of this persuasion, few were more outspoken in their dismissiveness of their institutions' collegiate programs than Columbia's redoubtable John W. Burgess. "I confess," Burgess wrote in his 1884 pamphlet *The American University: When Shall It Be? Where Shall It Be?* "I am unable to divine what is to be ultimately the position of colleges which can not become universities and will not become gymnasia. I cannot see what reason they will have to exist."[81]

Late-nineteenth-century Harvard and Columbia both had their vocal College Agnostics. The difference was that at Columbia such anti-College views
could expect a sympathetic hearing from the president. Long before Burgess
arrived on the scene, Barnard was already contemplating a Columbia where the
numerically moribund College was subordinated to the rapidly growing professional schools. This was the growth that could enable Columbia to become
the national presence that Barnard envisioned. His own statistical research
proved that no college, and certainly not Columbia College, could expect to
enjoy more than modest increases in undergraduate enrollments. For trustees
less enamored of the prospect of rapid growth and more comfortable with
things as they were, these modest increases might suffice, but not for Barnard,
a president in a hurry. In 1886, when undergraduate enrollments dropped for
the second year running, Barnard told the trustees that the College was not
likely to grow much. "Nor perhaps is such increase greatly to be desired," he
added complacently. "The chief usefulness of the institution is to be found in
the future, mainly in its professional schools and in its graduate department."[82]

Both Barnard's skepticism about the College as a growth center and his opti-
mism about the drawing power of Columbia's professional schools were borne
out by the numbers. In its first twenty-five years of operation (1858–83), the
Columbia Law School enrolled more students than the College had in its entire
130-year history. Within five years of its founding, the School of Mines was
enrolling larger classes than the College. When Barnard arrived at Columbia in
1864, the Law School and the College each accounted for about half of the total
enrollments. By 1880 both the Law School and the School of Mines accounted
for more than two-thirds of all university enrollments. And by the end of
Barnard's presidency in 1889, the College's share of total enrollments had
dropped to below 20 percent. If we follow Barnard's practice of including
Physicians & Surgeons numbers in the total, the College's share of enrollments
dropped during his presidency from over 50 percent to 13 percent of total
Columbia enrollments.[83]

It is revealing that Barnard, despite the fact that the College of Physicians &
Surgeons was throughout Barnard's presidency, by his own characterization,
"substantially an independent institution," always insisted on including P & S
statistics in his university tallies. Doing so allowed him to boast, as he did in his
1876 report, that the combined enrollments of the College (173), Mines (230),
Law (573), and Medicine (410) exceeded "by nearly 200 the attendance at any
other university on this continent." Three years later, he made the same point
about Columbia's enrollments, which had climbed to 1,436, as "exceeding that
of any other educational institution" and provided the comparative totals to
prove it: Michigan (1,372), Harvard (1,332), and Yale (1,022).[84]

Qualitative considerations also entered into Barnard's relegation of the College. Its graduates in his day were not particularly impressive. Even as enthusiastic a backer of the College as Trustee and College alumnus the Reverend Benjamin Haight, upon looking over the 1876 graduating class, declared them "a pretty motley crew." (A member of that particular class, the future economist Richard T. Ely, in a memoir written six decades later, offered no evidence to the contrary.) Morgan Dix was equally hard on the next year's class, which he declared "the poorest they have had at Columbia for many years: it numbered about 24, mostly poor sticks." Nicholas Murray Butler's description of his own class of 1882, which began with seventy-eight but ended up with fifty graduates, suggests no surfeit of brilliant classmates. While crediting them with "a love for the college that have never since been equaled," Butler allowed that the five hundred students who passed through Columbia College between 1875 and 1885 "included eight or ten who subsequently rose to a very high plane of productive scholarship and who left behind them noteworthy reputations as intellectual leaders."[85]

Contemporary comparisons between students of the College and those of the Law School and School of Mines seemed always to favor the serious-minded latter ("digs") over the adolescent former ("butterflies"). Barnard tried to raise the intellectual level of the College by instituting a prize program modeled after that of Oxford and by introducing a carefully calibrated grading scheme. Neither worked. A pattern quickly developed where two or three students in any class took all the prizes, while the rest remained indifferent to their studies. In a rare admission of defeat, he told the trustees, "There are marking systems and marking systems." Burgess came to the same conclusion immediately upon arrival.[86]

There was also the putatively deleterious impact the College had on faculty whose teaching was entirely given over to it. On this, too, Barnard and Burgess were of one mind: that to reduce the amount of undergraduate teaching expected of its professors was to increase their usefulness to the university and to their discipline. Both regarded Drisler and Van Amringe, who identified with the College, as throwbacks to an earlier era, men effective enough in what they did in the College but of no help with the larger purposes of the university. Moreover, insofar as they eschewed specialization and identified with what Barnard took to satirizing even before Burgess's arrival in 1872 as the "time-honored system of rounded culture," they represented obstacles to progress.[87]

The potency of such obstacles to progress at Columbia, the so-called collegiate party, remains a matter of dispute. A half-century after the battle ended with his university side triumphant, Burgess remembered its epic qualities, in which "enemies and critics beset us on all sides." In his view, faculty identified with the College contested every step he and his colleagues on the Faculty of Political Science took in the direction of offering an advanced curriculum. Only a sense of humor, the notoriously humorless Burgess wrote, and the knowledge that "we were animated by a broader patriotism towards Columbia than they were" saw them through the decade.[88]

In retrospect, it is the unevenness of the battle that is most striking. Those favoring moving in the direction of a university, whatever the consequences for the College, enjoyed most of the crucial advantages. For starters, having the president firmly in the university camp made Burgess's efforts much easier (and less dangerous) than the task faced by opponents organizing in defense of the College. "The time has come," Barnard declared in 1879, "for [graduate] instruction of this superior kind." Contrast this with the most determined faculty backers of the university idea at Harvard confronting the fact of President Eliot's refusal to sacrifice the interests of the college, as he understood them, to further their cause. At Yale and Princeton, unshakable identification with the college was a presidential hallmark under both Noah Porter and James McCosh, as the outgunned university supporters among their respective faculties and alumni well understood.[89]

A further advantage enjoyed by those favoring a university was that those opposing it were largely limited to the College faculty, and not to all of them, while the deans and faculties of the professional schools could be counted on to support the university party. Although he had run-ins with both, Burgess numbered Theodore Dwight and Charles Chandler among his allies in doing battle with the "reactionary forces" supporting the College. Here, too, time favored the university party, which could expect to gain adherents with every new faculty appointment, especially as they increasingly went to non–Columbia College men.[90]

On other campuses, faculty ready to defend the undergraduate mission of the institution against those were trying to make it a university could look to trustees and alumni for crucial backing. So it had been at Amherst in the mid-1870s when Burgess gave it up as a lost cause. And so it would be at Dartmouth, Oberlin, Brown, Wesleyan, Williams, and a dozen other colleges that ranked ahead of Columbia College in terms of numbers and eminence in the 1860s but then chose to finish out the century remaining strictly collegiate enterprises. At Yale and Princeton, boards of trustees dominated by ministers and alumni effectively slowed their transformation into universities. And when their transformation got under way in earnest (at Yale in the 1890s; at Princeton a decade later), the undergraduate programs were assured places at the institutional center. By contrast, the decentering of Columbia College, well under way early on in Barnard's presidency, was a fait accompli by its close in 1889.[91]

It was not that the Columbia trustees in the Barnard presidency lacked ministers suspicious of the intentions of university professors, or alumni loyal to the College of their youth, or both. The board did lack, however, members elected directly by the alumni and therefore beholden to them, as was by then becoming common elsewhere. (Such an arrangement had been proposed by Columbia alumni in the wake of the Gibbs controversy in 1854 but would not be implemented until 1908.) Still, Columbia had a respectable number of alumni who, then as now, being concentrated in and around New York City, were theoretically mobilizable in defense of "Old Columbia."

The question remains: Why, as happened elsewhere, did significant trustee or alumni opposition to transforming Columbia into a full-fledged university, in which the undergraduate college was subordinated to the needs of its professional and graduate programs, not materialize at Columbia? I propose three possible reasons. First, by as early as the 1880s (and not including the graduates of P & S), the majority of Columbia's living graduates had become graduates of its professional schools, not of the College, as was the case for all of its peers.[92]

Second, the undergraduate experience of most nineteenth-century Columbia College alumni was not sufficiently memorable or subject to ex post facto mythologizing to call forth the kinds of passions enlisted in the cause of "old Yale," or "pre-74 Princeton," or other of the era's more successful alumni crusades against change. Theirs was, after all, a commuter's experience rather than a residential one, and not all that life-altering, given the continuing impact of family life and the competing attractions of New York City. One need only compare Owen Johnson's fictional account of turn-of-the century undergraduate life in *Stover at Yale* or Henry S. Canby's memoir of Yale of the same era, *Alma Mater: The Gothic Age of the American College*, with John Erskine's memories of "The College on 49th Street" in the 1890s to appreciate the cultural disjunction.[93]

A third reason that trustee and alumni sentiments did not dissuade its presidents and faculty from successfully promoting Columbia's transformation into a university was that, even had such antiuniversity sentiments existed, neither trustees nor alumni were in the habit of backing their sentiments with substantial benefactions. Here the contrast with Harvard is instructive. By the 1870s the gifts and benefactions of living Harvard graduates could regularly be counted on to cover upward of one-third of Harvard's operating budget. Accordingly, the views of such donors mattered. So, too, did Yale and Princeton graduates direct a goodly share of their worldly earnings alma mater's way. But, after citing several recent gifts from alumni to Harvard, President Barnard noted dryly in his 1880 report, "Columbia College has been the recipient of hardly a single benefaction of this description." A quarter-century later, John W. Burgess was making much the same point to one of New York's leading "men of affairs," the Wall Street merchant banker James Speyer: "Whenever a Boston man of affairs conceives a large educational project, he almost always so executes it as to increase the prestige of Harvard University. I hope the time will come when our New York men of affairs will think of Columbia in the same way that the Boston men think of Harvard."[94]

The largest benefaction to Columbia in the Barnard era and the largest to that time came from Barnard himself. His entire estate, upon the death of wife, some eighty thousand dollars, went to Columbia, to support fellowships "for encouraging scientific research" and the library. The first substantial monies Columbia would receive specifically in support of the undergraduate program would not be forthcoming until early in the twentieth century, when a drive among College alumni to underwrite a College building on the Morningside Heights campus (later, Hamilton Hall) got under way. By then, several other buildings serving the professional, graduate, and research needs of the university had been funded and were up and running.[95]

After making the case why effective opposition to Columbia's transformation into a full-fledged university did not materialize, one can turn this essentially negative argument around. Absent a conservative countervailing force, the university-building forces proceeded largely unimpeded. Another way of putting it, looking a little ahead: Columbia became a world-class university as rapidly and as fully as it did because it was not held back by what Barnard and Burgess viewed as the dead weight of a collegiate past. It was Barnard, after all, and not Burgess, who used what turned out to be his penultimate annual report to argue "inferentially, at least, the expediency of abandoning the undergraduate School of Arts [i.e., the College] entirely, and devoting the whole strength of the institution to its superior work."[96]

Columbia was simply freer than more successful antebellum colleges such as Yale, Princeton, Amherst, and Union College to make itself over into a university. It was very nearly as free to do so as Cornell, Johns Hopkins, and Chicago, which came into being fully intending to be universities. It was like Harvard but more so, in that it was more willing than Harvard to subordinate its collegiate past in the process. Columbia did not so much evolve into as it was reborn a university.[97]

And unlike Harvard, where President Eliot, generally thought to side with the university builders, was followed by Abbot Lawrence Lowell, a decided advocate of Harvard College, all of Barnard's next seven successors, except

Dwight Eisenhower, who came to Columbia thinking he would be presiding over a college, were in varying degrees College Agnostics. Thus, when, on two subsequent occasions, after World War I and in the late 1980s and 1990s, well after the triumph of the university builders, some Columbians wished to renew and reemphasize Columbia's earlier mission as an undergraduate institution, it would become necessary to reinvent Columbia College. In the first instance, the effort was undertaken without either the initiative or support of President Nicholas Murray Butler. The recent effort of recentering the College has enjoyed presidential backing, so its prospects would seem to be promising. But this really is jumping ahead.

CHAPTER 6

The Aspect of a University

Thus at one stroke Columbia ceased to be divided into fragments, and took upon herself the aspect of a university.

Seth Low, 1890

As Columbia grows more and more complex, it is certain that the Trustees will have to leave the educational policy of the College more and more in the hands of the educators. This, I think, is a tendency not to be deprecated but rather encouraged.

Seth Low, 1892

The First Multiversity

COLUMBIA COLLEGE changed significantly during the twenty-five-year presidency of F. A. P. Barnard. Yet the Columbia University to come, including the Columbia of today, was only partially discernible in 1889. The College Seth Low inherited in 1890 bore resemblances to the earlier Columbia, but changes in the next decade would effectively end most similarities with Columbia's downtown collegiate past so that by 1900 the shape and character of the modern university was largely set. Even before the new century had begun, Columbia had become a recognizable prototype of what the chancellor of the University of California, Clark Kerr, would call seven decades into the twentieth century a "multiversity."[1]

Several developments at Columbia in the 1890s helped separate, or at least dramatize, the break with what had gone before and what would come later. The first was a formal change in name, giving the institution the fourth in its history. It began in 1754 as King's College and became in 1784 and remained for three years thereafter Columbia College in the State of New York. From 1787 until 1896 Columbia was officially Columbia College in the City of New York, until, by trustee resolution on May 2, 1896, it became Columbia University in the City of New York.[2]

Another change was in locale. From the opening of College Hall in 1760 until its demolition in 1857, Columbia resided at Park Place, fifteen blocks north of the Battery. For the next forty years, Columbia occupied a so-called temporary site fronting on Forty-ninth Street, between Madison and Fourth

Avenue (now Park), along with the School of Mines after 1864, the School of Political Science after 1881, and the Law School after 1882. In 1897 Columbia relocated all these entities, along with the newly constituted Faculties of Philosophy, Pure Science, and Applied Science, to the upper reaches of Manhattan's West Side, between 116th and 120th Streets. Accompanying Columbia were Teachers College (which actually preceded Columbia by migrating to Morningside Heights from University Place in 1896) and Barnard College, which, before moving in the fall of 1897 to 120th Street east of Broadway, had since 1889 rented a brownstone on Madison Avenue four blocks from Columbia College.[3]

Whereas the name change was symbolic in its implications and the change in locale was spatial in its impact, the third development, an accelerating rate of growth in the sheer size of the institution, was structural and sociological in its consequences. Columbia grew significantly in quantifiable ways between 1864 and 1889, especially after 1875. Still, the 1889 numbers could be understood as extrapolations of the 1864 numbers. The growth occurring in the 1890s, at rates never experienced before or since, makes the numbers for 1900 fit more naturally at the start of a pattern of growth that extends to the twenty-first century than at the end of a period that began in the nineteenth century. Columbia became today's Columbia in the 1890s.[4]

Another development was a fundamental reordering of the internal power structure within the new university. This marked the rise of the faculty estate to a position of effective parity with the heretofore dominant board of trustees. Indeed, as long as the faculty's enhanced standing enjoyed the active support of the president, which in turn could secure the tacit acquiescence of the trustees and no opposition from students, the faculty could and did lay claim to being first among the three principal university estates. This was not an ascendancy that would go uncontested for long, but while it lasted, through the 1890s and into the new century, it constituted the first florescence of the Columbia faculty.[5]

The "Great Harmonizer"

Never one to pass up an opportunity to set the historical record straight, Nicholas Murray Butler, in a 1940 interview, summed up the accomplishments of his presidential predecessor, Seth Low, during his nine years as a trustee before becoming president: "He negotiated higher rents on some Upper Estate parcels." And then, lest his interviewer infer parity between his own considerable diplomatic and linguistic accomplishments and those of Low, Butler recalled Low's one venture into international diplomacy. It was as a delegate to the 1897 Hague Conference, which he spent bicycling around Holland because his ignorance of French made most of the conference proceedings incomprehensible. "Low had a New York (or Brooklyn) commercial mind," Butler said of the man who had labored mightily to assure his own succession. "He would have been good running a steamship company or a manufacturing firm."[6]

In choosing for president a graduate of the College, a self-described New York Knickerbocker, an Episcopalian, and a nonacademic, the trustees in 1889 were, after a quarter-century with the academic outsider Barnard, reverting to tradition. Seth Low was unquestionably a graduate of the College and a nonacademic. But in point of genealogical fact, his Lows were not old New Yorkers and certainly not Knickerbockers. They were sixth-generation New Englanders who had been part of a substantial migration to New York in the early nineteenth century. They had lived as fishermen and maritimers along the north shore of Massachusetts until the father of Abiel Abbot Low (1811–93), Seth Low's father, left Salem for Brooklyn in 1829. They had been Congregationalists and latterly Unitarians. Once in Brooklyn, young Abiel shipped out on a China trader as an able-bodied seaman and soon thereafter became a business agent. In the early 1840s he opened A. A. Low and Brothers, which quickly became New York's leading house in the China trade. Abiel married in 1848, and in 1850 his wife died a week after giving birth to their only son, Seth.[7]

Low remarried in 1852 and continued to prosper as a China merchant with a fleet of clipper ships, later branching out with investments in the first transatlantic telegraph cable and, after the Civil War, the Baltimore and Ohio Railroad. Seth was raised in the comfortable circumstances of upper-class Brooklyn and in 1868 enrolled in Columbia College. Four years later, he graduated with the class of 1872, having spent his senior year taking courses at the Law School. Following graduation, young Low converted from his father's liberal Unitarianism to his stepmother's liberal Episcopalianism, without ever becoming a demonstrative churchman. After making the expected grand tour of Europe and entering his father's business, he shortly thereafter used family resources to try his hand in the insurance business, while pursuing cultural and civic activities in Brooklyn.[8]

In 1880 the thirty-year-old Low almost simultaneously married, became a Columbia trustee, and was elected to the first of two two-year terms as the reform mayor of Brooklyn. When in 1885 he declined to stand for a third term, Low walked away with a reputation for efficiency, integrity, and civic disinterestedness that he retained for the rest of his life. In 1887 the senior Low sold A. A. Low and Brothers for ten million dollars, the proceeds to go to Seth upon his father's death.[9]

Low was interested in the Columbia presidency when it became vacant upon Barnard's retirement in 1889, though he was by no means the leading candidate. President Barnard had two other possibilities in mind, one an outsider, Francis

A. Walker, president of MIT, and one an insider, the trustee Dr. George Agnew. But because neither was an Episcopalian, Barnard knew their chances were slim. (What he did not acknowledge was that they were slimmer for being seen by trustees as his choices.) Another trustee frequently mentioned was the attorney George L. Rives. But because his recent marriage to a divorced woman in a Dutch Reformed service (his fellow trustee and rector of Trinity Church Morgan Dix refusing to do the honors) was so certain to be opposed by Dix and the other Episcopalian clergy on the board, he declined nomination. That left the choice on October 7, 1889, between Low and Professor Henry Drisler. In the formal balloting, Low received seven votes to Drisler's six and was duly elected Columbia's next president.[10]

That the seventy-year-old Drisler came within one vote of being elected is surprising. He had been teaching Greek at Columbia for forty-five years, with the last fifteen or so as the faculty leader in opposition to Barnard's modernization project. Some trustees may have supported him for his longevity, others for his politics, but his supporters most likely intentionally wasted their votes on him rather than vote for one of their own whom they viewed as not the most qualified. Whatever the reasons, the seven trustees who elected the thirty-nine-year-old Seth Low as the eleventh president of Columbia made a splendid choice, every bit as good as that made twenty-five years earlier and with none of the subsequent second-guessing and conflict that followed on that more decisively positive vote.[11]

In settling on one of their own—and not by any means one of the most outspoken among them—the trustees may have been hoping for a return to the days when presidents saw themselves as the "get along or get out" agents of the trustees. After Barnard, they may have looked forward to having a president who would be both amiable and deferential. If so, they got half of what they hoped for. Low proved to be singularly attuned to the feelings and sensitivities of those with whom he dealt, including his fellow trustees. When asked during his presidency what he least liked about the job, he promptly answered: "Giving necessary offense." Dean James Earl Russell of Teachers College reminiscing about Low in the 1920s, remembered him as "the Great Harmonizer." But Low also knew when to seize the vocal lead. In an early exchange with a faculty member complaining about a newly hired mathematician from Michigan, Low informed the complainant: "Professor Cole and you are colleagues and that is the end of it."[12]

The Greater University

Two days after being installed as president on February 3, 1890, the thirty-nine-year-old Low called together the entire Columbia faculty at the President's

House on Forty-ninth Street for the first of two meetings. He wished to know their views on the reorganization of the university. Anyone who had witnessed the haphazard growth of the faculty in the 1880s was aware that some kind of reorganization was sorely needed, but there the consensus ended. Nicholas Murray Butler later remembered of the meeting that, as the most junior faculty member present, his views were the first solicited and later became the president's own. Whatever its origins, the reorganization plan Low presented to the trustees the following fall was one with which a minority of faculty initially identified (among them Butler and Burgess) and which the senior member of the faculty, Henry Drisler, openly opposed. In choosing it, the new president made clear the distinction in his mind between full consultation and executive decision making.[13]

The new organization that began to take shape in late 1891 divided the university's instructional staff into four coequal faculties (with some joint membership): the newly constituted Faculty of Philosophy, which included those faculty teaching primarily in "the College proper"; the Faculty of Political Science; the Faculty of Law; and the Faculty of Mines. Shortly after that, with the merger of Columbia and the College of Physicians & Surgeons, the Faculty of Medicine was added. Two years later, the Faculty of Pure Science was constituted from faculty in the physical sciences and mathematics heretofore in the Faculty of Mines, which in 1896 itself was renamed the Faculty of Applied Science. The result was that the constituent faculties of Columbia University now numbered seven. They were, by order of their founding: Columbia College (1754), Medicine (1767), Law (1858), Political Science (1881), Philosophy (1890), Pure Science (1892), and Applied Science (1864–96). "Thus at one stroke Columbia ceased to be divided into fragments," Low had announced in 1890, getting a bit ahead of himself, "and took upon herself the aspect of a university." Six years later, it had the name to match the aspect. And thus it was Low who gave the Columbia faculties the basic nomenclature and shape they would retain, with a few additions, into the 1970s.[14]

Each of the faculties in Low's Columbia had at its head a dean, elected from among and by the members of that faculty. He and another elected faculty member would serve on the newly constituted University Council, which was chaired by the senior dean and charged with making decisions that involved more than one faculty and with advising the president on matters touching the academic operations of the university. Although the University Council would, by the second decade of the twentieth century, be dominated by appointed deans and other administrators and long before the 1960s be dismissed by faculty as a rubber stamp for the administration, during the 1890s it both served the university's needs and contributed to the faculty's growing power.[15]

By its very composition, the University Council, as College-based critics such as Drisler well understood, heavily favored the professional schools and those faculty in arts and sciences of the university persuasion. This was quite intentional on the part of Low, who wasted no time in conveying his views to the trustees on College-university relations. "The College is indeed the seed out of which has grown the University," he acknowledged, "but the tree, which is the University, does not exist for the sake of the seed, but the seed for the sake of the tree." Thus spoke Columbia's second president as College Agnostic.[16]

For all the clarity with which he declared the interests of the College subordinate to those of the university, Low elicited little open criticism from trustees or faculty identified with the College. Especially after Drisler's retirement as the College's first in-all-but-name dean in 1896, when he was replaced by the easily placated John H. Van Amringe, the College took its further relegation largely without complaint. An occasional rearguard action against efforts by Low or non-College faculty to expand the electives available to undergraduates, to facilitate transfers from the College to the professional schools, or to increase the enrollments of the College for purposes of financial reasons (some things never change), pretty much constituted the limits of the political program of those faculty identified with the College during the Low presidency. Other faculties did not accept the new structure so obligingly.[17]

The Law School and the Revolution of 1891

Seth Low's first official contact as president with the sixty-eight-year-old Theodore W. Dwight was to inform his former teacher that henceforth all formal communications about the Law School should be directed to the president, not, as before, to the trustees. Eight months later, Dwight had retired, a new dean was in place, and the Columbia Law School had been "revolutionized"; critics said "Harvardized."[18]

Dwight had enjoyed a long, professionally satisfying, and personally remunerative thirty-two-year run as head of Columbia's Law School. From its founding in 1858, it vied with Harvard's older law school in numbers of graduates, while its enrollments quickly doubled those of Columbia College. Columbia Law School was also an immediate revenue generator, with its profits split between the Law Faculty (i.e., Dwight) and the College. Thereafter, Dwight proved an effective politician in thwarting or delaying most of the reforms proposed by trustees concerned with the "come one, come all" atmosphere prevailing at 37 Lafayette Place and then at 8 Great Jones Street. Dwight himself acknowledged a decided preference for teaching "men of average ability."[19]

Apparently, Dwight's inclusiveness did not extend to women. There is no evidence of his supporting applications for admission in 1869 from three women, which the trustees, led by George Templeton Strong, who referred to the applicants as a "clack of possible Portias," rejected out of hand.[20]

As early as the mid-1870s, trustees were expressing concerns with what they described as excessive enrollments in the Law School and the absence of any discernible entrance requirements. An 1875 proposal to require knowledge of Latin for admission would have limited applicants to those with some college experience, but insofar as knowledge of Latin was not needed to complete the law curriculum and requiring it would reduce enrollments and tuition revenues, Dwight, with President Barnard's support, successfully resisted its implementation. Prior collegiate experience did become increasingly common among Columbia Law School students in the 1880s—as in the cases of Brown graduate (1877) Charles Evans Hughes and Harvard graduate (1880) Theodore Roosevelt—but Dwight resisted making it a requirement. In 1890, 40 percent of the students attending the Law School were college graduates.[21]

A second reform Dwight resisted throughout his tenure as head of the Law School was the addition of a third year to the curriculum. As long as graduates enjoyed automatic admission to the New York bar, a third year made no sense to Dwight or most of his students. And even when the "diploma privilege" was rescinded in 1883 and Columbia law graduates had to take the state-administered bar exam, Dwight could effectively argue that the courses proposed did not bear directly on what a lawyer needed to know for the exam or to practice his profession. Not surprisingly, then, when a third year was added to the Law School curriculum with the class entering in 1888, most members of that class and the next (among them future Supreme Court justice Benjamin Cardozo) left after the second year and went directly into practice.[22]

A third reform Dwight effectively put off as long as he was in charge of the Law School was the introduction of teaching methods other than formal lectures, a delivery system that commended itself to Dwight both because of its economy and because, by all reports, he was himself a splendid lecturer. Here, too, the introduction of other approaches to teaching the law, including the case method that was being used at Harvard, would require hiring more faculty, which in turn would have a depressing effect on the income of current faculty. Dwight was the rare professor who almost never met a prospective colleague he did not think he could do without.[23]

Perhaps the proposed reform that was most subversive of Dwight's inclusive and practical view of legal education was the board's insistence that the Law School abandon its downtown site on Great Jones Street, hard by the courts, and relocate to the Forty-ninth Street campus. Here, Dwight was outmaneuvered, and the transfer was effected in 1884 after the completion of a building on the Forty-ninth Street campus that the trustees designated for the Law School. With the move, as Dwight predicted, enrollments temporarily slumped.[24]

There was a coherent idea behind these various reform proposals, as became clear after their comprehensive implementation after 1890 and the development of legal education at Columbia since. It held that the study of the law under university auspices ought to reflect those auspices by the academic rigor—as opposed to simply the professional utility—of that study. Law professors should possess academic as well as professional qualifications, with the former alone in some cases sufficient but never the latter. The law ought to be studied full-time and at some remove from the hurly-burly of the courts and the law offices downtown. Moreover, those who took up such studies ought to bring to them a measure of cultural sophistication that in America was/is thought to be a by-product of college going. And, finally, those entrusted with the education of lawyers must hold firmly to the concept of the law as a learned profession not accessible to all.[25]

This was an elitist, exclusive conception of the law, which when followed also had the effect of reducing the likelihood, as George Templeton Strong feared was happening back in 1867 thanks in no small measure to Dwight's policies, that the New York bar would soon be filled with "little scrubs (German Jew boys mostly) whom the School now promotes from grocery counters on Avenue B." Insofar as the reforms effected at Columbia Law School in 1891 all pointed in the other direction, they would have made earlier Columbia lawyers such as Gouverneur Morris, John Jay, and Alexander Hamilton, legal elitists all, proud of alma mater.[26]

But there was also a coherence to Dwight's inclusive and democratic vision of the Law School, no less defensible for having been on the losing side of the 1891 revolution at Columbia and elsewhere. When William A. Keener (1890–1902) was brought in from Harvard in 1890 by Low, it was clear that he was to be the broom by which Low and the trustees rid the Law School of all vestiges of the Dwight regime. Keener brought with him from Cambridge the case method and recommendations for new hires that solidified his position as the Law School's Harvardizer, as did his election as dean (1891–1901) after Dwight's retirement the following year. Those law faculty identified with Dwight—Professors Robert D. Petty and Benjamin F. Lee—resigned their Columbia positions and went downtown to establish New York Law School, where older, poorer, part-time students with no college experience remained the major clientele.[27]

In 1893 Columbia made the possession of a bachelor of arts degree an admission requirement for all non-Columbia College students wishing to enter its

Law School. Columbia College students could enter the Law School in their fourth year (as could those who transferred to Columbia in their third year) and would get their A.B. along with their law degree. After a dip following imposition of a third year, enrollments soon returned to levels that were economically satisfactory to the university and allowed the Law School to become increasingly selective in admissions. Meanwhile, three faculty appointments made in 1891 and one in 1894 of men in the Keener scholarly mold—Francis M. Burdick, George F. Canfield, George W. Kirchwey, and John Bassett Moore— would carry the Columbia Law School into the 1920s before confronting another revolutionary moment. As with so many other parts of Columbia University, the Law School acquired much of its contemporary shape in the 1890s.[28]

In 1901, as if to confirm the permanence of these changes, Columbia joined with a handful of other law schools committed to increasing their admission requirements and more generally to lifting the tone of legal instruction to form the openly elitist Association of Law Schools. But that it did so even as it continued to be a means of upward mobility, especially for the sons of New York Jewish and Catholic working-class families, many of them graduates of CCNY and the region's Catholic colleges, testifies both to the ambitions of those sons (and later daughters) and to the staying power of Dwight's inclusive vision.

Columbia Reacquires a Medical School

When Seth Low assumed the presidency in 1890, Columbia had been without a medical school since 1813, when the trustees closed it. For the next three decades, New York City made do with the successor to Columbia's medical school, the College of Physicians & Surgeons, which had been chartered by the New York Board of Regents in 1807 and absorbed the few Columbia medical faculty left in 1813. In 1841 the medical department of the University of the City of New York (later, NYU) began offering instruction, first in rented quarters on Bond Street and after 1851 in a new building on Fourteenth Street near Third Avenue. It is with P & S, however, that Columbia's history became entangled during the second half of the nineteenth century, and it was the acquisition of P & S in 1891 that put Columbia back into medical education.[29]

The College of Physicians & Surgeons operated during its first two years in a rented house on Robinson Street, within a block of Columbia College. After another temporary move, it moved again, this time to a house on Barclay Street, this time staying put for twenty-five years (1813–37). It then moved to Crosby Street (1837–56). In 1856, within months of Columbia's move from Park Place uptown to Forty-ninth Street, P & S moved to Twenty-third Street, in Chelsea.

During all these years, the Medical School either prospered or struggled accordingly to how its faculty, presidents, and trustees (some of whom were faculty) managed the delicate task of providing the College with adequate operating funds and assuring its faculty proprietors a sizable chunk of the income derived from tuition. The College was regularly criticized for charging excessive tuition for what was essentially a series of lectures on various aspects of medicine and medical practice. Its entrance requirements were nugatory, and its examinations perfunctory. Before the Civil War, the College offered little in the way of clinical experience or more than rudimentary instruction in the basic sciences.[30]

It was with the prospect of offering more science instruction that P & S entered into a formal relationship with Columbia College in 1860. But the real reason behind its deciding to redesignate itself the medical department of Columbia College was to free itself from the direct control of the New York State Board of Regents. Otherwise, the arrangement had few practical consequences for either P & S or Columbia, aside from allowing Columbia to count P & S graduates as their own when it served Columbia's purposes (e.g., to increase the number of Columbia's Civil War veterans). P & S retained its own board of trustees, its faculty continued to be paid on a proprietary basis, and Columbia faculty who taught at P & S, such as the ubiquitous Charles Frederick Chandler, did so as outside contractors. In 1875 President Barnard called on his trustees either to make the corporate relationship with P & S meaningful or to sever it. He favored the former, as did Dr. George Agnew, who served on both the Columbia and P & S boards, but a majority on both boards was not prepared to do more than continue the 1860 arrangement.[31]

All this changed a decade later, when P & S came into some money. In 1884 its president, Dr. James McLane, persuaded the terminally ill New York railroad magnate William H. Vanderbilt to make a gift to P & S. This took the form of a deed to a half block of New York City real estate located between Fifty-ninth and Sixtieth Streets and Ninth and Tenth Avenues, on Manhattan's West Side, adjacent to Roosevelt Hospital, which had been in the neighborhood since 1871. In addition to this land, valued at $300,000, Vanderbilt also gave P & S $200,000 with which to build a new medical school on the site. He died a year later, but in January 1886 Mr. and Mrs. William Sloane, Vanderbilt's daughter and her husband, donated $300,000 for the construction of Sloane Maternity Hospital on the southwest corner of Fifty-ninth and Tenth. Four months later, the Vanderbilts' four surviving sons donated another $250,000 for the construction of Vanderbilt Clinic.[32]

The opening of the new building for P & S in 1888 was also the occasion for introducing two important reforms. The first was to require passing entrance examinations for all applicants who had not completed three years of college. (About a third of those entering P & S in 1890 did so with A.B.s.) The second extended the curriculum of the school from two to three years. Both reforms had the intended effect of slowing the growth in enrollments, which by the late 1880s had reached average class sizes of around five hundred, while the second reform required the appointment of more faculty. Increased cost of instruction and added expenses attending the maintenance of the larger facility prompted P & S trustees and faculty alike to seek out an institutional alliance that would assure the school a greater measure of financial security.[33]

On March 24, 1891, President Seth Low of Columbia University and Dr. James McLane of the College of Physicians & Surgeons signed an agreement by which all the assets of P & S (assessed at $1,652,850) passed to Columbia University in exchange for Columbia's assuming responsibility for all future expenses in the operation of those assets. By this agreement, P & S acquired the deep pockets it needed, plus privileged access to the scientific facilities of the university. For Columbia, the agreement meant that it was once again, after a lapse of three-quarters of a century, back in the business of providing medical education.[34]

If no would-be university could be considered a real university on the level of Harvard or Yale or Johns Hopkins without a medical school, Columbia again had itself one. It would not be until the 1920s that an alliance underwritten by the philanthropist Edward S. Harkness, joining Columbia, P & S, and Presbyterian Hospital, permitted the move to 168th Street that put Columbia's Medical School in a position to challenge Harvard and Johns Hopkins as one of the country's leading providers of medical education. But the integration of P & S into the larger university in the opening months of the Low administration at least put Columbia back in the hunt.[35]

Low, Barnard College, and the "Woman Question," Part 2

When the trustees rejected President Barnard's call for the admission of women to Columbia College in 1883, Seth Low apparently voted with the majority, there being no recorded minority votes save Barnard's. He also likely shared the view that Columbia College should not become coeducational and certainly did nothing during his presidency to change its standing in this regard. In 1894 he informed Harvard's President Eliot, who had heard that Low favored undergraduate coeducation, that he and the trustees remained of the opinion "that it is inexpedient to attempt to educate the sexes together at Columbia College." On the issue of whether Columbia should provide more educational opportunities for women enrolled at Barnard College, he and his trustees were of a mind that it should. And as an effective advocate of such a policy, he proved to be considerably more successful in providing women educational opportunities than his redoubtable but often off-putting predecessor.[36]

The first decade of Barnard is primarily the story of a dozen or so women, themselves beyond college-going years but committed to the idea that New York City should have an institution ready and able to provide collegiate instruction to women, who successfully underwrote the College's operations. Some did this with a commitment of time and labor, as in the cases of the fundraising publicist Annie Nathan Meyer and the Vassar graduate Ella Weed, the College's first acting dean from 1889 to her death in 1893, and the Bryn Mawr– and Girton-trained classicist Emily Jane Smith, who in 1894 at the age of twenty-nine became the College's first official dean. Following the decision to move the College from 343 Madison Avenue to Morningside Heights in the wake of Columbia's decision to move uptown, other women, such as Mrs. Van Wyck Brinckerhoff, Mrs. A. A. Anderson, and Mrs. Josiah M. Fiske, came forward with the funds to build Barnard's first three buildings, Milbank Hall, Brinckerhoff Hall, which abutted Milbank along its east wall, and Fiske Hall, which became Milbank's west wing and provided Barnard with dormitory space. It is also, of course, the story of the young women who attended Barnard during its first decade, approximately two hundred of them, and of the women faculty, beginning with the appointment in 1891 of the Zurich-trained botanist Emily Gregory, who taught them.[37]

Among others who figured prominently in Barnard's early history number Jacob Schiff, the College's first treasurer and underacknowledged benefactor of Barnard Hall, and his much longer serving successor as treasurer, George A. Plimpton. But perhaps no one so effectively secured Barnard's future as part of the larger Columbia University as did Seth Low.[38]

Characteristically, he did so by turning a problem with securing Columbia faculty to teach courses at Barnard into a means by which Columbia could in turn look to Barnard for some of its essential faculty. The problem first surfaced, predictably enough, in dealings with the Faculty of Political Science, whose dean, John W. Burgess, manifested his opposition to all matters relating to the higher education of women by banning Barnard College seniors from graduate courses, even when his teachers were willing to admit them and in spite of the fact that the Faculty of Philosophy regularly did so (the Faculty of Pure Science did not follow suit until the late 1890s). Burgess also begrudged having any of his faculty teach at Barnard and made that increasingly difficult. The future of Barnard College, Low told Burgess in 1894, was "one of the very few subjects in regard to which we probably do not agree." Seven years later, when Low told Burgess why he had not been named his successor, Burgess's views on Barnard College were among the reasons given.[39]

Low's solution was as ingenious as it was personally generous. It involved his making an anonymous gift of thirty-six thousand dollars to the Barnard trustees to underwrite the salaries of three new professors for three years, with Barnard College assuming the costs thereafter. The appointments were to the Barnard faculty but were to be made to individuals acceptable to the Columbia Faculties of Political Science and Pure Science, where they would be expected to commit a share of their time to offering graduate courses. The three men appointed were the economist John Bates Clark, a close acquaintance of Burgess's who willingly traded his place at Amherst for one in New York; the European historian James H. Robinson, from the University of Pennsylvania; and the mathematician Frank N. Cole, from Michigan. Each added luster to the Columbia faculty while giving Barnard not only a share of his time but the right to teaching by other Columbia faculty in exchange for the teaching Clarke, Robinson, and Fiske did at Columbia. Low intuitively understood that the relationship between Columbia and Barnard, as with any of what his successor called the institutions that made up the "extended cofederation of the Greater University," needed to be mutually beneficial and two-way to overcome the structural problems involved.[40]

In June 1900 Low moved to capitalize on his good relations with the Barnard trustees (his wife being one) and with Dean Smith (now Dean Smith Putnam, after having married publisher George Putnam) to formalize a long-term intercorporate agreement. By its terms, Barnard would retain its own board of trustees (with Columbia's president a member) and its financial independence. It would have its own faculty, with permanent appointments to be approved by Columbia, and its own curriculum. Provisions were made for allowing Barnard students to take upper-level courses at Columbia. Barnard graduates would receive a Columbia degree. The head of Barnard would be a dean within the university and have a seat on the University Council, as would an elected representative of the Barnard faculty.[41]

With occasional adjustments in the way payments were calculated for Barnard enrollments in Columbia courses, this 1900 agreement established the relationship between Columbia and Barnard for the next eight decades. A byproduct of the agreement was that it perpetuated the disinclination among Columbia trustees, faculty, and alumni to admit women to Columbia College. It also allowed many at Barnard to see positive benefits in a women's college and to turn away from the original goal of President Barnard for full coeducation in favor of the "separate but equal" compromise Low worked out or even of total independence. But perhaps most important from the perspective of the greater university, the agreement assured the presence of women undergraduates, women faculty, and women administrators in numbers on Morningside Heights throughout the first two-thirds of the twentieth century, otherwise in short supply at Columbia proper. If not yet (and not for another eight decades) offered a full place at the high table, Columbia's women, thanks to the founders of Barnard College and Seth Low, were at least assured a room of their own.[42]

Founding/Enfolding Teachers College

Another intercorporate agreement Low effected in 1900 was with the trustees of Teachers College. Like that with Barnard College, it partially realized an initiative of President Barnard's that had earlier failed to win the support of his ever-doubtful trustees. Just as in 1881 he had advised a young Columbia College student scouting around for a promising career to "do something distinctive, something new and constructive," by which he meant getting into education, he so advised his trustees. But whereas the student, one Nicholas Murray Butler, took Barnard's advice, the trustees wanted nothing to do with their president's proposal that Columbia introduce courses in pedagogy.[43]

How Columbia in 1900 came to offer such courses is a story that began in 1880 with the founding of the Kitchen Education Association, one of the several philanthropic initiatives of Miss Grace Hoadley Dodge, daughter of the wealthy businessman William Dodge (and granddaughter of David L. Dodge, A. A. Low's principal competitor in the China trade), directed at substituting miniature versions of kitchen utensils for the toys of kindergarten-aged girls of humble circumstances. In 1884 the Kitchen Education Association changed its name to the Industrial Education Association, in keeping with its broadened target audience, which now included boys and parents, opened new quarters on University Place next to Union Theological Seminary, and began offering courses in industrial drawing, clay modeling, and cooking. With Miss Dodge its effective leader, the Industrial Education Association continued, a mixture of philanthropic impulse and what later came to be called vocational training.[44]

Meanwhile, at Columbia, the once-wunderkind and now-doctor Nicholas Murray Butler (CU Ph.D., 1884) had returned from a year's postdoctorate fellowship in Germany, where he heard all manner of lectures on the science of pedagogy and the philosophy of education. President Barnard remained as interested as ever in making educational courses available at Columbia. After again encountering resistance from the trustees in the fall of 1885, Barnard encouraged Butler, who held an appointment as assistant in philosophy and psychology, to develop a series of lectures on pedagogy that might be offered to New York City school teachers on Saturday mornings. The lectures attracted more than two hundred subscribers, proof that a market existed for teacher training and that young Butler was the coming man in the field.[45]

But when Barnard and Butler reported the results that fall to the Columbia trustees, they again rejected the idea of offering such courses as part of the regular Columbia curriculum, not least because doing so would inevitably bring women in numbers onto the Columbia campus (90 percent of Butler's subscribers were women). At this point, the heretofore separate histories of Miss Dodge and Dr. Butler converged when, with financial backing from William Vanderbilt Jr. and with Miss Dodge's support, Butler was offered and accepted the presidency of the Industrial Education Association. In 1887–88 the IEA employed six instructors, enrolled thirty-six juniors in the first year of its two-year program plus eighty-six special students, and operated a model school for sixty-four youngsters where the latest theories in pedagogical science were tested under laboratory circumstances and where the curriculum was "designed to equip students thoroughly for the profession of teaching." Reflecting Butler's intentions far more than Miss Dodge's philanthropic impulse, the Industrial Education Association changed its name in 1888 to the New York School for the Training of Teachers.[46]

Butler remained president of the School for the Training of Teachers until 1891, when he resigned to become the first dean of Columbia's Faculty of Philosophy. While president, he founded and undertook to edit the *Educational Review*, which he did for the next quarter-century. Butler merits inclusion among the three principal founders of Teachers College, along with Grace Hoadley Dodge and Dean James Earl Russell. His role, however, hardly justifies the title of the chapter in his autobiography, "The Founding of Teachers College." It was not a one-man undertaking.[47]

In 1892 the school changed its name again, this time to Teachers College. It was then that Butler let trustees of the school in on Columbia's plans to acquire the Bloomingdale Asylum site, enabling them to buy an adjoining site before public notice increased the cost. Teachers College then weathered some mid-decade financial difficulties brought about in part by the withdrawal of support from early backers (but not Grace Dodge) whose philanthropic interests did not square with the direction of the College. At one point in 1893, the trustees of Teachers College offered to sell out to Columbia, an offer the Columbia trustees rejected because of the coeducational complications. These problems notwithstanding, Teachers College became the first of the new educational residents of Morningside Heights when it opened for business on the corner of 120th Street and Broadway in 1895. Two years later, its trustees appointed the thirty-year-old German-trained and Butler-vetted psychologist James Earl Russell as dean, a position he held until 1927. A provisional agreement with

Columbia in 1898, followed by the more comprehensive one in 1900, established Teachers College as Columbia's "professional school for the training of teachers." And so, while often in the next century expanding its mandate into such areas as nursing and international studies, even while contributing to the scholarly eminence of Columbia in such academic fields as psychology, anthropology, and history, it has remained.[48]

The Rise of the Faculty Estate

Several factors helped bring about a shift in the internal power structure within the university in the 1890s, all to the effect of enhancing faculty agency. One was the growth of the faculty in sheer numbers; a second was a change in the credentials expected of Columbia faculty, particularly the rise of the Ph.D. as a job requirement; a third was the increased role played by outside evaluations in determining faculty hiring; and a fourth was the role that perceptions of faculty quality came to play in determining the relative standing of American universities. Each of these, the veritable building blocks of the American multiversity we have inherited, needs to be considered in turn.

Between 1889 and 1900 the size of the Columbia University faculty more than quintupled, from forty-five full-time faculty members at the time of Low's appointment to approximately two hundred fifty at the turn of the century. This represents a doubling of the faculty every four years. Such growth had never before been experienced at Columbia, nor has it since. Nor has it likely been matched on other campuses except in start-up circumstances. For an established institution, midway through its second century of existence, suddenly to experience such growth has to be viewed as unusual—and consequential.[49] As Columbia's faculty became more numerous, they became more differentiated in rank and specialization. As recently as 1864, all but one of the eleven faculty were professors, with the lone adjunct professor so designated to note his transitional status as the second man in a given teaching area. Columbia College made almost no use of the subordinate ranks of instructor or tutor regularly used elsewhere. In 1875, on the eve of Burgess's arrival, the three Columbia faculties still consisted of only thirteen professors and two adjunct professors. By 1889, especially in the Faculty of Mines, the ranks of instructor and tutor had become common and accounted for perhaps a quarter of the teaching faculty. By 1900 faculty ranks, not counting those of the Medical School, included professors, adjunct professors (soon to be changed to assistant professors), lecturers, instructors, tutors, and assistants, with professors and adjunct professors making up less than half the faculty. Rather than being synonymous with faculty, professors were now a privileged minority perched atop an academic ladder with the majority holding to rungs below, with uncertain prospects of moving up.[50]

Just as faculty became increasingly differentiated by rank in the late nineteenth century, so they became identified by finer and finer distinctions in their academic specialties. This process was already under way in the sciences by the 1860s, when the idea only a decade earlier of James Renwick's covering physics, chemistry, geology, and engineering mechanics had become unthinkable. By the 1890s specialization had proceeded to the point that the field of chemistry had divided itself into several subspecialties (organic, physical, and biological chemistry and chemical engineering), while the engineering faculty consisted of mechanical, civil, electrical, and mining specialists. Mathematics and astronomy, joined in a single professorship from the founding of King's College to the 1850s, had long since gone their separate ways. In 1864 Columbia had four professors in the sciences; in 1890 nine; in 1900 twenty-three.[51]

The process began later in the social science and humanities but was well under way at Columbia in the 1890s. What had begun as political science with Burgess's arrival in 1876 had become by the early 1890s, in addition to the much narrowed specialization of political science and public law, statistics, economics, history, and, in 1896 with appointment of Franklin Giddings, sociology. Among the modern social sciences, anthropology also made its appearance at Columbia in the mid-1890s in the person of Franz Boas, but its pre-Boasian history at Columbia was as an offshoot of philosophy, as was psychology, and as such both were considered to be among the humanities and housed in the Faculty of Philosophy. Such divisions were formalized in the 1890s by the creation of departmental units in which these specializations, all within the Faculty of Political Science, were further divided.[52]

The humanities were the slowest to break up into the departmentally differentiated specialties recognizable today but break up they did. Whereas before 1881 no one at Columbia had exclusive responsibility for English literature, it being part of what the professor of moral philosophy taught, after 1881 it became the responsibility of the first professor of English literature, Thomas Randolph Price, who came to Columbia from the University of Virginia. By 1900 English had been further differentiated into English literature, which included its own professor of dramatic literature, Brander Matthews, and comparative literature, with its own professor, George Woodberry. There was also a further division, rhetoric, to which junior faculty teaching in the College were assigned.[53]

Philosophy and psychology parted ways in 1891, while the ancient languages, earlier limited to Latin and Greek, came to include additional offerings (and professorships) in Semitic languages and Sanskrit. Whereas before the 1870s, only German among the modern languages was regularly offered, and the Gebhard professorship stood alone in the field, in the 1890s all the major romance languages had professorial representation. Some of this departmentalization was less a reflection of scholarly developments than local personalities and politics, as with the arrangement in English keeping George Woodberry and Brander Matthews at arm's length. It is also true that much the same process was under way at other would-be universities. But what is unique here is that the process was especially rapid at Columbia and relatively uncontested.[54]

The Ph.D. as Meal Ticket

Who were all these academic specialists joining the Columbia faculty in the 1890s, and where did they come from? As in Columbia's earlier history, a few were from abroad, usually with training from one of the major European universities. More common, especially in the first years of Columbia's expansion, were Americans who had studied in Europe before returning to America and academic positions (Joy, Chandler, Rood, Burgess, et al.). But by the boom years of the 1890s, more and more of the recruits to the entry ranks of the faculty were from the half-dozen American universities with sizable Ph.D. programs. Yale was the first to confer the degree, in 1861, followed a decade later by Cornell in 1872 and Harvard in 1873. The Johns Hopkins University, upon opening in 1876, immediately became and remained for fifteen years both the most prestigious and largest American Ph.D. producer. By the mid-1890s, however, Columbia graduate programs conferring the Ph.D. had pulled abreast of Hopkins in annual output and sufficiently even with Hopkins, Harvard, and the University of Chicago, which opened in 1892, in perceived quality of its Ph.D.s for the university to be increasingly able to fill its junior faculty ranks with its own Ph.D.s.[55]

Columbia did appoint a handful of new Ph.D.s from other American universities to junior positions in its faculty, but its overwhelming tendency was to appoint Columbia Ph.D.s from among the 243 (including 8 women) conferred between 1875 and 1900. Of these, 99 went on to academic careers, 38 at Columbia (including Barnard and Teachers College). Of the 38, only 17 had been undergraduates at the College. Hiring our own at late-nineteenth-century Columbia—and since—meant hiring from among Columbia Ph.D.s, who may or may not also have been graduates of Columbia College, rather than, as it meant at Harvard and Yale, hiring graduates of the College who also had Harvard or Yale Ph.D.s. Such discounting of undergraduate origins worked to Columbia's advantage in attracting ambitious graduate students. "To a graduate student coming to Columbia from some other college," a Ph.D. candidate from Bowdoin wrote in 1893, "the most striking characteristic of the student life is the fact that the whole body is not dominated by the undergraduates, that the university is not dwarfed by the college."[56]

Securing an entry position on the Columbia faculty in the early 1890s had become largely a matter of demonstrating sufficient scholarly promise as a Columbia graduate student to attract the attention of senior faculty in one's department. The backing of a single senior faculty member might have been enough to secure an initial appointment. But, after that, the future was uncertain. The odds were also that, as the rank structure became more formalized, the period of uncertainty before receiving a permanent appointment lengthened.

In the launching of academic careers in the late nineteenth century, timing mattered. When a Ph.D. came on the academic market was critical. To do so when there were more faculty openings than qualified applicants was best, and in such cases inside advancement occurred quickly. This situation existed in the mid-1880s at Columbia, when such freshly minted Columbia Ph.D.s as Nicholas Murray Butler (1884) and Edwin R. A. Seligman (1885) came along. Butler's graduate studies consisted of two years spent at Columbia following graduation from the College (1882), reading under the guidance of Archibald Alexander and writing a seventy-five-page dissertation entitled "A Study in the History of Logical Doctrine," since lost. He then used the third year of his graduate fellowship for a postdoctorate year in Germany. In 1885 he returned to Columbia as a fellow and assistant. In 1888 he became an adjunct professor to assist the ailing Alexander. Alexander's resignation in 1889 opened up a professorship to which Butler was appointed, he then being twenty-seven.[57]

A similarly meteoric rise characterized the early Columbia career of E. R. A. Seligman. His three-year sojourn in Germany came between graduating from the College in 1879 and returning in 1882 to commence Ph.D. studies. These studies completed in 1885, with submission of a dissertation entitled "Medieval Guilds in England," he became an adjunct professor in 1886 and in 1891 the first Columbia professor to hold a chair in economics. He was then thirty and, thanks to his family's banking interests, independently wealthy. He was also Jewish, though in a residual more than an active way. Over the next three decades of his career, he became one of the two or three leading American academic economists, a respected American participant in the international economics community, and the prototype of the economist as expert witness, especially in matters relating to taxation.[58]

By the early 1890s the inside road to Columbia professordom had lengthened appreciably, as in the cases of the mathematician Thomas S. Fiske (CC 1885) and the historian Herbert Levi Osgood. Fiske's first faculty appointment was as an assistant, a rank he held throughout his three years as a graduate student. After completing his Ph.D. in 1888, he became a tutor. Three years later he was advanced to Instructor and three years after that to adjunct professor. In 1897 he was made professor of mathematics, this after twelve years of teaching and at the relatively advanced age of thirty-five.[59]

Osgood's route was even more circuitous. He came to Columbia for graduate studies after having graduated from Amherst nearly a decade earlier (1877). He had started graduate studies at the University of Berlin but was obliged for economic reasons to return to his native New England to teach school. A fellowship brought him to Columbia in 1887 where, now married and without private means, he continued to teach high school. Only when his dissertation was completed, in 1889, did he begin his ascent up the Columbia academic ladder, and not until 1896, at age forty-three, did he become a full professor.[60]

Several early Columbia Ph.D.s became junior faculty elsewhere and then went on to distinguished academic careers far removed from Columbia. Among some of the more prominent examples are the Chicago political scientist Charles E. Merriam (CU Ph.D. 1900), the Chicago and later the California Institute of Technology physicist and Nobel Prize winner Robert A. Millikan (CU Ph.D. 1895), the Harvard Semiticist William Popper (CC 1896, Ph.D. 1899), the Harvard economist William Z. Ripley (CU Ph.D. 1893), and the Yale astronomer Frank Schlesinger (CU Ph.D. 1898). Columbia's graduate programs in the 1890s had become excellent places to begin academic careers, if not necessarily Columbia academic careers.[61]

While continuing to depend heavily on its own Ph.D.s to fill the junior ranks, Columbia in the 1890s turned increasingly to other universities and colleges to fill senior positions. By then, the expectation had become, and has remained so since, that most junior members of the faculty would not be promoted but have to find professorships and pursue careers elsewhere. Moving on simply became the normal career trajectory for junior faculty at Columbia. In the seller's market for credentialed academics that existed in the 1890s and early 1900s, where such faculty experienced little difficulty finding permanent places elsewhere, this came to be accepted as a fact of professional life.[62]

The regularity with which Columbia turned to outsiders to fill gaps in its faculty ranks in the 1890s marked a turning point in the history of the Columbia faculty and in the academic profession. Henceforth, at the leading universities and especially at Columbia, academic careers would be less institutionally grounded than they would be reputationally powered. To that extent, those coming from the outside often enjoyed a reputational edge over those who had always been where they were. Columbia necessarily turned to outsiders when embarking on the development of a field not previously represented on its faculty. Sometimes this was a field—geology, for example—that nineteenth-century Columbia had neglected but that other institutions, academic and governmental, had taken the lead in developing. More often, however, it was a field just then being recognized by leading universities as distinct from its antecedents and therefore meriting more focused study.

Biology was an instance of a field in which Columbia made a belated entry. Back in the 1830s the unemployed botanist Asa Gray was in New York looking for work and would have gladly taken a job at Columbia. But Columbia's loss proved Harvard's gain when Gray went there in 1842 and on to a distinguished career as a world-class botanist and American popularizer of Darwinian evolution. Yet five decades later, at the time of Gray's death in 1888, Columbia still was without a professorial presence in any of the biological sciences. In 1881 a proposal made by President Barnard and Trustee Agnew to appoint a botanist in the School of Mines had been rejected. Six years later, Nathaniel L. Britton, after teaching as an adjunct since 1879, was finally appointed an instructor in botany.[63]

The situation changed dramatically in 1891, when two outside faculty appointments began a process that within fifteen years would catapult Columbia into being the world's leading research center and training ground in genetics. Henry Fairfield Osborn and Edmund B. Wilson were both in their midthirties when they came to Columbia that year, and both would live out their distinguished scientific careers in New York City, Wilson at Columbia and Osborn first at Columbia and after 1908 as head of the American Museum of Natural History. Osborn came from wealthy, well-connected New York City circumstances (he was the nephew of J. P. Morgan), and his move from Princeton in 1891, where he had taught since 1880, to establish a biology department at Columbia and take a joint appointment at the American Museum of Natural History was a homecoming of sorts.[64]

For Wilson, a midwesterner raised in modest circumstances, Columbia represented the sixth and last stop on an academic journey that had included three years as an undergraduate at Yale (Ph.B., 1878) and another three of graduate studies at Hopkins (Ph.D., 1881), followed by brief teaching stints at Williams (1881–83) and MIT (1884–85), before landing a professorship at Bryn Mawr College (1885–91). But at Bryn Mawr, where his heavy teaching schedule kept him from his research in the structure of cells, he was on the lookout. When a Columbia offer held out the prospect of his getting on with his work, he seized it. Four years after his arrival, he published his first major book, *The Cell in Development and Inheritance* (1896). He thereafter became recognized as one of the most important cytologists of the twentieth century. Even more than Osborn, who later became involved in eugenics and a critic of unrestricted immigration, it was Wilson who transformed Columbia from a backwater in the biological sciences into a leading center for research and graduate training a decade before the arrival in 1904 of another distinguished scientific outsider, Thomas Hunt Morgan, who would make it for the first quarter of the twentieth century the country's preeminent center for biological research.[65]

The field of psychology developed at Columbia as an offshoot of philosophy but a half generation after it did so at Harvard and Johns Hopkins. Butler's mentor in philosophy, Archibald Alexander, did double duty in the 1880s as Columbia's lone teacher of psychology. Needless to say, the psychology Alexander taught was not scientific in the sense either that it was based on experimental work or that it was quantitative. With Alexander's resignation in 1889, the situation quickly changed.

The discipline we recognize today as psychology came to Columbia in 1891 from the University of Pennsylvania in the person of James McKeen Cattell (1860–1944). Like Osborn, Cattell came from a family of social distinction and economic means. His father was president of Lafayette College, from which young Cattell graduated in 1880. He then spent two years studying in Germany, where his initial interest in philosophy shifted to scientific psychology under the influence of Wilhelm Wundt at Leipzig. A year's fellowship at Johns Hopkins followed, but when it was not renewed Cattell went back to Leipzig and Wundt, with whom he completed his doctorate in 1886. By then, he had become well regarded among English social scientists such as Francis Galton and Alexander Bain. After marrying in 1888, he returned to the United States to take up a short-term appointment at Bryn Mawr and then another at the University of Pennsylvania, where he filled the first American professorship wholly in psychology. It was at Penn that he developed an interest and conducted experiments in the measurement of behavior. In 1891 he was invited to Columbia.[66]

Cattell was neither the effective founder of academic psychology in America (that distinction more properly belongs to Harvard's William James or Hopkins's and Clark's G. Stanley Hall) nor its influential theorist (again, the nod properly goes to James). His distinctions as a psychologist was two part: During his twenty-six years at Columbia, he trained more psychologists than anyone else, including a dozen or so who became leading psychologists of the next generation, among them his subsequent Columbia colleagues Robert S. Woodworth (CU Ph.D. 1899) and Edward L. Thorndike (CU Ph.D. 1898); he also helped effect the marked statistical turn in psychology, both by his own and his students' quantitative research in the measurement of mental capacities and by featuring the statistically based research of other psychologists in the many journals that he founded and edited, such as the *Psychological Review* (1894–1907), *Science* (1894–1932), and *Popular Science Monthly* (1900–1917).

Although Cattell's own research had ceased by 1905, he thereafter remained influential in his field by virtue of the eminence of his students and his position as an editor. When he came in 1891, Columbia had no standing in the emerging field of psychology; when he left in 1917, the Department of Psychology, including its members on the Barnard and Teachers College faculties, contained the most distinguished collection of psychologists in the country.[67]

Among Cattell's other contributions to Columbia was his urging in 1896 that Franz Boas be brought in to establish the university's presence in another new field, anthropology. In both England and the United States, anthropology had remained a primarily nonacademic pursuit through most of the nineteenth century. While the earlier work of E. B. Tyler and Sir Henry Maine in England and Henry Lewis Morgan in the United States represent the scholarly beginnings of the field, it first appeared at Columbia in 1893, when Dr. Livingston Farrand (his "Dr." was in medicine) taught an introductory course in anthropology under the auspices of the School of Philosophy.[68]

Boas was born, raised, and trained in Germany. Having begun as a physicist, he moved his scholarly focus first to physical geography and then to anthropology. Even before migrating to the United States in 1888, when he took a teaching position at Clark University and from which four years later he received the first American Ph.D. in anthropology, he had conducted extensive fieldwork in the Pacific Northwest. After leaving Clark in 1892, he became involved first with the World's Columbian Exposition in Chicago in 1892 and a year later with the founding of Field Museum there. Two years later, he left the Field Museum to become a curator at the American Museum of Natural History and in 1896 accepted an appointment at Columbia as a lecturer in physical anthropology. In 1896 he became Columbia's first professor of anthropology. During the ensuing four decades of Boas's involvement with Columbia (for a twelve-year period after World War I, he located himself primarily at Barnard), the university became the leading center of anthropological studies in America, its principal competition coming from Berkeley, where the Boas-trained Alfred Kroeber was the leading light. Before his retirement in 1936, Boas sponsored some forty dissertations in anthropology, including those of most of the leading women in the field, among them Ruth Benedict (CU Ph.D. 1924) and Margaret Mead (BC 1924; CU Ph.D. 1929).[69]

Present at the Creation

Running through these professional profiles is the inference that the on-campus standing of a faculty member was influenced, if not determined by, his off-campus reputation. Some Columbia faculty in the 1890s and since have been reckoned as forces in the university for their political skills, administrative talents, links to trustees and benefactors, or agreeable temperament. But from the Low presidency onward, even much of one's local standing was derived from one's reputation among peers, especially those located at other leading universities. Columbia was not alone in having external evaluations by fellow academics outweigh those of trustees, students, or alumni in establishing the relative worth of a given faculty member; this was part of what becoming a university involved. What was unusual about Columbia in the 1890s was how fully its faculty participated in creating the mechanisms through which these evaluations were made—and how accepting the trustees were of them.

In the 1890s the scholarly reputations of faculty at Columbia were built primarily on the positive reception by peers of the published results of their research and through their participation in the organizational affairs of their disciplinary specialties. Thus the development of disciplinary societies, scholarly journals, and university presses was crucial to the process by which reputations were made. Up until the 1870s, however, Columbia faculty had been conspicuously absent from the early forerunners of such undertakings. For example, of the three principal scholarly societies formed before the Civil War—the American Oriental Society (1843), the American Association for the Advancement of Science (1848), and the American Social Science Association (1861)—Columbia faculty played almost no role in their founding or early operations.[70]

Here, too, however, the Barnard presidency represents a turning point at Columbia. Barnard himself was an active member of the AAAS and its past president. As noted earlier, the American Chemical Society came into existence in 1876 at the urging and through the personal efforts of Columbia's Charles Frederick Chandler. Ten years later, the founding meeting of the Modern Language Association also took place at Columbia. The young E. R. A. Seligman played an important role in the founding of the American Economics Association in 1885 and an even more instrumental role five years later in directing it away from its initial reformist (some said populist) agenda and transforming it into a thoroughly professional organization. He was in the 1890s joined in this second effort by his Columbia/Barnard colleague John Bates Clark. The historian William A. Dunning played a similar role in the early doings of the American Historical Association after its founding in 1884, Cattell in the organization of the American Psychological Association in 1892, Boas in the American Anthropological Association in 1902, and Giddings in the American Sociological Association in 1905. All these Columbia professors became presidents of their respective scholarly associations.[71]

The first modern scholarly journal to appear under Columbia auspices and editorship (not counting Samuel Mitchill's *Medical Repository* in 1801) was Chandler's *Chemical News* in 1876. It was followed by the *School of Mines Quarterly* (1881). Next came the *Political Science Quarterly*, which began publication in 1886 under the editorship of E. R. A. Seligman. Butler's *Educational Review* began in 1891, followed by the *Physical Review* (1893), *Columbia University Germanic Studies* (1899), *Columbia University Contributions to Oriental History and Philology Series* (1901), *Columbia University Studies in Romance Philology and Literature* (1901), the *Columbia Law Review* (1901), and the *Journal of Philosophy, Psychology, and Scientific Method* (1904), later the *Journal of Philosophy*.[72]

In these publications regularly appeared articles by Columbia faculty members, reviews of their books and published research, and reviews by them of the books and published research of colleagues elsewhere. By 1900, along with Harvard, Chicago, and Johns Hopkins, Columbia provided a home for most of the campus-based journals of any scholarly significance. By then, too, the Columbia University Press was up and running, having been founded in 1893 and already publishing most of the monograph-length dissertations produced by Columbia Ph.D.s. Its charge was to "promote the study of economic, historical, literary, scientific and other subjects; and to promote and encourage the publication of literary works embodying original research in such subjects." The *Columbia University Quarterly* was founded in 1898, to inform a more general audience of the doings on Morningside Heights. There were to be no scholarly lights kept under bushel baskets at turn-of-the-century Columbia.[73]

Just as scholarly reputations of individual faculty came to matter much more than they had, so did the scholarly reputations of individual departments at a given university figure into its overall reputation. And here again, no late-nineteenth-century American university was more attentive to its scholarly reputation than Columbia. Having come from far back in the collegiate pack, it displayed all the characteristics of what came to be called in the era after World War II the prototypical university on the make, not least of which was an incessant curiosity about the competition. As recently as 1876, the Columbia faculty, or so Burgess found on joining their company, "did not know, or care to know, what any other college in the United States was doing." Yet by the late 1890s Columbia's faculty and its graduate and professional students had become preoccupied with the university's relative ranking. Today, when Columbia officials decry the role such rankings as those of *US News and World Report* play in American higher education, it is perhaps chastening to remember that a century earlier Columbia lived and thrived on such rankings. It also bears remembering that it was a Columbia faculty member, James McKeen Cattell, who in 1906 offered the first comprehensive ranking of "American Men of Science" that aspired to statistical validity. When grouped by institutions training and employing America's leading scientists, Columbia, he reported, was second and closing fast.[74]

Ranking was not exclusively a faculty preoccupation. In 1900–1901 the Education Committee of the Columbia trustees devoted several meetings to a systematic review of the relative standing of each of the university's major arts and sciences departments. It did so with the clear intention of using the results to determine where to put additional resources to strengthen Columbia's overall standing among the country's leading universities. Given that in the 1890s there were only a half-dozen universities with departments that could compete with Columbia's and the fact that even the largest of these seldom contained more than a half-dozen senior faculty, the migration of one star to or from Columbia could make a crucial difference. In mathematics, for example, the recently hired instructor, Thomas S. Fiske, could report to President Low that Columbia's current place in the pecking order—around fifth—could be instantly advanced by three or four positions by the raiding of Professor X from Y.[75]

Competition at the upper reaches of American academe in the 1890s increasingly turned on hiring away from other universities those faculty who were nationally recognized as leaders in their fields. Thus nothing so clearly marked Columbia as a comer than its success in recruiting such already nationally known scholars as James McKeen Cattell and James Harvey Robinson from Pennsylvania, Henry Field Osborn and Franklin Giddings (and later Thomas Hunt Morgan) from Bryn Mawr, John Bates Clark from Amherst, Frank N. Cole from Michigan. But recruiting away faculty from elsewhere was only half the competition; there was also the challenge of fending off the competition when they came after Columbia's own faculty. While such raids represented a considerable challenge to Columbia's administrators, they were welcomed by the targeted faculty. How better to prove one's local standing than for another university to come bidding for one's services? And what better confirmation of a university's standing than for it to succeed in holding just such a star?

The Wooing of William A. Dunning

The historian William Archibald Dunning's slow advance through the Columbia faculty ranks was a source of considerable consternation to him in 1899, thirteen years after joining the faculty. A graduate of the College (1881) and recipient of one of the first Columbia Ph.D.s (1885), in history—his dissertation was called "The Constitution in the Civil War and Reconstruction," and it was completed under Burgess—he began teaching at Columbia in 1885 as a tutor. Three years later, he was promoted to instructor and, three years after that, to adjunct professor. At that level he remained eight years later, when he wrote to Low to complain about his thirty-five-hundred-dollar salary and to remind the president that his promotion to full professor had been for several years "relentlessly opposed" by Drisler and others who correctly viewed him as too closely aligned with Burgess in favor of making Columbia over into a university. "The University is now a fact," he lamented, "but I am still suffering for having been connected with a department that wanted it." Low responded promptly, but only to say that the university's current deficit was thirty thousand dollars and nothing could be done that year.[76]

Four years without a raise later, in the summer of 1903, Dunning, in a letter to President Butler, was still complaining about the deleterious consequences for him of the "Drisler regime," but now in the context of an offer he had just received from Johns Hopkins, inviting him to succeed the retiring Herbert Baxter Adams as the senior man in American history there. This was no small honor, because it was at Hopkins that American history first became a serious subject for university study, and it was Adams who had made it so. He numbered among his more illustrious Ph.D. students Woodrow Wilson and Frederick Jackson Turner. More to the point, Hopkins was offering Dunning "salary and dignity" not currently his at Columbia. And, anyway, this native of Plainfield, New Jersey, allowed, Baltimore was probably a better place for him to be in light of his interest in southern history. He awaited Columbia's response.[77]

Butler promptly wrote back acknowledging Dunning's letter "concerning the Hopkins call" and asked for time to formulate a university response. Meanwhile, several of Dunning's Columbia colleagues in the Faculty of Political Science weighed in on his behalf, among them Richmond Mayo-Smith and the chairman of the history department, William M. Sloane, who pointed out that "it is Dunning who has worked up the fine southern constituency of graduate students which we now have." Others declared Dunning one of three first-rank U.S. history professors currently teaching at American universities, along with Andrew C. McLaughlin at Chicago and Turner at Wisconsin (soon off to Harvard), and that "his going from Columbia to Johns Hopkins at this time would be construed unfavorably to our interests." Butler, initially cool to Dunning's demands, now warmed to the challenge and informed the chair of the trustees' Committee on Academics, Francis S. Bangs, that Columbia must not lose him. Moreover, Butler reported, Dunning "would likely stay with $5000 retroactive to July."[78]

On October 6, 1903, President Butler wrote to Dunning that his salary had been retroactively increased to five thousand dollars by an action "unprece-dented in the history of the Board." Assurances were also made on the score of "dignity," when the next year Dunning was appointed as the inaugural holder of the Francis Lieber Professorship of History. Dunning stayed at Columbia another fifteen years, became president of the American Historical Association in 1913, and continued to sponsor more dissertations in American history than any two professors elsewhere, albeit many of them advancing a critical interpretation of Reconstruction history that has since been discredited by, among others, subsequent Columbia historians Eric L. McKitrick and Eric Foner.[79]

Three notes on Dunning's wooing: First, the discussions appear to have been carried on free of calls on him by Butler or colleagues to factor into his calculations his personal ties to Columbia, which at the time stretched back twenty-four years as student and faculty member. What Dunning confronted, and what Columbia's president, trustees and other senior faculty understood him to be confronting, was a career judgment that properly transcended local loyalties.

It is also interesting to note the risk Dunning took in communicating the Hopkins offer to Butler. Had Columbia not responded as it did, it would have behooved Dunning to go to Baltimore, a prospect that the club-going New Yorker must have regarded with a degree of trepidation. Waving offers around was not without its risks. Butler and his deans might have concluded that "our interests" were best served in letting him go.

Finally, one is struck by how little has changed in the century since. Doing what Dunning did in 1904 has become something of a post-tenure rite of passage for Columbia's most sought-after faculty. Much the same scenario had earlier been played out when Seligman received an offer from Harvard in 1890, which prompted Burgess to urge Low to "make his position here as gratifying as that to which he has been invited." For good measure, Burgess upped the ante: "I have long known it to be a purpose of President E[liot] to disrupt, if possible, our School of Political Science—and it must be foiled at the outset. If Seligman goes, so too Osgood and Monroe Smith." When the biologists Henry Hunt Morgan and E. B. Wilson were approached in 1907, the Trustees responded with assurances that they should "suffer no financial or other disadvantages from declining the proffered professorships elsewhere." With similar celerity, the trustees beat back offers from Virginia to John Bassett Moore, Berkeley for Franz Boas, and Chicago for the mathematician Edward Kasner. While some trustee grumbling attended these early negotiations, they quickly came to be generally accepted as the cost one paid for maintaining a world-class faculty.[80]

Matching offers inevitably led to gaps in the compensation between sought-after faculty and faculty without outside offers, which in turn produced some griping. Yet this was the route that Columbia set for itself when it determined to be a university second to none in the United States. Here, again, the wonder of it a century later is how unequivocal and how unattended by second thoughts of senior faculty, trustees, students, or presidents that determination was.

The Move to Morningside

While the Columbia faculty were reconfiguring the university's power arrangements more to their liking, principally by making their appointments every bit as self-perpetuating as the trustees', the trustees were usefully occupied elsewhere. It was to them that fell the responsibility for moving the Columbia campus from Forty-ninth Street to the Bloomingdale Asylum site on what came to be called Morningside Heights. This division of labor seems to be very much what Low had in mind when he informed his fellow trustees that "as Columbia grows more and more complex, it is certain that the Trustees will have to leave the educational policy of the College more and more in the hands of the educators. This, I think, is a tendency not to be deprecated but rather encouraged." The trustees, meanwhile, set themselves to securing and enhancing the material well-being of the university.[81]

The move to Morningside was in an obvious sense a physical and architectural undertaking of immense proportions, much larger than any Columbia had engaged in before or has since. It was also at least the occasion, if not the cause, of the trustees' moving away from their direct involvement with both the curriculum and faculty hiring, now the acknowledged domain of the faculty. It also occasioned their completely handing over the day-to-day operations of the university to the president, his deans, and the administrative staff. Not that the trustees would never again directly involve themselves in curricular matters, faculty appointments, or operational details: subsequently they would, with mixed results. It is, however, reasonable to argue that the primary concerns of the Columbia trustees of today—the plant and the endowment—became their focus in the 1890s. Again it was Low who showed the way.

For all its so-called temporary character, the eighty-five-thousand-square-feet Forty-ninth Street campus by the early 1890s contained an impressive array of buildings. They included, in order of their construction, the twenty-two-room President's House (1858); a four-storied L-shaped building that wrapped around the northeast corner of the site that was home to the School of Mines (1874, 1880, 1884); Hamilton Hall (1879–80), which fronted on Madison Avenue and provided the first dormitory accommodations the College had offered since the 1790s; a six-story library (1881–83) at midblock on Forty-ninth Street that also housed the Law School; and a chapel, which backed onto Fiftieth Street. Most were designed by the architect Charles Coolidge Haight, a nephew of the trustee Rev. Benjamin I. Haight (1843–79), and all were in the approved Collegiate Gothic style of the day.[82]

President Barnard's constantly berating the trustees in the early 1870s for their unwillingness to invest in the site deserves some credit for their eventually doing so. But a more compelling factor seems to have been that all the construction undertaken on the Forty-ninth Street campus in the 1870s and 1880s was paid for with money in the bank. That is to say, Columbia's second campus was built without recourse on the part of the trustees to fund-raising or borrowing. The longtime chairman of the trustees, Hamilton Fish, preferred it that way. As George Templeton Strong recorded the prevailing trustee view on the subject in 1869, "It is irregular for any of its members or committees or for anybody else to take the liberty of asking anybody to buy a valuable collection and give it to the College, without first obtaining leave of the trustees. How the governors of every other college in the country would grin at the suggestion of such a rule."[83]

By Low's installation in 1890, it was generally conceded that the Forty-ninth Street campus would not accommodate any more construction. Moreover, many of its original deficiencies, including the noise and soot emanating from the New York Central tracks running into Grand Central Station that skirted the Park Avenue side of the campus, had only worsened with time and surrounding development. Some trustees still held the thought that additional space might be economically secured adjacent to the current campus, and others to the older and even more economical idea of moving Columbia out of the city. But Low was committed to finding Columbia a larger campus within the city, and this meant coming up with new money to do so. "I hope it will not escape the notice of any in the city who are working to associate their names with some conspicuous gift to the cause of education," he stated in his second annual report, "that right here in New York there is a need for a great building to enlarge the faculties of Columbia in the great career which is certainly opening before her."[84]

In May 1891, a special trustees' committee on site was created. Its members included the three richest members of the board, William C. Schermerhorn, Cornelius Vanderbilt, and Low, along with two other of its more effective members, George L. Rives and the Reverend Morgan Dix, who, as rector of Trinity Church, oversaw one of the city's largest landholdings. Quickly discarding the options of staying at Forty-ninth Street, dispersing throughout the city, or moving to the country, the committee sought a new site that would "permit the university to retain its essential character as a university in the heart of the city of New York." Even before the committee's report had been printed in December 1891, that site was identified. John B. Pine, newly elected clerk of the board, informed the committee in August 1891 of the pending sale by New York Hospital of the grounds of the Bloomingdale Asylum up on 116th Street and the Boulevard, later Broadway. Within days, Columbia had secured an option to buy two-thirds of the available site for $2 million and launched a fund-raising campaign for that $2 million plus an estimated $4 million more for buildings.[85]

There was at this time no tradition of active fund-raising on the part of Columbia trustees and even less expectation that they themselves would contribute funds. Nor was there a tradition of alumni giving. As of 1890 the two largest benefactions to Columbia, the twenty-thousand-dollar bequest from Frederick Gebhard in 1843 to endow a chair in German and eighty thousand dollars from F. A. P. Barnard's estate in 1889 for science fellowships, had both come from nonalumni. The bequest that year of one hundred thousand dollars from the estate of Charles Da Costa (CC 1855, trustee 1886–90) for a professorship in biology was the first sizable gift to Columbia from either a graduate or a trustee.[86]

Annual gifts in the $5,000 to $10,000 range for specific Columbia undertakings beginning in the late 1880s from the Seligman and Schermerhorn families may have heralded the change in alumni and trustee giving that followed. Even so, the largest benefaction in hand at the time of the launching of the fund-raising campaign in 1892 was a $200,000 bequest from Daniel B. Fayerweather, who had never attended Columbia and whose gift was one of several he provided for in his will to various colleges and New York institutions. What really broke new ground was the eighteen solicited gifts totaling $427,150 made in 1892 for the purchase of the Morningside site. They ranged from two gifts of $100,000 each from J. P. Morgan and Cornelius Vanderbilt, plus a third for the same amount from William C. Schermerhorn, to $150 from a member of the class of 1882, along with those from fifteen other contributors, among them six Columbia alumni, including one for $5,000 from President Low.[87]

President Low's father, A. A. Low, contributed another $15,000 to the 1892 fund. But it was his death the following year and his son's decision to use $1 million of his father's $10 million estate to erect in his honor the first building commissioned for the Morningside site that marked a turning point in the history of the Columbia trustees and in Columbia giving. When Low announced his gift at the board meeting on May 6, 1895, Chairman William Schermerhorn promptly followed it up with another gift of $450,000 of his own for a building for the natural sciences. There followed building-naming gifts from Samuel P. Avery, William E. Dodge, the Havemeyer family, and Adolph Lewisohn, not all Columbia graduates or trustees or graduates, to be sure, but all aware that Columbians figured prominently among the big givers.[88]

What Low and Schermerhorn put into local practice was the since-tested fund-raising truism that those who do the asking should already have done some of the heavy giving. However slow to catch on to what the Columbia architectural historian Barry Bergdoll called "the politics of philanthropic speculation," Columbia's board of trustees quickly became adept practitioners. By Low's resignation in 1902, the Morningside campus consisted of seven impressive buildings all arrayed in keeping with the architectural vision of Columbia's architects Charles Follen McKim and Stanford White. And more to the point here, all had either been fully paid for or were being carried by a $3 million mortgage, with annual payments of $120,000. The trustees had built a campus for Columbia worthy of its highest aspirations, without saddling it with a debt equally for the ages. When William James visited Columbia in 1907, coming up from the Harvard Club on the recently opened "magnificent space-devouring" IRT subway, he wrote to his brother Henry James, who had many cross things to say of New York in his just-published *American Scenes*, that the Columbia scene represented "the high tide of my existence, so far as *energizing and being 'recognized'* were concerned."[89]

In the City of New York

In 1883 chairman of the board of trustees Hamilton Fish, not long back from Washington and his labors as Grant's secretary of state, took it upon himself to upbraid the citizens of New York City for failing to support Columbia College. While Harvard, Yale, and Princeton enjoyed generous support from many of New York's wealthiest families, he complained, "Columbia is lost sight of." To this lament, E. L. Godkin, the publisher of the *Nation*, responded that Columbia had only itself to blame for this state of affairs. He went on to question Fish's assumption that Columbia was a "city college." For it to be so, Godkin said, it must "endeavor to increase in every way possible the number of points at which it can come into contact with the life . . . of the city."[90]

Godkin, a Scot who had come to New York in 1856 at age twenty-five and who, as editor of the *Nation*, had since become a cultural spokesman for the city's educated class, was not the first New Yorker to pose this question to Columbia. William Livingston had when he voiced doubts in 1753 about whether King's College intended to serve any of the needs of the city's non-Anglican majority. The founders of New York University in 1830 were sufficiently skeptical about Columbia's interest in serving the city's "middling classes" that they created NYU for that explicit purpose. The Irish immigrants participating in the Draft Riots of 1863 gave every indication that their New

York City and Columbia's seldom overlapped. So, too, a century later, did some critics in 1968 fault Columbia for its lack of connectedness with its immediate neighborhood and the larger city. As the urban historian Thomas Bender has nicely put the question, it is whether Columbia University, to be sure "*in* the City of New York," has also always been, or even was, as NYU's founding documents describe it, "*of* the City of New York."[91]

It is a fair and important question and one that any serious history of the university must confront. Yet, as even Bender, who has provided an essentially negative answer, finding Columbia too often turning its back on the city, has acknowledged and amply documented, the decade in which the strongest case can be made for Columbia as *citoyen engagé* and net contributor to the city's civic culture was during the presidency of Seth Low. There was nothing accidental about this. "On the academic side I could be of small service to Columbia," Low acknowledged at the time of his election. "The one thing I think I could do is to bring the College into closer touch with the community; and this happens to be the one thing which especially needs to be done at this time."[92]

Low's civic reengagement project was actually well along at the outset of his presidency, thanks in considerable part to the involvement of the faculty and graduates of the School of Mines in the physical makeover of post–Civil War New York City. Virtually every large late-nineteenth-century municipal project in sanitation, water purification, transportation (including plans for the subway system), civil engineering, and electrification had as its director or lead consultant a Columbian. Professor James F. Kemp was consulting geologist for the Water Board of New York and helped with the construction of the Croton Dam. The merger of P & S with Columbia in 1891 similarly increased the role of Columbians in projects relating to the city's public health and child welfare, although even earlier Charles F. Chandler had been president of the New York City Board of Health. He and fellow Columbia chemist Pierre Ricketts also involved themselves heavily as consultants to several of metropolitan New York's largest chemical plants and in all manner of popular education efforts outside Columbia in their self-assumed roles as civic chemists. An 1895 science Ph.D., Harrison G. Dyar, wrote a dissertation entitled "Certain Bacteria from the Air in New York City," while an 1899 Columbia Ph.D. in biology, Elmer W. Firth, upon submitting his dissertation "Micro-organisms in the Air of Public Buildings," went to work for the New York City Bureau of Sewers.[93]

This same impulse toward civic engagement is reflected among several of Columbia's social science faculty and their graduate students. The city's growing and ever-changing immigrant population, for example, was the subject of several dissertations completed in the 1890s, as were various labor movements.

Ph.D. students in history and public law studied the history of the New York City charter, municipal land ownership, and the provision of public education. Some of these pursuits were combined with direct involvement in the city, as graduates and undergraduates alike participated in various mayoral campaigns (including President Low's in 1897 and 1901) and in the settlement house movement. A few years later, a young Columbia historian, Charles A. Beard, urged the establishment of a professorship in municipal government with the argument: "The duty rests upon all universities to help, but upon us especially. And we have the best laboratory in the United States at hand. By cooperation with other agencies in New York we could become a great school in municipal engineering, combining political and physical sciences."[94]

In these activities, Columbians had Low before them as the personification of civic engagement, albeit of the "best man" variety. In his case, however, it could be argued that, as a nonacademic, he encountered fewer conflicts than others trying to combine a life of civic engagement with an academic career. But right behind Low was the example of Dean Nicholas Murray Butler, whose involvement with efforts to consolidate the city of New York and to overhaul its public education system, as well as his regular attendance at Republican presidential conventions, he had no difficulty squaring with his role as a disinterested academic. This easy interpenetrability would not always exist, either among Columbia professors generally or Butler in particular. But while it lasted, Columbia's claims to being "of the City of New York" were impressively secure.

UNLIKE IN 1897, when the trustees were willing to give Low a leave of absence from the presidency when he unsuccessfully ran for mayor of New York, in 1901 they insisted that he resign should he win. Several weeks before the November election, Low submitted his resignation. Whether it would have been ignored had he lost is not clear. But because he won by a substantial margin, becoming the second mayor of the consolidated city of New York, his tenure as the eleventh president of Columbia was over. He was then only fifty-two years old and in excellent health. One consolation he derived at the time of giving up the job that had fully occupied him for eleven years for a position from which he would be ousted the very next year regarded the matter of his succession. When Nicholas Murray Butler's election as the twelfth president of Columbia University was announced on January 6, 1902, Low allowed himself an uncharacteristic self-congratulatory remark: "It isn't everyone who gets to pick his successor." But then the forty-year-old president-elect Theodore Roosevelt was still referring to admiringly as "Nicholas Miraculous" was virtually everybody's pick.[95]

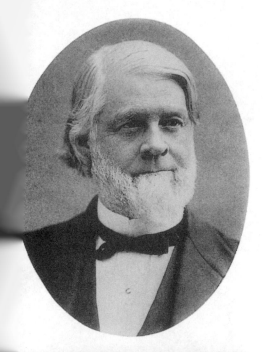

FIGURE 3.1 Theodore William Dwight (1822–92), first dean of Columbia Law School (1858–1891). Photograph.

Source: Julius Goebel Jr., *A History of the School of Law, Columbia University* (New York: Columbia University Press, 1955), opp. 34.

FIGURE 3.2 Charles Frederick Chandler (1836–1925), chemist and first dean of the Columbia School of Mines (1864–1997).

Source: James Kip Finch, *A History of the School of Engineering, Columbia University* (New York: Columbia University Press, 1954), opp. 32, lower right.

FIGURE 3.3 Frederick A. P. Barnard (1809–89), graduate of Yale (1828), scientist, tenth president of Columbia College (1864–89), namesake of Barnard College. Portrait by Eastman Johnson.

Source: Columbia University Archives—Columbiana Collection.

FIGURE 3.4 John W. Burgess (1844–1931), political scientist, Columbia professor (1876–1912), and dean (1880–1912). 1878 sepia-toned photograph.

Source: Columbia University Archives—Columbiana Collection.

FIGURE 3.5 Seth Low (1850–1916), Columbia College graduate (1870), eleventh president of Columbia College/University (1890–1901) and mayor of New York City (1901–3). 1901 photograph.

Source: Columbia University Archives—Columbiana Collection.

FIGURE 3.6 Franz Boas (1858–1942), German-born anthropologist, Columbia professor (1896–1936). Photograph taken in 1890s.

Source: Columbia University Archives—Columbiana Collection.

FIGURE 3.7 Thomas Hunt Morgan (1866–1945), geneticist and professor at Columbia (1904–28), received a Nobel Prize in physiology in 1933 for work done at Columbia, after moving to California Institute of Technology.

Source: California Institute of Technology.

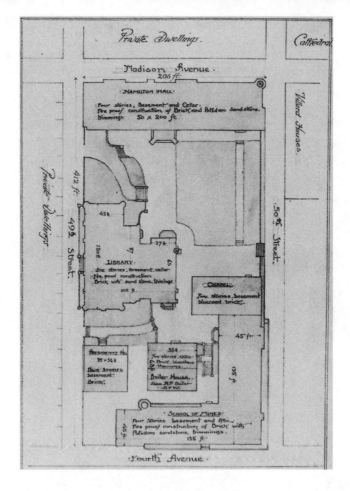

FIGURE 3.8 Site plan for Columbia College campus on Forty-ninth Street and Fourth (Madison) Avenue, 1885.

Source: Barry Bergdoll, *Mastering McKim's Plan: Columbia's First Century on Morningside Heights* (New York: Miriam and Ira D. Wallach Art Gallery, Columbia University, 1997), 26, fig. 12. Original photograph in Columbia University Archives—Columbiana Collection.

FIGURE 3.9 View of upper campus shortly after the opening of the Morningside campus in 1897.

Source: *American Architect and Building News*, 1898, copy in Avery Library, Columbia University, reprinted in Barry Bergdoll, *Mastering McKim's Plan: Columbia's First Century on Morningside Heights* (New York: Miriam and Ira D. Wallach Art Gallery, Columbia University, 1997), 50, fig. 26.

FIGURE 3.10 View of Morningside campus, 1910.

Source: Columbia University Archives—Columbiana Collection.

CHAPTER 7

Bolt to the Top

It is hoped that none of the universities included in this table is entering into competition with its fellows for mere numbers.

Registrar Rudolph Tombo, 1905

We are here to celebrate the growth of the greatest university on earth. Ten years ago there were 3500 students at Columbia. Today there are nearly 8000. We have at last passed Berlin.

Toastmaster remarks, Columbia Alumni Dinner, 1911

"Nicholas Miraculous"

NICHOLAS MURRAY BUTLER was the dominant personality in Columbia University's history in the first half of the twentieth century. He was also the best-known university president of his era and for most of it the academic whose pronouncements on matters domestic and international were assured closest attention in the national and world press.[1]

Some of Butler's conspicuousness can be attributed to Columbia's location in the nation's media capital and some to his own sedulous courting of the press. But some surely also had to do with the assurance, and often arrogance, with which he projected himself into so many different public venues beyond academe over so many years. Who else would, without a scintilla of ironical intent, devote an entire chapter of his autobiography to the subject "On Keeping Out of Public Office"? There seems no purpose in questioning the fact of his personal outsizedness or even his strong claims to being the last of America's "presidential" university presidents. What remains a live question is whether Columbia was the better for his extended imperium.[2]

"An ancestral record," Nicholas Murray Butler wrote of his own, "which abounds in scholarly endeavor, in religious ardor, in patriotic devotion and public service." What the record did not abound in was wealth or Knickerbocker connections. Neither the Butlers nor his family on his mother's side, the Murrays, were New Yorkers. The more credentialed Murrays were New Jersey Presbyterians, whose eighteenth-century American beginnings barely qualified their great-grandson for membership in the Order of Cincinnatus. This was also the side of "religious ardor," grandfather Murray, a graduate of Princeton and ordained minister, having acquired the sobriquet "the Presbyterian Pope of New Jersey."[3]

Butler's father, Henry, came to the United States from England in 1835, at age two. He settled in Paterson as a young man and became a rug manufacturer. In 1860 he married Mary Murray; two years later, the first of their five children who lived into adulthood, Nicholas Murray Butler, was born. As father of a young child, Henry sat out the Civil War. He later became active in New Jersey Republican politics and president of the Paterson school board. In the early 1890s his rug company went bankrupt, and his son became the family's principal provider.[4]

Young "Murray" graduated from Paterson's public high school in 1875, at the age of thirteen. A postgraduate year and two more in private reading at home were needed to prepare for college. Two generations of Murray boys had gone to Williams, but this was not feasible in his case because of cost. Princeton was a possibility, if also a financial reach, but as Butler told it, all thoughts of Nassau Hall ended when he saw Columbia defeat Princeton at the 1877 collegiate regatta in Poughkeepsie. Athletic enthusiasms may have been determinative, but the economy of being able to live with relatives in Brooklyn during his first two years at Columbia also helped.[5]

Butler entered Columbia in the fall of 1878. Some one hundred boys had sat for the required entrance exams, sixty-two were admitted, and fifty eventually graduated. His class had a dozen or so scions of Knickerbocker families (a Livingston, two Parsons, a Rives, a Van Cortlandt). It also had a half-dozen Jews. After his first semester, a combination of competitive scholarships, journalism, and tutoring rendered him financially independent. During his four years, when tuition was $100 in his first two years and $150 in his last two, he managed to save $1,000. Even with his substantial commute during his first two years and multiple jobs, Butler became a class officer, a member of the Peithologian, and editor of *Acta Columbiana*, the forerunner of the *Columbia Spectator*. Too slight for football or crew, he became reasonably adept at cricket. He did not pledge one of the undergraduate Greek fraternities. In sum: a "medium-sized man on campus."[6]

Butler's course of study and his dissatisfaction with it have been described earlier, but whatever its deficiencies the curriculum allowed him to shine. He quickly became a favorite of his teachers, most notably Professor of Philosophy and Psychology Archibald Alexander, for whom he substituted during Alexander's frequent neurasthenic illnesses. He also caught the eye of newly arrived Professor of Political Science John W. Burgess. President Barnard was sufficiently impressed with Butler's promise that in 1881 the seventy-two-year-old president took the eighteen-year junior aside and offered (rather as Dustin

Hoffman's prospective father-in-law did in *The Graduate*) some pointed career advice: "Think Education."[7]

Abandoning thoughts of a legal career, after graduating in 1882 Butler stayed on at Columbia as one of the university's first graduate students in philosophy. A five-hundred-dollar fellowship for three years and a stipend as Alexander's assistant allowed him in two years of resident graduate study to save another thousand. His course of study was largely self-mentored, although officially overseen by the ailing Alexander, who turned over more and more of his own teaching to his ambitious student. In his second year, Butler completed a seventy-two-page dissertation on Kant's philosophy of education, entitled "Outline of History of Logical Doctrine," which he defended at Alexander's bedside in the spring of 1883. As Butler tells it, the dissertation was then deposited in the Columbia library, where it was lost.[8]

Ph.D. in hand, Butler used the third year of his fellowship for study and travel in Europe, which he called "A Voyage of Discovery." There, he attended lectures of two of the University of Berlin's luminaries, the philosopher Edouard Zeller and educational theorist Frederick Paulsen. Otherwise, the year had more the character of an academic *Wanderjahr* than one of intense study. It was also one in which, according to Butler's biographer Michael Rosenthal, he suffered a romantic rebuff by a young American woman that left him emotionally on guard thereafter.[9]

Back in New York, Butler joined the National Educational Association, published an article entitled "The Post-Positive *Et* in Propertius" in the Johns Hopkins–based *American Journal of Philosophy*, and got himself appointed an assistant in philosophy at his alma mater. When Alexander resigned for medical reasons a year later, Butler was promoted to tutor; in 1889 he was promoted to adjunct professor. The next year, he became professor of philosophy, ethics, and psychology. Meanwhile he became the founding editor of the *Educational Review*, the head of the New York College for the Training of Teachers (later, Teachers College), and a presence in New Jersey Republican politics. He was twenty-eight.[10]

At Columbia, Butler aligned himself with Burgess and the pro-university faction then doing battle with the outgunned if not outnumbered College faction. Stopping short of favoring the abolition of the College, he saw it functioning as a three-year vestibule to the university's various professional schools. Drisler and Van Amringe correctly pegged Butler as one of the College Skeptics, a position from which he never really deviated.[11]

In 1887 Butler married the daughter of a New Jersey munitions manufacturer, Susanna Schuyler, acquiring a Knickerbocker connection in the bargain. He had been confirmed into the Episcopal Church in 1883. Their only child, Sarah, was born in 1895.[12]

Upon the creation of the Faculty of Philosophy in late 1890, Butler was promptly elected its first dean by faculty colleagues. Thereafter he continued to work in tandem with Burgess, dean of the Faculty of Political Science, but without becoming identified with some of Burgess's more reactionary positions, such as prohibiting members of his faculty from allowing women in their graduate classes. Butler continued to teach through his twelve years as dean, but his interests and energies were clearly not in the classroom. His favored format was the large formal lecture, such as those he gave to admiring schoolteachers on Saturday mornings in the late 1880s.[13]

Butler was one of those rare academic administrators who never felt the need to assure everybody that he regretted putting teaching and scholarship behind him. His formal graduate training in philosophy at Columbia had been cursory at best and far less than what was available at Hopkins, Harvard, or Yale. He subsequently showed little interest in other academic philosophers or the questions and methods that occupied them. Some issues in the philosophy of education did attract his attention, but these were not the major concerns of contemporary philosophers. Although no one said so, Butler was a philosopher by credential rather than by temperament and commitment. In later years, he could always muster the appropriate sentiments about the nobility of scholarship, but he could also be privately dismissive of faculty who stayed closeted in the library with their narrow scholarly projects and did not venture beyond them. Neither teaching nor scholarship ever engaged him as much as academic finance and the higher arts of university administration and institutional governance.[14]

Young Butler was the very prototype of the early-twentieth-century academic administrator, the master of multitasking a century before the term came into use. Those who encountered him in the 1890s came away impressed with his ability to transform academic ideas into plans and plans into academic realities. The philosopher George Santayana, Butler's almost exact contemporary at Harvard but in all others ways his polar opposite, could have had Butler in mind when in 1892 he described his fellow Ph.D.s: "Many of the young professors . . . are no longer the sort of persons that might as well have been clergymen or schoolmasters: they have rather the type of mind of a doctor, an engineer, or a social reformer; the wide awake young man who can do most things better than old people, and who knows it."[15]

Between 1886 and 1895, by Butler's own count, he was offered the presidency of eight state universities; he was twice offered the Berkeley presidency. "In addition," Butler added modestly, "Governor Stanford did his best to get me to become the first president of Stanford University in 1891." His easy command of financial and organizational matters were such that both Edward Harriman and J. P. Morgan offered him the presidencies of their railroads. Andrew Carnegie attested to his executive prowess by appointing him to several positions in his gift. The trustees did not make the mistake of confusing him with one of the faculty.[16]

Even as a young academic administrator, Butler preferred the company of the nonintellectual wealthy and the politically connected (to Republican pals he was "Murray") to academic friendships. Later, he cultivated foreign dignitaries, not least Kaiser Wilhelm II and Benito Mussolini. Although a member of all four, he much preferred the Bohemian Club to the American Academy of Arts and Sciences and the Century Club to the American Philosophical Society. He was less an intellectual's intellectual than a nonintellectual's intellectual. He not only tolerated his trustees' occasional fits of anti-intellectualism, he sometimes instigated them. In responding to a trustee's complaint about some public indiscretion by one of Columbia's leading scientists, Butler expostulated on our "so-called scientific men. Their littlenesses are so numerous and so conspicuous that they go far to hide their greatness."[17]

Among the chinks in Butler's armor discernible early on was his need to be found among New York's rich, powerful, and socially credentialed. Harlan Fiske Stone later called it his "ubiquitous currying of favor." It was well understood by publishers of biographical directories that Butler expected his entry to be longer than anyone else's, a condition made easier by his courting of honorary degrees and memberships in honorary associations here and abroad. "I am sorry to say that there are certain Americans who seem to be wholly unable to withstand contact with royalty," Theodore Roosevelt wrote in 1915, "and I know probably a dozen men of some little prominence who have been profoundly affected by meeting the German Emperor and having him be courteous to them. Nicholas Murray Butler is a striking example. Of course, in this matter he is much more royalist than the King himself."[18]

For evidence of Butler the notorious namedropper, his autobiography serves: "It is literally true, I think, that beginning with Mr. Gladstone, Prince Bismarck, Cardinal Newman and Pope Leo XIII, it has been my happy fortune to meet, to talk with and often to know in warm friendship almost every man of light and leading who has lived in the world during the past half century."[19]

Evidence of this need to signify among "men of light and leading" was a series of attachments with older and powerful men, among them F. A. P. Barnard, John W. Burgess, Seth Low, Theodore Roosevelt, Andrew Carnegie, Elihu Root, and Trustee William Barclay Parsons. (In later life, he became enamored of the self-made and culturally aspiring founder of IBM, Thomas J. Watson.) Some of these relationships, like the one with Burgess, survived disagreements and endured, but others, like that with Roosevelt, which began during TR's governorship of New York when "NMB" became "one of my right-hand men," broke up in mutual acrimony a decade later. "I never knew a man," TR wrote of Butler in 1910, "so completely belie the promise of his youth and middle age." Some who knew him at Columbia, like Stone and Trustee George Rives and Nobel Laureate Harold Urey, never trusted him, while others who did, like Low, later regretted doing so.[20]

The Low estrangement reflects poorly on Butler. Unlike in 1897, when the trustees were willing to give Low a leave of absence from the presidency when he unsuccessfully ran for mayor of New York, in 1901 they insisted that he resign should he win. There is some suggestion that Butler, with his standing offers elsewhere, pressured the trustees to do this. Low stayed on the board until 1912, when the last of several disagreements (this one over making St. Paul's Chapel available for Jewish events) led him to resign. By Low's death in 1916, he and his successor had long since stopped talking to each other.[21]

Yet Butler's election was not yet the done deal he and the trustees later implied. On November 11, 1901, four weeks after a trustee committee on nomination had been appointed, Chairman George Rives proposed to the committee a president/provost arrangement similar to that of President Harris and Provost Mason back in 1810, with Butler as provost and himself as president. When this scheme was presented to the entire board, Low objected to the idea as "entirely impracticable," and Rives dropped it, but only after voicing his reservations about "My Dear Butler."[22]

On December 30, 1901, the Education Committee unanimously endorsed the recommendation of the Nomination Committee of the then thirty-nine-year old Nicholas Murray Butler as the university's twelfth president. A week later the board did likewise, and, because Low was staying on the board, Trustee Frederick Coudert Sr. vacated his own seat for the incoming president. The formal installation on April 19, 1902, was attended by the president of the United States, Theodore Roosevelt (CU Law 1880–81), New York governor Benjamin Odell, the presidents of all the major universities, and three thousand other invited guests. Extending his personal congratulations and those of Yale, President Arthur T. Hadley, noting the relative youth of Columbia's new president and the newness of its five-year-old campus, placed the 148-year-old institution squarely "on the morningside of life."[23]

The Most Ideal Body Known to Civilization

One part of his job where Butler began at a relative disadvantage to his predecessor was dealing with the trustees. Whereas Low entered the presidency after a decade's service on the board, possessed social credentials fully equal to those of other board members, and was richer to boot, Butler had neither personal experience as a trustee, or the social standing that commanded the respect of old Knickerbockers, or money.[24]

As with so much else in his long presidency, Butler's relationship with his trustees went through three distinct phases. During the first ("Early Butler"), which covered the first fifteen years of his presidency, he proceeded cautiously lest he give offense to trustees who were not about to delegate their ultimate responsibility for the welfare of the university to its chief administrative officer. One should not read back into the outset of Butler's presidency either the influence over the trustees that he acquired midway through his presidency ("Middle Butler") or the dominance he exploited in his last years ("Late Butler") to such unfortunate effect for Columbia.

The twenty-three trustees Butler inherited were easily the most distinguished collection ever to have served Columbia. They included an impressive mixture of the city's Knickerbocker elite and its professional leadership. They were experienced as well, with an average tenure of more than fifteen years. The longest-serving member, William C. Schermerhorn (CC 1840), had been on the board since 1860 and chairman since 1887. Only two years junior to him in service was the Reverend Morgan Dix (CC 1848), the rector of Trinity Church. Ten members had been elected during the Barnard presidency, and eleven during Low's. All were older than Butler, all but two by more than a decade.[25]

Sixteen of the trustees were professional men—lawyers (nine), ministers (four), physicians (two), and an engineer. The other seven were businessmen, involved in shipping, railroads, real estate, and manufacturing. Many, like Seth Low, Gerard Beekman, and the Schermerhorn brothers, William and Frederick, came from old New York money, as did the banker John Crosby Brown, the manufacturer Abram Hewitt, the lawyer George Rives, and the engineer William Barclay Parsons. Some combined inherited wealth with more made on their own, while others, such as the lawyer W. Bayard Cutting, had more social standing than money. The only self-made men of moderate means were the four ministers.[26]

The trustees were overwhelmingly mainline Protestants, either Episcopalian (fourteen), Dutch Reformed (two), or Presbyterian (three). With the resignation of Frederick Coudert Sr. (to provide a seat for Butler), the board went without a Catholic member until the election of his son, Frederick Coudert Jr. (CC 1890; Ph.D. 1894), in 1912. In 1902 it had been eighty-seven years since the board had its first Jewish member; it would be another twenty-six before it would have its second. All but one of the trustees appeared in the *New York Social Register*; seventeen were members of the Century Club. Several were members of genealogical societies that required proof of American ancestry dating back, in the case of the Holland Society, to the seventeenth century.[27]

Butler's inherited board was more heavily dominated by Columbia graduates than earlier or later boards. All but three had either attended Columbia College (eighteen) or one of the professional schools (two), while ten attended both. Two of the non-Columbians were clergymen with informal ex officio seats, and the third, the realtor Hermann Cammann, was the only trustee not to have gone to college.[28]

In sum, the board had no reason to defer to their new president on social grounds. And while not unmindful of Butler's standing in the world of higher learning, the trustees were hardly in awe of him on that account. Those most clearly immune to presidential deference included his chief promoter for the presidency, Seth Low, and the recently elected chairman of the board. Just eight months into Butler's presidency, William Schermerhorn died, and the lawyer George M. Rives became chairman of the board. A graduate of the College (1868) and the Law School (1873), Rives had joined the board when Butler was a sophomore. He had expressed interest in the presidency back in 1890 but lost out to his fellow trustee Low in part because of his recent marriage to a divorced woman. Rives had little enthusiasm for Butler's candidacy in 1902, again showing personal interest in the job. During his fourteen years as board chairman, Rives liked nothing more than taking wind from Butler's sails. On the occasion of Butler's tenth anniversary, Rives's introduction of Butler to an alumni gathering was noticeably cooler than the adulatory remarks that preceded his: "We all know Butler."[29]

As one of the acknowledged aristocrats on the board, a New York Barclay on his mother's side and of an old Virginia family on his father's, Rives may have been sensitive to the arriviste Butler. A recorded assessment allows as much: "Butler is a great man, but the damnedest fool I know; he values himself for all his worst qualities." There is nothing in the record to suggest that Butler ever took Rives on, as he later did less socially formidable and more politically isolated trustees.[30]

Butler's luck in trustee chairs did not improve much when in 1917 Rives was succeeded by the board's other undisputed aristocrat, William Barclay Parsons (CC 1879; Mines 1882). Besides twenty years of service on the board, Parsons brought to the chairmanship impeccable social credentials (his great-great-grandfather was Trinity Church rector and King's College governor Henry Barclay), a worldwide reputation as an engineer (NYC subways; Cape Cod Canal), and the title Colonel, from his Spanish-American War service in the Corps of Engineers. For frontline service in France during World War I, he became General Parsons. Parsons served as chairman from 1917 until his death in 1933.

Thus it would not be until Butler's thirty-first year as president that he would finally have a board on which one no one could tell him how things were done before his presidency.[31]

While it may be an exaggeration to suggest that Early Butler was intimidated by his trustees, there is little question that their credentials and experience put him on his guard. He certainly never challenged them collectively the way Barnard had. To his credit, neither did he adopt the Uriah Heep posture favored by his mentor, John W. Burgess. In 1909, upon his appointment by the board as the first dean of the Graduate Faculties, Burgess confessed to his employers that "I have always regarded the Board of Trustees as the most ideal body known to civilization."[32]

Butler proceeded cautiously and respectfully, even deferentially, while alert to opportunities for altering the board's composition. The deaths of William Schermerhorn and Abram Hewitt created two openings on the board during Butler's first year, and within the next three years two more openings occurred. His choices signaled the kind of Columbia board he envisioned. Three of his new trustees were bankers, each having been approached by the president-elect for financial support in the weeks before his installation. The best known was Jay Pierrepont Morgan, although the other two, John Stewart Kennedy and Horace W. Carpentier, were also known to be immensely wealthy. Morgan soon lost interest in the board, leaving it in 1912, but Kennedy and Carpentier remained and became generous Columbia benefactors. Among his several gifts, Kennedy underwrote the construction of Hamilton Hall.[33]

Butler made no bones about his belief that Columbia needed to enhance its financial standing and that the best way to do so was to recruit more "men of means" for the board. He began his presidency with a list of prospects, a veritable top-thirty among America's richest men, most of whom had no connection to Columbia, and systematically paid each a visit. Sometimes he was warmly received, as in the cases of Kennedy and Carpentier and initially Morgan, who pledged one million dollars to Columbia on the spot. Or so Butler understood. Morgan later remembered it differently.[34]

Others received the new president's entreaties less warmly. Andrew Carnegie, despite admiring Butler personally and later using him in various philanthropies, declined to support Columbia because he was "very critical of some matters in the history of the University." Edward Harriman was even cooler, declaring that presidential solicitations were "not considered quite dignified or entirely appropriate."[35]

The outcome of Butler's visit to John D. Rockefeller goes unnoted in the record, but the fact that the Rockefellers, despite their generosity to both Barnard and Teachers College, gave virtually nothing to Columbia during

Butler's presidency suggests it did not go well. There is some suggestion that Butler's cold reception by the likes of Carnegie, Harriman, and possibly Rockefeller
was related to their resentment of some Columbia trustees, among them the
Schermerhorns and Cornelius Vanderbilt, who had slighted them upon their
entry into New York society. But then Butler, himself an interloper, would not
likely have been privy to such upstairs sensitivities.[36]

Butler was also less than nimble in his early fund-raising efforts among
board members. It clearly embarrassed longtime trustee William Bayard Cutting (1880–1912) to decline a direct request from the president that he underwrite the organ for St. Paul's Chapel, much as he had a decade earlier a similar
request from Low: "My capacity . . . does not entitle me to stand in the ranks of
some of the other trustees who are such liberal benefactors of the institution."[37]

Butler's early naïveté among the monied classes extended to dealings with
trustees he brought onto the board. Marcellus Hartley Dodge (CC 1903) was
elected to the board in 1907 at twenty-nine, the youngest trustee ever but old
enough to inherit control of the family's Remington Arms Company and marry
a daughter of John D. Rockefeller, a union that created what the New York press
called "the world's richest couple." Dodge's family had already endowed Earl
Hall and later Hartley Hall, and Dodge became over forty-seven years as a
trustee one of Columbia's most generous benefactors. (The Fitness
Center/Gym bears his name.) In 1915 Butler approached Dodge for a sizable
gift with the suggestion that the war in Europe "has been sufficiently kind to
our great and good friend the Manufacturer of Munitions to make you willing
to consider it." Dodge clearly did not appreciate the imputation of wartime
profiteering, especially from someone opposed to American entry into the
Great War. He coldly informed Butler that Remington's increased revenues had
gone into costly plant expansion and there was no such "surplus." "The way
matters stand now it is therefore impossible for me to help the University in the
way you suggest."[38]

Butler's dealings with Horace W. Carpentier went better. Unlike John Stewart Kennedy, a dour Scot, Carpentier was a Columbia College graduate (1848).
He had gone west with the forty-niners and made his fortune in Oakland, California, only to return to New York in the 1890s. He had declined an invitation
from Seth Low to join the board in 1901, citing his age, seventy-one, but in
1906, at Butler's urging, the seventy-six-year-old Carpentier accepted.[39]

Throughout his fourteen years as the board's oldest member, Carpentier was
also its most progressive. His proposals for the board included direct alumni
representation and the election of Jews and Catholics to the board. He favored
opening the Law School to women and all university courses to Barnard undergraduates. His general outlook is suggested in a 1907 letter to Butler, in which

he proposed that the mayor of New York be made an ex officio member of the board:

I am not forgetful of the excellent rule to let well enough alone, and it may be urged that Columbia has got along very well hitherto keeping itself aloof from entanglements and holding on in its even way under its ancient privileges. But its life in the past has not been lived as it must be in the future among intense competitions and in the midst of a crowded population of five or more millions. Does not the best conservatism admonish us to adapt policies to changed and changing conditions?

In all his efforts, Carpentier was vigorously opposed by the board's ranking young fogeys, Gerard Beekman and the Reverend Edward B. Coe. And except in the instance of alumni representation, he failed to win over a majority of the trustees. Most viewed the octogenarian much as Boston admirers did the philosopher William James, as "a sort of Irishman among the Brahmins."[40]

For all the rebuffs Carpentier experienced in trying to diversify the board and the student body, he persisted in seeing himself as a coconspirator with Butler in transforming Columbia into "a Great Democratic University." "It is already great and national," he reminded Butler in 1907, "but it must also be democratic. To this end very many things are needed, some of them seemingly negligible but in truth far-reaching and important." This view is hard to reconcile with what Butler was saying about many of Carpentier's proposed reforms to more hardheaded trustees such as Pine and Parsons, but it does speak to the care Butler took to avoid alienating Carpentier's good will, even as he agreed with other trustees who dismissed him by saying that, while he was "always full of interesting and helpful suggestions, . . . he is not very closely in touch with the actual realities of University administration."[41]

If not the reformer that Carpentier credited him as being, Butler was equal to the hypocrisy required in trying to be all things to all trustees. This made possible Carpentier's series of generous and effectively targeted benefactions, from the first in 1901, establishing the first endowed chair in Chinese studies at an American university, to a scholarship fund for Barnard students. On the occasion of his $100,000 gift of the Dean Lung Chair, Carpentier characteristically allowed: "I am not a Chinaman or the son of a Chinaman . . . but it would seem to be time for us to know something more about the 700 millions inhabiting Eastern Asia and its islands—beyond the somewhat vague notion that they are a mass of opium-smoking and pig-tailed barbarians or of devil-worshipping savages."[42]

Perhaps the most problematic relationship Butler had with an inherited trustee was that with Francis S. Bangs (CC 1877; Law 1880). "Teddy" Bangs was asked to join the board in 1900 in part because of his abiding interest in athletics, having rowed as an undergraduate and Law School student. On the board, he became one of the most assertive members, especially in matters relating to university finances and the College. Bangs's two sons attended Columbia College, and for the eleven years of their overlapping matriculation (1902–13), they provided him with an inside source of information about the state of faculty-student relations, which, according to Harry (CC 1906) and Francis Sedgwick (CC 1910; Law 1913), were not good. Reports from his sons of atheism and socialism being promoted in the classroom, plus his own self-acknowledged streak of anti-intellectualism ("much that goes on under the name of education is far beyond me. I don't see the use of it.") soured Bangs on the Columbia faculty and left him suspicious of Butler's loyalties as an ex-faculty member. If Carpentier was the prototype of the trustee as progressive gadfly, Bangs was trustee as grumpy parent.[43]

Given the independent character of the board in Butler's first decade, the amount its members accomplished together is impressive. Perhaps Butler's greatest feat was to persuade them to accept direct representation of alumni on the board. The issue had been raised back in 1854 in the wake of the Gibbs affair but subsided during the next four decades, even while alumni representation on university boards of trustees elsewhere became commonplace. The issue surfaced again in the early 1900s, urged in part by alumni anxious to have their views on intercollegiate athletics represented on the board. The board's decision to withdraw Columbia from intercollegiate football at the end of the 1905 season only increased alumni pressure.[44]

Within the board, only Horace Carpentier and board secretary John Pine (CC 1877) initially supported alumni representation, the former on principle and the latter arguing that it would increase alumni financial support for the university. But elsewhere early opinion ran decidedly against it. Some trustees, Chairman Rives among them, objected on the grounds that it would violate the 1810 charter and put the university at risk of a wholesale charter rewriting by the New York State Legislature. Others objected simply because it represented change. Only Carpentier allowed the possibility that the overall quality of the board might be improved by a regular infusion of alumni-selected trustees.[45]

Butler sided with the reformers and helped bring over most of the initial opponents by devising a procedure for alumni election that did not require a change of the charter but satisfied the alumni and left the constituted board formally in charge of determining its membership. The procedure he proposed: dues-paying members of the various alumni clubs of Columbia University would nominate a member for the board, who would be assured election by the board, provided the nominee agreed beforehand to resign his seat in six years. This procedure would be repeated annually until the number of alumni trustees reached six. Thereafter, one alumni seat would turn over each year. When these procedures were formally voted on by the board in 1908, only Chairman Rives dissented, but quietly.[46]

The first alumni-nominated trustee, Benjamin B. Lawrence (Mines, 1878), was elected in 1909. By 1916 all six alumni seats were filled, and the board's subsequent apportioning of eighteen life trustees and six alumni trustees was set, an arrangement not altered until the 1970s.[47]

But the arrangement soon took on a signature Butler wrinkle. When Lawrence's term ended in 1916, rather then leaving the board, he was elected to a life trusteeship under the traditional rules. This co-option happened with seven more of the thirty-nine alumni trustees who joined the board during Butler's presidency. As a result, the expected rate of board turnover because of alumni representation with fixed terms of service was substantially reduced, even as the average tenure of trustees dropped. But, more politically important, the new dispensation meant that every year someone joined the board who would be gone six years later, unless he sufficiently impressed Butler to merit being kept on. By treating the six alumni seats on the board as a minor league where candidates tried out for the majors—a life trustee seat—Butler gained control over the board more quickly than he would have either under the traditional arrangement where, as Trustee Cheesman put it in 1916, "I had hoped to die with my boots on" or according to the intent of the 1908 reform. Meanwhile, the election to life trusteeships of men of Butler's own social acquaintance, such as the banker Stephen Baker in 1910 and college chums like the banker Willard V. King in 1909 and the international lawyer Frederic R. Coudert Jr.(CC 1890) in 1912, hastened the day when the board would be dominated by Butler's men.[48]

Another major accomplishment of the early Butler years that had the effect of increasing presidential authority was securing board approval for the funding of the $3 million debt incurred in the move to Morningside. While less controversial than alumni representation, securing the trustees' agreement for debt repayment over thirty years at 3.5 percent interest impressed the trustees with Butler's financial acumen. It also allowed him to solicit gifts for new buildings without first having to secure the hard-to-come-by funding to pay for old ones with names already attached.[49]

On another matter, however, Butler failed to get his way with the trustees. In 1906, at the suggestion of Columbia economist E. R. A. Seligman, he urged the board to sell the Upper and Lower Estates and to invest the proceeds in securities and government bonds. The intended effect of this would have been to make a larger proportion of Columbia's endowment, then tied up in real estate, available for capital expenditures of an academic nature. That this also would have meant the president commanded far greater resources than were then at hand was not lost on Butler or the trustees.[50]

Opposition to the sale of the Lower Estate was led by three board members—Bangs, Cammann, and William Barclay Parsons—all vestrymen of Trinity Church. Bangs was the most categorically opposed, arguing that his fellow vestrymen might very well forbid Columbia to sell what he called "our Trinity Endowment" and instead insist that the 1754 gift be returned to the church.[51]

Opposition to selling the Upper Estate turned on a different but equally time-tested Knickerbocker principle: institutions should never sell off property, least of all property providing a steady return. Trustee Edward Mitchell put the argument thus: "In my opinion the estates in real property will last and be retained long after those invested in personal property shall have been subdivided and dissipated." The trustees were not convinced by the two principal arguments developed by Seligman and pressed by Butler: that the returns on the Upper Estate were below that of government bonds, which were safer investments, and that so long as Columbia owned such a conspicuous piece of Manhattan real estate, few potential benefactors would believe Columbia deserved financial support. Butler's exasperation showed through in a 1908 letter to Bangs: "I am between the devil and the deep blue sea. Men will not give us new endowments because of the Upper Estate and because of the Trinity Church condition, and yet neither the Upper Estate or the Trinity Church condition can apparently be gotten rid of."[52]

It would be another fifteen years before most of the Lower Estate was sold and seventy-eight years before the Upper Estate went on the block.

For all the constraints placed on Butler by his strong-minded board, the collaboration by checks and balances worked well for Columbia. The result was better than in earlier days when the trustees dominated their presidents or in later, when Butler dominated his trustees. Of course, one factor that helped the board and president work effectively together during the early Butler years was their essential agreement as to what they were about: making an already good and already big Columbia University into the best and biggest university in the world.

Bigger is Better

Running through Columbia's long history has been an argument about optimal size. The governors of King's College were indifferent to large enrollments, did nothing to generate them, and took pride in providing "an education for those who can afford it." Similarly, they made no efforts at diversification, preferring to limit admissions to their own sons and sons of fellow churchmen. Only the Medical Faculty favored more students and greater social inclusiveness.[53]

Republican Columbia College viewed large enrollments and an inclusive student body more positively, not least because it looked to state support and understood that the College's utility would be judged by the numbers and diversity of its students. This strategy enjoyed some success in the 1790s, when enrollments, diversification, and state support all increased. Unfortunately, despite efforts by trustees to present the College as socially inclusive and pro-grammatically expansive, state funding soon ceased, enrollments dropped, and what little social diversity had existed among both students and faculty disap-peared.[54]

Knickerbocker Columbia, despite the occasional gesture toward making itself more attractive to more students, as at the founding of NYU in 1831, remained persuaded that it should not compete with the likes of more recruit-ment-minded Union or Yale. The result was predictable: four decades of flat enrollments, social stasis, and curricular atrophy.[55]

The arrival of F. A. P. Barnard in 1864 brought changes. He encouraged the six-year-old Law School and the about-to-open School of Mines to adopt admissions and curricular policies that would attract students in numbers. Each quickly outstripped the College in enrollments, strengthening Barnard's case that Columbia's future lay not in the stagnant College but in its rapidly growing professional schools. That these schools attracted not only more stu-dents but of a sort different from the Knickerbocker boys who had been the College's mainstay made Columbia, to Barnard's mind, better able to exploit both the demographic realities of late-nineteenth-century America and the College's urban locale.[56]

Barnard's expansive and inclusive vision was not entirely shared by his trustees or the faculty. Changes mandated by the trustees in the 1880s stiffen-ing admission requirements and lengthening the course of study at the Law School, contrary to both Barnard's and Dwight's wishes, went in the opposite direction. For the most part, however, those who disagreed with Barnard had limited success pressing their more exclusive vision. Moreover, Seth Low shared his predecessor's belief that Columbia's admissions policies and curriculum ought to make the university attractive to as many students as possible.[57]

To argue that a more exclusive vision of the university's mission failed to carry the day among Columbians in the late nineteenth century and that it held no appeal for either Barnard or Low is not to argue that it lacked adherents or that it would not command presidential support later on. It is, however, to sug-gest that had Butler, at the outset of his presidency, displaced the "bigger is better" strategy with a more exclusive one of his own, he would have been abandoning the strategy that enabled Columbia's steady ascent from midcentury mediocrity to turn-of-the-century eminence. This he did not do.

Who's Counting?

For his first fifteen years as president, Butler shared the view original to Barnard and embraced by Low that if Columbia was to become the best American university, it must also become the biggest. Accordingly, his early presidency was marked by the steady accumulation of data attesting to the university's growth and by internal estimates of its qualitative standing vis-à-vis the competition. Size and scholarly quality were reinforcing, or so Early Butler was determined to demonstrate. In the course of doing so, he gave Columbia every appearance of a university "on the make."[58]

Butler sought to dominate New York higher learning by two strategies. The first was by merger, as in the case of the successful affiliation agreements Columbia struck with the American Museum of Natural History in 1904, the New York College of Pharmacy in 1906, and the New York School of Optometry in 1910, as well as the failed efforts to merge with Cooper Union in 1903 and NYU in 1906. The second was duplication of existing coverage, as in the creation of a Law School annex in Newark in 1911 and the Business School in 1916, each in direct competition with NYU.[59]

Nor were Barnard College and Teachers College immune to Butler's consolidating plans. His practice of encouraging Columbia trustees to serve on the Barnard and Teachers College trustee boards was meant to ease the institutional takeovers when they came. True, the Teachers College board had grown "quarrelsome" in 1914 over the matter of collecting tuition income from jointly offered summer programs, prompting trustees on both boards to suggest total separation. Barnard, on the other hand, Butler told Chairman Rives, could not be more compliant: "The corporate absorption of Barnard would be an extremely simple matter. Miss Gildersleeve's tactful handling of administrative problems has done away with all the friction which her predecessor carefully developed, and whenever the Barnard trustees feel that they have carried their separate responsibility long enough, that college could be taken into the University without the slightest difficulty or embarrassment." Amalgamation, consolidation, and cutting into local competitors' market share all were strategies consistent with Early Butler's twin ambition to make Columbia the biggest and the best.[60]

The College, despite having doubled its size since 1900, remained relatively small. Comparisons for 1907–8 have Columbia, even with Barnard enrollments included, with an undergraduate component both the smallest in absolute terms and as a proportion of all enrollments of any of the other universities, with the exception of Johns Hopkins, where the undergraduate program remained an afterthought.[61]

The College continued to draw its students almost exclusively from New York City, a situation reinforced by its being unable to house undergraduates during its first decade on Morningside. Housing was less a problem at Barnard, which provided for student residences as early as 1899 and as a result attracted the daughters of some of the same New York families who were sending their sons to New Haven, Cambridge, or Princeton.[62]

But Columbia's attraction for professional and graduate students was undeniable. Much of this had to do with being in New York. Indeed, some of the reasons the city was viewed as an inappropriate setting for undergraduates worked in Columbia's favor for professional programs. The Law, Engineering, and Medical Schools all attracted graduates from the leading colleges of the Northeast but also less credentialed young men from the South and West. Many of these came intending to return home with a Columbia degree, but others came as part of a larger plan to pursue professional careers in New York.[63]

Columbia's professional and graduate schools differed from Harvard's and Yale's in being less dependent on the undergraduate college for students. Many Columbia College graduates went on to Columbia's professional and graduate schools, but they never outnumbered students from elsewhere. This was especially true of the graduate school, where non-Columbia graduates outnumbered Columbia graduates from the start. Although slow to get under way in the 1880s—when its output of Ph.D.s trailed Yale's, Harvard's, Cornell's, and JHU's—Columbia by 1900 had passed both Cornell and Hopkins in the production of Ph.D.s and had pulled abreast of Harvard, Yale, and the recently founded University of Chicago.[64]

Part of the change had been brought about by Columbia's introduction of graduate fellowships, open to Columbia and non-Columbia graduates alike. Part was also due to the recognition that New York provided unparalleled research opportunities and, thanks to such institutions as the New York Public Library, the Metropolitan Museum, the American Museum of Natural History, and the Bronx Botanical Garden, scholarly resources unmatched elsewhere. With graduate enrollments already approaching one thousand, more than those of any competitors, Columbia would soon become the nation's largest producer of Ph.D.s.[65]

The trustees endorsed Butler's expansionist strategy. Even as they devised new ways of carrying more debt, they remained bullish on Columbia's long-term prospects. Indeed, one of the few criticisms leveled by board members at the way the university was operated during Butler's first decade as president was that not all the professional schools had joined in the surge in enrollments occurring in the College, the Graduate Faculties, Barnard, Teachers College, and the summer session. With an eye to limiting access to their respective professions while strengthening their offerings, the faculties of the Law and Medical Schools increased their admission requirements and extended their programs from two to three years. Horace Carpentier, who made important gifts to both schools, questioned the decision of the Medical Faculty, in the face of stagnant enrollments and declining applications, to stiffen their admission requirements. Hearing in 1902 that the Law School would now require applicants to be college graduates, he noted sourly that this would have foreclosed both John Marshall's and Abraham Lincoln's attendance. Bangs was similarly upset by the decision of the Medical Faculty "to set up new barriers" when "candidates for admission are scarce now and growing scarcer."[66]

Butler might have been expected to defend his faculties against such criticism, pointing out that limits on enrollments raised the level of instruction and enhanced institutional prestige. Later he would, but early in his presidency he did not. On the contrary, he was second to no trustee in urging all parts of the university to expand. When a trustee questioned opening an extension program in Newark as a feeder for the Law School, in light of NYU's already having done so, Butler shot back that "we have been busy for ten years or more in turning away a certain very desirable class of law student. . . . I am anxious to get back this clientage and bring them into the University."[67]

In 1910 Butler reported to the trustees with obvious satisfaction that Columbia had just completed a decade of "growth *and* rising standards of admission," citing enrollment increases of 157 percent in the Graduate Faculties, 113 percent at Barnard, and 49 percent in the College. He then suggested, with an eye to the enrollments of such programs generated at the state universities in the Midwest, that Columbia consider opening a program in agricultural engineering—with plans for an experimental farm, no less. The following year, the toastmaster at an alumni dinner announced breathlessly, "We are here to celebrate the growth of the greatest university on earth. Ten years ago there were 3500 students at Columbia. Today there are nearly 8000. We have at last passed Berlin."[68]

Did Early Butler Matter?

Columbia's twelfth president inherited a thriving, self-confident academic enterprise, one that had enjoyed an unchecked upward trajectory for four decades and two presidencies. He began with an operating budget of just under

$1 million ($20 million in 2000 dollars), a new campus already largely paid for with private benefactions, steadily expanding enrollments in the College, Barnard, Teachers College, and Graduate Faculties, plus four thriving professional schools (Law, Medicine, Engineering, and Architecture). Columbia's endowment—$8 million in 1902 ($160 million in 2000 dollars)—was the largest of any American university. No Columbia president ever entered his office in more auspicious circumstances.[69]

One might argue, then, that Butler's job was simply to keep the good times going—and that his would be what students of the American presidency call a "continuation" presidency, requiring managerial energy and political skills more than great vision and new ideas. These first attributes Butler possessed in spades. During most of Butler's long presidency, he administered the university's affairs with striking efficiency and political adroitness. Even toward the end, when he was beyond supervising those who attended to the details, the personnel and administrative mechanisms he had put in place allowed the university to bump along without anyone in effective charge. It may have been, as successors later complained variously, that "he ran the University out of his top drawer," or from his "inside breast pocket," or even his "back pocket" but run it he did.[70]

On hiring a bright young Columbia College graduate, Frederick P. Keppel (CC 1902), as assistant secretary in 1903, Butler told him how he wanted the president's office to operate: "as in the case of a large business corporation downtown." And so it did. Incoming mail was date stamped to assure prompt action; few letters in Butler's early correspondence went unanswered more than two days, and most had responses the same day. Budgetary matters were administered with similar dispatch and efficiency. Standardized forms, experimented with in Low's day, became the norm. Most of the university's correspondence passed through Butler's hands, and much of it got his personal attention. Mistakes, whether by staffers or senior administrators, particularly those involving financial matters that came to the attention of the trustees, became occasions for Butler to remind the miscreants that their lapses embarrassed the office of the presidency.[71]

It is little wonder that Morgan, Harriman, and Carnegie all tried to hire Butler to help run their empires, for in many ways his managerial capacities matched theirs. Thorstein Veblen's intended put-down of university presidents, calling them "captains of erudition," though aimed at Chicago's William Rainey Harper, applied even more to Butler. He entered into his presidency with twenty-four years of experience in Columbia affairs. He knew the ins and outs (and operative vocabulary) of acquiring additional campus space, staging the construction of buildings, floating the university's debt, whatever. Eventually, of course, matters exceeded in their complexity his personal capacities and were parceled out to specialists in the administration or to outside consultants. But through the first quarter of the twentieth century, Columbia was better run than during much of the half-century that followed his presidency.[72]

A critic said that "numbers meant to Dr. Butler what he wanted them to mean"; more charitably, he valued their rhetorical power. Accordingly, his administration led the way in urging uniform counting procedures among American universities, the better to demonstrate Columbia's steady ascendance. Most of the early comparative statistics of turn-of-the-century American universities were compiled at Butler's direction by Rudolph Tombo, the Columbia registrar, and first published in the *Columbia University Quarterly*.[73]

At Harvard, Tombo's requests for data were taken seriously, both by President Eliot and Jerome Greene, the university secretary. In 1905 Eliot acknowledged the existence of what he called "the friendly rivalry" that now existed between Harvard and Columbia. But what neither Greene nor Eliot took seriously was Tombo's assurances that same year that, "of course, it does not make any difference whether Columbia happens to have more students from Arkansas in any one year than Harvard." And both would have found laughable Butler's assurances to his trustees in 1914 that "Columbia University declines to measure itself or to permit itself to be measured by quantitative standards."[74]

Butler inherited a Morningside campus of twenty-five acres (including Barnard and Teachers College) and seven buildings; by 1915 Columbia's properties had grown to fifty acres and sixteen academic buildings. To be sure, some of this added space—the six acres east of Amsterdam Avenue ("The East Campus") and the five acres at 168th Street (where the medical center would later be built)—was not immediately built on but acquired for future growth. Yet that very fact permits the conclusion that the early Butler, the Butler well into the second decade of his presidency, saw himself not as a caretaker or as a "continuator" but as a planner and a builder. He remained one with the Barnard vision of a Columbia that could be both the best and the biggest institution of higher learning in America. Indeed, Butler's vision reached further than Barnard's by making Columbia's competitive frame of reference the entire world. "We have at last passed Berlin!"

By 1915 Columbia by several measures had become the biggest university in the country. Its five professional schools (Law, Medicine, Engineering, Architecture, and Journalism) enrolled more students (four thousand plus) and conferred more degrees (eighteen hundred plus) than those of any other university. When Teachers College numbers (two thousand enrollments; eight hundred degrees) were included, the margin grew substantially. The Graduate Faculties constituted the largest graduate school in the country and conferred more arts and sciences M.A.s and Ph.D.s than any other university. To be sure, the College was smaller than Harvard's or Yale's or Princeton's or, for that matter, Dartmouth's or Amherst's. But between 1900 and 1912 its enrollments expanded faster than any of theirs. And when its 1915 enrollment of twelve hundred was combined with Barnard—seven hundred—Columbia's undergraduates outnumbered those of Princeton, Dartmouth, and Amherst. The Columbia Summer School and Extension Program were also the largest in the country, enrolling some twelve thousand students in 1915.[75]

But was Columbia the best? The Law School was no match for Harvard's, though it could lay claim to being the nation's second best. Nor was the Medical School the equal of either Johns Hopkins or Harvard. Nor was its Engineering School as good at MIT. These back-in-the-packs acknowledged, the rest of Early Butler's Columbia was right up there.[76]

The university's three graduate faculties constituted pre-World War I Columbia's best claims to national eminence. This was especially so in the case of the Faculty of Political Science, where all the constituent departments— public law, history, economics and sociology—could claim to being the best in the country. The key discipline builders—Burgess, Mayo-Smith, Dunning, Seligman, Clark, and Giddings—were still in place in 1910, while their students held prestigious professorships throughout the country. This was also true of anthropology, then part of the Faculty of Philosophy, under the leadership of Franz Boas.[77]

Prewar Columbia outproduced other American universities in Ph.D.s in all the social sciences. Indeed, there already existed among American social scientists a "Columbia School," known to stress the quantitative aspects of the specific subdisciplines and identified with the work and students of Boas, Giddings, and the economist Henry L. Moore. A similar "Columbia School" existed in psychology, identified with the work of Cattell and his students, Edward L. Thorndike and Robert S. Woodworth, where, again, an emphasis on rigorous measurement distinguished it from its more heuristically disposed competitors. So, too, the "New Historians," with their interests in cultural and social history, centered on James Harvey Robinson and including Charles Beard, Lynn Thorndike, and James Shotwell, conferred on the Columbia Department of History a prominence second to no other turn-of-the-century history department.[78]

The humanities were similarly imposing. Prewar Columbia offered more courses in English and modern European languages than any other American university. It was also strong in ancient languages, including Semitics and Sanskrit, as well as in Chinese and Slavic languages. In the big humanities disciplines, such as English and modern European languages, the principal competitors were Harvard and Chicago, and in the smaller subjects, such as classics,

Johns Hopkins. Columbia's philosophers were less distinguished than Harvard's until Dewey's arrival from Chicago in 1905. Two years later, William James reported on his visit to Columbia that "they have a *very* strong philosophic team—to be ranked by some, no doubt, more highly than our Harvard team." Only in the fine arts, especially after Edward MacDowell resigned his professorship of music in 1904, did Columbia's humanities departments lag behind their competitors.[79]

It was in its Faculty of Pure Science where prewar Columbia was most impressive. When psychology is included, it then being housed in the Faculty of Philosophy and strongly represented on the Teachers College faculty, Columbia's overall science offerings were both more extensive and more acclaimed than those of any American university, except Harvard. In the case of psychology and botany/zoology, the two fields in which Columbia clearly excelled, the principal competition came not from Cambridge, Massachusetts, but from Cambridge, England, and from Berlin.[80]

The point here is that, if not the best American university on the eve of World War I, Columbia had little cause to cede that distinction to any competitor. Moreover, there were many reasons to think that its long-term prospects were brighter than theirs. Wealth, locale, and presidential leadership all seemed to favor Columbia. This was essentially the conclusion Edwin Slosson came to in his 1910 comparative study of *Great American Universities*. After declaring Harvard's faculty "the most eminent," he allowed that much else on which Harvard's reputation was based "indicates the past rather than the present." Similarly, Yale was viewed as having "lost its chance of priority" and Hopkins as in "relative decline," whereas Penn was poor and Princeton's commitment to "homogeneity" limited its university potential. And there was Columbia, which, "situated in the largest city," Slosson stated, "has the best chance to become the greatest of American universities—and it is improving the chance."[81]

By 1914, four years after Slosson's book appeared, further changes only strengthened Columbia's claims to preeminence. Johns Hopkins, except in medicine, could not sustain the heady pace set for it by President Gilman and was settling into becoming a midsize university with shaky finances. Harvard no longer had Eliot as its president but Abbott Lawrence Lowell, whose priorities were not graduate studies and faculty research, which had been at the center of his predecessor's "friendly rivalry" with Columbia. The University of Chicago remained a serious competitor, but after the death of President William Rainey Harper in 1906 and the uncertainties of future Rockefeller largesse, by 1910 it ceded to Columbia first place in overall enrollments, graduate enrollments, and annual production of Ph.D.s. Yale, under Arthur Twining Hadley, remained uncertain about the comprehensiveness of its university aspirations. So, too, did Princeton, which had the additional burden of recovering from the battles over its fledgling graduate program that had brought down Woodrow Wilson's presidency in 1910.[82]

And there was Columbia, with an experienced, vigorous fifty-two-year-old Nicholas Murray Butler ready to lead his university deep into the twentieth century. Just how deep neither Butler nor his contemporaries imagined. But for the time being, and not least for its assumed edge in presidential leadership, the smart money was on Columbia.

CHAPTER 8

1917: Twilight of Idols

I cannot, however, undertake to turn my office into a sanatorium for academic hypochondriacs. La malade imaginaire belongs to the job of the Professor of Dramatic Literature. The fact of the matter is that a good many men who are in the academic career made a mistake in choosing it—everlasting fretfulness and faultfinding.

Nicholas Murray Butler, October 1910

The power of the Trustees to regulate the affairs of the University is absolute.

Trustee Francis S. Bangs, September 1917

The public get the impression that there was a state of war in Columbia between the Trustees and the professors.

Nicholas Murray Butler, October 1917

Faculty Power and Its Discontents

WHILE research-oriented faculty were the principal beneficiaries of changes attending the rapid growth of Columbia in the 1890s, their rising fortunes did not occur without grumbling from correspondingly diminished estates. Some trustees held to the traditional notion that faculty ought to be teachers, first and foremost, and that scholarship ought to supplement professors' teaching, not vice versa. For these trustees, the principal interaction they envisioned for faculty was with undergraduates in the classroom and on campus, not with disciplinary colleagues at far-off conferences or in learned journals that neither trustees nor students read. "I fail to understand why the heads of departments at the present day," Trustee Edward Mitchell complained to Butler in 1906, "should be unwilling to illuminate the path of the undergraduate student at least three or four times a year." Even as faculty assumed virtual control over the selection of Columbia's teaching staff, some trustees held to the earlier view provided for in the charter: that faculty appointments were theirs to make. Among these were a few trustees with the odd son-in-law, nephew, or law partner with scholarly aspirations and in need of a position who thought their own services to the university earned their recommendation serious consideration. Had that not been the way it worked in the past?[1]

Such grumbling would not have slowed faculty takeover of the appointments process as long as it lacked presidential support. None came from Low, who consistently supported the faculty's right to choose their own colleagues. As a nonacademic with no intellectual pretensions, he regarded assessing faculty qualifications as beyond his range of experience—and that of the trustees. Although squabbling that required his intervention did go on between faculty members during his presidency, struggles between trustees and faculty over the proper responsibilities of each estate were noticeably absent. By consistently siding with faculty assertions of their prerogatives, "The Great Harmonizer" oversaw the transformation of these assertions into institutional norms, if never quite God-given or charter-backed rights. Butler's role in the rise of the faculty estate was more complicated than Low's president-as-enabler, if for no other reason than that he played three different roles. As a young faculty member in the late 1880s, he had joined forces with the more senior Burgess and his contemporary E. R. A. Seligman in advancing the cause of the peer-selected credentialed scholar over that of the trustee-connected amateur. His contempt for the likes of Drisler and Van Amringe, whose loyalties to Columbia College harkened back to an earlier Columbia and a less career-minded professoriate, was complete. Moreover, as someone whose own rapid professorial ascent was by what his generation took to be universalistic rules, he had good personal reasons for preferring them.[2]

Butler's entry into academic administration in 1890 was similarly facilitated by recent policies favoring faculty self-rule. Rather than appoint the first dean of the Faculty of Philosophy, as Barnard had appointed Burgess dean of the Faculty of Political Science a decade earlier, Low directed the faculty to elect their own dean from among their ranks. In electing Butler, his colleagues had reason to regard him as their representative and not an administrative officer. Little he did during his dozen years as dean disappointed his faculty or put into question his role as their effective advocate. Moreover, the faculty he recruited, such as James McKeen Cattell from the University of Pennsylvania, E. B. Wilson from Bryn Mawr, and Franz Boas from the University of Chicago, came as catches with every assurance of having their way. Dean Butler had been the faculty's candidate to succeed Low.[3]

Butler began his presidency no less solicitous of the views of his faculty than he had been as dean. He remained on the lookout for world-class scholars, even if, as in the case of the geneticist Thomas Hunt Morgan at Bryn Mawr and the philosopher John Dewey at Chicago, they were known not to suffer administrators gladly. That was the price an aggressive university should be prepared to pay. He similarly encouraged ambitious junior faculty, such as historian Charles A. Beard, whom some of his elders in the Faculty of Political Science, among them Burgess, regarded as too much of a climber.[4]

And yet there were early signs that, as president, Butler regarded his assertive faculty differently from the way he had viewed them while in their ranks. He did not so much align himself with the grumbling trustees in a campaign to put faculty members in their place as soon come to agree with moderates on the board that the accretion of faculty power that had characterized Low's presidency had gone far enough.[5]

Some changes in the prevailing administrative structure were inevitable, whatever Butler's views on faculty-administrative relations. President Barnard had managed Columbia's administrative affairs by himself, with the assistance of two secretaries, the second hired only after some unseemly wrangling with the trustees in 1879. President Low carried the university into the twentieth century with an administration that included the deans of the three professional schools (Law, Engineering, and Medicine), the three graduate faculties (Political Science, Philosophy, and Pure Science), and the College. These were chosen by the vote of their faculties, and they reported directly to the president. In addition, the offices of bursar, registrar, and buildings superintendent were created, all appointed by the president. His personal staff consisted of a secretary and three clerks. In 1901 the entire administrative structure of the university consisted of perhaps fifty full-time positions.[6]

The other already-in-place layer of administration intervening between the president and the faculty was the University Council, established in 1896. It consisted of the deans and two elected faculty from each of the schools and faculties and advised the president on all academic matters touching on more than one school or faculty. With most of its members faculty and with even the deans faculty-elected, the University Council operated in its early years more as a faculty senate than as an arm of the administration. Academic departments were chaired either by their senior member or by some other senior member elected by his peers.[7]

Thus Butler inherited a functioning if schematic administrative structure that gave the faculty considerable voice in the administration of the university. He could have kept it in place. That he did not do so suggests that his vision for his presidency differed from his predecessor's. His first change was to transform the mechanism for filling deanships from election by peers to presidential appointment. This was accomplished in 1904 by trustee resolution. The second was to create, for each of the faculties and schools, assistant deans, each to have a seat on the University Council, which had the effect of thickening the administrative layer between faculty and president, even as it diluted the faculty voice on the council. This was accomplished in 1906. The third change occurred in 1908, when Butler appointed Burgess the first dean of Graduate Faculties and directed all the other deans to report to him. In 1911, at

Burgess's urging, Butler gave his dean of Graduate Faculties the power to override appointments of department chairs determined by election. The reintroduction a year later of the office of provost, responsible for all academic matters not involving faculty completed Butler's administrative makeover, for the moment at least.[8]

To these new administrative posts Butler appointed faculty members whose administrative skills and loyalties to him had been confirmed earlier by committee service. Burgess was the most distinguished scholar of these appointees. But by 1908 Burgess's relationship with Butler had metamorphosed from faculty mentor to fellow dean and presidential aspirant, to trusted adviser, to cheerleader. More typical of his administrative appointees was William H. Carpenter, professor of Germanic literature, whom Butler appointed provost. Carpenter had tired of teaching and research but adored Butler and was good at keeping track of things. So, too, Adam LeRoy Jones, appointed director of admissions in 1909, who until then had been a philosophy instructor with an uncertain future at Columbia.[9]

Butler's university secretaries, Frederick P. Keppel (1903–10) and Frank Fackenthal (1910–37), were men whose loyalties were clearly not to the faculty, or even to Columbia, but to Butler personally. Butler's selection of Keppel as the third dean of Columbia College in 1910, when Keppel was only thirty, was one of the best he made in forty-four years as president; it was also a certifiably safe one.[10]

Thus, in the first seven years of his presidency, Butler transformed an administrative structure notable for its looseness and accommodation of faculty autonomy into a multilayered, buttoned-up, top-down bureaucracy that inhibited faculty-initiated dialogue with the trustees even as it emphasized presidential authority. Some of the change can also be attributed to a growth in faculty size—from around 250 in 1902 to almost 700 by 1915—and to the increased bureaucratization of American public life generally. But much of it reflects a growing impatience on the president's part with his own faculty and his desire to put some distance between himself and them. "I cannot," he informed University Secretary Keppel in 1910, "undertake to turn my office into a sanatorium for academic hypochondriacs. La malade imaginaire belongs to the job of the Professor of Dramatic Literature. The fact of the matter is that a good many men who are in the academic career made a mistake in choosing it—everlasting fretfulness and faultfinding." What hastened Butler to this conclusion was steady contact with trustees and benefactors who came by their mistrust of faculty naturally. But it was also the product of his being a witness, and party to, what Keppel later characterized as a bizarre series of "academic suicides."[11]

Academic Suicides and Other Misdemeanors

Faculty miscreancy in early Columbia College took relatively few forms. Failure to maintain classroom order and subject-matter drift topped the list; poor attendance in the days of compulsory chapel ranked a close second. Instances of faculty alcoholism or adultery went unrecorded in the trustee minutes, as did cases of absconding with College property. Clearly the most embarrassing nineteenth-century case of faculty malfeasance was that of Richard McCulloch, who used of his position as professor of physics to spy for the Confederacy during the Civil War. Occasionally a faculty member wrote directly to the trustees about his salary, but more often complaining took the form of a letter signed by several faculty, who hoped thereby to avoid individual retaliation. They likely learned this survival tactic from their students.[12]

During the Barnard presidency, some faculty came in for criticism for spreading themselves too thinly between academic responsibilities and various outside jobs. Charles Frederick Chandler was cited on several occasions for neglecting his students in favor of one or another civic employment. Herbert Levi Osgood was said to hide in his library carrel out of reach of all but his most persistent students. But otherwise the faculty of early Columbia University led lives no less exemplary than those of early Columbia College.[13]

But with the increased numbers of faculty and increased prominence of turn-of-the-century Columbia came increased misdemeanors. In 1899 the recently retired professor of rhetoric John D. Quackenbos was censured by President Low for misrepresenting his connection with Columbia in advertisements offering his services as a psychic. Only Quackenbos's abject apology and some words offered in mitigation by Low kept the trustees from taking him to court.[14]

The first "academic suicide" in the Butler presidency was that of Professor of English George E. Woodberry. A Harvard-trained New Englander, he had come to Columbia in 1891 after several efforts by President Eliot and Charles Eliot Norton to find him a place had been thwarted by circumstances and Woodberry's own passive stubbornness. After being fired from a position at the University of Nebraska in 1881, he hung around Cambridge for a decade hoping that Eliot might make him Norton's successor. Then came the Columbia offer.[15]

Woodberry's appointment at Columbia went well at first. Some of the College's best students were drawn to his literature courses, as they would be throughout his tenure. But he soon tangled with a departmental colleague, Brander Matthews, the epitome of the urbane college professor, man of the world, and Columbia insider—all that Woodberry abhorred. Matthews was immensely productive, which his light teaching program and independent wealth facilitated. Woodberry, since coming to Columbia and being very involved with his students, had published little of interest to his departmental colleagues.[16]

Their clash began with their vetoing each other's choices for junior appointments in the English department. In 1900 Low decided to separate them by dividing the English department in two, with Matthews as professor of dramatic literature in the English department and Woodberry in the newly created Department of Comparative Literature. They then fell to squabbling about who got the departmental assistant, who taught whom, and on and on.[17]

Right after Butler's installation, Woodberry wrote to Harvard's President Eliot of his fear that Columbia's new president planned to force him out in favor of Butler's social confidante Brander Matthews. Eliot advised him to sit tight. Woodberry then took his complaints with Matthews, Butler, and Columbia to the press, writing of a "breach almost irreparable" between him and Butler.[18]

Surprisingly, Butler did not immediately go after Woodberry but instead accepted a mutual friend's assurances that Woodberry was not out to get him. "The poor fellow is not quite himself in respect to many matters," Butler in turn informed Trustee Bangs, who believed Woodberry's "tenure of office should be ended as soon as the dignity of the University will permit." Meanwhile, Eliot advised Woodberry that "something is due to any organization in which one has long served, at the outset of a new management." In July 1903 he commended Woodberry for "holding on at Columbia." But by Christmas Woodberry informed Eliot that he had determined to resign, certain that "I can not endure my surroundings at the University." He did so, effective June 30, 1904, never again to hold a university position.[19]

Butler may not have been as solicitous of Woodberry's feelings as Low had been, and he was indeed on cordial terms with Matthews. But he should not be blamed for Woodberry's professional self-destruction, as Woodberry admirers such as Upton Sinclair later did. Even Woodberry seemed to concede as much a year later to his Harvard friend, Barrett Wendell, in a postmortem of the affair: "This career of mine is a queer thing—irregular both in its beginnings and in its course. Temperamentally, perhaps, I could not have done things otherwise. There was no place to begin with: and all along I found myself confronted with tasks, which had to be done or refused, for which I knew myself far from prepared. I have done them all as well as I could, not shirking drudgery, but never fully confident that my own best deserved much respect." An earlier Columbia might have provided a safe refuge for Woodberry, as it had for two generations of Renwicks, McVickars, and Anthons, but a Columbia University in hot pursuit of academic eminence was certain to eat up anyone "never fully confident that my own best deserved much respect." Knickerbocker Columbia was Trollope's Barchester; turn-of-the-century Columbia, Darwin's jungle.[20]

A month after Woodberry submitted his resignation, Professor of Music Edward A. MacDowell submitted his. Unlike Woodberry's, which the trustees had expected, MacDowell's resignation came out of the blue. His resignation letter went on for eight pages of complaints with Columbia and its president. But it was his taking these complaints to the press that prompted trustee chair George Rives to seek an explanation from the president.[21]

Much as in the Woodberry case, Butler appears at first less the offender than offended against. According to the president's account, on January 21, 1904, MacDowell informed Butler of his desire to resign the teaching position he had held for eight years and to devote himself full-time to composing. Butler responded a week later by suggesting that MacDowell consider a continuing part-time relationship with the university that would allow him more time for composing. And then, on February 4, the *New York Times* published an interview with MacDowell in which he declared his frustration with Butler's unwillingness to create a School of Fine Arts and described his eight years on the faculty as "a great disappointment." He also expressed sympathy for the recently decamped Woodberry. When reproved by the trustees for going public, MacDowell denied having told Butler that he was considering resigning to have more time for composing. He then resigned.[22]

MacDowell's actions greatly embarrassed Columbia's president. After noting Butler's "difficulties dealing with poets and composers," Chairman Rives in the end accepted Butler's explanation. Yet he and some other trustees came away from the MacDowell affair only slightly more displeased with their mercurial composer than with their president. For his part, Butler cast himself a victim of the yellow press and faculty vindictiveness. The MacDowell episode, hard on the heels of the Woodberry brouhaha, conveyed a presidential lesson: faculty eccentrics posed a threat to the maintenance of good presidential-trustee relations.[23]

Then came Harry Thurston Peck, Anthon Professor of Greek and Latin, editor of the *Bookman* (1895–1902), prolific literary journalist, and downtown presence. In the summer of 1910, Peck was publicly charged with breach of promise of matrimony (to a stenographer, following a divorce from his first wife and remarriage). Once again, Columbia faculty were making unflattering newspaper headlines, this time accompanied by excerpts from the professor's love letters provided by the jilted stenographer.[24]

On this occasion, Butler showed no hesitation in demanding the resignation of a senior member of his faculty for embarrassing the university. When Peck declined to tender it, Butler, citing the 1810 charter provision of faculty service "during good behaviour," called on the trustees to terminate him, as his "usefulness to the University is at an end." "The Trustees may," he informed them, "lawfully terminate Professor Peck's employment at any time and for any reason they please; and he is not legally entitled to any notice, trial or hearing." On October 3, 1910, they did so. Following the vote, Trustee Low asked that Peck be paid for the rest of the academic year, an act of mercy that the meeting minutes do not indicate the president joined. Butler's outburst to Keppel about "academic hypochondriacs" came three days after the trustee vote. In 1914, the same year Keppel's *Columbia* appeared, in which he made reference to "academic suicides," Peck committed suicide.[25]

At the time of Peck's firing, Joel Spingarn (CC 1895; CU Ph.D. 1899) was a recently promoted professor of English who had studied with Woodberry and taught under him in the Department of Comparative Literature. Spingarn was also an activist in Jewish and interracial causes. In 1908 he unsuccessfully ran for Congress as a liberal Republican; a year later he helped W. E. B. Du Bois found the National Association for the Advancement of Colored People, with which he remained affiliated all his long life.[26]

In April 1910 Spingarn objected when Butler rejoined the comparative literature and dramatic literature departments into a single Department of English and Comparative Literature. Ten months later he fired off a letter to Butler—copies to the press—in which he was personally offensive to the president and harshly critical of the trustees' actions in firing Peck. Butler responded by eliminating Spingarn's position, an action he apparently undertook without specific trustee urging. Indeed, so precipitous had been Butler's action that Chairman Rives took the occasion of the announcement of Spingarn's firing in the New York *Sun* to remind Butler that "professors are not dropped by the President, but by the Trustees." Of independent means, Spingarn, after complaining that his academic freedom had been violated by the university's action, became a New York publisher, yet another casualty in the quixotic battle waged by Columbia faculty against what they saw as the high-handedness of their imperious president.[27]

If there is any discernible pattern to these "academic suicides," it is that they all to one degree or another implicated Butler personally and called forth his defensive response. But another is that, as far as the president and trustees were concerned, the precipitating event was not a faculty member engaging in some misconduct so much as his going public in defense of his conduct and thereby subjecting the university to the scrutiny of the New York press. Although assured the benefit of the doubt from the city's more respectable newspapers and magazines, the New York *Times* especially, Columbia could also depend on its dirty linen getting an unsympathetic airing elsewhere. Accordingly, were there a single lesson for Columbia faculty to draw from these incidents, it was that the unforgivable transgression was publicly embarrassing the university, which, in the realm of external affairs, meant the president and trustees. The reciprocal of this lesson, of course, was that if a faculty member really wanted to get a rise out of his "employers," taking his story to the press did the trick.

In the Matter of James McKeen Cattell

Just as the trustees were dismissing Peck and Spingarn was preparing to take up his cause, Secretary Keppel sent Butler a heads-up memorandum on the state of faculty morale. "There is," he wrote on September 24, 1910, "a certain undercurrent of dissatisfaction about the place, and it isn't all Cattell."[28]

By then, James McKeen Cattell had been at Columbia for nearly two decades. It had been Butler who recruited him away from the University of Pennsylvania in 1891 and Low who had agreed to Cattell's terms that he be on campus only two days a week, that he have no undergraduate teaching responsibilities, and that he was free to live in Garrison-on-Hudson, forty miles north of Manhattan. During Low's presidency, Cattell got along well with the authorities and his colleagues. Although he and Butler disagreed about where psychology fit into the Columbia scheme of things—Cattell wanted it included in the Faculty of Pure Science, while Butler kept it in the Faculty of Philosophy—they did not clash. It was Cattell who helped secure a second psychologist, Charles A. Strong, and from Strong's father-in-law, John D. Rockefeller, the funds to underwrite the appointment. Ever on the outlook for academic talent, he was also helpful to Butler in his efforts in 1896 to secure the appointment of Franz Boas and in 1904 John Dewey.[29]

Cattell got on less well with President Butler, who was two years his junior. Whereas Butler at the outset of his presidency seemed prepared to allow his star psychologist considerable autonomy in pursuing various research and publishing ventures, Cattell took it upon himself to become the president's nag. He became the prototype of the faculty buttinsky, urging reforms in the academic calendar, admissions policies, the rank structure, whatever. He also regularly provided unsolicited commentary on what the competition was up to, usually attended by the blowing of his own horn.[30]

In 1905 Cattell complained to Butler about his decision to appoint the deans of the various schools. The president informed him he was the only faculty member to have objected. The following year he complained when Butler decided that members of the College faculty should be appointed for fixed terms by the president, not elected by their peers as they had been in the past. Butler, in his response, pointed out that Cattell's terms of appointment specifically exempted him from all involvement with the College. When, rather than take the hint, Cattell used his position on the University Council to bring the matter of membership in the College faculty to a vote, his resolution to override the president's decision was defeated seventeen to twelve. He then suggested that the other faculty on the council were too frightened of Butler to voice their real opinions.[31]

In March 1906 Cattell used the pages of *Science*, which he owned and edited, to publish the first of a series of articles on "university control." Although his examples of autocratic behavior were not limited to Columbia, its trustees and president came in for more than their share of critical commentary. From this point on, several trustees, chief among them Francis S. Bangs and John P. Pine, regarded Cattell as a marked man.[32]

Having abandoned his research to devote himself to his publishing empire and the cause of "academic freedom," Cattell found more to complain about, even as he explained why so few of his colleagues joined him. "We are so used to the idea of a paternal president who takes care of us all," he wrote Butler in February 1907, "that there seems to be a certain lack of loyalty in questioning his plans for our welfare." Two days later Butler shot back: "You are quite mistaken in supposing that the President is the executive officer of the Faculties and subject to their direction."[33]

For all his autonomy, Cattell sometimes found himself in need of a favor from the trustees or the president. Such an occasion occurred in 1908, when he asked to be allowed to take back-to-back sabbaticals. The request was rejected, with Trustee Bangs perhaps taking a bit too much pleasure in its denial. A year later, Cattell, his many publishing ventures having made him financially independent, publicly took up the cause in *Science* of his less well-heeled younger colleagues, contending that the salaries the trustees paid junior faculty undercut the quality of the university. When Butler told him to stay out of trustee matters and "stick to your own severe tasks," Cattell told the president that his reproof was "reminiscent of the doctrine that the people should be humble and work hard and leave it to the King and his Lords to care for him."[34]

Ignoring Butler's warning, Cattell weighed in at the next opportunity. It came in the summer of 1909, when the chairman of the Trustee Finance Committee, Francis Bangs, decided to change the schedule of faculty salary payments from twelve per year to ten, eliminating the summer checks, which often went astray. Cattell complained to Bangs about the inconvenience wrought by this change, but Bangs defended the new arrangement on the grounds of efficiency. Cattell then went to Low, who went to Butler, who informed his predecessor that "Cattell is chronically opposed nowadays to anything that anybody does" but then persuaded the Finance Committee to return to twelve monthly payments.[35]

Bangs was now mad at both Cattell and Butler. He took particular offense when Cattell persuaded John Dewey to complain about the change in the payment schedule. "I am tired of serving on honorary boards," Bangs told Butler, "where I get pelted by everybody who hates a change, and I am regarded as if I were oppressing them to my own profit."[36]

That fall, occasioned by Burgess's appointment as the first dean of the Graduate Faculties, Cattell returned to his earlier complaint about Butler's appointing deans formerly elected by the faculty. He also bemoaned the proliferation of administrators in general. When Butler told Cattell it had become necessary to have more administrators to assume responsibilities the faculty was neglecting, Cattell would have none of it. "If professors sometimes leave undone those things which they ought to do," he wrote back, "administrative officers often do those things which they ought not to do."[37]

If Butler increasingly affected an imperious manner, Cattell could also be downright petty. In November 1909 he refused to fill out evaluations of his departmental colleagues, seeing some insidious purpose to forms devised by the University Council to expedite a departmental chore. A few months later he renewed his campaign on behalf of junior faculty and demanded an opportunity to make their case for higher salaries directly to the trustees. Among the data he intended to present, he told Butler, were the results of a poll that showed nearly all junior faculty (139 of 154) favored higher salaries.[38]

In 1910, with the Carnegie faculty pension plan newly in place, Cattell began dropping hints about retiring. Only fifty-three, he was scheduled to complete twenty-five years of teaching in 1913, which would make him eligible for a Carnegie pension. When Bangs heard of Cattell's plans, he urged Butler not to wait but to give him two years of terminal leave and be done with him. Butler was inclined to agree. "We should have to meet [the Carnegie allowance] for thirteen or fourteen years," he calculated, "but, in the judgment of most people, it would be cheap at the price." Bangs was all for the expenditure. "We have lost so many men of eminence," he wrote Butler, "that I don't believe a total loss of him will now hurt us." To this Butler responded that there was only one problem: Cattell "would not accept it voluntarily." They would have to wait.[39]

Meanwhile, Cattell's editorials in *Science* and letters to the New York press faulting Columbia for one policy after another continued to infuriate the trustees. By then, a fairly typical letter on Columbia's underpaying its assistant professors to the *New York Times* on March 14, 1911, prompted Bangs to call it "the most flagrant breach in confidence and evidence of disloyalty which we have yet had." On May 1, 1913, the trustees' Education Committee, on which Bangs and Pine sat, decided to act on Cattell's earlier retirement musings and voted to retire him under the twenty-five-year provisions of the Carnegie Plan, effective June 30. Only the fact that the trustees' action caught Cattell in the midst of publicly resigning from the Century Association and calling on all other Centurions (including the eighteen trustee members) to do likewise, following the association's rejection of the nomination to membership of the noted physiologist Dr. Jacques Loeb—presumably because he was Jewish—prevented him from objecting immediately. When he did, informing Chairman Rives that he had no intention to resign, he attached a ten-page, fourteen-point list of indictments "Contra NMB." Shades of William Livingston.[40]

Meanwhile, Cattell had roused colleagues to his defense, among them his departmental colleagues Edward L. Thorndike and Robert Woodworth, Professor of Philosophy Frederick J. E. Woodbridge, who had just succeeded Burgess as dean of Graduate Faculties, and most of the Faculty of Pure Science. Ex-president and recently resigned Trustee Seth Low also spoke up for Cattell. None of his supporters doubted he was difficult, but all argued that his noisy departure would hurt Columbia. Three weeks before his forced retirement was to begin, the trustees withdrew his name from the Carnegie list.[41]

For the next two-and-one-half years, even as he actively pushed the cause of faculty control of universities nationally, Cattell laid low locally. It was not until January 1917, in a letter to Faculty Club members, a copy of which he provided to the *New York Times*, that he renewed his personal attack on Butler. By then, his running complaints risked being drowned out by the debate on campus provoked by the war in Europe and arguments over the role America should take in it. Although Cattell later succeeded in securing himself a conspicuous part in that debate, he played no role in generating it.[42]

Columbia and the Great War

One of the ways the prewar Columbia faculty differed from the trustees was the conspicuous presence among the former of open admirers of German culture. Some faculty came by way of their Germanophilia by birth and some by subject matter, but many who neither were of German extraction nor taught German acquired a taste for Germany through youthful sojourns at German universities, where their subsequent career plans took shape. Of Columbia's one thousand officers of instruction in 1915, perhaps one hundred had studied in Germany, far more than had studied in either France or England. The university's science faculty were far more likely to read German than any of the Romance languages.

Although hardly an admirer of the kaiser, Franz Boas was sufficiently loyal to his birthplace to participate in the affairs of the Germanistic Society of

Columbia University. John W. Burgess was an even more comprehensive admirer of Germany, its universities, and its royal family. When chosen as the first Theodore Roosevelt Exchange Professor in 1906, he took some pride in the fact that, unlike American exchange professors from Harvard who had preceded him to the University of Berlin, he planned to deliver his public lectures in German. That he shared the anti-Semitism of many of his German hosts only confirmed him as a kindred spirit.[43]

By contrast, the Columbia faculty had fewer Anglophiles than did Harvard, Yale, or Princeton—or the Columbia trustees, where pro-British sentiment was the norm. The sociologist Franklin Giddings, an Englishman by birth, and the historian Charles A. Beard, a son of the American Midwest whose postcollegiate years were spent in London's Toynbee Hall and whose 1902 Columbia dissertation was entitled "The Office of Justice of the Peace in England," were the closest the prewar Columbia faculty came to resident John Bulls. Several faculty members of French and Italian birth, however, took leaves in 1914 and returned home to join the fight against Germany and Austro-Hungary.[44]

In August 1914, with the exception of the recently retired Burgess, few Columbians openly sympathized with the German cause. But neither were there many ready to follow Theodore Roosevelt's call for immediate American intervention on the side of the Allies. Majority sentiment well into 1915 adhered closely to President Wilson's early pledge that America would be "neutral in thought and deed" and opposed efforts to prepare for the possibility of entering the war. In 1915 Dean of Columbia College Frederick Keppel urged Columbia not to participate in the Plattsburgh Movement, a concerted undertaking by preparedness groups and interventionists that provided undergraduates with opportunities for military drilling.[45]

Keppel did this with Butler's approval. Indeed, few American public figures more prominently identified with what the interventionist Theodore Roosevelt called the "pacifist crowd" than Columbia's president. Like his mentor, Burgess, he was an admirer of German culture. His personal audience with Kaiser Wilhelm at the German royal family's summer residence in 1907 had been a high moment for this son of Paterson, New Jersey. Well into 1915, Burgess cast Germany as the victim of Allied aggression.[46]

Butler's noninterventionist views can be attributed to many factors: his involvement with the international peace groups sponsored by Andrew Carnegie; his political estrangement from the rabidly interventionist Theodore Roosevelt; the counsel of Burgess; and his own positive feelings about Germany and the kaiser. What they cannot be attributed to is subservience to the trustees, who in 1916 numbered among them not only Anglophiles of the first water but Francophiles, international bankers, and munitions manufacturers—in short, all those cited in the 1930s as being responsible for having "tricked" the United States into entering the Great War.[47]

In the early weeks of 1917, several developments converged to make that year one of the most traumatic in the university's history. The first development occurred in Berlin, where the German military command determined to break the two-year deadlock by an all-out assault on the Allies. This included the renewal of submarine warfare, which had been halted in 1915 after the sinking of the HMS *Lusitania* very nearly brought the United States into the war. The second was the shift by the Wilson administration away from its stated policy of armed neutrality and toward intervention.[48]

The movement toward intervention discernible among politicians in Washington in early 1917 had been anticipated by politically engaged New York intellectuals, prominent among them the editors of the *New Republic*, Walter Lippmann and Herbert Croly. Like-minded Columbia faculty included the sociologist Franklin Giddings, the economist E. R. A. Seligman, and the historians James Harvey Robinson and Charles A. Beard. Of all the Columbia conversions, the most conspicuous had been that of the philosopher John Dewey.[49]

It was Dewey's evolving support for American entry into the war, and then his opposition to conscientious objectors, that moved the recent Columbia graduate (CC 1912) and unreconstructed noninterventionist Randolph Bourne to respond in *The Seven Arts*. In two articles, "War and the Intellectuals" and "Twilight of Idols," Bourne laid bare the disillusionment he felt watching his Columbia mentors, above all his revered Dewey, apply their pragmatic methods and instrumentalist ways to justify a war he could not condone. Of these professors, he wrote, "there seems to have been a peculiar congeniality between the war and these men. It is as if the war and they had been waiting for each other."[50]

Butler's lack of enthusiasm for preparedness extended right up to the German resumption of submarine warfare in February 1917. His subsequent martial fervor may have been all the greater for its belatedness. On February 13, the day following the German announcement, he sent a telegram assuring President Wilson and the nation of "the loyal support of the University to the Government of the United States in all measures of national defense."[51]

Although more to his board's liking, Butler's telegram seems not to have satisfied his most militant trustees. On March 5, six weeks before the United States entered the war, trustees Bangs and Pine secured adoption of a resolution holding Butler's feet to the fire: "Resolved—The unqualified loyalty to the Government of the United States be required of all students, officers of administration and officers of instruction in the University as a condition of retaining their connection with the University, and that the President have authority to exercise the disciplinary powers of the University to carry this resolution into effect."[52]

The trustees need not have worried. Butler was now second to no American in his militancy. On June 6, six weeks after the United States entered the war, he used his commencement address to declare that Columbia would not countenance any opposition to the war effort. "What had been tolerated before became intolerable now," he told his audience. "What had been wrong headedness was now sedition. What had been folly was now treason."[53]

Meanwhile, and at first unrelated to these developments, James McKeen Cattell's January letter personally attacking the president of the university continued to occupy trustees' attention. Several judged his statements to be disloyal to Columbia and grounds for dismissal. Before voting on a dismissal resolution, however, the board, at Butler's urging, asked the University Council for its view of Cattell's behavior. The council in turn established an all-faculty "Committee of Nine," chaired by E. R. A. Seligman and including John Dewey and Frederick J. E. Woodbridge.[54]

On March 3 the Committee of Nine reprimanded Cattell for his assault on the president. It then agreed to work with the momentarily remorseful psychologist in preparing an apology acceptable to Butler. Meanwhile, as regards Cattell, Seligman urged the president to "take no notice" and to accept the forthcoming apology "in light of Cattell's ongoing usefulness." While recognizing the delicacy of his committee's position in these deliberations, Seligman was sufficiently optimistic about the prospects of a positive outcome to suggest that his faculty committee might be the solution to all Columbia's governance problems.[55]

The Committee of Nine composed the apology to Butler, which Cattell reluctantly signed on June 5. When the committee then released the apology to the press, Cattell charged Seligman with deceiving him about the letter's intended circulation and violating his "academic freedom." That did it for Seligman. "I desire to state emphatically that in my opinion academic freedom has nothing to do with your case," he informed Cattell on June 18 before pronouncing, "Your usefulness to the University is at an end." And so concluded a majority of the Committee of Nine, with only Dewey and one other member declining to join in the call for Cattell's retirement, effective June 30, 1917.[56]

Cattell's past behavior in the face of criticism provided a fair indicator of how he would react in this situation. Even as his fate was in Butler's hands, he promptly violated the president's June 6 declaration that any action by a member of the Columbia community against the war effort would be grounds for immediate dismissal. In May, Cattell's son, Herbert, a part-time student in chemistry, along with two other undergraduates—"a bright but flighty girl in Barnard College" and "a Hebrew with a respectable father on West End Avenue"—had been arrested for participating in an antiwar demonstration.

Cattell immediately took up their cause, arguing that his son and two friends had done nothing to warrant expulsion from the university, much less criminal prosecution for treason. At the trial in July, the students' actions were defended by the Socialist attorney Morris Hillquit and applauded by Cattell. Each was fined two hundred fifty dollars.[57]

Now fully engaged in the antiwar movement, Cattell proceeded in August to send several congressmen and senators a letter outlining his views on the legality and morality of sending American conscripts overseas. By using Columbia stationery and identifying himself as a member of the Columbia faculty, he made certain that Butler and the trustees became aware of his correspondence. A copy of the letter appeared in the *New York Evening Post* on August 18. Several offended recipients predictably protested to Butler that Cattell's claim that conscripts be allowed to decline overseas assignments interfered with the prosecution of the war and was a crime under the recently passed Draft Act. At the very least, they informed Butler, it violated his commencement prohibition of public statements detrimental to the war effort.[58]

The Committee of Nine, after reconvening on October 1, restated its position that Cattell's continued membership in the faculty "was not in the interest of University." A day later, Trustee Pine wrote to Parsons in France: "I was waiting until we had taken one or two scalps as evidence that we meant what we said. Yesterday we got them." As for Cattell specifically, "We have got the rascal this time and must leave him no loophole."[59]

At the first meeting of the trustees, on October 4, a resolution called for Cattell's termination, citing his "continuance as prejudicial to the welfare of the University." Unlike the 1913 forced retirement, this termination was to be without pension. For good measure, the board also terminated Assistant Professor of English Henry Wadsworth Longfellow Dana for sundry antiwar activities.[60]

Several trustees were disinclined to stop with Cattell and Dana. Francis S. Bangs saw the economic exigencies imposed by the war as a splendid opportunity for making more cuts. "A little academic freedom in changing the Departments of Economics and History," he wrote to Butler in the summer, "for the good of the University would not be amiss." He specifically had in mind Seligman, with whom he had clashed a decade before over selling university real estate and more recently over the power of the University Council to determine university policy. Another target was the historian Carleton J. H. Hayes, who had the misfortune of being forever typecast in the Bangs household as the unsympathetic faculty adviser to his son, Francis (CC 1910; CU Law 1913). Hayes had also been among those Columbia faculty who, as late as January 1917, had publicly opposed American military preparations.[61]

In September Bangs reiterated his views in a letter to Butler: "I am for making short work of Cattell and Dana, and in connection with next year's budget making a radical and sweeping change in the personnel of history, economics and politics. . . . The power of the Trustees to regulate the affairs of the University is absolute.[62]

Similarly disposed was the newly elected chairman, William B. Parsons, who, though off in France on war work during the summer of 1917, was kept well informed by President Butler. From Paris, Colonel—soon to be promoted to general—Parsons wrote to Butler in July, "Now that the country is actually at war, we should purge ourselves of all doubtful characters." It had been Parsons, in the spring of 1916, who had directed Butler to form a special committee "to investigate the teachings of the professors . . . to ascertain whether any . . . have taught . . . doctrines not consistent with the Constitution of the United States or of the State of New York." Back then, however, the "doubtful characters" Parsons had in mind were not critics of the war effort but critics of the American way. Chief among these was one of Columbia's most prominent interventionists, the historian Charles A. Beard. But before Parsons could get back from Paris to New York to add Beard's name to the list of expendables, on October 9 the historian resigned his Columbia professorship.[63]

In the Matter of Charles A. Beard

On several levels, Beard's action came as a surprise. He was not a friend or political ally of Cattell's. Nor had he been conspicuously engaged in the "academic freedom" debate. He had been and remained at the time of his resignation an enthusiastic backer of America's intervention in the war. He and his wife, Mary, a suffragette, were active in local politics. And, unlike Cattell, he had entered fully into Columbia campus life. Undergraduates liked him and he them; he regularly taught an extra course at Barnard. In 1912 a student poll named him their choice for the next president of Columbia. Moreover, from his first days as a young lecturer in 1904, he enjoyed a cordial relationship with President Butler, who then and later showed an avuncular interest in him. Beard was one of the few faculty with whom Butler talked politics. Two decades after his resignation, when Beard returned to Columbia to teach in the 1938 summer session, Butler said "that he is red headed on the inside as well as the outside." For his part, Beard directed his criticisms upon his resignation at the trustees, not the president.[64]

But if Beard had gotten along well enough with Butler, he had ruffled many trustee feathers. His opposition in 1909 to the appointment of William Guthrie, a practicing attorney and prominent Catholic, to the Ruggles Professorship of

Public Law had been duly noted by Guthrie's many Columbia friends. Among them was the retiring Ruggles Professor John W. Burgess, who hoped his successor would be "a lawyer and not a sociological tyro." And that's what the trustees had in mind. Ready to let their arts and science faculty appoint whom they wished, lawyers and Law School alumni on the board, such as John Pine, Francis Bangs, and, in this instance, the Catholic trustee-to-be Frederick Coudert Jr., who briefly considered the professorship for himself, believed themselves at least as capable of identifying legal talent as nonlawyers like Beard. Even though the Guthrie appointment went through, several trustees resented the struggle it required.[65]

Nor were they pleased with the publicity in connection with what they viewed as Beard's assault on the founding fathers in his *Economic Interpretation of the Constitution*, published in 1913 to generally critical reviews. The unsigned review in Butler's own *Educational Review*, possibly written by him, was among the milder the book received, allowing only that it represented "a good deal of labor without, we fear, any very important result. . . . We had thought that the myth of the Economic Man had finally disappeared."[66]

Beard came under the direct scrutiny of a special subcommittee of the board's Education Committee in April 1916 after the New York *World* reported his presence at a meeting of the National Conference of Community Centers, at which the phrase "To Hell with the Flag" had been uttered. Bangs and Coudert used the occasion to criticize the historian's scholarship as well as the political company he kept. Trustee Coudert faulted Beard for some disrespectful remarks about the Supreme Court that he had allegedly made in class. Denying any sympathy for the reported statement and minimizing his involvement with the organization, Beard came away from the encounter exonerated but shaken. In February 1917 a student reported to the authorities that Beard had used profanity in his class. Butler promptly had the matter looked into, and the accusation was withdrawn. "In this age of frenzied thinking and lying," the grateful Beard wrote the president, "the only encouraging sign is the few who call for proof and witnesses."[67]

Thus Beard's resignation eight months later was about more than Cattell and the war, as his resignation letter made clear. It was also about professorial autonomy and occupational status. "The university is really under the control of a small and active group of trustees," he wrote, "who have no standing in the world of education, who are reactionary and visionless in politics, narrow and medieval in religion." Nor, he allowed, was the problem peculiar to Columbia. "America, of all countries, has made the status of the professor lower than that of the manual laborer, who, through his union, has at least some voice in the terms and conditions of his employment." Beard closed his letter with assurances to Butler: "And to you, Sir, I am deeply indebted for the courtesy and thoughtful consideration that I have always received at your hands."[68]

Several trustees reacted to Beard's unexpected resignation much as did the *New York Times*, which ran an editorial headed "Columbia's Deliverance." In the same issue, Barnard College trustee Annie Nathan Meyer wrote that that Beard's resignation revealed "this bogey of academic freedom." Among the many letters in the Butler Papers congratulating him for ridding Columbia of Beard, the sentiments in that of a lawyer and "New Yorker of 50 years standing" were typical: "The idea that some of these gentlemen seem to have, that because they have been employed at so much a year to teach boys in a college, they are therefore qualified to undertake to teach grown men of the community how it should be governed, and to meddle with affairs of which they have no knowledge, seems to me most absurd."[69]

Reaction on campus to Beard's resignation went quite the other way. A petition signed by twenty-one Japanese and Chinese graduate students in the Faculty of Political Science praised Beard for his deep concern with their educational welfare. The Peithologian Society wrote to Butler to protest the firings of Cattell and Dana and the resignation of Beard. Barnard students held a protest meeting on Beard's behalf.[70]

Two days after Beard's resignation, the Barnard philosopher William P. Montague applauded his action in a letter to the New York *Tribune*. Montague's Barnard colleague, Henry R. Mussey, an associate professor of economics, who had come close to being fired in September with Cattell and Dana, resigned in November, giving as his reasons, in a letter to Seligman, whose Committee of Nine had defended him, not only the firings of Cattell and Dana but the faculty's supine response to them.[71]

Despite the firings of Cattell and Dana and the resignations of Beard and Mussey, Trustee Bangs remained unsated. He still had his eye on Seligman, citing him, as he informed the other trustees on December 13, 1917, for "creating the machinery which would forever prevent the Trustees from carrying out their charter powers and authority." Failing to generate much enthusiasm for cashiering Seligman, Bangs got the trustees to agree to terminate Leon Fraser, an instructor in politics and one of Butler's "bright young men," whose only error was failing to abandon his antipreparedness views at the same time Butler and Keppel did. When Keppel was informed of Bangs's vendetta against Fraser, he said simply, "Bangs is that kind of man." Indeed, Keppel, who wanted to return to his Columbia College deanship after wartime service in Washington, only to be told by Butler that there was no place for him, is also to be counted among the casualties of 1917.[72]

By this juncture, Butler, seeing how this could play out, was having second thoughts. "The public get the impression," he wrote to Trustee George T. Ingraham, "that there was a state of war in Columbia between the Trustees and the professors." But the war went on a bit longer. When the Columbia-trained philosopher Will Durant, a lecturer in the Columbia Extension Program, made a speech protesting the circumstances of Beard's resignation, his contract was not renewed. In the spring of 1919 Beard's mentor and colleague James Harvey Robinson resigned after sixteen years at Columbia, "to explore the potential of adult education." Along with Beard and Alvin Johnson, who had taught at Columbia from 1902 to 1906, Robinson had helped launch the New School for Social Research. Like Beard, Robinson left shortly thereafter and opted for the life of the independent scholar.[73]

Other faculty losses were no less serious, if not involving firings or resignations. John Dewey, after nearly leaving Columbia in 1918 to take a place at the New School, was never thereafter as involved in the workings of Columbia as he had been before the war. The same went for Franz Boas, a target of Bangs in 1918 for teaching "Anthropology, as construed from the German standpoint," who moved his locus of activities to Barnard in the 1920s. Only a concerted effort by Butler to reconnect him with Columbia on the occasion of its 175th anniversary in 1929 ended his decade-long internal exile.[74]

Not all, or even most, Columbians shared Boas's neutrality or even Dewey's misgivings about the Allied cause. A handful of students were reprimanded and at least one expelled for antiwar activities, but hundreds of others enlisted in one of the armed services or stayed on at Columbia in the Student Army Training Corps (SATC). The United States School of Military Cinematography was housed on campus. Dozens of faculty enthusiastically joined the war effort, either in uniform or in one of the many war agencies, among them the Committee on War Information and the National Board for Historical Service, which put academic "experts" to use. Nearly the entire medical faculty received military commissions and were assigned to military hospitals. Professor of History James Shotwell became a wartime member of the Inquiry, a research organization charged with the collection of reports and documents that would aid in the peace settlement. His younger history colleague, Carleton J. H. Hayes, served in the United States Army in France.[75]

In fact, it was the attempt by Bangs to block Hayes's promotion to full professor in the spring of 1919 that marked the end of the wave of trustee reprisals, faculty resignations, and mutual recriminations. Just back from army service in France, Hayes had signed a petition in support of the International Workers of the World ("Wobblies") then on trial in Chicago, and Bangs wanted him to pay for it. This time, Butler, who is not recorded as having voiced any objections to the earlier faculty reprisals sponsored by Bangs and others, stepped in.

"He committed a grave error in judgment," the president allowed of Hayes, but his having "so admitted" should end the matter. Butler then made a more general point about the future uses of forbearance: "The morale of the University will be strengthened and the Trustees themselves aided in securing the support of all parts of the University for any action it might in the future be necessary to to take if any such unfortunate cases as arose in the year 1917 should again occur." This statement was then approved by the trustees, with only Bangs dissenting. He thereafter stopped attending trustee meetings and died the following year. By then, negotiations were under way with Cattell that in 1922 would end with an agreement that gave him his pension. The war was over.[76]

Three cautionary conclusions might be drawn from Columbia's inner war in the midst of the Great War. First, it produced few heroes or unimplicated victims. The trustees have the strongest claim to the part of the heavy, but neither the president nor the faculty should escape blame. Another allowable conclusion is that, as competing theories of governance, faculty autonomy and trustee authority—and, as we saw earlier and will see later, student agency—all produce their discontents, and no one of them, unchecked, is immune to abuse. And, finally, human relationships have their own histories and help incite open clashes not to be wholly accounted for by the immediate circumstances that occasion them.

The crisis of 1917—and the collective memory of it—influenced what happened later. Support for this conclusion comes from two different faculty sources. The economist Rexford Tugwell, who taught at Columbia all through the 1920s, before leaving to join the Roosevelt Brains Trust in 1933, viewed the consequences of 1917 favorably. "The shadow of the Beard resignation, especially," he believed, "would deter those who might otherwise have undertaken to enforce conformity . . . for a whole generation. He [Beard] helped to protect all the rest of us." The literary scholar John Erskine, who was to resign his position at Columbia in 1927, offered a more neutral assessment: "It seemed to me that the Trustees, reacting from their impulsive mistake, became a cautious, harmless and colorless body, and that control of the University rested thereafter in the strong hands of President Butler."[77]

Both Tugwell and Erskine were right. Presidential power would grow in the interwar period and do so at the expense of trustee authority. For their part, most faculty accepted this arrangement. Indeed, at least one senior faculty member, the philosopher Frederick J. E. Woodbridge, who had served, in his capacity as the dean of Graduate Faculties, on the Committee of Nine that supported the firings of Cattell and Dana, concluded that Columbia's faculty lacked "a sufficient sense of corporate interest and corporate responsibility" to provide the university with effective leadership. "Our house can not be cleaned by the Trustees. . . . There can be only one leader and that is the President of the University. Efforts have been made to reform this place without his leadership and these efforts have failed. These efforts should stop. A new effort should be made under his leadership as chairman of a committee chosen from the University faculties to look into our condition."[78]

No such committee ever materialized, but the idea behind it did. For the next quarter-century, peace would be maintained among Columbia's recently clashing estates by the trustees staying out of faculty affairs and the faculty following Butler's advice to Cattell to "stick to your own severe tasks." Both, in effect, ceded to the president ultimate control over the university, with consequences to follow.

CHAPTER 9

Jews at Columbia

Young Ham Fish is going to Harvard!

Trustee John B. Pine, 1906

By far the majority of the Jewish students who do come to Columbia are desirable students in every way. What most people regard as a racial problem is really a social problem.

Dean Frederick P. Keppel, 1914

In other words, I suggest treating the candidate for graduation as one treats a candidate for admission to a club, that is, having his personal qualifications examined.

Nicholas Murray Butler, 1914

I do not believe that a College would do well to admit too many men of low mentality who have ambition but not brains.

Dean Herbert E. Hawkes, 1922

Columbia must be very different and very much less attractive in the winter session, when the girls are not here and there are many more Jews.

Summer session student, Milton Halsey Thomas, 1923

Academic Nativism

E ARLY-TWENTIETH-CENTURY academic anti-Semitism has not wanted for chroniclers. That Columbia figures prominently in this literature is largely due to a fine book by the historian Harold S. Wechsler (CC 1967; Ph.D. 1974). Its deceptively bland title notwithstanding, *The Qualified Student: A History of Selective College Admission in America, 1870–1970* (1977) offers a thorough treatment of the many ways Columbia between the world wars actively discriminated against otherwise academically qualified Jewish applicants to Columbia College, Barnard College, and the Medical School. It has been a model for subsequent studies of anti-Semitism at Harvard, Yale, and Princeton. Those familiar with Wechsler's work will recognize my indebtedness in what follows, which I hasten to acknowledge.[1]

In one sense, however, my purposes run in the opposite direction from Wechsler's. I intend to argue less that Columbia discriminated against Jews in admissions to the College, as Wechsler demonstrates it did, than that, despite such discrimination, interwar Columbia was more accommodating of and less hostile to Jewish students than were the other major eastern universities. Nationally, only the University of Chicago was as welcoming.[2]

Although present in small numbers earlier, Jews first became a remarked-on part of the Columbia student body in the 1860s, when the brothers Isaac and Felix Adler (CC 1868 and 1870, respectively) complained about Saturday exams. Nicholas Murray Butler's graduating class in 1882 numbered fifty, of whom a half-dozen were Jewish. By the turn of the century, Jews constituted between 10 and 15 percent of entering College classes, with comparable proportions enrolled at Barnard, the Law School, the School of Mines, and the Graduate Faculties.[3]

In the fall of 1917, following American entry into the Great War that spring, total enrollments dropped sharply when dozens of undergraduates left for military service, and the proportion of Jewish students in the College topped 25 percent, though subsequent estimates that the proportion reached as high as 40 percent lack documentation and credibility. Yet even during the 1920s, when discriminatory admission practices were being rigorously enforced at both Columbia and Barnard, and even more so at the Medical School, Jews made up at least a quarter of the university's student body. Among business and Law School students, the proportion was closer to half. Only at the Medical School did the enrollment of Jews during the interwar period drop below earlier levels. There, according to Kenneth M. Ludmerer, the Jewish enrollment between 1920 and 1940 dropped from 47 percent of the class to 6 percent.[4]

Among Columbia's peers, only the University of Chicago had as high a proportion of Jewish undergraduates. The next closest was Harvard, where, despite President Lowell's call in 1922 for a 12 percent quota in the College—which his faculty rejected as unseemly—the percentage of self-identified Jews stayed below 10 percent throughout the interwar period. For Harvard overall, the percentage was on the order of 15 percent. At Yale, there existed an unacknowledged 10 percent quota for Jews admitted to the college; at Princeton, Jews seldom exceeded 5 percent of interwar classes. Almost no effort was made to conceal the existence of these barriers. Among college-bound Jewish kids in Brooklyn in the late 1930, the Hebrew inscription of the Yale motto translated as "If you can read this, don't apply."[5]

The conventional wisdom in the 1920s, as a reporter for *Vanity Fair* put it, was that "all Columbia students are Jews." A fraternity song offered the following comparative analysis:

Oh, Harvard's run by millionaires
And Yale is run by Booze
Cornell is run by farmers' sons,
Columbia's run by Jews.[6]

While Columbia challenged this perception, it was not without some basis. A WASP upstater who enrolled in the university's summer program in 1923 decided not to register for the fall term, "when the girls are not here and there are many more Jews." The Jewish-sponsored *Menorah Journal* matter-of-factly reported in 1930 that the Columbia Law School "is predominantly Jewish" and that the College, its limits on Jewish students notwithstanding, "has an atmosphere that is unmistakable . . . that atmosphere is Jewish."[7]

The point here is not to dispute the claim that institutional anti-Semitism existed at interwar Columbia but to argue that, despite its existence, Columbia provided one of the least hostile environments in the upper reaches of the American academy. For an ambitious Jewish student, particularly one who was not religious, interwar Columbia offered a place where he could acquire the intellectual and social wherewithal—plus a cultural credential—to become someone else.

It can also be argued that the restrictions imposed in 1919 on the number of Jews admitted to Columbia College were not primarily intended to limit Jewish admissions, though they had that effect. Interwar Columbia was less about keeping Jews out than trying to hold places in the College for "our natural clientele" or "boys from good families," the sons of the long since decimated and decamped Knickerbockers. Official interwar Columbia had its version of a cargo cult: the Knickerbockers, having once come, would come again.[8]

Of course, the Jewish applicant denied admission on grounds other than academic ability and intellectual promise would not likely have been consoled by this difference. Nor would his being told that his rejection was based on the judgment that there were already enough Jews at Columbia and that any more would risk exceeding the tipping point at which Columbia's remaining WASPs would make a mass exodus.[9]

Yet from an institutional perspective, there is a difference between discrimination that is secondary and expedient and discrimination that is primary and principled. For starters, the expedient form is more susceptible to modification in light of changing conditions. Moreover, its restrictiveness need not be seen as directed against Jews as such, unlike that of anti-Semites, for whom the exclusion of Jews was primary. The discrimination against Jewish applicants to Columbia was not only wrong; it was counterproductive.

Thus, while Columbia's "Jewish Problem" was a real problem for Jews denied admission to Columbia, it was also part of a larger institutional problem of Columbia's own making. And because it is this latter problem that concerns me here, it requires telling from the perspective of the discriminators. Chief among these were the trustees but also involved were President Butler and his principal administrators, for whom the historical record is rich if not always dispositive.[10]

It bears recalling that Columbia's discriminatory efforts were of a piece with what was going on outside the university. The 1920s witnessed a cultural struggle between the "old" rural and small-town Protestant America and the "new" urban and non-WASP America in the making. The passage of restrictive immigration legislation in 1921 and 1924, a resurgence of the Ku Klux Klan, not only in the rural South but in industrialized cities of the North, efforts of Henry Ford to reconstitute a rural America (i.e., before automobiles and Jews) in Dearborn, Michigan, the offense taken at Al Smith's presidential candidacy in 1928—as a Catholic and a wet—all were part of a cultural counteroffensive to slow the so-called mongrelization of America. Thus Columbia's discriminatory actions against Jews, if manifestly less effective than those of Harvard, Princeton, and Yale, can be seen as part of this crusade by the older custodians of American culture to keep the 1920s from realizing what immigration restrictionist Madison Grant had predicted in 1918: "The Passing of the Great Race in America."[11]

Again, we have Wechsler to thank for putting Columbia's discriminatory history in a comparative context, declaring it "the first university with elitest pretensions to be confronted with a huge influx of Jews." But Columbia can just as accurately described as the first university to be confronted with the desertion of its original, or "natural" clientele. An important interpretive question, crucial in determining the direction of the causal link, is which came first? The argument here is that the problem early-twentieth-century Columbia had with "a huge influx of Jews" followed and was in large part a consequence of the antecedent "Problem of the Vanishing Knickerbocker."[12]

"Young Ham Fish Is Going to Harvard"

Down to the Civil War, most college-bound sons of New York's leading Knickerbocker families—pre-Revolutionary in American ancestry, Episcopalian or Dutch Reformed in religion—went to Columbia College. So did some sons of the city's Presbyterian elite, with others dispatched to Princeton or Yale. Antebellum Harvard attracted virtually no New Yorkers.[13]

The defections began after the Civil War, when prosperous New Yorkers took to sending boys away to rural boarding schools, among them St. Paul's, Groton, Andover, Lawrenceville, and St. Mark's. Once away, these adolescent New Yorkers had their range of college choices significantly broadened, not only by classmates destined for colleges other than Columbia but by headmasters with ties to Yale, Princeton, or Harvard. Late-nineteenth-century Columbia, perhaps primarily because it was a day school, had no feeder relationship with boarding schools, as Princeton, for example, did with Lawrenceville, which regularly sent a majority of its graduates there. Even the link with Columbia Grammar School, which had produced a steady trickle of boys for the College in the 1840s and 1850s, weakened after the Civil War and was severed with Columbia's move to Morningside.[14]

The desire to stay with school pals through the next round of education became a strong inducement for young Knickerbockers not to return to New York and Columbia. Doing so meant coming back under parental supervision, for nineteenth-century Columbia College, before the opening of Hamilton Hall in 1880, provided no on-campus housing. (Nor would it again between the opening of the Morningside campus in 1898 and the completion of Hartley Hall in 1905.) To be sure, some families' ties to Columbia remained sufficiently strong to pull back even the most determined defector, but in other Columbia families the prospect of a son going off to Amherst or Williams or Wesleyan was easily accommodated, often with the assumption that he would return to the city—and Columbia—for his professional studies.

Neither President Barnard nor President Low made much of the "Problem of the Vanishing Knickerbocker." For Barnard, whose interest was primarily in building up the professional schools, letting the rural Amhersts and Dartmouths prepare undergraduates for Columbia's professional schools seemed a fair division of labor and one that played to Columbia's strengths—and metropolitan locale. For Low, his standing in the city's Episcopalian establishment notwithstanding, retaining the older Knickerbocker families' loyalties to Columbia in the 1890s was of less concern than opening the College up to all New Yorkers.[15]

It was Low's trustees who first identified (without so labeling it) the "Problem of the Vanishing Knickerbocker," when their sons began announcing their intentions to go someplace else. Defections began in the late 1890s in the families of such prominent trustees—and certified Knickerbockers—as William Bayard Cutting, George Rives, and William Barclay Parsons, the last two being successive chairs of the Columbia board from 1903 to 1932, whose sons chose Harvard or Yale over Columbia. But the most spectacular defection occurred in 1906, when, contrary to earlier plans, Hamilton Fish III, the great-grandson of longtime board chairman Hamilton Fish (CC 1827) and grandson of Hamilton Fish Jr. (CC 1869), opted for Harvard over his "ancestral college." Board clerk John Pine's announcement to fellow trustees that "Young Ham Fish is going to Harvard" was delivered with the solemnity appropriate to declaring "The Queen is dead." Both statements were meant to mark the end of an era.[16]

In 1908 Columbia received other evidence that it was losing in the competition to attract the best boarding-school students, even those with familial ties to Columbia. This came from Virgil Prettyman, the headmaster of the Horace Mann School, which was affiliated with Teachers College and enrolled the children of some of New York's elite, along with a number of faculty children. Prettyman's report to the trustees was based on a survey of the college-going plans of students and their perceptions of the country's leading colleges. Their perception of Columbia was nothing if not explicit: it had become filled with the graduates of the city's public high schools, which made it unattractive to the graduates of boarding schools and New York's day schools.[17]

This was precisely the kind of unsolicited opinion certain to catch the trustees' attention, especially that of Francis Bangs and John Pine. Unlike Rives, Parsons, Cutting, or the Fish family, Bangs had compelled his two sons, Henry (CC 1906) and Francis (CC 1910), who had gone to St. Mark's, to attend Columbia. Both were active in athletics and in the Psi Upsilon fraternity but, judging from the frequent complaints about Columbia undergraduate life that they passed on to their father, were unhappy with their fate. During their years in the College, Bangs became insistent that Columbia make more "efforts to hold the children of our own," even though at times he seemed ready to throw in the towel.[18]

Prettyman's analysis, and the anecdotal corroboration it called forth from the trustees, made an already defensive Butler more so. To the extent that Columbia had become more welcoming to the graduates of the city's public schools—a third of whom in 1910 were Jewish—the responsibility rested squarely on his shoulders. As dean of the Faculty of Philosophy, he had supported the elimination of the Greek requirement for admissions; as president, he had supported the elimination of the Latin admissions requirement; and as the driving force behind the adoption of the common college entrance examinations (the college boards), he had made applying to Columbia simpler for public schoolers. The Combined Program, which allowed College students to transfer to one of the university's professional schools after as few as three semesters, was another Butler innovation attracting students in a hurry. Finally, it was Butler who pressed for the elimination of intercollegiate football in 1905 in the wake of several fatal injuries and eligibility scandals, which second-guessers among the trustees soon blamed for the disappearance of what little discernible college spirit Columbia possessed, even as it deprived the College of the athletically oriented students whom Ham Fish epitomized.[19]

How Butler felt about Fish's defection is unknown, but the fact that well-placed trustees were exercised made it a problem for him and his administration. "To have a Hamilton Fish go to Harvard just at this juncture, when we are proving so conclusively what we can do for College students and are making such efforts to hold the children of our own," he wrote to an irate Bangs, "would be a serious blow." Yet when Bangs cited the implementation of the common entrance exam as contributing to Columbia's problem, Butler disagreed. "What has hurt us in the College more than anything else, has been the fact that members of the Board of Trustees and members of the Faculty have sent and are sending their boys elsewhere."[20]

This raises one of the interpretive conundrums of Columbia's history in the Butler era: distinguishing between what Butler and his deans regarded as a problem and what the trustees identified as such. (There is a third option: it is conceivable that Butler, who controlled the available historical record during his presidency and was known to have destroyed some material while carefully preserving other documents during the last months of his life, retrospectively decided that a Butler-inspired initiative that went awry might better be laid at the door of deceased trustees.) This distinction is important, if appropriate responsibility is to be assigned for the conclusion that Columbia had a "Jewish Problem," which led directly to policies intended to resolve it. In the case of Columbia's anti-Semitism, while none escape blame, some effort should be made to distinguish anti-Semites of the principled sort from the expedient ones, those, as it were, just doing their jobs.[21]

Dean on the Spot

The first known reference to Columbia's "Hebrew problem" was made by the just-appointed twenty-nine-year-old dean of the College, Frederick P. Keppel (CC 1899), in the summer of 1910. In his first surviving communication as dean to President Butler (July 19, 1910), his boss and mentor, Keppel urged a "careful and sympathetic consideration of the Hebrew problem. It is obvious that most of the education which these students most need can not be organized into courses." He then proceeded to suggest how to deal with the problem: "Query a conference with a few of the younger Jewish alumni who have earned the good-will of the general student body, looking forward to an invitation from them and from some undergraduates of the same type to some distinguished Jewish alumni like Mr. I. N. Seligman or Mr. Oscar Strauss to meet the Jewish students of the University and to give them some much needed advice."[22]

A series of weekly updates followed throughout the early fall on how the incoming class was shaping up, the first prefaced by an upbeat but revealing assessment of the classes already in place: "Barring a handful of Eastsiders in each class, practically every student takes some part in the College citizenship." As for the incoming class, which numbered 101 on September 10, three weeks before classes began, Keppel informed Butler of his instructions to Adam Leroy Jones, registrar and since 1909 the first head of the College Admissions Committee: "I told Jones that I was not greatly interested in the matter of numbers and that where an undesirable citizen could, with justice, be left outside the walls, I was sure in the long run his room would be more advantageous than his company." He then went on to explain that "the particular trouble at this time is that a number of ill-prepared and uncultured Jews are trying to obtain a cheap College degree by transferring, usually in February, from the City College, which they entered after only a three year High School course." A week before the opening of the College, Keppel informed Butler: "We have registered 240 men, and the new ones seem to be a most promising lot—not 'high livers' but good wholesome boys on the rising social grade, and more I think than ever before from outside New York. I have used the scholarships available to get in these latter."[23]

These statements might be read as the smoking gun of a confirmed anti-Semite, who, for all his euphemisms, had set to the task of keeping Jews out of Columbia with the enthusiasm of a true believer. Or they can be read as a careful attempt by the new, ambitious, and relatively unprejudiced dean to minimize the magnitude of the "problem" he had inherited: that of an outsized and conspicuously Jewish contingent in the College. An admissions update at the opening of the College in 1914 also allows both interpretations: "Most of these [Jewish students] are excellent and desirable students, but the danger of their preponderating over the students of the older American stocks is not an imaginary one. This has already happened at NYU and CCNY."[24]

At the same time, Keppel, who was the son of Scotch-Irish immigrants with no claims to membership in the city's Episcopalian elite, had few illusions about reclaiming the lost sons of Columbia's traditional families for alma mater. As Butler's personal secretary in 1904 and as a recent graduate of the College, he had labored to keep the son of Trustee William Barclay Parsons, away at school at St. Mark's, in the Columbia fold. After corresponding with the young Parsons regularly for the better part of a year, Keppel acknowledged some discomfort in the assignment. "I do greatly hope that Barclay will decide to come to his ancestral college," he informed Colonel Parsons, "yet I should be sorry to have him feel that he must come because of pressure upon him from without." Young Barclay, along with most of his St Mark's graduating class, went to Harvard. A year later, the son of Trustee George Rives, F. Bayard Rives, another St. Mark's boy, went to Yale. Columbia had a legacy problem in reverse: not too many sons who wanted in, but too few.[25]

Trustee Pine was even more fatalistic about stemming such defections, as when he wrote to Keppel about Bangs's recommendation in 1912 that Columbia College henceforth limit its admissions to residential students: "To put it frankly, I do not think such a plan, or any other, will bring to us the sons of men like Mr. Rives, Mr. Cutting and Mr. Parsons." Keppel, who regarded any such residential requirement as suicidal, took to quoting Pine's remark privately as support for his view that there was not much he could do about Columbia's lost legacies.[26]

Between Keppel's appointment as dean in 1910 and the outbreak of war in Europe, several reforms in the admission system were proposed for Columbia College, all with the purpose of encouraging "the children of our own" to enroll in their "ancestral home." Most also had the not unintended if secondary consequence of making the College less accommodating to graduates of the city's public high schools, nearly half of whom were by then Jewish. The most radical proposal was Bangs's 1912 suggestion that admissions be limited to residential students, which would have instantly cut the current enrollment of one thousand by half, there being only five hundred beds in the dorms. It would also have all but eliminated those students currently commuting from home who could manage the tuition—$150—but not the additional cost of room and board.[27]

Both of these outcomes were acceptable to Bangs, who regularly complained about his own sons not having enough contact with their research-oriented faculty. But faced with the loss of hundreds of otherwise able students, the faculty on the University Council, at Keppel's urging, rejected the proposal as "suicidal." This endeared neither the faculty nor Keppel to Bangs; nor did it let Butler off the hook.[28]

For his part, Keppel proposed that the College cap the number of students admitted to four hundred per class. This, he hoped, would have two beneficial outcomes: assure a class size small enough to encourage the development of close friendships and the fostering of college spirit and allow the College to deal with any surge in applications, especially from would-be commuters and graduates from the city's public high schools, by having in place an advertised upper limit. He was also prepared to use the scholarship funds to attract desirable but financially pressed students. He did not, however, support the proposal made to change the terms of the Pulitzer Scholarships, which were limited to the graduates of Brooklyn public high schools (a majority of whom were Jewish) so that upstaters (and, likely, non-Jews) could be eligible.[29]

Both Keppel and his admissions director, Adam Leroy Jones, opposed another proposal that originated with the trustees but carried Butler's imprimatur: that all applicants to the College be required to have a physical examination. Butler envisioned such examinations weeding out those "of hereditary disease or other physical ailment [who] ought not to have good money spent on them." The thinking here was that the children of immigrants were, for genetic or environmental reasons, less healthy than those of established American families and that a physical examination would eliminate many of the former from further consideration. But as admissions director Jones in 1912 pointed out, to his eternal credit, had such an examination been in place in 1909, when Randolph Bourne (CC 1912), who suffered from a congenital spine deformity, applied to Columbia, this already distinguished young man of letters would never have been admitted. The idea was dropped.[30]

By this time, Keppel had gone public with his reflections on Columbia's "Jewish Problem." He did so in what Butler praised as "your wholly admirable book," *Columbia*, published by Oxford University Press in the spring of 1914. In the section "Students and Student Life," Keppel confronted the conventional wisdom by asking preemptively: "Isn't Columbia overrun with European Jews, who are most unpleasant persons socially?" He then assured his readers this was not the case and stated unequivocally that, despite his contention that "no records [were] kept on the religion of incoming students," there were fewer Jews now coming to Columbia than in the recent past—and many fewer than the general public imagined.[31]

As to the Jews who were at Columbia being "not particularly pleasant companions," he offered a rejoinder: "By far the majority of the Jewish students who do come to Columbia are desirable students in every way. What most people regard as a racial problem is really a social problem. The Jews who have had the advantages of decent social surroundings for a generation or two are entirely satisfactory companions. Their intellectual ability, and particularly their intellectual curiosity, are above the average."[32]

And what of those few "who have not had the social advantages of their more fortunate fellows"? "Often they come from an environment which in any stock less fired with ambition would have put the idea of higher education wholly out of the question. Some of these are not particularly pleasant companions, but the total number is not large, and every reputable institution aspiring to public service must stand ready to give to those of probity and good moral character the benefits which they are making great sacrifices to obtain."[33]

Here, again, Keppel sought to minimize the magnitude of the problem and to recast it as a social problem, amenable to solution. The "uncultured" first-generation Jewish students would simply learn the ways of American collegiate life and good citizenship from their numerous and more fully acculturated Jewish classmates, as well as from their Christian classmates, for whom college spirit and good citizenship were birthrights.

Keppel gave little consideration to the possibility that those "not particularly pleasant companions" might not wish to undergo such peer-managed acculturation. Nor did he consider that these traditional rituals of collegiate life and the demands of good citizenship might be distractions from their purpose in attending Columbia: to secure the credential of a Columbia degree and the access it assured to further professional training. Keppel saw the Jewish kids who came to Columbia on the eve of the First World War as open to—even actively seeking—social assimilation. He took his job to be to help them do so. Keppel was not a Boasian cultural relativist, much less a cultural pluralist of the Horace Kallen variety, but neither was he an anti-Semite.

Just where Butler stood on the question of the social composition of Columbia College and on the lengths he was prepared to go to shape it is unclear. One can reasonably locate him between Bangs, whose anti-Semitism was of a piece with his anti-intellectualism, and Keppel, who did not seek to exclude Jews per se, except by urging "ill-prepared and uncultivated" ones to consider the merits of CCNY or NYU. Early Butler was not an exclusionist, as Bangs in his heart of hearts likely was, but he did favor policies that made it difficult for some Jews to attend Columbia. A comment to Bangs in 1906 allows the view that Butler was playing to Bangs's biases, displaying his own, or both: "Our Hebrew friends . . . had pushed us very hard. . . . I finally told them that we were a Christian institution and could observe no calendar but the Christian calendar."[34]

Early Butler was probably not an anti-Semite by any rigorous definition of that term. But he was unquestionably a social snob of the first water, which in early-twentieth-century New York elite society resulted in much the same thing. Not surprisingly, the one restrictive proposal that bears Butler's imprint reeks of a snobbish anti-intellectualism scarcely more tolerable than Bangs's down-home anti-Semitism: "In other words," he wrote Keppel in 1914, "I suggest treating the candidate for graduation as one treats a candidate for admission to a club, that is, having his personal qualifications examined." This is a long way from where Keppel was on his good days and where admissions director Adam Leroy Jones was when that same year he proposed the heretical notion "that since intellectual training is after all the business of a university, other than intellectual qualities were never matters of primary interest to it."[35]

Like the proposed physical examinations, personal interviews as a prerequisite for graduation were never implemented, a casualty of the disruptions attending the onset of war and possibly Keppel's sandbagging. But, unlike the physical examination, the personal-interview requirement would be revived after the war. By then, however, Keppel was no longer dean of the College. Having gone off to Washington with the first military call-up in the spring of 1917, where he served in the War Department as an assistant secretary, he was informed by Butler in the summer of 1918 that Columbia could not await his return and that a new dean had been appointed. Keppel was part of the Bangs-directed purge that Butler in his case chose not to oppose.[36]

Butler recommended his ex-dean for several academic openings, including the presidency of the University of California, and he was almost certainly instrumental in securing Keppel's appointment in 1924 as president of the Carnegie Corporation. They maintained friendly contact thereafter, with Keppel often suggesting possibilities for honorary degrees and Butler regularly congratulating him on various philanthropic initiatives. Yet there is something about the epistolary tone of their post-1918 relationship that allows the conclusion that the circumstances of Keppel's departure from Columbia were not what Butler would have chosen, but neither were they to be revisited.[37]

Succeeding Keppel as the third dean of Columbia College was the Yale-educated Herbert Hawkes, a forty-seven-year-old mathematician who had joined the Columbia faculty in 1910 after his promotion at Yale was stalled because his department chairman thought he was devoting too much time to students. He was appointed to Columbia to teach in the College. He became acting dean in 1917 and dean the following summer. Some sense of the new dean's views can be inferred from the contrasting descriptions of the class he inherited in 1918 and that entering in the fall of 1919. As for the wartime class, he complained to Butler: "They have no use for college affairs and regard Columbia less as an Alma Mater than as an Efficiens Pater." As for the incoming class, however, he boasted to his predecessor, Keppel, that it was "the like of [it] you have never seen in this place. I would like to have you read a list of the Freshmen. You could pronounce every name without tying a double knot in your tongue."[38]

It was during Hawkes's quarter-century as dean that Columbia's soft anti-Semitic admissions policies acquired a harder edge and the personal interview became the centerpiece of a new battery of policies to limit the number of Jews admitted to the College. At this point, Heywood Broun's 1931 characterization of Butler (and Harvard's Lowell) "as the leaders of the movement for educational restriction of Jews" becomes undeniable.[39]

Ambition But Not Brains

America's wars bear an exaggerated burden explaining the impetus behind major social changes. But in the instance of Columbia's restrictive policies with respect to Jews, the First World War and its aftermath provided the immediate occasion and at least part of the cause for their perceptible hardening. The war produced a sharp drop in male enrollments throughout the university that was only partially offset by the increasing enrollment of women in the schools open to them. Enrollments in the College also dropped, but less sharply among Jewish students. Butler dismissively described the entering class of 1917 in a letter to Chairman Parsons, then in France on military assignment, as "largely made up of foreign born and children of those but recently arrived in this country."[40]

A statewide census of Jewish college students conducted by a Jewish organization in 1918 reported Columbia College well down on the list, with 21 percent of its enrolled students identified as Jews. As might be expected, CCNY (79 percent), NYU (48 percent), and Hunter (38 percent) all had substantially higher proportions of Jews than Columbia, though the fact that the Jesuit-run Fordham had 23 percent suggests the demand within New York's Jewish communities for locally available higher education irrespective of auspices. Still, the impression easily took hold among predisposed Columbians of WASP lads patriotically fighting and dying abroad to make the world safe while Columbia became inundated with Jewish noncombatants.[41]

The civil unrest that flared up in the immediate wake of the war also took on an anti-Semitic dimension. Jews were thought to be instigators of this unrest, a view that only confirmed the judgment of Columbia trustee chairman General William Barclay Parsons, who had noted darkly back in 1912 that it had been New York's Jewish precincts that provided most of the votes for the Socialist presidential candidate, Eugene Debs, and the mayoral candidacy of the Socialist (and Jewish) Morris Hillquit. So, to the image of the wartime Jew as "doughface" is added the postwar Jew as "bomb thrower," which did little to enhance his admissions prospects at Columbia.[42]

Another war-related element in the hardening of official Columbia's stance with respect to Jewish applicants was the introduction in 1919 of psychological testing as a means of screening out undesirables. The test used was a modified version of that used by the army, the Thorndike Intelligence Test, which was developed by a member of the Columbia (and Teachers College) faculty, the psychologist Edward L. Thorndike. While ostensibly an evenhanded test of intellectual promise, like most such tests it was riddled with cultural biases that significantly disadvantaged test takers unfamiliar with American culture or American life beyond the boroughs. In view of the real purpose of the test, its inherent unfairness only enhanced its anticipated efficacy.[43]

Proponents of the intelligence test acknowledged that it was designed to identify applicants whose high school academic record exceeded their "native abilities." Its aim was to cut out the overachiever, the grind, the curve breaker. Such pathologies were assumed to be rife among the city's top high school graduates—and blessedly absent among boarding-school graduates, where the ideal of the "Gentleman C" remained alive and well.[44]

In practice, the Thorndike Test proved to be a disappointment. It was administered by Benjamin D. Wood, one of Thorndike's Ph.D. students and later a popularizer of educational testing, first as director and later as professor of collegiate educational research, from 1924 until his retirement in 1962, when he became the first head of the Educational Testing Service. Although he wrote extensively on the virtues of testing, Wood seems not to have published anything on the uses of the Thorndike test at Columbia. It would appear that its imposition as likely dissuaded as many WASPs and prep schoolers with uncertain academic abilities from applying to Columbia as it kept "overachieving" Jewish students from being admitted. The test itself was quietly dropped in 1934, after some years when it could be waived at the discretion of the Admissions Committee.[45]

The effective screening devices used in the interwar period were more low tech. They included:

1. A cap of 550 on the size of individual College classes. This enabled Columbia even during the Depression to reject about as many applicants as it accepted; it also meant that Columbia remained the smallest of its university-college peers.

2. An application form that called for the applicant's family religion, father's occupation, parents' birthplace, professional intentions (plans to go on to professional school as soon as possible counted against the applicant), and photograph.

3. A personal interview with a member of the admissions board, which included Dean Hawkes and his assistant deans, none of whom was Jewish, where an applicant's personal suitability for a Columbia education could be evaluated. Like the intelligence test, these interviews could be waived for applicants from outside New York and from boarding schools.

4. An acknowledged policy of preferential consideration of applicants from outside New York City and an unacknowledged policy favoring applicants from private schools.[46]

That trustees took an early and ongoing interest in these efforts at social engineering is clear from the minutes of their meetings. In early 1920 the board formed a special "prep-schools committee" and put at its head the recently elected trustee Albert W. Putnam (CC 1897; Law, 1900), a noted collegiate athlete in his day and one of the earliest critics of the ban on intercollegiate football. The committee's first report stated unequivocally that the College was not getting "as high a class of school boys as many of the other colleges and universities are getting." "Columbia unquestionably now has the quantity," Putnam reported, before addressing a rhetorical question to the president: "Do you not think it is a proper time to institute steps to get the highest quality?" The trustee resolution that followed indicated the students the committee had in mind: "the best class mentally, morally and physically."[47]

Individual trustees and their families did what they could to advance the

Hawkes-expressed ideal "of making the undergraduate body homogeneous and unified in college life and spirit." One way was to establish fellowships that incorporated their prejudices. An early instance of this was the Bayard Cutting Travelling Fellowship, established by the widow of Trustee W. Bayard Cutting in 1916, which limited eligibility to Columbia students whose parents had been born in the United States. In 1926 the widow of Trustee Francis S. Bangs indicated that the fellowship she was endowing in her husband's name should "be given to a citizen of the United States, a white man and a Christian, and to be known as the F. S. Bangs Scholarship." The trustee resolution modified the eligibility terms without undercutting the message they conveyed: "to a qualified student of either the Anglo-Saxon, the Germanic, the Scandinavian or the Latin Race, and who shall be of Christian parentage." Two years earlier, the widow of Trustee John Pine endowed a scholarship in his name but limited its eligibility to "a son or grandson of a graduate of Columbia College," which his colleagues believed "fit in well with Mr. Pine's dominant interest."[48]

In 1927 the widow of deceased trustee George DeWitt (1899–1912) endowed a fellowship in the Law School on the condition that it be reserved for "a Columbia College graduate, a citizen, a white man and of Christian parentage." In this case, however, President Butler pointed out that the conditions—virtually identical to those of the Bangs fellowship—"expressly contravene the terms of the Charter," by which he meant its explicit prohibition of religious discrimination. Accordingly, the condition "of Christian parentage" was removed. The 1810 charter, silent on the matter of racial and gender discrimination, did not affect the other conditions. Paul Robeson (CU Law 1928), then attending the Law School, and the first two women admitted that year, Margaret Spahr and Elizabeth R. Butler (no relation), need not apply.[49]

Then there was the curious and truncated history of the Brooklyn-based Seth Low Junior College. Established in 1928, Seth Low, like the Schools of Business and Dentistry, had its origins in the Columbia Extension Program, which had for some years offered technical courses in the evenings over in Brooklyn (in cooperation with Adelphi). Such courses were also offered in the other boroughs and in nearby cities in New Jersey. Most of these extension students were immigrants or sons of immigrants, many of whom hoped to go on to Brooklyn Law School, which required two years of college. The creation of Seth Low Junior College thus constitutes an interesting part of the history of Columbia's involvement in the extension movement, yet because of restrictions placed on its students and the uses to which it was put, Seth Low is also part of the tangled history of Columbia's "Jewish Problem."[50]

In establishing Seth Low Junior College in 1928, Butler reassured skeptical trustees, already concerned about their fiscal responsibility for it, on what obviously was to them a more important matter: Seth Low students would not be allowed to transfer to Columbia College, although those who completed the two-year program were free to apply to Columbia's professional schools or to continue undergraduate studies on Morningside Heights as "University undergraduates." Some observers took its real purpose to be to keep college-bound graduates of Brooklyn's high schools from even applying to Columbia. In 1936, shortly after the opening of publicly supported Brooklyn College and in the face of economies mandated by the Depression, the Columbia trustees pulled the plug on Seth Low Junior College. It officially closed in 1938. During its last year of operation, it had enrolled some 176 students, including the science fiction writer Isaac Asimov, who never forgave Columbia for its ethnic profiling.[51]

If an intended function of Seth Low Junior College was to prevent Columbia College from being swamped by academically qualified but culturally and socially lacking applicants from the high schools of the city's largest borough, another acquisition in the late 1920s was intended to have the opposite effect. In July 1928 the Columbia trustees entered into an affiliation agreement with St. Stephen's College, a small and about-to-go-bankrupt institution in Annandale-on Hudson, fifty miles north of Manhattan, that had been founded in 1860 by leading members of the New York City Episcopalian community. The idea had first been broached by Trustee Bangs back in 1906, when he proposed affiliating with St. Stephen's as a means for Columbia to reach "a certain element that now sends boys to New England prep schools where they are led away to other colleges." The terms of the 1928 agreement called for St. Stephen's "to integrate with Columbia University on like terms with Barnard College." For Columbia board members, most of whom were still Episcopalians, including the bishop of New York and the rector of Trinity Church, the affiliation with St. Stephens constituted another attempt to reconnect Columbia with its denominational origins.[52]

Columbia's affiliation with St. Stephen's, which in 1934 became Bard College, outlasted by eight years that with Seth Low. Proposals for terminating it, however, began as early as 1931, when St. Stephen's turned to the Columbia trustees for financial assistance. The end came in 1944, when Bard went coeducational and its board assumed full responsibility for the College. During its affiliation with Columbia, Bard, under the direction of Donald Tewksbury, a historian at Teachers College, became a center for experimental education. What it did not become was a source of Episcopalian transfers to Columbia College. Indeed, by the time of the disaffiliation, Bard had experienced its own version of the disappearing WASP.[53]

What impact did all these interwar policies have on the composition of the Columbia College student body? In the case of their derived intention—to limit the number of Jewish students attending the College—the policies succeeded. There is no doubt that more Jews would have attended Columbia had the restrictive policies not been in place. Columbia may not have had the kind of explicit quota that Lowell tried to sell to his faculty—Butler enjoyed the political embarrassment attending this public display of Brahmin maladroitness—but the fact remains that those he charged with admissions decisions in the 1920s and 1930s consistently produced entering classes in which the proportion of self-identified Jews ranged between 8 and 10 percent of each class.[54]

In 1922, in the midst of the controversy surrounding President Lowell's call for a quota on Jewish students at Harvard and insinuations in the *Nation* that Columbia also had a quota, Professor of Zoology E. B. Wilson sought from Dean Hawkes an explanation of Columbia's policy. Hawkes responded in an uncharacteristically straightforward way. After the obligatory prefatory disclaimer that "I have no desire whatever to eliminate the Jew from Columbia College," he got down to numbers: "Situated as we are in New York we ought to furnish the very best education we can to a good many of them and as a matter of fact the cream of the Jews constitutes a very fine body of people in my opinion. I believe that we ought to carry at least 15% of Jews and I do not think that 20% is excessive for Columbia College."

As to the allegation Wilson passed along "that our Intelligence Examinations are intended to discriminate against the Jew and are fudged with that idea in mind," Hawkes declared it to be "an absolute perversion of the truth [that] does not do justice to the honesty or the decency of the people who are trying to administer these tests." To the anticipated question, "What, then, is the rationale for the mental examination and all the other admissions paraphernalia?" Hawkes replied: "What we have been trying to do is to eliminate the low grade boy. We had 1200 applications for admission last fall and could accommodate only 550. This meant that somebody had to lose out. We have not eliminated boys because they were Jews."

And why is this? Here, Hawkes, trained as a mathematician but now under a full head of epistolary steam, turned amateur social psychologist: "It is a fact that boys of foreign parentage who have no background in many cases attempt to educate themselves beyond their intelligence. Their accomplishment is well over 100% of their ability on account of their tremendous energy and ambition." The upshot: "I do not believe however that a College would do well to admit too many men of low mentality who have ambition but not brains. At any rate this is the principle on which we are going."[55]

The next reported occasion to assess the effectiveness of the admission policies occurred in 1934, shortly after the longtime director of admissions, Adam Leroy Jones, retired and was succeeded by Frank Bowles. In his first correspondence with President Butler, Bowles reported that whereas over half the non-

Jewish applicants who applied had been admitted, the admission ratio among Jewish applicants was one in six. The president must have regarded this differential as about right, because he told Bowles to keep up the good work.[56]

There is also anecdotal evidence to suggest that getting into Columbia was on the order of five times as difficult for a Jewish graduate of the New York City public schools as for someone not Jewish who came from outside the city. One such bright 1926 Jewish graduate of a New York City high school—Eli Ginzberg from DeWitt Clinton—calculated his chances of getting in on the understanding that the College took only twenty-five such students a year. The son of a German-born professor at Jewish Theological Seminary, Ginzberg (CC 1930; Ph.D. 1938) took his chances, got in, and, except for wartime service, never left Columbia.[57]

But hundreds of other interwar New York Jewish kids simply assumed that Columbia would not admit them and so stayed on the subway for two more stops after it passed Columbia at 116th Street, getting off at 137th Street, where City College took them in. City College's gain was Columbia College's loss (Barnard suffered a comparable one to Hunter). Some of these City graduates later found their way back down to Columbia as graduate students and faculty, among them the philosophers Ernest Nagel and Sidney Hook, the historians Richard Morris and Henry Graff, and the future Nobel physicist Arno Penzias, who as a graduate assistant at Columbia in the 1950s made much of his plebeian days at City College. Nagel, Morris, and Graff all eventually found permanent places at Columbia, but not before it had become a different Columbia.[58]

The First Post-Protestant American University

But if Columbia succeeded in limiting access for Jews, it failed utterly to reconnect the College to its historical constituency—what Hawkes called its "normal clientele." Comparisons with Princeton bear this out. Between 1928 and 1938 some 177 sons of Columbia graduates graduated from Princeton (205 if the sons of Barnard graduates are included), substantially more than the number who graduated from Columbia College during those years. Meanwhile, students from public high schools (50 percent) and students from New York City (also 50 percent) continued to outnumber students from private schools (20 percent) and students from outside the city (20 percent). Thus the typical Columbia College student in the interwar years was not Jewish, but neither was he a WASP prep schooler from outside the boroughs.[59]

In 1935, now confronted on all sides by determined student radicals such as *Spectator* editor James Wechsler, Dean Hawkes as much as admitted defeat in his effort to create "a compact and homogeneous body of students" when he lamented the disappearance of the "great events of undergraduate concern . . . the cane spree, the flag rush, the tug of war, and the somewhat crude attention paid by sophomores to the incoming freshmen." "Has youth," he asked plaintively, "become a different kind of creature?" After a quarter-century on Morningside, Hawkes was still confusing Columbia with Yale.[60]

The upshot of the restrictive policies represents one of the ironies of Columbia's history: the places denied Jews because they were reserved for WASPs came to be filled instead by Catholics. Much the same occurred at Barnard. As early as the mid-1920s, more than a quarter of the entering classes of Columbia College was composed of Catholics. While a few came from New York Catholic families long associated with Columbia and represented on the board by Frederick Coudert and Joseph Grace, most came from Irish and Italian families whose American lineage seldom exceeded those of the "culturally unprepared" Jewish applicants being systematically rejected. By the mid-1930s Catholics outnumbered every other religious grouping on campus, except that achieved by lumping all Protestants together, a practice of which Columbia's Knickerbockers of old would have scarcely approved.[61]

Why, then, no "Catholic Problem"? Several possible answers suggest themselves. First, New York Catholics who went to Columbia College did so in spite of urgings by their clergy to attend one of the many Catholic colleges in the city. Columbia's admission authorities, knowing this, were likely more disposed to admit these renegade Catholics than Jews who had fewer educational options and seemed more desperate. Back in 1909 the then secretary of the university Frederick Keppel wrote President Butler in search of the name of "some Roman Catholic who would be interested in providing a scholarship for a young fellow named E. L. McKenna," who, the secretary explained, "tried for the Pulitzer examinations but was not quite high enough to get one of these awards." Keppel then played to Butler's natural competitiveness: "McKenna tells me that he has been offered a scholarship in one of the small Catholic colleges of Brooklyn, but that he would rather come to Columbia if he can possibly arrange it." An Edward L. McKenna appears among the graduates of the class of 1913.[62]

It was also the case that Catholics, for the most part of Irish and Italian extraction, were less in a hurry to get through their undergraduate years and more willing to enter fully into the social life of the College. Catholic students, for example, were viewed as more likely to participate in athletics than were Jewish students but less likely to become involved in radical student politics. Whether or not these nonthreatening stereotypes approximated the interwar reality, they allowed Admissions Committee to look kindly on the prospect of letting in yet another Catholic.

It should also be said that Columbia, certainly as compared with Harvard but also with Yale and Princeton, had traditionally been welcoming to some kinds of Catholics. At least one had served on the Columbia board of trustees more or less continuously since the early 1850s; at one point in the 1930s, the board included three Catholics. On the faculty, Catholics were few in number, but those few, such as the longtime chairman of the history department, Carleton J. H. Hayes, were well placed and politically influential. Another member of the history department, Harry Carman, whom Jewish students and later junior faculty such as Eli Ginzberg and Henry Graff regarded as their rabbi-protector, was also Catholic. Long before he succeeded Hawkes as dean of Columbia College in 1942, Carman cast an ecumenical glow over Hamilton Hall.[63]

As Catholic chaplain to the university, from his appointment in 1928 until his retirement in 1946, Father George Barry Ford represented an attractive official face of Columbia Catholicism to hundreds of non- and even anti-Catholic Columbians. For twenty years, Father Ford, who was also pastor of Corpus Christi Church on 122nd Street, engaged in the intellectual as well as the spiritual life of Columbia, even as he did battle with the New York archdiocese and its redoubtable archbishop (and later cardinal), Francis Spelman. He defied the stereotype of the Catholic, especially the Irish Catholic, as provincial, closed minded, priest ridden, and anti-intellectual.[64]

To be sure, anti-Catholic sentiment existed among some trustees. Gerard Beekman, in opposing the idea of inviting a Catholic priest, Father Francis Clifford, to deliver the baccalaureate address in 1913, identified himself "as a Christian of the Reformation." When Clifford's name came up again in 1915, David Greer, the Episcopal bishop of New York, informed Butler: "Personally, I have no objection; but as I said to you the other evening, there is such a strong prejudice in the community against our Roman Catholic brethren that it might not be good policy to invite one of their number to perform such a notable and conspicuous Duty; and then too I am wondering whether they would reciprocate it. . . . My Christianity includes them but does their Christianity include me?"[65]

Never one to leave his biases unstated or even unranked, Francis S. Bangs weighed in on the Clifford issue: "I have no objection, but I foresee a lot of criticism to the effect that we have gone over to the Roman Catholics—where I wish some of our University community would go. Perhaps this will back fire to our Hebraic reputation."[66]

Finally, there was the president himself, who counted among his many international acquaintances Cardinal Newman and Pope Leo XIII and among his few campus confidants Father Ford. Moreover, Butler's second wife, Kate Montagne, a domineering force throughout their forty-year marriage, was conspicuously Catholic. In 1914 Butler suggested to Chairman Rives that Columbia award an honorary degree to New York's Archbishop Joseph Farley. "The more I see of Archbishop Farley the more of a man I think him to be," he wrote to Rives, "and I think it would be a very good chance to show our freedom from any sort of religious prejudice by giving him our highest honor." Nothing happened with the suggestion. But twenty years later, when Fordham University proposed an honorary degree for Butler, the Columbia president accepted it with evident pleasure.[67]

An unintended consequence of Columbia's interwar admissions policies intended to favor one group and discriminate against a second ended up easing the way for a third. The cumulative result was that by the early 1930s Columbia's student body ceased to be preponderantly Protestant. And since then no single religious group—not Jews, not Catholics, certainly not Episcopalians, and not even mainline Protestants collectively—has constituted anything close to a majority of the Columbia student body. This was a condition New York City arrived at a half-century earlier. Thus, after nearly two centuries "in the City of New York," Columbia had become one in spirit with the religious character of its native city, which Governor Thomas Dongan (a closeted Catholic) described back in 1687: "Not many of the Church of England; few Roman Catholics, but also Quaker's preachers, men and women especially, Singing Quakers, ranting Quakers; Sabbatarians; Anti-Sabbatarians; some Anabaptist; some independents; some Jews. In short, of all sorts of opinions there are some, and for the most part none at all."[68]

For all their efforts to assure a place for "the children of our own," the interwar trustees, their president, and his deans only hastened the day when now, some seven decades later, Columbia can lay claim to the distinction of having become America's first major post-Protestant university. The historian George Marsden has argued in *The Soul of the American University: From Protestant Establishment to Established Nonbelief* that the loss of the university's "soul," by which he meant its "de-Protestantization," is part of the modern condition to be critically considered, if not lamented. Yet Columbia's history since the 1920s suggests that it is a survivable condition—and not necessarily destructive of the religious impulse, ecumenically defined.[69]

As evidence to the contrary, we have the case of Thomas Merton. In *The Seven Storey Mountain*, one of the most affecting spiritual autobiographies of the twentieth century, Merton describes his conversion to Catholicism and the discovery of his priestly vocation while a student at Columbia (class of 1938). It was there that he drew cartoons for the *Jester*, edited the *Columbian* yearbook, studied Eastern religions, argued about the monastic life with Father Ford, reveled in his teachers' skepticism about all matters religious, not least that of the agnostic but sympathetic Mark Van Doren, and where his friends were nearly all Jews.[70]

CHAPTER 10

The Invention of Columbia College

Sound body, sound mind. Take your pick.

Tom Lehrer (1966)

If you want to win, you must first beat Columbia.

Cornell crew coach Charles Courtney, ca. 1883

In striking contrast to my Radcliffe and Harvard contemporaries, Lionel's Columbia contemporaries were well acquainted with the masterworks of modern writing and art and wholly at ease with the idea of modernism itself.

Diana Trilling, 1993

When Lions Roared

Two developments mark the interwar history of Columbia College: a temporary rise to athletic prowess and the invention of a distinctive undergraduate curriculum. Neither development stemmed from presidential influence or a continuation of the earlier faculty battle between the Burgess-led university faction and the Drisler–Van Amringe "College Men." That battle was long over, and Burgess had won. What happened to the College in the 1920s and 1930s was novel, creative, and not ongoing. It involved finding a role for the College and the cadre of discontented faculty aligned with it in the dominant university. The Columbia College that emerged was fundamentally a new undertaking, an institution as distinct from the old Columbia College as from the contemporary university enclosing it. It has remained so since.

The coupling here of the simultaneous rise of intercollegiate athletics and the invention of the core curriculum is intentional. Their histories, usually separated in the telling, were connected and interactive developments. Moreover, each is indirectly linked to the College's interwar efforts to limit Jewish enrollments in the wake of the mass defections of its original Knickerbocker constituency. In effect, big-time athletics and the core curriculum did battle with one another to become the distinguishing characteristic of a post-Knickerbocker—but not yet inclusively meritocratic—Columbia College.

Organized sports at Columbia began six years after the crew race between Yale and Harvard in 1852 that inaugurated the history of American intercollegiate athletics. With President Charles King's active support, a Columbia base-ball team was organized in 1858 and played several games against neighborhood teams. Columbia's first intercollegiate baseball game took place in 1860, when the team played NYU. Intercollegiate athletics commenced in earnest at Columbia in 1867 with baseball games against CCNY, Yale, NYU, and Prince-ton. The team was underwritten with a two-hundred-dollar allocation from the trustees. Thereafter, baseball remained a conspicuous part of Columbia's increasing involvement in intercollegiate athletics, even as its teams included future Baseball Hall of Fame players as Eddie Collins (CC 1907) and Lou Gehrig (1922–24).[1]

On November 11, 1870, a Columbia team traveled to New Brunswick, New Jersey, to play Rutgers in what is thought to be the fourth intercollegiate foot-ball game ever held. Columbia lost, six to three The team captain was Stuyvesant Fish (CC 1871). During the 1870s Columbia played its home games at St. George's Cricket Field across the Hudson River in Hoboken, New Jersey. The team compiled a record of eleven wins, eighteen losses, and four ties.[2]

Columbia's first intercollegiate crew team was organized in 1874. It came at the instigation of George L. Rives (CC 1868; CU Law 1873), who had been inspired by the Oxford-Cambridge athletic rivalries while studying at the lat-ter. The hastily put together team entered the inaugural Saratoga Lake regatta in July, where, with twenty-five thousand spectators lining the lakeside, it defeated eight other collegiate teams, including those of favored Harvard and Yale. The crew members returned to New York City triumphant, to be greeted by President Barnard, who assured them "that in one day or in one summer, you have done more to make Columbia College known than all your predeces-sors have done since the foundation of the college by this, your great triumph." Four years later, a Columbia crew team defeated both Oxford and Cambridge crews to win the Henley Regatta, the first non-English team to do so. In the 1890s the Columbia and Cornell crew teams came to constitute one of the great rivalries in intercollegiate sports as they did annual battle at the intercollegiate regatta at Poughkeepsie.[3]

In 1880 the Columbia Football Association was formed, with the under-standing that the team was to be student run and student financed. College sophomore Nicholas Murray Butler became the association's first secretary. Later that year Columbia joined with Harvard, Princeton, and Yale to form the Intercollegiate Football Association. In the round-robin that followed, Colum-bia won once and lost twice. Thereafter, for the better part of a decade, Colum-bia football struggled. No team was fielded in 1886, 1887, or 1888. The team's overall record for the 1880s was much as it had been in the 1870s: disappointing, with eight wins, seventeen losses, and four ties.[4]

And so it went through most of the 1890s. In 1891 a future Columbia trustee, T. Ludlow Chrystie (CC 1892), captained the football team, but it managed to win only one game. During the seven years between 1892 and 1898, Columbia again made do without an intercollegiate football team. In the spring of 1899, however, the University Football Association was formed, again at student initiative and with student assurances, based on anticipated gate receipts and sponsorships, that the team would be self-supporting.[5]

In 1899 George Foster Sanford, who had played and later coached at Yale, was hired as Columbia's football coach for fifteen hundred dollars. Manhattan Fields was rented for home games, and the team held preseason workouts in the Catskills. These elaborate preparations paid off. In 1901 the Sanford-coached team beat Yale for the first time. By then, Sanford was reported to be paid a salary of five thousand dollars, making him the highest-paid coach in the United States. Published reports that he paid players to attend Columbia led to his departure at the end of the season. He later coached at Rutgers. The following year, the team compiled an eight–three record, with Charles Wright (CC 1902) and Harold Weekes (CC 1903) named by the effective creator and promoter of American-style football, Yale's Walter Camp, to his second and third All-America squads. Wright and Weekes would again be named All-Americans the following year, as would five other Columbians, who played on the winning teams of 1903, 1904, and 1905.[6]

Of the thirty-five-member squad in 1902, only three members were enrolled in the College. A few players came from the Law and Engineering Schools, but several were outright ringers, young men from the neighborhoods of New York who were paid for their Saturday afternoon exertions. The practice of hiring outsiders to play on collegiate football teams was not limited to Columbia, but the size of its local talent pool did give the "Light Blue" an edge in illegal recruitment.[7]

Football as played at the opening of the century was exceedingly violent, with serious injuries a commonplace and fatal injuries a regular enough occurrence to provoke a public backlash against the sport. During the 1904 season, some twenty fatalities were attributed to collegiate football. Fights in the stands or between fans after the games were also a regular occurrence. In 1905 President Theodore Roosevelt called on the presidents of Harvard, Yale, and Princeton to convene at the White House to discuss ways to come with ways to eliminate the violence and dirty play that had come to characterize the game.[8]

At Columbia, those inclined to do away with collegiate football altogether included several Columbia trustees, including George Rives and Francis Bangs, who believed the attention football received undercut other sports, especially rowing, which they had both done as collegians. Even the football enthusiast and later trustee George Putnam (CC 1899) acknowledged that only in rowing had Columbia, "from tradition and actual results . . . stood on a parity with other larger colleges." Besides, he added, contrasting rowing with football, "it is such a clean sport."[9]

Other trustees resented having to bail out the student-run team whenever gate receipts did not cover the substantial expenses required to field a competitive team. The death of a Union College player, as the result of a cerebral hemorrhage, on November 25, 1905, the same day that a brawl at the Harvard-Yale game emptied the stands in Cambridge, combined with an article on intercollegiate football in *McClure's Magazine* by the muckraking journalist Henry Beech Needham, in which Columbia was conspicuously featured, seems to have decided the matter. At a meeting of concerned college presidents organized by NYU's Henry MacCracken, held in New York on December 8, 1905, the Columbia delegate informed the representatives of the twelve other colleges present that Columbia had decided to ban football and urged the others to do likewise. Two weeks later, Trustee Horace Carpentier congratulated Butler for his willingness to risk the wrath of undergraduates, alumni, and the press by his acceptance of the recommendation of the University Council to abolish football.[10]

Butler had not expected Columbia to be alone among the eastern football powers to abolish the sport. He hoped Yale, Princeton, and certainly Harvard would join in. In the event, Yale and Princeton decided against abolishing football, and even Harvard, whose President Eliot had been among the sport's harshest critics and who gave Butler to believe that he was with him, decided against abolishing football in favor of reforming its rules. By making this decision, Harvard followed its alumnus Theodore Roosevelt's own judgment that eliminating football would have been "doing the baby act"; it also confirmed the limits of Eliot's control over the social life of Harvard College. Alumni sentiment at Yale, Princeton, and Dartmouth kept suspension from ever being a real option. Other colleges dropped football in 1905, but Columbia was alone among the major eastern universities to do so.[11]

Despite pressure from students, organized alumni, some trustees, and the local press, Columbia remained out of intercollegiate football for a decade. In 1915 the sport was reintroduced on a trial basis and under faculty supervision. Rules developed since 1905 and adopted by the National Collegiate Athletic Association, which was founded in 1908 with Columbia as a charter member, had tightened eligibility requirements, while the introduction of the forward pass had made the game less violent. Other conditions required that all games be played on school grounds on Saturday or holidays; that all coaches be members of the physical education department; that only Columbia College students were eligible; and that for the first five years Columbia could not play Harvard, Yale, Princeton, or Pennsylvania.[12]

Some Columbians remained unpersuaded that football had a place at the university. When offered a box seat from which to watch the six games scheduled to be played on South Field in the fall of 1915, Chairman Rives responded, revealing a class animus likely shared by other trustees, "So far as I myself am concerned, I should not take the trouble to go across the street to see a foot ball game; I should as soon think of going to look at a horse race." Although undergraduate athletics were now to be overseen by a faculty committee, professorial support for the return of football was conspicuous by its absence.[13]

World War I delayed Columbia's return to big-time football, but in the 1920s the university again fielded nationally competitive teams. It now needed a suitable stadium. Plans for an athletic stadium across the Hudson River off Riverside Park at 120th Street had been briefly considered by the trustees in 1906, but the banning of football and the projected cost of $10 million led to their shelving. Between 1915 and 1922 the football team played its home games on South Field, using temporary stands and removable goal posts. In 1918 an alumni-sponsored plan to put up permanent stands had been rejected by the trustees, who declared that South Field was reserved for academic or income-producing purposes. Two years later, however, Columbia acquired land on the northern tip of Manhattan and, with a gift of $300,000 from George Baker, proceeded to erect a three-sided, 35,000-seat stadium, with a field house and practice fields worthy of a national football power. That it was five miles away from the main campus only later came to be seen as reflective of a gulf between sports and the "real" life of the university.[14]

In anticipation of the 1923 season in the new stadium, Columbia hired as its football coach the fabled Percy Haughton, who had earlier played and coached at Harvard (1908–16). Haughton fielded a winning team in 1923 and was on his way to a second when, five games into the 1924 season, he collapsed at practice and died. Columbia's 1922, 1923, and 1924 teams were captained by halfback Walter Koppisch (CC 1925), who made third-team All-America in 1923 and first-team All-America in 1924, when he led the nation in touchdowns. During the 1920s Columbia football teams, while playing the country's best teams, compiled a record of forty-one wins, twenty-nine losses, and five ties. They also earned inclusion in a report by Howard Savage for the Carnegie Foundation, *American College Athletics*, for being among the conspicuous abusers of the rules regulating intercollegiate football.[15]

In 1930 Lou Little (born Luigi Piccolo), a graduate of the University of Pennsylvania, where he had earned All-America honors in 1919 as a tackle, and for the past five years the coach at Georgetown, became the coach of the Columbia football team. Although he remained in that position for twenty-seven years, it was during the first decade of the "Little Era" that Columbia football experienced its greatest triumphs. They included a Rose Bowl victory over Stanford on January 1, 1934, with a team that included two first-team All Americas, Joe Ferrara and quarterback Cliff Montgomery. In 1936 Columbia again defeated Stanford, seven to nothing, on an opening kickoff touchdown return by George Furey (CC 1937), who later became the university's athletic director. One of Lou Little's only two losing seasons in the 1930s occurred in 1938, despite the efforts of junior Sidney "Sid" Luckman (CC 1939), his Brooklyn-reared, first-team All America quarterback, who was drafted after his junior year to play professional football with the Chicago Bears. Little's teams in the 1930s did even better than those fielded by Columbia in the 1920s, compiling an overall record of forty-seven wins, twenty-three losses, and six ties, while regularly playing such national powers as Army, Navy, Wisconsin, and Georgia.[16]

Football was not the only major intercollegiate sport in which interwar Columbia distinguished itself. Its baseball and basketball teams regularly excelled, drawing from the city's seemingly endless supply of athletic talent to come up with the likes of Lou Gehrig, who grew up in the Germantown section of Manhattan and played football and baseball for two years for Columbia (1923, 1924) before joining the New York Yankees in 1925. Another was George Gregory Jr. (CC 1931), Columbia's first black basketball player and a scholarship student from Harlem. The six-feet, four-inch Gregory was the captain and star of Columbia's 1930–31 team, when it posted a twenty-one–two record. Meanwhile, Columbia continued its long tradition as a force in intercollegiate rowing, even as it developed strong teams in such "minor" sports as fencing and track and field.[17]

The importance of intercollegiate athletics was stressed by such interwar trustees as ex-footballers Albert W. Putnam and T. Ludlow Chrystie, as well as by many of the College's most active alumni. They saw strong teams as a means of attracting a national pool of applicants. Athletics was also, or so fans such as Columbia College dean Herbert Hawkes argued, a principal means by which Columbia instilled college spirit and "manliness" into its students. If a student could not play at the level required by a competitive intercollegiate team, he could at least root for his classmates who could. Hawkes was convinced, for example, that the abolition of football between 1905 and 1915 had led directly to the physical and moral deterioration of the student body, even as it undercut Columbia's efforts to attract the "best kind of boys." His personal prejudice in favor of "jocks" over "grinds" extended to many of his assistant deans, several of whom had been athletes as Columbia undergraduates.[18]

Ironically, one fact that Hawkes and others supportive of Columbia's interwar athletic programs did not cite in their favor but that was almost certainly the case in the major sports was that Columbia's athletes were disproportionately first-generation college goers drawn from working-class, immigrant families and, in a few instances, like Gregory, from racially underrepresented backgrounds. The argument that a large athletics program provided a significant means by which Columbia could achieve higher levels of socioeconomic diversity was still several deans—and a social revolution—away.[19]

A strong athletic program was, however, seen as a means by which Columbia contributed to the life of the city. In an age before television (the first live sports telecast was of a Columbia baseball game at Baker Field against Princeton in 1939) and before professional football acquired its post–World War II popularity, a Columbia football game could be the hottest ticket in town. One did not have to go to Columbia to root for its teams; if they were winning, being a New Yorker was enough. Meanwhile, the sellout crowds drawn to Baker Field on a fall Saturday afternoon provided nearby shops and parking lots with customers and neighborhood kids with jobs selling peanuts, hawking programs, and scalping tickets. The rhetorical question in the Columbia fight song "Who Owns New York?" has nothing to do with institutional finances, and everything to do with local bragging rights conferred on those identified with the city's winning teams. While perhaps not the size of Notre Dame's "subway alumni," Columbia's nonmatriculating football fans in the 1920s, 1930s, and 1940s represented an important public constituency.

Attendance at football and baseball games at Baker Field was also seen as a means of bridging the social divide among commuting students, fraternity men, and dorm residents. It was also recognized—and on the whole applauded—that the tightest bonding among Columbia students occurred on its athletic teams and in the fraternities identified with particular sports. Even reading about the fate of Columbia's teams in the *Spectator*, where sports-page editor was one of the coveted posts, provided a less divisive alternative to the paper's political coverage, which by the early 1930s, under the editorships of Reed Harris (CC student 1932) and James Wechsler (CC 1935), had taken a decidedly leftist and confrontational turn. But this was not an either-or situation. Harris may have decried big-time football, but Wechsler, both as a radical student journalist and later as a curmudgeonly columnist for the *New York Post*, was second to no one in his loyalty to Columbia football.[20]

Yet big-time athletics did cease to be an institutional hallmark after World War II. In 1945 Columbia joined with seven other colleges in signing an "Ivy Group Agreement" that limited its future football schedule to the other seven signatories and two non-Ivy games. The agreement prohibited the awarding of athletic scholarships and placed other restrictions on recruitment and practice time. Although Columbia football still had its moments, most memorably the 1947 upset of an Army team that had gone undefeated for three years, it could no longer consistently field winning teams. During Lou Little's last decade of coaching (1947–56), Columbia football teams had a record of thirty-four wins, fifty-five losses, and one tie. During the 1950s and into the 1960s, Columbia produced a string of individually talented quarterbacks—Claude Benham (CC 1957), Archie Roberts (CC 1965), and Marty Domres (CC 1969)—but few winning teams. In 1961, with Bill Campbell and Russ Warren, Columbia tied for the Ivy League title, the closest it would come to winning it outright in the twentieth century.

Columbia's postwar reputation for football ineptitude culminated in the mid-1980s, when the team, which had not enjoyed a winning season since 1961, strung together over four seasons a record-setting losing streak of forty-four games. When the streak ended, on October 8, 1988, in a sixteen-to-thirteen defeat of Princeton, it merited front-page coverage in the Sunday edition of the *New York Times*. To be sure, in 1980, thanks to a $3 million gift from Lawrence A. Wien (CC 1925; CU Law 1927; trustee 1964–70), the rotted and unsafe wooden stands at Baker Field were pulled down and replaced by a new and attractive stadium, but one—reflective of diminished expectations—with sixteen thousand fewer seats. However unfairly, given the very respectable records of its teams in swimming, fencing, tennis, and soccer and the still more recent success of women's teams in swimming and volleyball, Columbia athletics had come to be regarded as an oxymoron.

Columbia's greatest basketball teams were those of the immediate postwar years. Among players on 1950s teams, Walt Budko, John Azary, Jack Molinas (CC 1953), and Chet Forte (CC 1957) were named to All America teams, with Forte earning the honor twice, the second time in 1957, when he was also named National Player of the Year. Columbia teams coached by Jack Rohan in the 1960s regularly vied for the championship of the Ivy League (organized in 1954) and just as regularly received invitations to postseason tournaments. In 1967–68 Columbia won the Ivy League championship, senior Dave Newmark and sophomore Jim McMillin were named All-Americas, and Jack Rohan was named Coach of the Year. The 1967–68 Columbia basketball team was the last to win the Ivy League in the twentieth century.

The question bears asking: Why did postwar Columbia abandon big-time athletics? Some of the explanation undoubtedly has to do with the space limitations under which Columbia operates, even as compared with other Ivy League schools, to say nothing of the Stanfords and Michigans and Georgias, with whom it once did gridiron battle. Some has to do with the cost of maintaining a competitive athletic program without big gate receipts from the flagship sports to subsidize the teams whose games and matches mostly attract family and friends of the players. Some has to do with the relatively small influence alumni of the College have on the university's strategic decision making. And so, too, some may have to do with concern—in the 1950s—lest Columbia be caught up in the 1951 gambling scandals that brought down the big-time basketball programs of NYU and CCNY. The case of the All-American Jack Molinas (CC 1953), the man who "almost destroyed the game of basketball," who later admitted to point shaving and dumping games in 1952 and 1953 and was eventually the victim of a mob murder, suggests such fears were no wholly unwarranted.[21]

But another factor also contributed significantly to the diminution of intercollegiate athletics in the larger scheme of university life. It has gone less acknowledged by Columbians who lament the disappearance of big-time athletics because it involves another favored—and also sometimes endangered—component of the College. As with maintaining its original Knickerbocker constituency, staying in big-time athletics stopped numbering among the university's ambitions when it ceased to be needed to justify a Columbia College within "the Greater University." By the late 1930s that responsibility had been seized by another, and more enduring, invention of the interwar era: the core curriculum.

The Moral Obligation to Be Intelligent

The historian Frederick Rudolph, an astute and sympathetic observer of American collegiate life generally and of the rise of football in particular, regularly reminded his readers and students of the uncontestable truth that "the curriculum was not taken seriously or should not have been." That he did so in a book entitled Curriculum only reinforced his stress on the importance of the extracurriculum—athletics, fraternities, clubs, nonacademic rituals—in the total collegiate experience. Rudolph's own reference points were Williams College, where he taught for thirty-eight years and about which he wrote his dissertation, and Yale, where he was a student.[22]

In his best-known work, The American College and University: A History (1962), Rudolph credited Columbia with launching the "general education movement." What he did not note was the possibility that interwar Columbia College provides an exception, or at least a limiting case, to his general rule as to the insufficiency of the curriculum to define a college. By the end of the 1930s, after two decades of tinkering, Columbia's core curriculum had very nearly become, if not "the College," its uniquely saving feature, its raison d'être.[23]

The Columbia Core has not lacked for its historians. In 1946 Jacques Barzun wrote about it in his *College Plan in Action*. The 1954 bicentennial history volume *A History of Columbia College on Morningside* contained two separate essays on the Core, one by Lionel Trilling and the second by Justus Buchler. In 1966 the sociologist Daniel Bell wrote *The Reforming of General Education: The Columbia College Experience in Its National Setting*.[24]

More recently, David Denby (CC 1964), in *Great Books: My Adventures with Homer, Rousseau, Woolf, and Other Indestructible Writers of the Western World* (1996), and Timothy P. Cross, in *An Oasis of Order: The Core Curriculum at Columbia College* (1995), have written of their direct experience with the Core, Denby as a second-time student in 1991–92, after first experiencing it thirty years earlier, and Cross as an instructor of contemporary civilization. Both accounts are valuable in their detail and critically admiring in their assessment. But as it was not their purpose to locate the Columbia College Core curriculum in the larger history of the university, neither addressed two questions: (1) Why did the Core develop when it did, in the 1920s and 1930s? (2) Why has the Core, in a form fixed in the late 1930s, survived into the twenty-first century pretty much intact?[25]

As most accounts of American higher education have it, the general education movement was a reaction against an earlier curricular movement, the free electives system. Generally identified with Harvard's president, Charles William Eliot, the elective system effectively gave over to students the responsibility for selecting their courses from among those faculty chose to offer. In the 1870s Yale's president, Noah Porter, waged an ongoing public battle with Eliot in defense of the traditional, faculty-determined set of prescribed courses, but his was a losing cause. By the 1890s even Yale students after their freshman year were largely free to choose their courses. Harvard students had only one required course for graduation, a first-year course in writing.[26]

President F. A. P. Barnard numbered among the earliest supporters of the electives system. His public endorsement in 1872 of Eliot's scheme drew fire in New Haven, where Porter had earlier lumped him among "the educational reformers who should know better." By the early 1880s Barnard had succeeded in establishing a system whereby about half the courses a Columbia student took were of his choosing and the rest at the direction of the faculty. But he could not get beyond this, and, indeed, in his last years as president, the number of elective courses was cut back by the faculty. By 1890 Yale students enjoyed more choice than did Columbia students. Twenty years later, the Columbia College curriculum still remained more prescribed than its peers were.[27]

The reasons for Columbia's coolness to the idea of electives are not immediately obvious, especially as resistance to the elective system has usually been associated with a defense of the American collegiate system as against that of the German universities. This was the case at Yale, where the defenders of the traditional college insisted on prescribing the curriculum for their students and university advocates insisted on teaching what they wanted. The war went on in New Haven into the opening decades of the twentieth century. But at Columbia the battle was over in the 1880s, with the Burgess-led university side the acknowledged winners over those he dismissed as "the College patriots."[28]

Why did there not occur at Columbia a rush to adopt the elective system? It was not for want of specialists on the faculty. Nor was it for want of money, which, even at Harvard, was cited as the reason that slowed full implementation. Late-nineteenth-century Columbia, remember, was rich.[29]

The answer may be that the victory of the "University side" was so complete at Columbia that the winners had no need for the compromise that an elective system represented. At Harvard in the 1840s, electives were introduced to allow faculty to do some teaching in their specialties at an advanced level and to avoid having to teach freshmen and sophomores. But what if substantial numbers of Columbia faculty could get out of teaching undergraduates altogether? An elaborate elective system held out no such attraction for Burgess and Co., but prescribing courses for undergraduates, and then designating others in their company to teach them, did. This left those exempted free to focus on their graduate students and on their own research. Why support an electives compromise that assured partial exemption from teaching undergraduates, with a full one so close at hand?[30]

Such a solution was more easily implemented at Columbia than elsewhere because Columbia College was so small as compared with the graduate and professional schools. In 1900, for example, the College still enrolled fewer than five hundred students, while the graduate and professional schools enrolled two thousand students. Of the nearly one hundred full-time faculty in the Faculty of Arts and Sciences, only about a third were needed to staff undergraduate courses. (When formally organized as a distinct entity in the 1894, the Columbia College faculty was limited to thirty-three.) As for the rest of the faculty, teaching undergraduates could either be on their terms, in graduate courses open to advanced undergraduates with the instructor's permission, or avoided altogether.[31]

By the early 1900s there were three kinds of Columbia faculty teaching undergraduates: junior faculty, who on appointment were temporarily assigned to the College by their departments; senior faculty who did not wish to teach graduate students (or whom departmental colleagues deemed ill-suited to the task); and faculty of all ranks who enjoyed teaching undergraduates. The prototype of the third kind was Professor of English George S. Woodberry, a self-described eccentric. The books he wrote at Columbia were directed at the informed general reader. His efforts were rewarded by student encomia second only to those offered later to Mark Van Doren, who followed in the Woodberry tradition. They also accounted for his colleagues in the English department being less than distraught in 1903 when, at age forty-eight and after thirteen years at Columbia, Woodberry resigned.[32]

One of the many Columbia undergraduates whose lives Woodberry influenced was John Erskine (CC 1899; Ph.D. 1903). Of the New York social elite, John's father, a silk manufacturer, was by his son's lights "only through moral obligation a businessman." The Erskines were musical and Episcopal, and John was for many years a vestryman of Trinity Church. He attended Columbia Grammar School, which was then on East Fifty-first Street and still connected with Columbia College. There, he was taught by Professor George C. Odell, who split his teaching duties between the school and the Columbia English department. Erskine entered Columbia College in the fall of 1896, among the last students to take classes at the Forty-ninth Street campus.[33]

Young Erskine found much to like about Columbia College, including Dean John Howard Van Amringe, who "gave an admirable performance of the part which undergraduates in those days thought a dean should play." For all his eccentricities, including favoring athletes, "he was a human and reassuring institution." Erskine also appreciated Edward A. MacDowell, whom he considered to be one of America's great composers. But it was George Woodberry who won his lifelong affection—through his formal teaching, his published poetry, and, most of all, the time he lavished on Erskine and his literarily inclined College mates, who included Joel Spingarn (CC 1895), Hans Zinsser (CC 1899), Frederick Keppel (CC 1899), and Virginia Gildersleeve (BC 1900). "For Woodberry," Erskine later declared, "literature was life itself."[34]

After graduating from the College in 1900, Erskine determined to become a teacher, though "not necessarily a professor." "A teacher deals directly with youth," he offered as a retrospective *apologia pro vita sua* that could have been lifted verbatim from Woodberry, "and I love youth." He stayed on at Columbia for three more years, studying with Woodberry and George R. Carpenter, and earned his Ph.D. in English literature in 1903. He then went on to teach at Amherst, expecting "that there, in all probability, my life would be spent."[35]

In the event, Erskine spent only six years at Amherst before returning to Columbia. His reasons for the change of heart are not clear, though they likely had something to do with his disappointment with his colleagues, whom he categorized as "Old Giants," "Middle Lazies," and "Young, Soon to be Gones." If John W. Burgess's arrival at Columbia from Amherst in 1876 marked a turning point in Columbia's history, when the ascendancy of professional and, later, graduate studies over the work of the College became irreversible, the return of John Erskine from Amherst in 1909 launched the movement among some Columbia faculty to reclaim the neglected College.[36]

While happy to be back in New York, Erskine was less pleased with what he found at "the New Columbia." He soon realized that his own interests in creative writing and teaching outside his assigned specialty of Elizabethan literature set him at odds with his department's expectations. But insofar as "undergraduate and graduate work were now clearly defined," he opted to teach undergraduates. This meant he had a teaching program of five sections of freshman English, plus an Elizabethan literature lecture course. His only graduate course could hardly be viewed as central to the department's offerings: "The Influence of American Writers in Europe." His undergraduate students included the historian Dixon Ryan Fox (CC 1911), the publisher Alfred Knopf (CC 1912), the journalist Randolph Bourne (CC 1912), and the writer Lloyd Morris (CC 1914); all of them later acknowledged Erskine's benign influence.[37]

Even with his heavy teaching program, Erskine found time to pursue his musical and religious interests, as well as write essays on general subjects, which he delivered to public audiences, rather as a latter-day Emerson. One of these talks, entitled "The Moral Obligation to Be Intelligent," first delivered in 1913 as the Phi Beta Kappa address at Amherst, soon became the ur-document of the general education movement. Its message was clear enough: Intelligence was clearly reckoned a virtue in Greek literature and French, but it enjoyed no such standing in Anglo-Saxon ethics. In the United States, for example, it was "possible to admire extremely stupid men if only they have pluck or are good to their parents." Erskine declared such tolerance inimical to a moral life.[38]

"The Moral Obligation to be Intelligent," first published in the London-based *Hibbert Journal* in the fall of 1913, caught the attention of Amherst's new and determinedly innovative president, Alexander Mieklejohn, prompting him to urge Erskine to come back to Amherst and put his ideas into curricular form. But by then Erskine had decided to test Columbia's receptivity to a course he was planning, to be focused on "a few great books."[39]

Erskine's first proposal, offered to the College Committee on Instruction in 1915, was for a two-year course in which one "great book" a week would be discussed. Erskine presented it as an intellectually exciting option to bright undergraduates in their third and fourth years who, for want of such prespecialized courses, had been transferring into one of the university's professional schools.[40]

Erskine also promoted the course as an opportunity for students from immigrant backgrounds—he mentioned specifically those from Russia and Central Europe—"few of whom have English or American literature in their background." Erskine had in mind a course that would acquaint these students with the "great Anglo-Saxon writers" he had encountered growing up. In addition to exposure to good books, the course would stimulate intelligent conversation.[41]

Several faculty colleagues, even his friend Dean Keppel, opposed Erskine's "Great Books" course on the grounds that it encouraged "dilettantism." Classicists objected to his intention to have students read Homer in translation because, as Erskine caricatured the argument, "to read Homer in translation would be the same thing as not reading Homer at all." That Erskine's students should acquire a "reading acquaintance" with the classics but not engage in their scholarly investigation struck some as contrary to the whole thrust of the university's work.[42]

The course proposal was set aside in the spring of 1917 when the United States entered World War I and Erskine volunteered for service in France, where he ran educational programs for the YMCA. It would not come up again until 1919, by which time Columbia's explorations in general education had taken a decidedly contemporary turn.

From Current Events to Old Ideas

The prime mover behind "Contemporary Civilization," Columbia's first venture into general education, was Professor of Philosophy and Dean of the Graduate Faculties Frederick J. E. Woodbridge. He was another Columbian with Amherst ties, having graduated in 1898 before going on to Union Theological Seminary. There, he decided against pursuing a ministerial career, opting instead for an academic life as a philosopher. After four years teaching at the University of Michigan, he came to Columbia in 1902, as Butler's replacement in the philosophy department. In 1912 he succeeded Burgess as Columbia's second dean of Graduate Faculties, a position he held until 1929. He continued to teach as the Johnsonian Professor of Philosophy until 1939, a year before his death. It was likely Woodbridge's own predilections that led to the adoption of the Socratic method in the new curricular undertaking. But this was not merely a matter of pedagogy. As a colleague later recalled, "Socrates was precisely the kind of man Woodbridge wanted us all to be—that is, Columbia professors."[43]

The course that Woodbridge got up and running in the fall of 1918 was called "War Aims," and it formed part of the academic program designed for members of the Student Army Training Corps (SATC), several dozen of whom were enrolled at Columbia. It was a course in Allied apologetics, with no pretense at objectivity or balance. Once the Armistice was in place, the Columbia Committee on Instruction briefly considered a sequel course, entitled "Peace Aims." By the following fall, this had become "Contemporary Civilization," a year-long course required of all freshmen.[44]

Meanwhile, Woodbridge secured the appointment in 1919 of a fellow UTS graduate, philosopher, and wartime colleague John J. Coss—who preferred still to be called "Colonel"—to direct Contemporary Civilization. Coss stayed on as director until his death in 1941, becoming a political force in the College, for a time proposed as a possible successor to Butler. He was an adroit administrator, ran the summer session for many years, published little, and openly disdained graduate teaching.[45]

Early on, Contemporary Civilization made no use of historical documents. The principal readings were textbooks written specifically for the course by two members of the teaching staff: Irwin Edman's *Human Traits and Their Social Significance* (1919) and Rexford Tugwell's *American Economic Life and the Means of Its Improvement* (1925). A third text was an adaptation and revision of a textbook written by the historian Carlton J. H. Hayes, *A Political and Social History of Modern Europe* (1916).[46]

In a further assault on legend, Contemporary Civilization was in its first decade exceedingly contemporary in coverage, going back no further than 1871. CC, as it promptly came to be called, underwent a substantive change in 1928, when it became even more presentist and reformist by expanding what had been the third part of the original one-year course, "Today's Problems," into a full second year, where the political and economic problems of the United States would be given a full airing. Behind this change was the reform-minded economist Rexford Tugwell, who taught CC throughout his teaching years at Columbia, before becoming a member of Franklin Roosevelt's Brain Trust in 1933.[47]

In the early 1930s Contemporary Civilization consisted of two year-long courses, "CC-A," for freshmen, and "CC-B," for sophomores. With more time to devote to the past, CC-A dropped its starting point back from 1870 to 1300. This made the course more attractive to historians and philosophers of the premodern periods. The decontemporization of Contemporary Civilization had begun.[48]

The next major interwar change to CC occurred in 1933, when CC-A acquired more content relating to the arts and music. Here, the influence of history instructor Jacques Barzun (CC 1927), about whom more later, is discernible. And here, too, one reason for broadening the subject matter was to attract faculty from the fine arts and music departments. It was not until after World War II that CC-A turned to the distant past and the use of primary texts. And only then were the originating ghosts of John Dewey, Charles A. Beard, and

James Harvey Robinson fully exorcised from an educational experiment launched in the heyday of progressivism, instrumentalism, and the "new history," which survived (and survives) into an era deeply suspicious of all three.[49]

But even as Contemporary Civilization evolved from a one-year course in current events taught mostly by social scientists to a two-year course more suitably taught by historians, philosophers, and classicists, the proposal made by John Erskine in 1915 for a "Great Books" course won a conditioned reprieve from a still skeptical faculty. In the fall of 1920 Erskine was allowed to offer a "General Honors" course in the form of a seminar open to upperclassmen by application. The format was a two-hour seminar for twenty students, to meet on Wednesday evenings, where a previously assigned "important work" would be discussed. A second section was sanctioned in 1921, also taught by Erskine.[50]

By 1925 there were eleven sections of General Honors, with most of them cotaught. Columbia faculty who joined Erskine included English department colleagues Joseph Wood Krutch, Raymond Weaver, and Mark Van Doren, the last of whom joined up with a junior member of the philosophy department, Mortimer Adler, to make a particularly memorable team. Though not formally required, General Honors became a must course for the brightest College students of the mid-1920s.[51]

For all its success in attracting willing instructors and eager students, General Honors was suspended in 1929, when Erskine abruptly resigned from the English department, ostensibly to become the president of the Juilliard Conservatory. The break had been coming for some time, as Erskine's ever-broadening and even popularizing interests clashed with the specialized concerns of most of his departmental colleagues and with the dominant ethos of the research university more generally. The publication in 1927 of Erskine's novel, *The Death of Helen of Troy*, which proceeded to ring up sales over the next two years that exceeded those of all the books published by his departmental colleagues, likely made permanent the mutual alienation. Irwin Edman, one of Erskine's less admiring "Great Bookies," dismissed the novel as a "potboiler," a characterization not to be gainsaid by its daring jacket cover.[52]

Erskine stayed on as president of Juilliard for seventeen years, though the better part of his time was spent as a literary journalist. His two volumes of memoirs, *My Life as a Teacher* (1948) and *Memory of Certain Persons* (1947), express much the same ambivalence about the academic life at Columbia evinced by his contemporaries George Santayana at Harvard, in *Character and Opinion in the United States* (1956), and Henry Seidel Canby at Yale, in *Alma Mater: The Gothic Age of the American College* (1936). All three were beaters against the academic current.[53]

What Erskine started and left behind was revived in the fall of 1932 by

Jacques Barzun as a "Colloquium on Important Books." This was the course that Barzun and Lionel Trilling regularly cotaught off and on to such memorable effect over the next three decades. It was not formally part of the Core. In 1934, however, discussions began among members of the Columbia College faculty about a freshman humanities course, which might follow the Erskine/Barzun-Trilling format of having faculty and students enter into a conversation focused on a "great" or at least "important" books drawn from the canon of Western thought. From these discussions, which extended over three years, emerged a proposal for a new sequence of courses, "Humanities A," which would focus on Western literature and be required of all freshmen, and "Humanities B," with a focus on music and fine arts, which would be offered in a lecture format as an optional sequence to sophomores. In 1941 Humanities B was divided into two one-semester courses, Humanities B1 (music) and Humanities B2 (fine arts). In 1946 the Humanities B courses abandoned the lecture format for the small-section and discussion format characteristic of the rest of the Core; a year later they too became required of all Columbia College students.[54]

Two Cheers for the Core

In the 1930s Columbia College was duly recognized as the birthplace of the general education movement in the United States. When the newly installed chancellor, Robert Hutchins, decided to introduce a "Great Books" curriculum at the University of Chicago, he imported two Columbia instructors to sell it to his resistant faculty. The first was Mortimer Adler, who, unwelcome in the Chicago philosophy department, was provided a Hutchins-extracted appointment in the Law School, from where he proceeded to challenge just about everything the university was doing. The other Columbia import was the Thomist philosopher Richard McKeon (CC 1920), who became Chicago's dean of the college. Continued faculty resistance led committed "Great Bookies" Scott Buchanan and Stringfellow Barr to leave Chicago and try again at St. John's, a small college in Maryland, where the great books curriculum achieved its fullest implementation.[55]

It was only with the 1945 publication by Harvard of its *Report on General Education* (or, as it became known, for its jacket color, "The Red Book") that President James B. Conant and the Harvard faculty came to be seen as the leading proponents of general education. In point of fact, the Harvard faculty then and again in 1978 showed little interest in going down the road Erskine, Woodbridge, Tugwell, and Barzun had earlier traveled at Columbia. In 1987 the head of the Carnegie Foundation for the Advancement of Teaching, Ernest L. Boyer, reported the results of a national survey of academic deans in which the five most frequently cited institutional exemplars of general education were Harvard University, the University of Chicago, Alverno College (Wisconsin), St. Joseph's College (Indiana), and Brooklyn College of the City of New York. Columbia College did not make the list.[56]

There is something unfair about Harvard's hijacking Columbia's only serious claim to curricular innovation, to say nothing of nearby Brooklyn College's doing so later. But it is also understandable, and not only because whatever Harvard does, however slow in the doing, constitutes news. It is also understandable because the development of the Core occurred at Columbia without either presidential or trustee involvement and without much institutional backing. Moreover, to the extent that it was almost wholly a faculty project, it was one in which a self-selecting minority of departmentally marginal humanities and social science faculty took the lead.

Almost to a man, the interwar faculty identified with the Core were at odds with the research ethos that permeated their departments. Most saw themselves, as Erskine did, as teachers and only incidentally as professors or, as Mark Van Doren saw himself, primarily as poets and writers. This was true of John J. Coss, Irwin Edman, and Richard McKeon in philosophy and of Joseph Wood Krutch, Raymond "Buck" Weaver, and Mark Van Doren in English; it was also true of Jacques Barzun in history, whose department did not offer him a graduate course until he had been teaching for fifteen years. It was also true of Rexford Tugwell, in economics.[57]

Mark Van Doren is an especially good instance of the type. A midwesterner with his B.A. from the University of Illinois, he later acknowledged that when he received his Columbia Ph.D. in 1920 and accepted an instructorship, "I still held out for a writer's life." For the next twenty years he spent three days a week in Greenwich Village at the offices of the *Nation*, where his departmental colleague Joseph Wood Krutch was drama editor. Two days were spent on campus, where he had an office in Hamilton Hall, which became "my own professional home that has never changed." When he received tenure in 1930, his department chair urged him to stop writing for the *Nation*, advice he did not take. It was not until 1930 that he was invited to offer his first course "across the street" in Philosophy Hall, where the graduate English department resided. His teaching loyalties were elsewhere. About Humanities A, Van Doren later wrote: "I helped plan the course, and taught it for fifteen years; and nothing I ever did with students was more fun." Meanwhile, he published some forty volumes of criticism, commentary, history, and poetry and seems to have led, but for the troubles with his son Charles's 1958 involvement in a rigged quiz show, a charmed life.[58]

Other faculty who identified with the Core, such as John J. Coss and Raymond "Buck" Weaver, despite being credited with the literary rediscovery of Herman Melville in the early 1920s, published little over long careers. But as Van Doren's case indicates, the polarity here was not simply between faculty who liked to teach in the College and did not publish and faculty who taught graduate students and did publish. Barzun is another instance of a much-published Hamilton Hall habitué, but one whose interest in music and science fiction and predilection for academic polemics set him apart from most of his department colleagues. The divide here was rather between Columbia faculty who directed their published work at fellow specialists, whence came professional recognition and advancement, and those who sought out a more general audience, whence, as with Erskine, Van Doren, and Barzun, came public notice and royalties. For this second kind, bright undergraduates were the local equivalent of that general audience and preferable to graduate students on the lookout for the as-yet-undiscovered dissertation topic or first teaching job.[59]

Among those who identified with the Core, there may also have been a higher value placed on the "good life" over the "successful career." Jacques Barzun's recollection of the silent reproof from senior colleagues upon their discovery of his regular attendance at the Friday matinee of the New York Philharmonic, while they presumably labored away in the library, suggests such a cultural divide. Erskine struck many of his departmental colleagues as something of a dandy, with an amateur's love of the arts, while Edman's colleagues saw him more as an essayist than as a "real" philosopher. Such critics looked down on grown men passing their time in Hamilton Hall conversing with young men about great books, big ideas, and the like. Their doing so might be confused with having fun, whereas the academic calling as practiced in Fayerweather and Philosophy Halls was serious business.[60]

The Core provided some Columbia faculty with a venue other than the graduate program in which to earn their academic keep. Junior faculty who taught in it often came to do so at the direction of senior colleagues. Teaching in the Core was something you did until an opening in the graduate curriculum occurred in your specialization. When it did, some erstwhile teachers of the Core were never again seen in Hamilton Hall. Yet for others, such as Van Doren and Barzun, teaching graduate students never displaced teaching undergraduates as their first calling.

Most of the faculty identified with the humanities Core, before music humanities and art humanities became required in 1937, came from three departments: English, history, and philosophy. Each was big enough to accommodate a handful of Core enthusiasts, especially as this freed the majority from having to teach undergraduates altogether. (This may be one reason that

Barnard did not follow Columbia in developing a core: there was no disposition or incentive among its senior faculty to avoid undergraduates.) Economics and public law also contributed importantly to the instructional staff of both the original CC and, after the 1928–29 split, to CC-B. By the later 1930s, however, these departments found volunteers in such short supply that, as the case of Grayson Kirk will illustrate later, they frequently eased the burden on their regular members by requiring visiting faculty to teach CC.[61]

In the years after World War II, and acutely in the 1960s, the staffing of the Core became the problem it has remained since. Not so in the 1930s, when the necessity of teaching undergraduates allowed departments to justify keeping on certain nontenured faculty members year after year. But in the 1960s, according to the then dean of Columbia College, David Truman, the situation had changed: "Many young instructors regard their obligation to teach Contemporary Civilization as the substantial price to be paid for employment at Columbia, not as an intellectual challenge to their professional skill." Those who actually volunteered to teach in the Core were dismissed by at least one of their colleagues "as potential failures or real suckers."[62]

Meanwhile, there was the disputed matter of the cost of the Core. It has been generally described as high. Though hardly as economical as the huge lecture courses offered freshmen at Wisconsin and Berkeley, however, the Core has likely been cheaper than the vast array of elective courses from which Harvard, Yale, and Princeton freshmen and sophomores choose their programs. Indeed, with somewhere between a quarter and a third of Columbia College courses required and with those constituting the Core assured twenty-five students in sections mostly taught by junior faculty or preceptors with heavier teaching programs than senior faculty, the instructional costs of the College were sufficiently modest to keep cost cutters at bay.[63]

As long as the staffing and budgetary aspects of mounting the Core were manageable, it was not likely to be opposed on those grounds by the central administration or the trustees. But how was it received in other quarters? Their own educational experience antedating its introduction, most interwar alumni took less interest in the recent changes in the curriculum than in the teams, social organizations, and extracurricular programs that had defined their years at Columbia. It would not be until the 1950s, when several decades of interwar graduates made up the organized alumni, that they became the doughty champions of the Core that they remain today.[64]

What, then, of the interwar students who took the Core? Here, some caution is in order, if one is to distinguish the immediate experience from the retrospective. But even allowing for the creative reconstruction that permits anyone who went to Columbia College between the wars to claim to have had Mark

Van Doren, Jacques Barzun, and Irwin Edman as their instructors in the Core, the available retrospective evaluations are strikingly positive. Then again, why shouldn't they be? The Core offered small classes, often enough with famous professors but almost always with interested teachers, where student views on the text and subject at hand were actively solicited and taken seriously. Students were not lectured to but encouraged, even prodded, to verbalize their reactions to questions that had been around since Socrates and deemed important enough by the Columbia College faculty to be asked of all one's classmates.[65]

To be sure, the Core was required and therefore limited a student's freedom to fashion his own academic program. Yet for students coming from high schools where the classroom operated as a one-way transfer point for information, the give-and-take of a Core course was liberating. But it was more than that. The idea that a teacher might find your views on a subject interesting enough to withhold his own in the pursuit of yours and then encourage you to defend your views in the face of questioning from other students carried with it an imperative: maybe you really did have a "moral obligation to be intelligent."

And then there was the subject matter: the great books and big ideas that had animated Western culture from Homeric times. True, all the authors were dead, nearly all were white, and most were males. But then most of the students and all the instructors were white and male. That the texts and ideas presented were mostly European, or at least Western, was a limitation, but not one felt unduly by instructors or students who were themselves for the most part European by ancestry and Western by cultural inclination if not tradition.[66]

Thus the parochialism with which the original Core texts have since been charged with perpetuating, while a fair criticism today, carried less force in its formative years, when as many as 50 percent of Columbia's undergraduates were the children of immigrants. Learning something about their adoptive culture was part of why they came to Columbia. In at least partial if unacknowledged flight from their backgrounds, most Columbia students understood well enough at some level that the Core was preparation for life as a deracinated American professional man, a preparation not to be had at home or even, the betting was, at CCNY or Fordham. When Erskine said that his purpose as a Columbia teacher was to provide "the basis for an intellectual life in common," he did not envision his students going home again.[67]

Two decades after his graduation, Norman Podhoretz (CC 1948) recalled this aspect of his Columbia education as a "brutal bargain" that required him to leave Brownsville and all the religious and ethnic baggage it entailed. He later came to regret having had to make such an either/or bargain. But he also acknowledged that when he showed up on Morningside Heights in the fall of 1945, it was a bargain he was ready to make.[68]

We should not exaggerate the harshness of the terms of the bargain. It did not require its students to become WASPs, much less Episcopalian WASPs. Erskine was a practicing Episcopalian who believed "that the successful teacher of the great books of Western Europe for the last two or three thousand years, must have some form of religious philosophy." Similarly, Raymond Weaver was later recalled by one of his undergraduate students in the 1920s as "in his demeanor . . . hieratic and even Episcopal, rather more in the Church of England than in the Roman way." Mortimer Adler suspected Coss of being an anti-Semite, while his Presbyterian-reared colleague Mark Van Doren "had the reputation of being partial to Jewish students." But others who taught in the Core, notably Trilling and Barzun but also Edman and Moses Hadas, either made do without a religious philosophy or kept theirs to themselves. The Core provided a neutral meeting place for Protestant, Catholic, and Jewish Columbia students, particularly if their religious identities were seen as part of a larger set of inherited ethnic and cultural identities they were in the process of reconsidering. The joke about the Core—"Where Protestant faculty taught Jewish students about Catholic philosophers"—speaks to its considerable if not comprehensive ecumenism.[69]

The Core did not require Columbia undergraduates to accept the texts and ideas they studied as doctrine; skeptical readings were encouraged and expected, and students who took a considered stand against the views contained in the readings were not seen as heretics so much as intellectually independent. That large numbers of interwar Columbia undergraduates went into academic life and into publishing and communications suggests that the intellectual give-and-take of the Core experience at its best was carried beyond the classroom into their careers. This was true as well of many of interwar Columbia's brightest Jewish students, who, like Lionel Trilling, were advised not to pursue a career in academe. As a young instructor, Trilling gave the same advice to at least one of his own half-Jewish students, Carl E. Schorske (CC 1937). Yet both may have taken away from the College not only argumentative skills but the intellectual self-confidence needed to face down the anti-Semitism they encountered early in their academic careers.[70]

As for the larger numbers of Columbia College students who transferred into one of the professional schools after two or three years or entered the workforce after graduation, the Core was as broadly educative as any set of self-selected courses likely would have been. In later years, these graduates could take satisfaction in the fact that their time as undergraduates had been more than merely occupational preparation for what came later. By the time of America's entry into World War II, Columbia College had found in its core curriculum its own justification. The College had become the Core, the Core the College. Not that a winning football team every once in a while wouldn't be nice, too.

That the Core won is clear enough today. It did so because, unlike big-time intercollegiate sports, the disappearance of which postwar Columbia students, trustees, and alumni, along with New York sportswriters and the newspaper-reading public, have all on occasion lamented, the Core served distinctive and important faculty purposes as well. The opportunity costs in eliminating big-time football came to be understood as less than those of eliminating the Core, especially when, with the advent of the Ivy League, doing so kept Columbia in such academically elite company. Accordingly, for the last half-century, good lit. hum. instructors and Nobel Prize winners have been more numerous on Morningside Heights than good linemen and All-Americans. But one should not overlook the fleeting moment in Columbia's history when for a few years they were all here in more equal supply.

FIGURE 4.1 Nicholas Murray Butler (1862–1947), graduate of Columbia College (1882), professor of philosophy, dean, and tenth president of Columbia University (1902–45). 1902 photograph taken at age forty at time of his installation as president.

Source: Columbia University Archives—Columbiana Collection.

FIGURE 4.2 Nicholas Murray Butler, on the beach in Santa Monica, California. Photograph taken in 1920, when Butler was in his eighteenth year as president and age fifty-eight.

Source: Columbia University Archives—Columbiana Collection.

FIGURE 4.3 Nicholas Murray Butler in 1942, when Butler was in his fortieth year as president and age eighty. Photograph of portrait by Lotte Jacobi.

Source: Columbia University Archives—Columbiana Collection.

FIGURE 4.4 James McKeen Cattell (1860–1944), psychologist and professor at Columbia (1891–1917) until he was fired for public opposition to World War I. Photograph dates from the 1890s,

Source: Columbia University Archives—Columbiana Collection.

FIGURE 4.5 Charles A. Beard (1874–1948), historian, political scientist, and Columbia professor (1904–17) until he resigned over trustees' actions limiting the academic freedom of faculty. Photograph circa 1910.

Source: Columbia University Archives—Columbiana Collection.

FIGURE 4.6 George E. Woodberry (1855–1930), writer, poet, and Columbia professor (1891–1904) until he resigned following a dispute with a colleague. Prefounder of the Columbia core curriculum. Photograph circa 1900.

Source: Columbia University Archives—Columbiana Collection.

FIGURE 4.7 John Erskine (1879–1951), Columbia College graduate (1899), writer, professor of English (1910–1927), and advocate of the teaching of "great books" to undergraduates. Photograph circa 1920.

Source: Columbia University Archives—Columbiana Collection.

FIGURE 4.8   Aerial photograph of Columbia Presbyterian Medical Center in 1930s.

Source: Archives and Special Collections, Columbia University Health Sciences Division.

FIGURE 4.9   Football on South Field: Columbia versus NYU, October 19, 1920. *Source*: Wesley First, ed., *Columbia Remembered* (New York: Columbia University Press, 1967).

Source: Original photograph in Columbia University Archives—Columbiana Collection.

FIGURE 4.10   Lou Gehrig (1903–41), Columbia College (1921–23), at bat on South Field, 1923, with Hamilton Hall in background. Gehrig later played for the New York Yankess (1925–39).

Source: Original photograph in Columbia University Archives—Columbiana Collection.

FIGURE 4.11   Columbia basketball in 1930, captained by George Gregory (CC 1931), front-center.

Source: Columbia University Archives—Columbiana Collection.

FIGURE 4.12   Ben Johnson (CC 1933–35, 1936–38), greeting Olympic gold medalist Jesse Owens at IC4A track and field championships on Randalls Island in 1937. Johnson was dubbed "the fastest man in the world" for the world record he set for the sixty-yard dash in 1938.

Source: Columbia University Archives—Columbiana Collection.

CHAPTER 11

Prosperity Lost

We have reached the end of an era in the development of the University.... The sources of constant benefaction through a long generation have been in large part destroyed.

Nicholas Murray Butler, 1932

The hope which we have had that the economic depression would come to an end and restore business conditions in a manner that would make possible the flow of gifts which the University formerly enjoyed, has been unhappily disappointed.

Nicholas Murray Butler, 1940

The Limits of Prosperity

COLUMBIA's wartime dislocations ended with the Armistice and the brief economic instability that attended demobilization. By 1920 enrollments were back up and gave every indication of a limitless potential for further increases. This growth occurred despite a 1919 increase in tuition for most parts of the university from $150 to $250. By 1928 student fees accounted for 56 percent of the university's total income ($5.3 million of $9.6 million), the largest percentage in the university's history. That year Columbia rejected some six thousand applicants.[1]

Commercial property values in New York City surged in the early 1920s, assuring Columbia higher rents as leases came up for renewal. On the gift-giving front, recently elected trustees such as the banker Barton Hepburn proved to be as generous as any Butler had earlier brought to the board. Of even more direct financial benefit, the disposition of the estate of Amos F. Eno, under dispute for a decade, was settled in 1922, with Columbia declared the principal beneficiary, making the university, after legal fees, some $10 million richer. Annual gifts during the 1920s averaged $4.7 million. Butler anticipated the return to financial well-being in his 1920 annual report, where he declared the university to be in a "more satisfactory condition than ever before in its history."[2]

The 1920s witnessed the second surge in building on Columbia's three Morningside campuses. The Faculty Club (1922–23), the Business School (now

Dodge Hall, 1923–24), Johnson Hall (now Wien, 1924–25), John Jay Hall (1925–27), Pupin Hall (1925–27), Chandler Hall (1925–28), Casa Italiana (1926–27), and Schermerhorn Extension (1928–29) were all constructed on the main Columbia campus. At Barnard, a second dormitory, Hewitt Hall (1924–25), was built; at Teachers College, an extension was added to Grace Dodge Hall (1922–24).[3]

For all these tangible signs of prosperity, Butler had second thoughts about the depth of the university's financial security. In 1921 he informed the trustees that the university needed to increase its capital stock by 40 percent. Four years earlier, Trustee Willard V. King had reminded him what the competition was doing to increase their capitalization. "Every Harvard class that has been out for 25 years is now contributing $100,000 to the University's endowment. In time this will give Harvard an enormous endowment." Nor was Harvard alone in doing this. "The Yale Alumni Fund, which has been raised on a different principle, is also fairly successful." Meanwhile, King noted, "at Columbia most of our important gifts have come from persons not Alumni."[4]

King was surely not the first at Columbia to point out what was going on in Cambridge and New Haven to raise operating funds from alumni. Beginning in the 1890s, reunion classes gathered in New Haven were expected to leave a substantial gift behind. In 1903 Harvard announced that the class of 1879 had collected a class gift of $100,000 to be given to the university at its upcoming twenty-fifth reunion, establishing a tradition that added hundreds of millions to Harvard's coffers.[5]

A year later, Harvard pioneered another strategy aimed at securing the financial support of its alumni: an endowment drive. Undertaken to mark Charles W. Eliot's thirty-fifth year as president, the 1904 endowment drive raised $15 million, effectively doubling Harvard's endowment. In the wake of World War I, several universities mounted fund-raising drives designed to cover wartime deficits and build their endowments. Harvard's 1919–20 endowment drive attracted seventeen thousand subscribers and netted another $15 million. In the 1920s university fund-raising had become a big business, with a handful of companies, most prominently John Price Jones, Inc., aggressively vying for clients. Before the close of the decade, Harvard, Princeton, Yale, and Chicago had all conducted successful fund drives among their alumni. By contrast, Butler tried to cover Columbia's wartime deficits by asking twenty-five individuals of his immediate acquaintance, most of them not alumni, for $10,000 each.[6]

The implied question Trustee King wanted answered was clear enough: Why hadn't Columbia turned to its alumni for the financial support that alumni elsewhere provided their alma maters? An answer that had been offered back in the 1890s and again in 1908 during the discussion over alumni representation on the board was that Columbia's alumni represented a less promising source of support than did Harvard's or Yale's or Princeton's.[7]

Those persuaded of this regularly pointed out that alumni-directed fund-raising elsewhere focused on undergraduate alumni, of whom Columbia had fewer than its peers. Columbia was also thought to be disadvantaged by the fact that most graduates from the College had been commuters and thereby less likely to have generated the bonding experiences with class and college that existed on residential campuses and years later produced generous gifts. Some even allowed that Columbia graduates might not have been as successful financially as those of Harvard, Yale, and Princeton, which attracted the sons of the already wealthy more than did Columbia. And then there was the all-too-apparent fact that many sons of many of Columbia's richest graduates now numbered among the alumni of the competition.[8]

Each of these rationalizations for not aggressively fund-raising among alumni was plausible enough, but together they constituted a self-fulfilling prophecy. The judgment that Columbia graduates wouldn't give generously to to their alma mater if asked could hardly be proved wrong if the request was never made. But these explanations obscured two others, which were less openly discussed.

The first is that increased alumni involvement in financing the university's operations would inevitably mean more alumni involvement in those operations. For all the money that Princeton, Yale, and Harvard alumni donated, those same alumni exacted the price of having an important (and, in Princeton's case, often a determinative) voice in their universities' decisions. Avoiding such involvement had to be worth something to Columbia's trustees and president, so long as alternative—and less intrusive—sources of revenue were available.[9]

A second possible explanation for Columbia's reluctance to launch a fund-raising campaign was that its trustees were not themselves prepared to make the kinds of financial contributions that would be expected of them during such a campaign. Although Butler's earliest efforts at trustee selecting had focused on nominees of wealth and expected generosity, his subsequent choices were less focused. This was also true of the alumni-selected trustees, who, by the 1920s, constituted a quarter of the board. Nothing could be expected from the clergy on the board, although they accounted for three or four seats during the interwar period. Add to these the several board members who, first elected as alumni representatives, were later elected to life memberships in recognition of their ability to get along with Butler, and the upshot was the board likely no longer commanded the personal wealth it had in the 1890s.[10]

To be sure, several trustees in the 1920s were men of wealth. But most had come by their wealth through their own exertions, rather than by inheritance, and were less likely to part with it without first providing for their children.

Other board members, including several estate lawyers, who had been nominated in part because of their contacts with wealth, proved unable to direct their clients' philanthropic largesse Columbia's way. And yet only occasionally does the record show Butler pressing the trustees to do more themselves. He may well have concluded that the board's goodwill and increasing deference to him could best be assured by not testing their willingness to pony up. Election to the Columbia board of trustees in the 1920s remained a recognition of professional success and social standing but carried with it less expectation of major giving.[11]

The university's ability to stay out of the unseemly business of asking its own alumni and trustees for money turned on Butler's ability to raise sufficient income from other sources. This task would have been simpler in the 1920s but for two factors, the first being Columbia's need to keep up with its competitors. These now numbered not only its traditional eastern rivals, Harvard, Yale, and Princeton, as well as the University of Chicago, but a half-dozen midwestern and western state universities, whose legislatures seemed prepared to provide them with however many millions it took to bring them abreast of Harvard, Columbia, and Chicago, the acknowledged leaders among American research universities. It was not enough for Columbia to pay its bills; it had to keep expanding. As Butler said in 1921, "We have arrived at a point where [capital resources] must be increased unless we are going to stand still—and we cannot stand still, because to stand still in this particular endeavor means to fall back."[12]

The other development that tested the limits of Columbia's prosperity in the midst of the "prosperity decade" was the trustees' decision to move Columbia to the forefront of American medical education by building, in conjunction with the board of Presbyterian Hospital and with the support of several major philanthropies, the world's first comprehensive medical center. While Butler helped initiate a plan in 1910 for what became the Columbia-Presbyterian Medical Center eighteen years later, presided over its opening on October 12, 1928, and could rightfully claim its creation as the signal accomplishment of his presidency, he was at every step of the project conscious of the magnitude of the undertaking and not a little concerned about the long-term financial and administrative consequences. He gave a hint of his concerns in an aside to trustees in 1921, when he allowed that "I have never encountered an estimate of costs relating to medical education that was high."[13]

The Loss of Mastery

The 1891 transfer of the ownership of the College of Physicians & Surgeons to Columbia involved the assumption by the university trustees of the College's outstanding debt of $300,000, in exchange for its physical assets, among them its campus on West Fifty-ninth Street, which included the Vanderbilt Clinic and Sloane Maternity Hospital. The staff consisted of fifty part-time faculty and the dean, James McLane, who received a salary. The faculty's income came from sharing whatever surplus income the College enjoyed, plus fees from patients. These proprietarial arrangements—akin to those of Dwight's Law School into the 1880s—remained intact following the 1891 merger. They help explain the large numbers of students the faculty was prepared to enroll— upward of five hundred in any given year since the Civil War—and for the large-lecture format that dominated the curriculum. In 1891 the program leading to an M.D. was three years in length and required no college preparation.[14]

At the outset of the Butler presidency in 1902, the College of Physicians & Surgeons enrolled seven hundred students in a four-year program (extended in 1894) that required only minimal college-level preparation in the sciences. The faculty had expanded to one hundred members, who were elected to their positions by other members of the faculty. They were the only Columbia faculty to enjoy this prerogative. McLane remained the dean.[15]

What had not come with the 1891 transfer, and was still missing in 1902, was a comprehensive hospital. Yet one was crucial if medical students were to acquire clinical experience and faculty to conduct clinically based research. Both conditions had become expected of any serious medical school, following their implementation in 1893 by Dr. William Welch and his colleagues at the Johns Hopkins University Hospital in Baltimore. It was at Hopkins that the utility of linking formal medical training as traditionally provided by medical schools with the clinical experience that could only be had if medical students had supervised access to patients in a hospital was successfully demonstrated. Access to patients also enabled Hopkins faculty to become the leaders in American medical research.[16]

One of the reasons the College of Physicians & Surgeons had moved to West Fifty-ninth Street in 1887 was to be near Roosevelt Hospital, which had opened in 1871. Hopes of an affiliation agreement that would allow Columbia's medical students full access to the Roosevelt wards remained high in 1902, amid signs that Columbia's new president was intent on improving the Medical School's national standing. In 1903 Butler supported the move by the Medical Faculty to raise admission requirements by requiring science-level college preparation (but not an B.A.). This led directly to a drop in enrollments from 797 in 1903 to 304 in 1908, with a comparable drop in tuition revenues and rise in trustee grumbling. Meanwhile, in 1904 the trustees entered into an affiliation agreement, similar to those with Barnard and Teachers College, with the trustees of the New York College of Pharmacy.[17]

Dr. Samuel Lambert became dean of the Medical School in 1905 and made completing the negotiations to secure access for his medical students and faculty to the wards at Roosevelt Hospital an early order of business. His first formal proposal was rejected by the Roosevelt trustees in 1908. Their reasons ranged from a stated concern that those in their care would be mistreated by legions of probing doctors-in-training to an argument between Lambert's father and the head of the hospital, Dr. James McLane, who were neighbors in suburban Dobbs Ferry, over the removal of a limb of a tree on the boundary between their houses. The request for access was resubmitted to the hospital trustees in 1910, only to be rejected again, despite the expressed willingness of one of the hospital's trustees, Edward S. Harkness, to underwrite the cost of the affiliation with Columbia.[18]

The day after the Roosevelt board's second rejection of the affiliation plan, President Butler wrote to the disappointed Harkness to suggest another way of effecting an affiliation between the Columbia Medical School and a teaching hospital: by replacing the unwilling Roosevelt Hospital with the willing Presbyterian Hospital. A month later, Harkness had resigned from the Roosevelt board, joined the Presbyterian board, and extended the same offer there. To this, he added another $1.3 million, to come from his mother, "to be used exclusively towards support of the scientific and educational work connected with the Hospital."[19]

Presbyterian Hospital, which had been founded in 1868, was then located on Park Avenue and Seventieth Street, across town from the College of Physicians & Surgeons. Affiliation would require either the relocation of the Medical School to a site adjacent to the hospital, or vice versa, or the relocation of both to a third site. This last was obviously the more expensive, but Butler recognized in Harkness, the principal heir of one of John D. Rockefeller's first financial backers, someone not likely to be put off his agenda by the daunting cost.[20]

Butler's first idea had been to build the new medical center on what became the East Campus, the four acres of land between Amsterdam Avenue and Morningside, running north-south from 118th and 116th Streets, which the university acquired in 1910 for $2 million provided by the Vanderbilt family. The Presbyterian board countered with a proposed site on East Seventieth Street, where New York Hospital–Cornell Medical Center was eventually built. Both of these were rejected as being too small. Meanwhile, Harkness simply went ahead and acquired an option on a twelve-acre plot of land in northern Manhattan that had been the site of the New York Highlanders (later, the Yankees) baseball park. On April 28, 1911, Columbia's trustees and the Presbyterian board signed an affiliation agreement that committed both institutions to raising $1.5 million to acquire the site and then proceeding with the construction of the world's first comprehensive medical center. They gave themselves five years to come up with the money.[21]

If matters were not complicated enough, even as the Columbia and Presbyterian boards were working out the terms of their affiliation agreement, both trying to estimate the depth of Harkness's pockets, other parties were declaring their interest in the project. The most visible of these was Abraham Flexner, a Johns Hopkins graduate whom the Carnegie Foundation had commissioned in 1908 to conduct a study of American medical education. His 1910 *Medical Education in the United States and Canada*, thereafter called the *Flexner Report*, if not the revolutionary document some have made it out to be, did have the effect of systematically cataloging medical education's "best practices," which turned out in almost every instance to be the practices followed by Johns Hopkins. That the *Report* came out under the auspices of the Carnegie Foundation and that its author was shortly thereafter made the principal consultant on medical education of the Rockefeller-sponsored General Education Board, two organizations that had emerged as the principal foundations engaged in medical philanthropy, made Flexner a reformer with a unique capacity to see his recommendations implemented. America's first medical-policy expert, he was someone Butler had to reckon with.[22]

Some of Flexner's specific recommendations fit neatly into plans already agreed to in the Columbia-Presbyterian preliminary discussions. These included physically linking a medical school with a hospital under university auspices, the provision of specific hospital wards for teaching purposes, and staffing of the medical school by regular university appointment. His more controversial recommendation, that all medical school faculty forgo private practices and subsist on university salaries, was another matter. It was this full-time requirement that proved to be a sticking point and eventually demanded modification before the realities of medical practice and medical education in New York City in the 1920s could be fitted into the procrustean mold struck in Baltimore in the 1890s.[23]

The 1911 affiliation agreement was followed by nearly a decade of bickering among the Columbia trustees, the Presbyterian board, Harkness, and Flexner. In 1915 Butler angered most of the parties by claiming that Columbia did not have its half of the cost of the 168th Street site—$750,000. He was expecting the Carnegie Foundation, then headed by his friend Henry S. Pritchett, to pick up Columbia's share. When it did not, Harkness and others on the Presbyterian board began to doubt Columbia's, specifically Butler's, commitment to building a medical center.[24]

The acrimony persisted into the war years, during which Butler actively discussed affiliating the Medical School with other New York City hospitals, including Lenox Hill. Finally, in 1919, when the Columbia trustees removed Butler as the university's principal negotiator, putting Chairman William

Barclay Parsons in his stead, the negotiations were renewed. Meanwhile, Flexner's negotiating position had been strengthened by his becoming a principal consultant to Harkness and his family's recently incorporated Commonwealth Fund, from which subsequent Harkness benefactions to the medical center were to come.[25]

Butler's diminished role was confirmed in 1919, when, after months of attesting to the indispensability of Dean Lambert, he agreed to Lambert's replacement by someone more acceptable to Flexner and to his reform agenda, Dr. William Darrach. Six months into his deanship, Darrach had drawn up a "Memorandum on the School of Medicine" that became the basis for the subsequent resolution of the standing disputes among the parties. Darrach finessed the issue of full-time faculty appointments by allowing professors appointed to the Medical School to maintain limited practices, with some of the fees to go to the university. Here, it was Flexner who compromised, but only after being informed that the full-time salaries offered Hopkins medical professors in Baltimore would have to be doubled to induce New York's leading medical educators to give up their private practices.[26]

On February 7, 1921, the trustees of Columbia University signed a new affiliation agreement with Presbyterian Hospital to build a medical center on 168th Street, with the Medical School to be built on the northern side, the hospital on the southern. Edward Harkness's Commonwealth Fund agreed to contribute $2 million to cover the cost of the land, while the Carnegie Corporation, the Rockefeller Foundation, and the General Education Board each contributed $1 million to help with the cost of construction. Columbia and Presbyterian were each to come up with $3 million in construction funds. Once built, the medical center's operating costs were to be borne equally by the Columbia and Presbyterian trustees, each to maintain a separate budget overseen by a joint administrative board.[27]

Yet all was not forgiven among the parties. Butler had long since acquired an abiding dislike of Flexner, which was returned in kind. Of Butler and his trustees, Flexner wrote in 1925, "They had not the remotest idea of what they had gotten themselves in for." At several points when it looked as if the project would have to be terminated, Butler seemed relieved. Much of what kept the project from stalling in the 1920s was the knowledge, as Chairman Parsons emphasized to the foot-dragging Butler, "that unless we begin to take serious steps . . . the Cornell people will build up a medical centre before us." They nearly did.[28]

On October 12, 1928, the Columbia-Presbyterian Medical Center opened, with the fanfare appropriate to a signal event in the history of American medical education and of Columbia University. In addition to the College of Physicians & Surgeons and the Presbyterian Hospital, the center included Columbia's School of Dental and Oral Surgery, which the university had acquired through the merger of Columbia's School of Dentistry with the College of Dental and Oral Surgery of New York in 1923. The Medical School included an Institute of Public Health, which was created in 1922 with funds from the DeLamar endowment fund, and oversight of Sloane Hospital and Vanderbilt Clinic, which relocated from Fifty-ninth Street. Similar moves were made by Babies Hospital, from Fifty-sixth Street and Lexington Avenue, and the Neurological Institute, from Sixty-seventh Street and Lexington, with each becoming affiliated with the new center.[29]

The entire cost of the medical center exceeded $11 million, only $3 million of which came from Columbia. But as Butler well knew, securing the other funding had not been cost-free: long-term deals had been struck, arrangements made, and expectations generated that would make the ongoing administration of the center far more complicated and idiosyncratic than that of any other part of the university. It would also be expensive. In 1910 the Medical School budget of less than $250,000 represented about 10 percent of the university's budget; in 1930 the operating budget of the Medical School was $1.5 million, nearly 20 percent of the university's entire budget.[30]

Neither Columbia nor Presbyterian Hospital had endowments to cover more than a fraction of the center's annual operating budget. The demand for admission to the Medical School so exceeded its capacity that it could charge the highest tuition in the university (five hundred dollars) in the midst of the Depression, even as it imposed the most stringent quota on Jewish applicants. But with entering classes of only 125 students, it was not clear that the school's income would exceed its expenditures. Moreover, its regular faculty required a steady infusion of research funding, which in the 1930s depended on the university's remaining in the good graces of the major foundations and their staffs, for many of whom Abraham Flexner remained a role model. Decades before the term acquired currency, the Medical School became the first of Columbia's academic and research enterprises to be primarily dependent on soft money, that is, funding generated through short-term grants for specific research purposes rather than from tuition and endowment. It remains so today but is no longer alone.

Butler almost certainly had misgivings about how the opening of the medical center would alter the character of his job. Henceforth, he would be presiding over a substantial segment of the university about which he had little knowledge and no direct personal experience. The same held for his trustees, including the two or three physicians among them, whose medical training was of an earlier and simpler era. Eventually, of course, such expertise would become more widely available and represented on the board, but as long as Butler was president and the trustees were of his choosing, the Columbia-Presbyterian Medical Center remained effectively outside the normal oversight exercised by the central administration in Low Library.[31]

It was not by chance that the first of the Columbia deans of modern times to operate with the virtual autonomy that later earned them the collective title of "barons" was Dr. Willard C. Rappleye, who succeeded the retiring William Darrach as dean of the Medical School in 1930. When he came to Columbia at age thirty-nine, Rappleye was, much like his Harvard counterpart, David Edsall, one of those rarities in American medicine: a medically trained research scientist with extensive administrative experience. He also exuded the self-confidence that some of his faculty, during his nearly three decades as dean, came to see as arrogance. Whereas, as recently as 1922, Harlan Fiske Stone had sought to exert a measure of decanal autonomy on behalf of the Law School only to be handed his hat, Rappleye's even greater insistence on autonomy in the 1930s was received by Butler with equanimity tinged with resignation. Asked to describe Rappleye early on in his deanship, Butler could only comment, "He's a corker."[32]

"Our Friends Downtown" Reconsidered

The imminent opening of the medical center and the operating expenses to follow prompted Butler to renew his call for more capitalization. The $30 million needed in 1921 had grown to $40 million by 1925, and, in the 1926–27 annual report, to $60 million. To stress the seriousness of the matter, he called on the nation's leading fund-raiser, the John Price Jones Corp., to survey the university's capital needs and propose a fund-raising campaign in conjunction with the upcoming 175th anniversary, in 1929. But, true to form (and likely to Butler's intentions), on May 2, 1927, the board voted unanimously to reject the plan proposed by the fund-raisers, declaring "it is preferable to continue the general policies in this respect which Columbia University has followed for some 40 years past." This meant celebrating the university's 175th anniversary without any serious attendant fund-raising. And, lest there be any doubt on this point, the minutes recorded the trustees repeating themselves as declaring it "not expedient to undertake on behalf of Columbia University a formal and highly organized plan of campaign to increase the capital funds of the University."[33]

Harumphing aside, what was the board—or, more precisely, the president—planning to do? The answer was vintage Butler. He asked the board to authorize him to form a small committee consisting of "a highly esteemed group of men of New York who are not themselves associated with the government of the University or in any way concerned in its activities." The proposed members, all to be "knowledgeable in the ways of New York money," varied with the telling from five to eight. The purpose of the committee was clear: to help the president "form new contacts and establish new lines of influence." The New Yorkers proposed or named to the committee included Henry S. Pritchett, the president of the Carnegie Corporation; Walter S. Gifford; Darwin P. Kingsley, the president of New York Life Insurance Company; Phillip Gossler, CEO of Columbia Gas and Electric; two attorneys, Morgan J. O'Brien and John V. Bouvier; and Bernard M. Baruch, a Wall Street investor with strong connections to the Democratic Party. University insiders quickly dubbed them Butler's "wise men."[34]

Although the idea may have been Butler's, it was his new advisers whom he credited with coming up with a proposal that appears in his 1927–28 annual report, the audacity of which is staggering: "The time should now have come when, after a century and 3/4s of service such as Columbia has rendered, no will should be drawn in the City of New York without containing some provisions, large or small, to strengthen the historic institution which has been doing its full share to make New York a real capital of men and not merely a busy center of industry and commerce." The logic was straightforward: having given to the city for 175 years, Columbia was unilaterally declaring payback time. What the city's other historic and private educational institutions might have to say about this was presumably outside the charge of Butler's "wise men."[35]

The presumptuousness of this proposal notwithstanding, the idea of a surcharge, payable to Columbia, on all probate transactions, a 1928 variation on the 1765 Stamp Act, revealed an implicit acknowledgement on Butler's part that Columbia's financial needs could no longer be met by the handful of Columbia families who had underwritten the College for most of its history. Butler had decided the university must look beyond its "natural clientele" to the city at large.

The composition of the "wise men" provided a clear indication of where Butler had decided to look for help. If the inclusion of the CEOs Gifford and Kingsley was a fairly predictable gesture to the still Protestant-dominated corporate elite of the city, that of the others was not. Pritchett's inclusion, as president of the Carnegie Corporation, spoke to the financial importance of the major philanthropic foundations. But it was Butler's inclusion of two leaders of the New York Catholic community, John V. Bouvier (CC 1886), the principal attorney for the New York Catholic archdiocese, and the Fordham graduate Morgan J. O'Brien (CU Law 1875), who was even more narrowly identified than Bouvier with "all things Catholic and all things Irish," that bespoke ethnic outreach to a previously ignored quarter. For the benefit of trustees who may not have crossed his path, Butler identified Morgan "as the most influential Catholic layman in the City." That this move came a full half-century after Irish Catholics had become New York's largest ethnoreligious community and the Catholic Church a major provider of the city's educational and medical facili-

ties can most generously be attributed to a reluctance on the part of the Columbia board to be viewed as opportunistic.[36]

Even more dramatically, the inclusion of Bernard M. Baruch, who, by his
service in the Wilson administration and his successes on Wall Street, was perhaps the best-known Jew in the United States, spoke to Columbia's turnabout.
His naming represented a calculated signal to New York's Jewish community
that Columbia was rethinking its earlier reluctance to welcome and properly
acknowledge Jewish support.[37]

As for the charge that Columbia and its president were anti-Semitic, Butler
now assured the newly elected trustee, Stephen G. Williams (CC 1881), whose
law firm numbered among its partners Irving Lehman (CC 1896; Law 1898),
there was no basis for it. "The statement that the University is anti-Semitic or
that I myself am anti-Semitic," he wrote to Williams in November 1927, "was
mischievously put in circulation downtown some fifteen or twenty years ago by
two men of some importance on Wall Street, both of whom knew it was untrue
and kept repeating it as if it were." The two to whom Butler referred were
almost certainly Jacob Schiff and James Speyer, by 1927 both dead.[38]

And if this didn't sufficiently mark a change in Columbia's attitude toward
the prospect of Jewish benefactions, there was the move afoot to elect Judge
Benjamin Cardozo (CC 1889; CU Law 1890–91) to a lifetime seat on the Columbia board of trustees. Cardozo had been since 1914 a member of New York's
highest court, the Court of Appeals and since 1925 its chief judge. He was widely
regarded as one of the country's important legal thinkers. He was also, with the
possible exception of Butler, Columbia College's most distinguished living
alumnus. But then again, since the 1890s, there had been at least another half-
dozen Jews, many of them alumni and all wealthier than Cardozo, who had
been mentioned as possible trustees—all to no effect. If anything, in the early
1920s interest among the trustees seemed to be less than it had been before the
war. Why then was Cardozo, in 1928, different?[39]

The documentary record is suggestive but not dispositive. It consists mostly
of trustees' correspondence before and immediately after Cardozo's unanimous election to the Columbia board on March 5, 1928. It allows the view that
Cardozo was deemed the right Jew for that portion of the board that had resisted earlier nominees because of his lack of connections with what Trustee Pine
called "Our Friends Downtown," by which he meant the German-Jewish banking and retail communities that dated their New York beginnings to around
the Civil War. The Cardozos were part of the New York's prerevolutionary
Sephardic community, which over the course of several generations had
become assimilated to the point where many regarded themselves as Jews only
insofar as others did.[40]

Cardozo's frequently expressed loyalty to Columbia, where he had attended both the College (CC 1889) and the Law School (1889–91), his reputation as a legal scholar, even his membership in the Century Association, all commended his candidacy. Each was likely invoked by Butler to persuade the board chairman, Williams Barclay Parsons, despite his long-standing objections to the election of a Jew to the board, not to dissent from what the president had determined would be a unanimous vote in favor.[41]

Ironically, Cardozo also commended himself to some trustees for a characteristic not shared by most earlier Jewish prospects: he was not wealthy. Indeed, some trustees viewed this as a crucial factor, not wanting to give the impression they were on the lookout for Jewish money. Trustee Stephen Williams voiced this concern in 1926 when he proposed his colleague Judge Irving Lehman (CC 1896; Law 1898) and his classmate Edmund E. Wise (CC 1883; Law 1885) as prospective trustees: that the board should elect someone "not too obviously for his money, as election of Otto Kahn would be." Lest he be misunderstood by Butler, Williams repeated himself: "I am opposed to the nomination of a very prominent and rich Jew." On March 3, 1928, Cardozo was unanimously elected to a life-term position on the Columbia board of trustees, thus ending a 114-year hiatus in Jewish membership.[42]

Six months after Cardozo's election, Trustee Willard V. King, who had been an advocate of electing a Jew to the board since he had joined it in 1910, urged Butler to add Solomon M. Stroock (Law 1894) to his committee of financial advisers, identifying him as "a very influential Hebrew . . . who had expressed deep satisfaction at the election of Judge Cardozo as Trustee." It was not a coincidence that it was at the board meeting before that at which Cardozo was elected that Butler declared several of the scholarships and fellowships established earlier in the decade, such as that offered the Law School by the widow of Trustee George DeWitt, which was to be limited to a Columbia College graduate of Christian parentage, to "expressly contravene the terms of the Charter."[43]

That same spring of 1928 Butler responded favorably to an offer by Linda Miller, a member of Temple Emanu-El, of a gift of $500,000 for an endowed chair in Jewish history. After a protracted search that took careful account of the donor's anti-Zionist views, the Russian-born historian Salo Baron was appointed to this chair. He became the first member of a history department at an American university to teach Jewish history. It had taken Butler a quarter-century as president to get to where Low was back in 1890: a recognition that Columbia's future could not remained tied to its Knickerbocker past if the university was to have an expansive future. But by 1928 he was nearly there.[44]

The End of an Era

Too little, too late. On October 29, 1929, only five weeks before the report of Butler's "wise men" on how to interest New Yorkers in supporting Columbia was
due, and the very week of the university's celebration of its 175th anniversary, the
stock market crashed. By November 13, about $30 billion in the market value of
listed stocks had vanished. Almost instantly some of the obvious prospects in
Columbia's upcoming "dignified search for funds" were, if not personally wiped
out, without resources that could be spared to help out Columbia. Some of the
"wise men" found themselves scrambling to avoid bankruptcy.[45]

The extent of the devastation among some of New York's wealthiest is sug-
gested by one instance involving a member of the Columbia board of trustees,
Stephen Baker, chair of the Finance Committee. At the time of the Crash,
Baker's net worth was estimated to be on the order of $50 million. A member
of the board since 1908, he had informed Butler of his intentions to leave
Columbia "a very substantial gift," which Butler was counting on to be in the
tens of millions. But Baker's assets were almost all in U.S. Steel stock, and the
Crash wiped him out. He died in early 1931. When his will was probated, there
was nothing left for Columbia. A year later, Butler declared "the end of an era
in the development of the University. . . . The sources of constant benefaction
through a long generation have been in large part destroyed."[46]

But from another perspective, Columbia entered the 1930s not that badly
positioned to weather a fairly protracted depression. Very little of its endowment
had been in equities, for example, so the Crash had less immediate effect on
Columbia than it did on Harvard and Yale. In addition, on the eve of the Crash,
the university had entered into a thirty-year lease with the Rockefellers whereby
they secured the right to build Rockefeller Center on the thirteen acres that then
made up the University's Upper Estate. The lease called for an annual payment
of $3 million to the university, a substantially greater amount than the $1.7 million it had been receiving annually for the property leased in several parcels with
differing rents. With a total budget in 1930 of $10 million, the university was able
to cover 30 percent of it with the Rockefeller rent alone. Columbia trustees of
old, such as Gouverneur Ogden, who had always insisted that the university's
real estate would be its financial salvation, looked to be proved right.[47]

Yet this silver lining had its cloud. The negotiations with the Rockefellers
had been conducted by Frederick Goetze, the university treasurer, who officially reported to the chairman of board's Finance Committee and operated
out of a Wall Street office but was clearly one of the president's men. Goetze had
driven a hard bargain, and when, only months after the deal had been reached,

the Rockefellers sought a reduction in the rent, citing the altered circumstances in the wake of the Crash, he refused. Then, by some accounts, as if doubting the Rockefellers' liquidity, he insisted that the monthly rent be paid in gold! Subsequently, changes the Rockefellers had requested in the lease terms were made, but not before some Columbia trustees expressed disapproval of the installation at Rockefeller Center of "a music hall," declaring it "not on as high a plane" as the original plans for an opera house on the site.[48]

A year later Columbia found itself, hat in hand, asking the Rockefellers for a loan of $7.5 million, for which the trustees put up the land under the just-completed Rockefeller Center as collateral. Forty years later, these dealings still rankled Nelson Rockefeller, and he cited them as accounting for his family's coolness to Columbia.[49]

Nine months after the Crash and at the point when even Wall Street optimists were hunkering down for an extended depression, Butler sized up the situation: "We have come upon very lean years as far as gifts are concerned, and we are going to face two or three more years of that sort. If we simply sit down helplessly because no adequate gifts are received, heaven knows what will become of our work at the end of the next five or ten year period. No wiser words were ever written than these: 'Where there is no vision the people perish.' "[50]

Still, 1930–31 was not a bad year for the university in terms of gifts. Over $20 million had been received, about half of it designated for the medical center. This was also the year that Edward Harkness agreed, following his gifts to Harvard and Yale to build their houses and residential colleges, to give Columbia $4 million to build a new library. It would be another two decades before Columbia enjoyed a better year of giving. Payment of the library gift was delayed until 1932, while Harkness dealt with a cash-flow problem of his own. By then, the full brunt of the Depression was being felt. In the 1920s Columbia received gifts at an annualized rate of $4,700,000; in the 1930s this dropped to $2,667,000, down 43 percent. The total gifts for 1938–39 dropped below $2 million, less than any year since 1917.[51]

Even with the Rockefeller site rental locked in, Columbia's overall income from its real estate holdings fell throughout the 1930s. The total rental income it earned in 1930—some $4.5 million—was not again matched until 1942. Overall university enrollments, including the several affiliates and the Extension Program, which had topped fifty thousand in 1930, dropped steadily thereafter, until by the end of the decade they were below forty thousand. Only Teachers College enjoyed rising enrollments during the Depression. Tuition income, again with the exception of Teachers College, fell accordingly.[52]

With reductions in all three principal components of the income side of the budget ledger—real estate income, gifts, and tuition—cuts on the expenditure

side soon followed. The operating budget for 1931–32—just under $11 million—
fell to $9.8 million in 1932–33 and to $9.2 million in 1933–34. There, it stabilized
for three years before going through another three-year succession of further
reductions at the close of the decade. By 1940 the operating budget was $8 mil-
lion, or nearly a quarter less than what it had been at the start of the decade.
Even so, during each of these years, the university regularly experienced budget
deficits, which were covered by drawdowns from its shrinking unrestricted
endowment.[53]

Two aspects of Columbia's interwar endowment story are clear enough. By
virtually any of the operative measures, Columbia's endowment, after growing
modestly in the 1920s, shrank significantly, perhaps by as much as a fifth, during the 1930s. Second, drawing on endowment-growth numbers calculated by
Roger Geiger for the country's nine major research universities, Columbia's
endowment was the only one that actually declined. Between 1930 and 1940 the
endowments of Harvard and Yale, already in 1930 larger than Columbia's, grew
by $30 million and $15 million, respectively, while Columbia's fell $5 million.
Columbia entered the Depression as the third most richly endowed university
in the country; it emerged from World War II in sixth place.[54]

There is some indication that the effects of the Depression not only cut
deeper but persisted longer at Columbia than elsewhere. During the second
half of the 1930s, annual budgets included substantially larger deficits than earlier ones, the largest being the $500,000 deficit included in the 1940–41 budget
of $7.5 million. "The hope which we have had that the economic depression
would come to an end and restore business conditions in a manner that would
make possible the flow of gifts which the University formerly enjoyed," Butler
informed Trustee Albert W. Putnam on April 2, 1940, "has been unhappily disappointed."[55]

Having faulted Columbia's peers for having no "fixed educational policy"
back in the early days of the "prosperity decade," Butler took budgetary
actions during the Depression that leave him open to the same charge. He
complained about the unfairness of it all, occasionally took to blaming the
trustees, and sometimes did both. "This situation has to change or we shall go
on the rocks," he wrote to Trustee Archibald Douglas in 1936, before chastising the board. "My experience is that there is any amount of money available,
but no one goes after it." Back in 1931 Douglas had urged that "we should not
expand, but carefully conserve and consolidate what we have." But five years
later Butler put the needs of the university at $300,000 more per year to over-
come "our failure to keep pace with the scientific and scholarly demands
justly made upon us."[56]

And yet, at the most fundamental level, there was a financial strategy operating. Some financial options were exercised, while others, exercised on other campuses, were not. In 1934 Trustee Albert Putnam suggested increasing enrollments at Columbia College from sixteen hundred to two thousand, "provided, of course, that we can get the proper kinds of students for such increase," but nothing came of it. Otherwise, he and his trustees were prepared to invade the endowment by tolerating increasing annual budget deficits, to be covered by selling off parts of the Lower Estate. What Butler was unwilling to do was impose the only kinds of cuts in expenditures that could have brought the budgets back into balance: the wide-scale dismissal of faculty and staff made redundant by the Depression-induced drop in enrollments.[57]

Afternoon on the Hudson

During the 1920s Columbia's teaching staff increased by more than two-thirds, from some 850 officers of instruction in 1920 to 1,500 in 1930. The number of full-time faculty of professorial rank throughout the university increased accordingly (from 400 to 700), while the faculties that made up the arts and sciences more than doubled in size. Some faculty growth continued in the early 1930s, though it was largely limited to the Medical School and Teachers College. During the late 1930s real shrinkage occurred, so that by 1940 the faculty was about 20 percent smaller than it had been in 1930 and, on average, substantially older.[58]

Yet, in view of the sharp drop in enrollments experienced throughout the university (again, excepting Teachers College), the wonder is that the faculty was not cut more sharply than it was. Cuts that did take place were mostly attributable to attrition rather than terminations. Even those not protected by tenure were for the most part allowed to hold their positions indefinitely, if they could afford it. In the absence of more remunerative nonacademic jobs, many managed to do so.[59]

But it was not easy, as instructor Lionel Trilling discovered, especially after he became responsible for the support of his ailing parents. Nor could he expect much help or even understanding. After describing his inability to survive on his salary to a senior member in the English department, Trilling received the following advice from his solicitous colleague: "invade capital."[60]

On the other hand, Columbia professors were relatively protected from the vicissitudes of the Depression. Salaries were frozen, but they were not cut, so that a professor earning the same salary in 1940 that he had received in 1930 found himself substantially better off after a decade of declining prices. Moreover, insofar as a substantial number of Columbia professors had income-

producing activities off campus (almost certainly more than professors elsewhere), some enjoyed a further measure of economic protection. And then
there were those with "capital" to "invade."[61]

Another aspect of the Depression some Columbia faculty found agreeable
was the muting of the intense competition that had existed among the leading
research universities and new contenders in the 1920s. By the available comprehensive measures, Columbia held its place in the top three throughout the
interwar period, along with Harvard and Chicago and with Berkeley closing
fast. But it became harder to keep up in all the fields in which Columbia once
presumed to excel. Moreover, there had been a few disquieting signs in the late
1920s that, for all its size and acknowledged eminence, Columbia was beginning to slip, especially in the sciences.[62]

Several of the faculty who had brought their respective Columbia departments to eminence in the 1890s retired in the 1920s. These included the historian William Dunning (1922), the sociologist Franklin Giddings (1926), and the
economist E. R. A. Seligman (1929), whose retirement occurred within months
of the death of his equally eminent sixty-one-year-old colleague, Henry Seager.
The biologist E. B. Wilson retired in 1929 at seventy-two, only a year after
Thomas Hunt Morgan left Columbia for Cal Tech and the death of their
Barnard colleague Herbert Maule Richards. Yet another prominent biologist,
Bashford Dean, also died in 1929, leaving Columbia's once preeminent biology
department with the challenge of starting all over again. Modern languages
were similarly affected by the almost simultaneous deaths of Henry Alfred
Todd in romance philology and professor of German William Carpenter.

Resignations also negatively affected the perceived quality of Columbia's
leading professional schools. The loss of the bacteriologist Hans Zinsser (CC
1899; M.D. 1903) in 1923 to the Harvard Medical School was particularly serious, given his long affiliation with the university and his international standing. Nor did the reasons he gave help matters: "I am impelled by many weighty
reasons, not the least of which are those concerned with taking my family out
of New York."[63]

The most serious faculty turnover had occurred in the Law School. No
sooner had the school established itself in the early 1920s as the birthplace of
American legal realism, a nonreverential view of the law much influenced by
the social sciences, than it became the target of successful faculty raids. In 1922
Columbia lost Walter Wheeler Cook (CU Law 1894) to Yale, only three years
after he had been recruited from there. Nor was his reason for leaving any more
reassuring than Zinsser's: "Only a sincere belief that I can be of more use to
legal education elsewhere leads me to do so." The following year Dean Harlan
Fiske Stone resigned in a dispute with President Butler, who the previous year

had complained that the Law School "has fallen into ruts." Huger W. Jervey became the school's fifth dean in 1924.[64]

The exodus continued, and the appointment of Jervey as dean did little to check it. In 1925 Thomas Reed Powell left to take up an appointment at Harvard. In 1927 a graduate of the Law School and future associate justice of the Supreme Court, William O. Douglas (CU Law 1925), was appointed a full-time member of the faculty. He stayed only one year, resigning when President Butler appointed Young B. Smith dean when Jervey resigned for health reasons. In 1929 the Law School lost two of its three leading exponents of legal realism: Herman Oliphant, who left for the legal institute at Johns Hopkins, and Underhill Moore, who joined the Yale Law Faculty at the urging of its enterprising dean, Robert M. Hutchins, the future president of the University of Chicago. Of the Columbia legal realists, only Karl Llewellyn remained.[65]

If Yale benefited the most from turnover in the Law Faculty, displacing Columbia as the principal competitor with Harvard, it was at Chicago where changes in the social sciences were put to the best competitive advantage. In 1927 the quantitative sociologist William F. Ogburn (CU Ph.D., 1911), after teaching at Barnard and Columbia for fifteen years, moved to Chicago, where he passed the rest of his long career. This marked the effective transfer of national leadership in quantitative social sciences from Morningside Heights to the Midway.[66]

Meanwhile, in Cambridge, following the appointment of James Bryant Conant as president in 1933, Harvard set out to reclaim a primacy in the sciences that it had lost under President Lowell. Himself a world-class chemist, Conant spent the first decade of his presidency forcing through, in the face of faculty and student resistance, changes in the prevailing junior-appointment policies that would allow Harvard to recruit most of its senior faculty from outside the university. Conant's "up-or-out" system, in place in Cambridge by 1939, would not become operative at Columbia until the mid-1950s and even then allowed for more internal appointments than it did at Harvard. Unlike Butler, Conant exploited the Depression to upgrade his faculty.[67]

Robert M. Hutchins also, though to less clear-cut effect, used the Depression circumstances in which he found himself at the outset of his presidency of the University of Chicago to challenge most of the institution's standing arrangements. Curricular reforms, structural innovations, and (some said) presidential overreach all quickly brought the university to a creative boil, especially as compared with the relatively hunkered-down Columbia campus. Among the state universities, the University of California at Berkeley, with Robert G. Sproul as president (1929–58), now posed a real challenge to Columbia, especially in the physical sciences, after Ernest O. Lawrence moved there from Yale in 1928, joined a year later by his fellow physicist J. Robert Oppenheimer.[68]

Columbia in the 1930s remained strong in political science, anthropology, and history, although in none of the social sciences did it dominate as it once had in most. The humanities remained a source of qualitative strength, even as the Department of English and Comparative Literature continued to produce more Ph.D.s than did its competitors. It was in the 1930s that the Department of Fine Arts (later, Art History) first acquired international standing, thanks in part to the arrival of émigré art historians Margarete Bieber and Julius Held at Barnard in 1934 and the permanent appointment of Meyer Schapiro (CC 1924; Ph.D. 1929) in 1936. Laboratory facilities built in the 1920s—Pupin, Chandler, and the Schermerhorn Extension—provided the university's physicists, chemists, and psychologists with adequate research space on the already crowded Morningside campus. But only in physics could it be safely asserted that Columbia science in the 1930s was not living off an eminence earlier achieved.[69]

Interwar Columbia provided one of the principal American centers for the study of the contemporary non-Western world, what was once called area or regional studies and, after World War II, international studies. Unlike most other American centers, Yale and Princeton, for example, Columbia came by its interest in Asia and the Middle East without benefit of any nineteenth-century missionary links. The impetus was more often commercial possibilities, as in Japanese studies or, in the earlier case of Chinese studies, the strategic gift of an endowed chair. Interest in Russia and Latin America, similarly, was stimulated by interwar political considerations but also, in the case of the founder of modern Latin American studies at Columbia, the political scientist Frank Tannenbaum, by social idealism. There was also the interest that Franz Boas had sparked in anthropological field studies that survived his retirement in 1933. When faculty in international relations are included, specifically James Shotwell in the history department, Parker Moon in public law and government, and Charles Henry Hyde in the Law School, Columbia had more faculty deeply studying more parts of the world than any other interwar American university.[70]

The early stages of foreign area studies at Columbia were mostly underwritten by individual grants to faculty that allowed them the opportunity to travel and study in "their" parts of the world. Some of these grants were administered by the university, drawing on funds from the Rockefeller Foundation, but others came from the American Council of Learned Societies and the Social Science Research Council. While at Columbia, these faculty would earn their keep teaching languages and mounting introductory lecture courses aimed at the nonspecialist. Graduate students were recruited to teach in the Core, as in the case of the future Columbia professors Donald Keene and William T. de Bary.[71]

The absence of discretionary funding, combined with the perception that the faculty was already overstaffed, likely accounts for Columbia's failure to take full advantage of the Nazi-induced intellectual migration of the late 1930s—along with the absence of any discernible inclination on the part of Butler or the trustees to take in these displaced scholars. Of the six hundred known academic refugees who fled Europe for the United States, most landed in New York, and many found employment at local universities. The New School for Social Research was especially welcoming but only somewhat less than NYU and the newer branches of the City College system, which substantially added to their intellectual stature in the process. Relatively few found their way to Columbia, perhaps fewer than a dozen, and fewer still stayed on after the war.[72]

Overall, then, Columbia cannot be said to have been wholly successful in developing a succeeding generation to the founding one. On the eve of World War II, it commanded a less competitive presence among the leading American universities than it had on the eve of World War I. But the interwar decline was so gradual as not to be widely noted beyond Morningside Heights. Nor did it provoke internal debate or much in the way of institutional self-assessment. It was almost as if everyone involved—the president, trustees, faculty, and students—had decided to wait out the Depression, then the prospect of war, and then the war by individually attending to what each did best. In the case of Mark Van Doren that meant, as his unofficial auditor Alfred Kazin remembered a half-century later, spending his late Tuesday afternoons teaching a class in the art of the long poem, reading Virgil's lines, "with a shy, straight, Midwestern pleasantness. As the early winter twilight crept over the Columbia campus, Van Doren's craggy face looked as if he expected the sun to come out because he was teaching Virgil. . . . The voice of the Poet's eloquence and of the poet's nobility was calm, easy, undismayed by any terror outside Philosophy Hall."[73]

Presidential Endgame

If the crisis in 1917 marks the transition from Early to Middle Butler, the full onset of the Depression in 1932 marks the transition from Middle to Late Butler. By then, he had been president for thirty years, during which he had helped build and sustain one of the world's premier universities. The challenge now, however, was keeping a university that, like him, was starting to show its age, from going on the rocks. He could, of course, have decided that three decades was enough and retired. No one would have faulted him as a fair-weather sailor. Indeed, at age seventy, it might even have been expected of him. The fact that instead he determined to stay on in the job—and that he was allowed to—bears consideration, for what it reveals about Butler, about the university's governance, and about the university during those years.

Butler did not stay on because nobody thought it might be better for the university if he left. Students in the 1930s joked openly and in print about their septuagenarian and then octogenarian president. So did university staff, though privately, as in the case of university archivist Milton Halsey Thomas, who wrote in 1937 that Butler "should have resigned as president some time ago, but he can't realize his usefulness is over." Some faculty, notably the chemist Harold Urey, made clear their views on the university's lack of vigorous leadership, but most kept such thoughts to themselves.[74]

For Butler, one of the key stratagems involved in protracting his presidency was keeping up the appearance of active engagement. Intervening in 1936 on behalf of Lionel Trilling against an English department that had determined to terminate him or bringing the Oxford don Gilbert Highet back with him from one of his European presidential tours in 1937 to head up the classics department constituted sufficient activism to keep the faculty at bay. Meanwhile, the appointment of the longtime university secretary, Frank Fackenthal, as university provost in 1937 was another point at which the faculty might have raised concerns about the effectiveness of the administrative leadership but did not. Fackenthal was not an academic and held no advanced degrees; for twenty-seven years his job had been to execute the president's orders. There was no reason to expect him to depart from this lifelong pattern as provost. He remained Butler's loyal "secretary," even to the point of assuring Trustee Marcellus Hartley Dodge in the fall of 1942 that his hospitalized boss "is getting along swimmingly and hopes to be home before a great while."[75]

The Fackenthal provostship suggests another way in which interwar faculty shared complicity in allowing the Butler presidency to continue beyond its effectiveness: they failed to cultivate within their ranks a plausible successor. Early in the Butler presidency, several faculty were identified as possibilities, among them Charles A. Beard, Frederick T. E. Woodbridge, Carleton J. H. Hayes, Philip C. Jessup, and John Coss. But, as Butler aged, few faculty were willing to declare themselves interested in administrative work, much less admit to presidential aspirations. By the late 1920s, the name most frequently invoked as Butler's successor, and with Butler's blessings, was Dixon Ryan Fox (CC 1911; CU Ph.D. 1917), member of the history department since 1919 and son-in-law of Columbia historian Herbert Levi Osgood. Fox had been put in charge of the university's 175th anniversary celebration in 1929 and had received plaudits for its dignified execution. Yet in 1934 Fox, then forty-seven, left Columbia to become the president of Union College. There was talk this was meant as a brief rehearsal for the Columbia presidency, but the call from Morningside to Schenectady never came, and Fox stayed on at Union until his death in 1944.[76]

But the principal responsibility for Butler's remaining in the presidency beyond his usefulness rests with himself and the trustees. And it is in his relationship with the board that Butler's self-perpetuating intentions are most clearly in evidence. Early and Middle Butler had been attentive to trustee relations and to the wishes of the board chairman, always with an eye to maximizing presidential authority, but Late Butler seemed less concerned with his authority than with his tenure. This, he concluded, was more likely assured by a passive and deferential board than an engaged and assertive one. The last thing he wanted on the board was new blood. And to this end he seems to have been ready to reverse himself on the matter of trustee selection.

The year 1932 presented the board with an unusually large number of life trusteeships to fill. The two most problematic followed on the resignation of Benjamin Cardozo and the death of William Barclay Parsons, the board's longest-serving member and for the previous thirteen years its chairman. The death of the rector of Trinity Church, Caleb Stetson, occasioned the third opening.

Butler's relationship with General Parsons was complicated. He seems to have had no reason to suspect, as with Rives, that the board chairman held him in anything but the highest regard. Still, Butler consistently deferred to him, never seems to have challenged him, even indirectly, and was gratified by Parsons's friendship. Butler's letters to the incapacitated and terminally ill chairman in 1931 are as close as he comes in all his official correspondence with his trustees to what must pass among these buttoned-up gentlemen as personal affection. With Parsons's death on May 9, 1932, Butler was at long last fully in charge, but he was also alone.[77]

Parsons's death marked the end of an era in the history of Columbia governance. Never since has a single trustee had such intimate knowledge of university affairs, such influence with his fellow trustees or such sway over a president, or as long a term to acquire such knowledge and exercise such influence and sway. If it was still some twenty-five years between Parsons's death and William Paley's advising fellow trustees that their principal charge was "Don't meddle," the operational aspects of this hands-off disposition were in place.[78]

As for Benjamin Cardozo, his trusteeship had proved uncontroversial. The board's minutes have him attending regularly but saying little that required recording. Nor is there any evidence that serious discussions were thwarted by his presence. But with his resignation in 1932, upon his appointment as the second Jew to serve on the Supreme Court (the 1913 Wilson-appointee Louis Brandeis was the first), the Columbia board confronted the question of what to do about its own Jewish seat.[79] Again, there was no shortage of prospects. Edmund Wise had been among several suggested before the Cardozo selection, as had Irving Lehman. An even more promising prospect from 1927–28 was the publisher of the *New York Times*, Adolph Ochs. His chief sponsor in 1932, as he had been five years earlier, was Trustee Marcellus Hartley Dodge.[80]

Dodge enjoyed considerable standing on the board. Although only fifty-two in 1932, he had been a trustee for twenty-three years, making him, after Parsons's death the most senior member excepting Butler. And since Pine's death in 1922, he had served as clerk of the board. He and his family had given the money for Earl Hall and Hartley Hall (his estate would later underwrite the Fitness Center named after him). On the question of electing a Jew to the board, Dodge seems earlier to have been in the camp of trustees who, like Stephen Williams, acknowledged the need "for one, but only one."[81]

In 1927, when the seat opened to which Cardozo was elected, Dodge had vigorously pressed the candidacy of Ochs, not only as a prominent member of the Jewish community but as someone he could personally speak for, having done business with him. Dodge had loaned money to the *Times* on at least two occasions when Ochs needed funds to advance the paper's competitive position. He was also on friendly terms with Ochs's daughter, Iphigene (Barnard 1914). Five years later, he tried again.[82]

Dodge launched his campaign on behalf of Ochs by approaching Butler, whom he seems to have assumed would be favorably disposed. "Of course," Dodge began, preemptively dismissing two likely criticisms, "I know his age, and they said we would be electing him for his wealth (nonsense to my mind). . . . I would rather have him with his mature judgment and acquaintance, for the few years he could give us than a lot of others at 50." Then, in a blatant play to the seventy-year-old Butler's vanity, the 52-year-old Dodge added on behalf of the seventy-four-year-old Ochs, "Old heads are what they are asking for these days!"[83]

Dodge sent a follow-up letter to Butler providing assurances as to Ochs's state of health and a further argument designed to appeal equally to Butler's competitive urges and to his vanity.

To elect Mr. Ochs to Harvard or Yale would be to elect him to a fine body of men. To elect him to Columbia would mean receiving [him] in the family. You have no greater admirer and Mr. Ochs is one who wears and improves on close range. His daughter (the real future owner of the *Times*, in spite of his general plans) is a part of Columbia, Arthur Sulzberger is a graduate. He has for a generation assiduously printed in full your own opinions and full news of Columbia. It would be a fitting adornment at the close of his career, and he would adorn Columbia anyway.

And a final plea, aimed at the president's institutional pride: "There is no harm in considering it. The Chemical Bank or the Allied Chemical Co. might not consider it, but Columbia can. That just illustrates the difference between a commercial company and a great university."[84]

But Butler was not buying it. Expressing concern that Ochs might again be subjected to an "apparent rebuff," a likely reference to 1928, he told Dodge that "the matter, therefore, is one upon which I advise going very, very slowly just now." As Butler did not say who might administer the rebuff, he may have been signaling his own intentions.[85]

Meanwhile, Butler proceeded to float the name of Thomas J. Watson, the head of the International Business Machines Corporation, describing him as "a very high class individual and a good type of man to have on the Board." Watson had no connection to Columbia. Moreover, he was already on the board of Lafayette College and the NYU Council. Of these commitments, Butler breezily informed Dodge, "I am sure he would promptly resign." Two days later, Butler told Dodge of his dining with Watson downtown and noticing "how he is esteemed by our friends in the business world."[86]

Dodge, acknowledging Watson as a catch and agreeing to support him, then proposed that Ochs be elected to the seat just vacated by the death of Trinity rector Caleb Stetson. But again Butler was not interested. "In my judgment we should not think of breaking the tradition which has existed since 1754, and which leads us always to elect the Rector of Trinity to a trusteeship." There is irony in the fact that Butler and at least some trustees were said to be reluctant to elect a Jew to the board so soon after Cardozo's resignation because it would confirm the existence of a Jewish seat but found perfectly acceptable the notion of a Trinity rector's seat. A week later, at the trustees meeting, Dodge went along with arrangements by which Watson would be elected to take Parsons's place, Stetson's seat saved for his as-yet-unnamed successor, and the Ochs candidacy dropped.[87]

When informed of his election, Watson told Butler that it was "the greatest honor that had come to him in life, and as great an honor as could possibly come at any time." He soon became, with Butler's acquiescence, the board's most powerful member. Given his extensive business dealings with the Third Reich throughout the 1930s, however, he was an unlikely prospect to press for the election of a Jew to the board. As for Dodge, a year after the failure of his attempt to secure his friend Ochs a place on the Columbia board, in responding to a request from Butler delivered by his secretary, he allowed as how "The President's wish is a command to me."[88]

Twelve years and twenty elections later, the Columbia trustees would elect Arthur Hays Sulzberger, Adolph Ochs's son-in-law and successor as publisher of the *Times*, then serving in the United States Marines, as the third Jew to serve on the board in 190 years. The record does not permit a definitive conclusion that it was Butler who blocked the Ochs election; it does show him orchestrating the realignment of the board in 1932 so as to maximize its submissiveness to him. Perhaps it was Trustee Archibald Douglas who expressed the expected view best, in a 1931 letter to Butler in which he urged closing Seth Low Junior College, when he said he would have no concerns that such matters were in good hands "if I had a guarantee that you could continue at the head of the University for the next half century."[89]

Another instance where Butler used his sway over the board in the early 1930s to assure his tenure was in the matter of choosing a successor to Parsons as chairman. Traditionally, the position had been held by a leading member of the New York Knickerbocker community and, at least since Hamilton Fish's long and frequently in absentia chairmanship (1846–93), by seriously engaged and forceful individuals. This was certainly so in the instances of the last three chairs, the merchant William Schermerhorn (1893–1903), the lawyer George Rives (1903–17) and the engineer William Barclay Parsons (1917–32), all of whom were also acknowledged as leaders in their respective professions. Thus the election of Frederick Coykendall (CC 1897) as the board's nineteenth chairman on January 9, 1933, requires some explaining.[90]

Coykendall's seventeenth-century Dutch ancestry, financial independence, club memberships (Century, New York Yacht Club, Downtown, Grolier), and standing as a bibliophile met the social expectations of a board member. Unlike Parsons or Rives, however, whose wealth and public standing derived primarily from their professional activities, Coykendall inherited his grandfather's business, the Cornell Steamboat Company, and seems to have devoted little time to its management, considerably less than to the affairs of the Columbia University Press and to his bibliophilic activities. Marcellus Hartley Dodge, who as the hands-on head of Remington Arms was a very different sort of CEO, said of Coykendall on the eve of his election as chairman, "He has been in business, but his real interest has been the development of this great institution."[91]

At his election as chairman in 1933, the sixty-year-old Coykendall had served on the board for sixteen years, having been elected as an alumni trustee in 1917 and becoming a life trustee six years later. At some point during their three centuries in America, the Coykendalls had become Baptists. That idiosyncrasy aside, Coykendall was as dependably conservative in his politics as in wardrobe. (He was reported to have been the last trustee to attend meetings in a morning suit. He can usually be spotted in commencement pictures into the 1950s wearing a bowler hat.) Again, it was Dodge who best grasped the crucial Coykendall qualification from the president's perspective: "I believe he is the meekest member of the Board."[92]

The new chairman's response to his election was one of genuine surprise. "I feel myself quite out of place in this position," he told his fellow board members, "but I assume you have considered all these things and think you are acting in the best interests of the University." Whether or not his twenty-three years as chairman were in the best interests of the university, his first dozen passed with no record of his having questioned Butler's decision that, as he put it at an April 2, 1937, dinner on the occasion of his thirty-fifth year as president: "I intend to stay until I die."[93]

Butler's decision reflects less an as-yet-unfulfilled agenda than the absence of alternative ways to pass his last years. Deep into his sixties, he had seemed to be in the best of health. Regular lunchtime handball games with the university's athletic director, Ralph Furey, and frequent afternoons on the golf links had kept him in physical trim. But as he entered his seventies, his impaired vision, first diagnosed in 1925, limited his mobility, as his increasing deafness did his social interactions. What the Columbia historian James Shotwell called "his pontifical quality," present early on, toward the end may have become a coping strategy to cover for his loss of hearing. So, too, his drinking, which Diana Trilling noted he did in place of eating at the dinner staged to inform the English department that her at-risk husband had the president's imprimatur. However celebratory in intent, the annual parties hosted by trustees and senior faculty marking Butler's birthday and the anniversary of his presidency—in 1932 his seventieth birthday and thirtieth anniversary; in 1934 seventy-second and thirty-second; in 1937 seventy-fifth and thirty-fifth; in 1940 seventy-eighth and thirty-eighth—increasingly took on the maudlin character of anticipatory wakes as they became occasions for such preemptive utterances as that reported in the New York Times on the eve of Butler's eightieth birthday: "President of Columbia Insists That If He Resigned He 'Would Die Right Off.' "[94]

For someone dismissive of faculty who had only their work to interest and stimulate them, Butler found himself in the 1930s with little more than his university job to occupy him. His five-decade involvement in the inner doings of the Republican Party is a case in point. The last incumbent of the White House with whom he got on had been Warren G. Harding. Hoover could not abide him (the feeling was mutual), and Franklin Delano Roosevelt felt no obligation to be solicitous of a lifelong Republican who once admonished him to return to Columbia to complete his law degree. The last Republican convention he attended as a delegate was in 1932, where he must have been regarded as a relic of the McKinley era. After that, save for an occasional campaign appearance on behalf of New York mayor Fiorello La Guardia, Butler's politicking days were long over. One suspects that, for all his guff about successfully avoiding public office, he missed them.[95]

The same went for his role as international statesman, which received its fullest recognition in 1931, when he shared the Nobel Peace Prize with Jane Addams for his work securing the 1928 Kellogg-Briand Treaty outlawing wars. But two years later, with the rearmament of Germany under way and Japanese aggressions in the Pacific, Butler's brand of international relations was already hopelessly unequal to the task of maintaining the peace. Unwilling to forgo his internationalism in favor of isolationism and yet not in favor of disarmament either, he found himself with little to offer the world's leaders, even those who out of habit continued to accept his calls on them.[96]

Nor did his family life offer attractive alternatives. His second wife had discouraged his relationship with his daughter from his first marriage, and he was reduced to meeting her on the sly. Few friends from the old days remained, and even those fifteen years younger, such as his golfing pal Frederick Coudert, were tending to their own uncertain health. Gone were the Saturday evenings at the Century, the golfing holidays at Augusta National, and the campside weekends in California at the Bohemian Grove. With the coming of war in Europe in 1939, his travels abroad ended.[97]

To be sure, the Columbia presidency still allowed the occasional grand show that Butler had always reveled in and, as he aged, required. June 10, 1939, surely so qualified, when the king and queen of England, George VI and Elizabeth, appeared on campus to accept honorary degrees, to be bestowed on them by the seventy-seven-year old Butler, resplendent in his scarlet Cambridge University gown and pancake black velvet hat. A mural in Butler Library preserves the moment. Theodore Roosevelt was right: Butler was more royal than the royals.[98]

The 1942 dinner honoring Butler's eightieth birthday and his fortieth year as president found the honoree not only deaf and partially blind but ill enough to put his presiding over the commencement the following month in doubt. He rallied enough to be there, though, after being helped to the platform, he lost his place in his prepared speech and concluded it extemporaneously. Trustees wrote to congratulate him on his performance.[99]

The endgame persisted. At the opening of classes in September 1944, the eighty-two-year-old president wrote to Trustee Frederick Coudert, who, at seventy-five, was himself convalescing in Florida: "My Dear Fred—it was a fine beginning of what I hope will be another great year of service." Shortly thereafter, Thomas Watson, with Chairman Coykendall in tow, went to 60 Morningside Drive to tell the bedridden president the time had come. On April 12, 1945, forty-three years to the week after being inaugurated the twelfth president of Columbia University, Nicholas Murray Butler announced his retirement, effective in October. Fackenthal was named acting president. The long Butler imperium was over.[100]

CHAPTER 12

Columbia in the American Century

Not every comparable institution had suffered the long interregnum that put Columbia at a disadvantage in the early fifties.

Jacques Barzun, The American University (1968)

Nothing injures a University so much as to give the University itself and the public reason to believe that the President looks upon his position as a stepping-stone to political office.

Nicholas Murray Butler to Theodore Roosevelt, 1904

1945

O N April 13, 1945, in front-page headline, the *New York Times* reported "PRESIDENT ROOSEVELT IS DEAD." Roosevelt was sixty-three years old and had been president of the United States for thirteen years. Eleven days later, the *Times* reported, in a headline on the top left front page (the top right was preempted by "RUSSIANS BORE INTO BERLIN"), "Dr. Butler Resigns as Columbia Head: 44 Years in Office."

Coming within days of each other and within weeks of the Allied victory in Europe, these announcements shared certain features. Editorial commentators remarked on the singular longevity of the respective presidencies. Just as Roosevelt's leadership was described as having extended beyond the United States to include the entire Allied cause, so Butler's leadership was seen to extend beyond Columbia to all of American higher education.

The respective announcements also had differences. Roosevelt's place was quickly taken by Vice President Harry S. Truman in the manner prescribed by the Constitution. Butler's retirement would not take effect until October, when Provost Frank D. Fackenthal became acting president and a search for Butler's successor could begin. Butler would remain on the board of trustees, where he was to be kept informed on the search for his successor.

By October 1945, with the war over, important new questions faced Americans, American higher education, and Columbia University. All had reason to fear that with the end of the war would come a return to antebellum status quo. On the national level, cessation of hostilities with Germany and Japan brought about a rapid demobilization and raised the prospect of United States withdrawal from the international arena. Peace might also end the federal spending and high employment induced by the war and bring on the resumption of the Depression.[1]

While there was little prospect of the United States subscribing to the inter-war isolationism defined by its internationalist critics, it remained unclear in the months after the creation of the United Nations what role the United States would assume in the postwar era. By 1947, however, that role had been defined as one in which the United States would assume the leadership of the free world in a cold war against the Communist bloc led by the Soviet Union. Similarly, the national economy, after some initial uncertainty, quickly achieved levels of consumer-driven prosperity that made it the envy of the world. Both develop-ments seemed to confirm the declaration of the publisher of *Time*, Henry Luce, that the postwar era would be the "American Century." Historians have since adopted this characterization in describing the two decades after World War II, often, as here, with qualifying quotation marks to indicate their dissociation from Luce's triumphalism.[2]

For American higher education, especially its flagship research universities, the immediate postwar uncertainties turned on the prospect of federal support of war-related research programs ending with the restoration of peace. Again, not to worry. American higher education in the truncated "American Century" enjoyed unparalleled growth, popular approbation, and increases in material support not imagined before and not experienced since. All sectors of higher education benefited, but the leading research universities enjoyed the greatest expansion of their influence over the rest of American society. The era marked both what Harvard's president, Nathan Pusey, declared to be the "Age of the Scholar" and what the historian-administrator Richard Freeland has since called "Academia's Golden Age." Less favorably disposed renderings have linked the university's development during this period to the exigencies of the cold war.[3]

At Columbia, those who saw an uncertain future in 1945 had three principal areas of concern: financial viability; capacity to attract students; and capacity to attract and retain talented faculty. Columbia had managed to pay its bills during the war by engaging in federally funded research, much of it secret and nearly all of it war-related, by training some five thousand naval officers and military attachés, and by enrolling large numbers of tuition-paying women. By war's end, Columbia ranked as the fourth largest recipient of wartime federal support ($29 million), after only MIT ($117 million), Caltech ($83 million), and Harvard ($31 million).[4]

Meanwhile, Columbia's nongovernmental financial resources had all diminished. The endowment in 1945 was 20 percent less than it had been in 1930, with most of it tied up in lease arrangements with Rockefeller Center extending into the early 1950s. During the Depression, fund-raising came to a virtual stop. No additions to the physical plant had been undertaken since 1932, when ground was broken for the new library. It opened in 1935 as South Library and was renamed Butler Library in 1945. Both the Morningside campus, with several buildings now in their sixth decade of use, and the medical campus, its buildings entering their third decade of service, suffered from the consequences of long-deferred maintenance.[5]

Financial concerns were linked to the direction enrollments were likely to take in the postwar years. Columbia's annual enrollments peaked in 1931 at around fifty thousand and thereafter declined until they bottomed out at thirty-five thousand in 1945. The sharpest drops occurred in Summer School and Extension enrollments, as the Depression made both increasingly unaffordable. Yet more than just a return to the levels of the 1930s would be needed to assure Columbia the needed tuition revenues to break out of its fifteen-year holding pattern.[6]

Passage of the G.I. Bill in 1944 assured American universities at least a temporary surge in enrollments, as was the case at Columbia, when eight thousand veterans appeared on campus in the spring of 1946. More than fourteen thousand registered in the fall. In 1946–47, half of the twelve thousand students in Columbia College, the Graduate Faculties, and the School of General Studies (created in 1946 as the successor to the Columbia Extension Program) were enrolled under the G.I. Bill, with the vast bulk of the undergraduates in General Studies. Whatever the logistical problems these veterans, often accompanied by families, represented, their federally paid tuitions were as welcome as they were needed. Still, the declining birth rate in the late 1920s and 1930s remained a long-term concern, as did the prospect that Columbia's higher tuition and urban locale might price it out of the postwar market, which was likely to be increasingly dominated by tax-supported public universities.[7]

The third uncertainty turned on Columbia's faculty, most of whom were away during the war serving in the military or in government service. Many senior faculty who had stayed on during the war were now ready to retire. Some faculty decided to remain permanently in public service after the war, while others lingered on in government jobs for a year or two, making their ultimate return uncertain. Still others, who had been assigned duties at other universities during the war, decided to shift their academic allegiances there. These included the Nobel chemist Harold C. Urey and the Nobel physicist Enrico Fermi, both of whom decided to stay at the University of Chicago, where they had gone in 1942 when the Manhattan Project was dispersed, rather than return to postwar Columbia. The question remained: would postwar Columbia be able to attract—and retain—world-class faculty?

Similar doubts infused the thinking of even the most self-confident and well-heeled private universities. Indeed, the leaders of many of them set about vigorously lobbying to secure positive answers to each of these questions. Yes, the federal government would continue to help underwrite the research programs of leading private universities. Yes, students in numbers would continue to seek access to America's leading private research universities. And, yes, provisions would be made to assure leading private research universities had a steady stream of talented and professionally ambitious faculty.[8]

In these successful postwar efforts by private universities to assure themselves an important place in the "American Century," Columbia's voice is conspicuous by its absence. This is all the more striking for the fact that for most of the previous half-century the prevailing academic wisdom on any subject had been largely determined by what Nicholas Murray Butler last had to say about it. That role now fell to Harvard's president, James B. Conant, to MIT's Arthur Compton, to President J. E. Wallace Sterling and Provost Frederick Termann of Stanford, to Robert G. Sproul of the University of California, to Lee A. Dubridge at Cal Tech, and to Robert Hutchins of the University of Chicago, the academy's reigning skeptic.[9]

Even in matters within New York State, Columbia's postwar voice could barely be heard. In the struggle to persuade the legislature to provide support to the state's private universities, for example, as New York belatedly embarked on strengthening the state university system, it was not Columbia, as one of its representatives in Albany acknowledged, but "the Catholic colleges [who] saved us." And so Columbia would remain on the sidelines until it found itself a president.[10]

Waiting for Ike

Early in his presidency, Butler frequently spoke of the time when someone would take his place. By 1945 many of those once mentioned, such as Frederick J. E. Woodbridge (d. 1940) and John J. Coss (d. 1940) were dead, while most of Columbia's serving senior administrators were too old to be considered. This may have been what Butler intended by keeping them on, hoping thereby to block the appointments of possible successors. When, for example, Virginia Gildersleeve announced her desire to retire in 1942, at age sixty-five, he insisted that she stay as dean at Barnard until he left Columbia. Always solicitous of Butler, she acceded. Dean of the Graduate Faculties George Pegram, a year older than Gildersleeve, was another Butler administrator pressured to stick around; Frederick A. Goetze, university treasurer since 1916, was still another. Gildersleeve retired in 1945 at sixty-eight; Goetze in 1948 at seventy-eight; Pegram in 1950 at seventy-two. Wartime Columbia was administered by a gerontocracy.[11]

Where to look for a president? Columbia had in the dozen previous instances found most of its presidents nearby. Samuel Johnson, William Samuel Johnson, William Harris, William Duer, and Charles King were all known at their elections to members of New York City's Anglican/Episcopalian establishment. Benjamin Moore, Nathaniel Fish Moore, Seth Low, and Nicholas Murray Butler were graduates of the College. Only Myles Cooper, the no-show Charles Wharton, and Frederick A. P. Barnard were outsiders to Columbia and New York. But the first and third of these had at least been academics.[12]

Between October 1945, when Nicholas Murray Butler's retirement commenced, and the summer of 1948, Columbia made do with an acting president, Frank Fackenthal. It is a measure of the frustration attending what Jacques Barzun called the "long interregnum" that, a year into his acting presidency, some faculty proposed electing the sixty-two-year-old Fackenthal president. That he had faithfully served President Butler in a series of administrative positions—he began as a clerk in the president's office in 1902, then served as university secretary, and in 1938 became provost—was generally acknowledged. Moreover, he was someone, it was said, "who could interest himself in details." He was also a graduate of the College, class of 1906, a self-described "gentleman's C" student and fraternity man. Of Pennsylvania Dutch background, he could even, in a pinch, lay claim to a latter-day Episcopalianism.[13]

But not even his warmest admirers viewed Fackenthal during his forty-five years of service in Low Library as more than an efficient administrator who was devoted to Columbia and to Butler. There is some question as to whether the devotion was reciprocated. On being informed that the trustees had elected Fackenthal to the board in 1946, Butler upbraided board chairman Coykendall for violating the tradition that of Columbia's active officers only the president could be elected a trustee. When rumors persisted that the trustees intended to tap Fackenthal, Butler told Coykendall, "Oh, for heaven's sake, don't name my clerk as President."[14]

Among the university's other senior administrators, the picking was thin. The dean of the Graduate Faculties, George B. Pegram, was a Columbia Ph.D., a longtime faculty member in physics, and an experienced administrator but also well into his late sixties. The dean of the Medical School, Willard C. Rappleye, was more the right age—a forceful administrator in his late forties—and had held important public positions during World War II. He was Butler's personal choice but practically no one else's, being largely unknown on the Morningside campus and widely disliked uptown.[15]

Then there was Harry Carman, the popular dean of Columbia College, a

Columbia Ph.D. (1925) and member of the history department for more than a quarter-century. He had been raised upstate and attended Syracuse University. But Carman was Catholic, perhaps not Catholic enough to satisfy the archbishop of New York, Francis Cardinal Spellman, who passed him over for various public positions that required his informal concurrence (a seat on the New York City School Board among them), but Catholic enough to remove him from serious consideration for president. He stayed on as dean until 1949 and then retired. He died in 1962.[16]

Perhaps the best prospect among faculty with administrative experience was Albert C. Jacobs, professor of law and Fackenthal's acting provost. His successful handling of the many problems attending the immediate postwar surge in enrollments was a testament to his administrative skills. Tall, handsome, and in his midforties, Jacobs had been a Rhodes Scholar upon his graduation from Michigan in 1921 and came to the Law School in 1927. He was also an active Episcopalian.[17]

In the fall of 1945, a University Council–appointed faculty advisory committee chaired by Dean Pegram brought forward four faculty names for presidential consideration. Included among them were two historians, John A. Krout and Jacques Barzun; a professor of government and public law and later a member of the World Court in the Hague, Philip C. Jessup; and the economist and dean of the Business School Robert D. Calkins. Krout later served in several administrative capacities, including dean of Graduate Faculties (1949–53) and provost (1953–56). In 1948 President Truman appointed Jessup the United States representative to the United Nations. Calkins went to the Rockefellers' General Education Board in 1947 and five years later became president of the Brookings Institution. Thus all three had estimable public careers after being passed over for the Columbia presidency.[18]

But it is the thought of Jacques Barzun becoming Columbia's thirteenth president in 1946 that makes the most intriguing might-have-been. In terms of his administrative interests, he was a protégé of Harry Carman and closely identified with the College, from which he had graduated in 1927 at the age of nineteen. He passed the war mostly at Columbia, teaching a course in naval history. At thirty-eight, he was only two years younger than Low and one younger than Butler when they assumed their Columbia presidencies. He was both more naturally elegant and less intellectually circumspect than either. He was a superb teacher and an excellent scholar and had administrative experience. He wrote beautifully on a wide range of subjects but on none so wittily as on higher education, as in *Teacher in America*, which appeared in 1945 and marked his national debut as the acerbic commentator on academic folkways that he has continued to be into the twenty-first century.[19]

"Jacques," admirers said of him, "does not lack self-confidence." For this reason, he might have given his trustees as much trouble as President Barnard had his, but with less shouting and more verbal playfulness. Of twentieth-century university presidents who might serve as functional equivalents of this president-not-to-be, there really are none, though the stormy tenures of Chicago's Robert Hutchins and Boston University's John Silber are at least suggestive.

But even had a faculty consensus developed around Barzun, it was unlikely that the trustees would have joined it. Theirs was a board historically predisposed against choosing its presidents from among the faculty. Instead, the five-member search committee, chaired by Thomas I. Parkinson, chairman of the Equitable Life Assurance Society, and including the retired businessman Marcellus H. Dodge, the Reverend Frederick Fleming, rector of Trinity Church, the retired banker George E. Warren, and board chairman Frederick Coykendall, ex officio commenced its search by approaching three types of outside prospects. The first consisted of public figures with international interests, including Senator J. William Fulbright, who briefly had been president of the University of Arkansas before being elected to Congress in 1942 and to the Senate in 1944. Still in his thirties, but already well known for helping to create the Fulbright Scholars Program and acting as a key foreign policy adviser to President Harry Truman, Fulbright briefly considered returning to academe before deciding to remain in politics.[20]

A contemporary of Fulbright's, the lawyer John J. McCloy, was another of his generation who had a good war as undersecretary of war and of whom much was expected in the contentious peace to follow. Accordingly, he became a possibility for the Columbia presidency. A member of the foreign policy elite and already in training for his subsequent role as one of the Unites States' foreign policy wise men, he would have made an interesting choice. Back in 1945–46, however, the fact that he was a Catholic likely kept his candidacy from going far. Like Fulbright, McCloy, an Amherst College and Harvard Law School graduate, had no ties to Columbia.[21]

When the search committee looked at outside academics, it favored those whose wartime experience made them familiar with Washington. One such prospect was Vannevar Bush, erstwhile dean of MIT's School of Engineering, Roosevelt's wartime head of the Office of Strategic Research and Development, author of *Science: The Endless Frontier* (1944), and currently president of the Carnegie Institution. Another was Bush's ex-colleague and MIT president, Karl T. Compton. Neither showed much interest in coming to New York. A third possibility was the president of Williams College, James Phinney Baxter III, who had seen wartime service in the Office of Strategic Research with Bush but who decided to stay at Williams.[22]

Besides Compton and Baxter, the trustees approached at least one other sitting academic chief executive, the chancellor of the University of California, Robert G. Sproul. Indeed, it was Sproul's making known in early 1947, while renegotiating his contract with the California regents, that he had been offered the Columbia presidency that gave public currency to the idea that the Columbia search was in trouble. This also seems to be the point where, in collusion with search committee chairman Parkinson and without the knowledge of the rest of the committee, Thomas J. Watson hijacked the search process.[23]

Shaken by Sproul's public rejection, the search committee reluctantly agreed to allow nonmember Watson to approach Dwight D. Eisenhower about the position. Watson had brought up Ike's name earlier in the search, but it went nowhere. An already scheduled ceremonial appearance in February 1947 on the Columbia campus to honor the military heroes of World War II provided Eisenhower with his first glimpse of the campus—and a chance to be shown around by Watson. When the possibility of his becoming Columbia's president was raised during the visit, Ike expressed no interest in the position.[24]

In May Watson renewed his courting of Eisenhower, this time assuring the general that his election would have the unanimous backing of the board (he had no such assurance) and that his specific duties as president were negotiable. An equivocal response sufficed to have Watson request authorization from the entire board at its June 2 meeting for him to do whatever it took to secure Ike's acceptance. Of the twenty-one trustees present, sixteen voted for such authorization. The five who did not included a majority of the search committee and the chairman of the board, Frederick Coykendall. The University Council's faculty committee on the presidential search was not consulted.[25]

One of the many apocryphal stories surrounding the selection of Eisenhower has it that the trustees confused General Eisenhower with his older brother, Milton, who was in 1947 president of Kansas State University (and about to become president of Pennsylvania State University). A variant on this story had a trustee asking for suggestions from the University of Chicago's chancellor, Robert M. Hutchins, and being told to "get Eisenhower," Hutchins meaning Milton.[26]

The frequent retelling of this story and even its adoption by Ike himself do not make it credible. First, there is little reason to think that the Columbia trustees would have been interested in Milton, who only later achieved national academic prominence as the president of the Johns Hopkins University. But, second, there is every reason to believe that the Columbia board was prepared to go a very considerable distance to lure to Morningside Heights the most internationally admired American of his generation.[27]

Ike's political potential was recognized not only by Republican and Democratic operatives in Washington but by politically active Republican trustees such as Arthur Hays Sulzberger and Democrats such as Watson (and Parkinson) on the Columbia board. They could see their respective political allegiances advanced by bringing Ike to Columbia, even if only to await national political developments. New York Republicans backing New York governor, Thomas Dewey, in 1948, for example, would certainly prefer Eisenhower tucked away at Columbia rather than heading up a Democratic ticket in the event that Truman was denied the nomination in 1948. Similarly, Watson wanted a chance to try to get Eisenhower to declare himself a Democrat. Meanwhile, Trustee Douglas Black, who had Eisenhower under contract to his publishing firm, Doubleday, to write his wartime memoir, *Crusade in Europe*, had his own reasons for wanting his would-be author close at hand.[28]

The question of why Columbia wanted Ike as president largely disappears when it is remembered that the choice rested with the trustees, not with the faculty. Unlike the faculty, the trustees had many reasons to see securing Ike as a coup well worth the wait. They were not focused on the university's internal problems but on burnishing its international reputation. This is clearly the case with Watson and Parkinson, who concluded that snaring Ike as its next president would more likely assure Columbia continued prominence than would anyone else mentioned for the job. That he was already a frequently mentioned prospect for the White House only guaranteed that his every move as president of Columbia would be national news. As for qualifications, should not someone who pulled off the invasion of Normandy be able to administer Columbia?

Not the least consideration was the favor Ike's selection would receive from Butler, who could hardly feel diminished by his being succeeded by the Supreme Military Commander of Allied Forces and liberator of Europe. The Eisenhower that the trustees envisioned—and Butler endorsed—bringing to Morningside is the Eisenhower in the portrait Trustee Marcellus Dodge commissioned in 1953 upon Ike's departure for Washington, which hangs in the main stairwell of Butler Library. It has Ike in formal military regalia, sash, and medals and, for all the approachability suggested in his face, assuming a stance almost Napoleonic.[29]

If Columbia's interest in Eisenhower is explainable in terms of trustees' motives, what did Ike see in Columbia? The second apocryphal story surrounding Ike's election is that he assumed the presidency of Columbia University would be like presiding over a small liberal arts college in the countryside. As this story goes, he expected his principal interactions as president would be with his undergraduates, "his boys," whose education he would advance through informal Mark Hopkins–like conversations at nether ends of a log, interspersed with unannounced visits of the general to classrooms, much like periodic visits with troops in forward positions.

This story actually bears some resemblance to Ike's expectations. He acknowledged as much to friends while considering Watson's offer. One doubts he was familiar with Donald Davidson's poem "Lee in the Mountains," but the notion of retreating to a respectable and not too demanding job on a rural campus in the wake of battle as a way of avoiding the din of public exposure clearly attracted him. That his first executive decision as president-elect was to secure the continued presence of Lou Little as the Columbia football coach by getting Yale to withdraw its offer to have him come to New Haven is suggestive of what Ike hoped he was in for. Columbia would be a sinecure, one that would maximize his control over his schedule, allow him to speak out on matters that mattered to him, and politically to see what happened next.[30]

To the extent that Ike's acceptance of the presidency reflected his own misreading of the job, it was a misreading aided and abetted by assurances made in June 1947 by Watson in the course of reeling him in. As he came closer to accepting the offer, Ike, in two remarkable letters, made clear his reservations and stipulations to Watson and Parkinson (who did not convey them to the board). One stipulation was that he would have no responsibility for fund-raising. Among the "other details" from which he specifically exacted exemption was presiding over faculty meetings.[31]

There was still the problem of his and Mamie's "dislike of New York as a residence." Watson, sensing a deal in the making, countered with assurances of guest memberships at golf clubs in Westchester and on Long Island, plus a weekend retreat upstate. And, of course, the summers were to be entirely theirs. Not since Samuel Johnson was Columbia to have a president so uncomfortable in the city, so unwilling to come to terms with its distinctive character, and so glad to flee it at first chance.[32]

Even so, there remained second thoughts. As Ike acknowledged to a boyhood friend, entering "a field so entirely new that my self-confidence is somewhat shaken. . . . I am afraid it is going to demand real intensity of effort." But by then he was too far into the negotiations to back out, particularly in light of the absence of a better offer as his government service drew to an end. So, with the exaction of one more condition—that Columbia would pay for Eisenhower's personal staff but that it would be understood that they worked for him—he gave Watson the go-ahead.[33]

On June 29, 1947, the Columbia trustees, most still in the dark about the accommodations agreed to by Watson, elected Dwight David Eisenhower Columbia's thirteenth president. He would not assume the responsibilities of the office until his release from the army the following spring, when he would also have completed his war memoir, *Crusade in Europe*. As Ike candidly explained to a friend that fall, "Whatever activity I entered, I would want some kind of an organization that would serve as a shield against the interminable and pressing demands that I do this and that and the other. All things considered, I finally came to the conclusion that Columbia would offer me opportunity for some kind of public service and would provide almost as good protection as anything else." A few months into the presidency, Ike complained to Dean Harry Carman, one of his few Columbia confidants, that he had been tricked into the job.[34]

Life with Ike

Released from the army by President Truman in February 1948 and with the *Crusade for Europe* manuscript at the publisher, Eisenhower arrived on campus in May. Following commencement, he promptly left for a two-month vacation. Not a propitious start, but prophetic.

As Columbia presidencies go, Eisenhower's was short. Only Wharton's no-show presidency and the subsequent interim presidency of Andrew Cordier have been shorter. It also passed largely in absentia. Between assuming his responsibilities in May 1948 and relinquishing them in January 1953—nine semesters—he was off campus for all or substantial parts of seven. His first extended absence, in Washington helping reorganize the military, occurred within a month of his formal installation in October 1948 and extended well into the following spring. The next academic year, 1949–50, was the only year when he was consistently on campus, although, ironically, it is then that complaints of his "absentee presidency" began to appear in the *Columbia Spectator*. The following fall he went to Paris as Supreme Commander of NATO, never really to return to campus, except in mid-1952, when he declared the President's House on Morningside Drive his base of operations for the ongoing fight for the Republican nomination and the presidential campaign to follow.[35]

Consistent with his understanding with Watson, Ike largely stayed clear of fund-raising efforts. Instead, the university hired its first full-time development officer, Paul Davis, to attend to that part of the president's job. Eisenhower did interest himself in three projects. One was the establishment of the American Assembly, which provided him with a personal forum from which to speak out on issues that interested him, as well as a conduit by which Republican fund-raisers could underwrite such efforts. Another was the manpower project directed by Business School professor Eli Ginzberg, a project that dealt in part with a longtime concern of Eisenhower's: military recruitment. The third was the acquisition of Arden House, the family estate of the Harrimans, forty miles up the Hudson, which the trustees accepted in October 1950, after the Harriman family provided an additional gift to help with its maintenance.[36]

Any second thoughts Ike might have had about getting involved in fund-raising were effectively squashed early in his presidency after he agreed to make a visit to the offices of the Rockefeller Foundation. When staffers began pressing him about the status of several active grants the foundation had recently made to Columbia and about which Ike was uninformed, the visit was cut short. And not replicated. Whereas one of the justifications for building the President's House back in 1912 was that it would be used by presidents for formal entertaining and fund-raising, Ike used it as a retreat where he socialized at bridge with wartime buddies and, at the urging of Winston Churchill, took up painting.[37]

Eisenhower did have people around him who could tend to the store. First among these was his provost, Albert C. Jacobs. A skilled and respected administrator, Jacobs became Ike's provost in May 1948. The internal workings of the university were his responsibility, along with Dean of Graduate Faculties George Pegram.

Nine months into his provostship, Jacobs announced his intention to resign in the fall to become chancellor of the University of Denver. Just before his announcement, Jacobs asked forty-five-year-old Professor of Government and Public Law Grayson Kirk to become his associate provost, a position Kirk accepted, in part, he later acknowledged, because "I was tired of teaching." When Jacobs decamped in the fall of 1949, Eisenhower named Kirk provost.[38]

They were not entirely strangers, Kirk having organized Eisenhower's formal installation the previous fall. But they were not and never would get to, as Kirk later put it, "sitting around exchanging war stories." When Eisenhower left Columbia in 1950 to go to Paris, Kirk found himself in the same position for the last two years of Eisenhower's presidency as Fackenthal had been for the three years preceding it: institutional caretaker.[39]

It is not clear that Eisenhower's relations with the Columbia faculty had to be as mutually unsatisfying an affair as they soon became. Jacques Barzun told a story that offers at least the possibility of another outcome. Eisenhower had been invited to a gathering of faculty at the Men's Faculty Club early in his presidency, and the conversation had turned to the Balkans. Ike offered an extemporaneous rendering of the region in terms of its military vulnerability that left his listeners, many of them European historians, awestruck by his erudition and historical sensitivity. Unfortunately, Barzun's story is most notable for its singularity.[40]

Part of the problem was that, even when on campus, Eisenhower was kept out of faculty reach by his staffers, Kevin McCann and Robert Schulz, neither of whom ever quite made the transition from military base to university campus. Faculty requests to meet with the president were frostily received and rejected sufficiently often to deter future petitions. Such inaccessibility left Ike with both time on his hands, which he was reported to pass reading Zane Grey novels in his office, and a clear desk, neither of which endeared him to faculty.[41]

Eisenhower never made an effort to figure out what made Columbia faculty tick. He had very few native informants, and those he did have were, by their wartime experiences or administrative responsibilities, atypical, among these, Grayson Kirk, Eli Ginzberg, and I. I. Rabi. In his limited dealings with the general run of faculty, even those who had served in the military, Eisenhower, with his top-down operating style and unabashed nonintellectualism, came across as someone who had little understanding of or regard for their folkways. And vice versa.[42]

Ike's politics did not help. Just before accepting the Columbia presidency, he declared himself a Republican. During his Columbia presidency, he opposed federal aid to higher education and was given to insinuations about those thought to be soft on Communism. Of course, not all Columbia faculty were Democrats, but in 1948 those who were not were more likely to be Wallace Progressives than Dewey Republicans.[43]

Eisenhower's closest friend on the faculty was Harry Carman, the patron saint of lost boys and nervous junior faculty. But Carman, despite his liberal politics, was as likely to share the general's exasperation with faculty behavior as he was to attempt to explain it away. The test of his friendship, as well as his political savvy, came in the fall of 1952, when Columbia faculty, led by Allan Nevins, Peter Gay, and William Leuchtenburg, all members of Carman's own history department, secured the support of 324 faculty for a political ad in the *New York Times* backing Eisenhower's Democratic opponent in the presidential election, Adlai Stevenson. Even before the ad appeared, Carman had signatures of 714 Columbians for an ad supporting Ike. When the organizers of the Stevenson ad complained that the Eisenhower ad did not contain many faculty signatures but was dominated by administrators and staff, the inferred elitism was not lost on the Republican commentators on the Morningside battle of the ads. The overall impression was of Columbia as a warring camp, with neither its faculty nor its president ennobled by the affair.[44]

A similar clash of expectations resulting in disappointment all round occurred when President Eisenhower appeared unannounced in various classes in the College. Some instructors did not welcome these visits, but what seems to have brought them to an abrupt halt was one drop-in to a General Studies class in which the students (likely with the instructor's connivance) started questioning Ike on the subject at hand. Nor did it help that the *Columbia Spectator*, under the successive editorships of David Wise (CC 1951) and Max Frankel (CC 1952), regularly criticized Ike's political pronouncements. And other than the occasional drive to Baker Field to observe the football team at practice, Eisenhower's hopes of engaging "the boys"—and theirs of engaging him—came to naught. It may have been his disappointment on this score that prompted Ike to admonish the typical Columbia student to "become a more effective and productive member of the American national team."[45]

That Eisenhower's Columbia presidency was a series of distractions from the university business at hand is not to suggest that the reorganization of the military, the two-year command of NATO, and his campaign for the White House were not serious matters. It is to suggest the possibility that had the trustees considered these sufficiently time consuming, he would have been encouraged to resign to attend to them. Whatever Ike's views on the matter, the trustees seemed perfectly ready to have him on semipermanent loan as long as he was willing. After he returned to the United States in January 1952, after the New Hampshire primaries, and after declaring himself a candidate for the Republican nomination, the trustees were still willing to have him use 60 Morningside Drive as his residential base for the campaign.[46]

On November 4, 1952, Eisenhower scored a substantial victory over Adlai Stevenson in the presidential election. Thirteen days later, he informed the trustees of his intention to resign, effective January 13, 1953, the day before he was to be sworn in as president of the United States. On December 5 the trustees accepted his resignation and elected Grayson Kirk Columbia's fourteenth president.[47]

Ike took only a few Columbians with him to Washington. They included university treasurer Joseph Campbell, who became comptroller general of the United States, and Barnard Professor of Economics Raymond Saulnier, who became a member and later chairman of the Presidential Council of Economic Advisers. Ike seldom returned to Morningside. At his funeral in 1969, only two Columbians were invited: Grayson Kirk and Joseph Campbell. For Ike, Columbia was a breather between epic undertakings; for Columbia, the Eisenhower presidency was a lost opportunity to catch the new beat of postwar academe.[48]

Reimagining Grayson Kirk

It is hard for those who observed him then to imagine Grayson Kirk as other than he appeared in the last months of his presidency, during the troubles of Columbia '68. The impression he left then is of someone out of touch with the forces shaking Columbia and painfully inadequate to the challenge of bringing them back under control. His retirement in August 1968 was greeted with almost universal relief, even by those Columbians who had supported him back in April.

This negative impression has been reinforced by the fact that his two successors, William J. McGill and Michael I. Sovern, had every reason to distance themselves from Kirk and, in doing so, have provided in the different ways each went about his own presidency a negative commentary on Kirk's. Indeed, his immediate successor, McGill, said of him: "He didn't like a fight. As a consequence, whenever the normal struggling that develops in an administration for leadership went on, Grayson's response to it was to decentralize." He also noted that Kirk "did not have a combative impulse in his body." Coming from the self-consciously pugnacious McGill, this was damning without cover of faint praise. News of Kirk's death in 1998, at age ninety-five, seemed to provoke on campus no reaction quite so common as surprise that he had survived so long after 1968.[49]

My attempt to reimagine Grayson Kirk is not meant to explain why he proved unequal to the events of 1968. Who among that year's front liners proved equal to them? It is rather to try to understand why he came to be selected as president in the first place and how it could be that through much of his long presidency he was considered, as one of his trustees recalled, "one of the ablest of the Ivy League presidents in an era of very good presidents." It is also an attempt to account for the view expressed by Barnard's president, Millicent McIntosh, in 1964: "I'm one of Mr. Kirk's greatest admirers. I think that he's made an excellent president for the University. He's a professor's president." And to make sense of the view of Douglas M. Knight, president of Duke and colleague of Grayson Kirk in the Association of American Universities, that the post-'68 popular image of Kirk was a "gross caricature."[50]

In an age that expected more formality in its academic leaders, Grayson Kirk exceeded the era's norm for presidential buttoned-upness. The stiffly starched impression he conveyed was perhaps unintentionally reinforced on campus by the fact that the Columbia Spectator's gallery of Kirk images over the course of his eighteen years as the university's chief administrator seems to have been limited to two equally formal poses in which the president's pencil-thin moustache, dark-rimmed glasses, and impressive dome sat bestride either a Saville Row double-breasted lounge suit or a tuxedo. A man without a nickname, who "never played the game of being young," someone who openly admired Nicholas Murray Butler for the way he carried himself, Grayson Kirk was universally acknowledged to be the very picture of a university president.[51]

When Jacques Barzun remarked apropos of American culture in the mid-1950s that "the concept of Roman gravitas would seem to be permanently at bay," he likely exempted Kirk from the generalization. Four decades later, Barzun, who served in Kirk's administration for a dozen years and who resented Kirk's handling of his ouster as provost in 1967, allowed that his long-time boss "looked the part of the president, even if he wasn't equal to it."[52]

Kirk's formality was in part a consequence of his lifelong stutter. He compensated by avoiding the use of the telephone except for family and trusted secretaries, by minimizing informal chitchat, especially with strangers, and by writing out even the most casual public remarks. The considerable reputation he acquired as a young lecturer to large classes at Wisconsin and the regularity with which he spoke to large audiences as president are testaments to his success in coping with the problem. Its persistence, however, helps account for his woodenness in even the most informal of settings (e.g., the firing-up of the Yule log in John Jay Lounge). It also helps explain why he remained unimpressed with the pedagogical arguments that privileged the active discussion in small classes favored in the College.[53]

Any reimagining of the Kirk presidency should note its length: officially fifteen years but nearer eighteen with his two years as acting president. This was Columbia's third longest presidency. But Kirk's presidency had the unfortunate timing in its later stages to cross one of the great generational fault lines in American history. Few of his presidential contemporaries successfully negotiated it; most stumbled publicly. Witness California's Clark Kerr, Cornell's James Perkins, Harvard's Nathan Pusey, Michigan's Harlan Hatcher, Stanford's J. E. Wally, and even, though he stayed on, Yale's Kingman Brewster. When Abby Hoffman urged his cogenerationists not to trust anyone over thirty, Grayson Kirk simply epitomized the type.

Thus framed, the question becomes less what made Kirk a casualty of the late sixties than what made him the trustees' unanimous choice in 1953. First, he was viewed as the right age for the job. Provost at forty-five, Kirk was acting president at forty-seven and president at fifty. This assured what the early Virginians called "seasoning" while holding out the prospect of a reasonably long and vigorous presidency.[54]

And so his was. Except for an illness in 1958, requiring stomach surgery, Kirk was an active and engaged president. He willingly traveled to meet with alumni and solicit benefactors. Junkets abroad for the State Department also became occasions to conduct university business. His traveling accelerated in the last years of his presidency, largely in the service of the first universitywide capital campaign. In residence, he and his wife, Marion, entertained or were entertained almost very night of the school year, thus reviving the Butler tradition of a social presidency that Ike had allowed to lapse.[55]

The manner of Kirk's selection differed markedly from his predecessor's. The contrast may well have been intentional on the part of the trustees, who would not have been immune to the second-guessing that began early on in the Eisenhower presidency. Whereas Ike emerged from a search that extended over three years and left the presidency vacant for thirty-seven months, Kirk was selected two weeks after Ike announced his intention to resign and assumed office the day Ike's resignation took effect.[56]

What passed for a presidential search in his case consisted of a couple of phone calls, one to Harvard president James B. Conant, who advised the Columbia trustees to stay with Kirk. An informal faculty committee that included I. I. Rabi agreed.[57]

Although startled when asked to become provost back in the summer of 1949, Kirk put himself on the inside track for the future presidency by accepting. When Trustee Thomas J. Watson arranged a luncheon downtown in January 1950, at which Kirk got to "meet everybody who mattered," the presidency became, should Ike depart, his to lose.[58]

For reasons unknown, Eisenhower, ensconced in Paris in 1951, had sufficient reservations about Kirk's succeeding him that he dispatched a trusted member of the Columbia faculty to urge Kirk to take the Rutgers presidency, which was on a standing offer to him, rather than stick around Columbia. The trustees' reluctance to make him acting president upon Eisenhower's departure for Paris bespeaks some possible reservations from that quarter as well, although it may have reflected nothing more than the board's effort to deny the reality of Ike's having left the building.[59]

If reservations existed among key trustees, Kirk was in a position to allay them by exercising his powers as acting president in a manner designed to please them. This he did on three fronts. The first involved the potentially explosive issue of radicals on campus. This issue took the form of two questions very much on the minds of Americans early in the cold war: Should a university tolerate Communists or reputed Communists speaking on campus? Should Communists or ex-Communists who declined to testify against fellow Communists be allowed to continue to teach? Columbia trustees clearly favored negative answers to both, while the more vocal students and a substantial portion of the faculty believed that the campus should be open to radical speakers and that faculty who declined to cooperate with the various investigations looking into Communist subversion should not be fired.[60]

On the first question, Kirk sided with the trustees when he banned the self-acknowledged Communist Howard Fast from speaking on campus in the spring of 1951. He did so quietly and with the acquiescence of the undergraduate group that had invited Fast. The second question prompted a more complicated response, though one that would placate trustees insisting that the faculty be rid of any Communists or Communist sympathizers. Kirk drew a distinction between faculty whose notoriety stemmed from their refusal to identify others involved with them in past radical activity and faculty whose public announcements allowed the conclusion that they remained loyal Communists.[61]

Into the first protected category fell the sociologist Bernhard Stern and the psychiatrist Harry Grundfest, two untenured faculty who were called to testify before the Senate Internal Security Subcommittee (the McCarran Committee) as to their past links to the Communists but whom Kirk made no move to remove from the faculty. So, too, with the radical but non-Communist C. Wright Mills, a tenured member of the sociology department, whose writings drew fire from anti-Communists but were, Kirk later indicated, "something we had to tolerate." Kirk similarly ignored criticisms of Mark Van Doren, though he agreed that when it came to politics the English professor "was awfully naïve." Unlike those elsewhere, Columbia's China scholars experienced no institutional censure for suspected sympathies with the Chinese Revolution.[62]

Into the second and more dispensable category fell Gene Weltfish, a Barnard graduate, a Columbia Ph.D., a nontenured lecturer in anthropology, and a Communist. In June 1952 Weltfish charged the United States with using chemical weapons in the Korean War, which allowed the inference that she adhered to the Communist line. Three months later she took the Fifth Amendment before the Senate's McCarran Committee. Trustees looked to their acting president to do something about her. Meanwhile, the FBI and the conservative columnist George Sokolsky provided Kirk with incriminating information about Weltfish, as did New York congressman Frederic R. Coudert Jr. (CC 1918; Law 1922), the grandson and son of Columbia trustees, and a leading local anti-Communist who had charged CCNY's administration with harboring Communists in its faculty.[63]

In the fall of 1952, Kirk proposed to the trustees a change in the statutes to limit to five years the period a lecturer could remain on the faculty in that rank. (This was Columbia's first move in the direction of the formalized "up or out" provisions more fully put in place by Provost Jacques Barzun in 1956.) As Weltfish had served as a lecturer since 1936, she clearly fell under this rule and, if not recommended for tenure by her department, would be obliged to leave after the spring term in 1953. During the discussion of this change at the board meeting on October 6, 1952, a trustee inquired whether it applied specifically to Weltfish, to which the acting president responded in the affirmative. It was then unanimously adopted, and an earlier resolution calling for Weltfish's dismissal was tabled.[64]

Kirk's handling of these questions gave him credibility with the trustees without infuriating the faculty. When asked thirty years later about pressure from the trustees to fire Weltfish, he described it as "very great" and allowed that, in its absence, "I think I probably would have procrastinated further on it."[65]

If not in the class of the broadcaster Edward R. Murrow or the attorney

Joseph Welch, Kirk held up better than many academic administrators in fending off the excesses of the McCarthy era. The sociologist Sigmund Diamond, who had been an active Communist organizer in the 1930s, always gave Kirk high marks for supporting his appointment to the Columbia faculty in 1953 after the then dean, McGeorge Bundy, dismissed him from the Harvard faculty as an unnecessary political risk. While highly critical of many of his peers, Ellen Schrecker, in the now-standard historical account of the McCarthy era on campus, *No Ivory Tower: McCarthyisn and the Universities* (1986), gives Kirk (and Columbia) what amounts to a conditional pass. MIT, Michigan, and Stanford fare considerably worse.[66]

Kirk also demonstrated his toughness, at least from the trustees' view, by refusing to countenance a strike in June 1952 of dining hall workers led by the labor leader Mike Quill. He not only rode out an eighteen-day strike but garnered some popular support for his opposition to union organizing on campus by arguing that he was protecting cafeteria jobs for students, the kind of a student job that had made it possible for him to work his way through college. Kirk's critical views about unionization, however, were not limited to cafeteria workers or even to the unionization of university employees. Perhaps not surprisingly, he later contended his antiunionism was confirmed by his experiences as a member of various corporate boards, among those Watson's IBM.[67]

What most appealed to the trustees in Kirk's candidacy was that it gave promise of continuing the Butler tradition of a prominent internationalist as head of Columbia. Both knew their way abroad and around the State Department. But whereas Butler had been an amateur in international relations, Kirk was a recognized scholar in the field, one of the so-called realists whose views would dominate the field and shape the country's foreign policy well into the 1960s.[68]

Indeed, if there was hallowed ground for Grayson Kirk, it was the Sixty-eighth Street brownstone that housed the Council of Foreign Relations. There, he first encountered not just notables from the academic and policy-making communities but all the "absolutely top drawer people in the New York community." His election to the presidency of the council in 1962 likely meant nearly as much to him as his election to the Columbia presidency. He clearly enjoyed the post more.[69]

Like Columbia's other twentieth-century presidents, Kirk rose from modest circumstances. He was born in southern Ohio in 1903, into a family with Virginia links going back to the early eighteenth century. His father was a farmer, his mother a schoolteacher. Neither had gone to college; both were Presbyterians, a denominational persuasion to which their second son subscribed in adulthood. As the first college-goer in the Kirk family, Grayson attended nearby

Miami University, where he combined serious study with a fraternity-centered social life. Then, as later, he was immune to the lure of athletic activity of any sort.[70]

His first job after college was as his fraternity's national secretary. He also taught in a regional high school. After marriage in 1925 to Marion Sands, a local girl from a family of means, he pursued graduate studies in international relations at the University of Wisconsin. At Madison in those days, the leading figure was Paul Reinsch, under whose direction Kirk wrote his dissertation.[71]

As his thesis, "French Administrative Policy in Alsace-Lorraine, 1918–1928," required research in France, Kirk and his wife set out for Paris and the Ecole libre des sciences politiques in the fall of 1927. For these heretofore heartland Americans, life would never be the same. They acquired a permanent attachment to France and things French, including a discerning palate for French wines. He later wore the lapel rosette of the French Legion of Honor, as had Butler before him. For her part, Marion acquired an interest in formal entertaining that was to be a hallmark of the Kirk presidency.[72]

Back in Madison, Kirk moved up the academic ladder as Reinsch's likely successor, a position confirmed by his publication in 1936 of a monograph on the Philippine independence movement. In 1939, by then a tenured associate professor, he was invited to Columbia as a one-year visitor and as potential successor to the recently deceased Professor Parker Thomas Moon.[73]

Kirk's first encounter with New York was not promising. "I was not overwhelmed by it," he recalled forty-six years later. He developed an immediate dislike for the Morningside neighborhood and judged it no place to raise a family. Nor was he all that impressed with Columbia's undergraduates, whom he compared unfavorably to Wisconsin's "more solid, athletic types." This was all the more disquieting for the fact that the government department had assigned him to the College, with its small-class-discussion format so unlike that of Madison's large lectures. He resented the fact that his office in Hamilton isolated him from the department's graduate faculty in Fayerweather Hall. A year later, when Columbia offered him a permanent appointment, he accepted on the condition that he would "get into the Graduate School and away from this obligatory work in these required courses in which I had relatively little interest." Behold, another Columbia College Skeptic.[74]

Hardly had his family unpacked in more suitable Scarsdale than the exigencies of the war sent Columbia's newest professor of international relations off to a series of postings in Washington and London. These culminated in an appointment to the State Department staff that prepared the way for the creation of the United Nations at the 1945 San Francisco Conference. At the conference, he encountered several present and future Columbians, among them

Lawrence Chamberlain, Philip Jessup, Andrew Cordier, and Barnard's dean, Virginia Gildersleeve, the sole American female delegate. One can easily imagine Kirk staying on in Washington as part of the emergent postwar diplomatic establishment.

Back on Morningside in 1946, Kirk became involved in the organization of the School of International Affairs. A year later, he produced, under the auspices of the Council on Foreign Relations, *The Study of International Relations in American Colleges and Universities.* This established him, along with Yale's William T. R. Fox, who came to Columbia in 1949, Harvard's William Langer, and Chicago's Hans Morgenthau, as one of the leading academic spokesmen for the once again thriving field of international relations, which gave promise in the 1950s of transforming American diplomacy. In sum, Grayson Kirk personified the about-to-be consummated marriage of the academy and the foreign policy establishment that would be a hallmark of the "American Century."[75]

The Kirk Presidency, Part 1

Kirk's presidency had no clear starting point. While officially assuming the office in January 1953, he had performed most of the traditional duties of the presidency since 1950. Even earlier, Eisenhower gave him wide discretion as provost in casting policy options into simple dichotomous choices, which Ike then made and left Kirk to implement. As the transition from provost to president proceeded incrementally, Kirk simply added new responsibilities. While this made for a smooth transition and gave the appearance of continuity, it deprived the new president of an opportunity to think through, much less articulate, a postwar vision for the university. "I didn't think about long-range needs," he acknowledged twenty years after his presidency had ended, "simply because I was overwhelmed with day-to-day problems." Not the least of these problems involved the planning and execution of the 1954 bicentennial celebration, which took up much of his first two years as president.[76]

Surprising in an academic, Kirk possessed little of the teacher's imperative to explain what he was about. Whereas Butler, throughout his presidency, used his annual president's report to the trustees and his convocation remarks to the entering class of Columbia College to address large issues affecting the world, the nation, higher education, and Columbia, Kirk did not. Indeed, he allowed the tradition of published annual reports, which went back to the early Barnard presidency, to lapse altogether, while turning over responsibilities for the College convocation to its dean. Throughout his presidency the trustees' minutes, always a cryptic medium, are uniquely uninformative of presidential intentions. The only internal study conducted during his presidency, that chaired by fellow political scientist Arthur MacMahon and published in 1958 as *Report on the Future of The University*, seems not to have been Kirk's idea at all but that of his graduate dean and later provost, Jacques Barzun. Kirk made little use of it.[77]

It was as if, finding more than enough that he was expected to do, Kirk skipped over the step of deciding what he wanted to do as president. To characterize his presidency as rudderless, as some have later seen it, might be too harsh, but it was clearly responsive to slight shifts in wind and tide. To the extent that a presidency can be both hands-on and nondirective, hardworking and unreflective, that's what Columbia experienced in the Kirk presidency.

This said, one should not conclude that a nondirective presidential style could not work well in the 1950s, even at a university that had been without effective presidential leadership since as far back as the mid-1930s. Nor should it be assumed that the university's various estates would not welcome such a style. One could argue that the Butler legacy of presidential autocracy remained sufficiently palpable in the 1950s to sustain several personally nonautocratic successors. One could also argue that what Columbia really needed in a president in the 1950s was someone who would allow the trustees to reacquire a measure of their authority over finances, the deans to build up their schools, the faculty an opportunity to get on with their work, and the students freedom to take full advantage of the cultural and social mobility that postwar Columbia made available to them. As Mencken said of President Calvin Coolidge, in a favorable comparison with his much more intrusive successor, Herbert Hoover, "he had no ideas, and he was not a nuisance."[78]

Kirk fully met the early expectations of the trustees who entrusted the presidency to him. If not quite on the order of Butler, he immediately established himself as an imposing personage among important New Yorkers and world figures. Even more regularly than during Butler's presidency, Columbia under Kirk (a registered Republican) provided the State Department with its New York venue for welcoming or seeing off visiting dignitaries. Such visitors occasionally ventured to Cambridge or Berkeley but far less often than they were photographed ascending the steps of Low Library to greet President Kirk and appropriate trustees, who awaited them in front of Alma Mater. Sometimes, for purposes of providing translation services, faculty would join them. Here, too, Kirk's by now wholly internalized formality and attention to protocol, traits that might not win him points among undergraduates in Hartley Hall or assistant professors congregated on Hamilton 6th, served Columbia's official purposes admirably.[79]

A more tangible benefit of the Kirk presidency, from the perspective of the trustees, was that the control of the university's finances once again reverted to them. It had always been, to some extent, so. That is, Columbia had traditionally operated as two distinct financial entities, with two sets of books, one for "uptown," the academic enterprise, and one for "downtown," which encompassed the university's real estate holdings and the management of its endowment. A surplus in one of these enterprises might be used to offset a shortfall in the other, but then again it might, as in the instance of income derived from real estate, be allowed to accumulate even as academic needs went unmet. And insofar as the two budgets were prepared at different times of the year, those charged with preparing the smaller uptown budget regularly did so in the dark with respect to its larger downtown counterpart.[80]

Earlier in the century, Butler had gained effective control over both enterprises, principally through his eventual dominance of successive Finance Committee chairs and their salaried treasurers, his unmatched command of the details of the respective budgets, and his monopoly over fund-raising. During his last years and through the interregnum, members of the Finance Committee returned to making crucial decisions in the absence of an involved president. They did so sufficiently to their satisfaction to see little need to stop upon the installation of a new president. Certainly, Ike wanted no part of managing the university's finances. Thus by the late 1940s the prevailing financial arrangements had reverted to those last seen in the early 1880s, when the treasurer, then a member of the board, made crucial financial decisions on behalf of the trustees and it was the president's responsibility to live with them.[81]

Ironically, Kirk's principal structural accomplishment with respect to the trustees—that of securing their agreement in 1958 to a retirement age of seventy (later raised to seventy-two) for life trustees—further undercut his authority. While the retirement rule did thin the ranks of what he privately called "the geriatric brigade," it also had the effect of bringing to the board several new and assertive trustees who were more than prepared to direct the financial affairs of the university. They were also little inclined to take suggestions from academics, even the academic president.[82]

Percy Uris, who, along with his brother, Henry, directed one of the largest building and real estate companies in New York, epitomized this new generation of financially decisive, hardheaded trustees. He was elected in 1958, after first becoming active in the affairs of the Business School, from which he had graduated in 1918. President McGill later described Uris as "someone who knew how to do things in the cold dark world provided by New York.... A totally willful man—he thought he knew all about the essential things that the academics did not know."[83]

Uris took as his model among the older trustees the nothing-if-not-aggressive Thomas J. Watson, not the diffident Frederick Coykendall. Of a piece with Uris was Trustee William S. Paley, who, for all his admonitions to fellow trustees in his 1957 *Role of the Trustees of Columbia University* "that overactivity [is] as great a sin as neglect," found it difficult to leave the executive decisiveness he possessed as the creator of CBS at the door of the Trustees' Room. The same could be said of the Wall Street lawyer Maurice "Tex" Moore, who succeeded Coykendall as chairman (1954–67). The trustees worked well with Kirk because he did not challenge their recently retrieved powers over the university's finances. He saw himself as an officer of the trustees. F. A. P. Barnard he was not.[84]

The Age of the Barons

Powerful deans were not new to Columbia, an earlier instance being the Law School's founding dean/warden Theodore W. Dwight, a formidable advocate of home rule and fierce protector of local autonomy. The first dean of the School of Mines, Charles F. Chandler, was equally indisposed to take direction from above. It was Low who first put the professional schools under effective centralized control, subordinating the powers of their deans in the process. Early Butler also sought to rein in his deans, a task made easier after 1905 by securing trustee support for his taking the election of deans away from the respective faculties and investing the appointive power in himself, "subject to Board approval."[85]

Yet, as the number of professional schools and affiliated institutions increased in the early twentieth century, even Butler had trouble keeping track of all their increasingly complex and anything-but-transparent doings. As a consequence, and as described earlier, he gave over far more authority to his Medical School dean, Willard Rappleye, than he had been willing to cede to the deans of the university's other professional schools. Their turn came with Butler's successors.[86]

Rappleye, who resigned in 1958 after taking umbrage with criticism of the Medical School contained in the *Report on the Future of the University* (the MacMahon report) sponsored by Provost Barzun, can be viewed as the twentieth-century prototype of the Columbia professional-school dean who in the postwar era came to be collectively referred to as the "barons." They included Law School Dean William C. Warren (1953–68), who succeeded Young B. Smith (1928–53), Business School Dean Courtney C. Brown (1954–69), who succeeded Philip Young (1947–53), and the dean of the Engineering School, John R. Dunning (1950–69). Their common modus operandi involved a maximization of local autonomy and a minimization of interference from what at some point in the 1940s came to be derisively referred to as "Low Library," by which was meant the president and his central administrators.[87]

The emergence of the barons may well have been necessitated by the leadership breakdown in the late Butler period and their immediate postwar prominence to the leadership vacuum in Low Library during the interregnum and the Eisenhower presidency that followed. But once considerable power accrued to the schools and their deans, only a very forceful president and/or a widely perceived institutional crisis were likely to pull it back. Neither existed at the outset of the Kirk presidency.

To the contrary, Kirk seemed quite willing to let his deans run their schools. One could even surmise that he wanted them to do so, judging by the fact that early on in his presidency he personally recruited the oil company executive and his Scarsdale neighbor Courtney C. Brown to succeed the departing Philip Young as dean of the Columbia Business School. A graduate of Dartmouth (1926), Brown had worked on Wall Street for a decade before coming to Columbia in 1935 as a graduate student in economics. In his third year, he began teaching in the College, and, in his fourth, in the Business School. He continued teaching at Columbia for a year after completing his Ph.D. in 1940 and then took part in the migration of Columbia economists to wartime Washington.[88]

After the war, Brown joined the Standard Oil Company, where he rose to the position of chief adviser to the CEO, Frank Abrams. When Brown left Standard Oil in 1954 for Columbia, he swapped an oil company executive's salary of $77,500 for that of a Columbia dean—$17,500—not to mention forgoing the perquisites that went with his former life—although, in his autobiography, Brown did lament in particular the absence of parking. Parking place or no, the hyperkinetic Brown meant to leave his mark on Columbia as its "campus entrepreneur."[89]

Brown immediately sized up the organizational culture of the Business School, one of fifteen in the university, as distinctly "second rate" and at risk of being swallowed up. His first challenge was to keep the recently reorganized School of General Studies, which shared space with the Business School in Dodge Hall, and its enterprising new dean, Louis M. Hacker, from appropriating much of the revenue-generating part of the business curriculum for General Studies. In this turf war, Brown quickly discovered that he could not look for assistance to Low Library, its prevailing view of the Business School, dating back to Butler and the school's founding in 1914, being on par with its perception of General Studies as an intellectually dubious cash cow.[90]

Accordingly, the new dean took it upon himself to raise the funds that would secure the financial well-being and proper housing of the Business School—and, in the bargain, his own autonomy. He actively solicited support from Business School alumni, such as Percy Uris, and from his many contacts on Wall Street. Conferences for the business community at Arden House became a regular feature of the school year. So did the offering of classes to midlevel executives on weekends or in concentrated summer programs. It is a fair statement that the era of post-Butler fund-raising began with Brown and the fund-raising staff he quickly put in place at the Business School, which included Peter Buchanan, who later took over Columbia's overall fund-raising in the 1980s.[91]

The faculty Brown inherited was not distinguished. It consisted of twenty-eight full-time members and the full-time equivalent of another fourteen part-timers. Its most research-active members, such as James C. Bonbright and Eli Ginzberg, held joint appointments in the economics department, but others, including the famed securities analyst Benjamin Graham, did not. Faculty salaries trailed those in arts and sciences, with all the attendant morale problems the widely acknowledged differential implied.[92]

The Business School had only recently—in 1949—abandoned its original undergraduate curriculum, with its emphasis on accounting, to become a strictly graduate school. It fell to Brown to attract a faculty capable of mounting a genuinely graduate curriculum and at the same time eliminate the undergraduate courses that continued to make up the bulk of the school's offerings. A series of faculty appointments beginning in the mid-1950s that included Neil Chamberlain, Roy Blough, and Arthur F. Burns and continuing into the mid-1960s with the appointments of Giulio Pontecorvo, Maurice Wilkinson, and Ray Horton made it possible for the Business School to raise its research profile and put in place its own Ph.D. program, separate from that offered by the economics department. Along the way the salaries for Business School faculty first caught up and then surpassed those of arts and sciences.[93]

With its enrollment income steadily climbing, with much of the curriculum delivered in large (and economically efficient) lectures and no offsetting obligations to contribute to the undergraduate curriculum, with its increasingly research-oriented faculty attracting outside support from corporate America and its own fund-raising apparatus attracting gifts from alumni and non-alumni alike, the Business School under Brown gave every appearance of being its own master. Thus, when its activities and ambitions outgrew its quarters in Dodge Hall, its dean simply cast about for someone who would underwrite the construction of its own building and then build it directly behind Low Library on the original site of University Hall.

In 1955, only a year after Brown entered into his deanship, he was appointed to a second and concurrent position, that of vice president of the university for business affairs (this may have been Kirk's original intention). In this new role, Brown played a part in attracting to Columbia the funds that went into the on-campus construction of Ferris Booth Student Center, Carman Hall, and the Seeley Mudd Engineering Building, as well as the Business School's Uris Hall, plus the new home for the Law School across Amsterdam Avenue. Even as others involved in these efforts sometimes questioned the extent of Brown's role in these undertakings, he did not. It is thus perhaps only fitting that he also took credit for proposing to university officials in 1959 the construction of a gym in Morningside Park, an idea proposed to him by a city official whom other sources identify as Robert Moses (CU Ph.D. 1919).[94]

However instrumental Brown was in getting Columbia's postwar fund-raising into high gear, his stint in Low Library proved short lived and mutually disappointing. It seems only to have confirmed his initial impression that "the way the University was administered was painfully simplistic." The experience also permanently soured him on President Kirk, whom he held "in supreme contempt" and mocked as having as his talisman the "avoidance of confrontation." By contrast, Brown was given to describing himself as, after a nasty session with his faculty, not at all adverse to "a little blood on the floor." A later dean of the Law School remembers him as "a tough guy."[95]

The experiment had gone no less badly for Kirk. Having brought Brown into the central administration to help with matters where his training as an economist and experience in the corporate world might prove helpful and appreciating him as a man whose energy knew no normal bounds, Kirk soon determined that Brown wanted his job and was prepared to take him on in front of the trustees to get it. This not even the confrontation-avoiding Kirk was prepared to tolerate. When Brown proposed a plan whereby he would take over the financial side of the presidency, leaving to Kirk the ceremonial duties (shades of the Mason-Harris arrangement of the early nineteenth century), the trustees backed Kirk, and Brown left Low Library in a huff to return to the Business School deanship full time.[96]

Thereafter, until his retirement in 1968, he effectively protected the Business School's interests against interference from Low Library. Although careful to maintain civil relations with Provost Jacques Barzun, as when he supported Barzun's plan to have Business School faculty nominations to tenure vetted by a universitywide ad hoc system (a proposal the Law School dean, William Warren, and his successors resisted), he took up a prominent place among the president's not-so-silent opposition. For his part, Kirk quietly tolerated Brown's second-guessing for eleven more years, though he was stung by the personal disparagement contained in Brown's 1983 autobiography, characteristically entitled *The Dean Meant Business.*[97]

John R. Dunning, nuclear physicist and dean of Engineering from 1950 to 1969, was another of the postwar barons who insisted on running his own school his own way. But unlike Brown's tenure as dean of the Business School, which was marked by an improvement in the school's place among the country's leading business schools, Dunning's deanship coincided with a decline in the Engineering School's competitive standing. Where he succeeded was in securing the personal support of potential donors to the building fund of the Engineering School, chief among them the millionaire Henry Krumb, who in the late 1950s made known his intentions to leave the school $10 million. "And so," Kirk recalled years later, "we all cultivated Henry."[98]

In 1959, when mounting evidence of mismanagement of the Engineering School and rumors of personal malfeasance persuaded the reluctant Kirk to ask for Dunning's resignation, Krumb intervened, informing Kirk that "if you insist on doing it this way, I'm going to change my will." "At that point," the president of Columbia University later acknowledged, "I backed down." Krumb's estate eventually gave $15 million to the Engineering School, resulting in the creation within the school of the Henry Krumb School of Mines, and Dunning stayed on as dean through the Kirk presidency.[99]

Not all of Kirk's deans treated him as dismissively as his barons did. Houston Merritt (1958–67), a neurologist drawn from the faculty who succeeded Rappleye as dean of the Medical School in 1959, got along much better than did his predecessor with both his own faculty and with Kirk, who in turn judged him to be "a very good dean." Clarence Walton, who became dean of General Studies in 1963 after the resignation of Clifton Lord, who four years earlier had succeeded Louis Hacker, was equally popular with his own faculty and with Kirk. Finally, among the affiliate institutions, Barnard's president, Millicent McIntosh, has already been cited as a self-acknowledged "big fan" of President Kirk. Not least of the institutional reasons for her being so was Kirk's willingness to let Barnard go its own curricular and fund-raising way while allowing Barnard students free access to courses throughout the university.[100]

It is clear from his oral history recorded in the mid-1980s, as well as from the testimony of his staff, that Kirk was not always happy with the trustee-imposed financial arrangements under which his presidency operated and was sometimes clearly irritated by the high-handed actions of some of his deans. But it is also the case that only in extremis did he question the former or challenge the latter. He may simply have subscribed to the managerial philosophy that if you show up every day ready for work you will eventually wear the buggers out. But then again, at least for the first decade of his presidency, there was no obvious financial imperative requiring him to take on either his trustees or his deans. To the contrary, these were years marked by what at the time seemed to be an appreciable easing of the straitened financial circumstances that the university first began to face in the late 1920s. This was thanks to the timely appearance of two new benefactors who seemed fully prepared to underwrite postwar Columbia's full intellectual realization.

FIGURE 5.1 Thomas J. Watson (1874–1956), founder of IBM and Columbia trustee (1934–56), with Dwight D. Eisenhower, upon securing Eisenhower's acceptance of the Columbia presidency in 1947.

Source: Columbia University Archives—Columbiana Collection..

FIGURE 5.2 Dwight D. Eisenhower (1890–1969), army officer, thirteenth president of Columbia University (1948–53), and president of the United States (1953–61). Photograph shows Eisenhower talking with the Columbia football team and Coach Lou Little at Baker Field.

Source: Dwight D. Eisenhower Library, Abilene, Kansas.

FIGURE 5.3 Grayson Kirk (1903–98), political scientist, provost, and fourteenth president of Columbia University (1953–68). Retired in wake of the spring 1968 campus disruptions.

Source: Columbia University Archives—Columbiana Collection.

FIGURE 5.4 I. I. Rabi (1898–1988), physicist, professor at Columbia (1931–68), and Nobel laureate, cooking hot dogs on the Columbia University cyclotron in Pupin Hall.

Source: Rabi Family Collection, copy in Columbia University Archives—Columbiana Collection.

FIGURE 5.5 W. Maurice Ewing (1906–74) geophysicist, oceanographer, and Columbia professor (1944–72), with Lamont Geological Observatory research vessel *Vema* in background.

Source: Columbia University Archives—Columbiana Collection.

FIGURE 5.6 Lionel Trilling (1905–75), literary critic and Columbia professor of English (1938–72), and Jacques Barzun (1907–), cultural historian, professor, and Columbia administrator (1932–75), coteaching their College colloquium on important books in the 1950s. Trilling is on the left, Barzun on the right.

Source: Columbia University Archives—Columbiana Collection.

FIGURE 5.7 Richard Hofstadter (1916–70), historian and Columbia professor (1946–70), speaker at the 1968 Columbia commencement. 1956 photograph.

Source: Columbia University Archives—Columbiana Collection.

FIGURE 5.8 Daniel Bell (1919–), sociologist and Columbia professor (1961–69) until he moved to Harvard after the 1968 Columbia disruptions. Early 1960s photograph.

Source: Columbia University Archives—Columbiana Collection.

FIGURE 5.9 Architecture students picketing dedication of the Business School's Uris Hall in 1964.

Source: Columbia University Archives—Columbiana Collection.

CHAPTER 13

A Second Flowering

What could be more different from Indianapolis?

Dan Wakefield (CC 1955), New York in the Fifties

Young Lady From Kent

ALTHOUGH recruited from the faculty, Grayson Kirk was hardly a campus insider. Half his eight years as a member of the Department of Public Law and Government had been spent in government service or on leave. His name had not been included among the presidential possibilities put forward by the faculty committee in 1945 and 1946. Until he was appointed provost in 1949, he remained largely unknown to faculty outside his department.[1]

Shortly after being installed as president, Kirk ventured from his office in Low over to the Men's Faculty Club. He then proceeded to the "long table," where unaccompanied faculty regularly gathered for conversation with whomever else turned up. Being a bit early, Kirk was the first to sit down. When, after a half hour, no one joined him, he left. There is no indication that in his subsequent fifteen years as president he repeated this early experiment in outreach. A shy man, who likely did not see his job as inspiring loyalty among his faculty, much less devotion, he thereafter kept his socializing to trustees, donors, and visiting dignitaries. As a result, few faculty dealt with him except in the most formal circumstances—the same went for him—and none could be counted on in a crisis to act as what Henry Graff has called his "president's men." With friendship denied him, Kirk practiced the offsetting virtue of leaving the faculty alone.[2]

In chapter 6, I made a reference to the term "multiversity," introduced in 1963 in the first of three lectures delivered at Harvard by the then chancellor of the University of California, Clark Kerr, and published a year later as *The Uses of the University*. In his second lecture, Kerr took up another and still newer institutional arrangement: the "Federal Grant University." Kerr did not name the dozen universities he indicated had already undergone the transformation from "private" or "state funded" to "federal grant universities." Instead, he provided three criteria: they were among the top recipients of federal research contracts, they had established specialized research institutes, and more than 30 percent of their annual income came from federal contracts. Columbia qualified as a charter member of this new club.[3]

The impact of federal dollars at postwar Columbia was all the greater for its novelty. Before World War II, it had received almost none of the little federal support provided higher education. New York State's share of the 1862 Morrill Land Grant Act went to the newly opened and already politically better connected Cornell. Similarly, with the Hatch Act of 1887, which underwrote Agricultural Experiment Stations, the Second Morrill Land Act of 1890, and the Smith-Lever Act of 1914, which created the Agricultural Extension Service and supported agricultural research, Columbia lost out to Cornell and to branches of the State University of New York. (The existence of this funding, however, explains Butler's interest in getting Columbia into agricultural research in 1915.) Columbia students received some funding through several New Deal programs in the form of work-study jobs, as well as, beginning in 1917, funding for student military training. Yet before 1940, when the physics department entered into a contract with the Office of Scientific Research and Development for $30,000 to build magnetrons, Columbia faculty had no real experience with federal dollars.[4]

By the end of World War II, that initial $30,000 contract had grown to two hundred contracts with fourteen different government agencies, totaling $43 million. At the height of the war, Columbia employed twenty-six hundred individuals in war-related research and teaching. The Columbia Radiation Lab alone employed twelve hundred people. Berkeley, Harvard, MIT, and the University of Chicago were even more heavily committed to the war effort, and each had more to show for it in added physical facilities when the war ended. But if the origins of the federal grant university are to be found in the contract arrangements worked out during World War II, Columbia was present at the creation.[5]

There was no assurance that Congress would continue these arrangements after the war. Both the military (especially the navy) and most of the universities who were the major recipients of wartime funding for science favored doing so. And so argued the head of the Office of Strategic Research and Development and ex-MIT dean Vannevar Bush in Science: The Endless Frontier, a 1945 report commissioned by President Roosevelt and submitted to President Truman that called for a permanent partnership between the federal government and the major universities to advance the cause of American science. It even called for some help for the social sciences.[6]

Not everyone was equally positive about such a partnership. Harvard president James B. Conant expressed reservations about federal support of higher education, arguing that such funds would have greater utility directed at secondary education, soon to become a special cause of his. (Skeptics took his opposition to reflect Harvard's concern that its edge in wealth would be offset by the availability of federal funding to its less highly endowed but no less aggressive competition.) Others, mostly Republicans, held that the federal government had no business subsidizing science or universities, especially private universities in peacetime. And finally there were those, West Virginia's Democratic senator Harley M. Kilgore being the most outspoken, who favored a far more equitable distribution of federal funding among universities than had been the case during the war or would be under the "best science" scenario favored by the leaders of universities with established research programs and experience with the wartime contract system.[7]

Columbia did not take as prominent a part in these debates as it might have had a president been in place. And when Eisenhower arrived in 1948, he opposed federal aid to higher education. Nevertheless, Columbia, as fourth largest recipient of funding among universities during the war and as a substantial beneficiary of funding from the Office of Naval Research in the years immediately thereafter, had a vital stake in the outcome, as Kirk, upon assuming the presidency in 1953, well understood.[8]

Throughout his presidency, Grayson Kirk consistently championed federal funding of scientific research at the "best" private research universities. To be sure, it was, as Harold Orlans described academic sentiment in 1962, "the judgment of the overwhelming majority of faculty and other institutional representatives, which we share, [that] the over-all effect of federal programs at universities and colleges has been highly beneficial." But even in such accepting company, Kirk stood out for having so few misgivings about federal funding. He saw his role as that of enabler. He imposed fewer barriers to classified research by faculty than did Harvard and Chicago, for example, and more readily acceded to release time arrangements than did Yale, freeing some science faculty from undergraduate teaching altogether. His ill-fated participation in the Institute for Defense Analysis (IDA), which critics in 1968 took as evidence of Columbia's complicity in the Vietnam War, Kirk saw, at the time he accepted membership in 1962, as another means of assuring Columbia its place at the federal banquet.[9]

In 1962 Columbia received from ten different federal agencies nearly $35 million for some seven hundred government-sponsored research projects involving no less than six hundred faculty in sixty-four departments. This represented Columbia's largest single source of income, almost 40 percent and covered most of the salaries for 30 percent of the faculty. A half-dozen other major research universities experienced comparable or—and in the case of science-heavy MIT, Stanford, and Johns Hopkins—even greater surges in federal funding and commitments of faculty to government-sponsored research. And most of these undertook elaborate reviews in the early 1960s to assess the implications of federal money on their overall programs. Columbia did not.[10]

These reviews generally concluded that, on balance, taking the money beat

declining it. But in reporting Columbia's 1962 figures to his trustees and offering the prediction that within two years income derived from the federal government would exceed all other income combined, Kirk assured them that "the
financial risks [were] minimal, including the risks inherent in any sudden contraction of this research." In 1964 the Harvard political scientist Don Price
offered a limerick to suggest the mindset of universities confronted with this
seemingly boundless federal largesse:

> *There was a young lady from Kent*
> *Who said she knew what it meant*
> *When men asked her to dine,*
> *And served her cocktails and wine;*
> *She knew what it meant—but she went.*[11]

Rabi and an Embarrassment of Prizes

Among Columbians in the postwar era who effectively pressed the case for federal funding of private research universities in general—and Columbia science
in particular—was Professor of Physics Isodor I. Rabi. His 1944 Nobel Prize for
work on the magnetic properties of atomic nuclei and his wartime service in
developing radar and advising on the construction of the atomic bomb assured
him a respectful hearing in Washington. In helping to organize regional con-
sortia and in advising on the creation of the Atomic Energy Commission and
later the National Science Foundation, Rabi later acknowledged, "I was always
manipulating for Columbia." Thanks in no small measure to him, unlike Yale,
which temporarily dropped out of the race for scientific eminence in favor of
focusing on the college, or Chicago, which Robert Hutchins took in different
directions, Columbia remained in the thick of the postwar scientific hunt.[12]

Federal funding of science did not benefit only Columbia's budgetary bottom line; it helped underwrite one of the most creative moments in the history
of American science. That the Columbians prominently involved were for the
most part physicists spoke both to the importance of the field, with its obvious
military implications, but also to the unexpected rise of physics at Columbia in
what can only be called "the Rabi era."

The great strengths of earlier Columbia science were in the biological sciences, especially genetics, psychology, and, to a lesser extent, chemistry and
geology. In 1925, when Butler provided the trustees with a comparative survey
of the university's major departments, physics appeared among the "second-
rank" departments. Not even the likes of Michael Pupin and George Pegram

gave off the candle power associated with the geneticist Thomas Hunt Morgan and the bacteriologist Hans Zinsser or the psychologists Edward L. Thorndike and A. T. Poffenberger, which made those fields, by Butler's accounting, "pre-eminent." Butler acknowledged as much in his unsuccessful efforts to lure Albert Einstein from Germany to Columbia in 1925, following earlier attempts to recruit Niels Bohr.[13]

Robert Millikan, the first American to win a Nobel Prize in physics (1923), earned his Ph.D. at Columbia in 1895 but then went off to Chicago. To be sure, Columbia had been since the 1890s home to the *Physical Review*, the leading physics publication in the United States. But its articles in the 1920s excited little interest in Europe, which was where the action in physics was.[14]

Ironically, the appointment that may have sparked the turnaround in physics at Columbia was not in physics at all but in physical chemistry. Harold Urey joined the Columbia chemistry department in 1929 as an associate professor, after teaching at Johns Hopkins. Once installed in Havemeyer, he set about research that culminated in 1932 in his discovery of deuterium, a heavy isotope of water. In addition to bringing him a Nobel Prize in 1934, Columbia's first and only the third awarded to an American scientist, Urey's work introduced the Columbia scientific community to the fringes of the "new physics" of quantum mechanics then revolutionizing the field in Europe.[15]

Columbia's more direct link to this revolution was I. I. Rabi, who arrived on campus in 1923 as an unfunded twenty-four-year-old graduate student in physics. He chose Columbia for its proximity to his wife-to-be, Helen, who was studying at Hunter College. Raised in Brownsville, Brooklyn, Rabi had come there with his orthodox Jewish parents at the age of two from Galicia, Austria-Hungary, and was educated in the borough's public schools. Rabi used a Regents scholarship to attend Cornell, which was known for its science courses and for being less unwelcoming to Jews than Columbia. (In the event, he encountered considerable anti-Semitism there.)[16]

Following his graduation from Cornell in 1920, with a major in electrical engineering and chemistry, Rabi returned to New York and tried a number of jobs, among them bookkeeping. After two years of random employment, he returned to Cornell to do graduate work in "that part of chemistry . . . called physics." A year later, with no fellowship forthcoming from Cornell, he transferred to Columbia. An instructorship at CCNY, which had him teaching twenty-five hours a week, allowed him to get by for two years without a Columbia fellowship.[17]

Rabi realized that something important was going on in physics, about which no one at Cornell or Columbia was in a position to say much. He organized a Sunday study group of Columbia and NYU graduate students to familiarize themselves with recent work in the new physics, but this only persuaded him of the need for direct interaction with those doing the work. Accordingly, Rabi rushed to complete his dissertation in 1927 so that he could go, Ph.D. in hand, to Europe. A two-year travel fellowship in science, underwritten by F. A. P. Barnard's legacy to Columbia, provided the necessary backing. In Europe, Rabi quickly met, worked with, and impressed many of the pioneers in quantum physics. These included the Dane Niels Bohr, whose 1913 discovery of the electronic structure of the hydrogen atom prepared the way for the birth of quantum physics a decade later; Wolgang Pauli, at Hamburg and Zurich; and Werner Heisenberg at Leipzig, who became Rabi's "rabbi."[18]

A side benefit to his two years in Europe was that Rabi met most of the young Americans there who would, with him, effect the transfer of quantum physics from Europe to America. These included Linus Pauling, J. Robert Oppenheimer, and Robert Condon. He also had occasion to meet the likes of Edward Teller, Hans Bethe, and Enrico Fermi, Europeans who would come to America in the intellectual migration in the late 1930s. It was Werner Heisenberg, however, who buffaloed the longtime chair of the physics department and dean of Graduate Faculties George Pegram into hiring the thirty-one-year-old Rabi, who, albeit a Jew, clearly met Pegram's need for "a hot shot in quantum mechanics."[19]

After a year back on Morningside, Rabi, without benefit of additional publications, was promoted from lecturer to assistant professor, thereby securing him the equivalent of tenure. He then proceeded to replicate the molecular beam laboratory he had set up earlier in Hamburg. The initial funding for the lab came from his senior colleague in chemistry, Harold Urey, who donated half his $7,600 grant from the Carnegie Foundation. "With Urey's money," Rabi later recalled, "I was free."[20]

The molecular beam laboratory, located on the fifth floor of Pupin, became the site of nearly a decade of research by Rabi and his first wave of graduate students, most of whom, like him, were Jews raised in New York, had gone to CCNY, and became physicists without knowing whether there would be jobs for them. They included future National Academy of Science members Jerrold Zacharias (CU Ph.D. 1933), William Cohen, Gregory Breit, Jerome Kellogg, and Sidney Millman.[21]

Most of the work to develop a resonance method of recording the magnetic properties of atomic nuclei that earned Rabi his own Nobel Prize in 1944 had been completed by 1940. He then turned his energies to a project that would be his principal preoccupation during World War II: the development of radar. This work began a year before Pearl Harbor, but at a time when the British, who had done much of the early work on radar, were under nightly attack from the

German Luftwaffe. Like many of his Jewish colleagues, as Rabi later recalled, "I took the war personally." Even before the United States entered the war, Rabi transferred his work to MIT's Radiation Laboratory as its associate director. He remained there throughout the war, except for visits to Los Alamos and other locales associated with the construction of the atomic bomb subsumed under the Manhattan Project, which had begun at Columbia in 1940 only to be dispersed in 1942 to less militarily vulnerable sites.[22]

Compared with MIT, the University of Chicago, and the University of California, Columbia was not a significant beneficiary of the war in terms of added scientific capacity. The University of Chicago acquired its reactor, and Berkeley its accelerator, whereas Columbia had only its Radiation Lab, which was an adjunct of MIT's and for which Rabi served as absentee director. When Nobel Prize winners Harold Urey and Enrico Fermi (who came to Columbia in 1938) decided to remain at Chicago, Columbia science showed signs of becoming a casualty of the war.[23]

Rabi's return was not a sure thing. With a Nobel Prize, a war record that earned him the respect of the military and national security leadership, and postwar discrediting of anti-Semitism, he had his choice of academic and governmental posts. He had also become over the years a skillful negotiator for science, physics, his students, and himself. And so he drove a hard bargain with Acting President Fackenthal, exacting such conditions as the department chairmanship for four years and a free hand in filling the department's five open professorships. The Fackenthal policy of letting Rabi do what he wanted would be scrupulously observed by Presidents Eisenhower and Kirk. In fact, into the 1970s a negative nod from Rabi was still enough to kill a proposal in the history and sociology of science, his preference being for doing science over studying it.[24]

Back on Morningside and in residence on Riverside Drive, Rabi addressed the two most pressing challenges facing Columbia physics and Columbia science more generally. The first was to deal with the lack of space for labs and, in nuclear physics, the problem of neighborhood resistance to the construction of facilities that had even the remotest potential for radioactive fallout. This he did by spearheading a consortium of eastern universities to persuade the federal government to pay for the construction of a nuclear reactor and then to make certain that Columbia would have a major say in its operation. The product of these efforts was the 1947 opening of Brookhaven Research Laboratory on eastern Long Island, which in its early years operated as an extension of Pupin Hall.[25]

At the same time, Rabi secured funds for the installation of a small cyclotron in the basement of Pupin, on which he would be famously photographed grilling wieners to convey its nonthreatening nature. In 1950 he oversaw the installation of a larger synchrocyclotron at Columbia's Nevis Laboratories, a research facility twenty miles up the Hudson, for which the Office of Naval Research provided most of the start-up costs. Even all these facilities could not keep Columbia from eventually falling behind in an era that increasingly rewarded equipment-driven Big Science, but they allowed Columbia to remain competitive in many areas of physics during the postwar years while acquiring preeminence in a few.[26]

The second challenge was to recruit the best scientific talent in a market that had become, especially for quantum and nuclear physicists, extraordinarily competitive. Just how competitive is suggested by Rabi's failure to hire either of his two wartime colleagues, J. Robert Oppenheimer and Hans Bethe. Oppenheimer opted for the Princeton Institute of Advanced Studies, and Bethe stayed at Cornell, which had taken him in on his arrival from Europe in 1938. Rabi's own student and eventual Nobel Prize winner (1955) Norman Ramsey (CC 1935; Ph.D. 1940) left Columbia in 1947 for Harvard. He did, however, succeed in hiring Polykarp Kusch in 1946 as an associate professor, whose collaboration with yet another Rabi appointment, Willis Lamb, later produced two more Nobel Prizes for work done at Columbia.[27]

Kusch stayed on into the 1970s, as did the Rabi-trained Lee J. Rainwater (CU Ph.D. 1946; Nobel laureate 1975); both were soon joined by Charles Townes (Nobel laureate 1964). Rainwater and Townes eventually received Nobel Prizes for work they did at Columbia in the 1940s and 1950s, as would later appointees Jack Steinberger (Nobel laureate 1988), who came in 1950, and T. D. Lee (Nobel laureate 1957), who came in 1953. Meanwhile the department attracted a generation of graduate students, graduates from the College, such as Frank Press (CC 1954; Ph.D. 1959), later president of the National Academy of Sciences, and Melvin Schwartz (CC 1953; Ph.D. 1958; Nobel laureate 1988), but equally often graduates from CCNY, such as Leon M. Lederman (CU Ph.D. 1951; Nobel laureate 1988), who was to teach at Columbia until 1978, and Arno Penzias (CU Ph.D. 1960; Nobel laureate 1978), both future Nobel Prize winners.[28]

What made much of the work of these men possible was the care with which Rabi attended to the financial and psychological needs of his colleagues and graduate students. What he did not provide, from all accounts, was an example of effective teaching. He was, his student and colleague Norman Ramsey remembered fondly, "pretty dreadful." Nor did he welcome women into the department, having decided early in his career that they were temperamentally unsuited for great physics. "I'm afraid there's no use quarreling with it," he once offered in explanation, "That's the way it is." He may have softened somewhat after the war, however: in 1946 he promoted Lucy Hayner to assistant professor, after eighteen years in the department as an unpaid lecturer.[29]

Part of Rabi's success turned on the federal funding his standing in Washington attracted to Columbia. The amounts were such that he later acknowledged that, in what must be a unique moment in the history of scientific entrepreneurship, "we had more money than we needed." Columbia physics in the postwar era was a classic instance of what the Columbia sociologist Robert K. Merton has called the "Matthew Effect," after Matthew 13:12: "unto those who have shall be given." But in the end it was not Rabi's salesmanship but the department's singular success in converting federal funding into Nobel-Prize quality research that produced this endless loop. When the Office of Naval Research in 1958 sought to justify the elitist pattern of its funding, it presented to Congress as evidence an illustration of the "Rabi Tree," with its myriad branches of important work, much of it already recognized with Nobel Prizes (twenty), all connected to a single trunk: Rabi and the Columbia physics department.[30]

The spectacular postwar rise of Columbia physics was not a departmental anomaly. During these years, other Columbia science departments, especially chemistry, but also several of the basic research departments at the Medical School—anatomy, for example, without benefit of a single charismatic leader and with less attendant notoriety, or biochemistry, under Erwin Chargaff—took advantage of generous federal funding policies, the popular endorsement of scientific research, and the absence of local administrative strictures to take their place among the leading centers of American scientific research and training. In the case of chemistry and biochemistry, they continue to do so.[31]

As I discuss in the next chapter, the scientific breakthroughs associated with the geophysical and oceanographic research at Lamont during the 1950s and 1960s constitute another of Columbia's postwar glories, or what Stanford's provost, Frederick Terman, called "steeples," those parts of a university distinguishable by their eminence. Yet by the 1960s the nature of scientific competition had become so intense that no single university could dominate, or even effectively compete, in all fields, as Columbia, Harvard, and Chicago once did. Even the Columbia physics department, through a combination of aging, faculty departures, and bad bets on newly emergent subfields, had ceased to be what only the ever-supportive Grayson Kirk assured trustees in 1963 it still was: "without question . . . the best in the United States." But that it arguably had been for a quarter-century was no small feat.[32]

Among the Philanthropoids

Private foundations were the second underwriters of postwar Columbia. They were not an entirely new source of support. The Carnegie and Rockefeller foundations had supported various interwar undertakings on the Morningside campus and at the Medical School. While these grants, which altogether amounted to something on the order of $500,000 by 1940, had often proved crucial in opening new areas of research and training, their overall impact on the university's finances was modest. It was in the postwar years that foundation support became so crucially important that cutbacks in the late 1960s prompted some Columbia officials to blame the foundations' earlier generosity for the university's financial troubles.[33]

Unlike federal funding, which, before the passage of the National Defense Education Act in 1958, was directed almost exclusively to the physical and biological sciences, foundation money was more widely dispersed. In the interwar period, for example, Rockefeller money went mainly into medical research but after 1928 also into funding the Morningside-based committees for research in the humanities and the social sciences. Carnegie money supported various undertakings in international relations. Both Carnegie and Rockefeller remained significant players in postwar American philanthropy, providing support to Columbia foreign-area programs into the 1950s. But by then the resources of each were overshadowed by a new player in the philanthropic world that so concentrated its largesse on universities as to prompt them to direct their more modest resources elsewhere.[34]

The Ford Foundation came into being in 1936 as a tax shelter for the fortune accumulated by Henry Ford Sr. during three decades of making automobiles. Established in Dearborn, Michigan, the family-controlled foundation initially supported local institutions such as the Dearborn Hospital and the Detroit Symphony. In 1947 wartime profits renewed congressional scrutiny, and the death of Henry Ford Sr. prompted his grandson Henry Ford II to reorganize the foundation by appointing to its board trustees from outside the family. A year later, with an infusion of $417 million in nonvoting Ford Motor Company stock, the foundation suddenly became the country's largest, larger than the combined endowments of Rockefeller and Carnegie, twice that of Harvard ($191 million), and larger than the combined endowments of the next three richest private universities.[35]

In 1950 an internal advisory committee chaired by H. Rowan Gaither, a wartime associate of Karl Compton, produced a report that provided the Ford Foundation with a five-point mandate:

1. The establishing of peace
2. The strengthening of democracy
3. The strengthening of the economy
4. Education in a democratic society
5. Individual behavior and human relations

If skeptics read the Gaither report as overly idealist and ambitious, more positively disposed readers since have characterized it as "the quintessence of the liberal, internationalist, socially concerned outlook of that period." Either way, it was a clear call to the foundation to get on with the spending.[36]

The Gaither report clearly indicated that the foundation's concerns and reach were to be international. This led directly to Ford's establishing offices in India and Africa through which millions of dollars in refugee relief and agricultural development soon flowed.

A less clearly stated reading of the report was that the foundation's domestic agenda would be best served—and draw the least criticism—by making grants not to those directly engaged in the improvement of social conditions but, where possible, through intermediary agencies. Given the rising regard with which American universities were held, plus the fact that many of the early Ford staffers were drawn from academe, it was hardly surprising that foundation officials should turn to them for help. No less surprisingly, the universities, when asked, gladly agreed. What is surprising, but indicative of the privileged place universities enjoyed in the postwar era, was the success universities had in attaching conditions to the ensuing partnership.[37]

Early Ford grants to universities reflected no settled ideology or pattern of giving. A program in 1956 that distributed $260 million in one-shot grants to some nineteen hundred colleges and universities to increase faculty salaries (of which Columbia received $8.6 million and Barnard and Teachers College another $1 million each) did not play favorites among private institutions (although it did exclude denominational colleges). A similar program the same year dispensed some $250 million to six hundred hospitals (of which Columbia-Presbyterian received $500,000). Such grants had the dual advantage of dispensing lots of money quickly and garnering maximum public approbation. If the need to spread the money around faded by the mid-1950s, as antifoundation and populist sentiment in Congress faded, the need to keep spending increased as the foundation's endowment continued to grow. By 1960 it had grown to $3.6 billion, at a time when the combined endowment of *all* American universities was only $5.4 billion.[38]

By the mid-1950s it was clear that major private universities would become the favored beneficiaries of what then seemed to be the ever-expanding Ford largesse. The question became what kinds of programs could most effectively link the foundation and these universities while furthering the foundation's internationalist objectives. The answer was almost immediately forthcoming: the International Training and Research Program. Established in 1952 as an offshoot of the foundation's then much larger overseas program, ITR was conceived initially as a means by which Americans could be trained to work in the various world areas in which the foundation had programs and secondarily as a program to train academic area specialists. But because it furthered the foundation's international purposes, which included contributing to the country's cold war interests abroad, even as it allowed the foundation to spend more of its money at home, ITR suddenly became the major conduit by which the foundation funneled money into major American universities. "The ITR Program clearly existed for the benefit of American universities," its director, John B. Howard, later recalled: "That's what it was for."[39]

Foreign-Area Studies: The Fat Years

For Columbia, the foundation's decision to invest heavily in the training and research of area specialists could not have been more fortuitous. But unlike their role in the immediate postwar campaign for federal funding of academic science, where they were at most supporting actors, Columbians actively encouraged the Ford Foundation's taking on major private universities with strengths in international studies. With the foundation's headquarters in New York City after 1949, it became convenient for Columbia faculty and deans to meet informally with and advise foundation staffers.[40]

Once the foundation made training foreign-area specialists a priority, Columbia became an obvious partner. This was because of its already established reputation in the field of non-Western languages and cultures. Of Columbia's 155 faculty in the humanities and social sciences in 1940, twenty-eight (18 percent) specialized in the study of regions of the world outside the United States and Western Europe. Between 1900 and 1940, some 15 percent of the humanities and social science Ph.D.s it awarded were in international studies. Only Harvard approached prewar Columbia in the global sweep of its intellectual interests.[41]

A 1947 census of American universities identified fifteen operational foreign-area studies programs. Ten universities had one or more programs; Columbia alone had three. The oldest of these was the Russian Institute, organized in 1945 with support from the Rockefeller Foundation ($250,000 a year for five years) and the Carnegie Foundation ($250,000). The institute's director was historian Geroid T. Robinson, who had taught at Columbia since earning his Ph.D. there in 1930. During the war he served in the OSS and later in the State Department. Philip E. Mosely was another significant figure at the institute, equally at home dealing with Washington Kremlinologists and foundation staffers.[42]

The East Asian Institute, although organized in 1947, again with Rockefeller funding ($250,000), traced its Columbia origins back to the beginning of the century and the establishment of the Dean Lung Chair in Chinese Studies. Between the wars, the Chinese scholars Cyrus H. Peake and L. Carrington Goodrich continued Columbia's engagement with East Asia, as did George Sansom, Ryusaku Tsunoda, and Hugh Borton in Japanese studies. Sansom, an Englishman with extensive consular experience in China, became the first director of the East Asian Institute upon its establishment in 1948. Tsunoda came to Columbia from Japan via Hawaii in the late 1920s to develop the library's Japanese holdings; he taught Japanese literature until his retirement in 1955. Upon Sansom's retirement in 1953, the directorship of the East Asian Institute went to Hugh Borton, who had come to Columbia in 1937 and served in the State Department from 1942 to 1948. By the late 1940s, another generation of East Asianists, among them the Chinese specialists C. Martin Wilbur and William T. de Bary (CC 1941), along with the Japanese poetry specialist Donald Keene (CC 1942), was in place.[43]

The third Columbia program identified by the 1947 census, though not yet fully meeting its demanding criteria, was the Near and Middle Eastern Institute, under the direction of Professor of Government Schuyler Wallace. As the first dean of the School of International Affairs upon its establishment in 1945, Wallace served as Columbia's point man in soliciting funds from the foundations for its area programs through the late 1940s and 1950s. When Wallace left Columbia in 1962, he become an officer at the Ford Foundation.[44]

The first Ford Foundation ITR grant to Columbia was made in 1953: $150,000 in support of its newly organized Near and Middle Eastern Institute. Thereafter, in quick succession, came larger grants to the more established Russian and East Asian Institutes. By 1963 Columbia had received grants from the Ford Foundation of more than $27 million, half of which was for international studies. By 1966 the total support from Ford from its ITR Program surpassed $21 million, distributed over fifteen years in eighteen grants. Meanwhile, dozens of Columbia graduate students fanned out across the world conducting area-based research under the auspices of the Ford-funded Foreign Area Fellowship Program.[45]

Columbia also established area programs—for which it received Ford funding—in areas where other universities were already strong. These included Latin American Studies, where Berkeley and the University of Texas were preeminent; South Asian Studies, where Pennsylvania and Chicago had highly regarded programs; and African Studies, where Northwestern and UCLA led. A Columbia program was also established in East European Studies and the Soviet System, which competed with the Russian Institute. Meanwhile, the university expanded programs in international relations, international economics, and international law. Of the major universities engaged in area studies during this period, Columbia had the largest number of separate programs. Some Ford staffers allowed that it might even have too many and that more selectivity was called for.[46]

In 1965 Columbia received an $11 million ITR grant to endow five professor-ships in area studies and to help with the construction of a building for the School of International Affairs. This grant made Columbia the number one beneficiary of Ford ITR funding to that point. When the program was discontinued in 1971, a final accounting by the foundation had Columbia receiving $21 million, or about ten cents of every dollar spent by Ford over eighteen years to raise the level of international understanding. Though directed primarily at the area programs and regional institutes within the Graduate Faculties, some of this largesse found its way to the Law School, the Business School, and Teachers College.[47]

Columbia's singular success in attracting Ford money came despite the fact that Columbians figured only modestly among foundation staffers, where a Chicago connection was more common, or on the board of trustees, where a Harvard tilt was discernible. Nor could Columbia safely assume it had in Henry Heald, the president of the Ford Foundation from 1953 to 1964, a natural backer. Heald's previous job had been as president of NYU, and it was in Washington Square, not on Morningside Heights, that his local loyalties remained.[48]

Some of Columbia's success is attributable to its lack of diffidence. All parts of the university regularly asked for funding, sometimes in direct competition with each other. Although Ford program directors regularly complained of these multiple proposals coming from Columbia, Kirk did little to discourage competitive submissions.[49]

In 1961, after major grants to Harvard, Columbia, Chicago, and Berkeley, Ford announced that its next round of ITR grants would not go to the already-provided-for haves but to a second tier of aspiring universities, such as Duke, Syracuse, and Michigan State. But in 1964 the Ford trustees decided to make a substantial grant from this program to the University of Chicago. No sooner had the Chicago grant been approved than the question arose among Ford offi-cials: "What will Grayson say?" To which the preemptive answer was: Give Columbia some money, too.[50]

When McGeorge Bundy succeeded Heald to the Ford presidency in 1965, he already had a long-standing relationship with Kirk, their dealings going back to the war years. But now that he had moved to New York City, he took a neigh-borly interest in Columbia as well. Among the first grants Bundy put through as president of the foundation were two for Columbia, $10 million in urban studies and $25 million as a matching grant to help launch Columbia's first capital campaign. Even as Bundy made it clear that Ford was getting out of the business of underwriting international studies programs at Columbia and elsewhere, these grants seemed to confirm Columbia's high standing among the still richest of the philanthropoids.[51]

Ford was not the only benefactor of Columbia's international studies programs. The Near and Middle East Institute received grants from the governments of Turkey, Pakistan, and Iran, as well as from the Jewish Agency on Palestine. When the East Central Europe Institute was established in 1954, under the direction of Zbigniew Brzezinski, it received funding from the Council on Foreign Relations and several federal contracts, including at least one from the CIA. With passage of the National Defense Education Act in 1958, which contained provisions for federal support of major area centers, several of Columbia's were so designated and funded. Indeed, one of the reasons the Ford Foundation thought that it could begin to pull back its funding of area studies in the mid-1960s was the assumption that Washington's increasing involvement assured the continued well-being of academic international studies at Columbia and elsewhere.[52]

To what institutional end was all this grant making? On this question there is some dispute. When outside funding of area studies all but stopped in the late 1960s, many at Columbia blamed the Ford Foundation for corrupting the university with soft money, money that underwrote new programs but provided little or no endowment (hard money) to assure their long-term financial viability. "Perhaps Ford did tempt," one of its officers later acknowledged, and as a result, with reference to expenditures of its own money on area programs, "perhaps Columbia did spend too much." Between 1960 and 1966 those expenditures amounted to about $6 million a year.[53]

In pursuing their own studies and supervising the work of graduate students, Columbia's area specialists saw to the buildup of library holdings, as well as the sponsorship of collaborative arrangements with universities and scholarly institutions in other parts of the world. Meanwhile, Columbia's commitment to international studies since the termination of the ITR Program and the cutback of NDEA national centers funding has been continued, much as McGeorge Bundy prophesied back in 1967, when he declared, upon announcing the foundation's intention to shift its focus away from training in international studies and toward the resolution of urban problems: "We have wrought a revolution: the study of Africa, Asia, the Middle East, and Latin America—above all the study of Russia and China—has become a necessary, built-in element of the American academic establishment. Intellectual fashions being what they are, these studies will have good times and bad. But they are here to stay." An internal Ford Foundation memorandum that which closed the ITR books on Columbia in 1973 acknowledged as much:

We supported area studies not because a university judged this to be . . . important . . . but because one or another of our regional offices judged the center to be an indispensable resource for the whole country.

It is a significant commentary, therefore, on the quality of the area studies activities that Columbia developed . . . that five institutes and part of another [of Columbia's eight] received renewed support when this new conception had emerged.

The memorandum listed as nationally indispensable resources the Russian and East Asian Institutes, the East Central Europe Institute, the Institute of African Studies, the Middle East Institute, and the Pakistani portion of the South Asian Institute. It then did the arithmetic to conclude that this number exceeded that of any other of Ford's favored universities.[54]

The next chapter will consider further the problematic aspects of outside funding. But here let me suggest some of the good that the Ford Foundation's $25 million in grants for international studies did. First, the availability of these funds allowed Columbia to attract and retain faculty in international and area studies as well as to train a substantial portion of the generation that currently staffs the international and area programs at Columbia and throughout the country. It also, insofar as such funding went primarily to the social sciences and humanities, provided a partial but important offset to the funding being lavished on the sciences. Without it, there would have been an even starker division between the "have" sciences and the "have not" humanities and social sciences.

More directly, this funding facilitated the scholarly work of dozens of Columbia faculty and graduate students, some in departments such as East Asian languages and cultures and Middle East languages and cultures, wholly given over to the comprehensive study of specific world regions or to anthropology, where their presence might be expected, but also in economics, history, political science, and sociology, where, without this external support, these subjects would have been pursued in a much more provincial way. By the mid-1960s, departments such as history and political science contained nearly as many non-Western area specialists as Americanists, and it was the Europeanists who complained of being neglected.[55]

It was also from among these area specialists whence came Columbia's post-war generation of professors as pundits and policy intellectuals. For every Richard Neustadt, a member of the political science department, expert on the American presidency, and New Frontier insider, or American historian Henry Graff, who served in the Johnson White House, there were several Columbia faculty with regional interests, such as the political scientists Jacob Hurewitz,

Zbigniew Brzezinski, and Marshall Shulman, who regularly shuttled back and forth between New York's Morningside Heights and Washington's Foggy Bottom.[56]

To be sure, some of these scholars came under sharp criticism in the late 1960s for their putative failure to speak out forcefully enough against American military involvement in Vietnam and for complicity in American covert activities elsewhere in the world. But also numbering among them were scholars who argued aggressively, albeit usually through the accepted channels, against just such policies. The point here is that, to the extent that noncloseted scholars are, if not a force for national good, at least a Columbia tradition, it was the university's international studies contingent that sustained that tradition through the truncated American Century. Finally, one might also allow, in the instance of the subsequent scholarly work and polemical activities of the Palestinian-born Edward Said and the literary subfield of postcolonial studies that his *Orientalism* (1978) help stimulate and to which his colleague Gayatri C. Spivak has made important contributions, however different their critical stance, that Columbia continues to maintain a signal place in what is now called global studies.[57]

Paul F. Lazarsfeld and the Bureau

If less significant than the funding from federal agencies or the major foundations, support from corporate America also helped underwrite some of Columbia's most important postwar research and training activities. This was so especially in the Business School, where corporate contracts paid for released time for faculty and provided tuition support for student research assistants. More often, corporate funding formed part of a larger mix of outside funding that entrepreneurially minded parts of the university used to pursue their own research objectives as they met their corporate clients' specific needs.[58]

Arguably the best-known instance at postwar Columbia of this marriage of academic research imperatives and the needs of corporate America was in the Bureau of Applied Social Research (known as the Bureau). In the Bureau's founding director, the psychologist-turned-sociologist Paul F. Lazarsfeld, Columbia had, to use the name he chose for his role, its prototypical "managerial scholar."[59]

Lazarsfeld was born in Vienna in 1901, into a family of educated Jews with leftist leanings. Following studies at the University of Vienna, where he earned his Ph.D. in 1923 in applied mathematics, he joined his socialist politics with his fascination with data analysis in a job devising, administering, and analyzing social surveys of adolescents and unemployed workers in rural Austria. The work was supported by the Psychological Institute, which was privately funded and loosely affiliated with the University of Vienna.[60]

When Lazarsfeld's study of unemployment in Marienthal was published in 1932, it attracted sufficient attention to earn him a Rockefeller Traveling Fellowship to study in the United States. News of the Conservative Party electoral successes in Austria, a prelude to the Nazi takeover, prompted him to stay. Upon completing his fellowship in 1935, he availed himself of the good offices of Columbia sociologist Robert Lynd to secure a job analyzing questionnaires at the Newark Research Center, a juvenile agency funded by the National Youth Administration. In 1937 he became part of the original staff of the Princeton-based Office of Radio Research, a joint venture of the Rockefeller Foundation and the radio industry.[61]

In 1939 Princeton relinquished its stake in the Office of Radio Research and allowed Lazarsfeld to move it to New York City. That fall, Lazarsfeld was appointed as a lecturer in sociology at Columbia. The following year, he became a regular member of the sociology department, along with the Harvard-trained Robert K. Merton. Two years later, the Bureau of Applied Social Research officially came into being. Lazarsfeld was its founding director, Merton its associate director.[62]

The Bureau served during the war as an adjunct of the Office of War Information, performing analyses of wartime propaganda, especially radio-transmitted propaganda. In 1944 it received permission from the Council for Research in the Social Sciences, Columbia's in-house underwriter of social science research, to accept outside commercial contract work, if "consistent with the purposes of the University." This not only marked the arrival of survey research as an academically respectable field of research; it represented a turning point in the history of American universities. In 1945, as if to confirm the significance of this new departure, the Bureau of Applied Social Research became a distinct research unit in the Faculty of Political Science, with its own space, staffing responsibilities, and arrangements with other departments in the Faculty of Political Science as deemed mutually satisfactory.[63]

The catch was that, unlike an academic department such as sociology, the Bureau was expected to be self-supporting. And so it was. At no time during the next quarter-century (the Bureau closed in 1972) did university funds account for more than 10 percent of its operating budget. The rest came from federal project grants, some foundation support, and commercial contracts. The Bureau was one of the beneficiaries of a short-lived Ford Foundation Program in Behavioral Sciences. Even after this program ran into resistance from skeptical foundation trustees in the early 1950s and was terminated, the Bureau continued to receive support from Ford and other foundations.[64]

The Bureau's success in securing support from corporations gave Lazarsfeld special pleasure. Anybody, he responded to faculty grumbling about the Bureau's taking funding from soap companies, can extract money from the government agencies and foundations whose business is dispensing money. The real test, he insisted, was when profit-oriented corporate America beat a path to your door. Early commercial underwriters included manufacturers of toothpaste, Bisodol, vitamins, whiskey and wine, Sloan's Liniment, and greeting cards.[65]

Lazarsfeld enjoyed tweaking the purists among his colleagues, sometimes going out of his way to trace the origins of an elegant theoretical finding to some crass commercial consideration. "In the course of studying why housewives buy a particular brand of soap" or "while trying to figure out why listeners skip around the radio dial" were among his favorite lead-ins, since they predictably prompted an audience reaction that allowed him to ask if better results would have been produced had the Bureau limited itself to research without commercial value. The dramatic effect of these exchanges was heightened by Lazarsfeld's lines being delivered in his heavily German-accented English.[66]

Some of the skepticism Lazarsfeld encountered came from administrators. By his own account, Jacques Barzun struggled to keep his personal disdain for statistical sociology from influencing his policies as provost, but he did not always succeed. At the Bureau's twentieth anniversary in 1958, with Provost Barzun in attendance, Lazarsfeld made clear his view that the Bureau's success was not because but in spite of Columbia. Once freed from the restraints of his provostship, Barzun responded in kind. C. Wright Mills, despite having some of his salary covered by the Bureau, complained of the insidious impact it had on the sociology department and the university and hinted darkly about financial irregularities. College faculty grumbled that the Bureau bought up faculty time that should have gone to teaching undergraduates.[67]

Lazarsfeld's own teaching was limited to graduate students. And among them there was some disagreement as to his effectiveness in that role. He may even had doubts on this score, as when he inquired of a sociology graduate student about his colleague Merton's teaching. After the student described in some admiring detail how Merton's classes went, Lazarsfeld exasperatedly responded, "You mean he prepares his lectures?"[68]

Still, President Kirk allowed Lazarsfeld and those who succeeded him as director after 1954 to take the Bureau wherever its research interests and outside funding opportunities pointed. Thanks largely to the efforts of his career-long collaborator and friend Robert K. Merton, the Bureau played a larger role in the affairs of the university than critics claimed. Bureau-sponsored projects and conferences brought together faculty from different departments and schools of the university in genuinely collaborative, interdisciplinary research. Occasionally, the research directly affected the workings of parts of the university, as in the Merton-directed study of medical education, *The Student-Physician* (1956), for which the College of Physicians & Surgeons served as the principal research site. Also, whenever new hires with mathematical interests appeared on campus, such as the young psychologist William McGill, who came from MIT in 1958, or the historian Lee Benson, they were quickly inducted into "the Lazarsfeld Mafia."[69]

For nearly three decades, the Bureau provided data and research tools for data analysis with which a generation of Columbia graduate students in the social sciences fashioned their Ph.D. dissertations and commenced their careers as social scientists. It also provided the first of these scholars with experience in a new framework for social inquiry that enabled them to build social research centers at other universities. These missionaries included Seymour Martin Lipset (CU Ph.D. 1949), at the University of California and later Harvard; Nathan Glazer (CU Ph.D. 1962), at Harvard; James S. Coleman (CU Ph.D. 1955), at the University of Chicago; and Juan Linz (CU Ph.D. 1959). Lazarsfeld and Merton were directly involved in founding the Center for Advanced Studies in the Behavioral Sciences at Stanford, another important promoter of social science research and in some ways the successor to the Bureau.[70]

The Bureau tail, with its one-hundred-plus member staff (including many Columbia-trained women Ph.D.s) in the early 1960s and its budget in the tens of millions often appeared to wag the twenty-member sociology department dog. But the rise of the department to national preeminence in the late 1940s and 1950s corresponded exactly with the heyday of the Bureau. Moreover, thanks largely to the efforts of Merton, whose intellectual interests were of a more humanistic turn than Lazarsfeld's, the department's acknowledged tilt toward quantitative sociology and survey analysis was partially offset by more theoretical concerns. Some competitors, including the Chicago sociologist Edward Shils, regarded the department's approach as mechanical and reductive, but they acknowledged that Columbia had become the world's leading center for social research. It certainly constituted another of Columbia's postwar steeples.[71]

The Apotheosis of Cosmopolitanism

Postwar Columbia was home for around fifteen professors, mainly in the humanities and social sciences, who ventured beyond their disciplines into the outside intellectual world. There, they engaged a larger audience, which one of them called "our educated classes," as public intellectuals. Peripherally included among them were the aforementioned I. I. Rabi and Paul Lazarsfeld. There, too, were the philosopher Ernest Nagel, the art historian Meyer Schapiro, the sociologist C. Wright Mills, and the political scientist David Truman. There was also a younger second generation, some students of the first, that included literary critic Steven Marcus, historian Fritz Stern, and philosopher Charles Frankel. The theologian Reinhold Niebuhr, at Union Theological Seminary, and the philosopher Sidney Hook, at NYU, were corresponding members. At the center of this group of Columbia intellectuals were five men: the literary critic Lionel Trilling, the cultural historian Jacques Barzun, the sociologist Robert K. Merton, the American historian Richard Hofstadter, and the sociologist Daniel Bell.[72]

The presence of faculty who actively participated in the intellectual life of the city and nation was hardly new to Columbia. Earlier, Brander Matthews, John Dewey, Mark Van Doren, Irwin Edman, and Allan Nevins all had regular access to magazines aimed at nonacademic readers. Other early-twentieth-century universities had theirs, as William James and George Santayana at Harvard and William Lyon Phelps at Yale attest. But what set the postwar Columbia intellectuals apart from their predecessors was two other factors: the distinctive character of their social origins and the mutually reinforcing nature of their views.

Among the core members, Lionel Trilling (CC 1925; Ph.D. 1938) was the first to acquire a Columbia connection. He appeared on campus in the fall of 1921, with his prescribed freshman beanie undoubtedly set at a stylish angle. Then seventeen, he was born in New York, although his mother had been born in Eastern Europe and came to the United States as a girl. His father, a tailor, had also recently immigrated from Poland by way of England. Both parents were Jewish. Young Trilling went to Columbia, rather than follow his DeWitt Clinton High School pals to CCNY, because his father detected in its studied aloofness from the immigrant communities a more effective vehicle for acculturation.[73]

Trilling's Columbia College career was not a series of triumphs. He took up with the literary crowd, which included Clifton Fadiman, Mortimer Adler, and, off to the side, Meyer Schapiro. Whittaker Chambers numbered among his non-Jewish literary friends. He quickly caught the attention of his professors, perhaps most significantly the young English instructor and aspiring poet Mark Van Doren. Still, young Trilling's lack of clear purpose separated him from his more focused classmates and marked him as a dilettante in the making. He was rejected for membership in the Philolexian, one of the College's two honorary literary societies. When, nearly fifty years later, Trilling allowed to the incoming president, McGill, that "a lot of undergraduates who never fully reach their potential . . . was a Columbia experience," he may have had his own collegiate career in mind.[74]

After graduation in 1925, he turned to composing short stories, while earning a living writing for the *Menorah Journal*, a liberal Jewish publication edited in New York by Elliot Cohen. In 1929 he married Diana Rubin, a Radcliffe graduate from a more thoroughly assimilated family than his own, and thereupon decided to go to graduate school at Columbia, though without abandoning hopes for a literary career.[75]

Eight years later, Trilling finally completed his dissertation on Matthew Arnold and was arranging for its publication. He had then been teaching in the College for four years. At this point, he came into conflict with his senior colleagues, who seemed determined to send him off, citing his Marxism, his Freudianism, and his Jewishness as ample reasons. This was followed, as his wife, Diana, memorably recorded in "Lionel Trilling: A Jew at Columbia," by the divine intervention of Nicholas Murray Butler, who, by cowing the department's senior members, secured Trilling permanence in the department forthwith. As the first Jew to be assured tenure in the English department—this was now 1939 and he was not promoted to associate professor until 1945—Trilling had the singularity of his situation impressed on him by his department chairman Emory Neff, who informed him, after the department acceded to Butler's fiat, that "he would not use [his appointment] as a wedge to open the English department to more Jews."[76]

During the many years between graduating from the College and securing a permanent place in the faculty, Trilling had occasion to compare his feckless ways with the straight-on purposefulness of another Columbia College student three years behind him, Jacques Barzun (CC 1927; Ph.D. 1934). By the time Trilling enrolled in graduate school, Barzun had been teaching in the College for three years and was well along on his dissertation. As graduate instructors, they together taught a section of the John Erskine–inspired honors seminar in "important books," which they would regularly teach together until the late 1950s, thereby forming one of the most famous and enduring classroom twosomes in American academic history.[77]

Unlike Trilling, child of immigrants, Barzun was himself an immigrant, the son of cultured French parents who came to the United States when Jacques was twelve. Quickly adapting to American ways, without ever abandoning an inbred Continental elegance, Barzun entered Columbia College in 1923, at sixteen. He served as a campus stringer for several New York papers, was elected president of the Philolexian, and ran a tutoring business. His first teaching opportunity came immediately following his graduation, when a Summer School section of European history lost a scheduled instructor and Barzun was recruited by the department's chairman, Carlton J. H. Hayes. That marked the beginning of forty-four years of continuous teaching at Columbia, with stints early on at Barnard (where he replaced a drunk) and Sarah Lawrence, including his thirteen years in administration, when he taught a course each year. In 1968 he was named a university professor, a rank he created in 1964 to honor Rabi and to which his friend Trilling was named in 1970.[78]

The third of the Columbia intellectuals was the sociologist Robert K. Merton. He was born in Philadelphia, educated in public schools, and attended Temple University, which was to immigrant Philadelphians what CCNY was to immigrant New Yorkers. Like Trilling, his parents were Jewish immigrants, but of lower economic standing. The family name was Schkolnick, which Robert (né Meyer) changed at fifteen to Merlin, hoping to advance a budding career as a magician, and on entering Temple, to Merton.[79]

Attracted to sociology by a Temple professor, after graduation Merton proceeded to Harvard, in the expectation of studying with Pitrim Sorokin. Once in Cambridge, however, he became more interested in the work of George Sarton in the history of science and the theoretical concerns of Talcott Parsons, then an assistant professor. In 1939 he submitted his dissertation, an early version of *Science, Technology and Society in Seventeenth-Century England*, parts of which first appeared in Sarton's journal *Osiris*. Ph.D. in hand but with no job prospects at Harvard, Merton went to Tulane University. Two years later, he came to Columbia, where he remained for the next thirty-three years, ending his active career as university professor in 1974, but remaining a formidable intellectual presence into the twenty-first century. He died in 2002.[80]

Another core member of the postwar Columbia intellectuals was Richard Hofstadter. He was born in 1916 in Buffalo, New York, where he later went to college. His father was Jewish, born in Eastern Europe; his mother was American-born and raised in the Episcopal Church. The family was not religious, and neither would the son be. In 1939 he entered Columbia's graduate program in history. By 1941 he was deep into the research, alongside his companion in the New York Public Library's Main Reading Room, Alfred Kazin, that would culminate in his dissertation and first book, *Social Darwinism in American Life* (1944). After two years of wartime teaching at the University of Maryland, he returned to Columbia in 1946 as an assistant professor. And here he remained until his death from leukemia in 1970, at the age of fifty-five.[81]

During his quarter-century of teaching at Columbia, Hofstadter wrote several of the most influential books to appear in American political and cultural history. Both *The Age of Reform* (1955) and *Anti-Intellectualism in American Life* (1963) were recognized with Pulitzer Prizes, while *The Paranoid Style in American Politics* (1965) contained some of the most provocative essays to be written by a historian of his generation. He also involved himself in the training of dozens of graduate students, some of whom, like Eric L. McKitrick and Eric Foner, went on to distinguished careers at Columbia.[82]

The sociologist Daniel Bell was the last core member to come to Columbia and the only one to leave. But then he was an acknowledged public intellectual years before he became a Columbia professor, which occurred when he exchanged journalism for academe in 1961, at age forty-two. Like Trilling, he was born in New York (the Lower East Side of Manhattan) and attended public high school; but, unlike Trilling, Bell went to CCNY, where he was part of the famous lunchroom "Alcove No. 1," where the anti-Stalinist left that included Irving Kristol, Seymour Martin Lipset, Nathan Glazer, and Seymour Melman reigned unchallenged.[83]

After graduation, Bell became a contributing writer for several magazines, generally on the left, before establishing a full-time connection with Henry Luce's business-oriented *Fortune* in the 1950s. In these years, the worlds of New York intellectual journalism and the Columbia intellectuals regularly intersected, as when Bell wrote a glowing review of Trilling's *Liberal Imagination*, or included Hofstadter's piece "The Pseudo-conservative Revolt" in his edited work *The Radical Right* (1955), or voiced his reservations concerning C. Wright Mills's *The Power Elite* in his *End of Ideology* (1960) and later dedicated *The Reforming of General Education* (1966) to him. One reason Bell may have been invited to join the Columbia sociology department in 1961, after his published work was accepted in lieu of a dissertation for his Ph.D., was that he provided a balance to Mills, who by that time was an enthusiastic backer of Fidel Castro and Che Guevera.[84]

Several factors permitted these highly individualistic professors to constitute themselves into a latter-day and academicized Clapham Sect. They enjoyed physical proximity, both at work and home. Trilling, Hofstadter, Bell, and Barzun (until he shifted to Low) all had offices in Hamilton Hall, which brought them into contact with each other more than with their departmental colleagues in Fayerweather or Philosophy Hall. They also lived near each other, with Trilling, Hofstadter, Merton, Ernest Nagel, and Fritz Stern all having apartments on Claremont Avenue or Riverside Drive, a block from campus. Barzun lived three blocks away on Morningside Drive. By contrast, Mills seldom used his Hamilton office, lived forty miles away in rural Putnam County, from which he commuted by motorcycle.[85]

While proximity facilitated social interaction, what really brought these intellectuals together was the fact that they read each other's work in progress, often at several points in the writing process. They helped each other get work published and saw to it that it was properly reviewed, sometimes doing so themselves. They cited one another in their prefaces, provided blurbs for dust jackets, and recommended one another for fellowships. Merton's position as a member of the Guggenheim selection committee was one instance where a certain amount of intellectual logrolling likely occurred. Trilling's and Barzun's coeditorships (along with W. H. Auden) of the Readers' Subscription (later, Mid-century Book Club), a book club founded in 1951, was another. All aimed at a larger audience than their disciplinary peers, even as that audience began with each other.[86]

There were stylistic similarities among them, which sometimes set them apart from disciplinary colleagues. They all took pride in their writing. Perhaps this is not surprising in a literary critic and would-be novelist like Trilling or a cultural historian like Barzun, but such attention to readability was less usual among social scientists, least of all sociologists. Yet Merton was a superb stylist, one who put his knowledge of world literature to use in conveying sociological concepts as literary treasures (e.g., "The Matthew Effect," "A Shandean Postscript"). Bell, if less elegant, wrote in a style more felicitous than that of the average sociologist. Hofstadter was known to labor over his footnotes, to the point that they were infused with his "skeptical raillery" no less than his text. The nonhistorians among them brought a historical consciousness to their work, perhaps most explicitly in Trilling's dissent from the ahistorical approach of the new criticism then in ascendance among his professional colleagues. As social scientists, Hofstadter, Bell, and Merton made little use of statistics or other quantitative methods, while Barzun thought the spread of such paraphernalia presaged the end of Western civilization.[87]

The interpretive essay was their preferred genre, even when ostensibly writing books. The ideas they tackled were complicated and many faceted, seldom reducible to categorical judgments. They were quite capable of simultaneously holding opposing views, with no apologies. Compared with Trilling, Barzun could be very judgmental, but less often in his major concerns than in the many subfields—music, detective fiction, American popular culture—where he reveled in his amateur status. Trilling, on the other hand, without ever using the phrase "on the other hand," was conspicuously two-handed in his pursuit of "variousness, possibility, complexity and difficulty." Hofstadter did little archival research, preferring to rely on the primary research of other historians and then taking their generously acknowledged work to higher levels of generalization and sophistication.[88]

Biography also bound them together, after a fashion. All were unreconstructed urbanites. The three who were not native New Yorkers (Barzun, Merton, and Hofstadter) came and stayed through their academic careers, while only Manhattan-born Daniel Bell went off to the less citified climes of Cambridge, Massachusetts. None of the five had much direct contact with the American heartland. Jacques Barzun could write that "to know the heart and mind of America you had better learn baseball" and eventually settle happily in San Antonio, Texas, but he never quite left the earlier boulevardier behind.[89]

None was the product of an American boarding school, none went to a rural residential liberal arts college or to any of the great midwestern state universities. Barzun's first wife was a Boston Lowell and Trilling's wife, Diana, had gone to Radcliffe, but their upbringing and educational experiences—and those of their spouses—were of the aspiring urban working class and petit-bourgeois rather than of the white-shoe and ivy-favoring establishment.

All but Bell, who left for Harvard in 1969, stayed at Columbia once they got there, despite many offers, which some entertained only to consolidate their places on Morningside. When asked by Alfred Kazin why he stayed at Columbia, Hofstadter said "because he found it so interesting a 'society.'" This Kazin took him to mean "a certain intellectual contentment" not to be found elsewhere in America. Much the same could be said of Rabi, Lazarsfeld, Schapiro, and Nagel, although the last ventured as far away as Rockefeller University on the East Side for a year as he neared mandatory retirement at Columbia. Trilling's active connection with Columbia extended over forty-nine years, Barzun's forty-eight, Merton's thirty-five, Hofstadter's twenty-nine.[90]

For all this longevity, the postwar Columbia intellectuals seldom betrayed excessive true blue loyalties or undue reverence for Alma Mater. Barzun, Trilling, and Bell all had warm spots in their hearts for Columbia College, though Hofstadter less so and Merton not at all. Hofstadter's contribution "The Department of History" in the volume *The Faculty of Political Science* in the 1954 bicentennial history is notable for its astringency, while Trilling's account "Columbia College in the Era of Van Amringe and Keppel" reflected his considerable animus toward other parts of the university. "The one thing that kept me going on the job," Trilling wrote to Dwight Miner, the editor of the bicentennial history, "was my anger at the long history of the College's being a football of University policy, and the way the administration periodically congratulated itself for not having destroyed the College in order to create the University!"[91]

Yet all five, in their different ways and unlike their progenitor John Dewey or their contemporary Rabi, were excellent teachers. Each conceived of the classroom as a place to try out new and still-in-the-shaping ideas on fresh and receptive ears. Merton explicitly taught the book he happened to be writing at the time, a practice that Hofstadter followed for some of his books. Many of Trilling's best essays grew out of classroom discussions of texts he taught over and over again. None, however, risked confusion with Mr. Chips.[92]

Their reticence in singing the praises of Columbia was in sharp contrast to the high value they put on the place of the university in postwar America. This was indicated by the extent of their writing on the subject. Hofstadter, in particular, with his coauthored (with Walter Metzger) *The Rise of Academic Freedom in the United States*, his coedited (with Wilson Smith) *Documentary History of American Higher Education*, and his 1963 essay "The Revolution in Higher Education," demonstrated an abiding interest. Barzun wrote even more extensively on American higher education, first in his *Teacher in America* (1946) and later in *The American University* (1968), both best-sellers. Merton's *The Student-Physician* and Bell's *The Reformation of General Education*, like Barzun's books drawing directly on the Columbia experience though providing it a "national setting," addressed issues affecting all of American higher education.[93]

There was also about most of these intellectuals a dislike of administrative responsibilities and a disinclination to assume them. Trilling and Hofstadter actively campaigned to keep from being elected department chairs. Merton, too, preferred working behind the scenes or on key appointment committees rather than actually chairing his department. Barzun was the exception, agreeing in 1955 to serve ten years in Low Library and then putting in twelve, though his insistence that he be allowed to keep teaching and his success in finding time to write suggest that he continued to regard these more highly than his administrative labors.[94]

Their view of the university was, like Rabi's, decidedly faculty centered. None spent time cultivating trustees or presidents. "They were people I called by their first names," Trilling allowed of Kirk and his administrators (Barzun excepted), "but they were not my friends." Hofstadter concluded *The Rise of Academic Freedom in the Age of the College* by approvingly quoting Williams College president Paul Chadbourne, writing in 1873: "Professors are sometimes spoken of as working for the college. They are the college." In his 1968 Columbia commencement address he called the university "the center of our culture." But perhaps Daniel Bell most explicitly made the case, albeit interrogatively, for the faculty-centered university in a university-centered culture in *The Reforming of General Education*: "Is it *hubris* to say that if one were to look back at the present from the year 2000 ... one would discern in the second half of the twentieth century the transformation of the university into a primary institution of the emerging post-industrial society, just as the business firm had been the most important institution in the previous century and a half?"[95]

However comfortable with each other, the Columbia intellectuals were less so with most Americans and American culture in the main. As such, they provided a distinctive perspective on the American Century, or, in a phrase

C. Wright Mills used when chastising Trilling for being a participant, "The American Celebration." The American intellectual historian David Hollinger implied as much in a fascinating comparison of the postwar Michigan faculty, of which he was at the time a member, and Columbia's. Michigan, he argued, with its midwestern and college town locale, its egalitarian tradition, its early commitment to the education of women and a straight-ahead research ethos, represented "the national mainstream of academic pluralism" and made it "one of the most persistently generic of the major universities in the United States."[96]

Hollinger then went on to contrast the postwar Michigan faculty's scholarship in the humanities and social sciences, which he characterized as concrete, technical, and "least likely to be mistaken for political advocacy, cultural criticism, or journalism," with Columbia's, which "articulated some of the central concerns of [its faculty's] respective callings in theoretical terms general enough to engage the attention of men and women of other academic fields." If Hollinger's Michigan was "the apotheosis of pluralism," postwar Columbia was by implication "the apotheosis of cosmopolitanism."[97]

Hollinger also suggested that one of the important differences between Michigan and Columbia, and a contributor to the latter's greater cosmopolitanism, was its greater success in adding faculty drawn to America by the exodus from Central Europe, refugees for the most part Jewish, or labeled so by the Nazis. Without providing precise numbers, he assumed that many more stayed in New York and at Columbia then went on to Ann Arbor and Michigan.[98]

But here Hollinger may have been only half right. Without question, one aspect of Columbia distinctiveness in the decade after World War II was the large number of Jewish faculty members. But the bulk of these were not immigrants. Of the fifteen faculty members who made up the periphery and the core of the postwar Columbia intellectuals, all but three (Barzun, Truman, and Mills) were Jews, but only Lazarsfeld qualified as a refugee. The rest were American-born or came to America as children, not as adults. Many of them forged their career-long links with Columbia back in the 1920s and 1930s, when it was less than welcoming to Jews from wherever.

Their Jewishness tended to be not of the observant variety. Trilling explicitly rejected the idea "of myself as a 'Jewish writer.'" He went on: "I do not have it in mind to serve by my writing any Jewish purpose. I should resist it if a critic of my work were to discover in it faults or virtues which he called Jewish." Alfred Kazin thought Trilling uncomfortable among certain kinds of Jews. Hofstadter, whose mother was Episcopalian, similarly made little of his Jewishness, although his sensitivity to American anti-Semitism was acute, as in his saddling the populists with this sin, perhaps excessively so.[99]

Like Trilling, the mature Hofstadter had long since replaced his Jewish heritage with a secular rationalism that his colleague Robert Cross thought left him "too easily liberated from religious behavior." So, too, Trilling's long-time friend William Barrett (a Catholic) wondered why it was that "Trilling was not visited by a religious imagination," only to conclude that for him "to be religious implied a step backward in history, toward ghettos and the pale and the exclusion generally from American life." The comparison Barrett drew was not with Trilling's Columbia colleagues Hofstadter, Merton, or Schapiro, all more or less apposite, but with an earlier and equally secularized New York Jew, Walter Lippmann.[100]

Hollinger was right to seize on the Jewishness of the postwar Columbia faculty luminaries, even if he unduly minimized their New Yorkness. (Then, again, he may have had in mind that in some outlying districts "cosmopolitan" means "Jewish.") It is as New Yorkers *and* Jews that the relationship of the Columbia intellectuals to the rest of America should be understood. There may not have been a postwar Columbia school of social criticism, as there was, say, a Chicago school of economics, but there was a recognizable Columbia stance.

This stance, with respect to the rest of the country, was not so much critical or even defiantly alienated as it was standoffish and intellectually detached. At home in the university, or at least at "Columbia University in the City of New York," Columbia intellectuals were less sure of their welcome elsewhere—but not all that concerned about it, either. They were not anti-American, though sometimes they were viewed as such. Hofstadter's first nationally acclaimed book, *The American Political Tradition* (1948), evoked the comment that his was an "American history without heroes." They did eschew American triumphalism and were resolutely antiutopian, the later predilection reinforced by the influence of Reinhold Niebuhr across Broadway at Union Theological Seminary.[101]

The Columbia intellectuals were at the top of their game when criticizing America's critics. They were natural counterpunchers. This is seen in Trilling's disillusionment with Communism as conveyed in his novel *The Middle of the Journey* (1947) and in *The Liberal Imagination*, where he took on the Stalinist critique of America by "look[ing] at liberalism in a critical spirit." It can be seen in Hofstadter's *The Progressive Historians*, where he subjected three American historians of the previous generation—Vernon Parrington (also a target of Trilling's), Charles Beard, and Frederick Jackson Turner—to a post-Progressive critique of sufficient sweep to constitute, in his own words, a "parricidal foray." In another example, rather than mount their own spirited defense of American society, Trilling, Hofstadter, Bell, Merton, and Truman all indirectly allowed that it worked pretty well by dissenting from their colleague C. Wright Mills's full-throated assault in *The Power Elite*. Similarly, Merton did not so much directly take on the master theorists of sociology, Marx and Weber and Veblen or their principal American advocates, as propose "middle range" theories that were fundamentally accepting of postwar American society. So, too, Daniel Bell's *The End of Ideology* was intended to take some air out of the theorizing on the imminent demise of the American republic. None was either Communist or anti-Communist; they were all anti-anti-Communists of the sort that abhorred McCarthy as much for his small-town boorishness as for his politics.[102]

Critics of the postwar Columbia intellectuals have not been wanting. Charges of elitism, of aiding and abetting a consensual view of American history and culture, and of anticipating the neoconservatism of the 1970s have all effectively been made. Others have properly pointed out that the views of many of them as to the intellectual equality of women were no better, and in some cases worse, than their contemporaries, even in the face of contrary evidence all around them. Others find their secular faith in the sanctity of the university and of its rightful place "at the center of our culture" both self-serving and misplaced. For all that, by their manifold talents, energies, and brilliance, these scholar-intellectuals provided not only Columbia but the international intellectual community of the postwar era with a model of collective intellectual vitality.[103]

A Long Way From Brownsville

Most Columbia students in the 1950s and early 1960s did not have many of these Columbia intellectuals as teachers. Max Frankel (CC 1952) took courses with Charles Frankel (no relation) and C. Wright Mills, for example, but not with Trilling, Barzun, or Schapiro. As Frankel, by then executive editor of the *New York Times*, later acknowledged, he "majored aggressively in *Spec*." Similarly, Roy Cohn (CC 1947) zipped through Columbia College in two-and-one-half years on his way to the Law School apparently without benefit of instruction from any of the College's luminaries.[104]

For students to whom it did matter, like the 1952 sophomore transfer from Indiana, Dan Wakefield (CC 1955), the prospect of some classes with them was enough to plan their schedules accordingly. Arriving as a sophomore, Wakefield signed up for classes with Mark Van Doren, whose repute among fellow midwesterners attracted him to Columbia in the first place, with C. Wright Mills, and, in his junior year, with Lionel Trilling, whom he found to be in person "as elegant as his prose."[105]

Wakefield represented one kind of student drawn to Columbia in the 1950s:

a kid from elsewhere who was ready to take a chance on Columbia because it was New York. Jack Kerouac, of French-Canadian background from New Bedford, Massachusetts, was another student as much pushed away from somewhere as pulled to Columbia.[106]

But if the WASP Wakefield and the Catholic-cum-Beat Kerouac represented a strain of postwar Columbia studentdom, it was not the dominant one. And given Kerouac's football scholarship, his indifference to ordinary class going, his subsequent adventures "on the road," and his eventual retreat back to New Bedford, he makes for less than a representative type. Wakefield again, quoting his boss at *Spectator*, Max Frankel: "I was surprised by the beats coming out of Columbia. That was a side of the College I never knew, and it was just a few years before me. We were such innocents." As he recalled his Columbia days some thirty-five years later, "I felt like the minority kid as a WASP from the Midwest."[107]

What made the Columbia College classes of the postwar era distinctive was not the occasional WASP from Indianapolis but the many Jews from Brownsville and other Jewish enclaves of Greater New York. This geoethnic character of the undergraduates distinguished Columbia (and Barnard) both from most peer institutions (Chicago being the closest) and from prewar Columbia, where Jews constituted a smaller and more self-effacing presence. This is not to suggest that postwar Jewish students, especially in the College, were free of any feeling of being "a member of a small minority." For some, a half-century later, the memory persists.[108]

Jews who came to Columbia College after the war were much like those who came before the war (as described in Trilling's early short stories in the *Menorah Journal*): the children of immigrant parents who had not gone to college, of parents who had come to New York and worked their way into moderate prosperity, who had not yet acquired upper-middle-class social graces to bestow as a birthright on their Columbia sons and Barnard daughters. They were also, in the main, if not socially assimilated then intellectually secularized. One Columbia College undergraduate of the late 1940s, and later its dean, Carl Hovde (CC 1950), recalls those years as ones when "there were many more Jews in the College than later." At the same time, this grandson of a Lutheran minister, himself "thoroughly Deweyized" by his undergraduate experience, allowed, "I knew no pious Jews at Columbia."[109]

It may have been that very similarity between the undergraduates and their Jewish teachers like Lionel Trilling or Meyer Schapiro (who was from Brownsville) that encouraged so many to emulate them. Sometimes, this emulation took the form of undergraduates deciding on academic careers in the same fields as their teachers: Steven Marcus (CC 1948) with Trilling in English;

David Rosand (CC 1959) with Schapiro in art history; David Rothman (CC 1958) with Hofstadter in history; Stephen (CC 1962) and Jonathan Cole (CC 1964) with Merton in sociology. Sometimes, it meant merely affecting their teachers' manners or dress, as Dan Wakefield found himself emulating Trilling's languorous smoking. More than three decades later, one student of the early 1960s still remembered his surprise, on arriving at Morningside Heights fresh from working-class Crown Heights, Brooklyn, in finding that many upper-classmen, some from his own high school, now spoke with British accents.[110]

What Columbia's Jewish faculty held out to their Jewish students was the prospect of leaving Brownsville or Crown Heights behind. There was no obligation to do so; it simply existed as a live option. And many eagerly exercised it. "To wean me away from Brownsville," Norman Podhoretz (CC 1948) wrote seventeen years after graduating, "all Columbia had to do was give me the superior education it did." What Columbia made this son of Orthodox Jews was "a brutal bargain," by which what he called "one of the longest journeys in the world . . . from Brooklyn to Manhattan," already commenced by high school excursions across the Fifty-ninth Street Bridge to the Metropolitan Museum of Art, four years at Columbia made complete and irreversible. There, he would be allowed, even encouraged, to succeed. There, he found among the faculty Charles Frankel, Moses Hadas, Meyer Schapiro, Henry Graff, and Ernest Nagel, the last two CCNY graduates, who saw something of themselves in even the least sophisticated kid from Brownsville. Such kids, if bright and with a lot of work and a little luck, stood at least as good a chance as they had, to borrow the title of Podhoretz's 1967 memoir, of "Making It"—if not as a famous professor, then surely as someone of public moment who met what John Erskine first declared and Lionel Trilling affirmed as the objective of a Columbia education: meeting "the moral obligation to be intelligent," with all the privileges and obligations thereto.[111]

In much the same way, the sudden appearance in numbers of Jews on the faculties of the university's professional schools provided tangible proof that fields once restricted were now more fully open to the ambitious sons of Brownsville, including those recently transplanted out to Long Island or over to New Jersey, providing they acquired the appropriate degrees and a modicum of social polish. The bargain was not limited to Jewish students. The occupational restrictions against Irish and Italian Catholics in business and corporate law were also giving way to a credential-bearing meritocracy welcoming Columbia graduates across the board.

To be sure, the bargain was not yet universally applicable, as even the best academically credentialed women students at Barnard and the professional schools continued to experience sexual discrimination regularly in the workplace, sometimes at Columbia. Nor was it yet available to blacks or Puerto Ricans, who by 1960 made up more than a third of New York City's total population but whose negligible numbers among Columbia students bespoke not so much active institutional discrimination as indifference to the city's changing demographics and political realities.[112]

Yet what four decades later remains striking about the 1950s and early 1960s at Columbia was the historically unique convergence of student aspirations with faculty realities. Supporting evidence is of two sorts. The first is statistical and points to the large and growing proportion of postwar graduates of Columbia and Barnard who went for Ph.D.s and into academic careers. Both colleges had long ranked high in the numbers of their students getting Ph.D.s, especially in the humanities and social sciences. (Both also did well in sending graduates on to medical and law schools.) Yet as long as the Jews among them encountered discrimination when they tried to secure academic positions at Columbia, Barnard, or almost any other respectable college or university, as they did through the 1930s, many found themselves instead pursuing careers in the New York City public schools or with city, state, and federal agencies. Such discrimination in academe only ended after World War II, when it became illegal, economically dysfunctional, and, perhaps most crucially, competitively self-defeating.[113]

The speed with which the previous restrictions on Jewish faculty gave way at postwar Columbia should not be exaggerated. Well into the 1950s, some departments attempted to maintain a semblance of their WASPish pasts. As late as 1958, the Law School made matched hires, pairing a Jewish appointee with a non-Jew. That same year, the philosopher Charles Frankel was not made dean of Columbia College, some said at the time because he was Jewish. Law suits filed against the Medical School in the late 1940s for discriminatory practices in hiring and admissions, plus the fact that the first tenure appointment of a Jew to the Faculty of the Business, Eli Ginzberg in 1947, was not followed for some years by another, suggest that what students observed was a university in the process of changing before their eyes.[114]

Postwar Columbia (1942–58) ranked third overall among men's colleges in terms of the number of graduates who went on to complete Ph.D.s in the humanities and social sciences. Barnard ranked second among women's colleges. When institutional ranking takes into account the number of graduates per institution, Barnard tops the list of women's colleges, and Columbia College was roughly tied with Harvard. Some 40 percent of the graduating class of Columbia College of 1961 proceeded directly to graduate school in the arts and sciences, with a slightly lower proportion of Barnard graduates doing likewise. John Updike once characterized the 1950s as a decade "when everyone was

pregnant." On Morningside Heights, it was more one when everyone was getting a Ph.D.[115]

What national surveys in the early 1960s found to be true of the career aspirations of undergraduates at the best colleges nationally applied with particular force to Columbia and Barnard College: "the academic world that produced
them has the greatest attraction for the students who are most successful in its
eyes." There is also anecdotal evidence that points to the attractiveness academic careers came to have for many of postwar Columbia's brightest undergraduates, perhaps especially for its first-in-family-to-college New Yorkers,
from Jewish families with public school educations, who went on to graduate
or professional school at Columbia and then either stayed on or soon returned
as faculty. Even a partial enumeration, based on the author's random collegial
acquaintances over thirty years, speaks to what proved to be, for a generation of
undergraduate Brownsville Columbians, an almost irresistible call to the academy. As late as 1966, Dean of Columbia College David Truman estimated that
85 percent of Columbia College graduates were planning to go to graduate
school, most to pursue their Ph.D.s.[116]

Such interest in academic careers in the 1950s and early 1960s was encouraged—and not only at Columbia—by a rapidly expanding academic economy
in which Ph.D.s were said to be in dangerously short supply. "The need for college teachers is already so great," Hans Rosenhaupt, the director of graduate
admissions at Columbia, reported in 1958, "that the output of our graduate
schools fails to meet the demand." The growing availability of fellowship
money from foundations and the federal government that followed on the discovery of this Ph.D. gap was another inducement that led to the national output of Ph.D.s doubling between 1950 and 1960—and then doubling again by
1966. The ranks of the national professoriat increased even faster, from total of
265,800 in 1958 to 547,700 in 1967.[117]

Meanwhile, postwar Columbia accommodated the ever-present gentleman
C student, the serious athlete, and the casual jock, undergraduates for whom
Columbia consisted of prep school pals, fraternities, and sports. Barnard had
students majoring in finding a husband. Both colleges also made room for the
grinding, in-a-hurry, premed and prelaw students drawn to them because they
were the quickest route to the university's Law, Business, and Medical Schools.
Both types of students existed at all the major colleges and universities in postwar America, and perhaps only local chauvinism prompts the undocumentable
suggestion that they were less numerous on Morningside Heights than elsewhere.

And then, somewhere well into this academically bullish postwar period,
what the Columbia sociologist Jonathan Cole has called the "limited opportu-

nity range" of smart kids from Brownsville (Jewish or otherwise) broadened to encompass distinguished undergraduate programs farther afield. The result was that more and more of the brightest New York public high school graduates went off to Michigan (where the movement can be dated back to the 1930s) and Berkeley and MIT, if not yet to Stanford, then certainly to Harvard and to Yale, rather than to Columbia, Barnard, Cornell, NYU, and Rochester, where proximity, local reputation, and Regents fellowships had previously drawn them. Nicolas Lemann, in his valuable book *The Big Test: The Secret History of the American Meritocracy*, tells a story that allows us to date the passing of this period of limited opportunity range to 1965. It was that year when staff from the Yale admissions office first visited Abraham Lincoln High School in Brooklyn, where they were greeted by its principal's crack: "Where the hell have you guys been all these years?" Up until then, Abraham Lincoln and Bronx Science and Stuyvesant and Music and Art—that is, New York's most academically demanding high schools—had been in the postwar period Columbia's unacknowledged feeder schools, its secret weapon in the meritocratic wars, the functional equivalent of Andover and Groton for Yale and Harvard. No longer. The secret was out.[118]

Columbia historian Fritz Stern (CC 1946) once observed only half jokingly in the 1970s that the worst thing to happen to postwar Columbia was the waning of anti-Semitism among the other Ivies. When this happened, Columbia's privileged access to local talent in that brief moment between shaking off its own interwar anti-Semitism (along with its WASP pretensions more generally) and the nationalization of the educational meritocracy disappeared. It was great while it lasted.[119]

CHAPTER 14

Afternoon on the Hudson

And thus was this poor church left, like an ancient mother grown old and for-saken of her children, though not in their affections yet in regard of their bodily presence and personal helpfulness; her ancient members being most of them worn away by death, and these of later time being like children translated into other families, and she like a widow left only to trust in God. Thus, she that had made many rich became herself poor.

William Bradford, Of Plymouth Plantation (1644)

The Cautionary Case of Lamont

A N institutional moment can be rich in accomplishments and at the same time beset with problems. So it was at postwar Columbia. Even the posi-tive conditions facilitating the accomplishments of the 1950s and early 1960s—a decentralized administration, outside funding, the presence of semiau-tonomous scholar-entrepreneurs, the advantages inherent in a particular moment in the city's ethnic history—contributed to problems that became manifest in the mid-1960s.

The relationship of the Columbia geology department and its offshoot, the Lamont Geological Observatory, represented an even more dramatic tail-wag-ging-dog phenomenon than did the Bureau and the sociology department. Part of the difference between the two instances was the extent of the physical sep-aration of their respective parts. After 1948 the Bureau was located on 115th Street, between Broadway and Riverside, only a couple of blocks from the soci-ology department in Fayerweather Hall. Lamont was situated across the Hud-son in Palisades, New York, some twenty miles from the geology department's offices in Schermerhorn Hall. The twenty acres on which the first buildings of the observatory were built had belonged to Thomas Lamont, a principal asso-ciate of J. P. Morgan, and were deeded to the university by the Lamont family in 1948. It was understood at the time of the gift, and agreed to by President Eisen-hower, that the land would be reserved for geological and oceanographic research.[1]

For all its subsequent success as a leader in postwar geophysical and oceano-graphic research, Lamont remained terra incognita for most of the Columbia community. Otherwise well-informed Columbians scarcely knew of its existence. It was only in 1971, when he became provost, that William Theodore de Bary, a member of the Columbia faculty throughout Lamont's existence and a resident of nearby Tappan, ventured inside its gates.[2]

This was not just a case of Morningside provincialism. Lamont intentionally operated at arm's length from the rest of the university. As with other university-affiliated postwar research facilities, such as Nevis and Hudson Laboratories, Brookhaven, and later the Goddard Institute for Space Studies, Lamont looked to the university's central administration for neither students nor funding. Its staff consisted of a few regular Columbia faculty with appointments in the geology department but mainly of research staff hired outside the university's faculty appointments system. The additional fact that Lamont carried on secret research for the navy and the Atomic Energy Commission and thus required security clearances for its staff only added to the self-imposed seclusiveness of Lamonters.[3]

Lamont operated as a research facility that provided some graduate instruction. While organizationally linked to the Morningside-based geology department and, for specific projects, with chemistry and the Engineering School, it was, other than its use of university-owned land, financially independent. It depended on federal grants, mostly from the navy in support of antisubmarine research, and corporate contracts, especially from the petroleum industry for help with offshore drilling. The teaching that went on at Lamont was graduate instruction in the specialties in which its faculty-staff were engaged: geophysics, geochemistry, oceanography. Graduate students who worked there were not paid stipends but salaries charged to the grants of their dissertation sponsors.[4]

The need for Lamont to pay its own way with outside contracts did not pose a problem. So numerous and generous did these contracts become that federal agencies and oil companies competed with each other for the facility's services. In such a seller's market, it was perhaps inevitable that the principals at Lamont would take to wondering what benefits the university relationship offered.

For the quarter-century after its opening, Lamont was the virtual fiefdom of Maurice W. Ewing, one of Columbia's scholar-entrepreneurs in the classic Chandler-Burgess mold. Ewing was born in West Texas in 1906 and went to Rice, where he received his B.A. (1926) and Ph.D. (1931) in physics. He then taught at the University of Pittsburgh and at Lehigh University. In 1944, while on wartime service at the Woods Hole Oceanographic Institution, he became an associate professor of geology at Columbia.[5]

During his subsequent twenty-eight years at Columbia, Ewing commanded resources for his work in oceanography and seismology second only to those of Rabi for physics. A prodigious and inventive researcher, he was one of the pioneers in the field of tectonics. His success in extracting geological data and inferences from ocean bottom cores was such that these cores came to be known as "Ewings." He regarded science as in its essence fiercely competitive and showed little patience for those finishing back in the pack. It helped that, by several accounts, "he never slept." He also never did any classroom teaching, turning over the occasional course he was listed as offering to one of his staff.[6]

Ewing was involved in the discussions that led to the establishment of the Lamont Geological Observatory in 1949 and became its first director. During the ensuing decade, through his own work and that of colleagues and students, Ewing thrust Lamont to the head of the rankings of American oceanographic research centers; he then spent the 1960s beating back challenges from Scripps and Woods Hole. He wrote over 340 scientific papers and trained more than two hundred graduate students. He pushed his students to excel, got maximum scientific use out of the various research vessels under his command, and took his own accomplishments seriously. The fact that there was no Nobel Prize offered in geology, for example, moved him in the late 1950s to solicit funds from friends in the oil industry to create the Vetlesen Prize for geological achievement, to be awarded annually by the trustees of Columbia University. Its first winner: Maurice W. Ewing. He undoubtedly deserved it.[7]

Ewing's competitiveness contributed to the productivity and visibility of Lamont scientists. It may also have fed a penchant for making headlines with arresting and sometimes errant pronouncements on such newsworthy matters as the continental drift, climate warming, the melting of the Arctic ice, and the imminence of a magnetic reversal at the poles. But as Frank Press (CU Ph.D. 1947), one of Lamont's bright young researchers and later head of the National Academy of Sciences, recalled the Ewing era at Lamont, there was little risk of any of "his boys" ever hiding their light under a basket.[8]

Ewing's aggressiveness also manifested itself in his relations with the geology department and the Columbia administration. Sometimes, the issue was who would teach undergraduates, with Ewing arguing that doing so was not Lamont's business. More often, the issue concerned what portion of the research monies flowing into Lamont should be redirected to the department and the university. Ewing fought hard to retain every cent that came in, arguing that he needed it to maintain Lamont's preeminence and expand its research capacity.[9]

It was Ewing, using an offer from MIT for leverage, who persuaded Eisenhower to let Lamont retain the funds from its government contracts to cover the university's indirect costs (overhead) rather than turn most of them over to the department or university to cover such items as undergraduate instruction, library costs, upkeep of the Morningside campus, and so on. This deal, which even in the fat times of the early 1960s attracted the envious attention of other federal grant–generating parts of the university, not least the Medical School, was a testament to Ewing's singular autonomy. Members of the geology department not involved in Lamont deeply resented this privileged status. Although Ewing's deal with Eisenhower was subject to revision by subsequent presidents, it was not Kirk's style to challenge it. That would fall to Kirk's combative and financially pressed successor. And when this happened, Ewing would react with predictable anger. But even in the seemingly flush early 1960s, the exceptional success of Lamont did not so much produce a halo effect for Columbia science overall as it prompted finger-pointing and charges of favoritism that contributed to a general loss of morale.[10]

Computing at Postwar Columbia

The case of computing lends credence to the general argument that Columbia was struggling in the postwar years to hold its earlier place among the leading centers of American science. Computing at Columbia is also a classic example of the university's having an early start in a field that in the postwar era became a vital element in the life of America's leading research universities but only playing a minor role in its subsequent development.[11]

The beginnings of computing at Columbia date from 1928 and the installation of three truckloads of punch card equipment in the basement of Hamilton Hall. This came about as the result of discussions between Benjamin D. Wood, director of the university's Bureau of Collegiate Educational Research, charged with scoring examination papers in large-scale testing programs, and Thomas J. Watson, the president of IBM, who was then aggressively seeking potential users for the various tabulating, punching, and sorting machines that made up his company's line. (The technology involved in these first IBM machines was derived from a counter developed by Herman Hollerwith in the 1890s to aid with the census and processing of immigrants at Ellis Island. Hollerwith, it turns out, was a graduate of both the School of Mines (1879) and one of Columbia's first Ph.D.s (1890, political science).[12]

Wood quickly put these tabulators and sorters to work in what became in 1929 the Columbia University Statistical Bureau. Other campus uses were soon found for them. In the astronomy department, Professor Harold Jacoby set them to interpolating astronomical tables, a chore previously done by hand. A year later, Wood convinced Watson to build a Special Difference Calculator, for such work as calculating sums of squares. IBM, in an early instance of label placement, subsequently promoted these as "Columbia machines." Later models were installed in the Rutherford Observatory in the attic of Pupin Hall. These machines, built by IBM to specifications set by another member of the astronomy department, Professor Wallace J. Eckert, have since been credited by historians of computing to have been the first computers to perform general scientific calculations automatically.[13]

In the early 1930s Eckert became the key figure in the developing relationship between the university and IBM. This association acquired added intimacy after 1934 when Watson, who had not gone to college, was elected a life trustee of Columbia University. In 1937 the Pupin astronomical lab was renamed the Thomas J. Watson Astronomical Computing Bureau. Three years later, in 1940, Eckert published *Punched Card Methods in Scientific Calculations*, the first book on computers.[14]

During World War II, the computing machines in Pupin were used to calculate aiming angles and weapon trajectories for the United States Navy. Meanwhile, similar IBM equipment was being used by the Bureau of Radio Research, under the direction of the recently arrived Paul Lazarsfeld, in its many war-related public-opinion and propaganda-assessment projects. Even before the war ended, Watson committed IBM to establishing a computing research laboratory on the Columbia campus, yet another, as he put it, "major forward step in the long and productive cooperation between IBM and Columbia University." On February 6, 1945, three months before V-E Day, the Thomas J. Watson Scientific Computing Laboratory at Columbia University officially opened for business, although it did not move into its quarters on West 116th Street in the Casa Hispanica until three months after V-J Day.[15]

Thus no American university was better situated at the end of World War II to move forward with computing as a major area of academic research than was Columbia. And for a while it looked as if it might do so. In 1946–47 the Watson Laboratory offered graduate-level courses in computer science, the first to be offered by any university. That same year, Watson Lab staff designed and built the massive IBM Selective Sequence Electronic Calculator, one of the first large-scale stored-program electronic computers. The first IBM computer to use a keyboard for interactive control, the IBM 610 Auto-Point Computer, was also built at the Watson Lab. A member of the Watson Lab staff at the time, John Backus, went on in 1954 to design FORTRAN, the first high-level machine-independent programming language. In 1953–54 the Watson Lab staff designed and built the Naval Ordnance Research Calculator, then the most powerful computer in existence and precursor to IBM's first commercial general-purpose computer. By then, Columbia researchers at Lamont Geological Observatory had joined Columbia astronomers, physicists, and sociologists in exploiting the research uses of computers.[16]

And yet, for all these accomplishments, the advocates of making computing a major academic enterprise on Morningside Heights failed to do so. On a personal level, Eckert, unlike Rabi, or Ewing, or Lazarsfeld, was neither an entrepreneur nor an empire builder. Similarly, much of Columbia's success into the early 1950s turned on its relationships with IBM and, even more directly, with Watson, relationships that could—and so proved—to be limiting, especially in 1956 when Watson was succeeded at IBM by his son, a graduate of Brown, who had none of his father's ties to Columbia. Even with President Kirk on the IBM board, relations between "Big Blue" and the university grew strained in the early 1960s. The divorce was formalized in 1970 when IBM transferred its research staff out of New York City and Columbia to its Yorktown Heights "campus."[17]

During these years, Provost Barzun kept whatever interest he had in computers to himself. Other Columbians were less circumspect. Some faculty and students questioned the university's involvement not only with corporate America, which the IBM link epitomized, but also with computers, which symbolized to them a repudiation of the university's humanistic ethos.[18]

There was also the perennial problem of finding space for computing on or near campus. Indeed, the failure to do so in 1957, when the National Science Foundation had made a grant to Columbia to install the new IBM 704, only to have Columbia discover that the machine was too large to fit in the lab's facility on 116th Street, required the university to return the grant and prompted IBM to turn to Harvard to host what was then the world's most powerful computer. By the late 1960s Columbia had lost its early place at the vanguard of computer science, despite installing in 1969 what was then the biggest, fastest computer on earth, the IBM 360/91, in a new facility in the basement of Uris Hall. While some externally funded faculty in physics, chemistry, and sociology continued to make use of what was then considered the immense computing capacity provided by the 360, others were denied access and turned in the mid-1970s to installing and maintaining departmental computers, which took up still more valuable space in Columbia's already cramped quarters. "By then," a member of the Watson Lab at the time later recalled, "I think nobody at Columbia cared."[19]

And as so often happened during this era, Columbia-trained individuals left Morningside to create competing centers elsewhere. Kenneth King and Joseph Traub, among the first recipients of Watson fellowships in computing in the late 1950s, are two cases in point. King left Columbia in 1971 to take a position first at the City University of New York and later as vice chancellor for computing at Cornell. Traub left Columbia to head up the computer science program at Carnegie-Mellon, which became in the late 1970s one of the centers for computing research in the United States. By then, Columbia's computer science department ranked sixtieth of the seventy departments nationally rated. The fortunes of computer science at Columbia would improve in the 1980s, not least with the help of the returning Traub, but its failure in the 1950s and 1960s to hold its early place as a pioneer in the field speaks to the increasingly straitened competitive circumstances of the sciences more generally at postwar Columbia.[20]

The "Two Cultures" Problem

When the mathematical psychologist William McGill arrived at Columbia in the fall of 1958, after a decade at Harvard and MIT, he was immediately struck by the difference between the prevailing ethos of the campuses he had just left and that of his new home. "Harvard and MIT," he recalled two decades later, "were about nature. Columbia was about books." He went on to opine that Columbia's antiscientific posture "reflected the attitudes of striving of the Jewish population of New York City, which somehow felt that mastering what was written down in books, so that one could manage it with utter ease, was the goal of all learning, and that original thought was not really required." Whatever one thinks of McGill's armchair sociology, his first take on Columbia as unwelcoming to science was one shared by others. It was, moreover, an initial criticism that six years of doing science on Morningside Heights did not soften.[21]

McGill's characterization of a tension existing between science and the humanities at postwar Columbia inevitably brings to mind C. P. Snow. Indeed, McGill likely had Snow in mind when he offered his institutionally specific, shorthand version of what Snow had coined twenty years earlier as the problem of the "two cultures." As Snow argued in 1959, the problem was one of communications between the two segments of advanced Western culture, in which one segment, the "literary," showed little interest in understanding the "scientific." He allowed that the reverse was also sometimes true, but less often and to less destructive effect. Moreover, it was the literary culture that enjoyed an unearned ascendance over the scientific in public affairs generally and within universities especially.[22]

Snow's arguments were widely challenged, perhaps most summarily in 1962 by the literary scholar F. R. Leavis, like Snow, a Cambridge don. But Snow was also taken to task later that year by Lionel Trilling, who, after dissociating himself from Leavis's ad hominem assault, was equally dismissive of Snow's central complaint that "it is the traditional culture ["literature"], to an extent remarkably little diminished by the emergence of the scientific one, which manages the Western world." Trilling went on to suggest that what Snow "seems to require for scientists is the right to go their own way *with no questions asked.*" And inso-far as Trilling saw the asking of questions as his job and that of his fellow humanists, this was an unacceptable demand. Accordingly, he declared *The Two Cultures* to be a book "which is mistaken in a very large way indeed."[23]

Yet Trilling's dismissal of Snow's central argument—that scientists get no respect—could be said to prove it, with Columbia as an institutional instance. Indeed, as Snow acknowledged privately, the "two cultures" idea came out of conversations he first had at Columbia with none other than his fellow physi-cist, Columbia's I. I. Rabi.[24]

To the extent that postwar Columbia reflected the discounting of science that Snow deemed endemic to Western culture, it was hardly unique among major American campuses. Yale and Princeton arguably had a more advanced form of it, their postwar science faculty feeling even less appreciated by their colleagues in the humanities and by their administrations than Columbia's. At Harvard, however, or so McGill believed, the sciences operated on equal terms with the humanities, social sciences, and the professional schools. Berkeley was a similar instance. And then there were MIT and Stanford, whose first and most prominent steeples were in engineering, and Cal Tech and Johns Hopkins, espe-cially in the medical sciences, where the sciences enjoyed a privileged place. If Columbia were to persist in what Barzun referred to in 1958 as its "pretensions" to comprehensive excellence, these science-centered universities constituted new and formidable competition.[25]

The argument that postwar Columbia was less committed to the sciences than many peer institutions has some statistical basis. Its faculty contained a smaller proportion of scientists than not only those of MIT, Cal Tech, Stanford, and Johns Hopkins but those of Harvard, Berkeley, Michigan, and Cornell as well. When one turns to the relative production of science and nonscience degrees, at both the undergraduate and graduate levels, postwar Columbia's tilt away from the sciences was even more pronounced.[26]

This had not always been the case. Much of the surge in faculty appoint-ments in the two decades on either side of 1900 occurred in the sciences, with the result that Columbia's output of science Ph.D.s increased along with its rep-utation as a center for scientific activity. In Cattell's 1908 rankings in *American Men of Science*, Columbia was second only to Harvard in the size and eminence of its science faculty. Only in the late 1920s, despite the expansion in the bio-logical sciences attending the completion of the medical center, did Columbia lose its place among the largest American employers of scientists and take to emphasizing not the size of its science departments but their "pound for pound" qualities.[28]

The absence of scientifically informed leadership helps account for the secondary place science has played through much of Columbia's history. Of Columbia's nineteen presidents to date, only two, Frederick A. P. Barnard and William McGill, have been scientists. In McGill's case, Columbia's only twentieth-century scientist-president, his considerable credentials as a scientist played no role in his selection and were seldom invoked during his presidency. This contrasts not only with Harvard, which had the presidential service of two chemists—Charles William Eliot and James Bryant Conant—for the last third of the nineteenth century and much of the first half of the twentieth, but also with Yale and Chicago, which, in the persons of James Rowland Angell and Max Mason at Chicago, had eminent research scientists as presidents in the 1920s. Down through the end of World War II, Columbia relied on Nicholas Murray Butler, whose scientific education dated back to the 1870s. Eisenhower, an indifferent student at West Point, had little interest in the doings of his science faculty. Kirk had less. Among the dozen names submitted by the faculty committee in 1945 as possible successors to Butler, not one was of a scientist.[28]

Nor had Columbia often sought out scientists to fill the administrative positions below the president. The university's twentieth-century chief academic officers into the 1960s include the philosophers Nicholas Murray Butler and Frederick J. E. Woodbridge, the "gentleman C" Frank Fackenthal, the law professor Albert Jacobs, the American historian John Krout, and the European cultural historian Jacques Barzun. The only scientists to serve for any length of time were the physicist George B. Pegram, who served as dean of Graduate Faculties from 1929 to 1949, and the chemist Ralph Halford, as vice president for special projects and dean of the Graduate Faculties from 1959 to 1967. Polykarp Kusch, a Nobel physicist, served as vice president for academic affairs and provost in 1969–70, but his entire tenure encompassed only sixteen months. George Fraenkel, a physical chemist, served as dean of Graduate Faculties from 1968 and 1983 but never considered himself part of central administration.[29]

The one postwar Columbia administrator to write about science was the historian Jacques Barzun, who served first as vice president and then as provost through all but the last year of the Kirk presidency. It might have been better had he not. Even the title of his book, *Science: The Glorious Entertainment*, published in 1964, sufficiently angered some of his science colleagues, the geologist Wallace Broecker among them, that they considered leaving. Criticism of Barzun as biased against science by Broecker, Lazarsfeld, and other Columbia faculty may have been unfair, but there was never much likelihood of confusing him with Stanford's Frederick Termann, MIT's Julius Stratton, or any of the other postwar champions of academic science.[30]

And as with much else at Columbia, the administration's putative neglect of science faculty is tied up with the physical constraints imposed by locale and space. By the 1950s much of the university's work in the sciences was conducted off the main campus. Most of the research in the biological sciences was conducted at the medical center fifty blocks to the north, while much of the work in the physical sciences occurred at Lamont Geological Observatory twenty miles away in New Jersey, at the Hudson Laboratory in Yonkers, at Nevis Laboratory in Westchester, and at Brookhaven, fifty miles away on the eastern end of Long Island. When the Goddard Institute for Space Science was added to the list of Columbia's affiliated science institutions, it took up space above a bank and bodega several blocks south of the Morningside campus. Columbia's oceanographers and seismologists spent more time at sea or at remote sites than they did at Lamont, almost none at Columbia proper.[31]

Meanwhile, the sciences on the Morningside campus were tucked away in the northwest corner of the campus, where few nonscience faculty or students had reason to venture. Nor were the science faculty all that likely to wander far from their labs. The chemist George Fraenkel taught undergraduates in a classroom in Chandler Hall for fourteen years before ever finding his way across 116th Street to Hamilton Hall, only five hundred yards away. By occupational default, then, the postwar Morningside campus was in the effective control of Columbia's humanists, social scientists, and nonscience professional school faculty and their students.[32]

A less quantifiable factor that may help account for the nonscientific ethos of postwar Columbia is the possibility that scientists as a group are less enamored of New York City than are their nonscience counterparts. The desire to get away from the city figured prominently among the reasons for leaving given by bacteriologist Hans Zinsser in the 1920s and physicist Charles Townes in the 1950s. The prospect of coming back to "the utterly hostile environment" of New York City, either as a young faculty member in 1957 or as president twelve years later, did not figure among the attractions of a Columbia job for either the psychologist William McGill or his family. "I don't want to leave here," his wife, Ann, allowed after four years in California, "but if you go, I'll go."[33]

Another important consideration has to do with the size and curricular orientation of Columbia College. One way scientists at postwar Harvard, Stanford, and MIT maintained a connection with the rest of the faculty and the university at large was through their shared responsibility for undergraduate instruction. This worked less effectively at Columbia for two reasons. The small size of Columbia College, which enrolled 2,500 students in 1960, as compared with Harvard College (5,000) or the undergraduate programs of MIT (3,600) and Stanford (5,200), meant that there were fewer undergraduates at Columbia for its science faculty to teach. Barnard undergraduates seldom took science courses at Columbia, relying on those offered by Barnard faculty. Students in

General Studies received most of their science instruction from faculty assigned and adjuncts hired for that purpose. Science faculty were well enough represented formally among the Columbia College faculty, but few did much undergraduate teaching, and many did none at all. Consequently, the provision of adequate space for undergraduate instructional laboratories did not figure among their highest priorities.[34]

Even more limiting a factor than the size of the College was its structured curriculum. The glories of the Columbia Core have been sung earlier here and by others elsewhere, so no offense is intended in suggesting that it has worked more effectively in some ways—and for some Columbians—than others. The Core has not been notably successful in producing students who at the end of their sophomore year decide to go on to major in one of the sciences, even among those who came to Columbia intending to do so. Its impact has been more often the other way: redirecting undergraduates who came to Columbia intending to major in the sciences into the humanities or social sciences. Efforts have been periodically undertaken by members of the science faculty to add a serious science component to the Core, but when introduced such courses typically have been short lived for reasons often having to do with staffing or the availability of instructional laboratory space. Daniel Bell's efforts in 1965 to address this problem in *The Reforming of General Education* were largely dismissed by Columbia's scientists as presenting a view of science fifty years out-of-date.[35]

The percentage of Columbia College graduates going on to Ph.D.s in the sciences, as compared with those in the humanities and social sciences, was equally indicative of the comparative state of the "two cultures." In the early 1960s the undergraduate flight from science accelerated sharply. In 1963 the proportion of Columbia College juniors and seniors majoring in the sciences and engineering constituted a third (396) of those classes; in 1968 it formed a fifth (236). One side effect of this was that Columbia scientists, already looking to the graduates of other colleges for the bulk of their graduate students (Stanford and MIT got many of theirs from Stanford and MIT), had even less reason to concern themselves with the undergraduate life of the university. This remove would become painfully obvious in 1968, when science faculty, more than their colleagues in the humanities and social sciences, were caught unaware by what protesting undergraduates had wrought.[36]

Not surprisingly, Columbia College undergraduates in the 1960s were especially resistant to the claims of Columbia scientists that federally funded research and defense-related secret research were not necessarily the devil's handiwork. Thus, when conflicts inevitably arose between the needs of Columbia scientists and the sanctity of the campus as a war-free zone or between the scientists and concerns of the neighboring community about the risks inherent in on-campus research, Columbia College students and faculty had less reason to consider the scientists' arguments than did their counterparts at MIT or Stanford. When your own university's students—along with your nonscience faculty colleagues—turn against you in matters vital to your life as a scientist, the inclination to go elsewhere becomes pretty powerful. And as more than one departing scientist probably said over his shoulder, "I never liked New York anyway."[37]

The Campus Banal

Postwar Columbia experienced an upsurge in on-campus building made all the more dramatic by the absence of any construction in the quarter-century since the 1934 completion of the South Hall Library (renamed Butler in 1946). In the sheer number of new buildings, it matched the two earlier waves of construction, that attending the move to Morningside in the late 1890s and early 1900s and the second in the 1920s that culminated in the creation of a second campus for the medical center. Between 1956 and 1965 some eight buildings were added to the university's Morningside physical stock. These included, on the main campus north of 116th Street, Seeley Mudd (1958–61), for the School of Engineering, and Uris Hall (1959–64), for the Business School. South of 116th Street, the first student dormitory to be built in thirty years, Carman Hall, went up in 1959, at the same time as the adjoining Ferris Booth Hall, originally conceived as a center for community activities but opened and operated as a more comprehensive student center.[38]

On the east side of Amsterdam Avenue, the completion of the Law School building (now Jerome Greene Hall) in 1961 allowed the school to escape the small and antiquated confines of Kent Hall. Next door to the Law School, ground was broken in 1966 for what became the School of International Affairs Building, which proved to be, fittingly, the last Columbia building embarked upon in the winding-down American Century.[39]

On the west side of Broadway, Barnard College experienced in the late 1950s a mini–building boom of its own. It added two new structures to its existing four (Milbank [1897], Brooks [1907], Barnard [1917], and Hewitt [1925]) with the completion of a library in Adele Lehman Hall (1959) and its third dormitory, Helen Reid Hall (1959). To these were added a student center, named after President Millicent McIntosh, and a science tower, Helen Altschul Hall, both completed in 1969. Teachers College was unusual in not undertaking any substantial construction in the immediate postwar period, which continued a half-century-long moratorium that stretched back to the completion of Russell Hall in 1925 and forward to the groundbreaking for Thorndike Hall in 1969.[40]

Virtually all the new buildings Columbia constructed in the Kirk years were criticized on aesthetic grounds. Campus wags referred to the Law School building as "a toaster," with Seeley Mudd "the box it came in." The opening of Uris Hall was picketed by School of Architecture faculty and students, while Carman and Ferris Booth were promptly declared unworkable as undergraduate habitats, a judgment of Ferris Booth confirmed in 1994 when it was demolished to make room for Lerner Hall. In 1964 the alumni magazine, *Columbia Today*, devoted an issue to criticizing the university's new buildings. Successive architectural editors of the *New York Times*, including the formidable Ada Louise Huxtable, criticized Columbia for its architectural sins. Most campus master plans for Barnard in the last three decades have begun with the happy prospect of demolishing McIntosh Center and Lehman Hall.[41]

Opinions on postwar Columbia architecture have not softened. Andrew Dolkart's invaluable *Morningside Heights: A History of Its Architecture and Development* (1998) uses no descriptive adjective more often to characterize the architectural features of these buildings than "banal." Some blame, he allows, might be put on the generally parlous state of postwar American institutional architecture, but, as he indicates, to do so fails to acknowledge the impressive buildings that went up during the same period at Yale and Harvard.[42]

Most of the blame belongs with Columbia itself. Jacques Barzun saw the shabbiness of Columbia's postwar buildings as being of a piece with its general disregard for physical amenities. Grayson Kirk later attributed the rash of ugly buildings to bad luck in the choice of architects, further assuring his interviewer that the models of Uris and Mudd had looked better than the real things. Barry Bergdoll, in his wonderful *Mastering McKim's Plan: Columbia's First Century on Morningside Heights* (1997), suggests that the failure either to follow the original master plan laid out by the original architects of the Morningside campus or to develop a bold new one resulted in part from a lack of coordination among the schools responsible for raising the funds, deciding what the buildings ought to look like, and seeing the construction through to completion. This fits with what we know about Kirk, his "barons," and their dealings with each other.[43]

Another factor that bears consideration in accounting for Columbia's architectural problems was that the university had about run out of space. New buildings often could not be effectively sited but had to be shoehorned between existing structures, as in the cases of Seeley Mudd and Uris Hall, the latter built on the footprint of the demolished University Hall. Comparisons with postwar Stanford almost always work to Columbia's disadvantage, but that between

Stanford's 8,200-acre campus, 85 percent of which was unbuilt on in the early 1960s, and Columbia's 30-acre main campus, where 55 percent of the square footage was occupied by buildings, was particularly disheartening.[44]

The other problem was money. Many of the buildings that went up had the appearance of having been built on the cheap. Not "cheap" in terms of the price paid, which always ran high because of building in Manhattan and on a site in full operation. But "cheap" in the relative amount that went into making these buildings more than functionally serviceable boxes within which a given educational enterprise might proceed. The John Dunnings and Courtney Browns who labored mightily to secure the millions needed to get their schools new buildings were not about to squander any significant portion of that hard-come-by money on aesthetic considerations or amenities. (William Warren was something of an exception here, as evidenced by the care that went into the Law School's classrooms and the Jacques Lipshitz sculpture adorning its entrance.) Having told his deans to go out and find the money to build their own buildings, even a more assertive Kirk would have been hard-pressed to hold them to the McKim master plan. As for the trustees, Percy Uris, the chair of the Buildings and Grounds Committee in the early 1960s—who, along with his brother, Harold, developed a fair portion of postwar New York City real estate, much of it uninspired white brick high rises—might well have regarded any of his money so spent wasted.[45]

The net effect of all this construction was to provide Columbia's professional schools with some much-needed additional working space but fell short of furnishing the universitywide psychological lift that more aesthetically pleasing or even exciting buildings might have offered. The criticism these buildings received only added to the sense that the campus was no longer a source of community pride but, in its latest accretions, yet another cause for embarrassment, another reason for institutional self-berating.

There Goes the Neighborhood

Nicholas Murray Butler told the story of driving around Morningside Heights in 1896 with trustee-to-be J. P. Morgan when the first buildings of the Morningside campus were going up. Butler advised Morgan that the university ought to buy up all the adjoining property from the Hudson River on the west to the Morningside bluff on the east and from the southern point around 110th Street to where the Heights ends, just beyond 123rd Street. The financial titan dismissed the young dean's idea by assuring him "that it will all be here for the buying whenever Columbia wants it." Butler's self-attribution of superior wisdom aside, the story effectively conveys what had long since become the conventional wisdom: that in not buying up more of Morningside Heights when Columbia moved there in the 1890s, its trustees had been penny wise and pound foolish.[46]

The completion of the subway to 110th Street in 1902 marked a turning point in Morningside's fortunes. Until then, the neighborhood consisted primarily of institutional structures, beginning with Grant's Tomb, under way in 1890, St. Luke's Hospital (1893), the Cathedral of St. John the Divine (1893), Teachers College (1894), Columbia University (1896), and Barnard College (1897). But access by subway sparked a wave of apartment building construction in the first decade of the new century. The north-south avenues on either side of the main Columbia campus, now Amsterdam Avenue and Broadway, were filled in by 1910, as were the two beyond them, Claremont Avenue to the west and Morningside Drive to the east. So, too, were the cross streets from 110th to 122nd, where once empty city lots had become the sites of the apartment buildings that still give the Heights its distinctive residential character. In the midst of all this middle-class respectability, there were still pockets for nighttime revelry, as on the corners of 110th Street and Broadway, where saloons and dance halls appeared in the 1910s.[47]

A second wave of apartment building in the 1920s filled in most of the east side of Riverside Drive with swanky apartments that looked out over the Hudson. They only confirmed the early reputation of Morningside Heights as a prosperous middle-class neighborhood, much classier, for example, than the still transitional Upper East Side. Columbia in the 1920s might not have owned as much of the neighborhood as its prescient president had wanted, but it enjoyed an eminently respectable address.[48]

All this began to change with the stock market crash of 1929 and the ensuing depression. Soon landlords found themselves with eight-room apartments designed for sizable families with live-in maids that their tenants could no longer afford. As a consequence, they chopped them up into smaller apartments, some into units that qualified as "SROs" (single-room occupancies). During the war, this subdividing, which had begun as a means of increasing rent rolls, acquired, in the face of a shortage of housing for single wartime workers, an added patriotic rationale. Among these single wartime workers were prostitutes who plied their trade on the cross streets immediately below Columbia, making them off limits to naval personnel living on campus. In the immediate postwar years, many of the wartime workers were replaced with clients of the city's various welfare agencies. The prostitutes stayed on.[49]

Some landlords, whose buildings generated rents insufficient to cover the costs of maintenance and taxes, simply walked away from them, leaving them to the banks holding the mortgage or to the city for unpaid back taxes. Citywide rent controls enacted during World War II also contributed to making these apartments a losing proposition for their owners. Abandoned buildings then became illegally occupied by squatters, some of whom mixed consumption of drugs with their dispensing either in dens in the buildings or on street corners and alleyways. Whether a building followed the SRO or the abandonment scenario, the cumulative effect was the same: a massive degentrification of a once-prosperous neighborhood on a magnitude in postwar New York City rivaled only by that occurring in parts of Brooklyn and the South Bronx.[50]

It is another commentary on the negative effects of Columbia's long interregnum in the late 1940s that its officials were slow to sound the alarm about the deteriorating neighborhood. Instead, the responsibility was taken up by then-thirty-two-year-old banker David Rockefeller in May 1947, when he organized a meeting of Morningside institutional residents, out of which came Morningside Heights, Inc. The Rockefellers had a substantial interest in the neighborhood, which was the home of both the Rockefeller-financed International House (1924) and the massive Riverside Church (1930), the family church, whose head minister, Harry Emerson Fosdick, was a trusted family adviser. They also envisioned the neighborhood as the site of a new family philanthropic undertaking, the construction of a building to house the national offices of the many Protestant church and missionary agencies then spread across the city. This hope became reality when in 1951 the Rockefellers bought property from Barnard College, the block south of Riverside Church, and began construction of what became in 1955 the Interchurch Center. Alas, it, too, has been criticized for architectural banality, although even a more exciting design might not have saved it from acquiring its local nickname: "The God Box."[51]

David Rockefeller presided over Morningside Heights, Inc., from 1949 until 1964. Its other members included Columbia, whose successive treasurers served as its treasurer during the Rockefeller presidency; Barnard, whose President Millicent McIntosh took an active role; Teachers College; Union Theological Seminary; the Jewish Theological Seminary; St. John the Divine; St. Luke's Hospital; the Juilliard School (until its move to Lincoln Center in 1969); and two neighborhood Catholic churches, Corpus Christi and the Eglise de Notre Dame. Early on, MHI worked closely with city and state officials, including Lawrence M. Orton, who simultaneously served as MHI's executive director and a member of Mayor O'Dwyer's City Planning Commission, and Robert Moses (CU Ph.D. 1919), who, along with his several statewide offices, was chair of the mayor's Slum Clearance Commission.[52]

MHI initially interested itself in all manner of good works, including a survey of the schools in the neighborhood and another on the quality of police protection. The latter was a particular concern at a time when juvenile gangs of a distinctly less romantic sort than the Jets and the Sharks depicted in Leonard Bernstein's *West Side Story* roamed the neighborhood. The Twenty-fourth

Precinct, which then encompassed most of Morningside Heights, was in the early 1950s one of the most crime-ridden precincts in the city. It probably did the neighborhood no good to have it identified as the research site for Lewis Yablonsky's *The Violent Gang* (1962) or that its author conducted his research while MHI's security director.[53]

But MHI's principal concern was the accelerating deterioration of the area's housing stock. It sought to counter this by supporting the construction of public housing on the northern edge of the neighborhood, between 123rd and 125th Streets (others considered this Harlem). Thus both the Morningside Gardens Apartments, a cooperative in which the tenants were shareholders, and the Grant Houses, a more traditional public housing complex, were built with the backing of MHI. They were at the time considered models of effective slum clearance and neighborhood rehabilitation. That they effectively placed a concrete barrier between Harlem proper north of 125th Street and the Morningside institutions south of 123rd Street was also noted.[54]

Another strategy MHI favored for combating neighborhood deterioration was pooling institutional resources to provide mortgages and construction money so that abandoned buildings could be bought by investors prepared to rehabilitate them. MHI did so through its own agency, Remedco, incorporated in 1949. When MHI found relatively few takers for these mortgages, some of its member institutions turned to buying up neighborhood properties on their own. By the late 1950s no one was doing this more aggressively than Columbia.[55]

Columbia offered two explanations for doing this. The first, essentially defensive, was that buying abandoned buildings and deteriorating SROs kept them from being trashed by squatters or used for illegal and locally disruptive purposes such as prostitution and drug dealing. The second, although this was not said openly, was that buying up these buildings precluded their use as dumping grounds by the city for its large and growing population of welfare and mental health clients.[56]

A further explanation was that properties acquired in the neighborhood could eventually be used should the university need, as it surely would, to expand. Thus a parcel of buildings on 122nd Street and Morningside was acquired with the stated intention of allowing Columbia to move its newly acquired School of Social Work from East Ninety-First Street to within a couple blocks of the main campus. Similarly, when Remedco bought "the notorious" Bryn Mawr, a once-elegant apartment building on Amsterdam and 121st Street that had become, after several downward iterations, an SRO and drug den, Barnard College was persuaded in 1966 to buy it as a future site for a dormitory. Plimpton Hall, completed in 1969, now occupies the space. That still left thirty SROs to go.[57]

In 1964 David Rockefeller stepped down as president of Morningside Heights, Inc., to focus his civic interests sixty blocks south in the area that became Lincoln Center. Grayson Kirk succeeded him as president and promptly installed the university treasurer William Bloor, who had been Columbia's chief acquirer of neighborhood properties, as MHI's principal operative. This may have given other institutional members cause to rethink the cooperative strategy in force since 1947, particularly in light of recent instances in which Columbia acquired properties that other members would have liked to have bid on. As MHI's largest institutional member and with what seemed to be the deepest pockets, Columbia appeared to some of its institutional neighbors the kind of friend who makes enemies unnecessary.[58]

By 1965 such internal tensions were the least of MHI's or Columbia's real estate problems. At least three neighborhood organizations had been organized to check what they saw as Columbia's attempted takeover of Morningside Heights and nearby Manhattanville, an area east and south of Morningside Park. Some who joined these organizations were undoubtedly Columbia baiters of dubious neighborhood standing, but others were lifelong residents who wanted limits placed on Columbia's expansion. Some, like Marie Runyon, who led the fight against evictions to make way for the transfer of the School of Social Work from East 91st Street to 122nd Street and Morningside, were a bit of both. When the university declined to discuss its plans for expansion in detail with these groups, stating that to do so would result in a run-up of prices, suspicions hardened into outright opposition.[59]

Nor did it help that Columbia's point man in the neighborhood was Stanley Salmen, whom Jacques Barzun had brought to Columbia from a Boston publishing house in 1956 to serve as coordinator of university plans. The provost greatly admired Salmen's skill in protecting Columbia's interests. He stayed in the job until 1967, leaving when Barzun resigned as provost. Others were less impressed with him, including President Kirk, who later remembered Salmen as someone "who always said what he had to say in the most irritating way possible." Barzun's own occasional attempts at neighborhood pacification were only marginally better, as when he characterized Columbia's desire for a neighborhood that "not be uninviting, abnormal, sinister, and dangerous."[60]

Whether troublemakers or concerned citizens, the members of these neighborhood organizations were voters. As such, their concerns became one with their locally elected officials', a fact that Columbia in the mid-1960s was slow to realize. Indeed, by then it had become incumbent on local politicians, from Congressman William Fitz Ryan to Manhattan borough president Constance Baker Motley (CU Law 1946) and city councilman Franz Leichter, to engage in a certain amount of Columbia bashing, if only to prove their independence.

Even citywide campaigns, such as John Lindsay's for mayor in 1965, treated Columbia as fair game in the effort to secure votes on the West Side.[61]

Two meetings President Kirk had with borough president Motley in late 1965 and early 1966 suggest the state of Columbia's political relations. The trustees minutes describe each as "not hostile" but "unproductive." Twenty years later, Kirk vividly recalled how Ms. Motley upbraided him for Columbia's unwillingness to open its neighborhood to its "fair share of the City's derelicts." She also told him that Columbia's further expansion into the neighborhood was unconstitutional. Upon returning to Low Library, Kirk informed his staff he would make no more such visits.[62]

The Era of the Packed Suitcase

An incoming psychology professor in 1957 found Morningside Heights "an utterly hostile environment." What he might have thought it in 1965 we do not know because he, William McGill, had decamped two years earlier for San Diego, where the state of California was in the process of building a brand-new campus with a view of the Pacific in suburban La Jolla. Fifteen years later, back on Morningside, he recalled thinking at the time he was going to "Nirvana."[63]

McGill was not alone in fleeing Columbia when the opportunity presented itself. The man whose position he took in the psychology department, Henry Garrett, left Columbia in 1956 for the University of Virginia "when the blacks got too much for him." During McGill's time in the department, several talented assistant professors took tenured positions elsewhere rather than await almost certain tenure at Columbia. Psychology was fairly typical of the university's departments and schools in the late 1950s and early 1960s, when Columbia found itself in what Provost Barzun called "the era of the packed suitcase."[64]

Faculty raiding had long been an accepted fact of life at the leading universities. The distinguished Columbia faculty over which Seth Low presided in the 1890s was to a substantial degree the result of raids on the faculties of Amherst, Bryn Mawr, and the University of Pennsylvania. Until World War I, Columbia was far more often the raider than the raided. In the 1920s the losses of the cytologist Thomas Hunt Morgan to Cal Tech, the sociologist William Ogburn to Chicago, the bacteriologist Hans Zinsser to Harvard, and several law faculty first to Johns Hopkins and then to Yale produced a more nearly balanced situation. The general slowing-down of the academic market in the 1930s correspondingly slowed the comings and goings on university campuses, including Columbia's.[65]

The trouble for Columbia began after the war, with the nonreturn of Harold Urey and Enrico Fermi from wartime postings at the University of Chicago providing a taste of what lay ahead. The departure of Columbia-trained and future Nobelist Norman Ramsey (CC 1935; CU Ph.D. 1940) for Harvard in 1947 was another. While most of the postwar raids were of individual faculty, others, like those of Columbia economists by the University of Chicago, in which Columbia lost three future Nobel Prize winners—Milton Friedman (CU Ph.D. 1946), George J. Stigler (faculty 1947–58), and Kenneth J. Arrow (CU Ph.D. 1951)—or that of the UCLA medical school's raiding of Physicians & Surgeons in the late 1950s, took on the character of mass abductions.

Specific cases suggest part of the general problem. Weather and parking aside, much of the lure of UC San Diego for McGill was that it offered him a chance to build a psychology department from scratch. No such possibility existed at Columbia, where his duties as chairman consisted largely of keeping the department's two entrenched factions from each other's throats. In such an environment, appointments and promotions were inevitably compromised by the need not to disrupt the department's political alignments. For the same reason, new specialties were avoided.[66]

Part of the departmental pathology McGill described had to do with individual personalities, but some of the problems also related to the fact that, compared with San Diego's, the Columbia psychology department had little potential for further growth. Postwar Columbia psychology, McGill quickly concluded upon his arrival, "was living off its legacy," but one could hardly say that of San Diego's department. As such, postwar Columbia operated at the same competitive disadvantage with upstarts like San Diego or with Stanford when it decided to compete in disciplines that it had earlier conceded to others, as did the other established eastern and midwestern universities. Fortune favored the young.[67]

Even in competition with the older universities, Columbia labored under other structural constraints. Unlike the great state universities, Michigan, Berkeley, and Wisconsin among them, Columbia had achieved its full size by the late 1920s. With growth came the opportunity to move into new areas rather than simply fill vacancies in already covered areas of a given discipline. Fortune favored the still growing.[68]

Unlike its traditional eastern competitors Yale and Princeton, which competed selectively, Columbia had from very early on in the century competed in virtually every academic and professional discipline known to Nicholas Murray Butler. Thus for postwar Yale to decide to build a world-class economics department or for Princeton to do the same in computer science meant two things for Columbia, neither good: more competition for Columbia in those fields; more incentive for Columbia faculty to go to Yale or Princeton.[69]

Columbia administrators responsible for faculty recruitment and retention were well aware of the disadvantages under which they operated. And they tried to offset them with moves of their own. Both President Kirk and Provost Barzun regularly urged the trustees to authorize early promotions and additional salary for sought-after faculty. They also acceded to requests from department chairs that such faculty be allowed to have reduced teaching programs and special leaves. As Barzun sardonically noted in the case of some sought-after faculty in the sciences, reducing further their already light teaching loads or increasing the frequency of leaves sometimes had the effect of taking them off the curricular books entirely.[70]

Deans and department chairs provided these new faculty with help finding jobs for their spouses and schools for their kids. Choice apartments on Riverside Drive or Claremont Avenue were other inducements for faculty to come and stay. In 1967 a twenty-eight-year-old assistant professor in history, David Rothman (CC 1958), only three years beyond his Ph.D., after the publication of his Harvard dissertation and with offers from Michigan and Wisconsin, was promptly promoted to associate professor with tenure. Between 1960 and 1968 faculty holding the rank of professor increased by almost twice the rate (42 percent) of associate and assistant professors (23 percent).[71]

During the era of the packed suitcase, faculty salaries acquired a sharply bimodal distribution, rather like a two-humped camel, with one hump at the lower end where low salaries were the norm and a smaller one at the upper end where the sought-afters were congregated. While matching the salaries of competitive bids was the order of the day in Low Library, the average salary increases were consistently less than those of Columbia's competition. In 1959 Columbia's faculty salaries ranked ninth in the overall AAUP listings; in 1964, seventeenth; in 1968, twentieth. In struggling to keep its most sought-after faculty, Columbia paid its other faculty substantially less than faculty elsewhere, including those teaching in New York's public universities. Thus the resultant drain occurred not only at the top of the faculty pecking order, where faculty left for more prestigious positions, but also in the middle and lower rungs, where faculty left for the various branches of the State University of New York such as Stony Brook and Binghamton for substantially more money.[72]

Columbia and the Rankings

An important indicator of a department's competitive ranking is its faculty comings and goings. This is especially so with rankings that are determined primarily by peer evaluations, which were the basis of the three widely reported rankings published in the 1950s and 1960s. In these, which departments are coming up and which slipping got decided in large part by respondents attentive to who was coming and who going. This being the case, faculty departures and rank declines are not only positively linked but mutually reinforcing: departmental rankings decline when faculty leave, and faculty leave when departmental rankings decline. But even if postwar faculty comings and goings and the postwar rankings of university departments were independent variables and their accuracy questionable, the rank slippage of postwar Columbia requires consideration. Given Columbia's role in the origins of university rankings back in the days of James McKeen Cattell and the involvement of its faculty in refining the methodology ever since, it would ill become Columbia to dismiss them out of hand.[73]

The MacMahon report, published in 1957, compared the most recently available rankings, those produced in a 1957 survey by Kenneth Keniston of the University of Pennsylvania, with the first such rankings survey, conducted in 1925 by Raymond Hughes, to buttress its argument that despite some ups and down in individual departments postwar Columbia seemed as firmly in third place as it had been twenty years earlier. Harvard ranked first in both surveys, and in the 1955 survey California displaced Chicago, which had dropped to seventh.[74]

The 1957 Keniston rankings very likely reflected a significant lag built into their methodological dependence on the perceptions of senior faculty in the respective fields. They may also have reflected a bias in favor of those departments that produced the largest numbers of Ph.D.s. Both of these factors help account for Columbia doing as well as it did. Their long-term effect, however, was only to defer the day of reckoning, which came soon enough. Rankings published in 1966, produced by Allan Cartter for the American Council on Education using data collected in 1964, showed declines in the standing of nearly every Columbia department. For some, such as physics and economics, the decline cast departments earlier ranked in the top five out of the top ten, while other departments, earlier in high single digits, found themselves in the high double digits and in a few cases—psychology, for example—out of the top twenty. The derived overall ranking for Columbia in these 1964 rankings was seventh, which meant that in the intervening seven years it had been passed by Yale, Stanford, Princeton, and Michigan. Although the 1964 ACE report did not say so, it was clear to its readers that Columbia was slipping fast.[75]

Some saw it coming. In 1959, after moving from dean of the Graduate Faculties to provost, Jacques Barzun used his first opportunity to address the trustees to sound the alarm: "Columbia cannot long sustain its work and its pretensions if the departments of instruction and their ancillary services are held to a regime of drastic self-denial in essential expense. It will soon be idle to speak of the University's academic parity with her great sister institutions on the East and West Coast. . . . I foresee despair overtaking our faculty and our administration if relief does not come soon."[76]

So, why didn't the trustees come up with the money? And if the answer was that they simply did not have it, where had it all gone?

Where Did All the Money Go?

At an unnoted but historic moment in the early 1960s, probably sometime in 1963, the annual income of Columbia University dropped below its annual expenses. Graphically, the upward slope of the annual income line flattened just enough and the upward slope of the annual expense line increased just enough that the two crossed. The rest, as the accountants later said, is history. It would take fifteen years and two presidencies to get them to cross back, so that income again exceeded expenses, as God intended.[77]

The uncertainty as to the precise point where Columbia went into structural deficit has to do with the way the university kept its books. In point of fact, there was no single set of books, but two. When presented to the trustees at their March meeting, each had its own distinctive format and typeface. First, there were the "downtown" books, which kept track of Columbia's nonacademic businesses and its endowment, which were the purview of the trustees' Finance Committee and the university treasurer, who reported not to the president but to the chair of the Finance Committee. Kirk's access to this side of the university, such as it was, came through a weekly Saturday morning meeting with the treasurer, often held downtown.[78]

Then there were the "uptown" books, which tracked tuition income, instructional costs, government grants, and the like. But, to further complicate matters, each of the schools kept its own books after its own fashion, so that, for example, those of the Business School and the Law School treated teaching adjuncts and office expenses differently, while the Medical School's books were inscrutable to all but the Medical School folks. Jacques Barzun, encountering this state of affairs upon becoming provost in 1958, set about to correct it. His principal mechanism for doing so, however—a regular meeting of the school deans to work through interschool transfer and all-university assessments—suggests that, when it came to the financial well-being of the university, President Kirk remained pretty much dependent on what his various deans told him it was.[79]

Even then, there was room for last-minute adjustments. Marion Jemmott, in the early 1960s the assistant secretary of the university, recalled a scene where Kirk and John Krout, vice president for academic administration, huddled over Kirk's desk forcing the Arts and Sciences Faculty's proposed budget into balance by eliminating the line of a professor thought to be terminally ill whose timely death would spare the budget his salary. For all of Barzun's efforts to bring order to Columbia's budgetary process, transparent it was not.[80]

But Columbia's financial disarray ran deeper than bookkeeping problems, though it had those aplenty, especially in the mid-1960s when the bursar and payroll offices attempted to shift over from manual to computerized record keeping. The more fundamental problem was that, through the first decade of his presidency, Kirk and his administrators relied on steadily increasing revenues from government contracts and foundation gifts to cover steadily increasing costs throughout the university. By the early 1960s some parts of the university not on the receiving end of these contracts and grants were not able to cover their expenses with tuition income or income from restricted funds. And the central administration had little or no uncommitted money with which to cover these shortfalls. Such was the situation many of the arts and sciences departments found themselves facing, even as other departments and some of the professional schools continued to enjoy the benefits of federal and corporate support.[81]

The disparity between what some parts of the academic enterprise got from external sources and what others got was not wholly unanticipated. In the case of the federal government's support of science, the expectation was that some part of its funding would go to help sustain the nonsciences. That's what indirect costs and overhead charges in government contracts were intended to do. But at Columbia, as the case of Lamont showed, actually retrieving the overhead from the departments receiving federal grants and schools to help with expenses in the tuition-dependent departments and schools required more centralized authority than President Kirk possessed.[82]

The problem of spreading the income received from the federal government around the university was real even in the years of steadily increasing federal income. It became much more severe beginning in 1964, when federal funding of the elite universities in the sciences leveled off as the government's interest in universities narrowed to those willing to produce military weaponry or conduct applied secret research rather than including those who wished to limit themselves to pure science and publicly conducted research. Columbia's scientists in the early 1960s fell overwhelmingly into the second category, to the university's credit, perhaps, but also to its financial disadvantage.[83]

Thus, Kirk's 1964 assurances to the trustees notwithstanding, any slowing of external federal and foundation funding inevitably had a serious impact on a university that had come to depend on it as much as Columbia had. What made the Columbia situation more exposed than other major universities' was what was simultaneously happening (or not happening) to the three other lines that made up the income side of a private university's balance sheet: tuition and fees, endowment management, and alumni giving.

Student-generated tuition and fees provided a major source of income available to postwar private universities. But here, too, Columbia had a problem. Insofar as tuition revenues are primarily a function of enrollments and only secondarily a function of pricing, increased tuition revenues are principally derived through increases in enrollment. In the case of postwar Columbia, its high-growth era was three decades earlier. Once the GI Bill–induced enrollment spike in the late 1940s subsided, Columbia enrollments were flat throughout the 1950s. And then in the early 1960s they started to drop, especially in the traditionally tuition-dependent arts and sciences.[84]

The enrollment losses within arts and sciences in the 1960s were concentrated in two areas: in General Studies and the humanities and social science graduate departments. In both cases, some of the reductions were intentional, meant to raise the quality of incoming students. Columbia's Extension Program had long drawn criticism from some quarters for offering undemanding courses in subjects far removed from the traditional arts and sciences regimen. In 1931, for example, Abraham Flexner reprovingly pointed to courses Columbia offered in " 'magazine articles,' 'advertising layouts,' 'story telling,' 'direct-by-mail selling and advertising,' And 'photoplay composition.' "[85]

Meanwhile, on campus, the presence of thousands of General Studies students with varying amounts of academic preparation trying to talk their way into courses open only to students in the College had prompted some members of the College faculty and alumni to call for the elimination of General Studies altogether. The 1958 MacMahon report came very close to doing so. In response, some GS administrators were persuaded that tightening their admissions policies would improve the school's standing within the university and eliminate the need for them to apologize for using adjuncts to teach courses in bookkeeping and millinery. By the late 1950s downsizing in the name of quality enhancement had become part of the conventional wisdom.[86]

There was also the economic reality that Columbia's high tuition priced its various extension and adult-learning programs out of a New York City market increasingly crowded with competing programs aggressively promoted by NYU, the New School, Cooper Union, and a proliferating number of for-profit schools and institutes, each with its own brightly colored street-corner catalog dispenser. Whatever the mix of causes, the effect was that the seven thousand tuition-paying GS students in 1959 was reduced by the mid-1960s to forty-two hundred. The positive qualitative impact of this change was arguable; the negative financial impact was indisputable. Even in the early 1970s, as an unfavorably disposed administrator acknowledged in 1970, "no matter what resentments persons may have about the School of General Studies, it is reasonably solvent."[87]

Columbia's graduate programs had long been famous (infamous?) for their willingness to accept more first-year and terminal M.A. students than did other universities of similar repute. "Factory" was only one of the terms applied to them, not least by their graduates. A per-course tuition plan had made part-time attendance over many years financially feasible. The result was that first-year graduate courses of 125 or so students were common in the history, English, and French departments into the early 1960s. Most of these students would leave after a self-financed year or two with or without an M.A. to show for their efforts; relatively few stayed—or were permitted to continue as Ph.D. candidates. Whereas some critics saw this come-one-come-all policy as wholly mercenary and consistent with Columbia's reputation as a degree mill, others defended it on the basis that Columbia provided a second chance for students with weak academic credentials or from undistinguished colleges to demonstrate their intellectual capabilities. Both critics and defenders acknowledged that the system did not allow for a great deal of mentor-student interaction, even between students writing their dissertations and their sponsors.[88]

On balance, most postwar faculty understandably favored the admission of fewer and more academically certifiable students with either full scholarships or the prospects of securing one after the first year over the traditionally more numerous and more variegated students. And so standards were raised. Entering graduate classes in history that in the late 1950s regularly exceeded 150 were less than half that large in 1968. Comparable drops occurred throughout most other social science and humanities graduate programs.[89]

Of course, enrollment drops of this magnitude, with their inevitable impact on the university's income, might have been accompanied by comparable cuts in faculty size, effecting a corresponding reduction in the university's expenditures. Unfortunately for the bottom line, the decrease in enrollments in the arts and sciences at Columbia in the 1960s was accompanied by a substantial increase in the size of the arts and sciences faculty. When this was pointed out in 1969, it seemed to come as a surprise.[90]

Endowment management was another potential source of added revenue for postwar Columbia. While no longer among the universities with the largest—it ranked fourth in 1960—an endowment of some $142 million might have been expected to produce a steadily increasing return, especially that part of it invested in the stock market. Unfortunately for Columbia, most of its endowment remained tied up in Manhattan real estate, and the biggest single part of that in what remained of the Upper Estate, the eleven acres of land underneath Rockefeller Center. The annual return on this property was fixed according to long-term leases between the university and the Rockefeller family. The first lease had been negotiated in 1929 and provided for a $3 million annual payment to Columbia. This was at a time when the university's expense budget was $8 million. When this lease was renewed in 1951, the fact that the Rockefellers had during most of the intervening twenty years lost money on Rockefeller Center led outside arbitrators to set the new rent again at $3 million, with an annual increment of $150,000. This meant that in 1960 the university's annual income from the site had climbed to only about $4 million, or just 25 percent more than it had been more than three decades earlier. Meanwhile, the university's expense budget had grown to $270 million, or more than thirty times more than it had been when the last lease renewal was negotiated. With the next lease renewal not due until 1971, Columbia had as the centerpiece of its endowment one of the most valuable properties in the world, over which it had little control and from which it derived little in the way of usable income. This situation would not be fundamentally altered until 1985, when the university sold the land to the Rockefellers.[91]

Whatever other money came in was put not into securities that could be expected to appreciate but rather into buying up apartment buildings around the university. "I was attempting," said Kirk, recalling the operative strategy of his presidency, "to acquire as much real estate around the periphery as I could." These buildings usually required more money to renovate. Forty years later, this investment can be said to have paid off by providing Columbia with buildings to house some of its faculty, staff, and graduate students and serving as a modest generator of income. In the 1960s, however, it represented yet another way of tying up a large share of the university's wealth in ways that made it inaccessible to those charged with paying Columbia's bills.[92]

Throughout the postwar era, Columbia's income from fund-raising efforts among its alumni, both in absolute terms and as a fraction of total income, ran well behind that of its peers. This had been the case since at least the 1920s, when the sophisticated strategies developed by Price, Jones Company and other professional fund-raisers made annual giving and periodic capital campaigns regular features elsewhere, even as they were shunned by Columbia's trustees. This remained the board's prevailing policy at the outset of Grayson's Kirk's presidency in 1953, when Chairman Coykendall gave him the following advice: "He wanted me to spend no time on fundraising whatever. He said spend your time on education. We've got income from student fees. We've got income from our endowment. Cut your budget to fit that income and don't worry about fundraising." As for gifts from trustees, there seems to have been throughout the 1950s an informal $1 million limit on them, which Trustee William Paley discovered when he offered to underwrite a multimillion-dollar arts program. The gift was declined.[93]

Meanwhile, unwilling to put the loyalties of Columbia alumni—and perhaps their own pockets—to the test in a universitywide capital campaign, the trustees only reluctantly went along in the 1950s with the fund-raising campaigns insisted upon by the deans of several of the professional schools. While these efforts paid for several new buildings and underwrote improvements in professional curricula, they did not do much to improve Columbia's overall financial picture, as practically none of the money raised went into the endowment. And by increasing maintenance costs, these new buildings represented yet another drain on general resources.

The fund-raising activities of the professional schools also did little to alter the situation of the chronically cash-short Graduate Faculties, which, according to Kirk, showed no interest in mounting campaigns of their own. What the fund-raising successes of the professional schools did accomplish was make the graduate faculty more acutely aware of their relative poverty. In 1950 Business School faculty salaries paid to economists were well below those paid to economists in arts and sciences; in 1965 they were substantially above. As for the College, its fund-raising efforts for a decade after 1958 were held hostage to the need to pay for an ill-fated undergraduate gymnasium, about which more later.[94]

It was only in 1964 that Kirk, twelve years into his presidency, at the urging of his vice president for academic administration, Lawrence Chamberlain, and likely against the advice of his provost, Jacques Barzun, decided reluctantly that the university had to undertake a capital campaign. With grants from "my good friend, Mac Bundy" at the Ford Foundation in hand, one of $10 million for urban studies and the other for $25 million for general purposes to be matched on a one-to-four basis, the time had come. At the founder's day dinner on October 31, 1966, President Kirk launched the first comprehensive capital campaign in the university's history and the largest ever undertaken by an American university: the $200 million Campaign for Columbia.[95]

Better late than never? Not necessarily. The decision to launch a major capital campaign in 1965 had an immediate impact on Columbia matters large and small, from the share of the president's schedule given over to off-campus fund-raising to a heightened sensitivity to press coverage of campus affairs. Both of these would play into the events of 1968. A year earlier, in the summer of 1967, the exigencies of the campaign were partly responsible for a major shakeup in Kirk's administration, one that saw Lawrence Chamberlain off to an early retirement and sent Jacques Barzun back to the faculty as university professor. In filling both positions with one man, the heretofore dean of Columbia College, David Truman, Kirk proceeded into the fateful academic year of 1967–68 with a thinly staffed and untested administration.[96]

The choice of Truman as provost had not been the president's. An offer of the provostship of Stanford to Truman and vigorous College lobbying among faculty and alumni for his appointment had precipitated it. Nor was the incumbent at all happy that Truman's elevation made him the odds-on choice to be his successor and that its timing implied that some of Truman's backers felt the sooner this change occurred, the better. Kirk already had some reason to think that Butler—and Barzun—were right: capital campaigns cost more than they are worth. He soon had more.[97]

The Alienation of The College

The long College deanship of Herbert Hawkes ended uneventfully in 1943, to be followed by that of Harry Carman, arguably the most beloved dean in the annals of Columbia history. Upon Carman's retirement in 1949, Lawrence Chamberlain, a member of the political science department, became dean of the College. His popular and successful deanship lasted eight years, until 1958, when a member of the law faculty, John Gorham Palfrey, succeeded him. (Chamberlain shortly thereafter was asked by President Kirk to resume administrative duties as his vice president for academic administration.) Palfrey served only three years, before going to Washington to join the Atomic Energy Commission.[98]

At this juncture, a faculty search committee, chaired by Lionel Trilling, recommended the appointment of another member of the political science department, David Truman, author of *The Governmental Process* (1951) and authority in the field of political organization. A one-time member of the Williams College faculty, Truman, in ten years at Columbia, had become a devoted member of the College faculty. Even so, with a considerable reputation as a scholar, he surprised some of his graduate colleagues when he enthusiastically agreed to take the administrative job. Several others, similarly identified with the College, had declined the position. With the approval of the trustees, President Kirk, who did not personally know Truman, appointed him dean, effective July 1, 1963. Members of the College faculty and active alumni greeted his appointment with enthusiasm and high hopes, seeing it as the best opportunity in the century to put the College back at the center of the university.[99]

Unlike the faculties of most of the professional schools, Barnard, and Teachers College, the Columbia College faculty drew its professorial members from other faculties, principally the Graduate Faculties of Political Science, Philosophy, and Pure Science. In practice, these designated faculty did part or all of their teaching in the College. This could be for a stated period of time, a three-year rotation being the norm, as determined by the faculty member or his department (no women taught in the College before 1965). A few voting members of the College faculty after 1959 owed their membership as preceptors directly to the dean of the College, but they were usually graduate students working on their dissertations. Deans and admissions officers of the College who worked in Hamilton Hall were also members, and some of these taught an occasional College course.[100]

The College faculty in 1960 consisted of 175 voting members. A third of these might be called complimentary members, faculty who occasionally attended a College faculty meeting and periodically served on a College committee but whose principal loci of operation were their graduate departments. This was the case with most of the scientists, with the exception of those specifically designated by their departments to concentrate their teaching in the College. Some graduate departments—philosophy, for example—made it a practice to have most of their faculty members of the College faculty, but other departments—sociology, for example—had only a few.[101]

Atop the faculty pecking order of postwar Columbia were the graduate departments, whose personnel committees controlled appointments and promotions, whose chairmen recommended salary adjustments and approved teaching programs, and whose principal concerns were providing graduate instruction and a suitable environment for faculty to carry on their research. A senior member of the history department once asked solicitously of Henry Graff, then teaching in the College, "When are you going to come across the street and join us?"[102]

At the bottom of the pecking order resided the General Studies faculty. While having the same subordinate relationship to their disciplinary departments as the College faculty, GS faculty, from the perspective of the College, labored under the burden of teaching students drawn from a decidedly mixed bag. The Faculty of General Studies had been established as a separate faculty in 1952, five years after the School of General Studies was created. Evidence of their subordinate position came in two forms: they were dependent on the graduate departments for recognition, advancement, and salary; they were where the few women with teaching appointments at Columbia into the 1960s were mostly concentrated.[103]

Some dispute existed over where the Barnard College faculty had a place in the hierarchy of Columbia undergraduate faculties. But given the fact that in the early 1960s twenty or so Barnard faculty held appointments in the Graduate Faculties, whereas some members of the College and most members of the GS faculties did not, it was at least arguable that the Barnard faculty fell somewhere between the College and the GS faculties. The Barnard faculty was more self-governing than was either the College or GS faculty and had more control over its own appointments and (until 1973) over the tenuring of its faculty. On the other hand, the fact that Barnard faculty were paid less and taught more and that they mostly taught young women all served to diminish, in the operative coin of the era, their standing.[104]

Teachers College faculty had an even more problematic standing among Columbia faculties. A few members, in history and psychology, for example, held appointments in their cognate Columbia graduate departments, but because most were in fields such as school administration and curriculum development that had no Columbia departmental equivalents, they had little contact with Columbia faculty. This did not keep some of the latter from occasionally engaging in a certain amount of the Ed School bashing that was in favor in the late 1950s. When Columbia faculty referred to 120th Street, which separates Columbia and Teachers College, as "the widest street in America," they were not above deriving some measure of protective satisfaction from its being so.[105]

Yet among Columbia College faculty loyalists such as the philosopher Charles Frankel, the literary scholar Carl Hovde, and the political scientist David Truman, GS and its faculty bore the closest watching. As a member of the McMahon review committee, Frankel had tried to secure committee support for the abolition of GS. Between the College's English department and that of General Studies in the 1960s, Hovde later recalled, there was "real tension . . . almost warfare." Both Carolyn Heilbrun and Joan Ferrante, then assigned to the General Studies wing of English, have since confirmed this characterization. When General Studies secured the right to grant the A.B. as well as the B.S. to its graduates in 1967, over almost unanimous opposition from the College faculty, Truman was reported to have been in tears.[106]

While the concept of a pecking order gets at some of the prejudices operative in the postwar Columbia faculties, it fails to convey the positive loyalties that one's place in the scheme could produce. The reality is more closely approximated by reference to class, or caste. The core of the Columbia College faculty consisted of faculty who were both intensely loyal to and identified with what the College stood for—what Erskine famously described and Trilling endorsed as "the moral obligation to be intelligent." And some were uninterested in or disdainful of the work of their graduate school colleagues. Harrison R. Steeves in the English department, for example, simply refused to teach graduate courses, while others, such as Sidney Morgenbesser in philosophy, Moses Hadas in classics, and Karl-Ludwig Selig in Spanish, devoted most of their energies to teaching in the College. Still others, such as C. Wright Mills in sociology and James Shenton in history, did so with the added understanding that their departments preferred it that way.

Some of these unrepentant College faculty were productive scholars, some were not, and others would become so but for the moment were caught up with the excitement of teaching in the College. They also responded positively to the collegial atmosphere of Hamilton Hall, as against the all-business character of their graduate departments. In some ways, their view of academic life was closer to that of faculty at Amherst or Williams or Swarthmore than those at Michigan or Berkeley—or elsewhere at Columbia.[107]

The College's faculty in the main regarded the teaching of undergraduates as a noble calling. But many also deeply resented the subordination of that place by their graduate school colleagues, by faculty in the professional schools, and by the administrators in Low Library. A certain degree of alienation from the rest of the university was the inevitable result. Nor was such alienation totally unwarranted. Not since Charles King in the 1850s (discounting Ike's good intentions) had Columbia known a president who was not in some way a College Skeptic. Barnard, Low, Butler, and Kirk were all very much suspicious of the Hamilton Hall ethos. A quarter-century later, Kirk recalled approvingly Justus Buchler's 1960 characterization of the College: "It is dormant, threatening to smother in its own piety."[108]

Thus it came as something of a surprise that in the summer of 1967 Dean David B. Truman, a College Believer if there ever was one, moved into Low Library as provost of the university and, in doing so, became the front-runner to be Columbia's next president. For his part, Barzun, after being offered the position of provost of the professional schools, left quietly. He had stayed longer than he had agreed to and, now viewed as too old to be considered for the presidency, perhaps saw no constructive purpose in staying on in administrative harness. His account of his experience as Columbia's provost, which is conveyed inter alia in *The American University*, was elegantly sardonic rather than bitter, but reflective of an alienation from the university and its "higher bankruptcy" that is virtually complete.[109]

Truman's unexpected appointment as provost also had the consequence of leaving the College in mid-1967 without a dean. Henry Coleman (CC 1946), who had been director of admissions since 1960 and, for a decade before that, assistant to the dean, was made acting dean, while a search committee looked for an official replacement. It proved to be a difficult task, with several members of the Columbia College faculty declining to be considered and at least two attractive prospects, Professors Theodore William de Bary and Fritz Stern, declining offers of the position, pointing to long-standing scholarly obligations. It was a job seemingly without takers, even among those who identified with the College. The following April, nine months after the vacancy occurred and the committee began its search, a viable candidate had still not been found. By then, it was April 1968, and the search was overtaken by events that emanated from the College but were of such disruptive force as to put the entire university's future in doubt.[110]

CHAPTER 15

Riding the Whirlwind: Columbia '68

> Worrying about the collapse of Columbia was the farthest thing from my mind.
>> *Strike Coordinating Committee member Mark D. Naison (CC 1966)*

> You know, for Christ's sake, this isn't the Winter Palace. This is cruddy little Fayerweather Hall.
>> *Strike Coordinating Committee member Rusty Eisenberg*

> We were riding the whirlwind.
>> *SDS leader Lewis Cole (CC 1968)*

> At 2:30 this morning, Columbia University died.
>> *SDS flyer, April 30, 1968*

The Revival of Student Activism on Morningside

A S ON other campuses, Columbia through its history has experienced two kinds of student misbehavior. The more common might be classified as simple rowdiness. Examples include the kinds of behavior George Templeton Strong regularly reported in his diary, such as rearranging classroom furniture, producing minor explosions in Renwick's lab, and carousing outside faculty quarters. In Butler's student days, rowdiness took the form of turning over horse carts on either side of the Forty-ninth Street campus. Beginning in the 1890s football rallies and the games themselves became occasions for one or another form of often inebriated student excess. In the 1920s fraternity rivalries provided other occasions, as did the panty raids of the 1950s and the seventies' phenomenon of streaking.[1]

While not without their occasional indulgence in rowdiness, Columbia students have been more closely identified with a second form of student misbehavior, that which is the byproduct of social activism and manifests itself in political protest. And only relatively recently has such student protest come almost exclusively from the left. In the 1770s, King's College students for the most part aligned themselves with their parents, faculty, and the College's governors in opposition to the revolutionary forces. Similarly, Columbia students protested against the embargo of 1807 and the War of 1812, understanding both to be schemes of the Jeffersonians to bankrupt New Yorkers and destroy the Federalist Party, with which early-nineteenth-century Columbia was aligned.

Columbia students did not join the Abolitionist protests of the 1830s, as few respectable New Yorkers did, but they were out in full force to protect the College and private property against the draft rioters in 1863. Their patriotism knew no bounds on the eve of the Spanish-American War, and their conflicted views took many demonstrative forms in the months leading up to the entry of the United States into the Great War. Even in the generally quiescent 1920s, during which most students were resolutely apolitical, Columbia students such as Whittaker Chambers could become fully engaged in a quixotic effort to rouse campus support for the 1924 presidential candidacy of Calvin Coolidge.[2]

The coming of the Depression and the specter of Fascism in the 1930s gave Columbia student protest its recognizable character and provides the immediate historical context for the revival of student protest in the 1960s. As such, several aspects of that earlier activism bear reviewing here. The first was that the 1930s campus activism came from the left—in support of unions, in opposition to rearmament, in repudiating Fascism, in urging the New Deal to do more to meet the needs of the needy. Students espousing Socialism, Communism, or some Marxist position in between encountered little opposition from students on the right. For example, although a vocal student contingent supported the Oxford Pledge and dismissed the New Deal as "merely political pragmatism," little was heard on campus from America Firsters or even Wendell Wilkie backers in 1940, whereas both were well represented by student groups at Harvard, Yale, Princeton, and elsewhere. Permanently gone, it seemed, were the days when Columbia students could be counted on to have a good word for the Loyalists, the Federalists, the Cotton Whigs, the Republicans, or the munitions manufacturers.[3]

Another aspect of student political activism in the 1930s was how easily it produced a demonized view of the university's administration. Columbia was not merely the place where protesting students happened to be and therefore the base for their efforts; Columbia, and specifically Nicholas Murray Butler and his trustees, became a target. In the eyes of protesting students, they represented not unreasonable exercisers of in locus parentis so much as the corrupt and discredited ruling class.

A third feature of student activism in the 1930s was how seldom it addressed specifically student issues. To the extent that they were included, as in asserting students' right to free speech on campus, it was to enable them to press an outwardly directed political agenda. They did not, for example, protest much about the curriculum or about parietal rules. Nor did they openly question admissions policies or tuition rates. Their complaints were not those of dissatisfied educational consumers but of agitated citizens and, in a few cases, revolutionaries in the making. Even the antifootball views of the *Columbia Spectator* under the editorship of Reed Harris spoke to the sport's capitalistic commercialization rather than to its impact on student life. Butler was to be editorially condemned—and depicted in a cartoon beating babies—not for what he did on campus but for such public acts as opposing a constitutional amendment prohibiting child labor.[4]

Accordingly, the 1930s student activists largely exempted the faculty from the criticisms they leveled at those who ran Columbia—despite the fact that few faculty openly sided with students in their arguments with Butler and the trustees. However humbling such an exemption was to those who believed "we are the university," Columbia faculty in the 1930s seemed grateful to be out of the direct line of student fire. That's what administrators got paid to do.

Student political activism subsided with the United States' entry into World War II, a decision, when it came, that was opposed by only a handful of on-campus pacifists. Nor were the immediate postwar years, with hundreds of veterans on campus, propitious for rekindling the political passions of the 1930s. The Korean War provoked no more opposition at Columbia than it did elsewhere, even as it occasioned a fresh wave of Columbia students drafted into and volunteering for military service.

By the mid-1950s, however, concern with what was viewed as an unduly aggressive nuclear strategy in the cold war and opposition to the construction of bomb shelters led to the establishment of a campus chapter of SANE. Air-raid drills on campus provoked scattered protests, as did a proposal in the mid-1950s to construct a bomb shelter for the university. Fidel Castro's success in Cuba produced a handful of Morningside Fidelistas, including the sociologist C. Wright Mills, who were cheered by his impromptu visit to the campus in 1959. But more typical of the political activism of the late 1950s was the support Columbia students (and faculty) gave the presidential campaigns of Adlai Stevenson in 1952 and 1956 and to that of John F. Kennedy in 1960. The alacrity with which several dozen Columbians volunteered for the Peace Corps upon its creation in 1961 spoke to their seriousness of purpose.[5]

Columbia students in the 1950s participated in boycotts of New York outlets of national chains such as Woolworths, whose stores in the South discriminated against blacks. Others belonged to an Upper West Side chapter of the NAACP. But serious agitation on the civil rights front did not begin until the summer of 1964, when the first major expeditions of northern college students went south to help with voter registration drives. One of these expeditions, organized by Columbia historian Jim Shenton, left its student participants deeply affected, not only by the injustice of racial inequality they encountered in the South but by the complicity of state officials and institutions.[6]

In 1964 Columbia College, under the direction of the dean of admissions, Henry Coleman (CC 1946), began to recruit black students. There had been black students at Columbia earlier, but now they were to be actively recruited with the twin purposes of providing them with a Columbia education and their white classmates with a more diversified educational and social environment. Some of the first recruited black students came from upper-middle-class and professional backgrounds, such as Hilton Clark (CC 1968), the son of the CCNY psychologist (and Columbia Ph.D.) Kenneth Clark, who was raised in upscale Scarsdale. But most others came from families in which they were the first to go to college and from economic circumstances that made necessary substantial financial assistance. Barnard also undertook a program to recruit black women students from among the graduates of urban high schools.[7]

By the second year of recruiting, 1965, the number of black students in Columbia College had increased to fifty. Another forty or so black women were attending Barnard. Together, they created their own social life. The men established two on-campus fraternities, Omega Psi Phi and Alpha Phi Alpha, while Barnard women organized BOSS (Barnard Organization of Soul Sisters). In 1965 Columbia black undergraduates formed the Society of Afro-American Students (SAS).[8]

Others among this first contingent of black students directed their organizational energies elsewhere. Some athletes centered their social lives around their teammates, black and white. Others looked off campus, specifically to Harlem, in an effort to maintain ties to the black community outside Columbia. This meant joining with Harlem community activists in organizing rent strikes, protesting police brutality, and participating in all manner of off-campus civil rights protests. As one who cast his lot with Harlem, William Sales (CC 1969) later recalled, Columbia's black students could either be "Columbians who happened to be black" or "blacks who happened to go to Columbia." It is not clear which of these persuasions had more adherents before 1968. What is clear, with hindsight, is that the events of 1968 turned many heretofore "Columbians who happened to be black" into "blacks who happened to go to Columbia."[9]

Columbia College's black students played a significant role in the events of 1968, though they were neither numerous nor the most comprehensively engaged in the events that led up to them. Indeed, until the spring of 1968, there was little reason to believe that black students had a political agenda. Some, like Bill Sales, were more interested in what was going on in Harlem than on campus. Others were involved in their fraternities and sports, and still others focused on their studies. The elected officers of SAS before those installed in the spring of 1968 were typical student leaders, in arguing for some specific issues, to be sure, but not so vigorously as to disrupt campus life or their own collegiate careers, much less bring the university to its knees. Columbia students ready to do this were to be found elsewhere.[10]

The Rise of SDS

In 1962 a twenty-one-year-old University of Michigan undergraduate, Tom Hayden, along with some like-minded Ann Arbor student activists, produced the *Port Huron Statement*. It laid out the founding principles of the organization they called "Students for a Democratic Society." The *Statement* effectively captured the predicament in which many young political activists saw themselves in the early 1960s, that is, disillusioned with the bromides of the old left and alert to Stalinist authoritarianism yet unwilling to settle for what they saw as the corporate liberalism of John F. Kennedy's New Frontier. SDS sought to provide the vehicle by which a campus-community-labor new left alliance could seize the ideological high ground and bring about permanent change in U.S. society, even as it checked U.S. aggression abroad.[11]

By 1964 some forty campuses had their own SDS chapters, each undertaking to educate those within hearing about the evils of capitalism, the plight of blacks, and the perfidies of the military-industrial complex. A year later, SDSers on campus began to focus on U.S. military involvement in Vietnam and to condemn plans to expand the already substantial U.S. presence there. It is at this point, on March 10, 1965, that a handful of Columbia undergraduates, including Ted Kaptchuk (CC 1968) and Dave Gilbert (CC 1967) established the fifty-second chapter of SDS. Asked how to account for the lag between the founding of SDS in 1962 and the forming of a Columbia chapter three years later, one SDSer later attributed it to a suspicion among his fellow Columbians of SDS's "midwestern origins." Ah, New York.[12]

Columbia's SDS chapter maintained a fairly low profile in its early months. Rather than attempt to command attention by some dramatic action, its leaders concentrated on building up membership through forums at which off-campus radicals and sympathetic faculty participated. Much effort went into investigating and publicizing the ties between Columbia and the defense establishment. This early strategy, identified with Ted Kaptchuk, was later referred to by its critics as the "praxis axis," as opposed to what later became the dominant strategy of confrontation, the "action faction" favored by Mark Rudd (CC 1965–68).[13]

SDS was by no means the only locus for student political activity. The Columbia Citizenship Council (CCC) was a Ferris-Booth Hall–based student-run organization founded in 1959 that provided tutoring for neighborhood children and help with rehabilitation efforts. By 1965 it had become involved with some political action groups in Harlem and had begun organizing tenant rent strikes. Like SDS, the students involved in CCC were nearly all white, although it did have a few Puerto Rican members, among them Juan Gonzalez (CC 1968), who later was active in the Puerto Rican Young Lords and eventually became an investigative reporter for the New York *Daily News*.[14]

With the escalation of U.S. involvement in Vietnam in 1965 came campus offshoots of national antiwar groups. Some of these were old-line pacifist groups who found themselves welcomed at Earl Hall, where the chaplains, except the Newman Club chaplain Monsignor John Rea, openly supported the antiwar movement. Students of a radical bent could all count on a sympathetic ear from the newly installed university chaplain, John Cannon; the adviser to Protestant students, the Episcopalian Rev. William Starr; and the adviser to Jewish students, Rabbi Bruce Goldman.[15]

Finally, there was what passed for the organizational successor to the College Student Council, which had by student referendum voted itself out of existence in 1961. The organization the referendum organizers intended to replace the council, the Student Assembly, never materialized. (By then, the deans in Hamilton and the administrators in Low were quite prepared to live without either.) What remained was the Columbia University Student Council (CUSC), made up of elected student delegates of all the university's sixteen schools, Barnard, Teachers College, and Union Theological Seminary. Its actions, however, were frequently dismissed by Low Library as those of a handful of self-interested students, many of whom were not even at Columbia (as opposed to Barnard, Teachers College, and Union). The absence of a genuinely representative student council in 1968 proved to be doubly damaging: it foreclosed the possibility of university officials negotiating with a student group other than those on one side or the other of the barricades, and it deprived the majority of students in the middle, who neither supported the actions of the protesters nor aligned themselves with the counterprotesters, of a medium through which their views could be given the weight to which their numbers entitled them.[16]

The students who joined SDS, CCC, and antiwar groups and who became sufficiently persuaded of the complicity of the university in the perpetuation of whatever evil they were protesting to move to shut it down were a minority within a minority. In the fall of 1967 some twenty thousand students were enrolled at Columbia University. Of these, approximately six thousand (30 percent) were undergraduates, twenty-seven hundred of whom were enrolled in Columbia College, eight hundred in engineering, eighteen hundred at Barnard College, and seven hundred enrolled full-time in General Studies. Radical student organizations that same fall probably had no more than a total of three hundred members, with another seven hundred or so expressing sympathy with their causes. SDS, for example, never had more than fifty core members, with another hundred or so who could be counted on to lend support to SDS actions. CCC was slightly larger, but by no means did most of its members favor disruptive protest. Both SDS and CCC had some members who were in the Law School and the School of Architecture or over at TC, and a substantial number came from the graduate school, but if students from the Business School or Journalism or Engineering or Physicians & Surgeons were involved, evidence of this has eluded me. The overwhelming majority of organizationally connected student activists on the Columbia campus were undergraduates.[17]

A substantial portion of the student radicals came from politically active radical backgrounds. This was especially true, for example, of many of the SDS leaders, among them Mark Rudd, Lewis Cole, David Gilbert, David Shapiro, Harvey Bloom, and Nancy Foner. These so-called red diaper babies mostly came from New York (or from the city's surrounding suburbs, where their parents had recently moved) and were likely to be Jewish. There were few intercollegiate athletes among them, and still fewer fraternity members. Many lived off campus. Relatively few majored in the sciences or were premed; those with identifiable majors were in history, philosophy, and English. Some were excellent students; others slid by.[18]

In helping me fill out this sociological profile, Lewis Cole, a leading member of SDS in the late 1960s and now a professor of film in the School of the Arts, offered the suggestion that he and a large number of his closest friends on the left got into Columbia in the mid-1960s under a policy by which the Columbia College admissions office reserved 10 percent of each class for students it was willing to bet on the basis of high test scores were bright but who had lousy grades, which could be attributed to high-school boredom. If so, there is a delicious irony in attributing some responsibility for the radicalization of Columbia undergraduates in the late 1960s to none other than Nicholas Murray Butler's creation, the college boards.[19]

Campus protest activity first turned confrontational on May 7, 1965. The occasion was the annual ceremony that marked the commissioning of the graduates of Columbia's Naval Reserve Officer Training Corps. Established in 1946, it annually commissioned some twenty-five regular officers who had enrolled at Columbia four years earlier on full-tuition grants provided by the navy, which the students repaid with three years (later, four years) of active service.

The navy hoped some of these Columbians would stay on for full careers, but few did. It also commissioned another twenty-five nonscholarship students who received commissions in the Naval Reserve and were expected to serve on active duty for two years. NROTC students wore uniforms to class one after-noon a week, took one course each semester in some aspect of naval science taught by naval officers who had courtesy appointments in the Columbia Col-lege faculty. Aside from keeping their hair short, they were scarcely distin-guishable from other Columbia students.[20]

While NROTC students figured in the athletic and fraternity life on campus, it is fair to say that they were not equally represented in the ranks of student political activists. When the May 7 commissioning ceremony was disrupted by shouting students carrying placards protesting the presence of U.S. military forces in Vietnam and the navy on campus, police were called.[21]

This was the start of what became over the next three years a kind of civil war within the undergraduate student body. Most of the subsequent coverage of that war focused on the disrupters, with little attention paid to the disrupted. While the activists' intention was not primarily to make campus life difficult for their fellow students, their increasing resort to disruptions of normal cam-pus life plausibly came to be read that way by some of their increasingly exer-cised classmates.[22]

This student-versus-student scenario characterized another form of protest to emerge in 1965 and 1966: obstruction of on-campus recruiters. Here, stu-dents who kept recruiters from the Marine Corps, the CIA, and corporations such as Dow Chemical, which produced napalm used in Vietnam, from talking on campus about job possibilities were not primarily focused on depriving classmates of gainful employment. What they were about was protesting what they saw as the cozy relationship between the university and these war-making entities. But their disruptive protests did have that effect. When one would-be Marine informed the student disrupters of his thoughts on the matter, in the midst of some shoving and pushing, it did not help matters when one of his classmates told this aspiring leatherneck that "no one should be allowed to join the Marine Corps."[23]

Responsibility for maintaining order on campus resided with the univer-sity's administrative officers. Yet, as President Kirk ruefully acknowledged, there were few mechanisms in place for determining what constituted disor-derly behavior, investigating instances of it, or disciplining those engaged. Past instances had been treated on a case-by-case basis, with the various deans in Hamilton Hall meting out "dean's discipline," which consisted of warnings, suspensions, and even expulsion, depending on the severity of the misbehavior. But the bulk of this case law applied to acts of rowdiness devoid of political content, not to disruptive protests that were viewed by the protesters as funda-mentally political and hence constitutionally protected.[24]

It was not only the absence of agreed-upon procedures that made Kirk and his deans slow to respond to the NROTC and Marine Corps disruptions in the spring of 1965. It was also that they had no wish to have these disruptions given press coverage at the outset of a $200 million capital campaign. Thus what became the administration's operative strategy for the next three years could be discerned in 1965: minimize the extent of any disruptions; extend to disrupters sufficient anonymity to avoid identification and disciplining; keep press reports to a minimum; hope that most of the protesters are graduating seniors. "We were trying," Kirk later explained, "to be as even-handed, as light-handed, as we could, hoping that things would not get out of control."[25]

Such a strategy might have worked had student protesters wanted immunity in exchange for not directly challenging the president's disciplinary authority. But it was precisely the latter that the protesters wanted. An early indicator of this was a demonstration on Broadway in the spring of 1966 to protest the State Department–arranged visit of Queen Fredericka and King Paul of Greece to campus. While the demonstrators included members of the New York Greek-American community opposed to the Greek monarchy, they also included Columbia students angry at President Kirk and the trustees for inviting them. A subsequent visit by Japan's prime minister produced a similar disruption, which left Kirk, both in his role as the State Department's official greeter and as president of the Council of Foreign Relations, embarrassed and chagrined.[26]

Two incidents in the spring of 1967 revealed the limits of the administration's bend-but-don't break strategy in the face of students determined to have their protests recognized as direct challenges to the president's authority. The first of these occurred on the afternoon of March 24, when as many as one hundred stu-dents entered Dodge Hall to protest the presence there of a CIA recruiter and to disrupt any interviews he had scheduled. Several campus security officers were dispatched from Low Library to clear the building of the protesters, but to no effect. Deans on the scene took the names of some of the protesting students, but it was not clear what point this was to serve when, after two hours of disruption and the departure of the CIA recruiter, Dodge Hall resumed business as usual.[27]

The second incident took place in John Jay Hall, on April 21, when Marine Corps recruiters had set up tables to talk with undergraduates. Antiwar pro-testers encircled the tables, and, before the afternoon was over, an estimated five hundred protesters were themselves confronted by a larger group of under-graduates demanding that they leave the building. Again, security officers were summoned, again deans took names, and again both groups dispersed after much pushing and shoving.[28]

By Columbia standards, the administration's reaction to the John Jay Hall melee was swift and serious. President Kirk prepared a statement to be promulgated at the start of the fall term banning all indoor demonstrations.

The Bough Bends

The 1967–68 fall term began with every prospect that the administration was going to get serious about students who disrupted the workings of the university. President Kirk's September 25 announcement prohibiting indoor demonstrations seemed clear enough, whatever its appropriateness. Meanwhile, the trustees had put to rest the charge made by students the previous spring that the university was cooperating with local draft boards by supplying them with the class rankings of Columbia students. (They did this by doing away with the rankings altogether.) A November student referendum sponsored by the class officers of Columbia College overwhelmingly supported (67 percent in favor) open recruiting on campus, including that by the armed forces, the CIA, and militarily involved companies such as Dow Chemical. This position was further supported by the recommendations of a faculty committee chaired by the sociologist Allan Silver. A report commissioned in November 1965 from the President's Advisory Committee on Student Life, chaired by Aaron Warner, had been submitted to the president at the beginning of the term, along with a "Minority Report of the Four Students." Some useful student-administrative dialogue might have been expected from the airing of all these views.[29]

It was also thought that SDS had lost much of its earlier capacity to raise a crowd. The outcome of the referendum on recruiting was clearly a repudiation of its disruptive actions the previous spring. SDS leaders showed little capacity to forge an alliance among Columbia's leftist student groups, much less to attract faculty support. There was also talk of SDS being torn by internal disagreements. On October 30, 1967, the *Columbia Spectator* editorialized on the "ineffectiveness" of SDS's disruptive tactics and credited the administration with successfully isolating the few dozen radical students on campus.[30]

The disarray among the student left gave the administration time to attend to a self-inflicted wound. In the spring of 1967 officers in the medical schools, including Associate Dean Donald Tapley, were approached by the freelance inventor Dr. Richard Strickman about marketing a cigarette filter that he contended reduced nicotine intake by as much as 70 percent, without affecting taste. Should Columbia and its prestigious Medical School attest to the filter's effectiveness, the result could be beneficial both to the university and to the marketability of the filter. The royalties, pegged at one cent a pack, were estimated to be worth $200 million annually to Columbia. With both the Medical School and the university running deficits, the Strickman filter seemed almost too good to be true.[31]

A press release in June 1967, announcing the deal between Strickman and Columbia and touting the health benefits of the filter, attracted considerable attention. A congressional committee invited President Kirk to tell its members more about the filter and the university's means of testing its effectiveness. By the time Kirk went to Washington in August, doubts about Strickman's claims were already circulating at the Medical School, leaving the president exposed to a grilling as to the university's motives in endorsing this commercial venture. He acknowledged that early claims about the filter's effectiveness may have been exaggerated. This public embarrassment was then followed by an editorial in *Science* questioning the filter's effectiveness and the motives of the university. Independent tests indicated the Strickman filter blocked no more nicotine than filters already in use. Others complained the resultant taste compared unfavorably with smoking hay. In December Columbia announced that it no longer had an interest in the Strickman filter and would write off the $300,000 invested in the venture. "It was, on my part," President Kirk later acknowledged, "a great mistake."[32]

While unrelated to issues that students were protesting, the Strickman filter fiasco did bring into question the integrity of the administration against which students protested. To the extent that the other issues acquired positive salience in direct proportion to the administration's loss of general credibility, Columbia's premature and ill-fated venture into the patenting of medical discoveries provided another opening for those who were determined to bring the university to account.

Time seemed to favor the administration, however. Low Library could simply outwait the radical students, knowing that, come June, some of them would graduate, while others might decide to get back to the books in order to do so. There was also the hope that majoritarian sentiment opposed to the protests of the previous spring would oblige SDS and other radical student groups to abandon their confrontational strategy. Those who held this happy thought had not read Lenin.

But for time to be on its side, the administration had to control not only the clock but upcoming events as well. And this it could not do, most clearly in terms of external events, such as the spring '68 Tet Offensive in Vietnam, the revolt of the anti-Vietnam wing of the Democratic Party against President Johnson, and the growing urban unrest discernible a few blocks away. But even in something as supposedly in its control as settling on the date to commence construction of an undergraduate gym in Morningside Park, time was not a friend to the administration.

The Issues, Part 1: A Gym in Morningside Park

Few Columbia trustees have pressed for a cause so long or strenuously as Harold G. McGuire pressed for a respectable gym for Columbia College students. Known to his classmates and friends as "Mickey," McGuire had been an athlete in the College (CC 1927) and had good reason in his day to complain about most of Columbia's intercollegiate sports facilities. The never-completed University Hall, on top of which Uris Hall had been built, had housed a pool and a basketball court, neither of them suitable for intercollegiate competition. The facilities for intramurals or just working out would have made a prep school boy cry. When McGuire was elected to the board of trustees in 1958, little had changed in the intervening twenty years, despite his efforts as a College alumnus. He made a new gym his first priority.[33]

A new gym was not a high priority for President Kirk, an unapologetic nonathlete. But with McGuire now on the board and other College alumni expressing interest, he and other trustees encouraged McGuire and the College Alumni Association to mount a campaign along the lines that had underwritten buildings for the professional schools. McGuire wanted the gym on the South Campus, hard by the undergraduate dormitories. But with only the two fields in front of Butler Library not built on, the trustees' Buildings and Grounds Committee declined to designate either for McGuire's purposes. Moreover, the open spaces on the northern edge of the campus, he was informed, were already committed to the sciences and engineering.[34]

At this point, in early 1959, Dean Courtney Brown of the Business School passed along the suggestion made to him by Robert Moses (CU Ph.D. 1919), the city parks commissioner under Mayor Wagner and New York's consummate power broker for forty years, that the university seek permission from the city to build its new gym in Morningside Park, two blocks south and one block east of Hamilton Hall. McGuire originally resisted the idea, on the grounds that the site was too far from the campus and that the permissions process would delay the building (little did he know). But with no other land available, McGuire dutifully set about securing the necessary permissions.[35]

Morningside Park was not entirely terra incognita to Columbians in the 1950s. The athletic department had sponsored neighborhood summer leagues and tournaments there and had put up a small shed for storing equipment near the 110th Street entrance. Thus, when public hearings were held in 1960 about the possibility of Columbia's building a larger facility, to which the neighborhood would have access, of the dozen or so organizations that commented on the plan, the only to object was the Landmarks Commission, which opposed any use of public park land for private use. Neighborhood groups supported the plan.[36]

Had Columbia proceeded to build the gym in the early 1960s, it would have faced little public opposition. By 1961 all the relevant elected officials at the neighborhood, borough, city, and state levels had signed off on it. Elected officials from Harlem were publicly supportive of the project and seemed satisfied with the original plans that called for 20 percent of the total space to be reserved for community use. What later came to be viewed as prima facie evidence of institutional racism—the fact that the College entrance to the gym was to be up on Morningside Drive and that for the community at the base of the building inside the park—was then seen as merely reflective of the topographical realities of the site.[37]

The gym did not get built in the early 1960s because the money to pay for it had yet to be raised from the College alumni and the Trustees were unwilling to risk having to underwrite the gym with money from the endowment. Whatever uncommitted funds Columbia did have in the early 1960s were going toward raising faculty salaries and buying up neighborhood properties. But as each year went by, the estimates went up, and by 1965 the $7 million cost projected in 1959 had grown to $11 million.[38]

By then, time was running out. Neither the permissions to build in the park nor the public sufferance that secured them were open-ended. The building plans submitted to the Parks Commission in 1959 were approved on the condition that construction began in November 1965. One extension had already been secured—to November 1967—and as this date approached, another extension was sought.[39]

The problem with extensions was that they provided opportunities for those who had earlier supported the plans to up the ante. One way to do this was for elected officials to insist on changes in the building plans that increased the space and amenities available to their constituents. The original plan for the gym had no community swimming pool; before a second extension was granted in 1965, an Olympic-size pool available to the community was added. The projected cost went up another $500,000.[40]

Elected officials were not the only non-Columbians taking a second look at the idea of Columbia's building a gym in Morningside Park. In September 1965 community activists in Harlem and the Morningside Renewal Council declared themselves opposed to the gym. Such opposition in turn made it increasingly uncertain that support from elected officials could be counted on indefinitely.

If Columbia's trustees needed further evidence that political support for the gym was disappearing, the mayoral campaign of John V. Lindsay in the fall of 1965 provided it. With Lindsay's support on the Upper West Side and in Harlem uncertain, Thomas P. F. Hoving, Lindsay's designated park commissioner, declared himself opposed to all private use of city park land. He specifically mentioned Morningside Park.[41]

With neighborhood opposition to the gym project growing and with political support cracking, the trustees determined that the project could not be delayed any further. Without anything close to the needed $13 million in hand, they decided to go ahead. A third and final six-month extension secured in the summer of 1967 stipulated that construction had to get under way no later than February 1968. This time, however, the extension was opposed by both of Harlem's elected officials, Assemblyman Charles Rangel and Senator Basil Patterson. Their opposition to a Columbia-built gym in the park had earlier been conveyed to Kirk, who decided to press on anyway.[42]

One of the ironies of the gym project was that, aside from McGuire and some College alumni, it had little support at Columbia. Kirk's coolness was matched by that of other trustees, who worried about the university's capacity to pay its bills but went along with the gym out of respect for McGuire's commitment to it. The *Columbia Spectator* endorsed the project in editorials but opened its pages to readers opposed to it. Similarly, the endorsements of the dean of Columbia College, David Truman, allowed the inference that he thought there were better things on which to spend College-generated money. Even many of the athletic coaches found the gym's layout unsuited to their purposes. That use of the gym was to be restricted to Columbia College undergraduates gave graduate and professional school students, as well as Barnard and Teachers College students, little reason to champion it. Columbia's faculty were united in not having a good word for the gym.[43]

If the gym had few champions, it nicely served those intent on dramatizing what they saw as Columbia's rapacity in real estate matters and its systemic racism. Black activists such as H. Rap Brown found it an irresistible target. Addressing a Harlem crowd in December 1967, he described the gym's layout— Columbia/white entrance above; community/black entrance below—as intentionally racist and proposed a simple solution: "If they build the first story, blow it up. If they sneak back at night and build three stories, burn it down, and if they get nine stories built, it's yours. Take it over, and maybe we'll let them in on weekends." Columbia's black students saw the gym as peculiarly their issue, a test of their self-identity. It was also freighted with symbolic meaning for those Columbia white students who, through CCC and other organizations, defined their politics in terms of serving the community beyond the campus.[44]

On February 18, 1968, heavy equipment moved into Morningside Park to begin excavation for the gym. Two days later, a demonstration by Columbia students and neighborhood groups at the gym site brought the work to a halt. Police were called to the scene, and several arrests were made. A fence was put up around the site, and a guard posted.[45]

SDS did not figure prominently in the gym-site demonstration, nor had it made the gym issue part of its 1967–68 educational program. It was instead engaged in an internal struggle, between the praxis-axis old guard personified by Ted Kaptchuk, which favored recruitment of members and education, and a new group of insurgents, the action faction, which favored direct confrontation of the authorities. This second group included Mark Rudd, a junior just back from a visit to Castro's Cuba. On March 13, Rudd was elected chairman of the Columbia chapter of SDS, on a platform entitled "How to Get the SDS Moving Again and Screw the University All in One Fell Swoop." But there was still no mention of the gym.[46]

Campus opinion varied about Mark Rudd. Even within SDS there was some inclination to dismiss him as a less charismatic leader than Juan Gonzalez, as less theoretically informed than Tony Papert (who later joined Lyndon La Rouche), and as less convincing a committed radical than John Jacobs. The Brooklyn-born Lewis Cole dubbed the New Jersey–reared Rudd "the first suburban radical" and questioned his intelligence but not his courage. Tom Hayden later remembered the Mark Rudd of 1968 as "absolutely committed to an impossible yet galvanizing dream: that of transforming the entire student movement, through this particular student revolt, into a successful effort to bring down the system." At the same time, Hayden thought, he was "sarcastic and smugly dogmatic." Some women in the radical camp thought his male chauvinism excessive even by prevailing standards on the left.[47]

Faculty opinion similarly varied from the conditional positive, as in the historian David Rothman's view that "he did not seem unreasonable" and that "he is not a loathsome young man," to the political scientist Bruce Smith's view of him as "an unbelievable arrogant schmuck." Some faculty, such as Immanuel Wallerstein, identified Rudd as "the moderate within the radical student group," while others, such as the historian Orest Ranum, saw him in the role of Melville's Ahab, keeping less committed students in the buildings by the power of his own convictions. That he was at times duplicitous and wholly dismissive of democratic procedures was acknowledged even by sympathetic faculty like Seymour Melman and Marvin Harris. And no one—not even Rudd, years later—defended what he became in the immediate aftermath of Columbia '68, a leader of the Weathermen bent on the overthrow of American society by any means.[48]

The fact remains that Rudd played a role in the events at Columbia in the spring of 1968 second to no one else. He proved far more adept at riding the whirlwind than did anyone in the administration or among the various faculty who sought to intervene. And if one sees him—not at first but earlier than most—as understanding that the events as they unfolded on campus provided a singular opportunity to discredit the administration in the eyes of those whose politics was diametrically opposed to the SDS, he must be accorded a measure of success.

The differences within SDS in the early spring of 1968 were actually quite small. Ted Kaptchuk and Co. did not oppose all forms of direct protest, and Mark Rudd and Co. did not abandon SDS's educational efforts. Indeed, it was to dramatize the findings of an SDS-research effort into Columbia's ties with the Institute for Defense Analysis that brought one hundred SDS-led students into Low Library on March 27 and gave the protest movement its second and third issues.[49]

The Issues, Part 2: IDA

As noted earlier, Columbia had joined the five-year-old Institute for Defense Analyses in 1959. President Kirk served as the university's representative on the IDA board. Columbia trustee William Burden, an occasional adviser to the government on aviation and intelligence matters, was also a member. By virtue of a rotating arrangement, he was also chairman. There was nothing secretive about IDA's mission: to serve as a forum where the leading research universities and the principal government agencies funding military research could discuss issues of mutual interest. IDA did not issue contracts, although its members viewed their participation as a means by which they assured that their universities were not overlooked by the agencies that did.[50]

Although Columbia officials readily acknowledged the university's IDA membership when confronted by SDS in 1967, they had not been forthcoming about the extent of defense-related secret research going on at Columbia. Vice President Ralph Halford first reported that no secret research went on, only to have to correct himself when it became known that contract work performed by the Institute of East European Studies for the CIA, involving the accumulation of economic data, was indeed secret. Shortly thereafter, President Kirk indicated that while this was the only secret work under way, the results of some other government-contracted work were not available to the public. Neither Kirk nor Halford could state categorically that Columbia faculty were not engaged in secret military research in contracted projects outside Columbia.[51]

Like the gym, IDA was both less and more than first met the eye. SDS research turned up nothing about Columbia's dealings with federal funding agencies that was not in the public record. Financial interests that individual trustees had with defense contractors were also part of that record. Still, the extent of these institutional ties and personal interests came as a surprise to many on campus. Nor did the administration's early fumbling response to these revelations reassure those inclined to think the worst of Low Library. The SDS demand that Columbia withdraw from IDA acquired added credibility when the faculties of the University of Chicago and Princeton voted to do so. Kirk's refusal even to consider putting the matter to a faculty vote became further evidence of Columbia's complicity in what Professor Seymour Melman called the "war economy" and others called "the ongoing genocide in Vietnam." In belated recognition that Columbia's membership in IDA was at least a public relations problem, President Kirk announced in January 1968 the creation of a committee on external relations, chaired by Professor of Law Louis Henkin, that would look into Columbia's links with the CIA, IDA, and the military services. It was to report its findings, with recommendations, to the president in June.[52]

The Issues, Part 3: Disciplining Student Protesters

The administration's capacity to bend without breaking was put to a serious test on February 23, when two hundred students marched into Low Library to protest the presence on campus of Dow Chemical recruiters. A splinter group of some eighty students proceeded to Dodge Hall, where they conducted a sit-in that disrupted the building's operations for several hours. While both actions were in direct violation of President Kirk's prohibition of indoor demonstrations and despite the presence of deans at both scenes, no one was charged, because supposedly none of the student demonstrators was identified.[53]

The reluctance of the administration to discipline those engaged in disruptive activities was not lost on SDS. At a March 20 meeting held to discuss the changes in the draft laws, the New York City director of the Selective Service, an invited speaker, had a lemon meringue pie pushed into his face by a student whom everyone on campus, except the deans in charge of maintaining student order, understood to be Mark Rudd.[54]

On March 27, two weeks after Rudd's election as chairman, SDS mounted a second demonstration in Low Library, in which one hundred students paraded around the second-floor corridors of the rotunda. Visibly frightened by this show of force, some of the secretaries made their concerns known to their bosses. President Kirk was not in his office at the time, but upon his return he announced that disciplinary action would be taken against the six students identified, all of them, it turned out, leaders of SDS.[55]

The disciplinary fate of these six promptly joined the gym and IDA as an issue with its own succinctly stated demand: "No disciplinary action against the Low Six." SDSers did not dispute that the six had in fact been in Low Library or that they were among the loudest in attendance. They admitted that their actions had violated Kirk's prohibition against indoor demonstrations. What they insisted, instead, was that their identification amounted to persecution for a political action protected by the Constitution of the United States.[56]

During the week after the Low demonstration, a rapid succession of events off campus served to heighten tensions on campus. On March 30 Lyndon Johnson announced that he would not seek renomination for the presidency but would use his time left to try to resolve the conflict in Vietnam. For some moderate antiwar Columbians already campaigning for Eugene McCarthy or Robert F. Kennedy, this was welcome news, but, for SDSers and others on the left past believing in the efficacy of electoral politics, Johnson's announcement confirmed their belief in the corruption of U.S. institutions, academic as well as political. It also meant that the McCarthy and Kennedy insurgent campaigns could, if allowed to capture Columbia's political attention, draw support away from SDS's more disruptive tactics and radical solutions.[57]

On April 4, Martin Luther King Jr. was assassinated while leading a strike of garbage collectors in Memphis, Tennessee. News of his death set off riots in the black neighborhoods of the United States' major cities, with one of the most destructive taking place in Washington, D.C., within blocks of the White House. Thanks to calming efforts by its political and religious leaders, as well as the conspicuous presence of Mayor Lindsay walking its streets, Harlem did not suffer anything like the rioting that occurred elsewhere. But racial tensions throughout New York remained such that no one doubted the possibility that another incident might well spark what James Baldwin called "the fire next time."[58]

For his part, Chaplain John D. Cannon decided that Columbia should observe King's death with a memorial service in St. Paul's Chapel. It is not clear that he intended that either President Kirk or Provost Truman should have an official role. He asked M. Moran Weston, the rector of Harlem's St. Phillips Episcopal Church and a Columbia graduate (CC 1930 Ph.D. 1954), to deliver the main address. When these plans became known in Low Library, Kirk and Truman were added to the program. The leaders of SAS decided not to participate.[59]

The well-attended service, held on the afternoon of April 9, went smoothly until, midway through some remarks by Provost Truman, Mark Rudd left his seat in the nave and proceeded to the pulpit where Truman was speaking. When

Chaplain Cannon made no effort to stop Rudd, Truman, perhaps in confusion as much as through inherent politeness, let Rudd commandeer the pulpit microphone. The SDS leader then proceeded to declare the service an "obscenity" given Columbia's systematic mistreatment of the blacks and workers King had lost his life championing. He then descended from the pulpit, walked down the main aisle, where he was joined by forty other attendees, and left the chapel. Those remaining in the chapel seem to have been in shock, a condition hardly eased by Chaplain Cannon's assuring them that St. Paul's welcomed the views of anyone "who sincerely believes that he's moved by the spirit." The Rev. William Starr, counselor to Episcopal students, said the walkout "expressed the feelings of a considerable segment of the community and University."[60]

Kirk and Truman were furious at the clergy's condoning Rudd's actions, as were some faculty in attendance. Professor of History Fritz Stern caught up with the departing Rudd and told him his actions in the chapel were akin to the takeover of Socialist meetings by Nazis in Weimar Germany. This would not be the last time this analogy was invoked in the weeks that followed.[61]

Cannon's blessing of Rudd's actions in the chapel foreclosed any disciplinary action being taken against him. Nevertheless, the incident seems to have marked for both the SDS leadership and Low Library a point of no return. This can be said with greater assurance of SDS, because of its actions immediately thereafter. On April 12 its twenty-five-member steering committee voted to mount demonstrations throughout the remainder of the spring term that would focus on the issues of racism and the gym, as well as on their standard issue, university complicity in the Vietnam War. On April 17 the SDS general assembly, with ninety to one hundred students in attendance, endorsed the steering committee's vote and set April 23, a Tuesday, as the date for the demonstrations to begin, to be kicked off with a noontime rally at the sun dial, directly in front of Low Library.[62]

Rudd took two additional steps to assure a crowd at the sun dial. On April 19 he published a "Letter to Uncle Grayson," in which he listed three nonnegotiable demands that SDS had settled on: the cessation of gym construction; Columbia's withdrawal from IDA; and no disciplinary action against the Low Six. The letter ended with a line of poetry from the works of Amiri Baraka (Le Roi Jones) with an eye-catching sign-off: "Up Against the Wall, Motherfucker."[63]

Rudd's other preparatory step for the rally was to meet with the new leader of SAS, Cicero Wilson (CC 1969), to see if SAS and SDS might cosponsor the rally and work together on demonstrations to follow. The details of the meeting are unclear, but events of the next day suggest they reached some agreement. This marked a new departure for SAS, which until now had avoided involvement in any campus issues that were not directly related to the circumstances of black students.[64]

The administration in Low Library was aware of the planned SDS rally and unspecified demonstrations to follow. The "Letter to Uncle Grayson" had been nothing if not specific. But insofar as a noontime rally at the sun dial fell within the limits of political action, nothing could be done to prevent it. Nor did the administration have authority to prevent the counterrally planned for the steps of Low Library by the anti-SDS Students for a Free Campus. The proximity of these two rallies, plus the placement of the counterprotesters between the sun dial and Low Library, which gave the appearance of an intention to block attempts by the protesters to enter Low, deeply concerned both the university administrators in Low and the College deans in Hamilton Hall. Above all, they wanted to avoid a repeat of the confrontation a year earlier in front of John Jay, when College athletes tangled with SDS protesters. Their only countermeasure was to see that Low Library was locked at noontime and to reserve McMillan Theater on the off chance that the sun dial crowd could be redirected to a meeting at which Provost Truman would answer questions.[65]

There is no evidence that administrators knew beforehand of the SAS leadership's decision to participate in the sun dial rally. That decision, however, and the involvement of most of Columbia and Barnard's black undergraduates in the events that followed, heightened fears of a racial student confrontation. The participation of Columbia's black students also raised the specter that blacks from the Harlem community might storm the campus to help their outnumbered brothers and sisters.[66]

We know with hindsight that the several confrontations between protesting and antiprotesting students during the week that followed the Tuesday sun dial rally did not escalate into serious violence. We also know that the several dozen nonstudent blacks who came on campus during the first day were largely gone by the second and were not the advance guard for a Harlem invasion. It is easy, therefore, to conclude from here that these fears—of student-student violence and of an ensuing campus-community racial confrontation—were overblown. At the least, they showed a lack of faith in the good sense of Columbia students and Columbia's neighbors. And it is easy to see how these became disabling fears, unduly limiting the range of responses the administration, faculty, and city officials were prepared to take to counter the actions of the protesters. But we can not dismiss either fear as unreasonable.[67]

Day One: Tuesday, April 23 (Bright and Sunny)

Strollers on College Walk shortly before noon on Tuesday, April 23, were not especially surprised by the sight of a rally in the making around the sun dial.

Such events had become common. What did give pause was the size of the crowd and its biracial character. Again, the presence of SDS placards protesting Columbia's ties with IDA was hardly novel, no more so than SAS placards protesting the gym in Morningside or CCC placards protesting Columbia's policies as Morningside's largest landlord: it was their combined presence that suggested something more than usual was afoot. So did the fact that, after greeting those in attendance, the better-known and usually voluble SDS chair, Mark Rudd, turned the megaphone over to lesser-known SAS chair, Cicero Wilson, who called on all within earshot to join SAS in its protest against the construction of the gym in Morningside Park.[68]

After a half hour or so at the sun dial, the crowd of perhaps two hundred students and assorted onlookers was urged by an unidentified speaker to proceed to Low Library, where the list of demands could be served on President Kirk. As the more direct route up the steps entailed confronting the crowd of antiprotesters in front of Alma Mater, the protesters approached the library from the southeast entrance, only to find the door there locked. After some indeterminate shuffling about, a shout of "To the gym site" from somewhere in the crowd gave the protesters renewed direction, and they proceeded out of the main campus and across 116th Street to Morningside Drive, which ran along the western edge of the park. Inside the park, a pair of New York City policemen stood guard outside the fence encircling the gym site. As the crowd approached, some first arrivals attempted to scale the fence. The police arrested one of these, Fred Wilson (CC 1970), and called for backup. At this point, perhaps sensing the threat the crowd and the outnumbered but armed police posed for each other, Mark Rudd directed the crowd to return to the sun dial. This would not be the last time that protest leaders, sensing how easily events could spin out of control, demonstrated a capacity to lower the ambient temperature, even while at other times they raised it.[69]

Once back on campus, the protesting crowd, rather than returning to the sun dial, turned left into Van Am Quad and spilled into the lobby of Hamilton Hall. For the next several hours, the rally continued in the lobby, as classes proceeded on the floors above and faculty and students came and went. Among those in Hamilton that afternoon was Henry Coleman, acting dean of Columbia College. Unlike the other denizens of Hamilton, Coleman and two assistant deans did not vacate the building when classes ended at 6:00 P.M. It is not clear whether this was his choice at first; even if it was, as darkness fell and what began as an indoor demonstration took on the character of a building occupation, Coleman's status mutated from that of persistent tenant to hostage. By late evening, access to Hamilton became by invitation only, and among the welcomed visitors were several dozen black activists from off campus, some of whom were reported to be armed.[70]

Around midnight, the SAS leaders held a caucus. They decided that an ongoing occupation of Hamilton—now Malcolm X Liberation College—should be a blacks-only project. When this decision was communicated to the SDS leaders in the building, it was first met with surprise and consternation. But Rudd did not challenge its legitimacy, and the white protesters agreed to leave quietly.[71]

There is no evidence that the occupation of Hamilton Hall was part of a larger preconceived plan and much to suggest it was spontaneous. Insofar as the protesting students controlled the pace of events during the first three days of the occupation, it is easy to attribute more calculation to their actions than they likely possessed. The charge made at the time with respect to the administration—"that they had no idea what they were doing," much less "what would happen next"—can be more universally applied.[72]

Day Two: Wednesday, April 24 (Rainy)

The second day of protests began at 5:30 A.M. with the two hundred or so white students being escorted out of Hamilton Hall. When one of the white evictees ruefully asked what their role was to be henceforth, he was told by an evicting black comrade, "Get your own building." This is just what some of them did.[73]

In the spring of 1968, the Columbia Campus Security Force consisted of 9 officers (it now numbers 120). Plans to supplement it came to naught in the weekend before the scheduled sun dial rally when it was determined that all the private security forces in the riot-prone city were otherwise engaged. Thus, when one hundred or so students evicted from Hamilton decided to enter Low Library by the southeast door next to the security command post at around 6:00 A.M., there was little the two unarmed guards on duty could do to stop them. From there, the students proceeded upstairs, where they easily gained entrance to the presidential suite on the second floor. There, they made themselves comfortable, fully expecting that with the start of the business day they would be arrested and carted off. Indeed, so certain were some of imminent arrest that the appearance of one security guard intent on nothing more than the removal of a Rembrandt painting from the wall of the president's office sent most of the occupiers scurrying out onto the window ledges from whence they jumped to the ground and ran away. These included most of the SDS leadership, including Mark Rudd.[74]

That the twenty-five or so students who remained went unchallenged for what turned out to be another six days surprised both those who jumped and those who stayed. It also gave some SDS leaders, Mark Rudd among them, now operating out of the CCC offices in Ferris Booth, their first inkling that the administration might be running scared. Still, when Rudd moved at a steering committee meeting later that afternoon that SDS occupy more buildings, he was voted down by such an overwhelming margin that he temporarily resigned as chairman. Meanwhile, in an unrelated action, graduate students in architecture, after being informed that Avery was to be closed at 5:30 P.M. to prevent its occupation, refused the directive to leave and, by staying put, made Avery the third Columbia building in two days to go out of business as usual.[75]

These developments further angered students opposed to the protest. Around 5:00 P.M., on Wednesday, several dozen antiprotesters gathered in front of Hamilton Hall, intent on reclaiming "their" building from those inside. Only the intervention of several College deans, one of whom later remembered distinguishing protesters from antiprotesters by their hair, and a "providential" downpour, allowed this "rather ugly" student-student confrontation to pass without violence. Later that evening, these same antiprotest students, following a meeting in McMillan Theatre and some sympathetic faculty, declared themselves the "Majority Coalition."[76]

Although less assiduously covered by the media, the Majority Coalition constituted a presence with which the administration felt obliged to reckon throughout the crisis. It should also be said that its leaders, among them Paul Vilardi (CC 1968) and Kenneth Tomecki (CC 1968), likely helped calm the frayed tempers of some of the more combative in their ranks. So did basketball coach Jack Rohan at a meeting of athletes on the third day of the crisis. Faculty, from C. Lowell Harriss on the right to Seymour Melman on the left, also helped keep a semblance of peace. As Melman said of faculty discussions with antiprotesting students, "We were heard, we were respected."[77]

Where, one might ask, were the administrators during all this? News of the demonstration inside Hamilton Hall and the detention of Dean Coleman reached President Kirk downtown, where he was chairing a meeting of presidents of the Association of American Universities. His first inclination was to call in the New York City Police. Provost Truman, however, citing the advice of Coleman and others in Hamilton, thought that the police were not required and the demonstration would break up of its own accord. Kirk deferred to those on the scene. When Truman asked one of his secretaries that first afternoon what she would do, she later reported advising him to take a security guard with him to Hamilton and demand Dean Coleman's release. Truman responded, "I think not."[78]

Representatives of the New York City Police Department under the command of Sanford Garelick came on campus the morning of the second day at the request of President Kirk, to advise him on measures that could be taken to end the occupations. Garelick promptly set up a command post in the unoccupied part of Low Library. Joining him were three representatives of the mayor's office, Barry Gottehrer, Jay Kriegel, and Sid Davidoff. They remained on campus throughout the subsequent events, trying to impose a degree of political rationality on the actions of the primary participants but never quite succeeding. In their wake came an invasion of television reporters and cameramen, who only added to the already surrealistic character of the campus.[79]

All this notoriety was new to Mssrs. Kirk and Truman and to Dean of Graduate Faculties George Fraenkel. Especially unsettling were their early dealings with New York's Finest. Thus, for example, it came as an unwelcome surprise to be informed that their request to have the police develop a plan to evacuate the students from Low Library but leave those in Hamilton alone would not be granted. The police, they were told, did not do selective building emptyings. If an illegally occupied building on campus was to be cleared of occupiers, all occupied campus buildings would have to be cleared.[80]

The logic behind the request to clear Low but leave Hamilton alone turned on two considerations: the possibility that a violent clearing of black students in Hamilton could produce a reaction in Harlem, a concern that both the police and Mayor Lindsay's representatives on campus shared, and the possibility that the black students could be persuaded to leave Hamilton peacefully. But with the prospect of selective emptyings scotched, Kirk returned to his earlier position of using whatever force was required to get all the occupiers out, while Truman continued to hold out for a negotiated end to the crisis. Kirk later said he understood that ordering the police on campus would "in all probability destroy my usefulness hereafter as president." But his more immediate concern was the urging of his own trustees and university presidents elsewhere for him to take decisive action. Thus, Day Two ended with the protesting students occupying three buildings and the antiprotesting students remaining outside, while members of the administration bunkered down in the unoccupied parts of Low Library, already at odds with one another, short of sleep, and, by several accounts, into the bourbon. Maybe tomorrow would be better.[81]

Day Three: Thursday, April 25 (Enter Faculty Left)

The first two days of the crisis were dominated by the actions of the protesting students, to which antiprotesting Columbia students and the Columbia administration reacted in ways that did not allow either to seize the initiative. The third day witnessed more of the same, with the seizure by several dozen graduate students of Fayerweather Hall, which was occupied around 8:00 P.M., after having been closed for the evening. Thursday, however, also marked the emergence of a portion of the Columbia faculty in a role in which they cast themselves as honest brokers between overwrought student protesters and a politically inept administration.

Most faculty had been caught unaware by the sun dial rally, although those with offices or classes in Hamilton Hall on Tuesday afternoon observed some of the early goings on firsthand. On Wednesday, those faculty with access to their Hamilton offices denied them took up temporary quarters in the graduate student lounge in Philosophy 301. Others soon began to gather there as well, if only to hear the latest gossip from occupied buildings and participate in the maneuverings in anticipation of an emergency meeting of the Columbia College faculty that had been called for that afternoon at 3:00 in 309 Havemeyer Hall.[82]

Those in prominent attendance at the College faculty meeting represented a range of political views. From the right, Professor of Government Warner Schilling urged his colleagues to support his resolution backing the administration; from the left, Professor of Anthropology Marvin Harris called for stopping the construction of the gym. While these motions were pending, Professor of Sociology Daniel Bell seized what passed for the center ground with motions that called on the students in Hamilton and Low to vacate those buildings immediately and for the creation of a faculty-student-administration committee to deal with all disciplinary matters consequent on these occupations. He also attached to his resolution the following statement: "We believe that any differences have to be settled peacefully and we trust that police action will not be used to clear University buildings."[83]

At this point, Dean Coleman walked into the meeting, apparently none the worse for his twenty-four-hour incarceration. His relieved colleagues then voted overwhelmingly to approve Bell's resolutions, narrowly approved Harris's call for suspending the gym project, and tabled Schilling's resolution endorsing the administration. President Kirk and Provost Truman were not pleased by either the even-handedness they read into these resolutions or their proscription on calling in the police.[84]

Events the following day also heightened the determination of faculty to intrude themselves further. The morning gathering in Philosophy 301 now took on the appearance of a faculty caucus. After hearing of a scheduled news conference called by the administration for 1:00 P.M., several faculty operating out of Philosophy 301 wrangled an invitation to attend from Provost Truman. At the news conference, President Kirk announced, without having informed any faculty, that classes would be canceled until Monday morning.[85]

Later that afternoon, at the urging of friends on the faculty, Provost Truman walked the hundred steps separating Low Library and Philosophy Hall to provide those gathered in 301 with an update of where matters stood. There was no good news and much that was disheartening. At one point in his somber rendering, Truman broke down and to some seemed to be crying. After stating his belief that at some point the police might have to be brought in to clear the buildings, he trekked back to the Low bunker. It was at this point that it dawned on at least one faculty member that "the people in Low Library were really not in control."[86]

The faculty did not take the news well. Even Truman's warmest backers were disappointed in his performance. Many found disturbing the hard line he had taken, others his questionable psychological state, still others both. At the suggestion of Professor of History Walter Metzger, the gathering moved to constitute itself as the Ad Hoc Faculty Group, to be chaired by Professor of Government Alan Westin and directed by an AHFG steering committee. Eligibility to serve on the steering committee required support of the two resolutions adopted by the College faculty the day before—suspension of the gym project and the creation of a tripartite disciplinary committee—plus a third: that should the administration call the police on campus, faculty would interpose themselves between the police and students. There was also talk of faculty withholding their services to force administration compliance with these resolutions, but it did not amount to a fourth resolution.[87]

The first business of the AHFG steering committee was to dispatch faculty members to the occupied buildings—Hamilton, Low, Avery, and Fayerweather—as well as to SDS strike central in Ferris Booth Hall. Another set of faculty were sent to a meeting of the Majority Coalition scheduled in McMillan for later that evening. The faculty so chosen seemed energized by the chance to do something constructive after two days on the sidelines. Those occupying the buildings, they reminded themselves, "were, after all, our students." Don Quixote never put it better.[88]

These forays met with varied responses. The students in Hamilton declined to meet with the AHFG faculty. Those in Low were prepared to talk endlessly with them, on the chance of converting faculty to their views. Those in Avery were not interested. Students in Fayerweather, however, seemed genuinely interested in what their faculty had to say and were sufficiently impressed by the argument that their successful halting of the university's business as usual constituted victory enough that they considered voting on whether to leave the building. Indeed, it was such wavering on the part of many Fayerweather occupiers, plus the presence among them of what one SDSer called "too many damn McCarthy buttons," that persuaded hardliners to leave Fayerweather and Low and join in the occupation of Mathematics Hall just before midnight. AHFG faculty would cut no ice in Mathematics.[89]

Perhaps the most surreal encounter between faculty and students Thursday evening was in Wollman Auditorium, where six to eight hundred students, including the leadership of the Majority Coalition, were gathered. There, faculty who opposed the demonstrators, such as C. Lowell Harriss and Warner Schilling, were applauded, especially after Schilling promised that "if Mark Rudd was still at Columbia in the fall, I will not be." But when AHFG members David Rothman and Walter Metzger suggested that students in the buildings should not be expelled and that faculty might prevent this from happening by refusing to teach, they were roundly booed. Metzger came away from the meeting with the thought that "these were Columbia students I did not know existed."[90]

Day Four: Friday, April 26 (Administration Exit Right)

By Friday, the days had begun to blend into each other. Faculty who hadn't pulled all-nighters since graduate school found themselves staying up around the clock. Many of those present at the founding of the AHFG Thursday afternoon were still on campus just after midnight, when, at the urging of Professors Trilling and Eugene Galanter, Provost Truman informed the faculty holed up in Philosophy 301 of the decision to have the buildings cleared just before dawn. Truman's tight-lipped announcement that police action was imminent and his advice to faculty to stay out of it was roundly booed and, when he stalked out of the room, faculty unwilling to let matters stand followed him out. As chance would have it, this rag-tag contingent of provost and faculty entered the southeast door of Low just as a contingent of twenty-five plainclothes policemen attempted to do likewise. A scuffle ensued, during which instructor of French Richard L. Greeman got banged in the head. When the accompanying faculty presented their bleeding colleague to Truman, they vowed to interpose themselves in front of the buildings if the police attempted to clear them.[91]

Visibly shaken, Truman retreated into Low Library to confer with President Kirk. The upshot of his discussion was that the imminent police action was called off, explicitly to give the AHFG's mediation efforts a chance to resolve the crisis. This decision Kirk later acknowledged to be a mistake, having personally "wanted very much to use the police on Thursday night." Instead, he again deferred to Truman, who "was extremely active in negotiations because he perhaps had more confidence than I had in the possibility that something might come of all this." Truman released the following statement: "The Faculty committee has persuaded the University Administration to postpone a request for police action on the campus while the faculty and the administration continue their efforts to effect a peaceful solution to the situation." From this point onward, the administration was without a part to play, except, when the faculty's efforts to resolve the crisis failed, to bring on the police.[92]

After the tumultuous events of early Friday, the rest of the day passed relatively quietly. With classes canceled and staff urged to stay home, the campus quiet was only momentarily broken at noontime when a noisy gang of black high schoolers tried unsuccessfully to gain access to Hamilton Hall. Hamilton was also the destination that afternoon of black activists H. Rap Brown and Stokeley Carmichael, who were allowed in around 4:00 P.M., only to leave shortly thereafter. Later Friday evening, AHFG faculty conducted a second round of visits to occupied buildings and met with SDS leaders in Ferris Booth. In these meetings, some faculty argued that what the occupiers now faced, were they to leave voluntarily, was what would virtually amount to amnesty. On one matter there was general agreement: nobody ever gets thrown out of Columbia. When Rudd indicated an interest in exploring how far the AHFG faculty were prepared to go to assure this virtual amnesty, a meeting between Rudd and the AHFG was set for 1:00 A.M. Saturday morning in Philosophy 301.[93]

Day Five: Saturday, April 27

Whatever hopes AHFG faculty retained that a peaceful resolution was at hand if faculty were given the opportunity to find it were dashed by Rudd's appearance in Philosophy 301 early Saturday morning. He stayed only long enough to tell them that any proposed solution they might fashion that did not include amnesty from all disciplinary action was "bullshit."[94]

Nine hours later, the trustees released a statement categorically opposing amnesty for the occupying students and insisting that the final authority in all disciplinary matters rested with the president and not with any tripartite concoction. Since David Truman has been given all the bad lines in this narrative thus far, it is only fair that his assessment of the trustees' stab at conflict resolution be recorded: "Everyone is shooting off their mouths, why can't the Trustees shoot off their mouths too?"[95]

Meanwhile, in the five occupied buildings, a weekend routine settled in. Some of the architecture students in Avery worked on their drawings. Those in Fayerweather first voted to dissociate themselves from the demand for amnesty and then voted to dissociate themselves from the earlier effort to dissociate themselves from the amnesty demand. Meanwhile, the building's social calendar included a wedding between two students, officiated by the Episcopalian chaplain, Rev. William Starr, who declared the newlyweds "children of the new age." The women cooked, and some availed themselves of Fayerweather's "drug dispensary."[96]

Hamilton Hall received a string of visitors and would-be mediators, among them the psychologist Kenneth Clark (CU Ph.D. 1956), whose son, Hilton (CC 1967), was one of the founders of SAS, and the labor negotiator Theodore Kheel. Once Clark and Kheel saw there was no chance of talking the students out of the building, they had a pleasant visit. Meanwhile, the hardliners in Mathematics, under the tutelage of outsider Tom Hayden, called for sexual abstinence and banned the use of drugs. Those not enforcing these arrangements occupied themselves soaping the stairs in anticipation of the police raid. The students in Low taunted and were in turn taunted by a cordon of tie and jacket–clad antiprotesters, who tried to keep food from being thrown up to the occupiers. Meanwhile, the College Alumni Association catered the Majority Coalition's Sunday lunch.[97]

Except for Hamilton, students moved freely in and out of the buildings throughout the weekend. On Sunday, a clear spring day, people picnicked on South Field. What did not happen, however, was any noticeable falling off in the numbers in the buildings. On the contrary, it began to look as if the occupiers had passed the point where this was still a lark and were settling in, with occasional breaks to take a shower, walk the dog, call home. Despite some disagreements among members of the Strike Coordinating Committee, the occupation at the end of its fifth day gave every indication of holding together. Rudd and the others leading what was now widely referred to as "The Strike" had proved themselves good at what they were doing, which by now seemed to mean keeping enough students in the buildings to ensure a bloody police bust.[98]

With all earlier efforts at faculty mediation and negotiation having failed, five members of the AHFG steering committee decided on Saturday night to devise a resolution plan of their own. This plan, by the force of its logic and the moral standing of its creators, would then be imposed on the protesting students and recalcitrant administration alike. At midnight, they set to work.[99]

Day Six: Sunday, April 28 (And God Rested)

The AHFG group consisted of sociologists Immanuel Wallerstein, Daniel Bell, and Allan Silver, plus historians David J. Rothman and Robert Fogelson. At some point in the early morning, they were joined by the economist Peter Kenen, who had created for himself a role as intermediary between Low

Library and the AHFG. Although Bell was the senior member of this group, Rothman remembered Wallerstein as "its evil genius." By 8:00 A.M. Sunday, they had fashioned a package of five resolutions, which, if adopted by a vote of the AHFG, would be communicated to the students and administration for their unamendable acceptance or rejection. They included:

1. Cancellation of the gym construction.
2. Columbia's withdrawal from IDA.
3. Establishment of tripartite disciplinary procedures.
4. Acceptance of the principle of collective punishment for the building occupiers.
5. The disavowal by the faculty of either party, students or administration, that refused to accept these resolutions.[100]

The first three of what came to be called the "bitter pill" resolutions are familiar enough. By the fourth—collective punishment—the AHFG draftsmen intended that no participant in the buildings occupations could receive a more severe punishment than any other participant. This would protect the ring-leaders from serious reprisals, on the assumption that neither the university nor any tripartite committee would wish to expel hundreds of students. This reso-lution, as the draftsmen informed their AHFG colleagues, provided for amnesty without using the word.[101]

The fifth resolution was even trickier. It committed the faculty to a dis-avowal of either the administration or the occupying students should either refuse to accept the four earlier resolutions. It was also intended to put the administration on notice that, if the students accepted the first four "bitter pills" and the administration rejected any of them, then, by the AHFG's lights, the students would have command of the moral high ground and the adminis-tration would be discredited. But did the resolution also mean that, should the students reject and the administration accept the four resolutions, the faculty would endorse the use of police to clear the buildings? This was not clear, as was intended.[102]

The two hundred AHFG members present in 301 Philosophy when the "bit-ter pill" resolutions were presented for consideration at 8:00 A.M. Sunday morning enthusiastically endorsed the drafting group's handiwork. A delega-tion, which included Peter Kenen and Daniel Bell, was then dispatched to Low Library to present the resolutions to Provost Truman. His reaction was swift and definitive: should these resolutions be presented for a vote at the 10:00 A.M. meeting of the joint faculties, he would resign. The AHFG delegation, not ready to abandon Truman, agreed not to bring them up for a vote.[103]

Those who had made 301 Philosophy their campus home during the previous five days were not limited to faculty who had lost their offices. They were not even limited to regular members of one or another of Columbia's faculties. They included, depending on the time of day or night, teaching assistants and graduate students, faculty spouses, and sundry campus hangers on. Still, as of 8:00 A.M. on Sunday morning, the AHFG gatherings in 301 Philosophy constituted the closest thing Columbia had to a representative faculty assembly. That was part of the problem.[104]

In 1968 the teaching staff of Columbia University were organized into sixteen separate faculties, each with its own admissions requirements and procedures. By statute, the president of the university presided over each of them; in practice, the deans of the respective schools or faculties or, in the case of Barnard and Teachers College, their presidents, presided. Thus, for example, on the main Morningside campus, faculty could be members of the following faculties: Political Science, Philosophy, Pure Science, International Affairs, Law, Engineering, Architecture, Journalism, Business, Columbia College, General Studies, Barnard College, Teachers College. While, again, many faculty were members of more than one faculty, few knew the members of more than their own faculty. Virtually all interfaculty transactions occurred between deans, a state of affairs that dates back to the early Butler era when the University Council, a creation of the Low presidency that allowed for substantial faculty involvement, became inundated with administrators. A vestige of the University Council still existed in 1968, but not even President Kirk was prepared to defend it as a representative body of the faculty.[105]

For that matter, the meeting of the joint faculties convened on Sunday morning, April 28, itself had only a dubious constitutional standing. It was only the second time since World War II that such a meeting had been convened. Rules for determining membership were hard to come by and out of date. Were, for example, members of the Barnard and Teachers College faculties members of the joint faculties, or was membership limited to those within the Columbia Corporation? There was also the question of the membership status of instructors, lecturers, and the hundreds of clinical appointees in the Medical School.[106]

However constitutionally questionable, the convening of the joint faculties represented a belated attempt by President Kirk and his embattled administration to reclaim the initiative from both the occupying students and what he regarded as the meddling AHFG. Some senior faculty, among them Sigmund Diamond and Herbert Deane, had earlier urged Kirk to seek support for his hard-line policies from a larger and more sympathetically disposed circle of faculty than those directing the AHFG. They had in mind members of the professional schools faculties as well as senior faculty in the arts and sciences, many of whom resided in the suburbs and had not been on campus since classes had been canceled. There was also reason to believe that federal contract–dependent science faculty might not be as keen on the disavowal of IDA, with its more sweeping implication for all kinds of federally sponsored research, as were their social science and humanities colleagues, who dominated the AHFG.[107]

The joint faculties meeting, with some four hundred in attendance, proved to be as Kirk's advisers promised: an assembly of moderates unwilling to repudiate their president or condone the student occupations. A number of innocuous resolutions put forward by Peter Kenen, which had the administration's support, were discussed and adopted. Each of the AHFG's "bitter pill" resolutions was discussed but, as agreed, they were not joined together in a single resolution to be voted up or down. Before adjourning, a second meeting of the joint faculties was scheduled for Tuesday at 3:00 P.M. Kirk's performance throughout what was a nonhostile and even proadministration meeting, however, gave little comfort to those who hoped that the administration could regain control of events. He and Truman were visibly exhausted.[108]

Later Sunday afternoon, the Majority Coalition formed a cordon around Low Library to prevent the resupplying of the occupiers. The insistence of some faculty that they interpose themselves between the antiprotesters, who formed a tight cordon, and the occupiers of the window ledges a dozen feet above them made for much pushing and shoving. The photographs of this set-to that later appeared in *Life Magazine* convey the latent danger of the scene. That no one was seriously injured was another fluke in a weeklong series of instances of luck beating the odds.[109]

Day Seven: Monday, April 29 ("The Day of Decision")

With its "bitter pill" resolutions now widely circulated, the AHFG leadership understood that time was running out for a peaceful solution to the crisis. The Monday headline of the *Spectator* read "List of Six Proposals by Ad Hoc Faculty Panel Apparently Rejected by Administration, Strikers." This was to be, AHFG chair Allen Westin told his colleagues, "the day of decision." Members of the steering committee were privy to the fact that the administration had arranged with the New York City Police to clear the buildings within the next twenty-four hours, most likely early Tuesday morning. They decided not to share this information with the AHFG rank and file.[110]

Elsewhere on campus, the Strike Coordinating Committee in Ferris Booth struggled to maintain a united front. The occupiers in Fayerweather remained a problem, unable to decide where they stood on the amnesty demand, having rejected it in a vote taken Sunday afternoon, only to vote early Monday morning to endorse it. There was also concern about whether the occupiers of Hamilton Hall, never all that cozy with the strike leadership, would cut a separate deal with the administration. Meanwhile, the Majority Coalition cordon around Low Library had come to constitute a potent student counterforce, or at least was being described as such by the conservative media, including, in this instance, the *New York Times*, which had been covering Columbia since the first occupations as a front-page national story.[111]

Meanwhile, a semblance of normal times could be found over at Barnard, where at 10:00 A.M., the College's sixth head and third president, Martha Peterson, was inaugurated, with the pomp and circumstance appropriate to the occasion. Even President Kirk put in an appearance.[112]

But here, too, the times were out of joint, as indicated by the Barnard students picketing the installation. Their reasons for picketing were only indirectly connected with the events going on at Columbia. Shortly after Peterson arrived on campus in January, a Barnard junior, Linda LeClair, decided, after initially misrepresenting her living arrangements, to challenge the Barnard regulation that prohibited her from living with her boyfriend in an off-campus apartment. That fact that Columbia had no such rule with respect to its male undergraduates gave an interesting gender-bias twist to what was otherwise a straightforward assault on parietal rules. Not a little of Peterson's first year was taken up with the LeClair affair. Meanwhile, on the day of Peterson's installation, some three hundred Barnard women—about 15 percent of the student body—were among those occupying five Columbia buildings.[113]

Late Monday afternoon, President Kirk issued a response to the "bitter pill" resolutions that allowed the interpretation that he and the trustees were open to some fine-tuning of them. He proposed an alternative set of steps that he said would "carry out the essential spirit of the [AHFG] proposals." They were not repudiated out of hand.[114]

Shortly thereafter, The Strike Coordinating Committee repudiated the AHFG resolutions. Speaking for occupying students of Low, Avery, Fayerweather, and Mathematics Halls, The Strike Coordinating Committee stood by Rudd's earlier position that any deal that did not specifically include amnesty was "bullshit." Separately, the Hamilton Hall leaders also rejected the AHFG resolutions. Ironically, the only party to accept them was the Majority Coalition, which reluctantly did so later Monday evening and then withdrew its cordon from around Low Library, though not before a final shoving match with the would-be suppliers of Low Library that again very nearly turned bloody.[115]

There was now little to do but wait for the police. Some AHFG faculty tried throughout Monday to get either New York City mayor John Lindsay or New

York governor Nelson Rockefeller to intervene to prevent a police action. Neither was interested in doing so. "The day of decision" ended with the administration and some AHFG faculty knowing the police were already preparing for an early-morning assault on the occupied buildings and with the thousand or so occupiers, while not knowing precisely that they were only a couple of hours away from being forcibly removed, sensing that their removal could not be far off.[116]

Day Eight: Tuesday, April 30, 1968 (The Bust)

The preceding week, members of the Columbia administration had received a crash course in what police do when called in to remove trespassers from private property. They will do so when formally called upon by the rightful owners of the private property, in this case the trustees, but in a manner that was theirs to decide. Fortunately, the police in charge, Inspector Sanford Garelick and Assistant Chief Inspector Eldridge Waith, the highest-ranking black in the NYPD, were excellent teachers and amazingly tolerant of academic folkways. They also had every interest in minimizing the violence attending the removal of students from the buildings. But they were even more concerned not to put their overworked policemen in a situation that might turn violent.[117]

That is precisely what had happened four weeks earlier on March 22, when an understaffed police operation trying to keep order at an Abbie Hoffman–orchestrated antiwar demonstration in Grand Central Station devolved into what even observers sympathetic to the put-upon cops called a "police riot." Accordingly, one of the mayor's advisers, Barry Gottehrer, on campus since Wednesday, advised Mayor Lindsay not to allow the police to be used because it could "result in a massacre." But when Lindsay called Yale president Kingman Brewster for advice, only to hear that "the very future of the American university depended on punishing the strikers," he decided to let the police proceed.[118]

In calling on the police to clear the buildings, the administration ceased to have any operational say in the manner of the clearing. As David Truman later remembered, "It was like deciding to take an airplane ride and having to leave everything in the air to the pilot." George Fraenkel's thoughts about his discussions with the police took a more historical turn: "I felt out of place, and sort of wondered what a political commissar in the old days of the Red Army felt like."[119]

The plan called for the city's elite tactical police force as well as regular beat cops to clear the buildings one at a time. This was done to maximize command supervision but also to avoid spreading the police too thinly across the campus. The thousand-man force assembled was significantly smaller than the three-to-one ratio police procedures considered adequate to control the actions of the likely more than twelve hundred uncooperative occupiers of five different buildings. The administration had underestimated and the *New York Times* underreported the numbers of students in the buildings. Nonetheless, Garelick agreed that his police would enter the buildings without guns and with their badges displayed for identification purposes. It was also agreed that the students removed from the buildings would immediately be put in police vans parked on College Walk and driven to several different precincts for booking. Finally, spectators would be restricted to the South Campus, well away from the occupied buildings.[120]

For all their preparations, both the police in charge of the evacuation and the administrators who authorized it realized the dangers inherent in such an action. Both had every reason to believe that some students (and heart attack–prone faculty) outside the buildings would attempt to stop the police from entering and that, once inside, they would encounter active resistance from some students. They also had reason to fear that policemen facing such resistance, or even the verbal abuse likely to come from occupiers of both sexes, might go beyond their orders to effect the peaceful removal of those calling them "pigs" and worse. Accidents were bound to happen with police and students thrashing around on darkened staircases. Guns, having been reported in Hamilton earlier in the week, might also be present there and in other buildings when the bust came. One can only imagine how unarmed and verbally put-upon police might react to being fired on by those they took to be the sons and daughters of privilege. Grayson Kirk later recalled a conversation with a police officer during the bust, who allowed that he was now glad that his kids had not had the chance to go to a college like Columbia.[121]

In spite of these reasonable fears, the bust began at 2:00 A.M. nonviolently. It did so in the case of the first building cleared, Hamilton Hall, because the black students inside agreed beforehand to leave peacefully at the first incursion. The police entered the building by an underground tunnel, thereby precluding a struggle with those outside on the steps. At precisely 2:15 A.M., eighty-six students who had occupied Hamilton Hall for seven nights and six days marched smartly out the main entrance of the building and into awaiting police vans parked on College Walk. One down, four to go.[122]

The second removal, of the student-occupied parts of Low Library, occurred at 2:25 A.M. It went off without undue violence. Again, the police gained unobstructed access to the building through the underground tunnels. As one of the student occupiers recalled, "We all gave passive resistance and were dragged out—heads were banged, clothes were torn, some people were bleeding. Nothing serious though." Ninety-three students were arrested. Three to go.[123]

The clearing of Avery Hall began at 2:30 A.M., after a call on the students to remove themselves went unheeded, by a direct assault on its locked front door. Inside, the police encountered scattered resistance, and both police and students incurred minor injuries. Forty-two occupiers were arrested. Two left.[124]

The clearing of Fayerweather Hall, which commenced at 2:45 A.M., after the same call encouraging occupiers to leave produced no takers, required the police to climb over dozens of faculty and students gathered in front of the two main doors. This led to several injuries, including a bloody head wound incurred by Professor of History James Shenton. Once inside, the police spent a considerable amount of time corralling students refusing to cooperate in their own removal. Some students reported being hit as they passed through a police gauntlet on the stairways between floors. In the end, some 286 were arrested from Fayerweather. Only Mathematics remained.[125]

As expected, Mathematics Hall proved to be the most difficult to clear. Barricades obstructed the police as they made their way through the darkened building, and stairways made slick by liquid soap made even walking dangerous. In addition, some students actively resisted removal and, in doing so, were bloodied and bruised. Had Mathematics been the norm, rather than the exception, the injury count for the bust would have been much higher. Two hundred and three occupiers were arrested.[126]

The entire evacuation operation was attended by 148 reported injuries to students and police. The most serious was to a uniformed policeman, whose injuries resulted from a student falling or jumping on his back in Fayerweather and left him permanently disabled. Scalp wounds were common, particularly among sympathizers who had sought to block police entry into Fayerweather Hall.[127]

All five buildings had been cleared within an hour and fifteen minutes. But while this was happening and being reported over the campus radio station, WKCR, a large crowd had gathered on South Field, near where the police vans were parked. Some in the crowd were clearly sympathetic to the students being hauled off and so informed the police stationed on College Walk. Objects may have been thrown at the police. What is certain is that the crowd also consisted of Columbians drawn to the campus out of concern with what was happening, including faculty and their families who lived in the neighborhood, some in pajamas.[128]

Yet it was this crowd, not the students removed from the buildings, who experienced the police at their worst. Apparently on a call from uniformed officers overseeing the police vans, a phalanx of police charged the spectators in South Field, forcing them to retreat south and west until they were backed up against Ferris Booth Hall and Butler Library. Because the gates at that end of the campus were locked, they could not remove themselves from the path of the charging police. It was here and in the spillover onto Broadway, where mounted policemen were assigned, where the worst and most inexcusable violence occurred.[129]

One faculty member thought to be knowledgeable about police matters, the historian Robert Fogelson, later attributed the South Field stampede to an internal police rivalry between the "wiseacre Jew" Garelick about to pull off a career-making operation and disgruntled "Irish Mafia" precinct officers on College Walk determined to put their own stamp on it. Whatever its cause, this last event in the otherwise remarkably peaceful operation only served to point up the violent forces that can be set loose in any large-scale police action. "Even those of us who were intellectually ready for the police action," Peter Kenen later acknowledged, "were not emotionally ready for what we saw."[130]

April 30—The Morning After—Rearranging the Deck Chairs?

The stampede and the injuries to innocent parties that the South Campus assault produced had the immediate effect of inflaming extant feelings that the principal responsibility for these injuries and others rested with the administration. The alternative view, that responsibility rested with the students whose occupation of the buildings and disruption of the university's life required the police action, while not unheard the morning after, was clearly a minority one. From early on in the occupation, SDS leaders had believed their cause could only benefit from the police being called on campus, and now they were being proved right. A poll conducted among Columbia faculty and students only days after the bust revealed a substantial shift in opinion (17 percent) among the general Columbia population against the administration after the police action; among direct observers, the swing in favor of accepting the student demands was 30 percent.[131]

Within hours of the police's removal from campus, the Strike Coordinating Committee called for a student strike and demanded that the trustees fire President Kirk and Provost Truman. Later that morning, the Columbia University Student Council voted twenty-two to nine to support the strike and the call for the resignations of Kirk and Truman. By noon, 450 law students had signed a petition in support of the strike and for the censuring of Kirk and Truman. Hundreds of students walked about with black armbands signifying their support for the strike. Few were ready to dispute the claim of a SDS flyer circulating since before dawn: "At 2:30 this morning, Columbia University died."[132]

Meanwhile, after suspending classes for the rest of the week, Provost Truman and Dean Fraenkel walked across the campus early Tuesday morning to survey the damage. The condition of Mathematics Hall especially distressed Truman. Protesters later blamed broken furniture and toppled bookshelves on the police, contending they actively set about making the building look as disreputable as their time in it allowed. Still others, familiar with the building, suggested that Mathematics looked no worse after the bust than before. On his walk back to Low, Truman heard all along the route demands for his resignation.[133]

Later that morning, at 11:00 A.M., the AHFG steering committee, after meeting privately beforehand, called a meeting of the AHFG rank and file. It was held in McMillan Theater, with as many as one thousand faculty and others in attendance. Attendees were, as one participant recalled, "hanging from the rafters." Alan Westin chaired the meeting, which turned directly to the matter of a faculty response to the Strike Coordinating Committee's call for a strike and for the firing of Kirk and Truman. Opposition from Bruce Smith, one of the several conservative junior faculty in the political science department, but also from the historian Fritz Stern and Professor of Law Michael Sovern, both generally thought to be of the liberal left, must have given Westin pause. Just at the time a resolution to support the strike was being called for, he announced, "I will have nothing to do with it," indicated he could not continue as chair, and left. His departure was then followed by all but 150 or so faculty. Those who remained behind reconstituted themselves as the Independent Faculty Group and endorsed the student call for a strike.[134]

At 3:00 P.M., the second meeting of the joint faculties was convened, this time in St. Paul's Chapel. Some six hundred faculty attended, including instructors and lecturers who were allowed in the meeting but asked not to vote. President Kirk chaired the meeting until a resolution calling for his resignation was put forward, at which point he turned the chairmanship over to the dean of the Law School, William Warren. A counterresolution was offered by Professor of History Richard Hofstadter, supportive of the administration's actions. This was followed by a series of resolutions put forward by Professors of Anthropology Morton Fried and Marvin Harris, condemning the administration's actions but stopping short of calling for resignations. At this point, Professor of Law Maurice Rosenberg put forward a fourth set of resolutions, the lunchtime handiwork of two of his law colleagues, Michael Sovern and Kenneth Jones. It was this set of three resolutions that the meeting decided to debate.[135]

The first resolution called for a short moratorium of classes, its purpose, one of the formulators later explained, to preempt the call for a strike. The second expressed support for the tripartite disciplinary procedures that Professors Eugene Galanter, Lionel Trilling, and Carl Hovde had been working on and to which by now the administration (if not yet the trustees) had more or less acceded. The third was to call for the creation of an executive committee of the faculty that would be granted sweeping powers by the trustees "in our University's hour of anguish."[136]

Dean Warren had shown the "Rosenberg Resolutions" to Provost Truman before the meeting. The provost expressed disappointment in them and declined to support them. Truman's disappointment was understandable, in that the resolutions avoided endorsing administration actions and were "in fact though not in form a motion of no-confidence in the President." Meanwhile, Sovern showed them to members of the AHFG steering committee, who reacted more positively, not least because four of their members were suggested for places on the proposed executive committee of the faculty.[137]

The Rosenberg Resolutions were designed to identify a centrist faculty majority somewhere between the AHFG on the left and the administration backers on the right. They did so by initially calling for a ten-person executive committee of the faculty to "be composed of such people as the following" and then proceeded to name four liberal members of the AHFG, including its chair, Allan Westin, and then four conservatives, "such as" Ernest Nagel, William Leuchtenburg, Eli Ginzberg, and Polykarp Kusch, and then a liberally disposed non-AHFG faculty member (i.e., sympathetic to student concerns) "such as" Lionel Trilling. The tenth "such as," Professor of Law Michael Sovern, was added at the urging of William Warren, presumably to assure that the committee included a lawyer. After relatively little debate, the Rosenberg Resolutions were then adopted by a voice vote estimated to be three hundred for and two hundred against. The resolution describing the membership of the committee was then amended to drop all instances of "such as," thereby making those named the elected members of the committee. "E.g." became "i.e." With that bit of punctuational legerdemain, the second meeting of the joint faculties adjourned, leaving to the ten-member committee the thankless job of trying to save the university.[138]

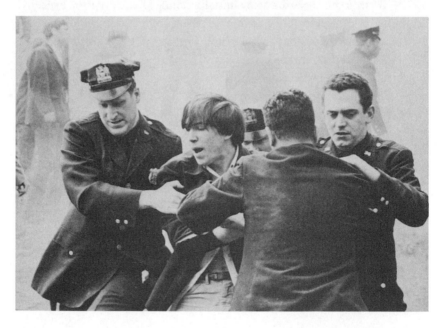

FIGURE 6.1 Mark Rudd speaking at the sun dial rally, spring 1968, flanked by other SDS members: Ted Gold, to Rudd's left; to his right, Nate Bossen, Nick Freudenberg (partially hidden), and Ed Hyman. Photograph by David Finck.

Source: Columbia University Archives—Columbiana Collection.

FIGURE 6.2 New York City police with Columbia College sophomore Fred Wilson in tow, outside fence surrounding Morningside gym site, April 23, 1968. Photograph by Craig Ellenbogen.

Source: Columbia University Archives—Columbiana Collection.

FIGURE 6.3 Columbia College sophomore David Shapiro in Grayson Kirk's office, April 24, 1968.

Source: John Fried, Don Stillman, Jim Grossman, Don Shapiro, Robin Reisig, April Klimley, and Tom Ehrich, "Mutiny at a Great University," *Life* 64, no. 19 (May 10, 1968): 36–37.

FIGURE 6.4 The Ad Hoc Faculty Group at an early meeting, April 25, 1968, in Philosophy Hall. Photograph by Richard Howard.

Source: Columbia University Archives—Columbiana Collection.

FIGURE 6.5 Antiprotest Columbia College students in the Majority Coalition attempting to cordon off Low Library to prevent the resupply of protesting students inside, April 27/28, 1968.

Source: Columbia University Archives—Columbiana Collection.

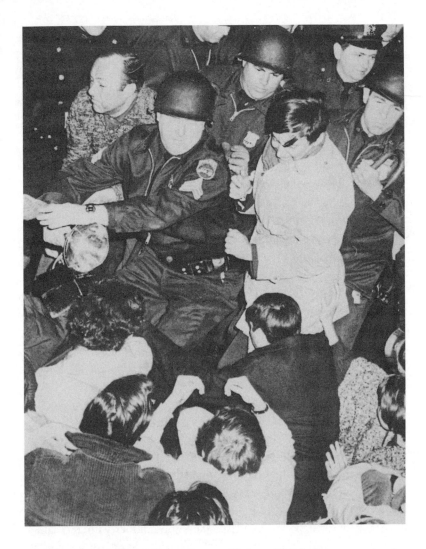

FIGURE 6.6 Nighttime police action outside Avery Hall, before evacuating the building of students, early on the morning of April 30, 1968. Photograph by Tom Metz.

Source: Columbia University Archives—Columbiana Collection.

CHAPTER 16

It's About Columbia

You see, I still can't understand why [students] give a good god damn about how the University runs. I didn't. Why should they?

Lionel Trilling, May 23, 1968

What kind of people would we be if we allowed this center of our culture and our hope to languish and fail? That is the question I must leave with you.

Richard Hofstadter, "214th Columbia University
Commencement Address," June 4, 1968

In the instance of both faculty and students the uprising demanded that one choose, simply, between conservatism and revolution.

Diana Trilling, spring 1969

Faculty Bestirred

THE fundamental political split within the faculty in 1968 was never between those who supported the protesting students and those backing the administration. In point of fact, of the twenty-five hundred or so Columbia faculty, only a few dozen throughout the university actively identified themselves with Kirk after the bust, perhaps the same number with Truman, and they were largely limited to Columbia College faculty. Similarly, no more than a dozen faculty openly aligned themselves with SDS and the Strike Coordinating Committee. A self-described contingent of "Radical Faculty" consisted of a half-dozen members of the anthropology department and hardly anyone else. Similarly, the ranks of what Henry Graff later referred to as unrepentant "king's men" were scarcely more numerous. But if narrower than the gap separating the positions staked out by the most radical students and the most conservative trustees, that dividing faculty was not necessarily more bridgeable.[1]

On one side, herein the left, were the fifty or so faculty in the Independent Faculty Group. They were persuaded that Columbia deserved to be shaken to its foundations and that the radical students had served a useful purpose in pointing up the university's relationship with the governmental war machine. Some were also persuaded that the university's real estate practices and admission policies were racist. Others felt that the legitimacy of some student demands should not be denied because of the incivility of the students' disruptive actions. Others, while not condoning the manipulative tactics of SDS, were prepared to cede their students considerable moral authority and legal responsibility for putting the university right. These faculty were for the most part located in the humanities and social science departments in the arts and sciences and in the Schools of Social Work and Architecture. Although disproportionately from the junior ranks, they included a fair number of newly tenured faculty and a few full professors.[2]

On the other side, the right, was a larger body of faculty, a majority in most of the professional schools, who were unwilling to entrust the retrieval of the university to either the protesting students or their erstwhile faculty allies. Polykarp Kusch's characterization of his position during the occupations—"to support the office of the presidency without limit"—reflected the separation between the office and the man that many faculty defenders of the presidency shared. They supported the need for the assertion of administrative/executive authority, without necessarily supporting Kirk. Indeed, Kusch found that Kirk's behavior during the building occupations reflected "a lack of insight into the realities of what was going on . . . [that was] totally preposterous."[3]

This conservative group included William T. Fox, Herbert Deane, and Bruce Smith in political science, Fritz Stern and William Leuchtenburg in history, Sigmund Diamond in sociology, C. Lowell Harriss in economics, and Charles Frankel in philosophy. Only Harriss would have been comfortable being so labeled. Many of these faculty later helped form, under Frankel's leadership, the International Council on the Future of the University. It became the council's mission to bring together like-minded professors—C. Vann Woodward of Yale, Edward Shils of Chicago, Oscar Handlin of Harvard, Charles Townes of Berkeley, and Allen Bloom of Cornell-Chicago, among others—as a lobby on behalf of the restoration of order on American and European campuses. On campus, they circulated signatures on statements and raised funds to pay for ads in the New York Times defending the academic mission of Columbia.[4]

Whatever their off-campus politics, these faculty shared a deep suspicion of the tactics and motives of their colleagues in the Ad Hoc Faculty Group, especially those imputed to its chair, Alan Westin. Warner Schilling, a colleague of Westin in political science and one of the more vocal conservatives, faulted Westin, Bell, and others on the AHFG for attempting a "power play" that turned an otherwise manageable student-administration confrontation "into a disaster" brought about by "the behavior of the faculty, and in particular of the actions of this group." Another of Westin's colleagues, Herbert Deane, was more damning, charging that the AHFG, "partly through good intentions, partly through ambition, partly through naivete, played an incredibly destructive role in the whole enterprise . . . a kind of objective arm of the SDS."[5]

So strong were intradepartmental disagreements about the events of spring '68 that collegial relations were soured for years. They figured in the decisions of several faculty to leave Columbia, among them Peter Gay in history, Juan Lintz and Immanuel Wallerstein in sociology, Alexander Dallin in political science, and Serg Lang in mathematics. The classicist Gilbert Highet remained on the faculty until retirement in 1975, but for all intents and purposes, according to one observer, "he ran away." Much the same was said of Lionel Trilling in the wake of 1968: he had "no stomach for fighting with these barbarians."[6]

Trilling briefly considered leaving Columbia. Although he ultimately turned down an offer from Oxford in 1970, he never reclaimed his earlier position as a moral and intellectual leader of the faculty. When not declaring that he did not "give a good god damn about how the University runs," he bemoaned the loss of the civil comity that he identified with pre-'68 Columbia. In an interview he gave to the *Partisan Review* in the summer of 1968, he predicted that "academic life will soon be made impossible."[7]

Yet in his last completed book, *Sincerity and Authenticity* (1971), which began as the 1969–1970 Charles Eliot Norton Lectures at Harvard, Trilling took as his subject the alienation of American intellectuals, a condition of concern to him since the late 1940s but that he now judged to be nearly total. "We must take it to be significant of our circumstance," he began the final paragraph, "that many among us find it gratifying to entertain the thought that alienation is to be overcome only by the completeness of alienation, and that alienation completed is not deprivation or deficiency but a potency." For those so disposed, he went on, "the falsities of an alienated social reality are rejected in favor of an upward psychopathic mobility to the point of divinity, each one of us a Christ."[8]

But then came his closing dissent, in which he offered his audience—perhaps his university?—an alternative Christ: one who "accepted the inconveniences of undertaking to intercede, of being a sacrifice, of reasoning with rabbis, of making sermons, of having disciples, of going to weddings and to funerals, of beginning something and at a certain point remarking that it is finished." Trilling died in 1975.[9]

As for Columbia's other fabled public intellectuals, Daniel Bell, after registering his views on Columbia and the new left in an article of the same title in his new journal, *The Public Interest*, departed Columbia for Harvard in the spring of 1969 without so much as a ceremonial bargaining session with Low Library. Merton remained, despite an offer from Chicago, and, as campus life settled down, resumed his preferred role as quiet adviser to the powers. Barzun, made university professor upon his departure from the provostship in June

1967, took no part in the events of 1968 or their aftermath. Ironically, his book *The American University: How It Runs—Where It Is Going*, a typically elegant and sardonic account of what he called "The Higher Bankruptcy" of academe, came out only weeks after the building occupations and the police bust. These events, he noted in an addendum to his introduction, had "disrupted the work of Columbia University." No matter. "I have since then found no reason to change or add to the substance of what I had written months earlier." Barzun retired from Columbia in 1972 and remained in New York City for another two decades before moving to San Antonio, Texas.[10]

Perhaps the most dispiriting denouement was that of Richard Hofstadter, who, like Trilling and Merton, declined offers to go elsewhere. But unlike them, he briefly departed from the role of behind-the-scenes operative to come forward and deliver the commencement address at the official graduation exercises in June 1968. The address provided another occasion to declare his oft-stated belief "in the ultimate reality that the members of the faculty *are* the university," but in circumstances that made it less a tired academic truism than an understated call to arms. Yet, still in character, Hofstadter acknowledged two weeks earlier, "I felt like Kerensky—that history had passed me by. . . . My main plans are to get back to my work, if I can." Shortly thereafter he was diagnosed as suffering from leukemia. He died in 1971, at the age of fifty-four, with what would have been his tenth book, on American colonial political culture, unfinished and the fate of his university still in question.[11]

To the extent that the faculty would have an opportunity in the wake of spring '68 to prove that they were the university, the primary responsibility fell not to the intellectual luminaries of the 1950s and early 1960s but to a younger, less well known generation, who, unlike their more detached elders, determined to set their work aside for the time being and to "give a good god damn about how the University was run."

The Executive Committee of the Faculty came into being by vote of the Joint Faculties on the afternoon of the police bust, May 1, 1968; it disbanded a little over a year later, on May 29, 1969, after the establishment of the University Senate, following a universitywide referendum of faculty and students. Twenty-eight faculty served as ECOF members, five of them throughout its thirteen-month existence. Their labors provided the university with the time and the political running room to focus on the consensus-demanding process of putting itself back together. If these particular faculty had not stepped up to the job, others might have. Yet it is hard to imagine who other than faculty could have done so and still harder to imagine their doing the job better. In this particular moment in Columbia's history, the faculty *was* the university.[12]

The original ten-person Executive Committee of the Faculty reflected a split between those who were said by their critics to be soft on students and the so-called hard-liners. It included four members of the Ad Hoc Faculty Group sympathetic to student demands (Alexander Dallin, Alan Westin, Walter Metzger, and Daniel Bell), as well as four faculty known for their conservative views (Polykarp Kusch, William Leuchtenburg, Eli Ginzberg, and Ernest Nagel). Lionel Trilling was included as the iconic man in the middle. Michael Sovern, whose general political persuasion was liberal and whose views on the local situation were not well known, became the committee's tenth member. At its first meeting, as if to acknowledge the balancing act that secured them their places on the committee, Westin and Sovern were elected cochairs.[13]

However politically balanced, the original membership slighted other faculty divisions. That the committee included members of two of the ten professional schools (Ginzberg in Business and Sovern in Law) was more a matter of chance than a conscious effort at representativeness. The other eight members all came from the arts and sciences, with three identified with the College. The inclusion of only full professors—all male and mostly Jewish—suggests the original slate makers had much to learn about constituting a representative faculty body under the new dispensation.[14]

The additional members, as well as the elected replacements for three original members who resigned, gave the Executive Committee a democratic and procedural legitimacy it had initially lacked. But it did something else at least as significant: it shifted the political orientation of the committee to the right. Of the newly enfranchised faculties, only the Columbia College junior faculty elected a colleague (Samuel Coleman, an associate in philosophy) who was publicly sympathetic to the student protesters. Several faculties chose colleagues known to be distinctly unsympathetic to them. The election of William Theodore de Bary, whose sympathies with the Majority Coalition were well known, as the representative of the Faculty of Philosophy, in place of the ambivalent Lionel Trilling, was a case in point. Alan Westin's resignation in the summer of 1968 both consolidated Michael Sovern's position as chairman and put the Executive Committee permanently in the control of its center-right majority.[15]

Call it what you will—and a community steeped in revolutionary history had no end of labels: Thermidor, Restoration, "return of the Mandarins"—the ascendance of the Executive Committee's center-right majority by September 1968 and the growing political activism of conservative senior faculty generally marked an important step back from the edge of the cliff that, five months earlier, the more radical members of the AHFG, with their call for virtual amnesty and support of a student strike, had momentarily contemplated going over.[16]

Two dozen or so faculty to the left of the Executive Committee continued to express themselves through the Independent Faculty Group (IFG). But even these faculty found they had fewer and fewer disagreements with the Executive Committee as it went about its business transforming earlier students demands—on the gym, on secret research, on neighborhood expansion, on NROTC, on disciplinary rules—into negotiable positions that the trustees could be persuaded to accept. Equally disarming was the committee's warm endorsement of the election of an Independent Faculty Group member, Professor of English Carl Hovde, by an extrastatutory vote of the College faculty, as dean of Columbia College.[17]

By fall, the Executive Committee had effectively persuaded most left-leaning faculty of the integrity of its intentions. Meanwhile, faculty to its right were cheered by the isolation of the Ad Hoc Faculty contingent within the committee and the mellowing of the Independent Faculty Group without. Still far from united, the Columbia faculty returning to campus in the fall of 1968 were better prepared to cope with the ideologically charged and threatening scene than when they had left four months earlier. For this, they had largely the summer-long efforts of their Executive Committee to thank.

Trustees Mobilized: Learning New Tricks

Establishing its nonrevolutionary bona fides made the Faculty Executive Committee's early dealings with the trustees possible but by no means easy. To a man, the trustees had resented the Ad Hoc Faculty's meddling during the building occupations. Several viewed Westin in particular as the rogue leader of an attempted putsch. When AHFG members had openly spoken of "withholding services," urged acceptance of "amnesty-without-the-word," and supported the first calls for a strike, trustees consigned them to the same camp as SDS.[18]

Trustee Harold "Mickey" McGuire was particularly insistent that the half-dozen faculty arrested during the bust be prosecuted to the full extent of the law—and then fired. His reprisal efforts extended beyond the faculty to members of the administration. A case in point: he wanted to sack the admissions officer who, back in 1965, admitted Mark Rudd to Columbia, demanding of fellow board members, "Did Harvard know more than Columbia in turning Rudd down?"[19]

Yet if the trustees were going to have a role in restoring the university to order, their best bet was to align themselves with the efforts of whatever faculty group could claim a measure of representativeness. From this perspective, the Faculty Executive Committee was far more acceptable than the Ad Hoc Faculty had been. Most of the trustees quickly accepted this reality and, after a meeting with the committee on the evening of May 6, warily endorsed the creation of Executive Committee of the Faculty.[20]

The trustees' own seriousness of purpose was confirmed by its decision at that same meeting to create a six-person special trustee committee, to be chaired by outgoing trustee Alan H. Temple and the newest member of the board, Robert Lilley. To help the committee with its charge "to study and recommend changes in the basic structure of the University," the trustees hired a management consultant firm, Cresup, McCormick, and Paget.[21]

Of the original Faculty Executive Committee members, only Professor of Business Eli Ginzberg was personally acquainted with any of the trustees. He knew Frank Hogan and Allan Temple as summer neighbors on Martha's Vineyard. Through Ginzberg, Sovern came to know Hogan and Temple and, through them, developed links to other key trustees, among them Lilley and another newly elected member, Charles Luce, both of whom took leading roles in the special trustee committee. Not since the halcyon 1890s had members of the trustees and the faculty worked so directly with each other. Butler would not have been pleased.[22]

The evolving relationship primarily involved the Faculty Executive Committee's convincing the trustees to put aside their inclinations to punish students and instead focus on getting the university going again. This was not easy. The first two substantive actions by the committee—to endorse the tripartite committee created by the Columbia College Committee on Instruction to devise provisional disciplinary rules for political activities on campus and to recommend that the university drop criminal charges against the students arrested on April 30—encountered trustee opposition.[23]

In view of the fact that the Disciplinary Committee, chaired by Professor of English Quentin Anderson, was already at work devising interim rules, the trustees decided not to press their earlier view that discipline was exclusively a responsibility of the trustees, which they delegated to the president. But the dropping of criminal charges was another matter, and one that exercised the passions of the several lawyers on the board.

It was widely assumed that Trustee Frank Hogan, district attorney of New York and by reputation and demeanor very much a law-and-order guy, opposed dropping criminal charges. Yet it was he who guided Ginzberg and Sovern in fashioning proposals for dropping criminal charges against the arrested students that would be acceptable to a majority of the board. Hogan also helped secure the trustees' acceptance of Hovde's appointment as dean of the College. Meanwhile, the chairman of the board, William E. Petersen, proved helpful in keeping Harold McGuire and other trustee hard-liners at bay. Finally, Westin's resignation from the Faculty Executive Committee in June, leaving the pragmatic lawyer Sovern in charge, persuaded the trustees that earlier suspicions that "we might be wild men" could be put to rest.[24]

Between April 30, the day of the bust, and the start of its regular schedule in September, the full board met thirteen times. The Temple-Lilley Special Committee struck some of its vacation-deprived members as being in continuous session. Even for veteran trustees, these meetings constituted their first serious encounter with the university's manifold problems. While the situation was worse than even the pessimists among them imagined, at least they now knew what it was. For new members, particularly Charles Luce, who had become a trustee in the spring, the experience must have been akin to boarding a boat about to capsize. Serious bailing was the order of the day. A few trustees despaired and took their eleemosynary interests to less troubled institutions. But, overall, the actions of the trustees in the three months following on the bust were those of a board becoming, for the first time in a half-century, fully and constructively engaged in meeting its charter-given responsibilities to sustain the university. It did so fully realizing that the trustees would have to undergo the restructuring they urged on other parts of the university, making them part of what was becoming an all-Columbia project.

Since 1909, when it had made provisions for six alumni-nominated members, the Columbia board of trustees had made only one major change in its procedures. That occurred in 1955, when the board imposed a mandatory retirement age of seventy on members, which it shortly thereafter raised to seventy-two to accommodate William Paley. Yet, in the two years after 1968, the board made the following changes to its procedures:

- It eliminated the category of life trustee by limiting the term of membership for all trustees to a six-year term, renewable only once, which meant that no trustee elected henceforth could serve more than a total of twelve years.
- It designated six more seats on the twenty-four-member board—in addition to the six selected by the alumni—to be filled by the vote of a representative body of faculty, students, and administrators.

The intended effect of these changes was to lower the median age of the trustees, increase turnover, and facilitate rapid diversification of the board. And that's just what happened.[25]

The principal nonstatutory change in the postwar board had been an increased openness to Jewish candidates for membership. The election in 1944 of Arthur Hays Sulzberger (Journalism 1919), the publisher of the New York Times, was followed three years later by that of CBS head William Paley. In the spring of

1968, the board had at least seven Jewish members. From one perspective, Arthur Ochs "Punch" Sulzberger's succession in 1967 to the seat held by his father seems a throwback to the hereditary successions of the nineteenth century.[26]

Within months of the spring disturbances, the Board elected its first black trustee, the Rev. M. Moran Weston (CC 1930; Ph.D. 1954), pastor of Harlem's St. Phillip's Episcopal Church. At the time of Weston's election, the trustees considered several other, more nationally prominent blacks, among then the head of the Urban League, Whitney Young, and the University of Chicago historian John Hope Franklin, who declined. When Trustee Benjamin Buttenweiser urged the prompt election of "at least two Negroes," Chairman Petersen, in words reminiscent of the debate in the 1920s over the election of a Jew to the board, reminded his colleagues that "trustees should not be selected merely because they are black." But this time the moral imperative to alter the racial composition of the board by electing more than one black prevailed. Weston's election was quickly followed by the alumni election of a second black trustee, Franklin A. Thomas (CC 1955; CU Law 1958). In 1973 the trustees elected the first woman, Martha Muse (BC 1948; CU M.A. 1955) to the board, only months before the University Senate elected the second, Katherine Auchincloss (CU Engineering 1961).[27]

Given the board's historic capacity to resist change, these were radical and audacious moves. Gone were the days when the board in gentlemanly fashion took up the Jewish Problem or the Woman Question or the Black Issue without the presence of a Jew, a woman, or a black in their company. As a silver lining in the cloud that was Columbia '68, the rapid and uncontentious diversification of the Columbia board of trustees qualifies. The post-'68 trustees reinvented themselves just in time to play a crucial role in the reconstruction of Columbia in the 1970s. In so doing, they merit positive comparison with their equally effective but less crisis-beset predecessors of the 1890s.

Students Engaged

Persuading trustees that they were not "wild men" complicated the other obligation pressing on the Faculty Executive Committee in its early days: securing legitimacy in the eyes of skeptical students. The strategy the committee adopted mirrored the one SDS devised for faculty during the building occupations: divide and co-opt. It sought to separate the most radical students—those in SDS and the Strike Coordinating Committee who did not care if Columbia went under and were, as SDSer Lewis Cole put it, "way beyond that"—from the larger number of other exercised students who did care. These the Executive Committee hoped to engage in the project of restructuring the university, thereby further isolating the radicals. Like faculty conservatives, the few student conservatives, the committee reasoned, would go along with just about any changes short of turning the place over to Rudd or the Ad Hoc Faculty Group.[28]

The notion of university restructuring had its genesis in the interminable discussions that took place during the occupation of Fayerweather Hall. It referred to internal reforms that were revealed as necessary by the disturbances. Chief among them was an increased role for students and faculty in university decision making. Ardent SDSers immediately recognized calls to restructure the university as likely to divert attention from their concerns and so disparaged the restructuralists as "student leaders." The Faculty Executive Committee, however, saw restructuring as a way to redirect student concern away from global or neighborhood issues and back to on-campus matters. Unlike SDS, the Faculty Executive Committee welcomed the restructuralists and gave every early indication of wanting to work with them. Thus the battle between the committee and SDS/SCC for the support of the left-center of the student body was joined.[29]

Here, the Faculty Executive Committee got some unintended help from the two most visible radical student groups. SDS's high-handed methods of maintaining control during the building occupations had secured the agreement of the SAS blacks in Hamilton Hall not to vacate short of a police action. SAS also went along with the Strike Committee's call to boycott classes. Yet SAS was soon operating independently of and increasingly at cross-purposes with SDS/SCC doings. Lionel Trilling aptly characterized the difference between the black occupiers of Hamilton and the white SDSers in Mathematics: the whites "were wholly political in their motives—not concerned with the University—simply destructive," whereas "the black students wanted in."[30]

SAS demands in the wake of the bust reflected the immediate and local concerns of Columbia's black students. They included:

- greater control over admissions of blacks, including a separate admissions committee on which black students would constitute a majority;
- control over the interim committee charged with creating a Black Studies Institute at Columbia;
- more financial aid for black students;
- a black lounge in the dormitory space previously occupied by the NROTC;
- more black faculty.[31]

In advancing these demands over the next several months, black students occasionally engaged in disruptive activities, such as blockading Hamilton Hall for several hours on April 14, 1969, when their demand for a separate admissions committee for black applicants was rejected. But they also proved willing to negotiate with the Faculty Executive Committee over more reasonable demands, including having a significant role in efforts to recruit more minority students to Columbia. The freshman class recruited in the spring of 1969 included 260 black, Hispanic, and Asian acceptances, up from 145 the year before.[32]

What Columbia's black students decided after 1968 was to see how much could be won by battling within the system. This meant pressing for more courses in African-American studies and more black faculty. One SAS member told the Faculty Executive Committee that where the SDS wanted to "apply a gangrene" to American society in order "to destroy it," black students wanted "to test the tolerance of the society, . . . to see how much play it allowed." That's what the Faculty Executive Committee was doing, too. And if, in the course of proving the university's "play," it disrupted the SDS-SAS alliance of convenience that had doomed the Kirk-Truman efforts to resolve the building occupations crisis, so much the better.[33]

Meanwhile, SDS/SCC calls to take the struggle off campus after the bust angered some students who had supported the occupations and the boycotting of classes but were not ready to take to the streets. Some of these decided that the overtures coming from the Faculty Executive Committee and the Temple trustee committee to join them in their restructuring project were worthy of consideration. On May 7 several students on the Strike Coordinating Committee broke with the SDS-dominated majority to join similarly minded radical students to form Students for a Restructured University, or SRU. This group included several history graduate students who had been part of the Fayerweather colloquy, among them Mike Wallace and Rusty Eisenberg, plus a third-year philosophy graduate student, John Thoms. When rebuked by Mark Rudd and Lewis Cole for forgetting that "the internal structure of the university cannot be separated from the University's social and political function in society," they remained determined to find that out for sure.[34]

One should not exaggerate the magnitude of the initial disagreement among student radicals. Many in SRU remained committed to the use of disruptive protests as an effective tactic and continued to back the boycotting of classes. As an SRU spokesman, John Thoms, assured an audience of radical GS students on May 16, "Those of us who left have not broken faith with our mentors in SDS."[35]

On May 17 Rudd-led SDSers made good on their call to carry their protest off campus by joining community activists in the aborted takeover by squatters of a Columbia-owned apartment building on 114th Street. Police were called, and 130 arrests were made, among them 61 Columbia and 21 Barnard and

Teachers College students. SRU members condoned this action, even as they set course in a different direction.[36]

The 114th Street demonstration did not mean that SDS had abandoned the campus just yet. On Tuesday night, May 21, an SDS-led crowd of 200 students stormed into Hamilton Hall to protest the suspension of four SDS leaders who had refused to report to their deans for disciplinary proceedings. President Kirk promptly called the New York City Police to clear the building, which they did early the next morning. They arrested 177 occupiers, 115 of whom were were students, among them Mark Rudd. This time the police, sensitive to criticism of their behavior three weeks earlier with respect to spectators, had tried to clear the campus before removing the students in Hamilton through the tunnels that led directly to Amsterdam Avenue. Even so, bystanders suffered minor injuries and major indignities.[37]

Unlike the reaction to the first bust, the general response to Hamilton II was unsupportive of the occupiers. Theirs had been a conspicuously whites-only undertaking, with no participation from SAS. The actions of supporters of the occupation, who broke windows with pavement stones and set fires in other buildings, struck many as gratuitous and at odds with the widely accepted view of the first occupation as a disciplined civil rights action. To the contrary, Hamilton II seemed to be about demands by SDS leaders that they be exempted from any disciplinary action.

Faculty support for Hamilton II was conspicuously absent. Some professors sympathetic to student protests were given pause by reports that occupiers had used their time in Hamilton to break into an office and destroy a decade's worth of research by Professor of History Orest Ranum, an outspoken critic of SDS. The Faculty Executive Committee promptly and unequivocally condemned the occupation and the trashing of Ranum's office, as did several student organizations. But perhaps the most telling reaction was that of SRU, which, while it retained its radical bona fides by asserting that "the burden of guilt lies with the administration" and faulted ECOF for accusing radical students of setting the fires, did "regret that SCC found it necessary to seize Hamilton Hall."[38]

Hamilton II did not mark the end of SDS's hold over radical student opinion on campus. On November 19, 1968, for example, a Law School hearing into disciplinary charges against Gus Reishbach (CU Law 1970) was disrupted by Jonah Raskin (CC 1963), then teaching at Stony Brook. But Hamilton II did mark the beginning of the end of the occupation-induced and bust-reinforced unity of the Columbia student left. Without leaving their radical credentials at the door, students redirected their political energies to working with less radical students, faculty, and trustees. Some would inevitably be disappointed in the modest restructuring that did occur, but the effort itself was salutary and co-optive.[39]

Meanwhile, when Rudd's efforts to take over the national SDS convention in June were rebuffed by delegates from other campuses, he and eighteen others—by the count of one SDS member, Paul Berman (CC 1969), who stayed behind—"left the chapter and the University to join the weather adventure." They then embarked on a downward spiral that included intermediate stops at the Weathermen-orchestrated "Days of Rage" protests in Chicago in the summer of 1969, the founding of the avowedly violent Revolutionary Youth Movement, and alignment with the Black Panthers and their campaign of "offing the pigs." The most tragic stop occurred on March 6, 1970, in an Eleventh Street townhouse, where three people were killed, including SDS member Ted Gold (class of 1968), blown up by antipersonnel bombs containing roofing nails.[40]

Several Columbia Weathermen implicated in the townhouse explosion, among them Mark Rudd, fled to Canada. Others persisted in various forms of what Berman characterized as "radical thuggery," including David Gilbert (CC 1966), who almost a decade later participated in the holdup of a Brinks armored truck in upstate New York, during which two policemen and a security guard were killed. Gilbert was sentenced to twenty years in Attica State Prison.[41]

As for conservative students, a handful sued the university for ending classes in violation of the academic calendar. A few others transferred to what they expected to be less radically beset campuses, only to find that in the next two years student unrest and political disruptions were endemic on the national academic scene. Others, among them Abbe Fred Lowell (CC 1971), offered rejoinders to the *Spectator*'s anti-administration editorials. But still others, including those who reconstituted the Majority Coalition as Students for Columbia University took up the invitation of the Faculty Executive Committee and various trustee committees to join erstwhile enemies to the left in the restructuring effort.[42]

Some conservative—or, more precisely, antiradical—students even found their way onto the editorial board of the *Spectator*, which remained during the successive editorships of Robert Friedman (CC 1969) and Paul Starr (CC 1970) resolutely critical of the administration and suspicious of the Faculty Executive Committee. By then, however, it had grown impatient with SDS excesses. Columnist Michael Stern (CC 1971) wrote an editorial condemning the Weathermen in the wake of the Eleventh Street explosion. With the election of Martin Flumenbaum (CC 1971) as editor-in-chief in April 1970, the *Spectator* took up the unfamiliar cause of opposing further student disruptions and occasionally crediting Columbia with doing some things right.[43]

Exit Kirk

For the Faculty Executive Committee, establishing a working relationship with both conservative-minded trustees and reform-minded students was crucial to its prospects of knitting the university back together. Getting along with the incumbent, wounded administration in Low Library was not, particularly if doing so compromised the committee's independence.

More than space considerations prompted the committee to pass up the offer of offices in Low Library. It decided instead to set up shop on the third floor of the Men's Faculty Club. This was just one of its early actions explained in part by the desire to distance itself from the administration. Kirk and Truman felt that the committee represented a challenge to their already compromised authority. President Kirk, on being told by one of its cochairs on May 4 of the committee's decision to convene an outside commission to investigate the recent events, informed the messenger to "take your witch hunt and go to hell."[44]

Among the many areas of the university traditionally the responsibility of the president and his administration that the Faculty Executive Committee increasingly took over was how the university presented itself to the outside world. To say that Columbia had a public relations problem in the wake of the spring disturbances was to put it mildly. Much of the animosity directed at Columbia antedated the events of 1968. Murray Kempton's "Thoughts on Columbia," in the *New York Post* on the day of the police bust is atypical only in his admission of an anti-Columbia bias: "I have hated it as long as I can remember . . . and am no judge of its agony. . . . [My] dream for Columbia is that it fall into ruin like the Roman Empire." Even Kempton's colleague, fellow liberal and long-suffering Columbia football enthusiast, James A. Wechsler (CC 1935), could muster little good to say on behalf of Columbia's handling of the April disturbances, except to applaud the evenhanded coverage of the student radio station, WKCR.[45]

Although the *New York Times* continued to be supportive of the Columbia administration and trustees in the months after the bust, other journalists, including the *Times*'s own Harrison E. Salisbury, so questioned the paper's reporting during the occupation as to make suspect everything it wrote of Columbia. Meanwhile, the national weekly magazines, *Life*, *Newsweek*, and *Time*, gave extensive and often cover-story attention to the Columbia troubles, typically balancing their hostile rendering of the actions of Columbia's radical students with pointed criticism of Columbia's administrators.[46]

The photographs of bloodied students and faculty accompanying the *Life* story, largely written by six Columbia Journalism School students on assignment, were especially evocative of a campus in chaos. Television coverage, technologically abetted by new lightweight shoulder cameras easily hauled up from midtown studios, produced footage that portrayed the nighttime clashes of police and students in building hallways as surreal exercises in brutality.[47]

The older opinion magazines on the left, such as the *Nation* and the *New Republic*, were predictably hard on Columbia. The *New Republic*'s reporter on the scene, Dotson Rader, was particularly imaginative, conjuring up encounters that apparently occurred only in his fertile mind. Meanwhile, a leading organ of the new left, *Ramparts*, gave over its back page to Mathematics Hall occupier Tom Hayden's Che Guevara–inspired musings on "Two, Three, Many Columbias." Of Columbia's student radicals, Hayden assured his readers, "they want a new and independent university standing against the mainstream of American society, or they want no university at all." Yet another critical voice was heard from the literary left, from Norman Mailer, whose daughter at Barnard had been among the occupiers of Mathematics Hall, when he informed the SDSers who had shut down Columbia, "I approve of your methods, but not your aims."[48]

Nor could Columbia find support among conservative journalists. William F. Buckley, in both his syndicated column in the *New York Post* and his own *National Review*, delivered several obituaries on Columbia, without the usual regrets and condolences common to the literary form. In his May 4 *New York Post* column, "In Defense of the Police," Buckley declared that if Columbia did not suspend the students and fire the faculty who participated in the disruptions, "it ought not to survive as a university." On one matter, at least, the Wolverine Hayden and the Old Eli Buckley agreed: Columbia was dispensable.[49]

Several Columbia faculty rushed into print accounts of the campus events and reflections on their meaning, in some cases without benefit of having been on campus. None of those first into print were prepared to offer a supportive word for Columbia's administration or venture a brief on behalf of the university's survival. Among these participant-observer-chroniclers were Daniel Bell, Zbigniew Brzezinski, Dankwart Rustow, and Marvin Harris. When not openly critical of Columbia, as was Harris, they favored a tone of academic detachment.[50]

Columbia's public relations problem was compounded by the fact that the roles the president, provost, and trustees played in calling in the police ill-suited them to conduct the damage control the situation demanded. Initial efforts to get out their side of the story only confirmed the difficulty. Truman's several press and television interviews, in which he declared, "This University is not going to die," however heartfelt, were neither convincing or reassuring. On the other hand, Kirk's "Letter to Friends of Columbia" and even more the Trustee

McGuire–sponsored defense of the Morningside gym project, "Partners in the Park," both of which were prepared by the public relations firm Hill and Knowlton, "made more enemies than friends." Neither did anything so much as allow readers to draw comparisons of Columbia's leaders with the Bourbons, who "never learned and never forgot."[51]

However personally offensive they found it, Kirk and the trustees had no choice but to accede to the Faculty Executive Committee decision on May 4 to bring an outside fact-finding commission to campus to investigate the events and underlying causes of the April disturbances. Three days after the trustees agreed to fund the five-member fact-finding commission, with ex–solicitor general of the United States and Harvard law professor Archibald Cox as chairman, the commission was on campus and inviting testimony.[52]

The composition of the fact-finding commission spoke to the ECOF's determination that its report not be viewed as an administrative white paper. Its membership included thee lawyers—Cox, Anthony G. Amsterdam, law professor at the University of Pennsylvania, and Simon H. Rifkind, a former United States district judge—a physician, Dana Farnsworth, director of the Harvard Health Service, and Hylan G. Lewis, a black Brooklyn College sociologist. The only Columbian was Judge Rifkind (CU Law 1925), though, as the transcript of the hearings makes clear, he would be none too sympathetic to those currently running his alma mater.[53]

On August 5, midway through the hearings of the Cox commission, before which he had declined to appear, President Kirk informed the trustees of his desire to retire before the opening of the fall term. In the interim, the trustees would appoint an acting president in his stead.[54]

While Kirk's departure had been expected, the trustees' decision not to make Provost David Truman acting president surprised and disappointed Truman's many Columbia friends. Only thirteen months earlier, he had been considered Kirk's heir-presumptive. But in making him provost, the trustees may also have made Truman's ascendancy difficult in even the best of times. Kirk had not favored Truman's abrupt insertion, nor had the bumped Barzun, nor had the deans of the professional schools. The fact that Truman continued to run the College, where Coleman had been installed as acting dean, after assuming both the provostship and the vice presidency (vacated by Lawrence Chamberlain, who left with Barzun), struck some observers as a monopolization of offices not seen since colonial times.[55]

During his opening months as provost, Truman alienated several professional school deans, among them William Warren of the Law School, Courtney Brown of the Business School and Andrew W. Cordier of the School of International Affairs, by his aggressive championing of the arts and sciences and, even more so, the College. (Nor did it help matters that, by one account, Truman's devoted secretary took it upon herself for his first four months in Low Library to make sure that the provost's "bad news" mail was set aside unread.) That these deans had reason to blame the spring disturbances on precisely those parts of the university with which Truman was most closely identified did not make the prospect of his becoming president any more palatable. When Kirk informed the other deans that Truman might well become the acting president if they did not voice their objections, they did so. Meanwhile, the Faculty Executive Committee, which favored one of their own for the acting presidency, Polykarp Kusch, enlisted in the deans' "Anybody But Dave" campaign.[56]

Some of Truman's admirers on the faculty admitted that he had lost stature during the crisis, through both his abruptness in dealing with friends and his obduracy in confronting critics. That he refused to distance himself from Kirk cost him points with some faculty; that he seemed to do so in private hurt him with others. Still others found his emotional swings, which left him shaking with rage one moment and reduced to tears the next, made him a serious risk. When interviewed in August by the Faculty Executive Committee, Truman struck one member from the Medical Faculty as so "psychologically damaged" by the experiences of the spring as to be unsuited for the acting presidency. Thus, when the deans urged the trustees to make acting president one of their own, Andrew W. Cordier, the dean of the School of International Affairs, the Faculty Executive Committee went along.[57]

Even after Cordier's appointment as acting president in late August, the Faculty Executive Committee remained the principal political force on campus. A week before classes began, this was confirmed at a meeting of the Joint Faculties on September 12, convened to consider the disciplinary rules devised by the tripartite committee chaired by Quentin Anderson. It was the acting sixty-seven-year-old president who greeted the five hundred faculty gathered in McMillan Theater and received much applause, but it was thirty-seven-year-old Michael Sovern, the chairman of the Faculty Executive Committee and still relatively unknown to most faculty outside the Law School, who ran the meeting.[58]

While some of the planning for the meeting had gone awry (drafts of an early proposal for what became the University Senate were late in arriving), the contrast between the orderliness and parliamentary probity of these proceedings and the participatory chaos of the AHFG sessions back in April was not lost on those who had participated in both. For some faculty, just back on a campus very much the worse for wear since the spring, the meeting was an acid test of the ability of the Faculty Executive Committee, and the senior faculty more generally, to get the university back on track.[59]

Following a report from Sovern on the Faculty Executive Committee's summer activities, including its dealings with the trustees and plans under way for a university Senate, the meeting turned to the principal business at hand: consideration of the interim rules of discipline drawn up by Anderson's tripartite committee. These rules adhered to Columbia's traditional practice of allowing nondisruptive political dissent but placed limits on picketing and subjected those engaged in disruptive activities to disciplinary action. The debate proceeded civilly, with a handful of faculty sympathetic to student protest questioning this or that provision. Dankwart Rustow of the Independent Faculty Group had a list of amendments. No one moved to make the proposed rules more restrictive or punitive, though Paul Kristeller and other conservatives objected to any moves to soften them. Members of the Anderson committee spoke in defense of each the challenged resolutions. All proposed amendments intended to weaken the rules were voted down by substantial margins.[60]

The meeting then took up alternate resolutions proposed by Sidney Morgenbesser of the Independent Faculty Group that would have the faculty "accept" the interim rules without "endorsing" them. This would allow, its sponsors suggested, rules to be put into effect without committing the faculty to defending them. A student member of the Disciplinary Committee, Eric Witkin (CC 1969) then spoke against these resolutions, declaring the issue to be "whether this faculty is going to take the responsibility of voting on approving disciplinary measures." He sat down to applause, and the question was called.[61]

Then, from the back of the room, came word that students outside were demanding to speak at the meeting. There was also some intimation that if they were not let in the faculty would not be let out. An audiotape of the meeting indicates that the pounding on the doors and the shouting from the students made proceeding difficult. Some of the faculty who had earlier proposed changes to the resolutions urged that the students be invited in. Others called for the meeting to adjourn. SDS leaders outside sent in a message that the faculty "had three minutes to admit them or they will attempt to break in." To this, the chair responded, "We will not be moved by such ultimatums."[62]

At this point, Sovern invited a motion from Faculty Executive Committee colleague Eli Ginzberg to close debate, vote on the Morgenbesser resolution, and then proceed directly to a vote on the Anderson-proposed interim rules. The Morgenbesser resolution was defeated 272 to 129. The faculty then proceeded—it now being 2:30 P.M. and at the outer limit of the agreed-upon time for the meeting to adjourn—to adopt the interim rules by a show of hands by the four hundred or so faculty still present. "I see about ten hands raised," the chair announced after calling for those opposed. "The resolution is carried." He then thanked the committee for its efforts, the gathered faculty for their participation, and declared the meeting adjourned. Test passed.[63]

The Cox Commission: Facts and Then Some

The Cox commission held twenty-one days of hearings, heard testimony from seventy-nine witnesses, and compiled 3,790 pages of transcript. Virtually everyone who wanted to was allowed to testify, including several neighborhood residents who provided color but shed little light on the matters under consideration. The leadership of the Strike Coordinating Committee, SDS, and SAS all refused to testify, despite Cox's urging. (Rudd occasionally attended.) Otherwise, a wide array of student opinion was made available to the commission. Provost Truman testified in two lengthy appearances. Some twenty faculty of every political persuasion also testified, sometimes lecturing the commission and sometimes being lectured at by Judge Rifkind.[64]

The testimony of Chaplain/Rabbi Bruce Goldman, openly sympathetic to the student protesters, tested Rifkind's patience, not least when Goldman suggested that the judge had a conflict of interest because he had publicly supported a reduction of clergy on campus. When Assistant Professor Mark Kesselman complained about junior faculty being overworked, Rifkind pointed out that "seventy-hour weeks are nor unusual for a professional man" and called it the norm at his law office. The fact that the commission was taking testimony on May 22, the day of the Hamilton II bust, and also on the morning after Robert Kennedy was assassinated in Los Angeles on June 5 gave the proceedings an added element of serious purposefulness. Only once did Cox lose his temper, when a self-invited testifier planted his feet on the table around which the commission sat. Otherwise, a courtroomlike decorum prevailed.[65]

On September 26, just seven weeks after the hearings ended, twenty-five thousand copies of *Crisis at Columbia: Report of the Fact-Finding Commission Appointed to Investigate the Disturbances at Columbia University in April and May 1968* were published in a 222-page paperback edition. A glance put to rest all but the most cynical doubts about a white paper in the making. After briskly noting the existence of outside forces at work on the Columbia campus, the Cox report focused on the internal causes, ladling out blame with a steady, unsparing hand.

The administration was judged slow in responding to student concerns and inflexible in matters relating to the neighborhood. The Ad Hoc Faculty Group was faulted for undercutting the authority of the president and for holding out to the occupying students the prospect of their joining in a sympathy strike. Senior faculty were chastised for demonstrating throughout the crisis that they "preferred individual autonomy to collective responsibility." The trustees were reproved for their disregard of shifting community sentiment with respect to the gym. Perhaps the harshest criticism was directed at the chaplains, who were found, with the exception of Monsignor Rea, to have openly supported the protests. Only the black students occupying Hamilton Hall escaped serious censure.[66]

The Cox report delved at length into "quality of student life" issues. The scruffy dorms reminded the commission chairman of "a run-down rooming house." Unfortunately, some of the "hard truths" contained in the report were undercut by a tone throughout, and by the chairman's remarks on releasing it, that suggested Columbia's problems were of Columbia's making and something to which other universities—read Harvard—were immune. Upon reading the report, several trustees demanded the university draw up a response to it, but both Acting President Cordier and the folks at Hill and Knowlton urged Columbia to take its lumps in silence.[67]

The wisdom of this advice was confirmed the following February, when the editor of *Columbia College Today*, George Keller (CC 1951; Ph.D. 1959), published his lengthy account "Six Weeks that Shook Morningside." The article was not so much a defense of the administration (it was in fact sharply critical of Kirk) as it was a critical analysis of the motives of the student protesters and those Keller regarded as their erstwhile faculty allies on the Ad Hoc Faculty Group. Three decades later, Keller's "Six Weeks" can be read as a powerful piece of journalistic advocacy, by no means even-handed but no more partisan—and far more factually reliable—than the dozens of "I was there" accounts or firehouse analyses offered up by faculty, students, and outside observers in the immediate wake of the disturbances. Even so, it cost Keller his job.[68]

Some faculty members complained to Columbia College dean Carl Hovde, in effect Keller's boss, about the antiradical character of the article and what they took to be anti-Semitic remarks. Rabbi Goldman threatened to take the issue to the state authorities. *The Owl*, an undergraduate journal associated with General Studies, published a critique of it, calling *Columbia College Today*'s editorial policy that of "telling the alums what they want to hear." Hovde's reprimand of Keller—not for the article's content but for failing to clear it with him in keeping with their understanding—prompted Keller to resign. Thirty years later, Hovde recalled the incident as the most personally wrenching of his deanship.[69]

For all the critical commentary its publication produced, the Cox commission's report served the intended purpose of the Faculty Executive Committee: to promulgate a factual version of Columbia's troubled recent history that might allow the university to get on with forging a better future. It was followed two months later by the publication of the well-received *Up Against the Ivy Wall: A History of the Columbia Crisis*, by *Spectator* editors Jerry Avorn and Robert Friedman, both CC 1969, as well as the more idiosyncratic but engaging

Strawberry Statement: Notes of a College Revolutionary, by James Kunen (CC 1970). Their appearance assured the university a second round of critical press coverage. Columbia's troubles qualified as one of the national media's top half-dozen stories of 1968.[70]

Nor was the Cox report the most critical booklength account of Columbia to appear in the months after the disturbances. That distinction likely goes to *The Battle for Morningside Heights: Why Students Rebel* (1970), by Roger Kahn. Here, the principal responsibility for Columbia's troubles in 1968 is placed on its tradition of genteel anti-Semitism and its WASP deans, which Columbia's radical students courageously took on, armed only with their close reading of Marcuse and Marx.[71]

However unkindly it treated the just-departed President Kirk and the present but sidelined Provost Truman, the Cox report did nothing to undercut the authority of the Faculty Executive Committee. Indeed, by stressing the absence of effective channels of communication linking Columbia's administrators, faculty, and students, the report implicitly endorsed the committee's plan for a representative university senate. Moreover, the report also came as close to providing the recently installed acting president and his successor with as clean a slate as they would be likely to get in those downbeat days.[72]

Our Man in the Congo

Physically, Andrew W. Cordier was a rumpled and jowlier version of Grayson Kirk. Two years older, he, too, was a son of the Middle West, raised on a farm, in a community of abiding Protestants and Republicans. Whether Manchester College in Cordier's case or Miami University in Kirk's, theirs were undergraduate experiences as unlike Columbia's as imaginable. In contrast with Kirk, the young Cordier had been an excellent athlete, the quarterback on his college football team. He was then, and remained for the rest of his life, an observant member of the fundamentalist but nonabstaining Church of the Brethren. More informal than Kirk, he urged casual acquaintances to call him "Andy." His secretaries favored "Poppa."[73]

Upon graduation from Manchester in 1923, Cordier proceeded directly to the University of Chicago to study medieval history. After two years at Chicago, where he received his Ph.D. in 1926, he returned to Manchester and commenced a teaching career that proceeded smoothly until 1944. He then accepted a government assignment as part of the U.S. team preparing for the San Francisco conference that would bring the United Nations into being. Like Kirk, once away from the Midwest, he never returned.

Cordier joined the newly organized United Nations staff in 1946. Over the next fifteen years, he served sixteen General Assembly leaders as their right-hand man and assembly parliamentarian. He also supervised the UN headquarters staff of some thirty-five hundred employees. He was regularly sent to trouble spots around the world to deliver messages and to review local conditions for Secretaries General Trygve Lie and Dag Hammarskjöld. In the late 1950s many of these missions involved the Congo. He was the UN representative there at the time of the death of the country's Marxist leader, Patrice Lumumba. The insistence of the Russian delegation in 1961 that, in the aftermath of the death of Secretary Hammarskjöld, he had become too forceful an American presence in UN affairs, led to his retirement at age sixty.[74]

It was Cordier's wartime associate and friend Grayson Kirk who, after the retirement of Schuyler Wallace, invited Cordier to become the third dean of the School of International Affairs. As dean, Cordier focused on securing SIA its own building, an undertaking that seemed assured when the last major international studies grant from the Ford Foundation in 1965 included funds for a building. Otherwise, as compared with the Business School's Courtney Brown or the Law School's William Warren, Cordier was less aggressive in his exertions on behalf of his own school and, correspondingly, viewed more favorably by Low Library as a team player. This reputation made him a more acceptable interim president to both Kirk and the trustees than either Warren or Brown. Upon assuming the acting presidency, Cordier took the occasion to refer to his experiences as an international diplomat: "I have been in tough, tight situations before in which many of the elements we find here today existed. I never failed. And I don't intend to fail now."[75]

Cordier presided over Columbia University for just under two years, ten months as acting president and another eleven as Columbia's fifteenth president. Throughout this period, his planning horizon seldom exceeded twelve hours. He came in daily from his Long Island home before dawn, held an 8:00 A.M. meeting in Low 210 with his administrative team ("the dawn patrol"), and then worked through the day until 5:00 P.M., when the team would reconvene in the president's suite for a tumbler or two of bourbon and a toast to their having survived the day. Cordier would then proceed to a trustee function or to a student gathering, which often ran late enough into the night to make returning to Long Island senseless. A room in Butler Hall frequently sufficed. The next morning at 7:00 A.M., a little more rumpled for the night away from home, he was back at it. Men twenty years younger and eighty pounds lighter were abashed at his stamina.[76]

Cordier's sixteen years at the UN admirably prepared him for his job as he construed it: being parachuted into one of the world's current hot spots, Morningside Heights, and charged with responsibility to effect a cooldown. He set about doing so by agreeing to meet, talk, and listen to all the interested parties until exhaustion required them to quit. Unlike Kirk, who shied away from unstructured meetings with students, local politicians, or the press, Cordier filled his days with them. Fred Friendly, an experienced reporter and later dean of the School of Journalism, marveled at Cordier's capacity to "spread foam over the whole campus." Carl Hovde awarded Cordier the prize for "the man who could talk longer and say less than anybody I've ever known." Still others compared his modus operandi to "a fog machine."[77]

He proved equally effective in calming down overheated trustees who saw Western civilization crumbling if they abandoned the Morningside gym or withdrew criminal charges against student protesters and students convinced that barricading Fayerweather Hall would bring an end to world hunger or halt the bombing of North Vietnam. One trait this wily bureaucrat shared with the participation-minded new left was an endless capacity to sit through open-ended discussions at which the last to leave win.

But there was more to Cordier than guff and a firm seat. As even his often critical successor, William McGill, granted him: "Sitting as a general to watch a situation evolve, making cold-blooded decisions, bargaining with demonstrators—that was his métier. He was superb." There was also in Cordier—and perhaps this was a sign that it should matter in a university president—an ample measure of physical courage.[78]

Among the many shortcomings McGill later attributed to Cordier was the poor quality of his administrative appointments. But this was not entirely fair. Some of Cordier's administrators he inherited and kept on to provide a semblance of continuity. Others were hired when applicants for administrative positions at Columbia were in short supply. Still others, recruited from the faculty, wore themselves out, finding the long hours and endless meetings of the administrator's life, as one put it, "hell on my sex life."[79]

What Cordier expected and got from his staff was not brilliance or professional competence as much as personal and institutional loyalty. And when a dean showed the least hint of disloyalty, the acting president brought him up short. He was not an intellectual and not even much of an academic administrator; he was a combat veteran of the bureaucratic and ideological wars endemic to the United Nations, who willingly put his experience in the service of Columbia. He had few illusions about students and fewer still about faculty or trustees—and he was determined to get through the day. Moreover, in deciding to work with the Faculty Executive Committee, rather than challenge its only recently acquired and statutorily dubious power, he sacrificed whatever long-term presidential aspirations he had for the sake of the university.[80]

The Demands Addressed

Columbia survived in the wake of the spring 1968 disturbances in part because of changes in tone, in procedures, and in the personalities who came forward to speak for the university. Comparable changes on the part of students and faculty also helped. But what made these changes more than rearranging the deck chairs was that they were accompanied by substantive responses to the demands that, if they had not sparked the spring disturbances, gave them substantial post hoc legitimacy in the minds of moderate Columbians.

Mark Rudd boasted to a *Boston Globe* reporter on October 1, 1968, that "we [SDS] manufactured the issues. The Institute for Defense Analysis is nothing at Columbia. Just three professors." He went on: "And the gym is bull. It doesn't mean anything to anybody." But for the Faculty Executive Committee, the interim president, trustees, and students concerned with the university's survival, these issues became a crucial checklist of matters requiring prompt resolution. Successfully resolving them constituted another test of the restructuring project. Whatever the sources of these demands, they were, as Diana Trilling observed in her spring 1969 essay "On the Steps of Low Library," "necessarily useful and, more, . . . the future good of Columbia depends on the readiness of the University to concede their worth."[81]

Demand 1: Columbia Out of IDA! On May 31, 1968, the long-awaited Report of the Columbia University Committee on Relations with Outside Agencies, chaired by Professor of Law Louis Henkin, was published. The *Report* defended the university's maintaining relations with outside agencies, including government agencies. It also confirmed the administration's contention that very little secret research went on at Columbia and none that directly involved weaponry. "This committee," the *Report* stated, "sees nothing sinister in nonprofit research corporations such as IDA."[82]

But then the Henkin report went on to assert that all relations with outside agencies should advance the essential purposes of the university and not just serve the agencies' purposes or those of the faculty involved. It concluded by making three recommendations that went a long way toward answering the criticisms embedded in the protesters' demand that Columbia get out of the Institute for Defense Analysis:

1. The adoption of universitywide procedures for supervising and controlling outside relations, the specifics to be worked out by a faculty-administrative committee

2. A discontinuation at Columbia of all government classified research

3. A discontinuation of the university's membership in IDA[83]

In a related outside-agency decision, on May 15, 1969, the trustees accepted the recommendations of a faculty-student committee, sponsored by the Faculty Executive Committee and chaired by Professor of Political Science Harvey Mansfield, that the NROTC program be discontinued on the Columbia campus. What had been hailed at the program's inception in 1946 as an instance of university-government cooperation and had subsequently allowed some six hundred young men to attend Columbia College on full scholarships and another one thousand Columbians to take up commissions in the Naval Reserve had become, on the far side of the American Century, politically expendable.[84]

Demand 2: No Gym in Morningside!   At their meeting on March 3, 1969, the trustees voted to abandon the Morningside Heights gym project. The corollary agreement to absorb the costs of canceling the construction and filling in the excavation effectively brought to a close this well-meant if ill-starred venture in town-gown cooperation. Some trustees and College alumni who had raised $7 million for the gym and had only reluctantly gone along with the idea of putting the gym in the park were angered with this outcome and would require years of recultivating. The gym's principal defender, however, Trustee Harold McGuire, remained on the board until 1978, when he reached the mandatory retirement age of seventy-two. He died three years later.[85]

Demand 3: Amnesty   Neither the Faculty Executive Committee nor the trustees were willing to grant total amnesty to students who participated in the illegal spring protests. At the September 12, 1968, meeting of the Joint Faculties to consider the interim rules, a resolution to do so (an early version exempted those responsible for destroying faculty papers!) was defeated by a vote of 242 to 163. At the Faculty Executive Committee's urging, however, the trustees did come around to accepting the wisdom—or at least the utility—of having the university drop all criminal charges against students arrested on April 30.[86]

University disciplinary charges were not dropped, but the punishment in nearly all cases where the students submitted to university disciplinary procedures amounted to no more than letters of admonition. Only in instances where multiple charges were made and where the accused refused to report to his dean, were students suspended for a semester. The interim disciplinary rules adopted in September 1968 by the faculty and confirmed by a student referendum allowed for sterner punishment for disruptive protests than any imposed on spring 1968 protesters. Nevertheless, the shift of the disciplinary function from the hands of the president to the collective control of faculty, students, and administrators represented a historic change. At the same time, it reaffirmed the principle that Columbians could not operate outside the rules of the university without being subject to them.

Toward a University Senate

While not specified as such by the building occupiers, the demand for restructuring the governance machinery of the university was no less a challenge to those in the aftermath of the occupations who committed themselves to the notion that the university was worth saving. Its upshot was the University Senate.

There is little to suggest that the original members of the Faculty Executive Committee, at the outset of their deliberations in May 1968, had anything in mind approximating the creation of the University Senate they found themselves urging on the university community twelve months later. Having taken on the task of persuading disparate elements of the community to compromise their particular interests for the greater good, they found themselves obliged to modify their own ideas of what the restructured governance arrangements ought to be in light of those of other interested parties. On one side stood the trustees, the administration, and the organized alumni, concerned that traditional presidential authority not be so compromised as to make the university ungovernable; on the other were students calling for a far more participatory system than had heretofore been seen at Columbia.

The proposal for a university senate that Michael Sovern outlined at the Joint Faculties meeting on September 12, 1968, called for "a policy-making and legislative body with full jurisdiction and power to deal with all matters of University-wide concern." Its proposed membership of ninety-two members included seventy faculty (fifty tenured and twenty junior faculty), seven representatives of the administration, five alumni, and ten students, these drawn from a separate student assembly whose jurisdiction would be limited to student matters.[87]

The senate as first envisioned by the Faculty Executive Committee would have elected its own presiding officer, which, given the allocation of seats, would likely be a member of the faculty and not the president. Thus it seemed to be suggesting a permanent legislative body not so different from the Faculty Executive Committee—bigger but still one in which senior faculty were firmly in control. That this early version also contained the provision that university professors (there were three in 1968) would be ex officio senators attests to the persistence of "the faculty is the University" shibboleth and the dubious assumption that the university's most distinguished scholars would make its best statesmen.[88]

But then something quite extraordinary happened. On October 10, 1968, the *Columbia Daily Spectator* published a special "Restructuring Supplement" that included not only the Faculty Executive Committee's proposals for a university senate but those of the Students for a Restructured University, which had students playing an equal role with faculty in a single legislative body. It also included the interim report of the Temple trustee committee on restructuring, which envisioned an important role for the president and his senior administrators in any senate, along with selections from a report authored by the newly elected alumni trustee and attorney Lawrence E. Walsh, on behalf of the Columbia University Federated Alumni Association, which opposed handing over so much power to the faculty and the students and called for a larger role for the alumni in the affairs of the university. What followed was a university-wide debate that was joined by all of Columbia's estates.[89]

Equally extraordinary were the procedural niceties and general goodwill that attended the debate. Eight open meetings were held in the fall under the joint sponsorship of the Faculty Executive Committee, the Temple trustee committee, and the SRU, at which the various ways a university senate might be organized were debated. An SRU-sponsored student survey, to which 3,440 students responded, had a considerable impact on increasing the representation of students on the senate from the original ten first proposed by the Faculty Executive Committee in September to the twenty it unanimously endorsed in February. In successfully lobbying for the enlargement of the role of students in the senate, SRU became more fully committed to seeing the evolving University Senate proposal through to enactment.[90]

By the first week of April 1969, a proposal for a university senate that had the support of the Faculty Executive Committee, the trustees, and SRU was presented as a referendum to be separately voted upon by tenured faculty, non-tenured faculty, and all registered students. The proposed senate was to consist of one hundred members:

forty-two tenured faculty;
seventeen nontenured faculty;
twenty students;
seven administrators;
six representatives of affiliated institutions;
six staff representatives;
two alumni representatives.

Additional provisions were that:

- the Senate select six nominees to the board of Trustees;
- the president of the university preside over the senate;
- the senate be "a policy-making body which may consider all matters of University-wide concern and all matters affecting more than one faculty or school";
- acts of the Senate be final on passage unless trustee concurrence is required;
- the senate supersede and replace the powers and functions of the Faculty Executive Committee and the moribund University Council.[91]

On April 8, 1969, the referendum of faculty and students overwhelmingly approved creation of the University Senate. Of the students voting, 89.3 percent approved; of senior faculty, 92.4 percent; of junior faculty, 90.4 percent. Elections were then scheduled by the constituent groups and plans made for convening the senate. Predictably, SDS, which had opposed the referendum, repudiated its outcome.[92]

Instead of the onus for defending the senate falling on the administration, the trustees, or even the Faculty Executive Committee, it was the Students for a Restructured University who, on April 18, repudiated their one-time SDS mentors by blanketing the campus with flyers proclaiming "Let's Change the University, Not Destroy It." The text described the senate as "an alternative to police violence and SDS revolutionary tactics." The required turnout of 40 percent of the eligible voters for the senate elections was in every instance met, and all balloting proceeded unchallenged.[93]

On May 29, 1969, the first meeting of the hundred-member University Senate convened in the Faculty Room in Low Library, adopted its bylaws, and got down to business. Those members of the Faculty Executive Committee who had not stood for election to the senate, chief among them Committee Chair Michael Sovern, greeted the new senators with pleasure and relief. And then, bearing no more physical resemblance to Cincinnatus than his beloved Law School did to a farm in the Campagna or his IBM Selectric to a plow, the now ex-chair walked back across Amsterdam Avenue to work earlier put aside. Columbia wasn't out of the woods just yet, but a clearing had been made for the pitching of a snug tent.[94]

CHAPTER 17

A Tough Place

> New York is a tough town and word had gotten out that Columbia could be
> pushed around. I have had to use what I learned on the streets, which was the
> ability to fight to show people, firstly, that we could not be pushed and, secondly,
> that our hearts were in the right place.
>
> William J. McGill, Address to the St. Nicholas Society, December 12, 1976

One Tough Mick

A NDREW CORDIER'S appointment as acting president in August 1968 was
conditioned on his not being a candidate for the presidency. By the time
the trustees acknowledged his important service by electing him president in
August 1969, the search for his successor had been underway for ten months.
The process involved two committees, one of trustees chaired by Robert Lilley,
which would make the formal decision, and a nine-member faculty committee,
which included three members of the Faculty Executice Committee—Michael
Sovern, Professor of English Robert Gorham Davis, and Polykarp Kusch—and
was chaired by Professor of Chemistry Ronald Breslow. Only David Truman
and Kusch were given consideration as insiders by the faculty committee.
Sovern excited some interest, but he was thirty-eight, Jewish, and recently
divorced, so his admirers set him aside for another day and looked instead for
an outsider. On July 1, 1970, he became dean of the Law School.[1]

The trustees were equally committed to finding an outsider, even after
Alexander Heard, chancellor of Vanderbilt, declined consideration, as did the
ex-secretary of health, education and welfare, John W. Gardner. An insider/out-
sider in whom some interest developed was Martin Meyerson (CC 1942), then
the chancellor of SUNY, Buffalo, and a veteran of the Berkeley 1964 campus
wars, where he had been vice chancellor. Meyerson would have been the first
Jewish president of an Ivy League university, a distinction his appointment as
president there later bestowed on the University of Pennsylvania. Meanwhile,
Columbia turned not to an alumnus, but to a one-time faculty member, a scientist of national repute, a Catholic, but who later recalled his principal credential as being, "Here's a live body, let's grab it."[2]

William J. McGill was born in East Harlem, New York City, in 1922. His parents were Irish and Catholic. His father came from Liverpool to New York as a

boy, learned to play the trombone, and in the 1920s made a good living as a member of the Paul Whiteman Orchestra. The well-paying gigs at the Hotel Biltmore ended with the Depression, and he thereafter struggled to make family ends meet as an organizer for the musicians' union. Growing up in the 1930s, McGill remembered his father as embittered and beaten.[3]

McGill's mother came from more prosperous second-generation circumstances. Not quite part of New York's lace-curtain Irish-American elite, she was what my mother would have classified as "T.T.I." (Two-Toilet Irish) and worked as a nurse. McGill was raised a boy of the boroughs, in the Bronx, living at times as close in as Fordham Road and as far out as Throgs Neck, where he made boyhood friends of the future archbishop of New York, Terence Cardinal Cooke, and the business executive David Mahoney.[4]

Like Cooke and Mahoney, McGill was a product of New York's "other" school system: the Catholic parochial schools. He attended grammar school at St. Francis de Chantel, then Our Lady of Mercy for junior high school, and then Cathedral Boys High School on Sixty-Seventh off Third Avenue in Manhattan. Cathedral was the archdiocesan school for "bright kids" run by La Salle Christian Brothers, what Catholics called their Bronx Science. He graduated with honors in 1939, having divided his high school years between studies and working after-school jobs in Manhattan before taking the train home to the Bronx.[5]

With his mother insisting he go to "a good Catholic college," McGill enrolled at nearby Fordham University, where he spent four years under the intellectually demanding supervision of its then predominantly Jesuit faculty. Informed that he had "a good quantitative mind," he majored in psychology. After graduating in 1943 and being exempted from the draft for physical reasons, he spent the remainder of the war in California in defense work.[6]

In 1946 he returned to Fordham for graduate studies in psychology. A year later, he transferred to Harvard, arriving in Cambridge just as cognitive psychology was struggling to gain a place in the Harvard and MIT scheme of things. In 1953 he completed his Ph.D. in communications theory and took a teaching job in the MIT economics department, where he became fast friends with George Schultz, Paul Samuelson, and Robert Solow.[7]

In 1956 McGill was recruited by the Columbia psychology department. Two years after his arrival, McGill was promoted to associate professor with tenure; one year later, he became a full professor; a year after that, department chairman. Meanwhile, he had become part of the "Lazarsfeld mafia," a community of Columbia quantifiers linked to the Bureau of Applied Social Research and to its founder, Paul Lazarsfeld.[8]

For all this institutional recognition, McGill found life in the Columbia psychology department unsatisfying. About the only matter on which his two feuding departmental elders, Fred Keller and Clarence Henry Graham, agreed was an unwillingness to commit departmental resources to the kind of cognitive work McGill did. The department, he concluded, once so distinguished, "was beginning to decline." While he got along personally with Jacques Barzun, who tried to interest the young psychologist in a Columbia administrative post, McGill saw no disposition on the provost's part to commit university resources to reviving the psychology department. Deciding that "I didn't want to go downhill simultaneously with Columbia," McGill began to consider some of the several outside offers that regularly came his way. In 1963 he went to Stanford on a research fellowship and while there accepted an offer to head up a new Department of Psychology at the University of California, San Diego. There, at least, unlike Columbia, he expected to find "no obsequies to the past."[9]

At San Diego, McGill became involved in campus politics. The troubles at Berkeley in 1964 had sent ripples through the California system, which found itself with few administrators prepared to operate within the new confrontational environment. On election to the statewide University Senate in 1966, McGill identified himself as someone prepared to do so, and, a year later, when the incumbent chancellor resigned in the face of campuswide disruptions, he agreed to become acting chancellor of the San Diego campus. In the spring of 1968 he was appointed chancellor, just in time to confront a campuswide strike led by the black Marxist graduate student Angela Davis and abetted by her mentor, the Marxist philosopher and visiting professor Herbert Marcuse. Leading the call for an immediate crackdown on the strikers—and the dismissal of Marcuse—was Governor Ronald Reagan, whose campaign for the governorship two years before had featured his hard-line views on campus disruptions and weak-kneed academic administrators.[10]

In these trying circumstances, which he later described in *The Year of the Monkey* (1982), McGill proved to be a tough, imaginative and politically adept crisis manager. "I'm operating in a sense of genuine fear," he later described his state of mind in 1969, "for what I saw as a collapsing society." But it came at a cost. "I tore up my faculty roots, parted company with old friends, and did what I had to do." Not least of these was learn to cope with ex-colleagues who enjoyed seeing him put in tight places. "Hi, Billy," he remembers one greeting him on the outer edges of a campus melee into which he was about to thrust himself, "How do you like your shiny new big-ass job now?"[11]

Not surprisingly, McGill's success at San Diego brought him to the notice of the Columbia presidential search committees. In November 1969 the Faculty Search Committee chair, Ronald Breslow, inquired as to McGill's availability. "We've had some bad problems here," Breslow wrote. "If you're not serious, say so now." McGill agreed to come east and meet with the faculty and trustee committees in December, in part, he later admitted, because "I was just so flattered."[12]

McGill recalled his first meeting with the trustees as "terrible . . . but we impressed one another." The one with the faculty committee, which included Robert Merton and Eli Ginzberg, friends from his Columbia years, went better. A visit to California by Breslow in January to assure McGill he was the faculty committee's choice and the fact that Breslow himself was "so utterly committed to the place" persuaded McGill to accept should he be asked. He proved an easy sell to the trustees, who, as McGill read them, "were interested in me because I'd grown up in New York City, and was not frightened of the racial tensions." On February 4, 1970, the trustees formally elected William J. McGill Columbia's sixteenth president.[13]

Making His Bones

There is a double irony in the trustees turning to McGill in part because of his New York City rearing—and the psychological mettle that was thought to produce. The first is that McGill's New York was the Catholic outer boroughs, not the lower Manhattan inhabited by generations of Knickerbocker trustees or the Upper East Side or Central Park West favored by its younger trustees. With the exception of Frank Hogan, another Irish Catholic West Sider, the trustees' New York and that of their new president were not simply physically separated by the East and Harlem Rivers but culturally distinct worlds.

But the second irony is that McGill was at best a disaffected and alienated New Yorker. When he came to Columbia in 1956, he chose not to live around the university but in the Westchester suburb of Dobbs Ferry. And part of his reason for leaving Columbia in 1964 was that "I thought the Upper West Side was deteriorating very rapidly . . . and I felt the problem at Columbia was not Columbia but New York City, and that what I could do would be to sort of change my base completely and go west where I could get a fresh start." Neither his wife, Ann, nor his son, who attended Columbia in the 1970s, ever put down roots in New York. Whether because he knew it in an earlier time, what he remembered as "the golden city" of the 1930s, he never sentimentalized New York life in the 1970s.[13]

The myth of McGill the street-savvy New Yorker was one part reality, one part trustees' wishful thinking, and one part McGill's invention. He did nothing to dissuade those with whom he dealt that he was, among other things, "a tough Mick." By no means tall and on the wide side, he walked with the hint of a swagger. His white hair in retro crew cut gave him the appearance of a seasoned state trooper, which he sometimes reinforced with aviator sunglasses and which even his bow ties did nothing to undercut. Sometime between leaving New York in

1964 and returning in 1970, he invented the "don't mess with me" character of the academic enforcer. What he called "a harsh combativeness" served him well in the student strike at San Diego, so he had no intention of leaving it behind when he came back to New York. "I understand the City intimately," he told a gathering of New Yorkers in 1977. "I have never really been afraid of it."[15]

Even before taking office in July, on a campus visit in April, McGill struck his hosts as positively eager to mix it up with student protesters. Yet his confrontational ways were not natural but learned. After being badly frightened by his first encounter with a mob of truculent San Diego students, after which he had collapsed, he discovered that getting in among the protesters was the best tactic, and not particularly dangerous. Once at the center of the melee, he would reason with the protest leaders, not with any prospect of converting them but to impress them with his personal courage and those on the outer fringes of the mob with his reasonableness.[16]

This was a tactic he had ample occasion to deploy in his first two years at Columbia. The mere hint of a crowd gathering at the sun dial or in Van Am Quad would bring McGill out of Low Library to the scene of the gathering. Sometimes accompanied by a staff member or two, occasionally by a security detail, often he weighed in alone. With a hint of braggadocio, he allowed in 1973 that he and his team had learned "to run rings around the protesters" and that the word was out "don't mess with McGill."[17]

Just how much this was a role he played is suggested by McGill's later remarks about recurrent nightmares of encounters with mobs that did not go so well. These began even before he took up residence on Morningside Drive. On April 4, 1970, "at the risk of being overly dramatic," he said at a news conference to announce that he was coming back to New York, "I lie in bed and think about Columbia. So many people know my face. Some day some psychotic person may take aim at me. But I'm ready to do it." Eight years later, on the tenth anniversary of the 1968 building occupations, a noisy but hardly life-threatening protest in front of the president's house on Morningside Drive was enough to trigger the physical revulsion and nightmares. Six years later, retired and safe twenty-four hundred miles from Morningside Heights in La Jolla, McGill's nightmares continued: "Those bastards are at it again."[18]

On one occasion in April 1972, when Hamilton Hall was temporarily besieged by a mob of mostly non-Columbians who not only were unintimidated by the president's arrival but viciously taunted him, McGill retreated to Low Library sufficiently shaken to indicate that he could not continue as president and that "I must resign." His staff urged him to go home and rest while they dealt with the situation. The mob subsided over the weekend, and McGill returned to Low Library three days later, ostensibly no worse for the wear, but with his reputation for imperturbable toughness, at least among his inner circle, dented.[19]

Whatever the psychic cost, McGill reassumed the point position in stemming student disturbances on campus. By 1973 these had largely ceased, with subsequent occurrences during his administration taking on the character of half-hearted homages to protests past rather than the real thing. Some have attributed this cessation of student protest to national developments, not least to President Nixon's abandonment of the draft, others to changes in Columbia admission criteria, wherein the problematic "10 per centers" and "red diapers" were replaced with more compliant kids from suburban Catholic high schools and Jewish day schools. Still others, of a Dionysian turn, have pointed to the virtual disappearance of parietal rules and the introduction of coed dormitories. Whatever the causes, McGill could pronounce as early as 1973, "The kids who come along now do not have the skills of Lewis Cole and Mark Rudd and Mario Savio had. We can run rings around them."[20]

There remained other uses for McGill's confrontational ways. Local politicians who, as he recalled a quarter-century later, had discovered in the 1960s that it was good politics to run against Columbia found its new president unwilling to let them do so. Perhaps because he seemed so much more one of them than the distant Kirk or the patrician Barzun, politicians from Harlem congressman Charles Rangel to New York governor Nelson Rockefeller became dependable allies of McGill and soon valuable friends of Columbia. It also helped that Columbia under McGill cut back on real estate acquisitions in the neighborhood and, when complaints were raised by local residents, abandoned plans for a second, larger nuclear reactor on campus.[21]

McGill was also successful in enlisting the support of Republican senator Jacob Javits, especially in matters relating to the Medical School, and of Javits's successor, Alphonse D'Amato. Although he could never win over those he castigated as "Upper West Side Socialists," such as Bella Abzug and Saul Alinsky, his relations with New York City officials during later years of the Lindsay administration and those of Abraham Beame's mayoralty moved from adversarial to mutually supportive. In the 1970s both the university and New York City, famously informed by President Gerald Ford, as the *Daily News* had it in 1975, to "drop dead," needed all the friends they could get.[22]

In Washington, during the Nixon presidency, the university's relations were less good. Even during the Carter administration, with McGill a Democrat, things could have been better. Part of the problem here was that the Carter staff had McGill on their list of "prominent ethnics," which resulted in White House invitations to all manner of Irish or Irish-American occasions rather than to events to which other university presidents and scientists were invited. This instance of ethnic stereotyping really bothered him. Capable of sporting the emerald and spouting the blarney when the spirit moved or the occasion required, McGill hated being required to do so on call.[23]

Finally, McGill's combativeness served him very well presiding over the University Senate in its formative years. Acknowledging to the trustees that there was more than a little "guerrilla theatre" in the behavior of some student senators, he nonetheless defended the senate's usefulness. Occasionally, he indulged in some legislative histrionics of his own, if only to show that he took no guff.[24]

Broke and Then Some

Bringing an end to violent student protests and mending neighborhood fences were among the immediate tasks McGill undertook. These he largely accomplished early in his presidency. He also knew from the start that there were important financial problems. What he did not know was just how bad Columbia's finances were and how much of his presidency it would take to put them right.

The roots of Columbia's financial troubles went back to the late 1920s. Beginning then, the absence of effective fund-raising among alumni, an endowment that failed to grow and yield at the rate of its peers, and the cost of doing business in New York City began to erode the university's wealth. The general prosperity of the postwar era masked these problems, while Kirk's heavy reliance on federal and foundation support to balance budgets, plus the spending of money on shoring up the neighborhood that otherwise might have gone into upgrading the campus, further exacerbated them. So did the decision in the early 1960s to limit enrollments in General Studies and cut back on self-financed graduate students. Kirk's last two budgets (1966–67 and 1967–68) contained deficits of $2 million and $4 million, respectively, a cumulative debt of $6 million, or about 5 percent of the upcoming $120 million 1968–69 budget.[25]

The '68 disturbances had both immediate and long-range financial consequences. The unbudgeted cost of cleaning up the campus, legal fees in handling suits filed against the university, and added security ballooned the initially projected deficit for 1968–69 of $2 million to an actual deficit of over $9 million. The university's debt then stood at $15 million.[26]

What had become a chronic financial problem midway through Butler's forty-four-year presidency and worsened during the last years of Kirk's eighteen-year presidency became nearly fatal in Cordier's twenty-two-month incumbency. Part of his success as a crisis manager in the short run flowed from his disregard for the long-term financial implications of his stopgap measures.

In this, he followed Keynes's dictum that "in the long run we will all be dead."[27]

The gym provides an example. The suspension of construction during the building occupations was not taken to be the final word by its alumni backers. Indeed, Trustee Harold McGuire used his appearance before the Cox commission to defend going ahead with the project. In part to placate McGuire and other College alumni not ready to see their project a casualty of occupations or the $11 million raised put to other uses, Cordier suggested constructing a gym on campus beneath South Field. The architect I. M. Pei was approached, and Pei proposed doing a $600,000 feasibility study.[28]

When Cordier brought Pei's proposal to the already strapped Finance Committee, its members refused to authorize any more than $200,000 for any feasibility study. They also made clear their disinclination to proceed further with plans that could only be implemented by the expenditure of tens of millions of dollars that Columbia did not have.[29]

Cordier was equally cavalier about calling on the university's outside counsel, Profitt and Thatcher, which during his tenure billed the university for some $700,000 in legal services. (One of McGill's early moves was to "turn off the meter" by creating an in-house legal office.) When in late 1969 it was discovered that many of the university's principal outside vendors had not been paid in fifteen months because the paperwork had been mislaid, Cordier directed that the University have its vendors resubmit bills based on how much they thought they were owed. His successor's exasperated judgment on Cordier: "Possibly the least gifted administrative figure I have ever met in my life."[30]

But it was in constructing the two budgets for 1969–70 and 1970–71 where Cordier's willingness to spend beyond the university's means came close to putting the university under. The 1969–70 budget contained a planned deficit— the fourth straight—of $9 million, on a total of $130 million. The 1970–71 budget, prepared in the spring of 1970, as his successor was being chosen, projected a deficit of $17 million. Cordier inherited a debt of $8 million; he left McGill two years later with a debt of $34 million—and it was growing.[31]

Another ploy of Cordier's was to promise the same money to multiple parties. Thus the same $100 million generated by the capital campaign to match Ford Foundation gifts was committed to pay for a new biology building, as promised to Professor of Biology Cyrus Leventhal, to match a construction grant for an oceanography building at Lamont (or so Maurice Ewing understood) and to pay for the completion of the SIA building grant, a project dear to Cordier's own heart.[32]

In these financial straits, Cordier proposed that the trustees sell the land beneath Rockefeller Center, which he thought might fetch upward of $125 million. The book value was at the time $75 million, about 25 percent of the university's entire endowment. A majority of the trustees initially favored the sale, until two of the most financially savvy members, Percy Uris and Arthur Krim, urged against it. It would give too much the appearance, Uris argued, "of a fire sale." And should it be sold and the proceeds turned over to Cordier and his administration, Krim added succinctly, "They will just piss it away."[33]

When the trustees elected McGill to the presidency in February 1970, they did not apprise him of the magnitude of the financial straits in which the university found itself. They might not have fully known it themselves. But some facts were known. The $5 million deficit Uris had projected midway through the 1969–70 budget year had grown to $9 million before the fiscal year was out. Moreover, the 1970–71 budget Cordier presented to the board in April 1970, which McGill would have to live with, contained a whopping $16.5 million projected deficit. Arts and Sciences alone had a projected deficit of $6–8 million. At its September meeting, the trustees informed McGill of the situation and then gave him the rest of the year to come up with a plan for balancing the budget and eliminating the accumulated debt, then approaching $40 million.[34]

McGill may later have exaggerated just how primitive Columbia's budgetary procedures were in 1970, but likely not by much. There was no capital budget, no system of amortization, and no capital campaign. Responsibility for constructing the university budget was divided between competing administrative offices and the chief financial officer, who, by McGill's lights, "could not write a budget or analyze a computer program." Overriding all these deficiencies were three long-term structural problems, the chief being that the president of the university did not have control of the entire budget but only that part relating directly to the academic mission. The treasurer of the university, William Bloor, reported not to the president, as McGill discovered upon asking him for some numbers, but to the chair of the trustees' Finance Committee, Percy Uris.[35]

The second problem was that the individual schools kept their books in their own way, which made centralized administrative oversight almost impossible and squirreling of resources by schools temptingly easy. Just how much spendable income each school had in its restricted accounts and how much each collected in tuition were the kinds of basic questions for which the new president could get no answers. Provost Peter Kenen, upon being asked at the April 6, 1970, board meeting by Alumni Trustee Frode Jensen (P and S M.D. 1937) "how much of a deficit there would be if the Medical School was not included in the budget," responded by "confessing ignorance of the Medical School budget." He went on to say that he "felt confident that the Morningside campus budget would not be a great drain on general income." To which newly elected Trustee Weston inquired: "Does this mean invading the endowment?"[36]

The trustees' charge to McGill to return Columbia to financial stability enabled him to make important changes in the way the university conducted its business. The first occurred at the January 1971 board meeting, when the trustees assigned all tuition revenues from the professional schools to the president instead of the schools' deans. Henceforth, it would be Low Library that gave back some portion of the tuition fees to the schools that generated them, not, as in the past, the schools giving back a portion of those fees to Low Library.[37]

Michael Sovern, the new dean of the Law School in 1971, experienced this shift firsthand when Vice President Kusch passed him a note at lunch with the amount the Law School could expect from the university in 1971–72. (In the days of the barons, the note passing went the other way.) When the dean indicated that the amount fell far short of the school's expenses, Kusch agreed and told him to make up the difference from the income from restricted funds to which only he had access. Subsequent haggling allowed the professional school deans to get back a portion of whatever increases their schools generated in tuition, either by charging more or increasing enrollments, which provided an incentive to do both.[38]

As expected, the new financial arrangements did not sit well with Maurice Ewing, the director of what in 1968 had been renamed the Lamont-Doherty Geological Observatory. The name change followed a $7 million gift solicited and secured by Ewing from the Doherty Foundation to underwrite oceanographic research. Coming in the midst of the spring disturbances, the gift and its assorted strings were gratefully accepted by President Kirk on behalf of the trustees and later confirmed by Cordier. When closely examined, however, the Doherty gift required the university to provide $3 million more to Lamont as a match and to continue to waive all claims to overhead income generated by future Lamont contracts. The attorney for the Doherty Foundation, a close friend of Ewing, also insisted that the university set up a separate account where the matching grant would be protected from raids by Columbia's trustees. In sum, Lamont-Doherty was henceforth to be about as autonomous as the Medical School had been before 1891. It would manage its own endowment, answer to its own board, and decide its future as its director saw fit.[39]

When McGill met with the Doherty Foundation attorney in 1971, it became clear that the foundation and Ewing were prepared to insist on every condition agreed to by McGill's two predecessors. In the event of any reneging by the university, Ewing was prepared to accept an appointment at the University of Texas, where he threatened to take everyone and everything at Lamont that could be moved or sailed to Galveston. When McGill refused to turn over the direction of Lamont to the Doherty Foundation board, insisting that it belonged to the trustees of Columbia University, Ewing announced to his staff that he was leaving for Texas—and urged them to come with him.[40]

The 1971–72 Lamont-Doherty crisis was more than two strong-willed individuals locking horns, although it was surely that. It was also more than a quarrel about overhead and indirect costs, although it surely was about that, too, especially with the Medical School and other federal-grant sectors of the university ready to insist on arrangements comparable to those Ewing was demanding for Lamont. At bottom, the question was whether the university—read McGill—could require the tuition-rich or contract-favored professional schools to help cover the deficits of the tuition-poor and/or contract-challenged schools, until the latter could be squeezed into financial equilibrium. As McGill recalled the stakes a quarter-century later: "We cannot permit this kind of independence or it will break out all over the entire University. If Lamont could become functionally autonomous, P & S would follow a year later."[41]

The second structural reform McGill imposed to bring the university back into financial equilibrium was to seize control of the "downtown" portion of the budget, which related to the nonacademic aspects of the university and the endowment. Here, the personal struggle was not so much with Treasurer Bloor, whom McGill later described as "one of the most marvelous characters I ever met. He is out of Dickens." It was with the man to whom Bloor reported, the chair of the trustee Finance Committee, Percy Uris. McGill characterized Uris as the most powerful man on the board, "someone who knew how to do things in the cold dark world provided by New York." "A totally willful man," McGill elaborated, "he thought he knew all about the essential things that the academics did not know." It was Uris whom McGill blamed for Columbia's failing in the 1960s to utilize New York Dormitory Authority mortgage money provided to private universities by Governor Rockefeller, preferring instead "to carry zero debt on decaying facilities."[42]

Columbia was spared an otherwise inevitable McGill-Uris donnybrook by the fact that, when the trustees in early 1971 gave McGill the authority over the entire budgetary process, Uris was already ill; he died before the year was out. Bloor thereafter reported to McGill, who worked directly with Arthur Krim, Uris's successor as Finance Committee chair and later board chairman. In 1973 Krim and McGill renegotiated the lease for the Rockefeller site, increasing the annual rent to Columbia from less than $4 million to $9 million, with scheduled adjustments to bring it to $13 million in later years of the lease.[43]

Financial Stability Regained

The process of returning Columbia to financial stability was pretty straightforward. Referring to the principal budgetary questions, McGill later described the process: "I decided them and then forced them down the throats of the parties."[44]

The first step was to have central control of the numbers. Here, McGill was assisted not only by able budgeteers operating out of Low Library, such as Bruce Bassett, an assistant professor on loan from the Business School, but by deans who understood and shared their president's belief in the power of numbers. Within Low Library, the dean of Graduate Faculties, George Fraenkel, so qualified, as did Deans Paul Marks at P & S, Boritz Yavitz at the Business School, and Michael Sovern at the Law School. All worked effectively together on the deans' Budget Review Committee, which McGill created in 1975.[45]

Once the numbers were agreed to, those parts of the university that were in the black were offered incentives to increase income, while those in the red were told to cut costs. In the first category, by virtue of high tuitions and steady demand, were the Law and Business Schools. Within the deficit-ridden Arts and Sciences, the School of International Affairs and General Studies were identified as tuition generators and were urged to become more so. Meanwhile, the rest of Arts and Sciences underwent a substantial contraction in faculty size and program offerings. Between 1968 and 1979 the Arts and Sciences Faculty was cut by 15 percent, from more than six hundred full-time faculty to fewer than five hundred. Part-time positions were cut even more sharply.[46]

Cuts in Arts and Sciences involved the elimination of two departments, linguistics and geography. They also involved the elimination of such university-wide publications as *The Forum* and reducing *Columbia College Today* from a glossy quarterly to an occasional newsletter. The School of Library Service, although not closed until 1991, saw its operating budget substantially reduced. Plans to move the School of Pharmacy to Morningside Drive were canceled in 1971, and the affiliation terminated in 1973. The university's relationship with Barnard College came under the close scrutiny of McGill's budgeteers as an area where additional savings might be exacted.[47]

The intention of this exercise was to bring expenditures into line with income without permanently gutting the university in the process. In 1971 McGill thought it could be done in three years, an estimate that might have been optimistic even without the intervening international oil crisis and a near fiscal collapse of New York City. The 1973–74 deficit did get down to $2.6 million, only to jump back the following year to over $4 million. Revised planning then put off the date for balancing the budget to the start of FY 1975–76, but this target date came and went with that year's budget still $5 million in the red. Finally, in 1978, President McGill could report to the trustees that Columbia's financial equilibrium had been restored. The projected budget for 1979–80, just under $291 million, was the first in fourteen years to be submitted to the trustees in balance.[48]

Lightning Down the Hall

It would be ennobling to be able to describe this decade-long battle to put Columbia's financial house in order as one conducted by the principals with quiet fortitude and camaraderie. Alas, it was more like a family feud, where as one occupant of Low Library during these years recalled it, nothing was so fervently wished for those with whom he did daily battle than "lightning down the hall." For most of those who ventured into academic administration in those years, life took on a Hobbesian cast: "nasty, brutish and short."[49]

The Nobel laureate Polykarp Kusch, who succeeded David Truman in the spring of 1969 as the university's executive vice president for academic affairs, was an early administrative casualty. Four months into McGill's presidency, he despaired of Columbia's future. A school-by-school review he had conducted at McGill's direction led him to recommend the closing of the School of International Affairs, the Engineering School, and the School of Architecture. He was equally damning of several departments in the Arts and Sciences as unlikely ever to pay their way or justify their existence in terms of academic distinction. When Kusch's recommendations met with opposition, both from the targeted deans and McGill, who feared cutbacks of such magnitude would bring more unfavorable attention to Columbia, Kusch resigned and went to the University of Texas. In doing so, he ended his brief and unhappy tenure in Low Library, an edifice he had taken to calling long before he began his administrative labors there: "the gray building."[50]

Kusch's successor as chief academic officer was William Theodore de Bary, who became vice president and provost in 1971. An East Asian scholar and specialist in Chinese neo-Confucianism, de Bary had long been prominent in the affairs of Columbia College and served as the first chairman of the Executive Committee of the University Senate before moving to Low Library. De Bary survived as provost for seven years, but in almost continuous conflict with several other senior administrators. He also had to cope with McGill, who, though he shared de Bary's Catholicism and admired his fund-raising skills, regarded him as too "mystical" for the heavy lifting administrative work required.[51]

Some in Low Library faulted de Bary for never wholly giving himself over to his administrative job, for keeping his hand in East Asian studies, and for championing the humanities. For his part, de Bary found life in Low Library "a nest of vipers" and administration "hardly what I wanted to spend the rest of my life doing." In 1978 he resigned, glad to return to the faculty as the inaugural John Mitchell Mason Professor, a chair named after Columbia's first provost and created, McGill only half jokingly allowed, to protect ex-provosts from reprisals by surviving administrators.[52]

De Bary's principal nemesis was George K. Fraenkel, the dean of Graduate Faculties. Theirs was a clash both of personalities and of differing responsibilities as each perceived them. De Bary saw his job as protecting and promoting those parts of the university that had in the past, did now, and might in the future bring intellectual luster to Columbia. Fraenkel saw himself as engaged in a form of academic triage, where the best that could be said of him was that he spread the pain evenly. De Bary favored planning retreats at Arden House, whereas Fraenkel's weapon of choice was long, often unsolicited memos bristling with statistics. De Bary was an aggressive fund-raiser, and Fraenkel did not raise a dime but managed the funds assigned, as McGill acknowledged, "with consummate skill."[53]

Fraenkel had the distinction of being the only senior administrator or dean in place at the start of the McGill presidency who survived it. His durability was all the more remarkable in that his was arguably the most trying of all the jobs: to effect the shrinkage of the Arts and Science Faculty without doing irreparable damage to its competitive standing and future prospects. The first part of his charge was met by slashing the number of untenured positions, by cutting back tenure appointments from fifteen to twenty per year in the late 1960s to six to eight by the mid-1970s, and by allowing positions vacated by retirement and the departure of raided senior faculty to remain unfilled.[54]

Some of these cuts were accommodated by consolidating previously separate departments within departments, such as existed with English, where in the 1960s Chaucer was taught by faculty assigned to the College, to General Studies, and to the Graduate Faculties, as well as at Barnard. Fraenkel directed the English Department to make do with one Chaucer scholar. Much the same duplication occurred elsewhere in the humanities and was by no means uncommon in the social sciences, where survey courses in American history were taught in three different venues. However rational and overdue such consolidation was, it adversely affected some individual careers, ended long-standing teaching arrangements, and increased class sizes, all of which the affected faculty resented.[55]

Even as professional school deans and senior administrators insisted that Fraenkel was too protective of Arts and Sciences, de Bary and others worried about the damage his cuts in Arts and Sciences did to Columbia's academic reputation. But Fraenkel usually gave as good as he got—and always with numbers to back his position. What kept Fraenkel at the job was not so much an inherent combativeness as another quality McGill attributed to him, as well as to his nemesis de Bary and to the vice president for administration, Paul Carter: "a deep sense of loyalty and honor."[56]

McGill himself did little to lessen the strain and stresses of life in "the gray building." Some suggested he exacerbated them by pitting one administrator against another, even as he projected an "us against them" view of the world. When in later years he described the relationship of Fraenkel and de Bary as "locked in mortal combat," it is hard not to infer that he had derived some pleasure from watching them go at it. Another hint of a Manichaean mindset comes through in a passing remark he made about Columbia in his *Year of the Monkey*: "Nor was there any gentle way to extract Columbia from the near-catastrophe into which it had fallen in 1968. The fiscal measures necessary to pull the university back from the brink were brutal and nearly every pressure group with a stake in Columbia's operations objected to them."[57]

Perhaps because McGill worked so doggedly to accomplish what he had taken on and derived so little pleasure in the doing, he simply assumed that others were comparably wired. Staffers who fell by the wayside were judged by him to have lacked "the stomach" for their jobs; those who hung in won accolades for their ability "to cope with stress." His principal budgeteer, Bruce Bassett, whom McGill credited with devising the budgetary system that pulled the university back from the brink, and Martin Gleason, whom McGill called admiringly "the administration's dogface," wore themselves out on the job.[58]

Someone who worked for McGill, in trying to account for the nastiness of his administration, placed responsibility with the president's Catholicism and declared it "his 'mea culpa' thing." But if Catholic theology offers an explanation, it might have been less the guilt implied in "mea culpa" than the low expectations implicit in his postlapsarian "vale of tears" thing. Regularly surprised by how loyal and caring his associates in the main were, he remained unwilling to risk the fate of the university on their best intentions, knowing the road to hell to be so paved.[59]

For nontheologically disposed veterans of the McGill era, more earthbound assessments had to serve. "While we hated each other's guts," one of them allowed, "we helped save the University."[60]

A Note on McGill's Catholicism   McGill was the first Catholic—and an Irish Catholic, to boot—to be president of Columbia University. He was not by disposition what my father dismissivley called a "professional Mick" and even less a "professional Catholic." His Irish Catholicism was a cultural inheritance, what he once called "a way of life," acquired from his mother, who McGill later concluded was "sanctimonious but not religious." Another maternal acquisition: "When I was a boy, my mother told me everything I needed to know about the

Cathedral of St. John the Divine. 'They look like us, Billy, and they have candles on the altar, but don't let them fool you. They are Protestants.' "[61] McGill was not, as compared with two contemporary Columbia converts, Thomas Merton and William T. de Bary, a theologically curious Catholic. He was, however, sufficiently observant to take some credit, when it became known that he attended early Sunday mass at the Church of Notre Dame on Morningside Drive, for the upswing in churchgoing among heretofore lapsed Catholics in his administration.

One might conclude that McGill's Catholicism made no difference in his presidency. He certainly made no effort to insinuate it into the affairs of the university. Indeed, when asked by Catholic Columbians to extend Pope Paul VI an invitation to the campus at his visit to New York in 1976, McGill refused, saying to do so would mean extending the same invitation to Iran's Khomeini should he come to town. McGill fit well into the Columbia tradition of non-proselytizing believers.[62]

That McGill's successor was Jewish and in turn succeeded by a Presbyterian with Buddhist inclinations suggests something more comprehensive: that in the last quarter of the twentieth century the personal religion of Columbia's president, originally mandated by the charter to be that of the Church of England, a provision rigorously adhered to for 150 years and then only broadened slightly at midcentury to accommodate three non-Episcopalian Protestants, was now a matter between the president and his/her Maker. When I asked about the religion of Columbia's nineteenth president shortly after the announcement of Lee Bollinger's election in October 2001, neither the university's public relations office nor the executive director of the search committee could tell me. The question, I was told, "never came up."

Turnaround on 168th Street

In the spring of 1977, when McGill informed his trustees that the struggle to bring the university's budget into balance was being won, he noted one of the effects of the decadelong effort: "a general growth in influence of the professional school faculties." This, he allowed, flowed directly from "the recognition that they were the centers of operations which could ease the stress in the Arts and Sciences divisions." While the president referred to the professional schools in general, some had clearly made more significant contributions to the collective well-being of the university than others.[64]

Thanks to the widely acknowledged Ph.D. glut, some of Columbia's professional schools benefited from increased demand generated by students who a decade earlier would have enrolled in Arts and Sciences programs leading to academic careers. The Graduate School of Business was one such beneficiary. Others benefited from the stimulus of new and dynamic leadership that led to curricular overhaul. Here, the School of Architecture and the Dental School, with the appointments as deans of James S. Polshek and Allan Formicola, are examples. The Law School enjoyed the lift provided by both increased student demand and responsive leadership. So did the Medical School, which, because the 1970s marked a crucial turning point in its history and in Health Sciences generally, merits further consideration here.

From the perspective of at least one medical student in those years, the mid-1950s represented a "golden age" for the Faculty of the College of Physicians & Surgeons. Not only were the heads of many of its departments world acclaimed in their specialties, but their textbooks were assigned medical students elsewhere. Houston Merritt's *Textbook of Neurology*, first published in 1958, and Robert F. Loeb's *Textbook of Medicine*, coauthored with Russell L. Cecil, are cases in point. The faculty included two Nobel Prize winners, André Cournand and Dickinson Richards, who shared the Nobel Prize in 1956 for work they had done on cardiac catheterization. Erwin Chargaff and DeWitt Stetten were acknowledged to be two of the world's leading biochemists. Rustin McIntosh, the head of Babies Hospital, was a national figure in pediatrics.[65]

In addition, P & S had enjoyed the benefits of stable leadership for twenty-seven years, the period of Rappleye's long deanship. His authority was seldom questioned and almost never challenged by the three presidents under whom he had served or by the board of trustees, members of which sometimes complained out of his hearing that they knew nothing of went on up at the Medical School.[66]

But Rappleye's deanship (he became vice president for medical affairs in 1949) had not been without its problems, especially in its last years. Never himself involved in medical research, he did not view it as a particularly high priority for the Medical School. Moreover, he took little interest in fund-raising and was often away in his role as medical statesman. Some faculty resented his autocratic ways and resistance to changes proposed from below. A 1955 study of P & S staffing revealed considerable turnover among midcareer faculty. In 1957, *The Report of the President's Committee on the Educational Future of Columbia University*, created under the chairmanship of Arthur MacMahon, called for fundamental changes in the operation of the medical center, especially in keeping the faculty's responsibilities as teachers and scientists from being undercut by "opportunities for the remunerative treatment of patients." Rappleye retired the following year.[67]

Unfortunately, there was no one of Rappleye's caliber waiting in the wings to take up where he left off. Before his appointment as dean of the College of Physicians & Surgeons in 1958, H. Houston Merritt had been for a decade chair of neurology, a department in which he had taught for two decades. During that time, he had become the country's leading trainer of neurologists, with thirty of his students heading departments at medical centers from coast to coast. He had also made important discoveries in the pharmacological treatment of epilepsy.[68]

Merritt was less successful as dean than he had been as a researcher and teacher. During his eleven years as its head (1958–1969), the Medical School experienced increasing difficulty replacing its retiring giants with appointments of comparable promise. Some prospects simply declined to take offered positions in situations where their predecessors cast such long shadows. Others preferred positions where they had the chance to build their own departments, an option that appealed equally to some faculty already at Columbia but looking around. In 1962 the UC San Francisco Medical Center raided P & S for several of its most promising faculty in one swoop. Unwilling to fill important department chairmanships with less than world-class specialists, Merritt retired from his deanship in 1969 with sixteen of the school's twenty-five departments being overseen by acting chairs. A trustee review of the Medical School at the time reported that faculty morale was down. Although by the end of his deanship he was responsible for a budget of over $70 million, Merritt, according to McGill, had "run the medical school out of his desk drawer."[69]

Structural problems exacerbated those of leadership. Unlike many of its peers, Columbia's medical center was not owned by the university but operated under the governance of two separate boards of trustees, those of Columbia University, which controlled the College of Physicians & Surgeons, the School of Dentistry and Dental Surgery (separated from the P & S in the late 1950s), and the School of Public Health, and by the board of Presbyterian Hospital, which controlled the hospital and until 1937 the School of Nursing. In the best of times, this arrangement created problems, but, in an era of dramatic changes in the ways medical education and patient care were to be financed, it virtually assured an uncertain response to the challenges these changes posed. Merritt was unable to impose solutions on either his fractious colleagues or the two boards. Nor was President Kirk of any help. If aware of growing problems at 168th Street, he never moved to confront them.[70]

With the passage of the Medicare and Medicaid legislation by Congress and its signing into law by President Lyndon Johnson in 1965, the federal government became a principal player in the financing of medical education and patient care. It had already been an important source of funding for medical research, through such agencies as the reorganized National Institutes Science

Foundation (later, NIH) in 1948 and the National Science Foundation in 1950, whose grants had helped underwrite most of the supported research conducted at Columbia since the mid-1950s.[71]

But whereas both boards and faculty had welcomed research support, senior medical faculty and the Presbyterian board expressed real reservations about actively seeking the federal money that would bring with it radical changes in the way doctors conducted their clinical practices and hospitals provided patient care. Their resistance to federal funding was reminiscent of Eisenhower's a decade earlier, and equally self-defeating.[72]

"There's no question," recalled one member of the P & S faculty in the 1960s, "we missed the boat." In response to the proffered federal funding, he recalled, many of his senior colleagues "didn't want to take it. And the Hospital Board was worse." The point here is not that such opposition to what Kenneth Ludmerer has called "the second revolution in medical education" was without cause. Serious changes would be required of those institutions accepting federal funding, not the least of which affected the way medical faculty conducted their private practices and hospitals determined whom they would admit for care. The point is that any institution that wished to retain an important place in the hierarchy of American medical education could not afford such resistance, and for the Columbia-Presbyterian Medical Center to do so was to risk turning a modest reputational slide into an irreversible free fall.[73]

Thus the search for a successor to Merritt took on extraordinary importance. Launched in the immediate aftermath of the university's disruptions of 1968, it did not get off to a good start. Several potential candidates declined to be considered, while others insisted on conditions that either the Columbia or Presbyterian board were unwilling or unable to meet. The search committee, in what is sometimes a sign of desperation, then nominated not only a member of the faculty but the chair of the search committee, Dr. Paul Marks, to become the sixth dean of Columbia's College of Physicians & Surgeons. On May 4, 1970, the Columbia trustees, who back in January 1969 had acknowledged that the Medical School "has lost some of its luster," accepted the nomination.[74]

Paul Marks proved to be an inspired choice. A native New Yorker and graduate of Columbia College (1945), he had proceeded directly to P & S on a navy scholarship (M.D. 1949). While pursuing his medical studies, Marks began conducting research in biochemistry, working under the tutelage of DeWitt Stetten and Erwin Chargaff. After a fellowship at Cornell and house staff training at Presbyterian Hospital, Marks was recruited back to Columbia in 1955 as an instructor in medicine. In 1960 he became director of clinical hematology at Presbyterian Hospital; in 1967, professor of medicine; in 1969, chairman of the newly created Department of Human Genetics and Development. During these years, he pursued groundbreaking research in hematology and genetic blood disorders.[75]

At forty-eight, the powerfully built and aggressive Marks presented a dramatic contrast with his predecessor, who was sixty-eight at his retirement. He immediately became more involved with fund-raising than had either Rappleye or Merritt and in his enthusiasm for identifying new funding possibilities won the active involvement of President McGill. Together, they secured gifts from the oil magnate Armand Hammer (P & S 1923) and Percy Hudson (here, McGill's Catholicism apparently helped, Hudson being a fellow communicant). Both also sought out federal money wherever it could be found, an undertaking in which they enjoyed the active support of the New York congressional caucus.[76]

In 1974 Health Sciences was administratively reorganized, with Marks becoming vice president for Health Sciences (and director of the Cancer Research Institute), and with Donald Tapley made dean of the Medical School. They made an effective team, together cajoling and dragging their colleagues into the brave new world of publicly funded patient care.[77]

Whereas there was little that could be done with senior faculty who resisted abandoning their private practices and moving into group medical practices managed by the Medical School, all newly hired clinical faculty were expected to do so. Newly appointed department heads were also expected to encourage reluctant department members to do likewise. Between 1978 and 1982 the Department of Medicine went from having only two of its members in medical practice plans to forty. By the late 1970s income from these medical practices provided both the Medical School and the hospital (where the patient billing rates had not changed since the 1920s) with additional income to help underwrite changes in the medical curriculum and upgrades of hospital facilities. (In 2001 such plans accounted for over $300 million in income, or about 16 percent of the university's overall income.)[78]

Several of the appointments made in the basic medical sciences in mid-1970s immediately enhanced Columbia's scholarly reputation. They also increased its standing with federal funding agencies. These appointments included Isadore Edelman and Richard Axel (CC 1967) in biochemistry and Eric Kandell, as professor of physiology and psychiatry, who in 2000, seventeen years after his appointment, would win the Nobel Prize in medicine for his contributions to the field of neuroscience. They joined the microbiologist Sol Spiegelman, who came to P & S in 1969 as director of the Institute of Cancer Research. Many of these appointees came (or in Spiegelman's case, stayed) largely on assurances from Marks and Tapley that Columbia was coming back. By the late 1970s Columbia was again among the top half-dozen medical centers in terms of research funding from the NIH, even as Marks was being described by President McGill, who was not given to excess praise, as "the most brilliant medical administrator in the United States." Upon McGill's announcement that he was leaving in 1980, Marks became a serious inside candidate for the presidency of Columbia.[79]

When the presidency went to his colleague and occasional tennis partner on the dean's Budget Committee, Michael Sovern, Marks departed Columbia that same year to become CEO of Memorial Sloan-Kettering Cancer Center. He left behind on 168th Street a medical center still faced with serious problems, including a deteriorating neighborhood, a shortage of space, and chronic financial problems at the hospital. These noted, Health Sciences began the 1980s far more capable than they had been a decade earlier of responding to the still rapidly shifting circumstances and priorities within the overlapping worlds of American medical education, medical research, and patient care. They did so in ways that gave promise of their ongoing revitalization. The turnaround in Health Sciences was a harbinger of the university's larger recovery yet to come.[80]

CHAPTER 18

Bottoming Out

The University has from five to ten years to work out its difficulties.

William J. McGill, January 3, 1972

Forty years ago Columbia was generally perceived to be one of the very few distinguished universities in the United States. Today it is one among a larger number of universities in the first rank.

Steven Marcus, chairman, Report on the Presidential Commission on Academic Priorities in the Arts and Sciences (1979)

Gender Matters

A s MY Barnard colleague Rosalind Rosenberg details in her forthcoming study, the place of women achieved contested prominence at two distinct points in Columbia's history. The first, as noted earlier here, occurred in the midst of institutional expansion, financial good times, and the presidency of F. A. P. Barnard in the 1870s and 1880s. This resulted in the creation of Barnard College in 1889 and the opening of Columbia graduate programs to women. Teachers College was also an indirect beneficiary of this first wave of feminist agitation.

Yet, despite the backing of President Barnard, opposition from trustees, faculty, and students kept women out of not only Columbia College but the Engineering, Law, and Medical Schools as well. The net result, then, was what might be called the "Columbia Compromise," an eight-decade arrangement by which women created for themselves a limited but growing place at Columbia, primarily as students. By the 1960s this extended to all parts of the university except Columbia College. The "Compromise" allowed far less access for women faculty and senior administrators, with nearly all the instances limited to Barnard and Teachers College.[1]

The result was not outright exclusion so much as functional segregation. Compared with turn-of-the-century Harvard, Yale, or Princeton, Columbia in 1900 had lots of women around. Their presence only increased throughout the pre–World War I years as the enrollments at Teachers College and Barnard expanded faster than the College and the proportion of women in the graduate programs increased. Following a drop in male applications in 1917–18, the Medical School began admitting a restricted number of women. The Law School followed suit in 1927. By the eve of American entry into the Second World War, the only Columbia professional school not accepting women was engineering, which finally did so in 1942. Only the College remained off limits to women. In 1940 women students accounted for a fourth of all Columbia students; in 1960, for more than a third. If Summer School enrollments are included, by the late 1930s women constituted a majority of Columbia's students.[2]

The situation on the faculty front was another matter. Even including Barnard and Teachers College appointments who were members of one of the graduate faculties, women constituted less than 5 percent of the arts and sciences faculties in 1940. The professional schools, with the exception of Nursing, had even a smaller proportion of women on their faculties, with Law, Business, and Architecture having none.[3]

The first woman to be appointed to a Columbia department was Christine Ladd-Franklin (1847–1930), who taught in the psychology department as an unpaid lecturer from 1914 to 1930. Ruth Benedict (1887–1948), a student of Franz Boas and a Columbia Ph.D. (1923), who was appointed lecturer in 1925, became the first woman to hold a full-time faculty position when she was appointed an assistant professor in the anthropology department in 1931. She was promoted to associate professor in 1937, making her the first tenured woman faculty member. Margaret Mead (1901–78) a Barnard graduate (1923), Columbia Ph.D. (1928), and student of Boas and Benedict, taught a course in Columbia Extension in 1934–35 before making the American Museum of Natural History her permanent base.[4]

Another Barnard graduate (1919) and Columbia Ph.D. (1925), Lucy Hayner, had a position in the Columbia physics department comparable to Ladd-Franklin's in psychology: in 1929 she was appointed instructor; in 1940, associate; and in 1946, assistant professor. It was only in 1941 that Columbia made its first appointment of a woman at the full professor level. That year, the English department appointed Marjorie Hope Nicolson, a Yale Ph.D. who had been teaching at Smith College, where she wrote several books that earned her a trans-Atlantic reputation as a scholar of seventeenth-century English literature. On the eve of Nicolson's appointment, women made up less than 3 percent of the faculty appointed by the Columbia Corporation, about 5 percent when Barnard and Teachers College are included—about the same proportion as in 1900. Even so, the felt need to account for Nicholson's appointment, led her departmental colleagues over the next two decades to assure others that "Marjorie was the strongest man in the department."[5]

Unlike the proportions of women students, which climbed from 1900 to 1940 and, after temporarily flattening out during the G.I. Bill surge of male enrollments, resumed their climb in the 1950s, the proportion of women faculty holding regular Columbia appointments actually decreased between 1945 and 1960. This was clearly the case in the arts and sciences, which in 1960 still had only eighteen women, eleven of whom had a primary appointment in the Medical School, Barnard, or Teachers College.[6]

In the early 1960s most students at Teachers College, in library service, and in social work were women, as were practically all the students in the School of Nursing. Barnard women made up 40 percent of the university's undergraduate enrollments. In addition, a majority of the research staff both on the medical sciences campus and on Morningside were women. But only at Barnard and in the School of Nursing did women figure prominently in the upper level of the administrative structure of the university. In 1967 the highest-ranking woman in Low Library was Marion Jemmott, who had advanced through the ranks from secretary to the philosophy department to assistant secretary of the university. Her job of keeping a record of trustee meetings was made difficult by the fact that trustee committees often met at clubs where women were not allowed.[7]

Just under a third of those arrested in the buildings in 1968 were women. Most of these were Barnard undergraduates, but some were graduate students. During the occupations, women staffed strike central in Ferris Booth Hall, worked the mimeograph machines, and handled press inquiries. But Columbia women did not number among either the SDS or SCC leadership. (The SAS had a women's counterpart in the Barnard Organization of Souls Sisters [BOSS].) Nancy Bieberman, a Barnard student, did play a role in the Strike Coordinating Committee during the occupations, though she later remembered the prevailing attitude among the male SDS leadership whenever the police were expected was "chicks up front."[8]

Much as the first American women's movement in the 1840s and 1850s can be traced in part to the reception women received when they sought to join the Abolitionist and antislavery movement, many women active in the civil rights movement and Columbia '68 came away determined to focus on their own rights. In doing so, they found support from women elsewhere in New York, many of whom had attended Columbia and Barnard. A core group at Columbia included Joan Ferrante, Carolyn Heilbrun, Kate Millett, and Catherine Stimpson, each of whom had reason to believe that Columbia (specifically, the Columbia English department) had treated them unfairly as students and faculty, principally because, as Heilbrun later put it, "we were not guys."[9]

In early 1969 a larger group of women, some already meeting informally, came together in the main-floor lounge of Fayerweather Hall to form Columbia Women's Liberation (CWL). They were for the most part junior faculty teaching at Columbia, including the art historian Ann Sutherland Harris, or at Barnard, in the cases of Catharine Stimpson and Kate Millett, or graduate students, as with Harriet Zellner and Rachel Du Plessis (BC 1963). Some belonged to the National Organization of Women (NOW), and others were members of the more radical feminist group the Redstockings. The group's formation had been sparked by state hearings held in February 1969 to reconsider New York's abortion laws, to which the only woman invited to testify was a Roman Catholic nun. But the group's focus soon shifted to issues closer to home, particularly their own direct experiences of discrimination at Columbia.[10]

To buttress their own experiences and anecdotal testimony of Columbia discriminating against women, CWLers decided to seek out statistical evidence of Columbia's hiring patterns. Informed that the university had no such data, they decided to compile some on their own by going through the faculty listings in all the university's catalogs and identifying the gender of faculty by first names. Doubtful cases were resolved by phone calls. In December 1969 CWL issued its *Report of Committee on Discrimination Against Women Faculty*, with copies to President Cordier and to the *New York Times*.[11]

Its rough methodology notwithstanding, the CWL *Report* offered clear evidence in support of what most observers of Columbia long knew: very few women held faculty positions, and almost none of these held senior positions. But what really made the *Report* news—and strengthened its implicit argument of discrimination—was the department-by-department juxtapositions it offered between the high proportion of Ph.D.s Columbia awarded to women and the tiny proportion of women faculty. For example, in three departments where the proportion of Ph.D.s awarded to women exceeded one-third— French (44 percent), anthropology (44 percent), and psychology (36 percent)— there were no women faculty. The English department awarded 27 percent of its Ph.D.s to women, but its forty-person faculty included only one tenured woman faculty member and two assistant professors, both assigned to General Studies. Only in art history did women faculty make up a substantial proportion of the department. But even here, the proportion of Ph.D.s awarded to women (56 percent) was more than twice the proportion of women faculty (24 percent). The inference that Columbia willingly took the tuition money of women wishing to pursue graduate studies and just as readily certified their competence by awarding them Ph.D.s but resolutely declined to consider them for faculty appointments was hard not to draw.[12]

The CWL *Report* came to the attention of the Department of Health, Education and Welfare (HEW), which had responsibility for monitoring compliance with federal work rules among federal contractors. Before 1965 private universities had been exempt from federal antidiscrimination rules. That year, however, President Johnson's Executive Order 11246 made universities with federal contracts subject to the work rules as applied to minorities. In 1967, despite opposition from the higher education lobby, Executive Order 11375 made them specifically bound by rules prohibiting discrimination against women. Henceforth, the concept of affirmative action became the law of the land, and private universities with federal contracts were expected to comply.[13]

The first regulations applying affirmative action requirements to universities receiving federal contracts appeared in the *Federal Register* on May 28, 1968. Shortly thereafter, the Civil Rights Division of HEW began calling on universities with substantial federal contracts to provide employment data showing racial distributions. The first call Columbia received went to the Medical School on January 31, 1969; a year later, by which time HEW had the CWL's *Report* charging gender discrimination, Columbia had received more than two dozen such calls, none of which had been responded to.[14]

Part of Columbia's nonresponsiveness was attributable to the general administrative disarray that characterized Columbia in 1968 and 1969, some to the fact that neither race nor gender was systematically recorded in most employment records, and not a little to the resistance of some university officials to providing data from which quotas might be both devised and assigned. University counsel John Wheeler, for one, opposed ceding rights previously enjoyed by private universities. For still other administrators and faculty, statistically generated racial and gender quotas called forth memories of the anti-Semitic uses to which they had been put by the Nazis.[15]

For HEW, however, and particularly for the head of the Civil Rights Division in the Department of Labor, J. Stanley Pottinger, Columbia's noncompliance smacked of stonewalling and lent credibility to the CWL's charges. When further calls on Columbia in the summer of 1970 produced polite responses but still no data, Pottinger decided to make Columbia a test case of HEW's enforcement powers. On November 3, 1970, he wrote to McGill to inform him that in light of Columbia's noncompliance with some thirty separate calls for information on the hiring of minorities and women, he had ordered a suspension of all current federal contracts with the university.[16]

By putting some $33 million in federal contracts in jeopardy, Pottinger got Columbia's full attention. Five days after receipt of the letter, McGill appointed a faculty affirmative action advisory committee, chaired by Vice President Paul Carter. Data gathering commenced forthwith, as did regular discussions with the staff of HEW, to assure that the data would be provided in a form acceptable to the government. In April 1972 the university submitted to HEW a 300-page Columbia University Affirmative Action Plan that included employment data sorted by race and gender. Without acknowledging past discrimination, the plan committed Columbia to hiring almost nine hundred additional women and minorities in the next five years.[17]

With a virtual hiring freeze in place throughout the university and an aggressive retrenchment program in the arts and sciences, meeting this target would not be easy. The plan estimated that it would require, for example, that more than a quarter of all available appointments in the humanities and social sciences go to women and minorities. HEW accepted the plan, and the threat of suspending federal contracts was withdrawn.[18]

Even as McGill and his administrators assured the feds that discrimination against women at Columbia was over, Columbia's women faculty opened a second front in their battle for full equality: gender-based salary discrimination. The battleground in this instance, however, was not the corridors of Washington but the newly organized University Senate, which, in the spring of 1971, established the Commission on the Status of Women.[19]

By the conclusion of its deliberations in 1975, the commission included eight members, two observers, and six consultants. All but three of these sixteen participants were women, among whom Professor of Physics Chien-Shieng Wu, Professor of History Nina Garsoian, and Professor of Biochemistry Barbara W. Low, were the most senior. In addition, the commission included the participation of Catharine Stimpson, an associate professor at Barnard who had been active in the CWL, four female members of the reputedly misogynistic Columbia English department, and two veterans of the nonfaculty gender wars at Columbia, Frances Hoffman, director of the chemical laboratories, and Marion E. Jemmott, acting secretary of the university.[20]

One might have expected McGill's reaction to these basic challenges to inherited practices—hiring mostly men and paying women less—as, at best, distractions from the other problems he had to address or, at worst, hitting the university when it was down. One of his associates in Low Library recalled the president angry at being "blindsided" by these charges and as "not giving a damn about affirmative action."[21]

To be sure, there was little at first glance about McGill to distinguish him from the other Columbia "guys." His wife's reaction to his announcement that he had accepted the Columbia presidency—"in the style of Ruth—'wherever you go, I'll go. I don't want to leave here, but if you go, I'll go' "—hardly suggests that he was subject to feminist consciousness-raising at home. Little in his educational or professional biography suggest a sensitivity to gender discrimination; he encountered few women colleagues in what he called the "hard side" of psychology. During his ten-year presidency, he never appointed a woman to a senior administrative post and allowed the indignity of Marion Jemmott's remaining "acting" secretary of the university to persist for seven years after she took over the duties of the job.[22]

Yet dismissing McGill as just another of the "guys" does him a disservice.

During his years as a graduate student and a young professor, his wife, Ann, had worked evenings as a nurse while he took care of the kids. It also overlooks the constructive role he played in accommodating the demands, however inconveniently timed, that Columbia's women made on the university to correct past injustices. Rather than resenting the Commission on the Status of Women or subverting its efforts, he actively engaged its members in putting in place regulations and structures that would assure that past discrimination against women in hiring and compensation would not be carried on in the future.[23]

McGill established his immediate bona fides with the commissioners by asking them at their first meeting to identify the most egregious examples of salary discrimination against women, assuring them that he would look into them personally and take corrective action as necessary. One of the examples provided was that of Chien-Shieng Wu, the senior member of the commission. Her salary was adjusted upward forthwith, and the president gained an ally. Other instances of salary discrimination, often going back years, were uncovered and corrected.[24]

The first part of the commission's report, published in March 1975, focused on the faculty and reads very much like a collaborative effort between the president and the commissioners. Gone was the sharply accusatory tone of the CWL's 1969 *Report* and gone also was the defensiveness that characterized the university's early dealings with HEW and critics in the press. While the report was submitted not to the president but to the senate executive committee, its authors deftly indicated the president's role in their deliberations by quoting as their epigraph remarks made by President McGill in 1972 at the University of Michigan: "For too long we have been content with appointment practices at faculty level that have produced relatively few women faculty members, fewer blacks, very few orientals and almost no Puerto Ricans and Chicanos. Women, blacks, and latins are crying out for their full rights in our society." "There is no excuse," the epigraph concluded with not a trace of irony, "for pious or sanctimonious explanations of why these rights cannot be granted."[25]

At some level, McGill, as a member of a religious-ethnic group discriminated against in the upper reaches of American academe, may have identified with the cause of women and minorities. His mother had worked most of her life, and his older sister had worked throughout hers for the New York Telephone Company, rising to the position of top operator at the same time her brother was named to the Columbia presidency. (McGill joked that their simultaneous appointments got equal billing back in the Bronx.) More likely, he recognized early in his dealings with the exercised Columbia women faculty and staff, as he had with black students, that what they wanted was not the destruction or humbling of Columbia but acceptance as full members. The decision to provide equal treatment, though prompted by federal legislation and internal pressure, was another conscious choice on part of the president of the university to break with past policies of exclusiveness and redefine Columbia in terms of greater inclusiveness.[26]

Yet, even here, Columbia's past was not something to be entirely cast off in an attempt to move forward. Part of what made Columbia's accommodation to the demands of the feminist movement relatively smooth was that it had never been nearly as much a male preserve as had its peers. In 1971 women accounted for 18.2 percent of all Columbia faculty members (excluding Barnard and TC). This was three times the proportion of women at Harvard (5.5 percent), twice that at Chicago (7.3 percent), and better by half than the publicly supported University of California at Berkeley (11.4 percent). Columbia also did far better than these institutions in the lower ranks, where more than half (52 percent) of its instructors and more than a quarter (26 percent) of its assistant professors were women.[27]

Columbia's numbers improved significantly when they included Barnard and Teachers College faculty, a not unreasonable stratagem that the university adopted whenever the federal counting requirements allowed. Just as women from the 1880s onward represented a substantial portion of the university's degree holders, Barnard and Teachers College were affiliated institutions of higher learning where women, contrary to the stereotypes, performed as scholars, teachers, and administrators. Their faculties had long provided Columbia professors with placement opportunities for their best women students even as they remained close enough for ongoing collaboration. Two cases in point: In the 1930s the Columbia historian Evarts B. Greene secured his graduate student and research assistant, Virginia Harrington, a position in the Barnard history department, where she remained part of Greene's research team. In a variation on this arrangement, Annette Fox, the wife of Columbia Professor of International Relations William Fox, became a member of the Barnard political science department upon her husband's appointment in 1949. Such male-female trans-Broadway scholarly collaborations were just one of the many ways Barnard and Teachers College simultaneously reinforced and subverted the logic of gender discrimination on Morningside Heights.[28]

Between 1971 and 1973 the proportion of women faculty positions at Columbia grew from 18.2 percent to 18.9 percent, a net gain of just three women. This occurred, however, while the university cut fifty-four faculty positions and when departments and faculties were just beginning to change the way they recruited faculty. As these changes became institutionalized and as the freeze on faculty appointments thawed, the share of faculty positions held by women increased sharply. By 1990 the proportion of women faculty at Columbia would grow to 28 percent.[29]

In 2002 women held upward of 40 percent of the full-time faculty positions at Columbia, Barnard, and Teachers College, and Columbia alone numbered 1,014 women among its 3,046 full-time faculty (33 percent). Salary differences that correlate with gender persist, and women faculty are still more highly represented in the lower ranks. Yet the installation in the 1970s of affirmative action guidelines, regular monitoring of faculty salaries for evidence of gender discrimination, and, most important of all, the increased presence of senior women faculty—and women trustees—alert to signs of institutional backsliding allow the feminist revolution properly to claim Columbia as one of its success stories.

Reimagining the Barnard Connection

It was coincidental but not inconsequential that the first serious modification of the Columbia-Barnard relationship since 1900 occurred in the early 1970s, in the midst of the second feminist revolution. The earlier arrangements worked out by Columbia president Seth Low and Barnard dean Emily Jane Smith underwent only minor modifications for eight decades. This was as President Butler and Dean Virginia C. Gildersleeve wished it. Gildersleeve owed her 1911 appointment as Barnard's third dean in large part to Butler and decided early on, whether from feelings of deference or political calculation, that there was little to be gained by taking Butler on. During the thirty-five years during which their administrations overlapped, she never openly did.[30]

This is not to suggest that Gildersleeve was neglectful of Barnard's welfare or afraid to advance the cause of educated women, especially Barnard women. She simply saw advantages to both in keeping on Butler's best side. Thus, for example, Barnard was free to go its own curricular way, but when it came to admission policies, it followed those of the College, as in limiting the admission of Jews in the 1920s and 1930s. If anything, Gildersleeve may have been even more disinclined to hire Jewish faculty than Butler was.[31]

The 1900 intercorporate agreement with the trustees of Columbia University gave the trustees of Barnard College responsibility for faculty appointments. In practice, however, senior appointments throughout the Gildersleeve era were cleared with the senior members in their counterpart departments at Columbia. Similarly, which Barnard faculty were asked to teach graduate students was determined by the Columbia department.

Columbia departments sent many of their better Ph.D.s to Barnard and occasionally junior faculty for whom they had no permanent place. The cumulative effect of this was to create an interwar Barnard faculty made up primarily of Columbia Ph.D.s. In 1940 two out of three Ph.D. holders on the Barnard faculty (forty-eight of sixty-nine) were Columbia Ph.D.s. Thus Barnard faculty typically had relationships with members of their counterpart Columbia departments, which, however unequal, were familiar and reciprocal. The fact that Columbia exercised considerable control over Barnard senior appointments did not mean that the criteria for tenure were identical or that the faculties, except for the difference in size, were interchangeable. For one thing, the Barnard faculty had proportionally many more women than did the Columbia faculty. For some at Columbia, Lionel Trilling, for example, that fact alone brought their qualifications to teach Columbia men into question.[32]

The institutional relationship changed after World War II, when Barnard scrambled to replace a generation of faculty that had been hired in the 1920s but who had delayed retirement because of the war. Their replacements were less often handpicked by Columbia and less often Columbia Ph.D.s. This was as Gildersleeve's successor, Millicent Carey McIntosh, who became Barnard's fourth dean in 1947, wanted it. A Bryn Mawr graduate who had studied at Johns Hopkins for her Ph.D. before becoming headmistress of the Brearley School and marrying Rustin McIntosh, Columbia professor of pediatrics and director of Babies Hospital, she favored diversifying the Barnard faculty as part of a larger plan to increase Barnard's autonomy. Hence in 1952 the change of her title from "Dean" to "President." While several early appointments during her administration were made with Columbia's involvement, those of Bernard Barber in sociology and LeRoy Breunig in French being examples, others, such as Eleanor Rosenberg in English and Gladys Meyer in sociology, carried no such Columbia imprimatur.[33]

The American art historian Barbara Novak and Renaissance literary scholar Anne Prescott, both Barnard A.B.s, began teaching at Barnard years before completing their Ph.D.s at Columbia and owed their early appointments less to Columbia influence than to their success as Barnard instructors. Still others, among them the American historian Chilton Williamson, graduate of Columbia College and a Columbia Ph.D., transferred their loyalties to "little" Barnard as opposed to "big" Columbia. When in the early 1970s an inquisitive and recently arrived Barnard assistant professor asked a senior member of the Barnard English department what Columbia constituted in his intellectual life, he was told: "A great distraction."[34]

Barnard's smaller departments, such as classics and Russian, generally maintained close and cordial relations with their counterparts, not least because neither could staff a full curricular program without the cooperation of the other. Still other Barnard departments made a conscious effort to maintain ties with Columbia, such as art history, sociology, and anthropology. Thus the situation was far from comprehensive and mutual estrangement but rather one in which departments on both sides of Broadway had reason to be skeptical about the other's priorities. By the mid-1960s two out of three Barnard faculty were women. Some of these maintained close ties with Columbia, but still others in the early 1970s saw the enhanced autonomy of Barnard as part of the larger feminist agenda that they were loath to put at risk to Columbia's whim or financial vicissitudes.[35]

During the 1950s few Columbia College courses were open to Barnard women—and relatively few Columbia men took Barnard courses. Barnard seniors could petition to take graduate courses, and some did, especially those planning to go on to graduate school. But with the academic programs of Columbia College freshman and sophomores largely taken up with courses in the Core, which were closed to Barnard students, and with Barnard juniors and seniors concentrating on courses in their relatively more structured majors, there was little classroom interaction. Many Barnard students objected to the lack of access to Columbia courses, even while others reveled in classroom circumstances free of men.[36]

This relative alienation of Barnard went largely unnoticed by Low Library during the expansionary postwar years. Nor were the Barnard trustees especially cognizant of it. They continued to interact socially with Columbia trustees much as in the Butler era, when Columbia trustees regularly served on the Barnard board or had a relative doing so in their stead. But Columbia's straitened financial circumstances in the later 1960s and early 1970s provoked an extended season of Barnard scrutinizing. The Columbia scrutinizers came in three varieties: Low Library budgeteers; curricular and faculty consolidators; and a "cut her loose" contingent located in Columbia College. While all three wished to change Barnard, the Barnard each envisioned in the wake of the change was very different.[37]

A truism among these Columbia administrators was that Barnard had long enjoyed a free ride on the financial coattails of the university. President McGill had only been on the job four months before concluding: "Columbia in effect subsidizes Barnard"—this despite the basic fact that since 1889 the Barnard trustees had been wholly responsible for the College's finances. Services received from Columbia, such as steam or telephone, were paid for at going rates. Barnard faculty and administrative salaries, maintenance of plant, financial aid, and other expenditures were covered by tuition fees, gifts, and income from the College's own modest endowment. Barnard was then—and is now— much more tuition-dependent than Columbia.[38]

The "free ride" argument, however, gains credence in areas where Barnard drew on Columbia for services that Barnard would otherwise have had to provide its students and faculty or do without. Chief among these was access to Columbia's world-class research library. Before the opening of Wollman Library in Lehman Hall in 1959, Barnard had no real library of its own. Even with Wollman, advanced research by Barnard students and faculty required access to Butler Library and the university's many libraries. In 1970 Columbia's library budget approached $8 million; Barnard's was $500,000.

Another benefit involved the specialized courses offered at Columbia that were open to Barnard students, which Barnard on its own—or any other liberal arts college—could not have offered. Such access gave Barnard an important competitive advantage over other women's colleges, and one it was willing to pay for. Over the years, different arrangements had been tried by which Barnard paid Columbia for its students taking Columbia courses. At some points, Barnard's unfavorable balance of trade in cross-registrations was paid for by Barnard to Columbia in an annual lump sum; at other times, variously calculated per capita charges were exacted.[39]

During the Kirk administration, when Barnard's access remained limited to a select number of courses in arts and sciences departments and the Morningside professional schools, the difference in the cross-registration numbers was not considered worth haggling over. Neither was Barnard's access to Columbia's libraries. In these areas, postwar Barnard did indeed enjoy something of a free ride.[40]

In the early 1970s Low Library budgeteers blew the whistle on both practices. They were not opposed to having Barnard students and faculty use Columbia's libraries or Barnard students take Columbia courses but insisted that Barnard henceforth pay for both. They actually favored opening up more Columbia courses to Barnard students, seeing this as way of increasing enrollments in Columbia courses with tuition-paying Barnard students. They were also prepared to have Barnard open more of its courses to Columbia students, on the assumption that redundant courses could be eliminated and that the results of any such free-trade policy would produce a net flow of enrollments increasingly in Columbia's favor.[41]

As the budgeteers set about establishing what that compensation might be, the prospect of more Columbia students being taught by Barnard faculty prompted questions in other Columbia quarters. Just who were these Barnard faculty who would now be teaching Columbia students? Were they any good? What role did Columbia have in determining their appointments? Thus the issues of opening more Columbia courses to Barnard students and the qualifications of Barnard faculty became joined.[42]

About the scholarly credentials of the Barnard faculty there was some disagreement. Because the Barnard science faculty had little or no access to graduate students and limited laboratory facilities, they were seldom in a position to compete with science faculty at Columbia and other universities on anything like equal terms. Their researches were accordingly often on the fringes of their disciplines, where funding and rapid publication were less determinative. This said, the interwar research of Barnard scientists such as the physicist Margaret Maltby, the chemist Marie Reimer, and the psychologist Harry Hollingworth was of a caliber substantially higher than that found at even the best liberal arts college faculties. Yet it is also the case that many Barnard interwar science faculty conducted little publishable research beyond that derived from their dissertations. That the same could be said of some Columbia science faculty did not alter the stereotyping of Barnard as a teaching institution, Columbia a research institution.[43]

Among faculty in the humanities and social sciences, the disparities in scholarly output between interwar Columbia and Barnard were smaller. Several Barnard faculty, although working in areas of their disciplines at some remove from the main action, made significant contributions. The work of the sociologist Mirra Komarovsky, the economist Elizabeth F. Baker, and the art historian Marguerite M. Bieber are examples. Among the men, William Haller in English, William P. Montague in philosophy, and Julius Held in art history all brought distinction not only to Barnard but to Columbia. It was also the case that for many years Komarovsky's contributions to sociology were more fully recognized elsewhere than by her Columbia colleagues.[44]

Under the leadership of Millicent McIntosh, larger departments at Barnard such as English, economics, French, and psychology achieved greater autonomy from their Columbia counterparts than they had in the interwar years. In them, consultation with Columbia about hiring at the junior level became perfunctory or nonexistent, while Columbia's views on tenured appointments went unprovided, unsolicited, and sometimes unheeded. By the mid-1960s these Barnard departments had several tenured faculty who remained professionally unknown to members of their counterpart Columbia departments.[45]

These arrangements served both Barnard and Columbia well enough as long as each went its own way. But in the early 1970s some Columbia administrators began actively to consider a merger of the two faculties, some seeing such a merger as a prelude to merging the two institutions, others as an alternative to doing so. Here, too, the impetus was substantially if not totally financial, though the logic, unlike that of the budgeteers' having Barnard pay more for Columbia services, is less obvious. Why would Columbia, even as it was reducing its own faculty, actively consider absorbing Barnard's?

Part of the answer was that Barnard faculty were paid less than Columbia faculty yet taught more courses to more students. They were, in a word, cheap.

Barnard faculty were also less likely to be tenured than Columbia faculty (40 percent as against 70 percent) and therefore, in a crunch, more expendable. Whereas Columbia had instituted a virtual freeze on hires in the early 1970s, Barnard continued to make two or three tenured appointments a year. Thus, were Columbia to acquire the Barnard faculty, and the enrollments that came with them, it might not only save some money, it could use openings in the Barnard faculty to meet some in its own pressing needs.[46]

Thus, as the budgeteers and the consolidators converged on the Barnard faculty as a partial answer to some of the university's financial problems, it became important for Columbia to play a much larger role in determining who should and should not be granted tenure at Barnard. The most direct way to do so would be to subject all new Barnard faculty to the process already in place for Columbia's arts and sciences departments and some of its professional schools. This consisted of a review by a five-person ad hoc committee of senior faculty, selected by the provost, whose recommendation was advisory to the Columbia president. In the case of professional school tenure reviews, two of the five faculty on the ad hoc committee were drawn from the candidate's school, a provision that would also obtain for Barnard tenure candidates. If adopted, Barnard tenured appointments would henceforth not only have to be approved by Barnard's own review procedures but also by a favorable vote by a Columbia-appointed committee made up of three Columbia and two Barnard faculty and then by a decision by Columbia's provost and president to accept the vote.[47]

For all the subsequent second-guessing, Barnard had good reasons for supporting such an arrangement. It was the price to pay for securing Barnard students fuller access to Columbia undergraduate courses. But it was also hoped to end insinuations about the scholarly qualifications of Barnard faculty, which would now be judged in qualitative terms the same way as other Columbia tenure appointments. There was also reason to believe that, in the academic economy of the 1970s characterized by a comprehensive glut of Ph.D.s, Barnard could find individuals who could meet its own and Columbia's standards.[48]

The upshot was a 1973 intercorporate agreement between Barnard and Columbia more sweeping in its changes than any of the other half-dozen entered into since 1900. It consisted of four principal parts:

1. Barnard would pay Columbia an annual fee of $1 million as compensation for the expected imbalance in cross-registrations.
2. Barnard would pay Columbia a charge to reflect the difference between what Barnard expended on its library and what it would have expended (based on

library expenditures at the other Seven Sister colleges) if it did not have access to Columbia's libraries.

3. All future Barnard faculty candidates for tenured appointments would be reviewed by a university ad hoc committee and subject to the approval of the president of Columbia University.

4. Both institutions would cooperate to avoid unnecessary redundancy in faculty appointments and academic programs.

In the three decades since the 1973 agreement was reached, some 150 Barnard faculty have been reviewed by university ad hoc committees. Of these, more than 80 percent have been approved for tenure (about the same percentage as for Columbia-recommended faculty). A few negative decisions in Barnard cases have been occasion for controversy, often accompanied by claims that Columbia values published scholarship too highly and does so at the expense of effective teaching. But, on the whole, the system has worked smoothly and to the advantage of both Columbia and Barnard. The former has greater certainty about the scholarship of its Barnard colleagues, while the latter now has a faculty significantly more engaged in scholarship than it had been before 1973 and significantly more so than faculties at other liberal arts colleges.[49]

Coeducation Deferred

The 1973 intercorporate agreement has not lacked critics on either side of Broadway. Over the years, most have come from the Barnard side and have concerned disputed tenure cases. The first complaints, however, came from Columbia College faculty and administrators, who saw the agreement with Barnard as preventing the College from taking its destiny into its own hands by admitting women directly into the College. Viewed from Hamilton Hall, Barnard had become Columbia's "great distraction."[50]

Advocates of coeducation at Columbia College were thin on the ground into the 1960s. They would also have been advised to keep their views to themselves, so long as staunch defenders of a male-only College as Lionel Trilling and Jacques Barzun strode the land. Not until the late 1960s, after Princeton and Yale, followed by Bowdoin, Amherst, Williams, and Dartmouth, all began admitting women, did the issue acquire local salience. By the early 1970s, Columbia, which retained the distinction of being the smallest of the Ivy League colleges, now had the new one of being alone in not admitting women. The proponents of coeducation could no longer be put off.

In June 1972 the eighth dean of Columbia College, Carl Hovde, resigned to return to full-time teaching in the English department. During his four years as dean, however, he had been persuaded that the College's future would be best assured by admitting women. A look at the College's recent recruitment history suggests why. Like all colleges in the interwar era, including the other Ivies, Columbia accepted a high proportion of its applicants. Only applicants from New York City, and especially Jews from the city's public schools, had less than a fifty–fifty chance of admission. Out-of-town applicants, especially those applying from leading prep schools, were accepted pretty much automatically. So was the son of an alumnus, though, as Hovde once sardonically allowed, "we were never much burdened with the legacy question."[51]

With entering classes of five hundred, Dean Hawkes and his staff filled them from a total application pool seldom exceeding one thousand, with would-be transfers from CCNY making up the waiting list. When the GI Bill surge ebbed in the early 1950s, this prewar pattern returned. Thus, into the early 1960s, as long as the College remained small, there were enough qualified applicants who wanted to come to Columbia—for its distinctive core curriculum, its lead-in to the university's professional schools, its location, whatever—that filling a College class with bright and motivated students posed no serious problem.[52]

The situation deteriorated in the mid-1960s, when the College began experiencing difficulties getting accepted applicants to come to Columbia rather than go to other places where they had also been accepted. While still attracting—and now accepting more—Jewish applicants, Columbia College was no longer the principal Ivy League school to which academically able Jewish students from New York applied or went. As those close to the admissions scene began phrasing the situation, Columbia still attracted its share of the best students in any given year, as the quality of the top half of its entering classes consistently reflected, but the bottom quarter "left something to be desired."[53]

This bottom-quarter problem worsened in the wake of the 1968 disruptions. By 1972 the College was putting together its entering class of 750 students from under 2,000 applicants, with a share of these using Columbia as their backup. Thus any thought of increasing the size of the College, which Low Library's budgeteers very much wanted to do, bumped up against the harsh reality that those additional students could only be found deeper into the barrel than the College admissions staff and the College faculty were prepared to venture.[54]

A few observers suggested that the required core curriculum clashed with a generation of students in flight from requirements and might be part of the College's recruitment problem. But the more widely offered explanation was that the College was doubly disadvantaged by its all-male character. First, it deprived the College of the opportunity of considering women—or half of all those who applied to college. But, second, it lost men who chose to go where they would have women in their classes. The more College Believers thought about admitting women, the better it sounded. For example, should Columbia College enroll women, they would likely be highly qualified women seeking entrance into an Ivy League college, who would then take their places alongside equally able male admits (i.e., the traditional upper half). Admitting women might eliminate the bottom-quarter problem altogether.[55]

Such a strategy was not without problems, though some faced earlier by other Ivies were less worrisome for Columbia. For example, the alumni opposition to coeducation that first greeted the idea in New Haven, Hanover, and Princeton posed less of a problem, if only because alumni were less a force at Columbia than at Yale, Dartmouth, or Princeton. Whereas much of the opposition elsewhere reflected alumni concerns that the sons of alumni might lose their places to women (some, to be sure, daughters of these same alumni), here, too, the absence of a serious legacy problem at Columbia helped. Should the College have to increase its size in the wake of admitting women, as Dartmouth did, to keep the number of men from dropping, doing so could only cheer the hearts of the Low Library budgeteers. Indeed, some skeptics thought this was the whole point.[56]

The real problem with Columbia College's contemplating coeducation in the early 1970s was, what would happen to Barnard? Whereas Hovde was sufficiently concerned about this question, and sufficiently alert to the concerns of others in high places, not to put forward a plan for coeducation, neither concern prevented his successor from doing so.

Peter R. Pouncey, the ninth dean of Columbia College, was an untenured assistant professor of Greek and Latin in the summer of 1971, when he became associate dean. English by birth and trained by Jesuits for the Catholic priesthood before going off to Oxford, Pouncey was one of those recently arrived Columbians who immediately identified with the purpose and the mystique of the College. When appointed dean in 1972, he was already committed to advancing the cause of the College by having it begin admitting women as soon as possible, whatever the opposition. "We were young and high-strung. We shot at everything that moved," he later said of himself and his fellow Hamilton Hall sharpshooter, another untenured College convert, Associate Dean Michael Rosenthal. "We had perfect aim. . . . We chose our targets wisely and were never wrong."[57]

They also aimed high. Among those who came to feel they were targeted by Pouncey's Hamilton Hall were Provost de Bary and President McGill. Deferring to no one in his loyalty to the College but also protective of Barnard (his wife was an alumna), de Bary drew Pouncey's fire when he opposed coeducation even as he proposed increasing the size of the College by some four hundred male students over four years. Pouncey complained to McGill about de Bary's interference, McGill informed de Bary of the complaints, and de Bary and Pouncey stopped talking to each other.[58]

McGill's turn came in April 1975, when Pouncey, without informing the president of his plans but having apprised the *New York Times*, held a meeting of the College faculty at which a vote was taken to begin admitting women to the College in the fall of 1977. McGill promptly disavowed the vote and the College's dean, informing the *Times* and the trustees that such an action would spell "the end of Barnard." Shortly thereafter, Pouncey resigned his deanship and returned to the classics department. "A most charming scoundrel," McGill called him, after tempers had cooled. Friends allowed that he was "brashly candid to the point of embarrassment." Pouncey left Columbia in 1984 to become the successful but no less outspoken president of Amherst College.[59]

Although Pouncey overplayed his hand, he had held some high cards. The problem of the College was serious and growing worse, and solving it by admitting women was an idea whose time had nearly come. McGill staved it off, in part by holding out the hope that negotiations with Barnard at the trustee level would produce a way to make Columbia College more coeducational in the classroom without destroying Barnard—and thus avoiding the bad press sure to attend her demise. The problem with this compromise was that it proved unachievable and, in any event, would not have satisfied either the College faculty or the Barnard trustees. But if Columbia College was to become coeducational and Barnard expire in the event, it would have to await McGill's departure.[60]

"We Have Fallen"

In December 1979 a presidential commission of nineteen faculty members, convened in the spring of 1978 under the chairmanship of Professor of English Steven Marcus, submitted its report on academic priorities in the arts and sciences. It was the first such undertaking since the MacMahon report of 1957 and could hardly have been more different in tone or conclusions. Its opening two sentences made clear that this was not to be another exercise in self-congratulation and complacency: "Forty years ago Columbia was generally perceived to be one of the very few distinguished universities in the United States. Today it is among a larger number of universities in the first rank."[61]

The historical value of the Marcus report is a function of its timing and candor. It provides an unflinching overall assessment of the state of the arts and sciences after a decade of budgetarily mandated retrenchment and an even longer period of relative decline, when the qualitative standing of the arts and sciences core of the university, as a subsequent upturn allows us to conclude, bottomed out. It made for painful reading.

Of the seven science departments reviewed by the commission, only geology—earth sciences—was described as having been strengthened during the preceding decade. Others, such as mathematics and chemistry, were allowed to be "excellent" or "of high quality" in some respects but were also seen as too small to compete effectively with peer departments twice their size. That psychology had "declined precipitously" since the 1940s, when it became an "enclave of animal behaviorists," was directly acknowledged. As for the biological sciences, the judgment was as unequivocal as it was historically informed: "[Columbia biology] has not participated to any appreciable extent in the extraordinary research developments of the past twenty-five years, particularly in molecular biology. Thus the 'golden age of biology,' regrettably, bears no significant Morningside stamp. The flow of great discoveries in the area of gene expression has effectively bypassed this campus."[62]

The fourteen humanities and seven social sciences departments fared no better.

- Greek and Latin: "lacks both the highly visible luminaries of the past and the young innovators of the present";
- Italian: "by any measure, has essentially failed to capitalize on the potential of the field";
- Spanish: "In recent years the Columbia department has been in a valley";
- Philosophy: "At present, there is little likelihood that the department's standing in the field can be much improved."

To be sure, small departments like Slavic studies, East Asian studies, and Middle Eastern language and culture remained competitive with their peers, and art history was still "one of the pre-eminent departments in the country." But English, as late as 1965 "one of the four or five best departments" in the country, experienced such severe faculty losses in the 1970s—sixteen assistant professors—as to prompt the commission to lament generally on "the tendency to eliminate young minds from the present and future of the University."[63]

The Marcus commission's harshest judgments were reserved for the social sciences, which, it noted, had been "exceptionally pre-eminent" as recently as the late 1950s. "We have fallen. The evidence is unambiguous, and candor compels us to acknowledge that we no longer occupy a position of distinct pre-eminence. In several disciplines we have fallen below the first rank." The evidence was compelling: in the 1969 Anderson-Roose ratings, three of the seven Columbia social science departments (anthropology, history, and sociology) figured in the top ten of their respective disciplines; in a 1977 faculty survey conducted by Seymour Martin Lipset and Everett Carll Ladd Jr., less than 10 percent of the survey respondents ranked any of Columbia's social science departments among the top five departments nationally.[64]

Sometimes the problem cited was the impact of individual faculty, as in the retirement of Paul Lazarsfeld and the imminent retirement of Robert Merton in sociology or, contrarily, the outsized and continuing impact of Marvin Harris in anthropology, which caused the department to be perceived externally as dominated by one theoretical—and ideological—perspective, that of cultural materialism. (A softer version of this criticism had been offered in the instance of the impact of Michael Riffaterre on the French department.) Economics, history, and political science were all described as having been led astray in the 1950s by the momentary glamour and funding involved in area studies, while failing to sustain strength in the core concerns of these disciplines. Viewing the overall condition of the social sciences, the commission concluded: "The implication of slippage is inescapable." Were one to doubt this, it went on, "One need only consider the eminent scholars who have chosen to leave Columbia in the past twenty years."[65]

The judgments of the Marcus report did not soften when assessing the physical circumstances in which the Columbia community labored. But at least in reporting on these, one member of the commission, Professor of Psychology Stanley Schachter, who made the amenities portfolio of the commission his own, occasionally waxed poetic. "Our buildings grow shabby, our grounds tacky," he allowed, even as the university's "parking, apartments, loans and the like are controlled by quirky pixies." From there, the final heresy was within reach. "Morningside Heights outside the campus," this native New Yorker concluded on behalf of the commission, "is not attractive, and life on Morningside Heights is not commodious or particularly entertaining." William Livingston, Samuel Ruggles, James McKeen Cattell, Mark Rudd, and all the other Columbia iconoclasts had found in Schachter a late-twentieth-century kindred spirit.[66]

The Marcus commission's report was of a piece with the McGill presidency; indeed, it would be hard to imagine it seeing the light of day in anyone else's presidency. If anything, it likely overstated the competitive disadvantages Columbia labored under as it approached the 1980s. And it understated the importance of recently enacted structural and financial reforms on academic prospects. Moreover, because it was focused on the arts and sciences, the Marcus report said nothing of positive developments in the health sciences, even as it neglected the fact that the 1970s provided tough going for some of Columbia's competitors (e.g., NYU) as well. As McGill's recently appointed provost and odds-on successor, Michael Sovern, saw the report through its last editing, he could at least gain a measure of consolation from the thought that its unvarnished truth telling left the university with little place to go but up.[67]

Time to Go

When McGill accepted the presidency in 1970, he did so for a five-year term. Two years later, he was still planning to leave in 1976. "This job," had said in 1971 "just eats you up." But in 1974, when bringing the budget into balance proved to be a more protracted struggle than either he or the trustees had imagined, he agreed to stay on for a second five-year term. From then on, he and the board understood that he would be leaving no later than 1980.[68]

As that date drew near, McGill had many reasons to look back with pride on what had been accomplished. The oral history interviews he had with Professor of History Henry Graff in 1979–80 gave him that opportunity. On dealing with the four problems he faced at the outset of his presidency—the budget, the administration, student unrest, and community relations—he gave himself high marks. Even latterly, on the fund-raising front, especially with respect to the Medical School, he allowed himself some success. He took particular pride in his comprehensive upgrading of the caliber of the university's professional school deans, citing specifically his appointments of Peter Likins (1978) in engineering, Boris Yavitz (1975) in business, and James Polshek (1972) in architecture. Within Low Library, he took satisfaction from his recent appointment of the dean of the Law School, Michael Sovern, as provost, a year before his scheduled departure, which amounted to his choosing his own successor as well as setting the time of his departure, something no other Columbia president had managed to do.[69]

There were other reasons for McGill to leave. The jobs he had been hired to do had been done, and what now needed doing required a different kind of president. Even as the university emerged from the crisis circumstances of the early 1970s, he maintained full battle readiness. Although he and his wife, Ann, seldom got away from 60 Morningside, the president's residence, they only infrequently entertained there. Except for the annual dinner for recipients of honorary degrees, gone were the elegant dinners of the Butler era—the last in New York (Diana Trilling informs us) to require long gloves for the women guests—and the opera outings of the Kirk years. The felt need for economizing may have accounted for the lack of entertaining, as might his wife's discomfort

in formal social circumstances, but some of his social reclusiveness was probably attributable to the wearying strain of the job.[70]

Even McGill's oratories, annually on display at commencements, reflected
the hunkered-down quality of his presidency. In them, he sometimes aspired to
the "we shall fight them on the beaches" rhetoric of Winston Churchill or the
sardonic "life is sometimes unfair" accommodations of John F. Kennedy but
never the idealistic flourishes of Martin Luther King's "I have a dream." After
listening to more than a few commencement calls to arms, one regular platform attendee turned to another and allowed that Columbia's problem was that
"here it was the late 1970s and Columbia still had a 1960s president."[71]

Only fifty-eight at the close of his presidency, McGill was worn out. The job,
though it had not killed him as he thought it might, had aged him. As he put it,
"a decade spent trying to keep your head out of water" can do that. Chief among
the many qualifications he attributed to his successor was that, of all the administrators he had known, Sovern was "the most able to cope with stress." The syn-
tax of the statement allows the inference that he included himself in the comparison. One of Barnard College's founders, Annie Nathan Meyer, entitled her
autobiography *It's Been Fun*. McGill never did write an autobiography, but if he
had, her title was safe from plagiarizing. His would more likely have been along
the lines of *That Vale of Tears Thing*.[72]

So, on June 20, 1980, laughingly appointing his successor acting president for
the ten days remaining of his term, the sixteenth president of Columbia University left Morningside Heights to return to his beloved La Jolla with his wife,
Ann. There, he lived for another seventeen years, for a few years occupied with
government commissions and foundations but seldom venturing back to New
York and rarely to the Upper West Side. He died on October 20, 1997. In the
annals of the Columbia presidency, if the slogging job of saving the university
from financial destruction is to be as fully honored as successfully bringing it
to academic greatness, his remains second to none.[73]

CHAPTER 19

Columbia Recovered

We are now in a position to plan our future with confidence.

Michael I. Sovern, 1984

When something happens, someone is bound to ask, "Is this another '68?" All students and administrators use it as a benchmark for measuring failure and progress.

Robert E. Pollack, dean of Columbia College

The presidency is indeed a "bully pulpit," [but] it is a pulpit without intimacy, without the sustained dialogue of the nourishing teacher-pupil relationship.

Michael I. Sovern, 1997

"Soul Food at Last"

F OR all the credit due the McGill administration, its decade-long struggle to bring the university into financial equilibrium left much undone. It was not accompanied by a general uplift of spirits. Extended belt-tightening budgetary battles seldom are. But moreover McGill did not see tending to the psychological well-being of the university as his job. Life's tough. In handing his presidency over in 1980, he offered his somber assessment that it was going to take three presidencies to make Columbia right.[1]

On July 1, 1980, Michael I. Sovern became Columbia's seventeenth president. In many ways, his election represented a return to insider Columbia presidents. Like Butler, he was a graduate of Columbia College and had spent virtually all his professional life at Columbia. He was also a native New Yorker. In other ways, however, he marked a significant departure. He had grown up not in Knickerbocker Manhattan but in the Bronx, where he was born in 1931 and where he went to the Bronx High School of Science. His parents, neither of whom attended high school, were descended from East European Jews. He was also the first president to come from one of the university's professional schools.[2]

That these last two characteristics—his Jewish ancestry and his professional-school antecedents—did not block Sovern's way to the presidency speaks to changes at Columbia during his years there. When the seventeen-year-old Sovern arrived at Columbia College in 1949, remnants of the university's earlier anti-Semitism were, if less than at the other Ivies, still enough in evidence to prompt ambitious young Jews from the boroughs to proceed with caution. Not that such vestiges stopped him from achieving academic distinction and admission to the Law School after three years in the College. His A.B. was awarded a year later (1953), summa cum laude. Two years later, he graduated from the Law School first in his class and the winner of the Ordronaux prize.

Sovern then accepted an appointment to the Law Faculty at the University of Minnesota, where he spent two years and secured promotion to associate professor. In the fall of 1957 he returned to Columbia as a visiting assistant professor. That spring, he became an associate professor, although his appointment was intentionally paired with that of a Christian. In 1960, then twenty-eight, he was promoted to full professor.[3]

In the 1960s, along with a full teaching schedule and an active publication program in labor law and employment discrimination, Sovern became the legal adviser to *Time* and directed the NAACP Legal Defense Fund's training program for lawyers. He also helped found the Mexican-American Legal Defense Fund and the Puerto Rican Legal Defense Fund. His pivotal activities in the aftermath of the 1968 disruptions, as chairman of the Executive Committee of the Faculty, have been described earlier; it is enough here to say that these brought him to the attention of the larger Columbia community and prompted his being mentioned as a presidential possibility in 1970. Meanwhile, President Andrew Cordier accepted Sovern as the consensus choice of his colleagues to become the seventh dean of the Law School.[4]

Sovern proved an effective dean, successful both in involving the Law School in university matters and in maintaining faculty morale. Part of his success in the latter effort involved defending the school's autonomy, as in reclaiming control of the Law library and keeping the Law Faculty out of the ad hoc faculty system. During the 1970s the school made several significant faculty appointments (among them the first woman, Ruth Bader Ginsburg, in 1972), improved relations with the city's major law firms, and strengthened its standing relative to its traditional competitors, Harvard and Yale, as well as its local rival, NYU. In 1978 the Law Faculty offered to waive its ten-year term limit, imposed shortly before Sovern's election, virtually assuring him life tenure as dean.

Sovern had been one of several effective professional-school deans at Columbia in the 1970s; Paul Marks at the Medical School, Boris Yavitz at the Business School, and James Polshek at the School of Architecture were others. All demonstrated a willingness to work with the central administration on universitywide problems even as they advanced the causes of their schools. Indeed, the turnaround effected by Marks and Polshek at their more troubled schools exceeded the changes wrought by Sovern. But as President McGill looked around for possible successors in late 1978, it was on Sovern he fixed as his provost and unofficial president-designate. He saw something of himself in Sovern's ability to handle stress, but he also saw useful presidential traits he lacked. One of these he described admiringly: "Mike is the sort of guy who enters revolving doors after you, but emerges ahead of you." At a party honoring Sovern's provostship (and his pending presidency), the departing McGill said of the guest of honor: "What can I say to add—Columbia kveles over you" ("kveles" means "puffs out" in Yiddish—in other words, "gushes"). Among the invitees, Professor Emeritus Eli Ginzberg took particular note of the buffet spread, which included chopped liver, intoning, "Soul food at last." [5]

One of the striking aspects of the Sovern election is how little his being Jewish figured into it. McGill viewed it as a minor but positive consideration. A Jew following a Catholic in the presidency had symbolic significance but was also potentially helpful in fund-raising. (It should be noted that the other most frequently mentioned prospect for the presidency in 1980 was Paul Marks, also Jewish.) The trustees regarded the prospect of a Jewish president with equanimity, with some likely allowing, sotto voce, "it's about time."

In the event, Sovern proved to be singularly successful in attracting large gifts from individual Jewish benefactors, most notably Lawrence A. Wien, who, after leaving the board in 1971, had redirected his philanthropic interests to Brandeis, and Morris Schapiro. His fund-raising prowess, however, extended beyond the Jewish community, as in the cases of the Harrimans at the outset of the presidency and the Catholic John Kluge later on. On the matter of his own Jewishness, Sovern, like his predecessor and his Catholicism, made little of it. In opposing a petition from some Jewish undergraduates that major Jewish holidays be recognized as university holidays, he reminded the senate: "The Jews have survived over 5,000 years, including the last 230, without having Columbia adopt their holidays. I see no need for a change." Meanwhile, he comfortably presided over an administration of which many principal positions were staffed by Jews. The "Jewish Problem" had ceased to be a problem. [6]

Coeducation Realized

The early years of the Sovern presidency were marked by the disappearance of another once-consequential "problem": the prospect of women attending Columbia College. The idea was first proposed in the late 1870s, advanced by New York women and championed by President Barnard, and then again in the mid-1970s, endorsed by the Columbia College faculty and pushed by Dean Peter Pouncey. McGill's call in 1977 for the College and Barnard to work out arrangements by which de facto coeducation (comparable to that at the other Ivies) would be achieved for the College without compromising Barnard's status as the undergraduate women's college in the university only assured that the coeducation issue would return again for his successor to confront.[7]

The admission of women to Columbia College was not a high priority for the incoming Sovern. Like McGill, he had to be concerned with the impact it might have on Barnard College and with any negative publicity if Columbia was perceived to be improving its situation at the expense of Barnard. Little had changed since McGill's statement in 1975 that it is "generally believed that Barnard would not survive if Columbia began admitting women." A Columbia committee appointed by Sovern and chaired by Professor of Chemistry Ronald Breslow, had satisfied itself that Barnard could survive Columbia's admitting women and then concluded that the advantages to Columbia were so obvious that it had no other choice but to do so.[8]

Meanwhile, Barnard representatives in the discussions with Columbia had second thoughts about the impact of functional coeducation on Barnard. At the least, substantially larger numbers of Barnard women would have to take Columbia courses (and Columbia men take Barnard courses) than under the current free-trade cross-registration arrangements. In 1981 Barnard students took upward of 20 percent of their classes at Columbia, although the percentage varied widely by student majors. By one estimate, functional coeducation in Columbia's classrooms could be achieved only if Barnard women took more than half their classes at Columbia. This would have several effects, including the transfer of a substantial portion of tuition income from Barnard to Columbia to pay Columbia instructors and the reduced need for Barnard faculty.[9]

Meanwhile, presidential relations between Barnard and the university took a turn for the worse. In 1975 the Barnard trustees encouraged the resignation of President Martha Peterson, who left to become president of Beloit College, and embarked on a search for a new president. They wanted someone more academically credentialed (Peterson's academic training was in mathematics education, and most of her administrative experience had been in student services) and more cosmopolitan than the midwestern-reared and plainspoken Peterson. What the Barnard trustees did not fully appreciate at the time, but soon had reason to, was that Martha Peterson got along well with McGill, even as she played Barnard's weak hand with panache. Her interpersonal effectiveness even extended to the dean of the Graduate Faculties, George Fraenkel, whom rumor had it had been assigned the "Get Barnard" portfolio.[10]

The extended search for a successor to Peterson was concluded in November 1975 with the appointment of Jacqueline Mattfeld as Barnard's fourth president and seventh head. A respected musicologist who had taught at Sarah Lawrence and Boston University, who was dean of the faculty at Brown University when approached by the search committee, she seemed an excellent fit for the Barnard job. Even Barnard faculty who disapproved of the treatment accorded Peterson welcomed Mattfeld as a scholar with an impressive administrative résumé. In her early months as president, she proceeded to shake up the place, in matters large, in encouraging long-term financial planning, and small, by whistling monthly faculty meetings to order. She also appeared genuinely committed to improving the compensation of the Barnard faculty, which by the late 1970s had slipped substantially below that of Columbia's.[11]

Salary parity became an issue on which both Barnard's faculty and the new president agreed, although neither, trustees were soon pointing out, had any solid plan for achieving it short of bankrupting the College. In search of the additional revenues needed to approximate parity, Mattfeld enlarged the size of successive entering classes, which resulted in overall enrollments increasing from under two thousand in her first year to over twenty-four hundred in her last. This so-called Mattfeld bulge put a strain on student services, increased the proportion of commuting students, and contributed to a decline in selectivity, which lost the new president points with the faculty.[12]

But where Mattfeld ran into serious trouble was in her dealings with Columbia. After a couple of encounters, McGill determined that she could not be trusted and so informed the Barnard members of the joint trustee committee. Barnard's president was thereafter prohibited by her trustees from carrying on any direct discussions with her Columbia counterparts. All future contact with Columbia would be through the trustees. Mattfeld responded by trying to extend the same no-contact stipulation to all members of the Barnard faculty, some of whom were members of the Graduate Faculties and regularly taught on the Columbia side of Broadway.[13]

On May 28, 1980, two weeks after commencement and a little more than a month before Sovern was to assume the Columbia presidency in July 1980, the Barnard trustees fired their president. The immediate cause was the board's judgment that Mattfeld had understated the extent of faculty salary increases planned for 1980–81. In her temporary stead, the trustees appointed someone from their own ranks, Ellen V. Futter, a thirty-year-old Wall Street attorney, who had served on the Barnard board as its youngest member since 1975. Raised on Long Island and a graduate of Barnard (1972), she then went directly to Columbia Law School (1975), where she had Sovern as a teacher. In addition, her father, Victor Futter (CC 1939; CU Law, 1942), had long been active in Columbia alumni affairs. But perhaps most important, unlike Mattfeld, Futter enjoyed the confidence of the trustees then negotiating with Columbia.[14]

Futter inherited not only a divided board—some of the male trustees were ready to have Barnard folded into Columbia—but a divided faculty—some of whom, male and female, were persuaded that a merger with Columbia was not only inevitable but desirable. From their perspective, almost any deal with Columbia would be preferable to no deal. This was clearly a minority view. Moreover, expressing it subjected those who did so to recriminations about institutional loyalty and commitment to women's education. Championing the cause of "small Barnard" were the senior members of the English and modern languages departments. It was their opposition that blocked a plan developed by a joint faculty committee whereby Barnard faculty would be invited to teach and Barnard students enroll in the Core, with some of its courses replacing some of Barnard's general requirements.[15]

By the spring of 1981 it had become clear to those engaged in the negotiations that there was no middle ground where Columbia could be coeducational enough to satisfy the "admit women now" faction in the Columbia College faculty but leave Barnard autonomous enough to satisfy its "small Barnard" trustees and faculty. Acting President Futter, who in July 1981 became President Futter, acknowledged as much, when, after preliminarily endorsing a plan for greater cross-registration, drew back when it became unlikely that Barnard could meet the terms of the plan without transferring nearly 60 percent of its enrollments—and half its annual tuition income—to Columbia. A similar acknowledgement could be discerned on the Columbia side, when the Columbia trustees, previously reluctant to approve any moves that would put Barnard in jeopardy, voted on May 4, 1981, to have President Sovern develop a plan for the admission of women to Columbia College, "with or without the cooperation of Barnard."[16]

It is not certain whether Sovern had been waiting for this go-ahead or only reluctantly accepted the responsibility to act on it in the face of faculty, alumni, and trustee pressure. Support for the latter view can be inferred from his teacher-student relationship with Ellen Futter, his personal and professional friendship with Barnard trustee Helene Kaplan (BC 1953), and the fact that one of his daughters was a Barnard graduate. Ex post facto evidence is also inferable from the care he took to keep a public break from occurring when the Columbia trustees unilaterally announced, following a board meeting on December 7, that they had directed the president to develop plans to begin enrolling the first class of Columbia College women in 1983.[17]

In the trustee discussions that occurred in the immediate wake of the announcement of this decision, Sovern readily agreed to a change in the prevailing ad hoc tenure provisions, thereby giving Barnard something substantial to carry away from the table. Sovern's view of the matter, twenty years later: "I tried to do [what was right for Columbia] in ways that would minimize people's anger or discontent. The co-ed decision was the best example of that. I really am proud of having brought that about in a joint statement with Barnard rather than my going down in history as the butcher of Barnard." Others have suggested the president was indifferent to Barnard's fate. But even they acknowledge that his was a more benign view of Barnard than that held by his "take no hostages" College faculty.[18]

On January 26, 1982, the Columbia and Barnard trustees reached a new intercorporate agreement whereby Barnard tenure cases would be reviewed by ad hoc committees with equal numbers of Barnard and Columbia members and a fifth member drawn from outside. In exchange, Barnard quietly forwent its ninety-two-year monopoly on the education of undergraduate women within Columbia University. It had little choice. Still, it would take a decade before the Breslow committee's assurances that Barnard could survive Columbia College's admission of women were confirmed.[19]

The impact on Columbia, however, was immediately positive. With understandable exaggeration, the newly appointed dean of Columbia College, Robert Pollack, declared that, with the decision made to admit women, he "could now plan to make [Columbia] the pre-eminent college in the country." Applications for the entering class in 1982, the last before coeducation, numbered 3,650; those for the first coeducational class entering a year later, 5,500, with 45 percent of these from women. In a stroke, Columbia College replaced what for the past fifteen years had been its bottom quarter of academically chancy men with much better qualified women.[20]

Nor did the surge in applications prove to be a one-year spike: in 1987 applications rose to 7,000, or almost twice what they had been five years earlier. By the late 1980s Columbia found itself in the enviable position of selecting its students from a large pool of increasingly qualified applicants who, when accepted, were more likely to choose Columbia than had been the case in previous years. This was not a strictly female phenomenon. The male applicants got better, too, which made admission uncertain for all but the best qualified, including increasing numbers of male applicants from prep schools. Gone were the days of Columbia as the Ivy League safety.[21]

Other positive secondary effects accompanied the increase in applications. The pressure on the financial aid budget, which resulted from the uncertainties of the College's need-blind policy, was diminished when more families of admitted students were able to pay all or a substantial share of the cost of a Columbia education. At the same time, lots of applications made it possible to be selective in ways that resulted in making Columbia classes, according to Dean Pollack, "the most ethnically, racially, and geographically diverse in the

Ivy League" without compromising on other qualifications. It became easier to accommodate diversity when it exacted no cost in academic preparedness.[22]

Coeducation at Columbia College encountered strikingly little alumni opposition, especially as compared with the earlier experiences at Dartmouth, Yale, and Princeton. Some grousing could be heard that the football team would now have to fill its roster from only among fifteen hundred or so men, as opposed to the twenty-seven hundred before coeducation. On the other hand, Columbia women's teams quickly became competitive when a Columbia-Barnard Athletic Consortium was formed in 1985, allowing Columbia's women's teams to draw their players from both schools.[23]

Faculty, even critics of coeducation back in 1981–82, were soon acknowledging the positive impact. The presence of women in the classroom, especially in the Core subjects, was said to induce a spirit of general seriousness not always present in the all-male classes of old. This view that women had upped the academic ante received immediate support when the top two academic places in the class of 1987 went to women.[24]

Where the Money Is

The trustees had not made Sovern president to bring women to Columbia College, although his reputation as a labor negotiator commended him as someone with the skills to pull it off. What he was mostly hired to do was to raise the collective spirits of the university and to provide it with a more secure financial foundation. Fortunately, these two charges proved to be mutually reinforcing: renewed confidence begat increased financial support, and increased financial support enhanced confidence.

Sovern had proved himself an effective fund-raiser as dean of the Law School. Now, with Peter Buchanan as his VP for development and alumni relations, he set about to become the first Columbia president since early Butler to make filling Columbia's coffers a preoccupying responsibility.[25]

Sovern found money for Columbia where others before him had not even looked. One source he and one of his provosts, Robert Goldberger, identified within his first months as president was income to be derived from the patents on intellectual property created by Columbia faculty. Federal regulations introduced in 1979 allowed universities to patent discoveries made by their faculty whose research was supported by federal grants, but Columbia was among the first major universities to establish formal internal procedures for doing so. These were developed with the assistance and approval of the University Senate. By the summer of 1981 Columbia had its new intellectual property policy

COLUMBIA RECOVERED | 541

in place. The following year, Professor of Biochemistry Richard Axel and Columbia secured a twenty-year patent on a procedure developed in Axel's laboratory for a cotransformation of genes, which permitted the stable introduction of any gene into cultured cells. This procedure almost immediately came to be used by pharmaceutical companies to manufacture complex human hormones. By the late 1980s the annual royalties on this single patent payable to Columbia exceeded $10 million; in 2000, the last year before the patent expired, royalties from it were $143 million. In all, the Axel patent earned some $300 million for the university.[26]

A more controversial source of financial support for Columbia that Sovern aggressively tapped early in his presidency was the use of Washington lobbyists to secure $24 million to build new chemistry facilities on campus. The money came in the form of a federal budget line item. Columbia was not the first to benefit from such academic pork-barrel legislation—Tufts University and its president, Jean Mayer, did so a year earlier for a nutrition facility to be built in the congressional district of Speaker of the House O'Neill—but it was the first major research university to do so. When his fellow presidents complained that Columbia was subverting the peer-review system, Sovern justified Columbia's actions by pointing out that there was no federal facilities program, peer-reviewed or otherwise, and that Columbia was following the only possible route to federal financing. Besides, he added unapologetically, having sat out much of the 1970s tending to its internal repair, Columbia badly needed such facilities. And now, with both of New York's United States senators, the Democrat Patrick Moynihan and the Republican Alphonse D'Amato, as well as Congressman Charles Rangel, whose district encompassed both the Morningside campus and the medical center, disposed to help, Columbia continued to press for as much assistance as it could wrangle from Uncle Sam.[27]

Another source of found money was the 11.7 acres beneath Rockefeller Center, the Upper Estate first acquired by Columbia as a gift from the State of New York in 1814. Once this property started generating rents in the 1850s, the trustees insisted that it not be sold; even Butler failed to persuade his trustees otherwise in 1906. It is not clear whether the Rockefellers were prepared to buy the land from Columbia in 1929 to construct Rockefeller Center, but the lease that was worked out was in keeping with the Columbia board's disinclination to sell off capital. It provided for a reopening every twenty-one years for a renegotiation of the rent. The $3 million annual rent that represented a good return during the Depression had become far less so by 1951, when the first renegotiated lease, signed by President Eisenhower in 1951, provided for no increase in the annual payment.[28]

In 1969 President Cordier had urged selling the property for $150 million, only to have the deal blocked by trustee opposition. Two years later, President McGill renewed the lease with the Rockefellers at $9 million, which had risen to $11 million by 1980 because of the $200,000 annual increments. At the close of his presidency, McGill had begun to explore the possibility of selling the land to the Rockefellers.[29]

By the outset of the Sovern presidency, the board had come around to the idea of selling off the Rockefeller site—for the right price. As Sovern recalled the circumstances twenty years later, arranging for the sale was "not controversial, but difficult to execute." In 1981 Columbia was approached by Harvey Kreuger, the Rockefellers' investment banker, who renewed the offer made to McGill to buy the property for $200 million and then raised it to $220 million. President Sovern indicated that he expected to get $500 million for the property, if not from the Rockefellers, then from other interested buyers. Among those mentioned were the sultan of Brunei and various Japanese groups (one of which later did buy all of Rockefeller Center). When it became clear that Columbia was shopping the property around, the Rockefellers increased their offer to $300 million and, on February 5, 1985, agreed to pay $400 million. "Of course," Sovern later allowed, "I would have liked to have gotten the full $500 million."[30]

The sale of the Upper Estate occurred at the top of the 1980s market for New York City commercial real estate. A higher price could not have been fetched until well into the 1990s, if then, when Columbia trustee Jerry Speyer (CC 1962; Business 1964) became one of the owners of Rockefeller Center. Moreover, all the $400 million was considered unrestricted endowment and thus usable for any legitimate university purpose. This allowed Columbia to invest a much larger share of its endowment in equities, which, even with the crash in October 1987, grew at a far faster rate throughout the 1990s than did Manhattan real estate. Looking back at the Rockefeller land sale, its prime mover correctly described it as "the single most important financial event of my term, perhaps of any Columbia president's term."[31]

Sovern inherited a fund-raising apparatus little changed from that used by Butler. Columbia had sputtered along for the first eight decades of the twentieth century without ever mounting a single all-university capital campaign, except for the disastrous $200 million campaign that President Kirk had launched with such fanfare in 1966 and President Cordier terminated in 1970, $80 million short of its goal. McGill was a more effective fund-raiser than he was generally credited with being, especially in acquiring the wherewithal for projects relating to the Medical School and in securing corporate support, but it was not a principal preoccupation for him.[32]

Nor had McGill done much to improve the way Columbia went about the cultivation of alumni giving. (One of his counterproductive economies had been to reduce the alumni magazine, *Columbia Today*, from a glossy and award-winning quarterly to an occasional newsletter.) Relatively few of the regional alumni clubs raised more money than they needed to cover their own costs, while class giving existed more in rhetoric than in bankable gifts. A proposal made in 1975 that alumni voting for trustees be limited to dues-paying regional club members was blocked by the expressed concern of the Alumni Federation that it would reduce alumni participation to the vanishing point. During the 1970s only 18 percent of Columbia College alumni contributed to their alma mater on a regular basis, whereas elsewhere the percentage ranged from 26 percent (Harvard) to 45 percent (Dartmouth). More than a quarter of Columbia's presumed-to-be-living alumni during those years were carried on the Development Office's records as "lost." Nor, finally, did it likely help mat ters for McGill occasionally to let slip his view that "Columbia alumni are prone to give only advice." [33]

Although Sovern paid more attention to alumni fund-raising than his predecessors had, his principal energies went not to building a development infrastructure but to cultivating and landing individual gifts in the million-dollar-plus range. But even more than Butler, the university's last great "retail" fundraiser, he was at his best reselling Columbia to alums whose financial success began after graduation. [34]

Sovern the fund-raiser started fast from the gate. In his first year as president, Columbia received over $50 million in gifts, up from $30 million in McGill's best year. In October 1982 he secured a gift of $10 million from Averell Harriman and his wife to establish the W. Averell Harriman Institute for the Advanced Study of the Soviet Union, then the largest single gift in university history. Two weeks later, at a special kickoff dinner, he announced the launching of a $400 million "Campaign for Columbia," with Trustee Thomas M. Macioce (CC 1939; CU Law 1942) as chairman and Peter Buchanan as campaign director. [35]

The Campaign for Columbia went so well that in June 1985 its goal was raised to $500 million, without extending its duration. In May 1987 Sovern announced that the $500 million target had been reached eight months early, thanks to a gift of $25 million from broadcast mogul John W. Kluge (CC 1937), which then became the largest single gift in the university's history. By the time the books closed on the campaign in February 1988, it had raised more than $600 million, most of it through direct presidential involvement. [36]

That spring the *New York Times Sunday Magazine* ran a cover story entitled "Columbia Recovered," written by Queens College English professor Morris Dickstein (CC 1961), who, as a junior faculty member at Columbia in 1968 had been nothing if not critical of Columbia's "stiff-necked administrators who had no commitment at all to our idea of the university." Yet twenty years later he could write, "if any one person is responsible for Columbia's recovery it is surely Michael Sovern." Not the least of Sovern's recent triumphs that Dickstein noted was his fashioning of a resolution of the most potentially explosive issue to confront Columbia since 1968: South African divestment.[37]

Doing the Right Thing

What made the matter of South African divestment so explosive was its potential for pitting the trustees, conscious of their fiduciary responsibilities and personal ties to corporate America, against students and community groups demanding that the university do the right thing, which to them meant immediate divestment from companies doing business with the apartheid regime in South Africa. The issue actually antedated Sovern's presidency, having its Columbia beginnings in a board decision in 1978 to follow the so-called and widely adopted Sullivan Principles in deciding which companies doing business in South Africa were appropriate investments and which were not. At the same time, the board asserted its overriding obligation was to protect the university's financial well-being by investing in profit-generating companies irrespective of ethical reservations about their products, employment policies, whatever. This position was usually buttressed by citing responsible black South Africans who argued that total divestment would lead to the economic ruin of the country even as its black majority moved closer to self-government.[38]

This is where the matter stood when Sovern became president and where it remained into his fourth year in office, despite louder calls from students and civil rights groups for total divestment. By then, the University Senate, which had created an investment policy committee in the summer of 1970, had become deeply involved in the issue and called on the president and the trustees to take a more forceful stand by agreeing to make no new investments in companies doing business with South Africa. On May 7, 1984, the board agreed not to increase its current investments in such companies, then pegged at $40 million, but reiterated its opposition to total divestment.[39]

In July 1985 the board again rejected calls for total divestment. Yet just three months later, at a board meeting on October 7, the trustees, in a rarely recorded tally, voted twenty-one to zero (with three abstentions) to begin selling the $39 million in endowment currently invested in companies doing business in South Africa, with total divestment to be achieved within two years. The Barnard trustees quickly followed suit, although some were surprised by Columbia's decision to divest. Trustees elsewhere were even more critical of Columbia's caving in to student demands, while the CEOs of major companies affected by Columbia's divestment, such as Mobil and City Bank, wondered aloud whether Columbia was still interested in their corporate gifts. Sovern assured them that it was.[40]

Events in South Africa, where the apartheid regime had become more intransigent as international pressure on it increased and where earlier moderates among the black leadership were now pressing for economic measures that would bring down the regime, in part account for the turnaround. So does a shift in U.S. public opinion in the direction of supporting more aggressive action against the South African government. The University Senate's call for total divestment also played a part. Less clear was the impact of student protests, the most visible of which occurred on April 1, 1986, by which time divestment was well under way but when students unhappy with the pace of divestment constructed shanties on College Walk, vowing to stay until total divestment was achieved. Sovern allowed them to remain there until April 7, but they were dismantled on the fourth by protesters, who acknowledged they did so "because of lack of interest and support by the University community."[41]

Rather than directly confront the protesters in their shanties, his predecessor's modus operandi, Sovern "just sat them out." At commencement, he announced that the university's divestment was ahead of schedule. To be sure, not to have divested would have caused Columbia difficulties with its unions, who favored divestment, and hurt community relations, particularly with Harlem, where divestment was viewed as a civil rights issue. Moreover, Trustee Chairman Arthur Krim strongly favored divestment. But Sovern's role was crucial in determining the pace of the deliberations, slow enough to provide time to bring along hesitant trustees but fast enough not to exhaust the patience of the senate or provide an excuse for student-led disruptions. It is hard to imagine either Kirk or McGill containing the latent conflict embedded in the issue as well as Sovern did. The pride he subsequently took in the decision—"we were the first university with real money to divest"—is deserved. In the end—no, fairly early on, and with the quiet nudging of its president—Columbia did the right thing.[42]

The Audubon Accord

One explanation offered by a participant in 1968 as to how the Kirk administration allowed things to go so wrong was that there had been no rehearsals. Everything was happening for the first time. A striking aspect of Columbia in the 1980s is that events had a déjà vu character and were approached with the lessons of 1968 very much in mind. The divestment controversy was clearly a case in point, a successful replay of the IDA issue; the Audubon Ballroom was the Morningside gym redux.[43]

The medical center had exhausted the available space on the original 168th Street site with the construction of the Augustus Long Library/Health Sciences Center in 1976. These physical constraints were further exacerbated by the sharp decline in the Washington Heights neighborhood generally. The infestation by crack cocaine, accompanied as it was by homelessness and AIDS, manifested itself in many ways, including crime. Between 1970 and 1980 the murder rate in the two precincts encompassing Washington Heights increased by 218 percent, against an increase throughout New York City of 56 percent. Reported incidences of rape increased by 252 percent, against a 45 percent increase throughout the city; assault, by 125 percent, against 27 percent citywide. The armory, situated directly across 168th Street from the main entrance to the hospital, had become, with two thousand beds, the city's largest men's shelter. Meanwhile, the neighborhood suffered a sharp drop in population, exceeded only by the reduction in usable housing.[44]

Washington Heights was seen as an unsafe place to work, live, or even visit, a perception that contributed to the decisions by five neighboring volunteer hospitals to close. It was also cited by Medical School and hospital officials as having a negative effect on the recruitment and retention of students and staff. Thus in the early 1980s the medical center confronted yet another of those recurrent decision points in the history of "Columbia University in the City of New York": to stay in the city or to leave.[45]

In 1982 a long-range planning committee charged with considering the future of the medical center concluded that "CPMC is committed to remain in Washington Heights and to maintain and strengthen its position as one of the nation's leading research hospitals and medical schools." It was a close call, but once made it required the university to commit scarce resources to stabilizing the neighborhood through the construction of housing and the provision of additional security. It also committed Columbia to trying to attract into the neighborhood research-related companies whose presence would provide jobs even as they allowed the university to explore the entrepreneurial possibilities of linking university-based research with the biomedical industry. Which brought everyone back to the question of where to put such ventures.[46]

The Planning Committee identified the likeliest prospect for expansion to be a six-acre site of land east of Broadway, between 168th and 165th Streets. In 1982 it contained no residential buildings, which eliminated the problem of resettlement of tenants that had ensnared the Kirk administration two decades earlier in its redevelopments efforts on Morningside Heights. The site did contain five small businesses, but most of these indicated a willingness to accept help from the university to relocate.

That left only the Audubon Ballroom, a rundown and shuttered space but also the site of the 1965 assassination of Malcolm X, who, in the seventeen years since his death, had come to be viewed by some members of the black and Muslim communities as a martyr to the cause of black liberation and Islam. Although nothing much had been done to acknowledge the site's historic significance, the announcement that Columbia had acquired the six-acre property from the city produced immediate consternation in the neighborhood and in the city's black and Muslim population. Among many other New Yorkers whose memories extended back to the 1950s and 1960s, there was the equally predictable reaction: "Here they go again." [47]

Negotiations between Columbia and the city over what the university could build on the Audubon site began in 1984, when Edward Koch was mayor. These negotiations, as well as discussions with local neighborhood organizations, extended over several years, as Columbia developed plans for a series of institutes on the site while acknowledging its historic significance. The prospect of hundreds of new jobs in the neighborhood, plus the careful cultivation by Sovern, the dean of the Medical School, Herbert Pardes, and community affairs director Larry Dais of local politicians such as Congressman Charles Rangel and Koch's successor in 1990, David Dinkins, produced an agreement in 1992 to proceed with construction. Malcolm X's widow, Betty Shabazz, also gave her blessing. The last holdout was Manhattan borough president Ruth Messinger, but she came around in time for the construction to begin in the last months of Sovern's administration. Even Assemblyman Edward Sullivan, in the past a severe critic, complimented Columbia on how its community relations "had greatly improved in recent years." The Morningside gym redux, this time done right. [48]

Coda on the Limits of Student Protest   On December 14, 1992, Hamilton Hall was blockaded by black students and neighborhood activists to protest the start of construction on the Audubon site. Unlike 1968, however, the gathering was dispersed peacefully after six hours, thanks in part to the mediation efforts of the Rev. Calvin Butts, minister of the Abyssinian Baptist Church, who secured in the course of the negotiations assurances from the university that it would make some improvements at Harlem Hospital. Of the participants, forty-two students were disciplined, three of whom were suspended for a semester, in keeping with the University Senate's standing rules on student behavior. [49]

The failure of the 1992 protest against the Audubon project, like the 1986 student protest demanding immediate divestment, has been interpreted as reflective of a failure of the student nerve much in evidence in 1968. It has also been attributed to a combination of student apathy and administrative adeptness. It was likely attributable to all three. Unfortunately, these were not the only student disturbances during the Sovern years. On the night of March 21, 1987, a clash between white and black College students returning to the dorms led to charges by the black students that they had been racially assaulted. On April 21, when disciplinary procedures did not move with the speed they thought appropriate, forty-five black students chained themselves to the front doors of Hamilton Hall. The police were called, and arrests made.[50]

That summer, one white student involved in the fracas was suspended, a decision later reversed by a state court. This incident notwithstanding, it remains possible to argue that the hostility of students to administrative responses to student protests that helped bring about Columbia '68 and persisted into the 1970s was, by the late 1980s, no longer operative. The Columbia community had not become a peaceable kingdom, but its students had become properly suspicious of the uses of disruptive protest, particularly when the protest disrupted the lives of many members of the community to advance the cause of a few. Students were also more fully persuaded that those who disrupted had to take responsibility for doing so.[51]

Discordant Close

No Columbia president had ever enjoyed a honeymoon as extended as Sovern's. On September 10, 1985, at his fifth anniversary as president, the trustees expressed their complete delight in the job he was doing in a gala at the New York State Theater in Lincoln Center. A year later, when a middle states reaccreditation team visited the campus, its report declared that "hope and confidence have been restored" and then described President Sovern as the turnabout's "principal agent and personal symbol." Moody, the bond-rating agency, that same year upped Columbia's credit rating from AA, where it had been since the late 1960s, to AAA. Meanwhile, the computer science building (1981–83) and Uris Hall extension had been completed (1983–84), the Havemeyer extension was under way (1984–88), and plans were being developed for the Morris A. Schapiro Center for Engineering and Physical Science Research. So well in hand did matters appear that Sovern proposed and the trustees agreed that he take a sabbatical in the fall of 1987.[52]

Sovern on sabbatical was never much farther from campus than Cape Cod, from where he persuaded Dr. Herbert Pardes, then chairman of the Department of Psychiatry, to become vice president for Health Sciences. The sabbatical did, however, keep him away from the newly opened Lawrence A. Wien Stadium throughout the fall of 1987, when the Columbia football team experienced its third consecutive winless season. (the elusive win, after forty-four consecutive losses, finally occurred on October 8, 1988, against Princeton, 16–13.) He also missed the stock market collapse in late October. For all that, when Sovern returned in January 1988, "We were still going gangbusters." [53]

Yet there had been problems from the start, some of which did not go away. During his nine years as dean of the Law School, Sovern had been a smoothly effective administrator. He used his five years on the dean's Budget Committee to familiarize himself with other parts of the university. So, too, his year as provost had given him insight into the workings of Low Library. He came to the presidency, in sum, with more relevant administrative experience than any president since Butler. Yet in committing himself from the outset of his presidency to raising money wherever it could be found, Sovern found it necessary to entrust more of the daily operations of the university to others, principally his appointed deans and provosts, than had his predecessor. Even those otherwise wholly admiring of the Sovern presidency later allowed themselves the view that day-to-day administration was not Sovern's long suit. [54]

Some support for this view can be seen from the outset, when Sovern announced that the position of university provost would be divided into three: a provost for Arts and Sciences (including the College, the School of International and Public Affairs, General Studies, and the Graduate School of Arts and Sciences), another for the Morningside professional schools, and a third for the medical sciences. To the first provostship, Sovern appointed Fritz Stern, a distinguished historian, lifelong Columbian, and close ally in 1968. The provostship for professional schools went to Peter Likins, who came to Columbia in 1978 as dean of engineering. For provost of the Health Sciences, initially left vacant, Sovern appointed Dr. Robert F. Goldberger, who came to Columbia in the summer of 1981 from the National Institutes of Heath. Each one of the troika was to report directly to the president. [55]

The arrangement did not work. Its dismantling began in the summer of 1981, when Likins accepted the offer of the presidency of Lehigh University. Stern, who took the administrative job as a favor to the new president, stayed on for a second year before returning to the faculty. This left Goldberger, who in July 1982 became the university's single provost. Of course, had the troika worked or evolved into a two-provost system, one for Morningside and one for Health Sciences, Sovern might have been deemed an administrative genius for having concocted it. [56]

Also in the summer of 1982, another administrative restructuring was implemented with the creation of a new senior academic post, vice president of arts and Sciences. The position combined the responsibilities of the Arts and

Sciences provost and most of those of the dean of the Graduate Faculties that George Fraenkel had exercised for the past fourteen years. To this position, Sovern appointed Don C. Hood, a thirty-nine-year-old psychologist who had come to Columbia in 1969 and survived as one of those 1970s rarities, an assistant professor who got tenure. His interest in administration had been signaled by his success as chair of psychology and service on the College Committee on Instruction, where he was active in the coeducation campaign. One of his first duties as vice president was to tell the dean of the Graduate Faculties, George Fraenkel, that his responsibilities had been much reduced. A year later, Fraenkel resigned.[57]

A year before Hood's appointment, Robert E. Pollack was named the tenth dean of Columbia College. Like Hood's, Pollack's appointment was something of a surprise. He had been a member of the biology department for only three years when offered the deanship. His interest in undergraduate teaching, unusual in a midcareer scientist with a full research agenda, plus the fact that he was a graduate of Columbia College (1961), brought him to the attention of the search committee charged with finding a successor to Arnold Collery, an economist from Amherst who had succeeded Peter Pouncey in 1978 and resigned after four years. The other leading candidate for the job was the associate dean of the College, Michael Rosenthal, but his prospects were hurt by his past association with Pouncey and their frequent assaults on Low Library. So Pollack it was.[58]

As with Hood's stint in Low Library, Pollack's in Hamilton Hall began positively. Both brought new ideas to their respective offices. Hood was the first arts and sciences administrator in Low Library for decades to undertake long-range planning, while Pollack managed the successful integration of women, encouraged still greater diversity in the student body, and tapped new sources of gifts for the College. But both soon found working with Provost Goldberger sufficiently irksome to make their feelings known. In 1985 Hood indicated to Sovern his desire to go back to research but agreed instead to take a year's deferred leave with his return to Low Library left open. Five months into his leave, Hood decided to return to the psychology department upon its conclusion. In his place, Sovern appointed the sociologist Jonathan R. Cole, a College graduate (1964) and Columbia Ph.D. (1970), a student of Robert K. Merton, and another of those rare inside tenure appointments (by way of Barnard) in the 1970s. His directorship of the Center for the Social Sciences and work on the Marcus commission had given him visibility beyond his department. When Goldberger resigned in 1987, it was Cole whom Sovern tapped as his provost.[59]

Relations between the College and the central administration were not improved by the change in provosts, which suggests that the problem was more than a question of clashing personalities. By the late 1980s the College's overall situation had improved so markedly that it came to be seen—and saw itself—as a potentially significant contributor to the university's financial well-being. From the perspective of Low Library, the College could best help by sharing more of its fund-raising income with arts and sciences, from whence its faculty came, as well as by increasing the size of the College and thereby its tuition revenues. When Pollack resisted both proposals, his relationship with Cole soured as it had earlier with Goldberger. This time, however, continued resistance cost Pollack his deanship. In his place, Sovern appointed Jack Greenberg, a recent appointment to the Columbia Law School and an old friend from the president's long involvement with the NAACP and the Legal Defense Fund, which last Greenberg had headed.[60]

For some, Greenberg's appointment smacked of cronyism. That he did not assert the autonomy of the College as publicly as Pollack had seemed to them to confirm the suspicion that neither Sovern nor his new provost tolerated dissent within their administrative team. Much had changed since the 1970s, but some things had not: Columbia administration remained a blood sport.[61]

This said, structural factors were likely more responsible for the clashes of the late 1980s. Chief among these was the changing relationship between the arts and sciences and the rest of the university. It was opposition from the arts and sciences that helped bring the Sovern presidency to its discordant close. Back in the 1960s, the graduate faculties of the arts and sciences dominated university affairs. The Kirk administration had been staffed almost exclusively by arts and sciences faculty, with the deans of the professional schools kept well outside the inner circle. This began to change in the 1970s, when McGill and his budgeteers looked increasingly to the professional schools to increase enrollments and generate badly needed tuition income. Meanwhile, the arts and sciences had contracted, both in terms of staffing and enrollments and as a share of the overall operating budget. This was part of a national phenomenon, when academic openings in the humanities and social sciences had virtually dried up, but because Columbia remained one of the major producers of Ph.D.s in those fields, the Ph.D. glut hit it particularly hard. In 1970 Columbia awarded 278 Ph.D.s in the humanities and social sciences; in 2000, just 150, a drop of 46 percent. In 1970 arts and sciences accounted for 32 percent of Columbia's full-time faculty; in 2000, 22 percent.[62]

The election of a professional school dean to the Columbia presidency in 1980 may have marked one of those quiet turning points in the university's history. The shift away from the arts and sciences and toward the professional schools that it reflected occurred not only in terms of university leadership, enrollment, staffing numbers, and finances but also in a qualitative dimension.

In the 1980s, when the arts and sciences departments had yet to regain some of their lost national standing and the College's renaissance was still something of an inside secret, the Medical, Law, and Architecture Schools had all significantly advanced their relative standing among their peers. Not a few of the deans of these schools occasionally drew the conclusion that they were now carrying the arts and sciences. This view acquired operational form with the introduction of a new decentralized budget system in the mid-1980s that redirected money that might have been available for the arts and sciences to the professional schools.[63]

Only within this structural context can the revolt of the arts and sciences departments in the late 1980s be understood. Previously settled arrangements were now subject to hard bargaining. The apportioning of a department's teaching between its shrinking graduate programs and the expanding professional and undergraduate programs became a flash point. Replacement of retiring faculty was another. Financial aid for graduate students in departments where such aid could not be written into research grants and its absence meant that departments would not be able to compete for the best applicants was still another. Other schools did not automatically accept the logic of increased subsidization of graduate fellowships in the humanities and social sciences that were not available in sciences or in professional schools, where grants provided for fellowships or students took out large loans to cover their tuition.[64]

The structural reordering by which the professional faculties achieved full parity by the late 1980s would likely have been more readily accommodated by the Arts and Sciences Faculty but for two other developments, one planned and one unexpected. The former was the unification of the four arts and sciences faculties (Graduate Faculties, Columbia College, General Studies, and the School of International and Public Affairs) into a single faculty of arts and sciences. The fact that this had been coming for some time, at least since the creation of the position of vice president for arts and sciences in 1982, and was one the principal recommendations of the 1987 report of the Presidential Commission on the Future of the University, chaired by Provost Goldberger, did not make its implementation any the less controversial. This was especially so among arts and sciences faculty who were protective of the symbolism of a separate College faculty. Some of the more suspicious among them saw the new faculty arrangements as assuring that Low Library's designs on the College—Provost Cole had called for an "enhanced and expanded College"—would be implemented without effective opposition. Others saw it as of a piece with faculty identified with the College who had resided in Hamilton Hall being reassigned to buildings where their departments were housed.[65]

Among those to voice opposition to the unified faculty were ex-provost de Bary and ex-College deans Pollack and Hovde. At a College faculty meeting in the fall of 1987, with Acting President Goldberger presiding in Sovern's sabbatical absence, a motion by de Bary opposing the dissolution of the College faculty carried overwhelmingly. As one faculty member who voted with the majority stated after the tally, "The size of the vote in favor of Professor de Bary's motion was evidence of faculty suspicion that the administration planned to effect the proposed structural changes by fiat." Two years of discussions ensued, producing assurances that the College faculty was not to be abolished. The unified faculty finally came into being in 1990, but not before the controversy surrounding it identified another faction of arts and sciences faculty no longer enamored of their president and his provost. "As you know," Sovern later remarked, "friends may come and go, but enemies accumulate." [66]

The unexpected development was a serious budget crunch that began to be felt in 1988. Throughout the 1980s the university's budget grew steadily, even in after-inflation dollars. Increased revenues from tuition and gifts and a swelling endowment, which provided more endowment income, made it possible to avoid deficits. By 1987, however, these endowment drawdowns exceeded the 5 percent rule (by which no more than 5 percent of the endowment's total value be available for annual budgetary expenditures) that the trustees had adopted at Sovern's urging at the outset of his presidency. Higher drawdowns in turn kept the endowment from growing as rapidly as it would have had they been less. Another aspect of the financial situation was that much of the money coming in was earmarked by the donors for specific projects rather than for general endowment. Thus the Sovern administration found itself in the late 1980s in the anomalous financial position of having just completed the most successful fund-raising campaign in the university's history, which raised more than $600 million, and about to embark on another, the New Campaign for Columbia, in conjunction with Presbyterian Hospital, for $1.15 billion, but still spending more than it deemed prudent. [67]

No single development transformed these latent political and budgetary problems into a single crisis of confidence, but several factors contributed to doing so. On the income side, in the wake of a congressional investigation at Stanford, Columbia, along with all other research universities, felt pressure to reduce the indirect costs it attached to its federal grants. The Stanford investigation had turned up the embarrassing fact that some of the upkeep of a university-owned yacht used for ceremonial purposes was included in the indirect cost calculation, prompting the resignation of President Donald Kennedy and eliciting from Stanford's peers the reaction "there but for the grace of God . . ." Columbia's indirect costs on most federal grants dropped from 36 percent to 26 percent, for a loss of $7 million. [68]

Another contributing factor was the falloff of New York State assistance. In the late 1970s "Bundy money," the state aid to New York's private universities begun in the Rockefeller administration, amounted to as much as $13 million annually and was crucial in McGill's fight to achieve solvency. Under Governor Mario Cuomo, the assistance was cut annually, until by the late 1980s it was below $3 million. In such a stringent environment, even something as minor as an unexpected shift in the student cross-registrations between Barnard and Columbia in the late 1980s, which reduced Barnard's annual payment to Columbia from nearly $4 million to under $500,000, made life difficult in Low Library.[69]

On the expenses side, Columbia, along with other large employers in the late 1980s, was confronted with huge increases in medical insurance, which resulted in unplanned increases in the fringe benefits the university paid to its employees from 27 percent to 31 percent of their salaries. When these reductions in income and increases in expenses were tallied, Columbia found itself looking at an upcoming deficit of some $33 million. And when this was forcibly brought to the attention of arts and sciences department chairs preparing their own annual budget requests, which by their lights included only modest increases, push met shove.

One should not exaggerate the dimensions of the 1990 budget situation or the severity of the steps taken to cope with it. What occurred was a temporary slowing of the rate of growth: from 13 percent earlier on in the 1980s to 8 percent at its close. No budget was ever less than the previous year's, and no budget ever contained a deficit, although this second feat was accomplished by endowment drawdowns that approached 8 percent. Sovern later described what happened as "a very gentle retrenchment," amounting to only $80 million spread over three years out of a $1 billion annual budget. "That's why I say it wasn't a crisis; we managed our finances very well, but we caught a lot of hell from some faculty." [70]

The faculty raising hell included chairs of the arts and sciences departments, represented by David Helfand (astronomy), Donald Melnick (anthropology), and David Kasten (English). On being informed by Vice President of Arts and Sciences Martin Meisel that their departments would have to make up a looming shortfall in their revenues by effecting economies, twenty-eight department chairs threatened to resign. Meanwhile, the elected chair of the newly organized executive committee of the unified arts and sciences faculty, Don Hood, and Vice-Chair Kathy Newman insisted that the problems of the university's finances were not of their faculty's making but the result of Low Library's prodigal ways.[71]

On April 11, 1992, the New York Times reported that the Arts and Sciences

Faculty was considering a vote of no confidence in President Sovern and Provost Cole. On April 17, Hood and Newman met with both the outgoing chair of the board of trustees, G. G. Michelson, and his successor, Henry L. King, to discuss faculty complaints with the administration. On May 25, The *Times* carried a front-page special report on Columbia's financial problems and its likely need to dip into its $1.5 billion endowment to cover a looming $72 million deficit. The fact that all major universities were faced with similar financial difficulties did not go unnoted by the *Times*, but still, after a decade of consistently favorable press coverage, the story did not help matters on campus.[72]

Clearly the honeymoon was over. Still, Columbia presidents had survived bumpier moments. Both Cole and Greenberg advised Sovern to spend more time with the faculty, but, as he later acknowledged, "I found I no longer had the patience for it." There was also a personal consideration: the president's wife, Joan, was in the final stages of her battle with cancer. She died in September 1993. Time and psychic resources that might have gone into the job went to her. At the trustees' meeting on June 6, 1992, Columbia's seventeenth president announced his decision to resign in June 1993. "Had I encountered faculty discontent during my first years," he later explained, "I would have been out there explaining, justifying, persuading, but I just didn't have the motivation. And that's ultimately what caused me to quit. . . . I quit because I couldn't do it anymore, under any circumstances. Didn't want to do it anymore, actually."[73]

Having made the decision to resign, Sovern finished up his presidency by settling two politically explosive issues relating to faculty compensation. One was to reduce the university's contribution to the faculty pension from 15 percent, which the trustees had long regarded as exorbitant, to 12.5 percent; the other was to set up a health plan for faculty and staff that utilized Columbia medical faculty, thereby increasing the availability of top-flight medical care and reducing the overall cost of the plan. The lame duck Sovern also accomplished something else in his last year that indicated he was still the best negotiator in town. When it became clear that his personal choice for successor, Provost Jonathan Cole, lacked sufficient support among the faculty and the trustees, Sovern did not push his candidacy. He did, however, urge the disappointed Cole "to stick around" as provost, which he did, effectively serving under Sovern's successors for another ten years.[74]

The rap on Mike by his critics is easily come by and much of a piece. He was "too political, even when he didn't need to [be]," especially with the senate and the faculty. His fund-raising was of "the cherry-picking sort," failed to build an alumni-oriented infrastructure, and was too much given to securing spendable gifts funds rather than endowment. He did not always choose or nurture good administrators and was slow to fire incompetent ones. And last, a criticism that encapsulates the others, he was unable to put 1968 behind him, approaching many problems from the defensive perspective of someone determined that what happened to Kirk's university was not going to happen to his.[75]

Some of these criticisms, such as being too political, can be contested but not disproved. About his fund-raising priorities, however, the quadrupling of the endowment during his presidency suggests that his efforts were not limited to the easily acquired special-project gifts, although, to be sure, relatively little grassroots fund-raising was undertaken. With the faulting of his appointments, it bears noting that several of his decanal and senior administrative appointments (e.g., Herbert Pardes in Health Sciences and Meyer Feldberg in Business, Jonathan Cole as provost, and Richard Naum as vice president for development) successfully served on through his successor's nine-year presidency.[76]

And as for the last complaint, could one have expected, or even wanted, otherwise? In the 1980s Sovern was one of hundreds of Columbians who had been participant-observers in 1968. But he was only one of a handful still around who had been directly involved in the tortuous process of inching the university back from the postbust abyss. Political skills of a high order had been vital to his success back then. Moreover, as a dean in the 1970s, he knew first-hand the persistent precariousness of the university's finances. During these struggles, he came to place a high premium on personal loyalty and discretion. Perhaps more than anyone else, Sovern was the biographical link between Columbia's time of troubles and its full recovery in the 1980s.

If in the last years of his presidency Sovern struck others, as McGill had before him, as personally unable to free himself from what others regarded as history, it was his presidency that effectively consigned 1968 to the past. What McGill thought would take three presidencies, his immediate successor had mostly accomplished in one. His trustees said as much in their resolution of appreciation: "A man who helped shape this institution and leaves it, strengthened, to a rising generation." What Michael Sovern vouchsafed to his university was its future.[77]

CHAPTER 20

The Way We Are

If you want more structure, I suggest you go to Amherst or Princeton.

George Rupp

Charisma Optional

A FTER President Sovern's announcement in May 1992 that he would resign the following June, the trustees formed a search committee to identify his successor. Board Chairman Henry L. King (CC 1948) was selected to chair the committee, which, in addition to five other trustees, included a faculty member and one student. Provost Jonathan Cole and ex-vice president Donald Hood enjoyed some support on campus, but the search committee indicated early on that it was looking for an outsider with administrative experience and scholarly standing in the arts and sciences. Vartan Gregorian, the newly elected president of Brown, was a serious prospect until he declined to be considered. Others interviewed included the political scientist Nan Keohane, then president of Wellesley, who, by the time of her interview, had agreed to become president of Duke, and Judith Rodin, who would become president of the University of Pennsylvania and the first woman president of an Ivy League university.[1]

Another outside prospect materialized in October, when the fifty-year-old president of Rice University, George Rupp, announced his resignation at the end of the academic year. His reasons for leaving after eight years turned on a disagreement about the timing of a $200 million capital campaign that Rupp wanted to launch immediately despite the reluctance of some trustees. When a leading footdragger informed the president that "he had no choice" but to wait, he resigned. Although Rupp spoke of resuming his career as a teacher and scholar, he did not foreclose a presidency elsewhere. A vigorous and experienced president of an up-and-coming university, whose only problem was that his eagerness to raise money exceeded that of his trustees, was suddenly available.[2]

Rupp's name was likely on the search committee's list before his resignation, thanks to several Columbia faculty who had known Rupp at Harvard, where he had earned his Ph.D. (1970), taught (1974–77), and served as dean of the Divinity School (1979–85). These included members of the Columbia and Barnard religion departments, plus Caroline Bynum, a Harvard-trained medievalist who had joined the history department in 1988. With his resignation a front-page story in the *Houston Post*, the search committee was free to take up his candidacy seriously.[3]

Committee chair King met with Rupp in November and came away impressed with his interest in undergraduate education generally and in particular his views about the unrealized promise of Columbia College. Preaching to the choir, the College, the candidate said, had been historically "undersold," to its detriment and that of the university. A graduate of Princeton (1964), Rupp had at three different points in his academic career developed innovative undergraduate programs within larger institutional contexts. The first was at the University of Redlands, where he served for three years (1971–74) in his first job as a faculty member and then as dean of the university's experimental Johnston College; at the University of Wisconsin, Green Bay, he was dean of undergraduate studies; and at Rice where, as at Green Bay, the undergraduate programs in the sciences were especially strong, he presided over a university of 2,600 undergraduates and 1,300 graduates.[4]

Thus Rupp met the search committee's specifications for administrative experience and academic stranding in the arts and sciences, even as his interest in undergraduates impressed the committee's chairman. The candidate's other credentials similarly raised no problems. Married, the father of two daughters, he had grown up in New Jersey the child of German-speaking parents who had migrated to the United States in the early 1930s. He went to public schools, then attended Princeton, Yale, where he earned a masters in divinity, and Harvard. His politics were moderately to the left: he had been active in civil rights in New Jersey and in the antiwar movement in New Haven. During his graduate years in Cambridge, however, marriage and the need to press on with his studies kept him from the barricades. Taking his oral exams at the time of the Harvard student disruptions in the spring of 1969, Rupp stayed in the library. "Building disruptions," he later allowed, "were not my thing."[5]

Two events in these years depart from the normal career trajectory of a would-be academic. The first was his acceptance as a graduate student of a Danforth Traveling Fellowship that enabled him and his wife, Nancy, to spend 1969–70 in Sri Lanka, where he studied Buddhism, not with any intention of becoming a Buddhist specialist but to provide his work in Christian theology a comparative frame. The second occurred after he received his Ph.D. in 1971. On his way to his first teaching job in California, he accepted ordination by a Presbyterian Church in New Jersey. He would, in the event, become the sixth Columbia president to be an ordained minister, but like the last, F. A. P. Barnard (1864–89), he never took up a church. The other five, of course, had been Episcopalians, while he was of the church of William Livingston and a student of Buddhism to boot.[6]

The search committee was similarly unconcerned by Rupp's unfamiliarity with Columbia and New York City, which was limited to Sunday afternoon forays with parents through the Holland Tunnel to the McBurney YMCA to visit with German friends. He was clearly an outsider, hardly less so than Eisenhower. When so described, he later allowed: "An outsider like Ike, OK, but I understand universities." On February 2, 1993, now fifty-one, George Rupp was named Columbia's eighteenth president, his duties to begin July 1.[7]

Four weeks before assuming office, Rupp eliminated all prospects of the normal honeymoon allowed a new president by firing the dean of Columbia College, Jack Greenberg, and the dean of Graduate Faculties, Roger Bagnall. In Greenberg's place, he installed Professor of English Steven Marcus, who would also serve as vice president for academic affairs (a position vacated by Martin Meisel's resignation). Professor of Biology Eduardo Macagno replaced Bagnall as dean of Graduate Faculties, and Professor Caroline Bynum became dean of General Studies and associate vice president for undergraduate education, the second a new position. Whatever might be said about these changes—"drastic" and "forceful" were terms invoked regularly at the time—they attested to Rupp's determination to focus on fixing the problem between the College and Low Library.[8]

Like Sovern's troika of provosts at the outset of his presidency, Rupp's administrative shakeup failed to work. Combining the jobs of VP for arts and sciences and the dean of the College in Marcus, known for his loyalty to the College, was supposed to end the decade of bickering between the occupants of those two positions. Instead, having only reluctantly taken on both jobs because of uncertain health, Marcus disappointed College loyalists even as he struggled with a fractious Arts and Sciences Faculty. Caroline Bynum was equally frustrated trying to meet the dual responsibilities of keeping a hand in all undergraduate affairs, including Columbia College, while heading up General Studies. Eight months into her administrative assignment, Bynum announced her intention to return to the history department in July. Marcus agreed to stay on a second year, but the experiment had failed.[9]

Unlike Sovern's early administrative miscues, which came at little personal cost or loss of momentum, Rupp's made his a bumpy start. Initial encounters with faculty, the University Senate, the press, and even some trustees earned him a reputation for abruptness and prickliness. Moreover, except for dealings with undergraduates engaged in social service activities and with Harlem community groups, for which he and his wife did volunteer work, he projected little of the charisma that attended his immediate predecessor, and none of the bravado of McGill. Two years into his presidency, Rupp was still finding his way—and not much enjoying it.[10]

Three things saved the Rupp presidency. First, he stuck with the job of making an administratively cumbersome and opaque university more efficient and transparent. Here, he was helped by the quality of his nonfaculty administrative appointments, notably three vice presidents drawn from the public sector. Vice President for Administration Emily Lloyd had served in the Dinkins administration; Vice President for Finance John Masten had served in the Koch administration and at the New York Public Library; Allen Stone, the vice president for public affairs, had worked in the Clinton White House. Lloyd and Masten stayed throughout Rupp's presidency, while Stone left in its last year to take a comparable position at Harvard.[11]

Early missteps notwithstanding, Rupp eventually put together a solid cadre of academic administrators who remained throughout his presidency. Many were surprised he did not move quickly to replace Jonathan Cole as provost, as some faculty and trustees had urged. Instead, the two established an effective working relationship, which strengthened over time as Cole focused on the inside responsibilities of running the university, while Rupp set the agenda, established priorities, and raised money. The retention of several of Sovern's successful decanal appointments, among them Herbert Pardes in Health Sciences, Meyer Feldberg in Business, and Allan Formicola in Dentistry, gave Columbia during the Rupp years an unusual degree of administrative continuity.[12]

Add to these Rupp's own appointments of David H. Cohen as vice president of arts and Sciences and Austin Quigley as dean of Columbia College in the summer of 1995 and, a year later, with Cohen's involvement, those of Lisa Anderson as dean of SIPA, Robert Fitzpatrick as the dean of the School of the Arts, Peter J. Awn as dean of General Studies, and the conclusion is allowable that Columbia in the late 1990s was better administered than at any time since the 1890s. Only Fitzpatrick soon departed, to be succeeded by Bruce W. Ferguson as dean of the School of the Arts in 1999.

To be sure, Cohen and Quigley publicly clashed in 1997, which resulted in the temporary firing of Quigley and *New York Times* headlines. Quigley's restoration following a veritable sit-in at Rupp's office by prominent College alumni bespoke the new place the College enjoyed both within arts and sciences and in the university more generally. That Cohen and Quigley managed thereafter to work with one another through the remaining four years of Rupp's administration and into the first year of the Bollinger presidency speaks to Rupp's effective mediation, to their survival instincts, or to their commitment to their respective jobs. Likely all three.[13]

Another factor that permitted the Rupp presidency to overcome early missteps was the continuing revival of the fortunes of New York City. An important part of this was the widely shared perception that the city generally and both

Morningside and Washington Heights particularly had since the 1970s become safer places to work, study, and live. Families that twenty years earlier might have vetoed a son or daughter's expressed preference for Columbia or Barnard came to welcome the prospect and applaud the result. Columbia was not the only academic institution to benefit from the Giuliani renaissance, but because it was ready, Columbia's boat got an especially big lift from the rising tide.[14]

A third saving factor was the strength of the national economy throughout the 1990s. When Rupp took office in July 1993, the Dow-Jones stood at 3,500. At the height of the equities run-up in June 2000, it reached 12,000, and when he left in June 2002, it was still above 9,000. Columbia's internal situation made it possible to make the most of these good times. The sale of the Rockefeller site in 1985 had allowed the trustees to put most of the university's endowment into aggressively managed equities accounts. Thanks to moves made by his predecessor, Rupp inherited a board of trustees knowledgeable about Wall Street and a development team skilled at pursuing large gifts from alumni and nonalumni alike.[15]

Rupp assumed responsibility in 1993 for an endowment of $1.4 billion; the one he handed over to his successor a decade later was valued at $4.6 billion. During his first year as president, Columbia received $100 million in gifts; in his last, $300 million. When back in 1988 Moody's upgraded the rating of Columbia bonds from AA+ to AAA, many financial observers believed it to be more a testimony to President Sovern's persuasiveness than to Columbia's balance sheet. But when, midway through the Rupp presidency, Standard and Poor's upgraded its rating of Columbia bonds to AAA, the consensus was that Columbia had secured it the old-fashioned way, by earning it.[16]

For all its accomplishments, Rupp's presidency has an uncertain place in posterity. Part of the problem has to do with personality. His troubles at the end notwithstanding, the charismatic homeboy Sovern proved a tough act for the unimposing outsider to follow. Mike was said to "light up a room," whereas few granted George such candlepower. Sovern elicited through his presidency strong loyalties from many and strong animosities from a few; Rupp may have to settle for the consensual acknowledgment that his had been a successful watch. Even the judgment of several tough-minded trustees that "George was a superb CEO" doesn't quite assure him a place alongside Seth Low, his own favorite president. Yet the two presidencies have much in common, particularly in their outreach to the city, their fund-raising prowess, and the fact that both left Columbia stronger than they found it. An aspect of Columbia that first attracted Rupp, he later commented, was the challenge of its reputation for treating administrators roughly. This he thought he could manage, since he was "not unduly dependent on having everyone's love." Columbia did not disappoint. But Columbia does owe him its collective thanks.[17]

Tubs on Their Own Bottoms

A structural development of the 1990s that contributed to the decline of the personal presidency at Columbia was the professional schools' reassertion of the autonomy they had relinquished during the tough going of the early McGill regime. With the financial well-being of the university better assured, thanks in no small part to their efforts, several schools laid claim to a larger share of the revenues they generated. Health Sciences, by the early 1990s much the largest of the professional schools, in both income and staffing, but also with the most complicated relationship with the university, took the lead.[18]

The departure in mid-1980 of Paul Marks as vice president of Health Sciences was followed by seven years of administrative turmoil on the uptown campus. Replacing him appeared to go smoothly at first, when in the summer of 1981 Robert F. Goldberger, previously director of research at the NIH, was appointed vice president for Health Sciences. He shortly thereafter became the provost for the Medical Sciences under Sovern's troika arrangement. When that arrangement was abandoned in 1982, Goldberger became provost of the university, necessitating a new search for VP for Health Sciences. The position went to Robert Levy, a recently recruited faculty member from NIH. Tapley stayed on as dean of the Medical School.[19]

Unfortunately, Levy and Tapley soon found working together sufficiently difficult that each approached Goldberger threatening to resign if the other was not removed. This situation persisted into the summer of 1984, when, on a day remembered at the medical center as "Black Friday," Goldberger fired both Levy and Tapley. Henrik Bendixen became acting vice president for Health Sciences and dean of the Medical School. Much of the momentum generated during the Marks years was lost.[20]

In the fall of 1987 the search committee settled on Herbert Pardes as its choice for both vice president of Health Sciences and dean of the Medical School. Goldberger, with whom Pardes had worked at NIH, had recruited him from the National Institute of Mental Health to Columbia three years earlier as chair of psychiatry and director of the New York State Psychiatric Institute. Though on leave, President Sovern took an active role in the negotiations, giving assurances to the nominee that the first order of business for the new VP would be revisiting the financial arrangements between Health Sciences and the university. On March 1, 1989, Herbert Pardes became vice president for Health Sciences of Columbia University and dean of the College of Physicians & Surgeons.[21]

The promised revisiting of the financial relations began immediately. It was intended to allay concerns among uptown administrators that for several years

Health Sciences had been carrying the rest of the university. They had a point. By the late 1980s Health Sciences had become by far the university's biggest recipient of research funding from the federal government, as well as producing the indirect overhead income such funding generated. Pardes wanted more of this money to remain uptown, where it could be used to underwrite curricular development and ongoing capital refurbishment, not sent downtown, where it was thought to be used shoring up other parts of the university, such as the humanities and social sciences. Sound familiar?[22]

What occurred in the early 1990s was a replay of the 1969–71 Lamont-Doherty negotiations, with Pardes in the Maurice Ewing role and Mike Sovern as Bill McGill. Moreover, it was being observed by much the same audience: other professional school deans looking to piggyback on any deal the the most aggressive among them cut with Low Library. The outcome, however, was different. Unlike Ewing, who, failing to reach an agreement with McGill, departed for Texas, Pardes secured enough from Sovern, and then Rupp, to return uptown pleased with the outcome. It had not come easily. Pardes argued that the $5 million structural deficit of Health Sciences that he had inherited, which was being met by decapitalizing the Medical School's unrestricted endowment at a rate that would reduce the endowment by one-third ($13 million) in three years, was attributable to the university's keeping too much of the health science's tuition and research overhead revenues. Let Health Sciences keep these revenues and charge it for university-provided services, he urged, and the medical center would soon be out of deficit and could thereafter take care of its own needs. Sovern was too experienced a negotiator to make such a counterargument at the time, but when an interviewer later suggested that the rest of the university might have needed that money, Pardes responded: "So did Mother Theresa."[23]

It took three years for the change to be fully implemented, but by the beginning of the Rupp presidency, Health Sciences had achieved substantial financial autonomy. This was helped along by the imposition of a so-called dean's tax gradually increasing to 5 percent on all medical practice income generated by the clinical departments, which was then followed by another 10 percent tax on all gifts received by the clinical departments By the mid-1990s a third new income stream was created when Pardes secured for Health Sciences 25 percent of the income deriving from patents, most of which covered discoveries or procedures attributable to the Medical School.[24]

Money was now available to effect long-term changes. A building program stalled since 1975 was reinvigorated in the 1990s with the completion of three buildings, the Mary W. Lasker Biomedical Research Building (Audubon I), the Russ Berrie Medical Science Pavilion (Audubon II) and the New York Psychiatric Institute, and the groundbreaking for a fourth, the Irving Cancer Research Center (Audubon III). This was accompanied by a virtually complete turnover in the heads of the clinical and basic science departments, thereby assuring leadership well into the twenty-first century. During the 1990s Pardes and his department chairs successfully recruited leading scientists and clinicians from elsewhere, even as they responded to offers made to more than one hundred of their own faculty in ways that kept them at Columbia.[25]

Prosperity begat more prosperity. The forty endowed chairs that existed at the outset of the Pardes era grew to over one hundred by its close twelve years later. An endowment that stood at $250 million in 1989 was closing in on $1 billion in 2001. A fund-raising program that in the late 1980s raised about $23 million a year a decade later raised $125 million.[26]

Similar arrangements worked out between Pardes and the deans of the Schools of Dentistry, Nursing, and Public Health encouraged them to increase their revenues by allowing them to keep most of what they brought in. Allan Formicola aggressively sought private foundation support to underwrite the Dental School's community outreach programs; Mary Mundinger led the Nursing School into clinical and outpatient care; Allan Rosenfield, by focusing on HIV/AIDS, made the School of Public Health's research program the second largest in the university. In 1998 he and Pardes attracted to the school a name-changing gift of $33 million from the family of Joseph L. Mailman. Incentive capitalism had come to 168th Street.[27]

Meanwhile, Presbyterian Hospital struggled with chronic deficits and leadership turnover. The completion of the Milstein building in 1989 provided much needed space for inpatient care, but its finances remained shaky. These improved in the mid-1990s under President William Speck but at the cost of cutting back clinical services. By then, the Presbyterian board was looking to partner with another New York hospital. After discussions with New York University and Mount Sinai Hospital, Presbyterian decided in 1998 to merge with New York Hospital on East Sixty-eighth Street, the teaching hospital of Cornell Medical School. The result was New York Presbyterian Hospital, which became the primary teaching hospital of both the Columbia and Cornell medical schools. In these negotiations, as in those with Pardes earlier, Rupp was an active participant, earning among his uptown counterparts the distinction of being the first Columbia president who became seriously invested in their world.[28]

Among the close observers of these late 1980s negotiations were Deans Barbara A. Black of the Law School (who was succeeded by Lance Liebman in 1992) and Meyer Feldberg, who had become dean of the Graduate School of Business in 1990. Each had, invoking a metaphor for financial self-sufficiency long used at Harvard, "a tub" that each wished to be settled "on its own bottom." During the last years of the Sovern presidency, when calls had been made on both schools to provide help with the budget deficits they attributed to Arts and Sciences, the deans each undertook a risks-benefits analysis of the feasibility of their schools going off on their own. Neither did, although Dean Black, who held a Ph.D. in American history as well as law degrees, once compared the relationship of the Law School to the university administration in the late 1980s as that of "colonies and the crown, just before the Revolution." No break occurred, however, and both schools renegotiated relationships with the university that gave them substantial control over most of the revenues they generated.[29]

The beneficial results of this decentralized arrangement are illustrated in the case of the Graduate School of Business. When Meyer Feldberg arrived in 1990, the school had been operating without a dean for two years and without a system of financial controls for several. Its budgets had run deficits for ten straight years, accumulating $3 million in overdraft accounts that the school owed to the university. By 1992, with the decentralized system in place, the budget was in balance, and for the next ten years the school operated in the black. Meanwhile, the school's operating budget quadrupled in size, from $30 million in 1990 to $120 million in 2002.[30]

Between 1990 and 2002 the Business School's endowment increased from $16 million to $220 million. In those same thirteen years, the school raised some $300 million. Under the terms of the agreement with the central administration, the dean was able to use these funds to refurbish Uris Hall and to establish branches of the executive MBA program in Berkeley, California, and in London. The school was also able to hire new faculty (either singly or in collaboration with other parts of the university) and fend off raids on its own faculty. "I raised enough money," Feldberg explained recently, "so that I never have to turn to Low for money."[31]

In the early 1990s Columbia's less prosperous schools included the chronically deficit-ridden Graduate School of Arts and Sciences and the School of Engineering and Applied Science, which carried a substantial debt to the university and struggled with declining enrollments. Their deans were told to emulate the income-generating ways of their more prosperous peers. In the case of arts and sciences, this meant increasing enrollments in the School of International and Public Affairs and the School of the Arts. In Engineering, it involved increasing levels of federally funded research, on its own and in collaboration with other parts of the university. Successful fund-raising by Zvi Galil, who became dean in 1996, was highlighted by a name-changing $26 million gift from the Z. Y. Fu Foundation in 1997. Midway through Rupp's presidency, all fifteen of the schools under the Columbia Corporation were operating in the black.[32]

Other evidence attested to the university's improved financial standing in the late 1990s. When Rupp assumed the presidency in 1993, annual drawdowns from the endowment for operating funds had been running at over 7 percent for several years. By the late 1990s the percentage had been brought below 5 percent. During that same period, the central administration's budget grew at a much slower rate than did those of the schools and faculties. Meanwhile, the five-year capital campaign launched in 1995 exceeded its goal of $2 billion months ahead of schedule, and without the kind of single blockbuster gifts in the $100 million-plus range that many other universities received between 1999 and 2001. The laconic Rupp, however impatient with "the endless cultivation" that some potential donors required, raised more money for Columbia—nearly $3 billion—than all his seventeen predecessors combined.[33]

Financial stability and, in the case of Columbia's professional schools, greater autonomy have been accompanied by enhanced competitive standing. By the end of Rupp's presidency, the Medical, Business, and Law Schools all could cite evidence that each numbered among the top five in their fields. For the Business School, which counted itself behind only Harvard and Wharton in national reputation and ahead of both in global visibility, this was traveling in new company, having ranked fourteenth as recently as 1989. For the Medical and Law Schools, it represented a return to standings not enjoyed since the 1950s.[34]

During the 1990s the School of Dentistry, whose accreditation was in jeopardy in the 1970s, became the national leader in the development of community-based dentistry, even as it strengthened its standing in oral surgery and basic research. Similarly, the School of Architecture, under the deanship of Bernard Tschumi, built on the accomplishments of the Polshek era to permit the school to be counted among the top five schools in the country. Twenty-five years earlier, its accreditation had been at serious risk.[35]

The same case can be made for the School of International and Public Affairs, the School of Journalism, the School of the Arts, the School of Social Work, and the Mailman School of Public Health. Indeed, the only one of Columbia's professional schools that entered the twenty-first century not numbering among the top ten in its field was the Fu Foundation School of Engineering and Applied Science. But here, too, the recent positive effects of increased funding, decanal leadership, and interschool cooperation are discernible.[36]

One division of contemporary Columbia reflects not so much a return to an earlier eminence but new strength. Established in 1965, the School of the Arts struggled for recognition and resources in its early going. During the deanship of Schuyler Chapin (1971–86), the school achieved some prominence in the wider arts community, especially for its writing and theater arts program. Still, it was only the passionate commitment and political skills of his successor, Peter Smith (1987–93), that kept the school from being gutted during the financially straitened circumstances after 1989 when it was incorporated within the newly constituted Arts and Sciences Faculty. During the subsequent deanship of Robert Fitzpatrick (1995–98), the school broadened its program in film studies, especially in production and technical training, which it had previously ceded to NYU. In sublime indifference to its traditional claims to innocence on the charge of "who's counting?" Columbia has taken of late to including Oscars, Golden Globes, and Venice Film Festival awards among its trophies.[37]

Since 1998, when Bruce W. Ferguson became dean, the school's faculty, students, and graduates have achieved sufficient recognition for their work to lay claim to Columbia being "a premier arts institution" in the artistic capital of the world. A refurbished Dodge Hall and expanded facilities at Prentis Hall on West 125th Street have helped. Meanwhile, in collaboration with other parts of arts and sciences, especially the music and art history departments, and with Barnard College, which provides instruction in theater and dance, the university now offers a much wider array of undergraduate courses in the arts than was available as recently as 1990. In its recent incorporation of the arts into its educational and creative mission, Columbia has come a long way from 1904, when, following the almost simultaneous decamping of George Woodberry and Edward MacDowell, the chairman of the board of trustees, George Rives, could scotch any notion of establishing a faculty of fine arts by reminding the twice-burned President Butler that "we have had some experience already of the difficulties of dealing with poets and composers."[38]

It remains the case that much of an American university's overall standing is determined by the assigned ranking of its arts and sciences departments. And considerable evidence exists that Columbia exited the twentieth century as it entered it: near the very top and climbing. The most recent comparative assessment of arts and science departments of leading American research universities appeared in 1997, using data collected in 1995. The rankings Columbia received are consistently higher than those assigned by comparable assessments made in the late 1970s and early 1980s. The slide discernible in the rankings of the late 1960s and 1970s had been halted, and a climb back could be inferred to be under way.[39]

There are good reasons to believe that the upward trajectory indicated by these rankings has continued in the years since 1997. Subsequent appointments of economists Jeffrey Sachs from Harvard and Joseph Stiglitz from Yale, the political theorist Jon Elster from Chicago, the international relations scholar Michael Doyle from Princeton, and a wholesale raid on the Michigan anthropology department in 1997, which included the cultural anthropologist Nicholas Dirks, all bespeak Columbia's improved competitive position in the social sciences. So does the success enjoyed by the history department in retaining its most notable scholars, among them Eric Foner and the East Asianist Carol Gluck, in the face of offers from elsewhere. Finally, the establishment in 2001 of the Institute for Social Research and Policy gives promise of collaborative work in the social sciences not seen at Columbia since the 1950s heyday of the Bureau of Applied Social Research.[40]

It is in the sciences, however, which ranked eighth overall in the 1997 study, where the prospects for improved standing seem the greatest. Subsequent appointments of physicists Horst Stormer from Lucent Labs and Steven M. Kahn from Berkeley and the chemist Samuel J. Danishefsky from Yale suggest as much. But so, too, did a comprehensive external review of nine departments that make up the natural sciences, commissioned by Vice President Cohen and completed in January 2002. Its principal finding: while only Columbia's earth sciences/geology department currently numbers among the top five in its field, most if not all of the nine reviewed departments could be by 2010.[41]

Not since the 1910s has Columbia been perceived by its peers as advancing on so many fronts at once. "The question is not whether Columbia can make its way back into the top half dozen universities in the world," Provost Cole informed the trustees in 1999, "but whether we should try to make it into the top three." "Selective excellence," which came to be a euphemism for "managed decline" in the 1970s and still constituted a theme of the 1987 report of the Presidential Commission on the Future of the University, had been set aside for a return to the larger, all-encompassing ambitions of the early days of the university. Problems remained, not the least of which was securing space for expansion. Yet, as the *New York Times* allowed on November 1, 1999, even in a good time for elite universities, "Columbia seems to be particularly blessed."[42]

Whither Barnard?

The same could not be said of Barnard College. Rupp wasted little time, upon his arrival in mid-1993, making known his view of Barnard College as an institutional redundancy. Having served its purpose while the College remained men only, it had no place at the now-coeducational Columbia. In the second year of a five-year agreement with Barnard, Columbia appeared about to pull the plug on the affiliation of more than one hundred years.[43]

Meanwhile, Barnard had its own problems. Having weathered the 1970s somewhat better than other parts of the university, it really struggled in the

1980s. The leadership shakeup and disagreements among trustees over how to respond to Columbia's call for functional coeducation in the late 1970s set the stage for the hard times to follow. But it was the Columbia trustees' decision in early 1982 to admit women to the College that, however publicly accommodated, privately obliged Barnard trustees and the still new president, Ellen Futter, to consider several endgame scenarios. They quickly dismissed the idea of admitting men to Barnard, which was prohibited under the new agreement and would likely have involved severing all ties with Columbia. Only slightly less radical was the prospect of developing joint programs with other New York educational institutions, such as the American Museum of Natural History, the Jewish Theological Seminary, or the Manhattan and Juilliard Schools of Music.[44]

Whereas Columbia College's applications slide ended with the 1982 decision to admit women, Barnard's continued through the middle of the decade. Meanwhile, the College's endowment remained stagnant at $35 million, in part because what little income the endowment generated went to cover operating expenses, including monies owed Columbia under the intercorporate agreement. These increased significantly in 1988–89, when a sharp shift in enrollments away from Barnard and toward Columbia the year before left Barnard owing more than $3 million in cross-registration fees.[45]

Few at Columbia worried about Barnard's survival. Certainly, Hamilton Hall was otherwise occupied, as Dean Pollack labored to create for his women undergraduates "a room of their own" on the east side of Broadway and where admissions officials leaked Columbia's success rate in head-to-head competition with Barnard for admitted students. Some Columbia departments still welcomed Barnard faculty to teach graduate courses, but even here the prevailing financial arrangements discouraged doing so. In this environment, some departments, notably art history, simply raided their Barnard counterpart departments for faculty. Meanwhile, the Barnard trustees mandated a faculty planning profile that in theory placed a cap of 50 percent tenured on the Barnard full-time faculty but as implemented assured that the percentage would not get much above 40 percent, or about only two-thirds that of Columbia and most select liberal arts colleges. Already singularly demanding for a liberal arts college, because of Columbia's involvement in the process, Barnard's tenuring process became even more so.[46]

Barnard in the 1980s was a good illustration (the gender attribution aside) of the truth of Dr. Samuel Johnson's observation "Depend upon it, Sir, when a man knows he is to be hanged in a fortnight, it concentrates his mind wonderfully." Improvements in student recruitment and curricular reform, needed in their own right, became the response to the competition now posed by a coeducational Columbia College. To offset the expected loss of those young women who would now apply to Columbia, Barnard undertook to nationalize its recruitment pool. It also needed to attract a larger share of students whose families could afford to pay full or close to full tuition. In the early 1980s financial aid under the College's "need blind" policy grew to 16 percent of Barnard's operating expenses, which, with its limited unrestricted endowment, had to be covered by other tuition income.[47]

Curricular reform was linked to the recruitment efforts seeking a national pool of women applicants. The reforms adopted included senior research seminars, earlier available in a few majors but now required in all. First-year seminars, focused on writing and major texts, and seminars in quantitative reasoning were developed by senior faculty and directed at incoming students. This strategy represented a twofold gamble: in an era when colleges were abandoning requirements, that good students would be attracted to a curriculum front-loaded with required general-education courses (but less so than Columbia) and that senior faculty would be willing to teach such courses.[48]

Curricular changes made Barnard's offerings more attractive to prospective students but also to students already at Barnard, as well those as at Columbia. Here, the financial terms of the standing intercorporate agreements since 1973 came into the picture. Both Barnard and Columbia expected, in allowing their students to take courses offered at the other institution, that the net flow would be from Barnard to Columbia. Yet too great a flow to Columbia could prove financially disastrous for Barnard. It became imperative for Barnard to mount courses that met the needs of its own students even as they attracted a respectable share of Columbia students. Here, too, Barnard's efforts paid off. In 1987–88 there was a net flow of 7,400 credit points from Barnard to Columbia; three years later, the flow had dropped to 1,536 points.[49]

Many of these magnet courses covered mainline topics such as political theory or financial markets or European history, but others were in areas slighted by the Columbia curriculum. These included women's studies and environmental sciences, fields that in the late 1980s were just getting under way at Columbia but had been part of the Barnard curriculum since the late 1960s. Others were in the arts, especially theater, dance, and the visual arts, which had yet to secure a place in the Columbia undergraduate curriculum and which Columbia was willing to cede to Barnard. And then there was another category: new courses in architecture and urban studies that both Columbia and Barnard were determined to develop but, for reasons of economy and staffing, decided to do so jointly.[50]

Such joint programs served another purpose: to make Barnard a valued resource in the eyes of Columbia faculty and administrators. Curricular competition suited Barnard's short-term purposes in the financially strapped late 1980s, but curricular cooperation was more likely to secure a respected and stable place in the larger university and, at the same time, ensure a substantial measure of autonomy.

Like Columbia, Barnard benefited from the lift provided by New York City's revival. It also benefited from Columbia College's rapid ascent into the ranks of America's most selective colleges. It may also, as a selective women's college, have been a beneficiary of what the economists call "inelastic demand," that point when a given product—in this case, quality education at a woman's college—becomes sufficiently scarce through attrition of suppliers that those left are assured a sustainable demand.[51]

Another crucial factor in Barnard's survival in the 1980s was the unwillingness of President Ellen Futter and the Barnard board, particularly its chair, Helene Kaplan (BC 1953), to throw in the towel. It was Futter who kept the faculty from getting any more paranoid than befits their calling and Kaplan who kept open the communication channels with Columbia trustees. Together, in 1986 they urged on Barnard's cautious trustees a plan to borrow $20 million to build a dormitory, which would allow the College for the first time to offer housing to all accepted applicants. With an endowment of only $35 million, no bond rating to issue uninsured bonds, and no name donor up front, the board decided to bet the ranch on the still uncertain prospect that Barnard had a future within what Butler on his good days used to call "the greater Columbia University."[52]

The gamble paid off. The seventeen-story Centennial Hall, designed by the ex-dean of the Columbia School of Architecture, James Polshek, opened in the fall of 1988, just in time to accommodate a surge in applicants the following spring. A year later, members of the Sulzberger family made a gift of $5 million to the College in honor of their mother, Iphigene Ochs Sulzberger, a Barnard alumna (1914) and longtime trustee (1944–1960). The new dormitory was renamed Sulzberger Hall. Rather than a momentary spike, the attendant rise in applications proved to be the first evidence of the New York lift that would have the College's applications increasing for each of the the next fourteen years.[53]

Although the remaining cost of the building continued to be a substantial draw on Barnard resources, the psychological lift that attended its groundbreaking, opening, and renaming persisted throughout Ellen Futter's presidency. In the spring of 1993 she resigned to become the president of the American Museum of Natural History. Hers had been a presidency as saving for Barnard as McGill's had been for Columbia.[54]

On July 1, 1994, Judith Shapiro, a New York–reared and Columbia-trained anthropologist who had served as provost of Bryn Mawr College, became Barnard's sixth president and ninth head. She immediately set out to persuade

Columbia colleagues, not least the skeptical George Rupp—even as she reminded her Barnard colleagues—of Barnard's important place in the university. Thus, for all the tensions implicit in the relationship and the quite explicit strains at Barnard that flow from Barnard's agreement in 1973 to have its tenure nominations vetted by Columbia, Shapiro championed the strategy that longtime Barnard-Columbia watchers called "progressive entanglement," whereby should Columbia ever decide to severe its ties with Barnard, so many would exist that it would not know where to begin.[55]

In 1999 Barnard became the most selective women's college in the United States. The year before, a renewal of the 1973 intercorporate agreement assured the continuation of the unique Columbia-Barnard relationship well into the twenty-first century. Both institutions had come a long way in the intervening quarter-century, if not in precise tandem, along the same improving road.[56]

Teachers College Continued

The recent history of the relationship of Teachers College to the university differs from Barnard's. In 1976, when Lawrence A. Cremin, a distinguished historian of American education (CU Ph.D. 1948), became Teacher College's seventh president, relations between the two institutions were only somewhat less entangled than those of Barnard and Columbia. All Teachers College students received their degrees from Columbia, while several TC departments (e.g., psychology, history, anthropology) ran joint Ph.D. programs, exchanged faculty, and otherwise operated as if they were a single department located on both sides of 120th Street. TC students took courses at Columbia and vice versa.[57]

On two scores, however, Teachers College remained outside the Columbia orbit. Unlike Barnard, it retained full responsibility for selecting its tenured faculty. And when the Columbia libraries computerized the management of their collections in the 1970s, Barnard's modest holdings in Wollman Library were included, while Teachers College's more extensive collection in Memorial Library was not. The combined effect of these two nonconnects was that academic and curricular developments at Teachers College came to be of less moment to Columbia than those at Barnard.

Teachers College enjoyed more autonomy than Barnard for not being beholden to Columbia in these matters. Exempt from the ad hoc arrangements for tenuring faculty, for example, Teachers College has been able to reconfigure its faculty into more functional groups than the disciplined-based department structure at Columbia allowed. Where, into the 1970s, there were Departments of History and Education and Philosophy and Education, there is now a

Department of Art and Humanities; where once Departments of Sociology of Education and Developmental Psychology, now there is a Department of Human Development. TC has also been freer to move away from the traditional division of faculty into tenured and untenured toward an arrangement where most faculty are neither but rather serve as adjunct faculty.[58]

Upon Cremin's retirement in 1986, Michael Timpane became TC's eighth president. During his eight-year tenure, 120th Street, once called by Richard Hofstadter (who took graduate courses at TC with Merle Curti in the late 1930s) the widest street in the world, widened a bit more. Earlier student-exchange arrangements ceased to work to the satisfaction of one or the other institution and were cut back sharply. During the presidency of Arthur E. Levine, who succeeded Timpane in 1994, relations between Teachers College and Columbia University have not become noticeably closer. Recent surveys by *U.S. News and World Report* ranking Teachers College among the top three (with Harvard and Stanford) of the fifty U.S. schools of education surveyed, however, suggest that it entered the twenty-first century doing many things right.[59]

The Recentering of Columbia College

One factor that contributed to the different trajectories of the recent relationships of Barnard College and Teachers College with Columbia University stems from their different missions. Whereas Teachers College is a comprehensive graduate and professional school of education, Barnard's mission is to provide its women undergraduates with a residentially based liberal arts education. And, as it turned out, it was undergraduate education that became one of the university's major concerns in the 1990s. In 1996, looking back on the first years of his presidency, Rupp reminded the trustees: "The main emphasis at Columbia was to enhance undergraduate education, placing the College and SEAS [engineering] at the center of the University."[60]

Perhaps it took an outsider who studied at Princeton, taught at Harvard, and presided over Rice to bring to Low Library the conviction that no American university can achieve greatness if it is seen to neglect its undergraduates. Evidence that Columbia University had done this since the 1890s was undeniable, to the ongoing consternation of generations of College alumni. The College was not only the smallest undergraduate unit among the Ivies, but it was also the most administratively and financially beholden to its own university. The lament of the College's first dean, John Henry Van Amringe, that the College, with respect to the rest of the university, "was as in a shadow," could be heard from each of his successors into the 1980s.[61]

In June 1941 Lawrence Condon (CC 1921) brought these decadeslong sentiments to public notice in his *Survey of the Relationship of Columbia College to Columbia University*, ostensibly presented to the university as his class's twentieth-anniversary gift. "Funds and assets originally intended for the purposes of Columbia College," the *Survey* contended, "have been employed . . . [to build] a huge, many-sided University." As for Columbia College, Condon went on, "It seems fair to say that its best interests have not been served but have in fact been subordinated." Butler used his annual report in the fall of 1941 to rebut the charges, asserting that "it is the power of Columbia University which has brought into being the Columbia College of today." The bombing of Pearl Harbor produced a truce of sorts between Butler and his disgruntled College alumni but no resolution.[62]

As indicated earlier, Butler's four successors (Eisenhower, Kirk, Cordier, and McGill) did little to assure alumni that Columbia College occupied all their waking thoughts. Under Sovern, a graduate of the College, relations between the College alumni and Low Library warmed significantly, although grumblings could still be heard that the university was only interested in the College for its wealthy graduates. The firing of the popular dean Robert Pollack in 1988 was seen by some College alumni as an example of Low Library's getting up to its old tricks.[63]

That same year, Provost Cole—another graduate of the College (1964)—first articulated the policy with respect to the College of "enlargement and enhancement," only to have the policy decried by the College faculty, administrators in Hamilton Hall, and College alumni as yet another attempt by the university to make the recently application-rich College pay for a larger share of the university's operations. Even some trustees regarded Cole's expressions of fealty to the College with undisguised suspicion. In the event, the budgetary difficulties of Sovern's last years made it difficult to deliver on the "enhancement" aspect of the stated strategy, even as the "enlargement" part was widely felt to be proceeding all too well.[64]

So, too, Rupp's first pronouncements on the College, perhaps most spectacularly his comment that if everything at Columbia worked as well as "The College Core," the university would be in fine shape, elicited from the College Believers little more than suspended disbelief. This began to change, however, when he called for the demolition of the functionally and aesthetically challenged Ferris-Booth Hall, since the mid-1950s the locus of Columbia College extracurricular life, and set out to build in its place a more than $65 million state-of-the art student center. Doubting Thomases were also converted by a visit to Butler Library, where the $12 million renovations of the gloomy space previously occupied by the Library Service School transformed it into an elegant, inviting, and digitally sophisticated undergraduate library for the twenty-first century.[65]

At Columbia, more than on less highly congested campuses, space within the existing campus footprint is the coin of the realm. This remained as true in the 1990s as it had been in the 1950s, when College alumni calling for an undergraduate gym were consigned to the rocky cliff of off-campus Morningside Park and told to come up with the money first. In the 1990s the needs of the College were met with substantial allocations of on-campus property and, in the instances of the student center and the library, before naming gifts of $25 million from Alfred Lerner (CC 1955) and $10 million from the Milstein family were in hand. The $12 million upgrading of the Dodge Fitness Center in 1995–96 is another instance of a capital improvement aimed primarily at undergraduates. Two other new buildings just outside the campus footprint, the dormitory on 114th and Broadway and the Robert K. Kraft Family Center for Jewish Student Life, also directly addressed the needs of hundreds of Columbia and Barnard undergraduates.[66]

For all these recently added amenities, the Columbia campus today runs little risk of being confused with its Ivy counterparts, much less a pricey spa. As befits its urban setting, it is congested and noisy. Faculty learn to teach through sirens, jackhammers, and planes approaching La Guardia much as clergy preach through wailing babies. Newly arrived students—and not a few new faculty—note the emphasis placed on the adjectival component of the tough love they sometimes encounter from library and custodial staff. Nor are those experiencing initiatory disorientation always assured understanding from on high. "If you want more structure," President Rupp informed a *Columbia Spectator* reporter voicing these concerns, "go to Amherst or Princeton." Warm and fuzzy it is not.[67]

During the Rupp presidency, Columbia College expanded enrollments by 25 percent, from thirty-two hundred students in 1993 to four thousand in 2002. More than 80 percent of the entering class in 2002 came from outside New York State, with Californians constituting the second largest state contingent. It may still not be nationally representative, but the College's student body has of late acquired a distinctly bicoastal character.[68]

Even as Columbia College expanded, the social sciences and humanities departments continued the now two-decade process of downsizing their graduate programs. They did so by becoming more selective and in the early 1990s more generous, offering full fellowships for nearly all the students they admitted to their Ph.D. programs. Largely gone are the days of self-financed Ph.D. students who, because of multiple part-time teaching jobs or night shifts driving cabs, required ten-plus years to complete their dissertations.[69]

The shrinking of graduate programs has made more arts and sciences faculty available to teach undergraduates, both within the traditional Core and in upper-level undergraduate courses. Full-time faculty in the humanities and social sciences are now expected to teach at least one undergraduate course per year, with the norm expected to rise to two. Gone are the days when it was a point of pride among some senior faculty that they had no contact with undergraduates. Departments that slight their undergraduate responsibilities now do so at their budgetary and reputational peril.[70]

Columbia College in the 1990s became increasingly selective, with its apply-to-admit rate dropping from 30 percent in 1993 to 15 percent for the entering class in 2002. That year, among the nation's two thousand four-year colleges, only two (Harvard and Princeton) turned away a higher proportion of applicants.[71]

Yet no other highly selective private college admitted a more socially diverse class than Columbia College, where 50 percent of the entering class is made up of women, and self-identified minorities account for a third of the class. White Protestant native-born men, who, a century ago, made up 80 percent of an entering Columbia College class, now account for less than 20 percent. "Legacies" are more numerous than they were twenty years ago but still constitute a smaller portion of entering classes than they do at any of the other Ivies. Together with the School of Engineering and Applied Science, General Studies, and Barnard College, whose student bodies are all at least as socially diverse as that at Columbia College, the undergraduate divisions of Columbia University have become a much fairer approximation of the social diversity of the city whose name they bear, where 60 percent of these inhabitants are self-identified minorities and 40 percent are foreign-born.[72]

While the College still looks to the Arts and Sciences Faculty to staff most College courses, in other ways it has increased its autonomy within the university. One vehicle for doing so has been the College Board of Visitors, started by Dean Peter Pouncey in the 1970s and revived by Dean Robert Pollack, which includes several of the university's major benefactors, including prospective and past trustees. The visitors speak for the interests of the College or, as in the case of the 1997 standoff between Dean of Columbia College Austin Quigley and Vice President of Arts and Sciences David Cohen, for its dean. More often, the board serves as an effective fund-raising enterprise. Between 1990 and 1995 only four of the twenty-one endowed professorships (19 percent) created in the arts and sciences came from College donors; between 1995 and 2001 College donors, most of them actively solicited by Quigley, accounted for twenty-six of the forty-six new professorships (57 percent).[73]

As more College alumni come from classes post-1968 and many from the 1990s, when the needs of the College became more effectively attended to, the alumni can be expected to play a larger role in the university's affairs. In 1993 Rupp identified the College as the most underleveraged part of the university and then proceeded to leverage it to the hilt. His successor, Lee C. Bollinger (Law 1971), comes to a Columbia where the rate of alumni giving, 31 percent in 2001 (up from 18 percent in 1993) is still substantially less than at either of his last places of employment—Michigan, where he presided for seven years, and Dartmouth, where he earlier served as provost. He might well conclude that alumni involvement and alumni giving are areas at today's Columbia that hold out the best prospect of rapid turnaround.[74]

To be sure, Columbia faces difficult challenges at the outset of the Bollinger presidency. The long-term impact on New York's fortunes of the attack on the World Trade Center on September 11, 2001, remains unknown. So is that of an uncertain economy and a stock market that between 2000 and March 2003 had lost one-third of its value.

There are internal challenges as well, some of which the new president identified at his installation on October 3, 2002. These include the need to secure room to effect the necessary expansion of several programs that are constrained by the lack of space on Morningside or Washington Heights to accommodate them. Another involves the need to rethink the mission of some of Columbia's most distinguished professional schools, such as the Journalism School, where the search for a new dean was halted in August 2002 to allow such rethinking to proceed. The appointment as dean of Nicolas Lemann, an historian and staff writer for the *New Yorker*, in March 2003, bespeaks the School's new orientation. There is also the challenge of continuing to compete for the world's best scholars without further reducing the teaching expected from them. The list is lengthy, and it contains only the known challenges. But, for all that, a retrospectively informed perspective allows the view that Columbia's nineteenth president entered on his duties at a singular moment in the university's history, one marked by great recent achievement and still greater promise.[75]

FIGURE 7.1 Andrew W. Cordier (1901–75), United Nations ambassador, acting president (1968–1969), and fifteenth president of Columbia University (1969–70).

Source: Columbia University Archives—Columbiana Collection.

FIGURE 7.2 William J. McGill (1922–97), psychologist, Columbia professor (1957–64), and sixteenth president of Columbia University (1970–80), with Mayor John V. Lindsay on Broadway and 116th Street, early 1970s.

Source: Columbia University Archives—Columbiana Collection.

FIGURE 7.3   Aerial view of Columbia-Presbyterian Medical Center in 2003.

Source: Archives and Special Collections, Columbia University Health Sciences Division.

FIGURE 7.4 Michael I. Sovern (1931–), graduate of Columbia College (1953) and Columbia Law Scho[ol] (1955), law professor, dean, provost, and seventeenth president of Columbia University (1980–93).

Source: Morris Dickstein, "Columbia Recovered," *New York Times Magazine*, May 15, 1988, 35.

FIGURE 7.5 Christina Teuscher (CC 2000), Olympic swimming medalist in 1996 and 2000, competing the breast stroke for Columbia in 1999.

Source: Photograph by Gene Boyars, Columbia Sports Information.

FIGURE 7.6 George Rupp (1942–), religion scholar, academic administrator, and eighteenth president [of] Columbia University (1993–2002), with Columbia and Barnard students following a cleanup in Mornin[g] side Park.

Source: *Columbia University Record*, March 9, 2001, 4.

FIGURE 7.7 Alfred Lerner Hall, Columbia student center, designed by Dean of Architecture Bernard Tschumi and opened in 1997. Built on site of Ferris Booth Hall (1959–95).

Source: Andrew S. Dolkart, *Morningside Heights: A History of Its Architecture and Development* (New York: Columbia University Press, 1998), 337.

FIGURE 7.8 Lee Bollinger, right, and New York mayor Michael Bloomberg, on October 3, 2002, at the installation of Bollinger as the nineteenth president of Columbia University.

Source: AP Photo/Columbia University, Diane Bondareff.

Epilogue: Worth the Candle?

IN THE preface of their recent and estimable *Making Harvard Modern: The Rise of America's University* (2001), historians Morton and Phyllis Keller explicitly reject the job of determining "whether or not Harvard is as potent a force (for good or bad) as [its idolators and detractors] claim" as too "difficult to measure." "In any event," they state, "that is not what this book is about." Surely, a prudent course, leaving this messy, perhaps unanswerable question to others. Yet in explicitly acknowledging the question at the outset of their narrative, they embolden a less prudent historian at the close of his to consider briefly the eschatological implications of his subject: Is Columbia "worth the candle"?[1]

The candle in Columbia's case has burned for a quarter-millennium, during which time its consumption of human resources has included:

- 5,000 person-years of fiduciary service by some 400 trustees;
- 250,000 person-years of teaching and research by some 25,000 faculty and research staff;
- 600,000 person-years of studying by some 300,000 students;
- 500,000 person-years of employment by some 50,000 staf memmbers.[2]

Columbia, especially since the 1890s, has also consumed large amounts of capital expenditures, coming to it in tuition payments, private benefactions, and public grants, totaling on the order of $20 billion (in 2000 dollars). So, too, it has required the physical occupation at different times and for different durations of approximately one hundred acres of some of the world's most valuable property.[3]

And what have the city, the nation, and the world received for these substantial investments? For a start, one can point to the occupational services of Columbia's 150,000 graduates, whose training qualified them for responsibilities demanding intellectual preparation of a high order. These include lawyers, physicians, businesspeople, engineers and architects, nurses and dentists, social workers and journalists, writers and publishers, artists and diplomats, academics and scholars, schoolteachers and public servants. Absent the work of these talented and ambitious graduates, the world would be the poorer. Let a sampling of the public offices filled by Columbia alumni in 2003 suggest the ongoing magnitude: one member of the United States Supreme Court, three United States senators, three congressmen, three governors (New York, New Jersey, and California), a chief justice of the New York Court of Appeals, a president of the New York City Board of Education.[4]

Columbia can also take some credit for the products of the intellectual, scientific investigations of its students and faculty, including the thousands of scientific papers, essays, and books, the hundreds of inventions, and the gigabytes of scholarly discourse. Included here is the work (as of spring 2003) of the thirty-nine alumni and twenty-three faculty of Columbia who have won Nobel Prizes—a total of sixty-two, including five in the last six years. So, too, is the work that came out of the 1,184 Guggenheim fellowships Columbia graduates earned between 1925 and 2002 or that merited the election of 509 graduates to the American Academy of Arts and Letters and 254 graduates to the National Academy of Science. In the number of Nobel Prize winners, Columbia graduates are in a dead heat with Harvard's; in Guggenheim Prizes and American Academy memberships, Columbia is second only to Harvard; and in National Academy of Science membership, it trails Harvard, Berkeley, and Chicago.[5]

And then there are the contributions twentieth-century Columbians have made to the artistic and creative arts. They include novelists, poets, and essayists; composers, lyricists, and film makers; musicians, artists, actors, and dancers. Again, with the possible exception of Harvard, it is hard to imagine any other twentieth-century American university whose graduates and faculty have contributed more to the arts than Columbia's.[6]

A comparably weighty impact can be seen in the learned professions, in medicine, in law, in architecture, and in journalism. Banking and finance, the media, and industry all employ Columbians in substantial numbers. Approximately one hundred thousand Columbia alumni work in New York City alone, a fact brought home by the loss of forty-two alumni and students in the attack on the World Trade Center on September 11, 2001.[7]

Even as it sends its graduates out into the work world, Columbia has provided gainful employment to thousands of New Yorkers. A 1996 report on the economic impact of Columbia on New York City ranked it third among the city's employers and first in its two principal neighborhoods, Morningside and Washington Heights. It was also first among New York institutions in attracting federal research funds to the city.[8]

Consider also the direct assistance provided New Yorkers by the faculty, staff, and students of Columbia's professional schools, whether it be primary care treatment at the Allen Pavilion in northernmost Manhattan or dental care in Central Harlem, legal clinic services on Amsterdam Avenue, or entrepreneurial advice offered by the Business School. Yet another form of working with the community is the tutoring provided neighborhood kids by Columbia and Barnard undergraduates involved in Columbia's Double Discovery and Community Impact programs.[9]

Another benefit, less quantifiable but perhaps even more important, affects not only New York and the world, Columbia's favored venues, but also the American nation. It takes us back to an earlier theme of this book: the traditionally problematic Americanness of Columbia University. At the outset of its second quarter-millennium, Columbia provides Americans a working model of an old and conservative institution that has learned to operate successfully in the polyglot, multitudinous, and fast-paced circumstances of today's New York. In that these are almost certainly the circumstances that will increasingly characterize American life generally, Columbia finds itself in the historically novel yet instructive position of being what America is becoming.

Columbia has not always been—or wished to perceive itself as—an avatar of cultural diversity. The book chronicles many past efforts by official Columbia to keep it from becoming so. Yet I would argue that Columbia in the last part of the twentieth century has earned the sustained regard of Americans by its role in advancing the intellectual, social, and career mobility of many of those best able and most suited to provide leadership in a city and a world but also a nation where no one ethnic, racial, or religious group will constitute an effective majority.

That Columbia is meeting its inclusionary responsibilities can be inferred from recent changes in the demographic composition of its three principal estates. The board of trustees was, as recently as 1968, the preserve of twenty-four white males who, three decades earlier, could also be counted on to have been mainline Protestants, for the most part Episcopalians. In 2002 the board was so constituted (four women, three African Americans, two Asian Americans, ten or so Jews) as to place its white, male, American-born Protestants in a distinct minority.[10]

So, too, with Columbia's faculty. In 1968 its full-time female members accounted for less than 5 percent of the whole; in 2002 they account for 33 percent. In 1968 minority faculty constituted less than 2 percent of the faculty; in 2002, 20 percent of the faculty are minority members, with another 6 percent foreign nationals. Again, white, Protestant native-born males are a minority.[11]

In the student body, the effects of diversification have proceeded the furthest. While virtually all American academic institutions can point to some diversity on their campuses, the most cursory observation of Columbia today confirms that diversity has extended well beyond the point where the categories "male," "Protestant," and "white" obtain for a majority of Columbians. The Knickerbocker Columbian has become an endangered species.[12]

Columbia has not erased the edge that accrues to those who begin with wealth and social credentials or eliminated privileges that traditionally applied to white, male, and native-born Americans. But Columbia came to recognize over the course of the twentieth century that its responsibility extends to the intellectually talented who lack this edge and these privileges. It is as if Columbia has, more than two hundred years later, been persuaded of the truth uttered back in 1779, when King's College was finished and Columbia College had yet to begin, by the great nemesis of Knickerbocker Columbia, Thomas Jefferson: "Whence it becomes expedient for promoting the publick happiness that those persons, whom nature hath endowed with genius and virtue, should be rendered by liberal education worthy to receive, and able to guard the sacred rights and liberties of their fellow citizens, and that they should be called to that charge without regard to wealth, birth or other accidental condition or circumstance."[13]

But it will just not do to give the last word in a book about the history of Columbia University in the City of New York to a Virginian, graduate of William and Mary, founder of the University of Virginia, and avowed enemy of cities. Better the honor go to a Massachusetts-reared Yale graduate, Columbian by adoption and New Yorker at heart, Frederick A. P. Barnard. It was he, precisely a century after Jefferson, who held out the prospect of Columbia becoming America's first culturally inclusive intellectual meritocracy. And unlike Jefferson's vision, Barnard's extended to include women and racial minorities: "It is earnestly to be hoped," he implored his resistant trustees in 1880, "that no single and earnest seeker after knowledge, of whatever age, sex, or previous condition, shall be denied the privilege of coming here." At the start of the twenty-first century, that hope is in a fair way to being realized. "Stand, Columbia."[14]

Stand, Columbia! Alma Mater
Through the storms of Time abide
Stand, Columbia! Alma Mater
Through the storms of Time abide.

"Stand Columbia!"
Gilbert Oakley Ward, CC 1902 (1904)

Columbia College Trustees Minutes and Columbia University Trustees Minutes can be found in the Columbia University Archives–Columbiana Library. Unless otherwise indicated, all Oral History interviews are in the Oral History Research Office, Columbia University. Appendices can be found at http://www.columbia.edu/cu250

1. TORY PREAMBLE: THE SHORT HISTORY OF KING'S COLLEGE

1. William Livingston to William Livingston Jr., July 15, 1768, quoted in Milton M. Klein, *The American Whig: William Livingston of New York*, rev. ed. (New York: Garland, 1993), 341. On the 1702 dating of the letter, see John B. Pine, *King's College and the Early Days of Columbia College* (New York: University Printing Office, 1917), 2; Brander Matthews, ed., *A History of Columbia University, 1754–1904* (New York: Columbia University Press, 1904), 2–3.

2. Lewis Morris to John Chamberlayne, June 1704, in Eugene R. Sheridan, ed., *The Papers of Lewis Morris*, vol. 1, *1698–1730* (Newark: New Jersey Historical Society, 1991), 48. See Morgan Dix, *A History of the Parish of Trinity Church in the City of New York*, 4 vols. (New York: Putnam, 1898).

3. Ibid., 1:118, 135.

4. Ibid., 1:195.

5. See Sheridan, *The Papers of Lewis Morris*, 1:48. For quotations about Cornbury, see William Smith Jr., *The History of the Province of New-York* (1757), ed. Michael Kammen (Cambridge: Harvard University Press, 1972), 1:117–30. See Patricia U. Bonomi, *The Lord Cornbury Scandal: The Politics of Reputation in British America* (Chapel Hill: University of North Carolina Press, 1998), 6—9, 13–26, esp. 14.

6. Bonomi, *The Lord Cornbury Scandal*, 61–62, 79–82.

7. Lawrence C. Wroth, *The Voyages of Giovanni da Verrazzano, 1524–1528* (New Haven: Yale University Press, 1970), 137.

8. Edwin G. Burrows and Mike Wallace, *Gotham: A History of New York City to 1898* (New York: Oxford University Press, 19991), 18–19.

9. Ibid., 15–26.

10. Patricia U. Bonomi, *A Factious People: Politics and Society in Colonial New York* (New York: Columbia University Press, 1971), 1–2, 10–14.

11. Quoted in Edmund B. O'Callaghan, ed., *The Documentary History of the State of New York* (Albany, 1849–1851) 1:186.

12. Bonomi, *Factious People*, 56–57; Burrows and Wallace, *Gotham*, chap. 7.

13. Richard Hofstadter, *America at 1750: A Social Portrait* (New York: Knopf, 1971), 8–9.

14. Perry Miller and Thomas H. Johnson, eds., *The Puritans: A Sourcebook of Their Writings* (New York: Harper Torchbooks, 1963), 2:701. See Samuel Eliot Morison, *Three Centuries of Harvard* (Cambridge: Harvard University Press, 1936), chaps. 1 and 2.

15. Richard Warch, *School of the Prophets: Yale College, 1701–1740* (New Haven: Yale University Press, 1973), chaps. 1 and 2.

16. Beverly McAnear, "College Founding in the American Colonies, 1745–1775,"

Mississippi Valley Historical Review 42 (January 1955): 24. See Stephen Nissenbaum, ed., *The Great Awakening at Yale College* (Belmont, Calif.: Wadsworth, 1972); McAnear, "College Founding in the American Colonies," 24–44.

17. George E. Thomas and David B. Brownlee, *Building America's First University: An Historical and Architectural Guide to the University of Pennsylvania* (Philadelphia: University of Pennsylvania Press, 2000).

18. David C. Humphrey, *From King's College to Columbia, 1746–1800* (New York: Columbia University Press, 1976), 3–4.

19. Ibid., 5–17.

20. The principal biographical source on William Livingston is Klein, *The American Whig*, a revised edition of Klein's 1954 Columbia doctoral dissertation on Livingston. See also Dorothy R. Dillon, *The New York Triumvirate* (1949; reprint, New York: AMS, 1968).

21. Thomas Jones, *History of New York During the Revolutionary War, and of the Leading Events in the Other Colonies at That Period* (1879), ed. Milton Klein (New York: New York Times, 1968), 1:3.

22. Klein, *The American Whig*, chap. 3.

23. Ibid., 221–31.

24. Ibid., 88, 90.

25. William Livingston to New York Assembly, November 1, 1754, quoted in Herbert Schneider and Carol Schneider, *Samuel Johnson, President of King's College: His Career and Writings* (New York: Columbia University Press, 1929), 4:185–90, stating the reasons for his dissent as a Lottery Commission trustee, wherein he provided a timeline of events. For the members of the Lottery Commission, see appendix A, http://www.columbia.edu/cu25o

26. Columbia's historians have consistently favored Morris, as in John B. Pine, "King's College, Now Columbia University," *Half Moon Series* 2 (1896): 31–59.

27. The King's College controversy as a rehearsal for the subsequent revolutionary debates is discussed in Milton M. Klein, ed., *The Independent Reflector; or, Weekly Essays on Sundry Important Subjects More Particularly Adapted to the Province of New York* (Cambridge: Harvard University Press, 1963); and Donald F. M. Gerardi, "The King's College Controversy, 1753–56, and the Ideological Roots of Toryism in New York," *Perspectives in American History* 11 (1977–78): 145–96.

28. William Smith, *Some Thoughts on Education: With Reasons for Erecting a College in This Province* (New York, 1752); Herbert Schneider and Carol Schneider, *Samuel Johnson, President of King's College: His Career and Writings* (New York: Columbia University Press, 1929), 4:4–5.

29. Humphrey, *From King's College to Columbia*, 19.

30. Schneider and Schneider, *Samuel Johnson*, 1:337. On Samuel Johnson, see Joseph J. Ellis, *The New England Mind in Transition: Samuel Johnson of Connecticut, 1696–1772* (New Haven: Yale University Press, 1973); Norman S. Fiering, "President Samuel Johnson and the Circle of Knowledge," *William and Mary Quarterly* 28 (April 1971): 199–236.

31. Samuel Johnson to Bishop Sherlock, October 5, 1742, quoted in Schneider and Schneider, *Samuel Johnson*, 3:232.

32. Richard Warch, *School of the Prophets*, chap. 4.; Ellis, *New England Mind*.

33. William Samuel Johnson to Samuel Johnson, May 3, 1754, quoted in Schneider and Schneider, *Samuel Johnson*, 4:10. See ibid., 4:10–13, for the May 27, 1754, response.

34. On the effort to secure an American bishop, see Carl Bridenbaugh, *Mitre and Sceptre: Transatlantic Faiths, Ideas, Personalities, and Politics, 1689–1775* (New York: Oxford University Press, 1962). On Johnson's direct interest, see Bishop Sherlock to Samuel Johnson, September 19, 1750, quoted in Schneider and Schneider, *Samuel Johnson*, 3:237. On the loss of young men on their way to ordination in England, see Samuel Johnson to Dr. Bearcroft, December 21, 1757, quoted in Schneider and Schneider, *Samuel Johnson*, 4:42–45.

35. Samuel Johnson, draft of statement to the society, fall 1750, quoted in Schneider and Schneider, *Samuel Johnson*, 3:242; see 241–43.

36. On New York City's claims to be the seat of the Anglican see, see Samuel Johnson to the archbishop of Canterbury, September 29, 1741, quoted in Schneider and Schneider, *Samuel Johnson*, 3:229.

37. On Johnson's being mentioned as America's first bishop, see William Smith, "Some Impartial Thoughts Concerning the Settlement of Bishops in America," July 13, 1753, in Schneider and Schneider, *Samuel Johnson*, 3:248–53.

38. Quoted in Humphrey, *From King's College to Columbia*, 19. The principal source here is Klein, *The Independent Reflector*. For a contemporary account, written in 1783 by a New York Loyalist and émigré, see Thomas Jones, *History of New York During the Revolutionary War* (New York, 1879), 1:chap. 1.

39. William Livingston to Noah Welles, February 1753, quoted in Klein, *Independent Reflector*, 36–37.

40. Quoted in Klein, *The Independent Reflector*, 172, 176.

41. William Livingston, "A Continuation of the Same Subject," *The Independent Reflector*, no. 18 (March 29, 1753), quoted in Klein, *The Independent Reflector*, 178, 183.

42. Ibid.

43. William Livingston, "The Same Subject Continued," *The Independent Reflector*, no. 19 (April 1, 1753): 184–90; idem, "A Farther Prosecution of the Same Subject," no. 20 (April 12, 1753): 192, 194.

44. William Livingston, "Remarks on the College Continued," *The Independent Reflector*, no. 21 (April 19, 1753): 203.

45. William Livingston, "The Same Subject Continued and Concluded in an Address to the Inhabitants of This Province," *The Independent Reflector*, no. 22 (April 26, 1753): 209–10, 214.

46. Samuel Johnson to the archbishop of Canterbury, June 25, 1753, quoted in Schneider and Schneider, *Samuel Johnson*, 4:4.

47. William Smith, *A General Idea of the College of Mirana; with a Sketch of the Method of Teaching Science and Religion, in the Several Classes; and Some Account of Its Rise, Establishment and Buildings* (New York, 1753), 14; Johnson to the archbishop of Canterbury, 4:4. See Samuel Johnson to William Samuel Johnson, May 27, 1754, quoted in ibid., 4:12. For biography of William Smith, see Albert F. Gergenheimer, *William Smith, Educator and Churchman, 1727–1803* (Philadelphia: University of Pennsylvania Press, 1943).

48. Quoted in Klein, *The Independent Reflector*, 308, 279; see 40–44.

49. William Livingston to Samuel Johnson, January 7, 1754, quoted in Schneider and Schneider, *Samuel Johnson*, 4:7. See Humphrey, *From King's College to Columbia*, 47–48.

50. Nissenbaum, *The Great Awakening at Yale College*, 21, 199.

51. On Johnson's efforts to dissuade Whittelsey, see Samuel Johnson to William Samuel Johnson, May 27, 1754, 4:12.

52. Quoted in Klein, *The American Whig*, 285. See Dix, *History of Trinity Church*, 1:271.

53. William Livingston, "Twenty Unanswerable Questions," May 16, 1754, in Schneider and Schneider, *Samuel Johnson*, 4:185–89; Benjamin Nicoll, *A Brief Vindication of the Proceedings of the Trustees Relatings to the College* (New York: H. Gaine, 1754), reprinted in Schneider and Schneider, *Samuel Johnson*, 4:191–207.

54. Johnson advertisement, reproduced in Schneider and Schneider, *Samuel Johnson*, 4:222–24.

55. Ibid.

56. On "Billy" Johnson, see Humphrey, *From King's College to Columbia*, 116, 118.

57. William Livingston to Chauncey Whittelsey, August 22, 1754, quoted in Schneider and Schneider, *Samuel Johnson*, 4:21–23.

58. On charter conferral, see Humphrey, *From King's College to Columbia*, 52.

59. Theodore Sedgwick, *Memoir of William Livingston* (New York: J. and J. Harper, 1833), 111.

60. Quoted in Klein, *The American Whig*, 340, 341.

61. For the 1754 charter, see *Early Minutes of the Columbia College Trustees, 1755–1770* (New York: Columbia University Press, 1932).

62. See appendix A.

63. On Anglican efforts to include Dutch Reformed, Humphrey, *From King's College to Columbia*, 56.

64. Ibid., 56–58; Henry Barclay to William Smith, February 12, 1755, quoted in Schneider and Schneider, *Samuel Johnson*, 4:83.

65. Appendix A; attendance tallies in "General Biographical Data," in David C. Humphrey Collection, Rare Book and Manuscript Library, Columbia University.

66. On Samuel Auchmuty, see Dix, *History of Trinity Church*, 1:246, 307.

67. Samuel Auchmuty to Dr. Burton, SPGFP secretary, October 17, 1767, copy in Humphrey folder on Samuel Auchmuty, Rare Book and Manuscript Library.

68. On Lispenard and the financial management of King's College, see Humphrey, *From King's College*, 137.

69. Samuel Johnson to East Apthorpe, December 1, 1759, in Schneider and Schneiders, *Samuel Johnson*, 4:54–57.

70. On Cooper's selection, see Humphrey, *From King's College to Columbia*, 122–24.

71. On Cooper, see A. L. Jones, "Myles Cooper, Second President of Columbia," *Columbia University Quarterly* 1 (September 1898): 347–57; Clarence Hayden Vance, "Myles Cooper," *Columbia University Quarterly* 22 (September 1930): 261–86.

72. Jones, *History of New York*, 1:60; Samuel Auchmuty to Samuel Johnson, March 27, 1771, Connecticut Historical Society, Hartford.

73. Humphrey, *From King's College to Columbia*, 127.

74. On the "American University," see Humphrey, *From King's College to Columbia*, 140–51; King's College Governors to King George III, August 4, 1774, containing "Draft of Charter for the American University in the Province of New York," Columbia University Archives–Columbiana Library.

75. *Gentleman's Magazine*, August 15, 1785, reprinted in Jones, *History of New York*, 1:60–61.

76. On Samuel Johnson and science, see Fiering, "President Samuel Johnson," 199–236; Theodore Hornberger, *Scientific Thought in the American Colleges, 1638–1800* (University of Texas Press, 1945).

77. On Johnson as a teacher, see Humphrey, *From King's College to Columbia*, 116–17; Fiering, "President Samuel Johnson," 199–236.

78. On Daniel Treadwell, see Clifford Shipton, ed., *Sibley's Harvard Graduates*, vol. 13, *1751–1755* (Boston: Massachusetts Historical Society, 1965), 495–97.

79. Samuel Johnson to William Samuel Johnson, October 12, 1761, Robert Harpur folder, Columbia University Archives–Columbiana Library. See *Early Minutes of the Trustees*, May 13, 1766. On Robert Harpur, see Paul D. Evans, "Harpur, Robert, 1731–1825," in *Dictionary of American Biography*, 20 vols. (New York: Scribner's, 1928–36), 8:293–94.

80. Humphrey, *From King's College to Columbia*, 127; see 200–202.

81. Morris Saffron, *Samuel Clossy, M.D. (1724–1786), Professor of Anatomy at King's College* (New York: Hafner, 1967). On Cooper's indifference to science, see Humphrey, *From King's College to Columbia*, 128.

82. Samuel Bard was the first student to return to King's College as a professor, but Bard had not graduated from King's before going on to Edinburgh for his medical training. On John Vardill, see Dix, *History of Trinity Church*, 1:362. On Benjamin Moore, see Milton Halsey Thomas, "Moore, Benjamin, 1748–1816," in *Dictionary of American Biography*, 13:115–16; Dix, *History of Trinity Church*, 1:362–64.

83. Milton Halsey Thomas, "The King's College Building, with Some Notes on Its Later Tenants," *New-York Historical Society Quarterly* 39 (January 1955): 23–60; Humphrey, *From King's College to Columbia*, 111–15.

84. Andrew Burnaby, *Travels through the Middle Settlements in North America, 1759–1760* (London, 1798), 112.

85. Patrick McRobert, *Tour Through Part of the North Provinces of America in 1774 and 1775* (Edinburgh: 1776), reprinted in *Pennsylvania Magazine of History and Biography* 59 (April 1935): 59: 139–40. On Cooper's enclosure efforts, see Humphrey, *From King's College to Columbia*, 130.

86. Milton Halsey Thomas, ed., "The Black Book of King's College," *Columbia University Quarterly* 23 (March 1931): 1–18; *Early Minutes of the Trustees*, March 1, 1763.

87. Paul H. Mattingly, "The Political Culture of America's Antebellum Colleges," *History of Higher Education Annual* 17 (1997): 81.

88. On King's College enrollments and graduation statistics, see appendix B.

89. On enrollments at the Colonial Nine, see McAnear, "College Founding"; see also appendix B.

90. For Oliver De Lancey's query about "so many tutors and so few scholars," see Samuel Johnson to William Samuel Johnson, February 1, 1762, in Schneider and Schneider, *Samuel Johnson*, 4:78.

91. John Adams, entry for August 25, 1774, in *Diary and Autobiography*, ed. Lyman Butterfield (Cambridge: Harvard University Press, 1962), 2:110.

92. For Harvard enrollments and graduates in 1770s, see Beverly McAnear, "The

Selection of an Alma Mater by Pre-Revolutionary Students," *Pennsylvania Magazine of History and Biography* 73 (1949): 429–40.

93. On regional competition, see McAnear, "College Founding," 24–44; Edward Potts Cheyney, *History of the University of Pennsylvania, 1740–1940* (University of Pennsylvania Press, 1940); Mark A. Noll, *Princeton and the Republic, 1768–1822* (Princeton University Press, 1989); Richard P. McCormick, *Rutgers: A Bicentennial History* (New Brunswick, N.J.: Rutgers University Press, 1966).

94. On King's College dropouts, see "Matriculation Book," in Schneider and Schneider, *Samuel Johnson,* 4:243–61.

95. On Washington's stepson at King's College, see H. B. Howe, "Colonel George Washington and King's College," *Columbia University Quarterly* 24 (June 1932): 137–57.

96. On the social characteristics of King's College students, see appendix A..

97. On the endogamous character of the New York Anglican community, see Jean Paul Jordan, "The Anglican Establishment in Colonial New York, 1693–1783" (Ph.D. diss., Columbia University, 1971); Thomas, "Black Book of Misdemeanors," passim.

98. On the DePeyster family linkages, see Jordan, "Anglican Establishment," 16–18.

99. On the comparative youthfulness of King's College matriculants, see McAnear, "College Founding," 33.

100. On Antill's rejected proposal for scholarships, see Humphrey, *From King's College,* 87–89.

101. Beverly McAnear, "The Raising of Funds by the Colonial Colleges," *Mississippi Valley Historical Review* 38 (March 1952): 591–612.

102. Humphrey, *From King's College to Columbia,* 115.

103. On King's College fund-raising, see Humphrey, *From King's College to Columbia,* 121–23, 131–33; see also Columbia University, *Gifts and Endowments, 1754–1898* (New York: Columbia University Press, 1898).

104. On these differences, see Stanley Elkins and Eric L. McKitrick, *The Age of Federalism: The Early American Republic, 1788–1800* (New York: Oxford University Press, 1993), 21–25.

105. John Witherspoon, *Address to the Inhabitants of Jamaica, and the Other West-India Islands* (Philadelphia, 1772), 295.

106. [John Vardill], *Candid Remarks on Dr. Witherspoon's Address to the Inhabitants of Jamaica . . . ,* November 24, 1772 (Philadelphia, 1772), 347.

107. Ibid., 21, 39, 23–24, 42, 27.

108. Ibid., 57, 57–58; William Smith Jr., quoted in Humphrey, *From King's College to Columbia College,* 81.

109. On governors' occupations, see appendix A.

110. On King's College students' subsequent occupations, see appendix A.

111. Quoted in Richard B. Morris, *John Jay: The Making of a Revolutionary* (New York: Harper and Row, 1975), 39. On John Jay's occupational plans, see ibid., 43–47.

112. On the 1756 restrictions on entry into the New York bar, see Paul M. Hamlin, *Legal Education in Colonial New York* (New York: New York University Press, 1939); Milton M. Klein, "The Rise of the New York Bar: The Legal Career of William Livingston," *William and Mary Quarterly* 15 (July 1958): 334–58.

113. On "The Moot," see Sedgwick, *Memoir of William Livingston,* 152; on the 1764 com-

mencement and Cooper's gloss on it, see Milton Halsey Thomas, "King's College Commencements in the Newspapers," *Columbia University Quarterly* 22 (June 1930): 226–47.

114. For Jay and the almost-duel over the Dancing Assembly, Morris, *John Jay*, 116–18.

115. On efforts to limit access to the medical profession, see Bryon Stookey, *A History of Colonial Medical Education in the Province of New York, with Its Subsequent Development, 1767–1830* (Springfield, Ill.: Charles C. Thomas, 1962); Richard H. Shryock, *Medicine and Society in America, 1660–1860* (New York: New York University Press, 1960).

116. Humphrey, *From King's College to Columbia*, 247. On James Jay and the medical faculty, see ibid., 131–34.

117. Ibid., 247.

118. On the medical degrees available from King's College, see Humphrey, *From King's College to Columbia*, chap. 13; see also Frank Monaghan, "Samuel Kissam and John Jay," *Columbia University Quarterly* 25 (June 1933): 127–33.

119. On King's College medical graduates, see *Catalogue of the Governors, Trustees, and Officers, and the Alumni and Other Graduates of Columbia College* (New York: Columbia College, 1876), 99.

120. On Cooper's medical preferences, see Jones, *History of New York*, 1:60.

121. Humphrey, *From King's College to Columbia*, 258–59.

122. On the Medical School's latent inclusiveness, see ibid., 252. On Isaac Abrahams, see Joseph Rosenbloom, ed., *Biographical Dictionary of Early American Jews* (Lexington: University of Kentucky Press, 1960), 3.

123. Quoted in Jones, *History of New York*, 1:3. See Janice Potter, *The Liberty We Seek: Loyalist Ideology in Colonial New York and Massachusetts* (Cambridge: Harvard University Press, 1983). On the governors' revolutionary politics, see appendix A.

124. For Van Amringe on King's College's involvement in the Revolution, see his *History of Columbia University, 1754–1904; Published in Commemoration of the One Hundred and Fiftieth Anniversary of the Founding of King's College* (New York: Columbia University Press, 1904), 52–53. For Keppel's views, see Frederick P. Keppel, *Columbia* (New York: Oxford University Press, 1914), 2. John Adams on Witherspoon's patriotism is quoted in Richard A. Harrison, *Princetonians, 1769–1775: A Biographical Dictionary* (Princeton University Press, 1980), xxx–xxxi.

125. On the political loyalties of King's College students, see appendix B.

126. On the Crugers and their fellow merchants, see Virginia D. Harrington, *The New York Merchant on the Eve of the Revolution* (New York: Columbia University Press, 1935), 13, 34, 326. For a revisionist account of the second tier of New York merchants, see Cathy Matson, *Merchants and Empire: Trading in Colonial New York* (Baltimore: Johns Hopkins University Press, 1998). On New York during the Revolution, see Joseph S. Tiedemann, *Reluctant Revolutionaries: New York City and the Road to Independence* (Ithaca, N.Y.: Cornell University Press, 1997).

127. On the Philipses, see Matson, *Merchants and Empire*, 20, 57–5, 60. On the Kempes, see Ralph Ketchum, *Divided Loyalties: How the American Revolution Came to New York* (New York: Henry Holt, 2002), 306–7.

128. On the Barclays, see R. Burnham Moffat, *The Barclays of New York* (New York: R. G. Cooke, 1904). On the Auchmutys, see Henry Morse Stephens, "Auchmuty, Sir Samuel, 1736–1822," in *Dictionary of National Biography* (London: Oxford University Press, 1917),

1:718–20. On Vardill, see Ketchum, *Divided Loyalties, 307*; Milton Halsey Thomas, "Vardill, John, 1749–1811," in *Dictionary of American Biography*, 19:222–23.

129. John Adams to Thomas Jefferson, July 13, 1813, in Lester J. Cappon, ed., *The Adams-Jefferson Letters* (New York: Simon and Schuster, 1959), 354; Myles Cooper, *Gentleman's Magazine* 46 (1776): 326. The phrase "the right sort" is from Cooper's account of his departure, cited in James Thomas Flexner, *The Young Hamilton: A Biography* (Boston: Little, Brown, 1978), 78. On Hamilton's politics while at King's College, see ibid., chap. 7.

130. Carl Becker, "John Jay and Peter Van Schaack," in *Everyman His Own Historian* (New York: F. S. Crofts, 1935), 286. On John Jay and Peter Van Schaack, see ibid., 284–98; see also Henry C. Van Schaack, ed., *Life of Peter Van Schaack* (New York: Appleton, 1842).

131. Becker, "John Jay and Peter Van Schaack," 288. On Livingston, see George Dangerfield, *Chancellor Robert Livingston of New York, 1746–1813* (New York: Harcourt, Brace, 1968). On Morris, see Mary-Jo Kline, "Gouverneur Morris and the New Nation, 1775–1788" (Ph.D. diss., Columbia University, 1970).

132. Quoted in Becker, "John Jay and Peter Van Schaack," 285.

2. FLIRTING WITH REPUBLICANISM

1. Willis Rudy, *The Campus and a Nation in Crisis* (Madison, N.J.: Fairleigh Dickinson University Press), 18–20, 26–46.

2. Columbia College Trustees Minutes, May 16 1775, in *Early Minutes of the Columbia College Trustees, 1755–1770* (New York: Columbia University Press, 1932), copy in Columbia University Archives–Columbiana Library. See David C. Humphrey, *From King's College to Columbia, 1746–1800* (New York: Columbia University Press, 1976), 269–71.

3. Edwin G. Burrows and Mike Wallace, *Gotham: A History of New York City to 1898* (New York: Oxford University Press, 1999), 233–61; Morgan Dix, *A History of the Parish of Trinity Church in the City of New York*, 4 vols. (New York: Putnam's, 1898), 1:390–92.

4. Columbia College Trustees Minutes, March 13, 1777, in *Early Minutes of the Columbia College Trustees*.

5. Edward P. Alexander, *A Revolutionary Conservative: James Duane of New York* (New York: Columbia University Press, 1938), 176. See also Reginald V. Harris, *Charles Inglis: Missionary, Loyalist, Bishop* (Toronto: University of Toronto Press, 1937).

6. Harris, *Inglis*, 109–10. On King's College, Nova Scotia, see ibid., 109–10.

7. Sidney Sherwood, *The University of the State of New York* (Washington, D.C.: U.S. Government Printing Office, 1900), 49. See Edward P. Alexander, *A Revolutionary Conservative: James Duane of New York* (New York: Columbia University Press, 1938).

8. Humphrey, *From King's College to Columbia*, chap. 15.

9. Sherwood, *University of the State of New York*, 49. See Francis B. Hough, *Historical and Statistical Record of the University of the State of New York, 1784–1884* (Albany: Weed, Parsons, 1885).

10. Sherwood, *University of the State of New York*, 49.

11. On "Whig Episcopalians," see Dix, *History of Trinity Church*, 2:chap. 1.

12. Columbia College Trustees Minutes, May 5, 1784.

13. Columbia College Trustees Minutes, November 26, 1784. On Gershon Seixas, see

Herbert Solow, "Seixas, Gershon, 1746–1816," in *Dictionary of American Biography*, 20 vols. (New York: Scribner's, 1928–36), 16:564–65.

14. "Memorial of the Regents of the University of New York [1784]," in Columbia College Papers, 1784–1809, Rare Book and Manuscript Library; Benjamin Franklin to Regents, August 9, 1784, Columbia College Papers.

15. On Columbia faculty, see appendix A.

16. Evan Cornog, *The Birth of Empire: DeWitt Clinton and the American Experience, 1769–1828* (New York: Oxford University Press, 1998). The title translates as "On the utility and necessity of a liberal arts education."

17. Humphrey, *From King's College to Columbia*, 284. For enrollments and graduation statistics, see appendix B; Elizabeth McCaughey [Betsy Ross], *From Loyalist to Founding Father: The Political Odyssey of William Samuel Johnson* (New York: Columbia University Press, 1980), 260–62.

18. On 1787 charter, see Humphrey, *From King's College to Columbia*, 277–78.

19. For the change in trustee arrangements, see chap. /.

20. On New York Federalism, see Stanley Elkins and Eric McKitrick, *The Age of Federalism: The Early American Republic, 1788–1800* (New York: Oxford University Press, 1993), chap. 7.

21. On the roles of Columbians at the Philadelphia Convention, see McCaughey, *From Loyalist to Founding Father*, chaps. 13 and 14.

22. On Hamilton and *The Federalist Papers*, see Elkins and McKitrick, *Age of Federalism*, 22–23.

23. McCaughey, *Loyalist to Founding Father*, chap. 14; Robert Ernst, *Rufus King: American Federalist* (Chapel Hill: University of North Carolina Press, 1968), chap. 6.

24. On William Samuel Johnson as second lay president of an American college, see Frederick Rudolph, *The American College and University: A History* (1962), intro. John R. Thelin (Athens: University of Georgia Press, 1990), 170. The first was Dartmouth's second president, John Wheelock (1779–1816).

25. Alexander Hamilton to James A. Bayard, August 6, 1800, reprinted in Harold C. Syrett, *The Papers of Alexander Hamilton* (New York: Columbia University Press, 1977), 25:56. For Johnson's conciliatory ways, see McCaughey, *From Loyalist to Founding Father*, passim.

26. Sherwood, *University of the State of New York*, 142–43.

27. On early Columbia College trustees, see appendix A.

28. On Johnson's indifferent presidency, McCaughey, *From Loyalist to Founding Father*, 261–62. For a student perspective on Columbia College in the 1790s, see Daniel D. Tompkins, *A Columbia College Student in the Eighteenth Century* (New York: Columbia University Press, 1940).

29. On Johnson's departure, see McCaughey, *From Loyalist to Founding Father*, 265–73.

30. On the size and composition of the Republican Columbia faculty, see appendix A.

31. Columbia College Trustees Minutes, August 8, 1801. On faculty turnover, see appendix A.

32. On early Columbia College faculty by terms of service, see appendix A.

33. On the social origins of faculty, see appendix A.

34. On Tétard, see Julia Post Mitchell, "Jean Pierre Tétard, 1721–1787," *Columbia University Quarterly* 12 (June 1910): 286–89. On Gross, see John W. Francis, *Old New York; or, Reminiscences of the Past Sixty Years* (New York: Charles Roe, 1858), 47. On Kunze, see George Henry Genemer, "Kunze, John Christopher, 1744–1807," in *Dictionary of American Biography*, 20:26–27. On curricular interests parallel elsewhere, see Roger L. Geiger, "New Themes in the History of Nineteenth-Century Colleges," in Roger L. Geiger, ed., *The American College in the Nineteenth Century* (Nashville: Vanderbilt University Press, 2000), 1–36.

35. Courtney R. Hall, *A Scientist in the Early Republic: Samuel L. Mitchill, 1764–1831* (New York: Columbia University Press, 1934). See also John W. Francis, *Old New York: Reminiscences of the Past Sixty Years* (New York: Charles Roe, 1858), 87–96.

36. Columbia College Trustees Minutes, February 29, 1798. See Hall, *A Scientist in the Early Republic*, 61–62.

37. On Robert Adrain, see David Eugene Smith, "Adrain, Robert, 1775–1843," in *Dictionary of American Biography*, 1:109–10.

38. Ibid., 110. See Columbia University Trustees Minutes, November 7, 1825.

39. Quoted in Benjamin Haight (class of 1828), Robert Adrain folder, Columbia University Archives–Columbiana Library; T. W. Ogden (class of 1829), Adrain folder; Columbia College Trustees Minutes, August 4, 1823.

40. For the Columbia Medical School, see Humphrey, *From King's College to Columbia*, chaps. 13 and 14. See also Francis, *Old New York*, 102–3, 316–24.

41. On early-nineteenth-century faculty, see Francis, *Old New York*, 84–107.

42. John C. Dalton, M.D., *History of the College of Physicians and Surgeons in the City of New York; Medical Department of Columbia College* (New York: Columbia College, 1888), chap. 1.

43. Ibid., p. 31.

44. Richard Shryock, *Medicine and Society in America, 1660–1860* (New York: New York University Press, 1960).

45. For a list of early Columbia medical graduates, see *General Catalogue: Columbia University, 1754–1916* (New York: Columbia University Press, 1916), 309–10.

46. Richard H. Shryock, *Medical Licensing in America, 1650–1965* (Baltimore: Johns Hopkins University Press, 1967).

47. John T. Horton, *James Kent: A Study in Conservatism, 1763–1847* (1939; reprint, New York: Da Capo, 1969).

48. On the open-ended character of legal profession, see Richard Hofstadter, *Anti-Intellectualism in American Life* (New York: Vintage, 1963).

49. Alexander Hamilton to James A. Bayard, August 6, 1800, reprinted in Harold C. Syrett, *The Papers of Alexander Hamilton* (New York: Columbia University Press, 1977), 25:56. On Charles Henry Wharton, see Harris E. Starr, "Wharton, Charles Henry, 1748–1833," in *Dictionary of American Biography*, 20:26–27.

50. Starr, "Wharton," 20:27.

51. On Benjamin Moore's selection, see Clement Clark Moore, *The Early History of Columbia College* (1825; reprint, New York: Columbia University Press, 1940), 19.

52. On Hobart and Mason, see John McVickar, *The Early Years of Bishop John Henry Hobart* (New York, 1836).

53. Dix, *History of Trinity Church*, 2:238.

54. [Rufus King], "Report of Committee Charged with an Inquiry into the State of Columbia College (1809)," College Papers, Rare Books and Manuscript Library, Columbia University. See Ernst, *Rufus King*, 296–99.

55. On William Harris, see William B. Sprague, *Annals of the American Pulpit* (New York: Arno, 1969), 5:383–88. On the provost arrangement, see Brander Matthews, ed., *A History of Columbia University, 1754–1904* (New York: Columbia University Press, 1904), 97–98.

56. Columbia College Trustees Minutes, August 14, 1811; *The Trial of Gulian C. Verplanck, Hugh Maxwell, and Others, for a Riot in Trinity Church at the Commencement of Columbia College, in August 1811* (New York, 1821), copy in New-York Historical Society, 7, 10–11.

57. *The Trial of Gulian C. Verplanck*, 19, 13. On the "Riotous Commencement," see Cornog, *The Birth of Empire*, 92–94; *The Trial of Gulian C. Verplanck*; Robert July, *The Essential New Yorker: Gulian Crommelin Verplanck* (Durham, N.C.: Duke University Press, 1951). See also Class of 1811 to Trustees, August 8, 1811, Columbia College Papers, Rare Book and Manuscript Library. On campus violence elsewhere, see Steven J. Novak, *The Rights of Youth: American Colleges and Student Revolt, 1798–1815* (Cambridge: Harvard University Press, 1977).

58. Novak, *Rites of Youth*, chaps. 6 and 7.

59. On the redenomination of American higher education in the early nineteenth century, see Colin Burke, *American Collegiate Populations: A Test of the Traditional View* (New York: New York University Press, 1982); David B. Potts, "American Colleges in the Nineteenth Century: From Localism to Denominationalism," *History of Education Quarterly* 11 (winter 1971): 363–80.

60. "Report on the Senior Class," August 3, 1811; "Report on the Senior Class, July 18, 1814," Columbia College Papers, Rare Book and Manuscript Library.

61. On sources of income for early Columbia College, see appendix C; on the Columbia College neighborhood, see Milton Halsey Thomas, "The King's College Building, with Some Notes on Its Later Tenants," *New-York Historical Society Quarterly* 39 (January 1955): 23–60.

62. On Columbia College tuition shifts, see Columbia College Trustees Minutes, August 5, 1811, August 4, 1815.

63. On faculty receiving per capitum payments, see [King], "Inquiry into the State of the College (1809)."

64. Columbia College Trustees Minutes, July 24, 1843. On faculty complaints about their pay, see Kemp and Wilson folders, Columbia University Archives–Columbiana Library.

65. Columbia College Trustees Minutes, July 24, 1843.

66. *Gifts and Endowments—With the Names of Benefactors, 1754–1898* (New York: Columbia University, 1898).

67. On New York state support in the 1790s, see Franklin B. Hough, *Historical and Statistical Record of the University of the State of New York, 1784–1884* (Albany, 1884).

68. Codman Hislop, *Eliphalet Nott* (Middletown, Conn.: Wesleyan University Press, 1971), 154. On the state's cutting Union in on promised profits in 1802, see ibid., 144.

69. Ibid., 153–65.

70. Sherwood, *History of SUNY*, 209.

71. Petition to New York legislature, included in Columbia College Trustees Minutes, December 7, 1818. On the Hosack Garden grant, see John Henry Van Amringe, *History of Columbia University, 1754–1904; Published in Commemoration of the One Hundred and Fiftieth Anniversary of the Founding of King's College* (New York: Columbia University Press, 1904), 316. Some state money went to support Columbia Grammar School in 1830s; see Columbia College Trustees Minutes, October 7, 1839.

72. On Trinity Church's postwar revival, Dix, *History of Trinity Church*, 2:chap. 12.

73. Richard Varick to Trustees, March 4, 1816, Columbia College Papers, 1784–29, Rare Book and Manuscript Library. See Columbia College Trustees Minutes, May 6, 1816.

74. On William Duer, see Ernest H. Wright, "Duer, William Alexander, 1780–1858," in *Dictionary of American Biography*, 5:488; William A. Duer, "William Alexander Duer," *Columbia University Quarterly* 3 (June 1901), 221–29. See appendix A.

75. On family ties of the trustees, see appendix A. On re-Episcopalianization, see Thomas Bender, *New York Intellect: A History of Intellectual Life in New York City, from 1750 to the Beginnings of Our Own Time* (New York: Knopf, 1987), 91–92.

76. Columbia College Trustees Minutes, March 3 and 27, 1817. On Daniel Tompkins, see Ray W. Irwin, *Daniel D. Tompkins: Governor of New York and Vice President of the United States* (New York: New-York Historical Society, 1968).

77. Columbia College Trustees Minutes, March 24, 1818. On the impact of the removal of state capital from New York City, see Elkins and McKitrick, *Age of Federalism*, 186–93.

78. On New York City as a Federalist stronghold in the 1790s, see ibid., 732–33.

79. On Jay and Hamilton in the 1790s, see ibid., passim.

80. Ibid., 747. On Jay's refusal in 1800 to play politics with New York's electoral votes, see ibid., 734–36. On Hamilton's demise, see ibid., 745.

81. Thomas Jefferson, *Notes on the State of Virginia* [1781–83] (New York: Harper Torchbooks, 1964), query 19, 158, quoted in Morton White and Lucia White, *The Intellectual Versus the City: From Thomas Jefferson to Frank Lloyd Wright* (New York: Oxford University Press, 1962), 19; [John Vardill], *Candid Remarks on Dr. Witherspoon's Address to the Inhabitants of Jamaica . . .* , November 24, 1772 (Philadelphia, 1772), 354.

82. On Jefferson's desire to remove the capital from cities, see Elkins and McKitrick, *Age of Federalism*, 169–94.

83. Robert A. McCaughey, *Josiah Quincy: The Last Federalist, 1772–1864* (Cambridge: Harvard University Press, 1974), 48; Alexander Hamilton, "Federalist No. 27," *The Federalist Papers* (New York: New American Library, 1961), 174–77. On Quincy, see McCaughey, *Josiah Quincy*, 45–50.

84. Ann Douglas, *Terrible Honesty: Mongrel Manhattan in the 1920s* (New York: Farrar, Straus, 1995), 9–10.

3. KNICKERBOCKER DAYS: THE LIMITS OF ACADEMIC REFORM

1. Richard Hofstadter and Walter Metzger, *The Rise of Academic Freedom in the United States* (New York: Columbia University Press, 1955), 209; see 209–38, esp. 204 and 275.

2. Colin Burke, *American Collegiate Populations: A Test of the Traditional View* (New York: New York University Press, 1982); Hofstadter and Metzger, *The Rise of Academic Freedom*, 274. See Roger L. Geiger, introduction to Richard Hofstadter, *Academic Freedom in the Age of the College* (New Brunswick, N.J.: Transaction, 1996), xv–xxi.

3. On revising the revisionists, see Geiger, introduction.

4. Hofstadter and Metzger, *The Rise of Academic Freedom*, 209. On Columbia College enrollments, see appendix B.

5. On Columbia College students by ethnic and religious backgrounds, see appendix A.

6. On the novelty of a Jewish student at Columbia in the 1830s, see Allen Nevins and Milton Halsey Thomas, eds, *The Diary of George Templeton Strong* (New York: Macmillan, 1952), March 10, 1838, 1:82–83. Use has been made here of both the four-volume published version, indicated hereinafter by "GTS, *Diary*," volume number, and page; and the longer manuscript version at the New-York Historical Society, indicated by "GTS, Diary" and date of entry.

7. On Oberlin, see Robert S. Fletcher, *A History of Oberlin College from Its Foundation through the Civil War* (Oberlin, Ohio: Oberlin College, 1943).

8. On the debate over the declining demand for higher education in Jacksonian America, see Geiger, introduction.

9. See Charles Grandison Finney, *Lectures on Revivals of Religion*, ed. William G. McLoughlin (Cambridge: Harvard University Press, 1960).

10. Burke, *American Collegiate Populations*, chap. 2.

11. Hofstadter's principal source was a book by Teachers College historian Donald Tewksbury, *The Founding of American Colleges and Universities Before the Civil War* (New York: Teachers College Press, 1932).

12. On Union's aggressive recruiting, see Codman Hislop, *Eliphalet Nott* (Middletown, Conn.: Wesleyan University Press, 1971).

13. Ralph Waldo Emerson, "The American Scholar," in Mark Van Doren, ed., *The Portable Emerson* (New York: Viking, 1946), 28; Bancroft quoted in John William Ward, *Andrew Jackson—Symbol for an Age* (New York: Oxford University Press, 1962), 31; Henry David Thoreau, "Walden," in Carl Bode, ed., *The Portable Thoreau* (New York: Viking, 1947), 283; see 304–6. On Emerson, Bancroft, and Thoreau's discounting college going, see George Fredrickson, *The Inner Civil War: Northern Intellectuals and the Crisis of the Union* (New York: Harper and Row, 1965), chap. 1.

14. Faculty Report to Trustees, October 20, 1808, Columbia College Papers, Rare Book and Manuscript Library, Columbia University.

15. David F. Allmendinger, "The Strangeness of the American Education Society: Indigent Students and the New Charity, 1815–1840," *History of Education Quarterly* 11, no. 1 (spring 1971): 5.

16. Columbia College Trustees Minutes, February 2, 1830.

17. On the curriculum, reconstructed from GTS, *Diary*, vol. 1, passim. See also John A. Kouwenhoven, "The New York Undergraduate, 1830–1850," *Columbia University Quarterly* 31 (June 1939): 75–103.

18. On decline of instruction in modern languages, Olga Raguso, *Lorenzo Da Ponte in American Perspective* (New York: S. F. Vanni, 1996).

19. On the nonappearance of the social sciences, see Joseph Dorfman, *Early American*

Policy: Six Columbia Contributors (New York: Columbia University Press, 1960); John B. Langstaff, *The Enterprising Life: John McVickar, 1787–1868* (New York: St. Martin's, 1961).

20. For professional outcomes by college, see George W. Pierson, *The Education of American Leaders: Comparative Contributions of U.S. Colleges and Universities* (New York: Praeger, 1969).

21. Kouwenhoven, "The New York Undergraduate," 100. See also Wilson Smith, "Apologia pro Alma Mater: The College as Community in Ante-Bellum America," in Stanley Elkins and Eric McKitrick, eds., *The Hofstadter Aegis* (New York: Knopf, 1974), 125–53.

22. On the financial imperatives to limit and fix the curriculum, see entries of May 2, 1833, September 17, 1829 *The Diary of Philip Hone, 1828–1851,* ed. Bayard Tuckerman (New York: Dodd, Mead, 1927), 1:92, 17.

23. On the founding of NYU, see Thomas Bender, *New York Intellect: A History of Intellectual Life in New York City, from 1750 to the Beginnings of Our Own Time* (New York: Knopf, 1987), 92–97; Thomas J. Frusciano and Marilyn H. Pettit, *New York University and the City: An Illustrated History* (New Brunswick, N.J.: Rutgers University Press, 1997).

24. Quoted in Thomas J. Frusciano and Marilyn H. Pettit, *NYU and the City: An Illustrated history* (New Brunswick, N.J.: Rutgers University Press, 1997), 15. On NYU's early success, see GTS, *Diary,* 1:3, 78; and Frusciano and Pettit, *NYU and the City,* chap. 2.

25. Nicholas Murray Butler to Dwight Miner, December 11, 1946, Dwight Miner Papers, Rare Book and Manuscript Library; Bishop John Henry Hobart, *An Address to the Citizens of New York on the Claims of Columbia College and the New University To Their Patronage* (New York, 1830), 5.

26. Hobart, *Address to the Citizens of New York,* 5.

27. On the demise of the scientific and literary course, see Columbia College Trustees Minutes, July 25, 1843.

28. On NYU's problems, see Bender, *New York Intellect,* 104, 114.

29. [Henry Adams], *The Education of Henry Adams* (New York: Modern Library, 1918), 304–5.

30. See appendix A.

31. On Mason, see John W. Francis, *Old New York: Reminiscences of the Past Sixty Years* (New York: Charles Roe, 1858), 58–62; Paul P. Faris, "Mason, John Mitchell, 1770–1829," in *Dictionary of American Biography,* 20 vols. (New York: Scribner's, 1928–36), 12:368–69; Jacob Van Vechten, *Memoirs of John M. Mason* (New York, 1856).

32. On Nott, see Hislop, *Nott.* On Day, see Brooks Mather Kelley, *Yale: A History* (New Haven: Yale University Press, 1974), chap. 10. On Quincy, see Robert A. McCaughey, *Josiah Quincy: The Last Federalist, 1772–1864* (Cambridge: Harvard University Press, 1974), chaps. 8 and 9. On Matthews, see Frusciano and Pettit, *New York University,* chap. 3.

33. See William A. Duer, "William Alexander Duer," *Columbia University Quarterly* 4 (March 1902): 147–58; Ernest H. Wright, "Duer, William Alexander, 1780–1858," in *Dictionary of American Biography,* 5:488.

34. *Diary of Philip Hone,* September 17, 1829, 1:17.

35. GTS, Diary, May 17, 1837; GTS, *Diary,* March 14, 1864, 3:415.

36. On Nathaniel Fish Moore, see Milton Halsey Thomas, "Moore, Nathaniel Fish, 1782–1872," in *Dictionary of American Biography*, 13:134. On Moore's election, see *Diary of Philip Hone*, June 1842.

37. Nathaniel Fish Moore to Clement Clark Moore, June 4, 1849, Nathaniel Fish Moore Papers, Columbia University Archives–Columbiana Library.

38. Nathaniel Fish Moore to Columbia Trustees, June 4, 1849; Moore to Moore, June 4, 1849, Moore Papers.

39. On Charles King's interest in the presidency, see Hamilton Fish's notes of a communication he made to the trustees about a letter to him from Charles King, January 22, 1845, Charles King Papers, Rare Book and Manuscript Library.

40. Moore to Moore, June 4, 1849, Moore Papers. *The Warden* was published as volume 1 of *The Chronicles of Barsetshire* (London: Chapman and Hall, 1887–89).

41. On King's election and presidency, see John Henry Van Amringe, "Charles King, L.L.D.," *Columbia University Quarterly* 6 (March 1904): 121–37.

42. Quoted in Robert A. McCaughey, "The Transformation of American Academic Life: Harvard University, 1821 1892," *Perspectives in American History* 8 (1974): 248; GTS, *Diary*, November 6, 1854, 2:195.

43. On the Knickerbocker faculty, see appendix A.

44. Henry Drisler to Alumni, 1868, Charles Anthon Papers, Columbia University Archives–Columbiana Library.

45. Henry Drisler, *Speech to Columbia College Alumni on Charles Anthon* (New York: Van Nostrand, 1868), 10.

46. On Anderson, see *The Medical Register of New York, New Jersey, and Connecticut* (New York, 1876), 240–41.

47. On Anderson's conversion, see "Anderson, Henry James," in *National Cyclopaedia of American Biography* (New York: James T. White, 1897), 6:389.

48. James P. C. Southall, "Renwick, James, 1792–1863," in *Dictionary of American Biography*, 15:506–7; James Kip Finch, *Early Columbia University Engineers* (New York: Columbia University Press, 1929).

49. Washington Irving to Henry Brevoort, April 14, 1821, in G. S. Hellman, *The Letters of Washington Irving to Henry Brevoort* (New York, 1915), 2:163.

50. On Renwick as polymath, see Southall, "Renwick."

51. On Hackley's dismissal, see GTS, *Diary*, April 13, 1857, 2:331.

52. Ernest H. Wright, "Drisler, Henry, 1818–1897," in *Dictionary of American Biography*, 5:458–59.

53. On Tellkampf, see George H. Danton, "A Flippant Little Fellow," *New York History* 44 (1946): 471.

54. Ibid., 471.

55. On Henry Schmidt, see John W. Burgess, *Reminiscences of an American Scholar* (New York: Columbia University Press, 1934; reprint, New York: Arno, 1966), 166.

56. Columbia College Trustees Minutes, January 16, 1830.

57. Frederick Rudolph, *The Curriculum: A History of the American Undergraduate Course of Study since 1636* (San Francisco: Jossey-Bass, 1977).

58. Columbia College Trustees Minutes, June 5, 1826.

59. On student agency in antebellum colleges, see Roger L. Geiger with Julie Ann

Bubolz, "College as It Was in the Mid-Nineteenth Century," in Roger L. Geiger, ed., *The American College in the Nineteenth Century* (Nashville: Vanderbilt University Press, 2000), 80–90.

60. Milton Halsey Thomas, "The King's College Building, with Some Notes on Its Later Tenants," *New-York Historical Society Quarterly* 39 (January 1955): 23–60.

61. For early Columbia College enrollment, see appendix B.

62. These estimates are based on the author's analysis of 174 Columbia students who overlapped with the College-going years of George Templeton Strong, 1834–41.

63. On the persistent youthfulness of Columbia students, see appendix B.

64. For a discussion of the adolescent "psychosocial moratorium," Erik Erikson, *Young Man Luther* (New York: Norton, 1958), 100–104. GTS's diary during his College years is filled with commentary on fires, shipwrecks, and other New York City calamities.

65. On negotiated holidays, see GTS, Diary, December 21, 1835.

66. On the academic week, see Kouwenhoven, "The New York Undergraduate."

67. On classroom procedures and grading, see Maud Howe Elliott, *Uncle Sam Ward and His Circle* (New York: Macmillan, 1938), 33; Kouwenhoven, "The New York Undergraduate."

68. Andrew Dickson White, *Autobiography* (New York: Century,1905); Nicholas Murray Butler, *Across the Busy Years: Recollections and Reflections* (New York: Scribner's, 1939), 1:62–91; Hofstadter and Metzger, *Rise of Academic Freedom*, 222–37.

69. On the history of George Templeton Strong's diary, see Allan Nevins, "The Man and His Diarist," GTS, *Diary*, 1:ix–xli; see also Vera Brodsky, *Resonances: George Templeton Strong on Music, 1836–1850* (New York: Oxford University Press, 1988).

70. On GTS's unusual attentiveness to his studies, Diary, March 25, March 28, April 4, 1836; June 29, July 15, July 20, October 3, 1837; on cheating, ibid., April 4, 1837.

71. On Duer's son's failing the science exam, GTS, Diary, July 19, 1837; on Frederick Anthon, ibid., July 20, 1837; on faculty at exams, ibid., July 15, 1837; on the medal for his work on descriptive astronomy, ibid., October 3, 1837; on his difficulties with differentiations, ibid., November 7, 1837.

72. On the senior's suspension, GTS, Diary, May 16, 1836; on Strong's uncertain robustness, ibid., June 29, 1837, February 15, 1838; on his encounter with Quackenbos, ibid., June 18, 1837; on experimenting with drugs, ibid., January 2, 1838.

73. On Anthon, GTS, Diary, December 7, 1835, April 20, 1836, July 18, 1837; on McVickar, ibid., May 20, 1837, December 23, 1836; on Anderson, ibid., April 20, October 5, 1836, November 10, 1836.

74. On Anderson, GTS, *Diary*, October 7, 1836, 2:37–38; on Duer and his family, Diary, October 13, 1837, May 23, 1837.

75. On Renwick, GTS, Diary, June 6, 1837; GTS defending McVickar against his critics, ibid., June 6, 1838; at McVickar's death, GTS, *Diary*, October 30, 1868, 4:230.

76. On public speaking, GTS, Diary, May 12, 1837; on "our second alma mater," ibid., May 20, 1837.

77. On Columbia's' literary societies, see Kouwenhoven, "The New York Undergraduate," 75–103.

78. Titles culled from GTS, Diary, 1835–38, passim. On importance of extracurricula at antebellum American colleges, see Frederick Rudolph, *The American College and Uni-*

versity: A History (1962), intro. John R. Thelin (Athens: University of Georgia Press, 1990), chap. 7.

79. GTS, Diary, December 15, 1837. On Philolexian politics, ibid., November 27, 1835, February 10, May 6, June 30, October 27, December 15, 1837; February 9, 1838.

80. On Columbia fraternities, see GTS, *Diary*, June 7, 1836, 1:25.

81. On the semicentennial planning and festivities, GTS, Diary, January 13, February 3, April 13, 1837.

82. GTS, Diary, May 16, 1836.

83. GTS, Diary, December 21, 23, 1835, December 24, 1836; Columbia College Trustees Minutes, April 3, 1837.

84. For an instance where Strong's class declined to support another class's behavior, GTS, Diary, May 17, 1836.

85. On the occupational outcomes of Strong's collegiate contemporaries, see appendix A.

86. On the eminence of antebellum college graduates, see George Pierson, *The Education of American Leaders: Comparative Contributions of U.S. Colleges and Universities* (New York: Praeger, 1969).

87. Allan Nevins, *Hamilton Fish: The Inner History of the Grant Administration* (New York: Dodd, Mead, 1936), 1. See Lyon Richardson, "Blatchford, Samuel, 1820–1893," *Dictionary of American Biography*, 2:359–60; A. Everett Petersen, "Kearney, Philip, 1814–1862," in ibid., 10:271–72; Meyer Reinhold, "Anthon, Charles, 1797–1867," in *American National Biography* (New York: Oxford University Press, 1999), 1:541; Wright, "Drisler"; George B. Kauffman, "Gibbs, Wolcott, 1822–1908," in *American National Biography*, 8:925–28.

88. GTS, *Diary*, 4:52. See Victor Paltsis, "Duyckinck, Evert A., 1816–1878," in *Dictionary of American Biography* 5:561–62; Robert G. Albion, "Stephens, John Lloyd, 1805–1852, ibid., 17:579–80; Julius W. Pratt, "John H. O'Sullivan, 1813–1895," ibid., 14:89; A. Everett Petersen, "John Jay, 1817–1894," ibid., 10:10–11; Talbot Hamlin, "James Renwick, 1818–1895," ibid., 15:507–9.

89. GTS, *Diary*, October 4, 1830, 1:91. On GTS's Civil War experiences, see Fredrickson, *The Inner Civil War*.

90. GTS, *Diary*, January 8, 1849, 1:342.

91. On GTS's views on Catholicism and the Irish, see Diary, April 28, 1848; *Diary*, September 6, 1854, 2:182–83.

92. On GTS's anti-Semitism, see *Diary*, June 19, 1854, 2:97; November 6, 1865, 4:45. For his comments on slaves, see *Diary*, January 26, 1850, 2:5.

93. ON GTS's views on women, see GTS, *Diary*, September 8, 1853, 2:129.

94. GTS, Diary, October 8, 1839, February 26, 1867.

4. MIDCENTURY STIRRINGS

1. See appendix A.

2. For Columbia trustees by familial ties, see appendix A.

3. For trustees by tenure, see appendix A.

4. For trustees by educational sources, see appendix A. For the Ruggles complaint, see

Allen Nevins and Milton Halsey Thomas, eds, *The Diary of George Templeton Strong* (New York: Macmillan, 1952) (hereafter GTS, *Diary*), April 21, 1851, 2:43.

5. For trustees by occupation, see appendix A.

6. Columbia College Trustees Minutes, February 10, 1835. On trustee moves to supplement income by tuition deals, see Columbia College Trustees Minutes, January 16, 1830.

7. On finances as of 1851, see Columbia College Trustees Minutes, December 1, 1851.

8. On the trustees' financial strategy in the 1840s, see GTS, *Diary*, February 21, 1850, 2:8.

9. These discussions figure prominently in George Templeton Strong, Diary, New-York Historical Society (hereafter GTS, Diary), October 18, 1850, not least because GTS's father-in-law, Trustee Samuel Ruggles, was himself one of the city's principal real estate developers in the 1840s.

10. On the 1852 strategy, see Columbia College Trustees Minutes, December 6, 1852.

11. On Ruggles, see Daniel G. B. Thompson, *Ruggles of New York* (New York: Columbia University Press, 1946).

12. GTS, *Diary*, August 16, 1852, 2:103.

13. Robert A. McCaughey, "The Transformation of American Academic Life: Harvard University, 1821–1892," *Perspectives in American History* 8 (1974): 239–332.

14. On the concept of peer review, see chap. 6.

15. On Gibbs's credentials and links to Ruggles-Strong, see GTS, *Diary*, December 9, 1850, 2:30.

16. On Gibbs as a Unitarian, see GTS, *Diary*, December 15, 1853, 2:141.

17. On Ruggles securing Renwick's retirement, see GTS, Diary, March 9, 1852.

18. Richard Hofstadter's rendering of the affair, for example, wholly accepts the Strong-Ruggles version. See Richard Hofstadter and Walter Metzger, *The Rise of Academic Freedom in the United States* (New York: Columbia University Press, 1955), 269–74. For a more complete and balanced account, see Milton Halsey Thomas, "The Gibbs Affair at Columbia in 1854" (M.A. thesis, Columbia University, 1942).

19. GTS, *Diary*, January 16, 1854, 2:150; April 3, 1850, 2:165–66.

20. On the mobilization of the American scientific community, see Sally Gregory Kohlstedt, *The Formation of the American Scientific Community: The American Association for the Advancement of Science* (Urbana: University of Illinois Press, 1976).

21. Benjamin Peirce to Columbia Trustees, December 1853, among testimonials communicated to the Columbia Trustees on behalf of Dr. Wolcott Gibbs, January 9, 1854, Wolcott Gibbs Appointment, Columbia College Collection, box 7, New-York Historical Society.

22. Columbia College Trustees Minutes, January 9, 1854.

23. Edward Jones to Hamilton Fish, January 10, 1854, Hamilton Fish Papers, Library of Congress.

24. Newspaper coverage quoted in Thomas, "The Gibbs Affair."

25. Columbia College Trustees Minutes, January 17, 1854.

26. Charles King to Hamilton Fish, January 18, 1854; Fish to King, January 16, 1854, Fish Papers.

27. Columbia College Trustees Minutes, February 9, 1854; GTS, Diary, February 2, 6, 9, 1854.

28. On the attempt at a compromise, see GTS, *Diary*, February 11, 1854, 2:157.

29. Columbia College Trustees Minutes, February 14, 1854.

30. Henry James Anderson to Hamilton Fish, February 17, 1854, Fish Papers.

31. GTS, Diary, January 29, 1854; Anderson to Fish, February 17, 1854, Fish Papers; Columbia College Trustees Minutes, February 6, 1854.

32. Columbia College Trustees Minutes, March 6, 1854; Samuel Ruggles, *The Duty of Columbia College to the Community* (New York: John F. Trow, 1854).

33. Ruggles, *The Duty of Columbia College*, 13, 12–13, 13–14. On the reaction to Ruggles's pamphlet, see GTS, *Diary*, April 14, 1854, 2:168.

34. GTS, Diary, April 4, 1854.

35. On the alumni meeting, see GTS, *Diary*, April 22, 1854, 2:171.

36. *Report of the General Committee of the Alumni of Columbia College* (New York: Wm. C. Bryant, 1854); GTS, *Diary*, April 22, 1854, 2:171.

37. Gouverneur M. Ogden, *A Defense of Columbia College from the Attack of Samuel B. Ruggles* (New York: J. P. Wright, 1854), 12, 14, 13, 41

38. Columbia College Trustees Minutes, June 5, 1854.

39. On the alumni meeting proposing alumni seats on the board of trustees, see *New York Herald*, April 22, 1854.

40. GTS, *Diary*, January 16, 1854, 2:150; [Gouverneur Morris Ogden], *Review of the Proceedings of the Alumni of Columbia College; and an Answer to the Pamphlet Entitled The Duty of Columbia College to the Community; and Its Right to Exclude Unitarians From Its Professorships of Science* (New York, 1854), 22. Thomas, "The Gibbs Affair." On New York Senate hearings, see Columbia College Trustees Minutes, May 1, June 5, 1854.

41. On the shift away from trustee selection of faculty, see chap. 6.

42. On the New York State decision, see Brander Matthews, ed., *A History of Columbia University, 1754–1904* (New York: Columbia University Press, 1904), 129.

43. GTS, *Diary*, December 3, 1854, 2:200–201; December 1, 1856, 2:312.

44. On the subsequent career of Wolcott Gibbs, see George B. Kauffman, "Gibbs, Wolcott, 1822–1908," in *American National Biography* (New York: Oxford University Press, 1999), 8:925–28. Eliot took the rejection so much to heart that he very nearly left academe for a career in textiles. Instead, he went to Europe for more training, took a teaching position at MIT, and in 1869 returned to Harvard as president. See McCaughey, "The Transformation of American Academic Life," 267–68.

45. On the honorary degree for Gibbs in 1873, see Columbia College Trustees Minutes, May 5, 1873.

46. Samuel Ruggles to Hamilton Fish, February 11, 1854, Fish Papers.

47. GTS, Diary, January 8, 1854.

48. On the College's early financial fortunes, see chap. 1.

49. On the history of the Upper Estate, see William Bloor to H. Bronson Cowan, December 29, 1948, William Bloor Folder, Central Files, Columbia University Archives–Columbiana Library.

50. Columbia College Trustees Minutes, March 1, 1852.

51. On Ruggles and Strong's opposition to the development plan as a decade premature, see GTS, *Diary*, May 22, 1859, 2:174.

52. On acquiring the Forty-ninth Street campus site, see Columbia College Trustees Minutes, June 19, July 7, 1856.

53. Columbia College Trustees Minutes, June 19, July 7, 1856.

54. On income from the Upper Estate, see appendix C.

55. See also Edward Chase Kirkland, "The Higher Learning," in *Dream and Thought in the Business Community, 1869–1900* (Ithaca: Cornell University Press, 1956), 83–114. That sizable gift was for twenty thousand dollars, to endow the Gebhard professorship in German.

56. Morgan Dix, Diary, April 27, 1857, Columbia University Archives–Columbiana Library; GTS, *Diary*, May 10, 1857, 2:334.

57. See Milton Halsey Thomas, "The King's College Building, with Some Notes on Its Later Tenants," *New-York Historical Society Quarterly* 39 (January 1955): 23–60. The site is currently shared by the IRS building and a parking lot. See Nathan Silver, *Lost New York* (Boston: Houghton Mifflin, 1967).

58. Columbia College Trustees Minutes, June 15, 1857.

59. On the Forty-ninth Street site left unimproved into the 1870s, see chap. 5.

60. GTS, *Diary*, May 3, 1858, 2:399–400.

61. On the composition of the mid-nineteenth-century faculty, see appendix A.

62. Frank B. Freidel, *Francis Lieber: Nineteenth-Century Liberal* (Baton Rouge: Louisiana State University Press, 1947).

63. GTS, Diary, March 23, 1857, June 5, 1865; John W. Burgess, *Reminiscences of an American Scholar: The Beginnings of Columbia University* (New York: Columbia University Press, 1934; reprint, New York: Arno, 1966), 169, 170.

64. GTS, *Diary*, June 1, 1857, 2:339. Nicholas Murray Butler, *Across the Busy Years: Recollections and Reflections* (New York: Scribner's, 1939), 1:67.

65. On Knox's nomination of his son, see GTS, *Diary*, June 22, 1857, 2:345. On Haight's proposed appointment criteria, see GTS, *Diary*, May 7, 1866, 4:82.

66. Richard J. Storr, *The Beginnings of Graduate Education in America* (Chicago: University of Chicago Press, 1953).

67. GTS, *Diary*, March 3, 1858, 2:388; June 24, 1858, 2:<PAGE TO COME>. On the board's response to the proposed postgraduate program, see Columbia College Trustees Minutes, March 8, April 5, 1858.

68. The standard history of the growth of graduate education makes no mention of Columbia's efforts in the late 1850s; see Lawrence R. Veysey, *The Emergence of the American University* (Chicago: University of Chicago Press, 1965).

69. GTS, *Diary*, March 3, 1858, 2:388.

70. For Dwight's biography and the standard account of the Law School, see Julius Goebel Jr., *A History of the School of Law, Columbia University* (New York: Columbia University Press, 1955).

71. Ibid., 33–53.

72. GTS, *Diary*, December 21, 1859, 2:480.

73. G. Adler Blumer, "Ordronaux, John, 1830–1908," in *Dictionary of American Biography*, 20 vols. (New York: Scribner's, 1928–36), 14:50–51; Thomas T. Read, "George Chase, 1849–1924," in ibid., 4:25; Goebel, *The School of Law*, 49–50.

74. GTS, *Diary*, November 12, December 1, 1874, 4:542, 544.

75. [John B. Pine], *General Catalogue of Columbia University, 1754–1916* (New York: Columbia University Press, 1916).

76. Columbia University, *Supplement to General Catalogue, 1754–1894* (New York: Columbia University Press, 1898).

77. Willis Ruddy, *The Campus and a Nation in Crisis: From the American Revolution to Vietnam* (Madison: Fairleigh Dickinson University Press, 1996), chap. 2; Fon W. Boardman Jr., *Columbia: An American University in Peace and War* (New York: Columbia University Press, 1944), 37.

78. For Columbia enrollments, see appendix B.

79. Roger Howson to Fon W. Boradman Jr., July 6, 1944, box 1, Miscellaneous, Dwight Miner Papers, Rare Book and Manuscript Library, Columbia University; GTS, *Diary*, August 5, 1856, 2:287.

80. On the Draft Riots of 1863, see Adrian Cook, *The Armies of the Streets: The New York City Draft Riots of 1863* (Lexington: University Press of Kentucky, 1974).

81. GTS, *Diary*, April 19, 1870, 4:283. Columbia University, *Supplement to General Catalogue*, passim.

82. On Strong's service in the United States Sanitary Commission, see George Fredrickson, *The Inner Civil War: Northern Intellectuals and the Crisis of the Union* (New York: Harper and Row, 1965), 101.

83. Thomas T. Read, "Vinton, Francis L., 1835–1879," in *Dictionary of American Biography*, 19:282–83; Burgess, *Reminiscences of an American Scholar*, chap. 2; Freidel, *Leiber*, chap. 14.

84. On McCulloch, see GTS, *Diary*, October 11, 15, 1863, 3:362–64; Columbia College Trustees Minutes, October 15, 1863.

85. Columbia College Trustees Minutes, October 15, December 21, 1863; GTS, *Diary*, December 21, 1863, 3:383–84.

5. TAKEOFF

1. Thomas C. Cochran, "The 'Presidential Synthesis' in American History," *American Historical Review* 53 (July 1948): 748–59.

2. For timelines of late-nineteenth-century university presidents, see Laurence R. Veysey, *The Emergence of the American University* (Chicago: University of Chicago Press, 1965), 447.

3. Thorstein Veblen, *The Higher Learning in America: A Memorandum of the Governing of Universities by Businessmen* (1918; reprint, Palo Alto: Stanford Reprints, 1956), 72. See Hugh Hawkins, *Between Harvard and America: The Educational Leadership of Charles W. Eliot* (New York: Oxford University Press, 1972), 80–84, 96–105.

4. Ibid., 68–69; Robert A. McCaughey, "The Transformation of American Academic Life: Harvard University, 1821–1892," *Perspectives in American History* 8 (1974): 301–5.

5. Hugh Hawkins, *Pioneer: A History of the Johns Hopkins University, 1874–1889* (Ithaca: Cornell University Press, 1960); McCaughey, "Transformation," 287–92.

6. Cited in McCaughey, "Transformation," 314.

7. Hawkins, *Between Harvard and America*, 78–79, 143–48.

8. Quoted in John Fulton, *Memoirs of Frederick A. P. Barnard, 10th President of*

Columbia College in the City of New York (New York: Macmillan, 1896), 83. For Barnard's pre-Columbia biography, see William J. Chute, *Damn Yankee! The First Career of Frederick A. P. Barnard* (Port Washington, N.Y.: National University Publishers, 1978); for an account based on Barnard's papers collected by his wife, see Fulton, *Memoirs of Barnard*. See also Stacilee Ford Horsford, "F. A. P. Barnard: Reconsidering a Life" (Ed.D. diss., Teachers College, Columbia University, 1991).

9. Fulton, *Memoirs of Barnard*, 33. See Brooks Mather Kelley, *Yale: A History* (New Haven: Yale University Press, 1974), chap. 10.

10. Fulton, *Memoirs of Barnard*, 64–65.

11. Ibid., 70–81; Chute, *Damn Yankee*, chap. 7.

12. Fulton, *Memoirs of Barnard*, 83–88; Chute, *Damn Yankee*, chap. 8.

13. Chute, *Damn Yankee*, 98–101. On Barnard's marriage and dealings with forceful women, see Horsford, "F. A. P. Barnard."

14. Chute, *Damn Yankee*, chap. 12. On "Lazzaroni," see Sally G. Kohlstedt, *The Foundation of the American Scientific Community: The American Association for the Advancement of Science, 1845–1860* (Urbana: University of Illinois, 1976).

15. Chute, *Damn Yankee*, chap. 16.

16. Fulton, *Memoirs of Barnard*, 195–96.

17. Fulton, *Memoirs of Barnard*, 249. See William J. Chute, *Damn Yankee! The First Career of Frederick A. P. Barnard* (Port Washington, N.Y.: Kennikat, 1978), 168. See Fulton, *Memoirs of Barnard*, chap. 11.; Chute, *Damn Yankee*, chaps. 18 and 19.

18. Allen Nevins and Milton Halsey Thomas, eds, *The Diary of George Templeton Strong* (New York: Macmillan, 1952) (hereafter GTS, *Diary*), December 21, 1863, 3:383; February 27, 1864, 3:409.

19. Ibid., March 14, 1864, 3:415. See Columbia College Trustees Minutes, March 18, 1864; Morgan Dix, Diary, May 18, 1864, Columbia University Archives–Columbiana Library. For a discerning examination of Barnard's impact on Columbia, see Marvin A. Lazerson, "F. A. P. Barnard and Columbia College: Prologue to a University," *History of Education Quarterly* 6 (winter 1966): 49–64.

20. See appendix A.

21. This does not mean that all subsequent presidents availed themselves of the power of the office. Dwight D. Eisenhower, the university's thirteenth president, is a limiting case. See chap. 12.

22. On Barnard's nonbeholdenness, see Fulton, *Memoirs of Barnard*, 338.

23. F. A. P. Barnard to Dr. Hilgard, of Mississippi, November 30, 1865, copy in Dwight Miner Papers, box 1, F. A. P. Barnard folder, Rare Book and Manuscript Library, Columbia University.

24. GTS, *Diary*, March 2, 1868, 4:194.

25. Dix, Diary, April 21, 1882.

26. Hamilton Fish to Gouverneur Ogden, October 17, 1873, January 14, 1884, Hamilton Fish Papers, Library of Congress, copies in Miner Papers.

27. James Kip Finch, *A History of the School of Engineering, Columbia University* (New York: Columbia University Press, 1954).

28. Monte Calvert, *Mechanical Engineers in America, 1830–1910: Professional Cultures in Conflict* (Baltimore: Johns Hopkins University Press, 1967); Roger L. Geiger, "The Rise

and Fall of Useful Knowledge: Higher Education for Science, Agriculture, and the Mechanic Arts, 1850–1875," in Roger L. Geiger, ed., *The American College in the Nineteenth Century* (Nashville: Vanderbilt University Press, 2000), 153–68.

29. Thomas Egleston Jr. to the Board of Trustees, cited in Columbia College Trustees Minutes, April 6, 1863. See Finch, *A History of the School of Engineering*, 27. See also Edna Yost, "Egleston, Thomas, 1832–1900," in *Dictionary of American Biography*, 20 vols. (New York: Scribner's, 1928–36), 12:56; George Templeton Strong, Diary, New-York Historical Society (hereafter GTS, Diary), May 4, 1863, and June 5, 1865; [Thomas Egleston Jr.], "A Proposed Plan For a School of Mines in New York City," reprinted in *School of Mines Quarterly* (May 1914), quoted in Finch, *A History of the School of Engineering*, 28.

30. Marston T. Bogert, "Charles Frederick Chandler, 1836–1925," *Biographical Memoirs* (National Academy of Science) 14 (1931): 125–81; Elizabeth N. Shor, "Charles Frederick Chandler," in *American National Biography* (New York: Oxford University Press, 1999), 4:658–59.

31. For his many civic activities, see Charles Frederick Chandler Papers, Columbia University Archives–Columbiana Library.

32. For enrollment figures for the School of Mines, see appendix B.

33. Finch, *School of Engineering*, chaps. 3 and 4.

34. Columbia College Trustees Minutes, April 13, 1865; Frederick A. P. Barnard, President's Annual Report to Board of Trustees, 1865, copy in Columbia University Archives–Columbiana Library; Thomas T. Read, "Vinton, Francis, 1835–1879," in *Dictionary of American Biography*, 19:282–83.

35. Columbia College Trustees Minutes, January 6, 1873.

36. Barnard, President's Annual Report, 1865, 1872.

37. Barnard's first President's Annual Report was published on June 5, 1865, for academic year 1864–65 (hereinafter, 1865). William F. Russell, the dean of Teachers College, edited a selection of Barnard's reports, arranged topically, under the title *The Rise of a University, I—The Later Days of Old Columbia College* (New York: Columbia University Press, 1937).

38. Barnard, President's Annual Report, 1868; see also ibid., 1871.

39. Barnard, President's Annual Report, 1869.

40. Barnard, "Declining Popularity of Collegiate Education," President's Annual Report, 1865–66, June 4, 1866; President's Annual Report, 1870.

41. Barnard, President's Annual Report, 1865–66.

42. Fulton, *Memoirs of Barnard*, 368–76; Barnard, President's Annual Report, 1887.

43. For Barnard's complaints about the restricted academic work week, see President's Annual Report, 1869, 1871, 1876.

44. On Barnard's limited success in installing an electives system, see President's Annual Report, 1875, 1879, 1884. On the role of electives in the emergence of universities, see Frederick Rudolph, *Curriculum: A History of the American Undergraduate Course of Study Since 1636* (San Francisco: Jossey-Bass, 1977), 178, 191–96.

45. Noah Porter, *The American Colleges and the American Public* (1870; reprint, New York: Arno, 1969), 29–30. On the trustees withholding funds to publish Barnard's President's Annual Report, see Roger Howson, "President Barnard and the Trustees," MS, in Miner Papers.

46. F. A. P. Barnard to Benjamin I. Haight, November 20, 1873, New-York Historical Society, copy in Miner Papers.

47. Fish on Barnard, 1885, in Hamilton Fish Papers, Library of Congress, quoted in Howson, "Barnard and the Trustees." On Fish's and Ogden's complaints with Barnard, see notes for October 17, 1873 (for Fish's view), January 12, 1869 (for Ogden's view), and November 16, 1881, in Barnard Folder.

48. Henry Adams, *Democracy: An American Novel* (1881) (New York: Farrar, Straus, and Young, 1952), 7. For the state of Columbia's finances, see [Gouverneur Ogden], Columbia College Treasurer's Reports, 1859–1883 [1884], a bound volume of annually printed reports, Columbia University Archives–Columbiana Library.

49. On the Forty-ninth Street campus, see Barry Bergdoll, "Columbia Moves Uptown: Physical Relocation and Institutional Ascendance" (talk to University Seminar on the History of Columbia University, January 27, 1999).

50. On Barnard's standing up for his faculty on the matter of chapel attendance, see President's Annual Report, 1875. On faculty moonlighting, see President's Annual Report, 1870, 71–74.

51. John W. Burgess, *Reminiscences of an American Scholar: The Beginnings of Columbia University* (New York: Columbia University Press, 1934; reprint, New York: Arno, 1966); R. Gordon Hoxie, "John W. Burgess," (Ph.D. diss., Columbia University, 1950); Roger Bagnall, "John W. Burgess," *Columbia Magazine* (forthcoming).

52. William R. Leonard, "Mayo-Smith, Richmond, 1854–1901," in *Dictionary of American Biography*, 12:467–68. On Burgess as influential, see Thomas Bender, "E. R. A. Seligman and the Vocation of Social Science," in *Intellect and Public Life: Essays on the Social History of Academic Intellectuals in the United States* (Baltimore: Johns Hopkins, 1993), 49–77.

53. Burgess, *Reminiscences*, 179–80; Daniel G. B. Thompson, *Ruggles of New York* (New York: Columbia University Press, 1946), 176. See also Burgess, *Reminiscences*, 179–80, 194–95, chap. 7.

54. This unpublished analysis of the occupational outcomes of Columbia Ph.D.s, 1875–1900, is mine.

55. Burgess, *Reminiscences*, 207.

56. Burgess, *Reminiscences*, 164–73.

57. Finch, *School of Engineering*, 58; appendix B.

58. R. Gordon Hoxie, ed., *A History of the Faculty of Political Science, Columbia University* (New York: Columbia University Press, 1954); William James, "The Ph.D. Octopus," *Harvard Monthly* (March 1903), reprinted in *William James: Writings, 1902–1910* (New York: Library of America, 1987), 1111–18.

59. This account is a provisional assessment, awaiting a more definitive analysis by Rosalind Rosenberg in her upcoming *Changing the Subject: A History of Women at Columbia* (New York: Columbia University Press, forthcoming).

60. For use of the term "the best men," see John G. Sprout, *"The Best Men": Liberal Reformers in the Gilded Age* (New York: Oxford University Press, 1968).

61. Burgess, *Reminiscences*, 353.

62. Barnard, President's Annual Report, 1880, 262. Burgess, *Reminiscences*, 3–4..

63. Eric Foner, *Reconstruction: America's Unfinished Revolution, 1863–1877* (New York: Harper and Row, 1988), 609. This is not to suggest that blacks were welcomed at other

universities. Yet the fact that both Yale and Harvard did award Ph.D.s to blacks before 1900 (Edward A. Bouchet, 1876, and W. E. B. Dubois, 1895, respectively) indicates that they were not entirely closed out from graduate studies.

64. John W. Burgess to Nicholas Murray Butler, April 6, 1910, Burgess Papers, Columbia University Archives–Columbiana Library; Burgess, *Reminiscences*, 241–42.

65. Dix, Diary, January 18, 1884; Edgerton quoted in Rosenberg, *Changing the Subject*; Dix, Diary, May 29, 1887. The second woman to receive a Columbia Ph.D. was Anna Stockton Pettit in 1895, in ancient languages. By 1900 eight women had received Columbia Ph.D.s. See appendix B.

66. Dix, Diary, January 30, 1883; Class of 1884 Resolution Against Admitting Women to the College, in *Acta Columbiana*, October 1, 1881, p. 1, copy available in Coeducation folder, Dwight Miner Papers, Rare Book and Manuscript Library. See Dix, Diary, April 24, 1882.

67. Quoted in John Erskine, *The Memory of Certain Persons* (Philadelphia: Lippincott, 1947), 71.

68. Frederick A. P. Barnard, "Expediency of Receiving Women as Students," in *President's Report*, 1879, reprinted in Russell, *Rise of a University*, 1:249–59.

69. Barbara Miller Solomon, *In the Company of Educated Women: A History of Women and Higher Education in America* (New Haven: Yale University Press, 1985).

70. John W. Burgess to Charles William Eliot, November 11, 1894, Charles William Eliot Papers, Harvard University Archives. See Barnard, President's Annual Report, 1879; Burgess, *Reminiscences*, 78–79; Rosalind Rosenberg, "The Limits of Access: The History of Coeducation in America," in John Mack Faragher and Florence Howe, eds., *Women and Higher Education in American History* (New York: Norton, 1987), 107–29.

71. Barnard, President's Annual Report, 1879. On Barnard as a feminist, see Horsford, "F. A. P. Barnard."

72. Barnard, President's Annual Report, 1880, 1881.

73. Burgess, *Reminiscences*, 174.

74. Dix, Diary, March 7, 1883; Barnard, President's Annual Report, 1885. For the vote, see Columbia College Trustees Minutes, March 5, 1883.

75. Annie Nathan Meyer, *Barnard Beginnings* (Boston: Houghton Mifflin, 1935); Annie Nathan Meyer, *Nation*, June 26, 1888, reprinted in *Barnard Beginnings*, appendix C. On Meyer, see Lynn Gordon, "Annie Nathan Meyer and Barnard College: Mission and Identity in Women's Higher Education, 1889–1950," *History of Education Quarterly* 26 (winter 1986): 503–22; Robert A. McCaughey, "Meyer, Annie Nathan, 1867–1951," *DAB*, supp. 5, 487–88.

76. Dix, Diary, February 9, 1888; Columbia University Trustees Minutes, February 4, 1889. Relevant excerpts from Dix's diary are included as appendix A in Meyer, *Barnard Beginnings*. See Marian Churchill White, *A History of Barnard College* (New York: Columbia University Press, 1954), chap. 2.

77. Barnard, President's Annual Report, 1879, 54–55. See Columbia College Trustees Minutes, April 1, 1889; White, *Barnard College*, 19.

78. Schermerhorn's remark about Barnard is in the Hamilton Fish Papers, January 14, 1884, in the F. A. P. Barnard folder, Miner Papers.

79. Seth Low to Nicholas Murray Butler, March 13, 1896, Seth Low Papers, Columbia University Archives–Columbiana Library. See Laurence R. Veysey, *The Emergence of the American University* (Chicago: University of Chicago Press, 1965), 99–100; Butler, *Across the Busy Years*, 1:70–77; Nicholas Murray Butler, "President Barnard," *Columbia University Quarterly* 32 (February 1940), 12–16.

80. Roger Howson, "History of Columbia University, 1849–1913," Miner Papers, box 29. See also Roger Howson, *His Excellency, a Trustee, and Some Other Pieces* (New York: Columbia University Bookstore, 1946).

81. Cited in McCaughey, "Transformation of American Academic Life," 306; John W. Burgess, *The American University: When Shall It Be? Where Shall It Be? What Shall It Be?* (Boston: Ginn, Heath, 1884), reprinted as appendix 1 in Burgess, *Reminiscences*, 349–68 (the quotation is from 353).

82. Barnard, President's Annual Report, 1886, 13.

83. For enrollment statistics, see appendix B.

84. Barnard, President's Annual Report, 1876 and 1879.

85. Dix, Diary, June 13, 1877; Butler, *Across the Busy Years*, 1:63. See Richard T. Ely, *Ground Under Our Feet: An Autobiography* (New York: Macmillan, 1938), 31–36.

86. Barnard, President's Annual Report, 1887. See Burgess, *Reminiscences*, 179–80.

87. Barnard, President's Annual Report, 1872.

88. Burgess, *Reminiscences*, 210.

89. Barnard, President's Annual Report, 1879. See Hawkins, *Between Harvard and America*, chap. 5; Kelley, *Yale*, chap. 13; Thomas J. Wertenbaker, *Princeton, 1746–1946* (Princeton: Princeton University Press, 1946), chap. 9.

90. Burgess, *Reminiscences*, 207–10.

91. George E. Peterson, *The New England College in the Age of the University* (Amherst: Amherst College Press, 1964); John Barnard, *From Evangelism to Progressivism at Oberlin College, 1866–1917* (Columbus: Ohio State University Press, 1969); Marilyn Tobias, *Old Dartmouth on Trial: The Transformation of the Academic Community in Nineteenth-Century America* (New York: New York University Press, 1982); David B. Potts, *Wesleyan University, 1831–1910: Collegiate Enterprise in New England* (New Haven: Yale University Press, 1992).

92. For Columbia graduates in the late nineteenth century, see appendix B.

93. Owen Johnson, *Stover at Yale* (New York: Frederick A. Stokes, 1912); Henry S. Canby, *Alma Mater: The Gothic Age of the American College* (New York: Farrar and Rinehart, 1936); John Erskine, "The College on 49th Street," in *The Memory of Certain Persons*, 70–82.

94. Barnard, President's Annual Report, 1880; John W. Burgess to James Speyer, May 17, 1905, John W. Burgess Papers, Columbia University Archives–Columbiana Library. See Ronald Story, *The Forging of an Aristocracy: Harvard and the Boston Upper Class, 1800–1870* (Middletown: Wesleyan University Press, 1980), 175–76. For the sharp contrast between the Boston elite and its New York counterpart, see Sven Beckert, *The Monied Metropolis: New York City and the Consolidation of the American Bourgeoisie, 1850–1896* (Cambridge: Cambridge University Press, 2002).

95. *Columbia University in the City of New York: Gifts and Endowments, 1754–1898* (New York: Columbia University Press, 1898), 27. See ibid., 28; Andrew S. Dolkart, *Morn-*

ingside Heights: A History of Its Architecture and Development (New York: Columbia University Press, 1998), 168.

96. Barnard, President's Annual Report, 1887.

97. Hawkins, *Between Harvard and America*, 116–17.

6. THE ASPECT OF A UNIVERSITY

1. Clark Kerr, *The Uses of the University* (Cambridge: Harvard University Press, 1964).

2. Columbia University Trustees Minutes, January 8, 1912. The change was formally accepted by the New York State Board of Regents in 1912.

3. On Forty-ninth Street campus, see Barry Bergdoll, *Mastering McKim's Plan: Columbia's First Century on Morningside Heights* (New York: Miriam and Ira D. Wallach Art Gallery, Columbia University, 1997), 24–30.

4. For enrollment growth, see appendix B.

5. See chap. 8 for the challenge trustees mounted to growing faculty agency in 1917.

6. Nicholas Murray Butler (hereafter NMB), interview with Dwight Miner, December 5, 1940, Dwight Miner Papers, box 4, Rare Book and Manuscript Library, Columbia University.

7. Richard B. Morris, "Low, Abiel Abbot, 1811–1893," in *Dictionary of American Biography*, 20 vols. (New York: Scribner's, 1928–36), 11:494–95. See Robert G. Albion, *The Rise of New York Port, 1815–1860* (New York: Scribner's, 1939).

8. Gerald Kurland, *Seth Low: The Reformer in an Urban and Industrial Age* (Boston: Twayne, 1971). On Low's civic career, see David C. Hammack, *Power and Society: Greater New York at the Turn of the Century* (New York: Columbia University Press, 1982).

9. Kurland, *Seth Low*, 51.

10. On the jockeying for the presidency in 1889, see Columbia College Trustees Minutes, October 7, 1889; William R. Shepherd, "Rives, George Lockhart, 1849–1917," in *Dictionary of American Biography*, 15:634–35.

11. Ernest H. Wright, "Drisler, Henry, 1818–1897," in *Dictionary of American Biography*, 5:458–59.

12. James Earl Russell, as quoted in James Martin Keating, "Seth Low and the Development of Columbia University, 1889–1901" (Ed.D. diss., Teachers College, Columbia University, 1973), 209, 215; Seth Low to Thomas S. Fiske, October 22, 1895, Thomas S. Fiske Papers, Columbia University Archives–Columbiana Library.

13. John W. Burgess, *Reminiscences of an American Scholar: The Beginnings of Columbia University* (New York: Columbia University Press, 1934; reprint, New York: Arno, 1966), 237–39.

14. Seth Low, President's Annual Report, October 6, 1890, Columbia University Archives–Columbiana Library.

15. For deans of the various schools, see appendix A.

16. Seth Low, "Reorganization of the University," President's Annual Report, 1890.

17. On Van Amringe's feelings about the College, see Lionel Trilling, "Columbia College in the Van Amringe and Keppel Era," in Dwight C. Miner, ed., *A History of Columbia College on Morningside* (New York: Columbia University Press, 1954), 14–47.

18. Julius Goebel Jr., *A History of the School of Law, Columbia University* (New York: Columbia University Press, 1955), 140–41.

19. Goebel, *School of Law*, 34–36.

20. George Templeton Strong (New York: Macmillan, 1952) (hereafter GTS, *Diary*), October 9, 1869, 4:256.

21. Columbia College Trustees Minutes, June 1, 1874; Seth Low, President's Annual Report, 1890.

22. Burgess, *Reminiscences*, 207–9; Goebel, *School of Law*, 104–5, 135–58; Andrew L. Kaufman, *Cardozo* (Cambridge: Harvard University Press, 1998), 48–49.

23. Goebel, *School of Law*, chap. 7.

24. Ibid., 92–93.

25. Robert Stevens, "Two Cheers for 1870: The American Law School," *Perspectives in American History* 5 (1971): 405–548; Jerold S. Auerbach, *Unequal Justice: Lawyers and Social Change in Modern America* (New York: Oxford University Press, 1976).

26. GTS, *Diary*, December 1, 1874, 4:544; Goebel, *School of Law*, chap. 6.

27. Arnold J. Lien, "Keener, William A., 1856–1913," in *Dictionary of American Biography*, 10:285–86; Goebel, *The School of Law*, 152.

28. H. W. Howard Knott, "Burdick, Francis M., 1845–1920," in *Dictionary of American Biography*, 3:273–74; W. David Lewis, "Kirchwey, George W., 1855–1942," ibid., supp. 3, 420–21; Richard Megargee, "Moore, John Bassett, 1860–1947," ibid., supp. 4, 597–600; Goebel, *School of Law*, part 4.

29. On nineteenth-century medical education generally, see Joseph F. Kett, *The Formation of the American Medical Profession: The Role of Institutions* (New Haven: Yale University Press, 1968); Kenneth M. Ludmerer, *Learning to Heal: The Development of American Medical Education* (New York: Basic, 1985).

30. John C. Dalton, M.D., *History of the College of Physicians and Surgeons in the City of New York* (New York: College of Physicians and Surgeons, 1888); George C. Freeborn, *History of the Association of the Alumni of the College of Physicians and Surgeons, New York* (Lancaster, Pa.: New Era Printing, 1909).

31. Columbia College Trustees Minutes, "Relations of Columbia College to the School of Medicine," April 1, 1878.

32. Dalton, *History of Physicians and Surgeons*, chap. 9.

33. Seth Low, President's Annual Report, 1890. For enrollment and graduation statistics for the College of Physicians & Surgeons, see appendix B.

34. Seth Low, President's Annual Report, October 5, 1891.

35. For move to 168th Street, see chap. 13.

36. Seth Low to Charles W. Eliot, January 16, 1894, Charles William Eliot Papers, Harvard University Archives, Harvard University.

37. Marian Churchill White, *A History of Barnard College* (New York: Columbia University Press, 1954), chaps. 2, 3, and 4; Lynn Gordon, "Annie Nathan Meyer: Mission and Identity in Women's Higher Education," *History of Education Quarterly* 26 (winter 1986): 503–22. For numbers of early Barnard Graduates, see appendix B.

38. White, *Barnard College*, 16, 17, 25, 26, 71, 80; Naomi W. Cohen, *Jacob Schiff: A Study in American Jewish Leadership* (Hanover, N.H.: University Press of New England, 1999).

39. Seth Low to John W. Burgess, October 17, 1894, October 5, 1901, John W. Burgess Papers, Columbia University Archives–Columbiana Library.

40. Columbia University Trustees Minutes, November 5, 1906. See White, *Barnard College*, 31. My understanding of this transaction has benefited from discussions with Rosalind Rosenberg.

41. Columbia University Trustees Minutes, January 8, 1900. See also Marian Churchill White, *A History of Barnard College* (New York: Columbia University Press, 1954), 45–46.

42. For changes in the Columbia-Barnard relationship in the 1970s, see chap. 18.

43. NMB, *Across the Busy Years: Recollections and Reflections* (New York: Scribner's, 1939), 1:72–73. See Barnard, President's Annual Report, 1881.

44. Lawrence A. Cremin, David A. Shannon, and Mary Evelyn Townshend, *A History of Teachers College, Columbia University* (New York: Columbia University Press, 1954). On Grace Hoadley Dodge, see Ellen C. Lagemann, *A Generation of Women: Education in the Lives of Progressive Reformers* (Cambridge: Harvard University Press, 1979), 9–31; James Earl Russell, *Founding Teachers College: Reminiscences of a Dean Emeritus* (New York: Teachers College Press, 1937).

45. NMB, "The Founding of Teachers College," *Across the Busy Years*, 1:176–87.

46. Ibid., 1:183. See Cremin, Shannon, and Townshend, *Teachers College*, 9; see also 3–9.

47. Ibid., 10–40.

48. Seth Low, President's Annual Report, 1900, Columbia University Archives–Columbiana Library. See Columbia University Trustees Minutes, March 31, 1900. For Teachers College in the early twentieth century, see Bette Weneck, "Russell, James Earl, 1864–1945," in *American National Biography* (New York: Oxford University Press, 1999), 19:101–3; Geraldine Joncich, *The Sane Positivist: A Biography of Edward L. Thorndike* (Middletown, Conn.: Wesleyan University Press, 1968); Norman Cousins, "TC in the 1930s," in Wesley First, ed., *University on the Heights* (Garden City: Doubleday, 1969), 73–79.

49. For the growth of the Columbia faculty, see appendix B.

50. For rank differentiation data, see appendix B.

51. For disciplinary differentiation, see appendix B.

52. R. Gordon Hoxie, ed., *A History of the Faculty of Political Science, Columbia University* (New York: Columbia University Press, 1954).

53. Oscar James Campbell, "The Department of English and Comparative Literature," in John Herman Randall Jr., ed., *A History of the Faculty of Philosophy, Columbia University* (New York: Columbia University Press, 1957), 58–103; Howard Stein, "Brander Matthews and Theater Study at Columbia," *Columbia Magazine*, spring 2002, 20–27.

54. Randall, *Faculty of Philosophy*, passim. On the process generally, see John Higham. "The Matrix of Specialization," and Laurence Veysey, "The Plural Organized Worlds of the Humanities," in Alexandra Oleson and John Voss, eds., *The Organization of Knowledge in Modern America, 1860–1920* (Baltimore: Johns Hopkins University Press, 1979), 3–18, 51–106.

55. On the major American producers of Ph.D.s to 1900, see appendix B. See also *A Century of Doctorates* (Washington, D.C.: National Academy of Sciences, 1978).

56. Letter from H. C. Emery (CU Ph.D. 1896), *Columbia Literary Monthly* 2, no. 1 (October 1893): 145–46. See Robert A. McCaughey, "The Transformation of American Academic Life: Harvard University, 1821–1892," *Perspectives in American History* 8 (1974): 239–332.

57. NMB, *Across the Busy Years*, 1:134; Albert Marrin, *Nicholas Murray Butler* (New York: Twayne, 1976). All consideration of Butler here is tentative and awaits the more comprehensive study by Butler's current biographer, Michael Rosenthal.

58. Thomas Bender, "E. R. A. Seligman and the Vocation of Social Science," in *Intellect and Public Life: Essays on the Social History of Academic Intellectuals in the United States* (Baltimore: Johns Hopkins, 1993), 49–77; Laurence S. Moss, "Seligman, Edwin R. A., 1861–1939," in *American National Biography*, 19:620–21.

59. Thomas S. Fiske, Faculty Appointment Card, Columbia University Archives–Columbiana Library.

60. Dixon Ryan Fox, *Herbert Levi Osgood: An American Scholar* (New York: Columbia University Press, 1924).

61. Barry Karl, *Charles E. Merriam and the Study of Politics* (Chicago: University of Chicago Press, 1974); John H. Michel, "Millikan, Robert A., 1868–1953," in *American National Biography*, 15:532–36; John F. Stover, "Ripley, William Z., 1867–1941," in ibid., 18:540–42; Peggy A. Kidwell, "Schlesinger, Frank, 1871–1943," in ibid., 19:388–90.

62. On the academic boom in the 1890s, see Lawrence R. Veysey, *The Emergence of the American University* (Chicago: University of Chicago Press, 1965), 264–68.

63. A. Hunter Dupree, *Asa Gray, 1810–1888* (Cambridge: Harvard University Press, 1959), 50, 56; Nancy G. Slack, "Britton, Nathaniel Lord, 1859–1934," *American National Biography*, 3:577–79.

64. Ronald Rainger, "Osborn, Henry Fairfield, 1857–1935, *American National Biography*, 16:785–88.

65. Marilyn Ogilvie, "Wilson, Edmund, B., 1856–1939," *American National Biography*, 23:566–68; Charles E. Rosenberg, "The Social Environment of Scientific Innovation: Factors in the Development of Genetics in the United States," in *No Other Gods: On Science and American Social Thought* (Baltimore: Johns Hopkins University Press, 1976), 196–209; Eric R. Kandell, "Thomas Hunt Morgan at Columbia University: Chromosomes and the Origins of Modern Biology," *Columbia Magazine*, fall 1999, 29–35.

66. "Robert S. Woodworth," in Carl Murchison, ed., *A History of Psychology in Autobiography* (New York: Russell and Russell, 1961), 2:359–80; Andrew S. Winston, "Woodworth, Robert S., 1869–1962), *American National Biography*, 23:837–39; "Edward Lee Thorndike," in Murchison, *A History of Psychology in Autobiography*, 3:263–70; Joncich, *The Sane Positivist*, 219–21 passim; Michael A. Sokal, "Cattell, James McKeen, 1860–1944," *American National Biography*, 4:584–86.

67. Charles Camic and Yu Xie, "The Statistical Turn in American Social Sciences: Columbia University, 1890–1915," *American Sociological Review* 59 (1994): 773–805; Randall Collins, "Social Factors in the Origins of a New Science: The Case of Psychology," *American Sociological Review* 31 (1966)): 451–65; Steven P. Turner, "The World of Academic Quantifiers: The Columbia University Family and Its Connections," in Martin Blumer, Kevin Bales, and Kathryn Kish Sklar, eds., *The Social Survey in Historical Perspective, 1880–1940* (Cambridge: Cambridge University Press, 1991), 269–90.

68. Douglas Cole, *Franz Boas: The Early Years, 1858–1906* (Seattle: University of Washington Press, 1999); Shari Rudavsky, "Livingston, Farrand, 1867–1939," *American National Biography*, 7:734–36.

69. Keay Davidson, "Boas, Franz, 1858–1942," *American National Biography*, 3:83–86; Melville Herskovitz, *Franz Boas: The Science of Man in the Making* (New York: Scribner, 1953).

70. On the American Oriental Society, see Robert A. McCaughey, *International Studies and Academic Enterprise: A Chapter in the Enclosure of American Learning* (New York: Columbia University Press, 1984), 10–13. On the AAAS, see Sally G. Kohlstedt, *The Formation of the American Scientific Community* (Urbana: University of Illinois Press, 1976). On the ASSA, see Thomas L. Haskell, *The Emergence of Professional Social Science* (Urbana: University of Illinois Press. 1976).

71. On Charles Frederick Chandler, see Douglas Sloan, "Science in New York City, 1867–1907," *Isis* 71 (March 1980): 35–76. On Seligman and the AEA, see A. W. Coats, "The First Two Decades of the American Economic Association," *American Economic Review* 50 (September 1960): 556–73; Robert L. Church, "Economists as Experts: The Rise of an Academic Profession in America, 1870–1917," in Lawrence Stone, ed., *The University in Society* (Princeton: Princeton University Press, 1974), 2:571–609; Bender, "E. R. A. Seligman." On William Dunning and the AHA, see Elizabeth Donnan and Leo F. Stock, eds., *An Historian's World: Selections from the Correspondence of John Franklin Jameson*, Memoirs of the Society (Philadelphia: American Philosophical Society, 1956). On Cattell, see n. 67, above. On Boas, see n. 68, above.

72. Frederick P. Keppel, *Columbia* (New York: Oxford University Press, 1914), 193–95; Randall, *Faculty of Philosophy*, passim.

73. Henry H. Wiggins, *Columbia University Press, 1893–1983* (New York: Columbia University Press, 1983), 1.

74. Burgess, *Reminiscences*, 164–65; James McKeen Cattell, "A Statistical Study of American Men of Science," *Science* 24 (1906): 658–65, 699–707, 732–42, reprinted in A. T. Poffenberger, *James McKeen Cattell: Man of Science* (Lancaster: Science Press, 1947), 1:388–426. For Columbia's endorsement of another early ranking of academic institutions, see David S. Webster, "The Bureau of Education's Suppressed Ratings of Colleges, 1911–12," *History of Education Quarterly* 24 (winter 1984): 499–511.

75. Thomas S. Fiske to Seth Low, January 26, 1841, Fiske Papers.

76. William A. Dunning to Seth Low, January 1, 1899; Seth Low to William A. Dunning, January 30, 1899, William A. Dunning Papers, Columbia University Archives–Columbiana Library.

77. Dunning to NMB, August 27, 1903, Dunning Papers.

78. Ibid.; NMB to Dunning, August 27, 1903, Dunning Papers. All comments about Dunning are from NMB to Francis S. Bangs, September 29, 1903, Francis S. Bangs Papers, Columbia University Archives–Columbiana Library.

79. NMB to William A. Dunning, October 6, 1903, Dunning Papers. See Mark C. Smith, "Dunning, William A., 1857–1932," *American National Biography*, 7:104–5; Peter Novick, *That Noble Dream: The "Objectivity Question" and the American Historical Profession* (Cambridge: Cambridge University Press, 1988), 69, 75, 77–80.

80. John W. Burgess to Seth Low, May 17, 1890, Burgess Papers, Columbia University

Archives–Columbiana Library; Columbia University Trustees Minutes, May 6, 1907. See Columbia University Trustees Minutes, January 7, 1907.

81. Seth Low, President's Annual Report, 1897.

82. On the Forty-ninth Street campus, see Barry Bergdoll, "Columbia Moves Uptown: Physical Relocation and Institutional Ascendance" (talk to the University Seminar on the History of Columbia University, January 27, 1999); Talbot F. Hamlin, "Haight, Charles Coolidge, 1841–1917," in *Dictionary of American Biography*, 8:89. See also appendix D.

83. GTS, *Diary*, March 8, 1869, 4:243–44.

84. Seth Low, President's Annual Report, 1891.

85. Quoted in Bergdoll, *Mastering McKim's Plan*, 33; see 19–34.

86. Subcommittee of the Committee on Buildings and Grounds, "Columbia University in the City of New York: Gifts and Endowments, 1754–1898," 27–30, copy in Columbia University Archives–Columbiana Library.

87. Ibid., 36.

88. Columbia University Trustees Minutes, May 6, 1895; Andrew S. Dolkart, *Morningside Heights: A History of Its Architecture and Development* (New York: Columbia University Press, 1998), 137–38.

89. Bergdoll, *Mastering McKim's Plan*, 34; William James to Henry James, February 14, 1907, in Ignas K. Skrupskelis and Elizabeth M. Berkeley, eds., *William and Henry James: Selected Letters* (Charlottesville: University of Virginia Press, 1997), 481–82.

90. The Fish-Godkin exchange is detailed in Thomas Bender, *New York Intellect: A History of Intellectual Life in New York City, from 1750 to the Beginnings of Our Own Time* (New York: Knopf, 1987), 269–71.

91. Ibid., 92.

92. Seth Low, quoted in Gerald Kurland, *Seth Low: The Reformer in an Urban and Industrial Age* (Boston: Twayne, 1971), 53.

93. Robert L. Larson, "Charles F. Chandler" (Ph.D. diss., Columbia University, 1950); James Kip Finch, *A History of the School of Engineering, Columbia University* (New York: Columbia University Press, 1954); author's unpublished study of early Columbia Ph.D.s.

94. Charles A. Beard to NMB, May 24, 1913, Charles A. Beard Papers, Columbia University Archives–Columbiana Library.

95. Keating, "Seth Low," 264; E. Morison, ed., *The Letters of Theodore Roosevelt* (Cambridge: Harvard University Press, 1954), 83.

7. BOLT TO THE TOP

1. The biographical aspects of Butler's life here are largely dependent on his own account or on documents he preserved for posterity and thus used cautiously. He was known, on the testimony of university archivist Milton Halsey Thomas, to have in the last two years of his life directed a selected pruning of his official papers in what would seem to have been a clear effort at posterity management. Publication of the upcoming biography of Butler by Michael Rosenthal will permit a much clearer distinction between the real NMB and the constructed one. Butler's papers include 140 volumes of newspaper clippings relating to him and copies of some five thousand speeches.

2. Nicholas Murray Butler (hereafter NMB), *Across the Busy Years: Recollections and Reflections* (New York: Scribner's, 1939), 1:363–421.

3. Ibid., 1:chaps. 2 and 3.

4. Ibid., 1:36–38.

5. Ibid., 1:chap. 5.

6. Ibid., 1:83–91.

7. Ibid., 1:68–70, 72–73. Butler included full-page pictures of Burgess and Barnard in his autobiography, but none of Low.

8. Ibid., 1:chap. 5.

9. Ibid., 1:chap. 6.; Michael Rosenthal, "Nicholas Murray Butler" (talk to Friends of the Rare Book and Manuscript Library, Columbia University, March 8, 1999).

10. NMB, *Across the Busy Years*, 1:134, 137, 160; Lawrence A. Cremin, David A. Shannon, and Mary Evelyn Townshend, *A History of Teachers College, Columbia University* (New York: Columbia University Press, 1954), 18–27. See also Michael Rosenthal, "Nicholas Murray Butler, Captain of Erudition," *Columbia Library Columns* 44 (autumn 1995): 5–11

11. NMB to Charles M. Da Costa, April 5, 1889, reprinted in NMB, *Across the Busy Years*, 1:137–43; John W. Burgess, *Reminiscences of an American Scholar: The Beginnings of Columbia University* (New York: Columbia University Press, 1934; reprint, New York: Arno, 1966), 233–34.

12. Albert Marrin, *Nicholas Murray Butler* (Boston: Twayne, 1976), 34–36. Butler made no mention of his first wife and daughter in his autobiography.

13. NMB, *Across the Busy Years*, 1:161, 177.

14. Butler figures not at all in Bruce Kuklick, *The Rise of American Philosophy: Cambridge, Massachusetts, 1860–1930* (New Haven: Yale University Press, 1977), though several Columbia philosophers are cited.

15. George Santayana, *Character and Opinion in the United States* (New York, 1920; reprint, Garden City: Doubleday, 1956), 142–43.

16. NMB, *Across the Busy Years*, 1:148–49 The seven other state universities were those of Ohio, Indiana, Illinois, Wisconsin, Iowa, Colorado, and Washington.

17. NMB to Trustee Timothy Cheesman, May 12, 1905, Cheesman Papers, Columbia University Archives–Columbiana Library.

18. Harlan Fiske Stone, quoted in Marrin, *Nicholas Murray Butler*, 15; Theodore Roosevelt to Arthur Hamilton Lee, September 16, 1910, in E. Morison, ed., *The Letters of Theodore Roosevelt* (Cambridge: Harvard University Press, 1954), 7:129. See Alpheus T. Mason, *Harlan Fiske Stone: Pillar of the Law* (New York: Viking, 1956), 136.

19. NMB, *Across the Busy Years*, 1:3–4.

20. Theodore Roosevelt to J. B. Matthews, April 30, 1910, August 16, 1910, in Morison, *Roosevelt*, 2:1273; TR to Arthur Hamilton Lee, August 16, 1910, in ibid., 7:111–12. For the falling-out with Theodore Roosevelt, see Morison, *Roosevelt*, 7:112n.

21. Gerald Kurland, *Seth Low: The Reformer in an Urban and Industrial Age* (Boston: Twayne, 1971), 50–62.

22. Seth Low to George L. Rives, December 11, 1901, George L. Rives Papers, Columbia University Archives–Columbiana Library.

23. "Address of President Hadley," *Columbia University Quarterly* 4 (June 1902): 38; see 36–38. On Butler's election and inauguration, see "Programme of Exercises: The

Installation of Nicholas Murray Butler as President of Columbia University," April 19, 1902, bound volume in Columbia University Archives–Columbiana Library.

24. For Columbia trustees in 1902, see appendix A.

25. For the tenure of trustees, see ibid.

26. For occupations and wealth of NMB-inherited trustees, see ibid.

27. For trustees by religion and social credentials, see ibid.

28. For trustees by Columbia education, see ibid.

29. William R. Shepherd, "Rives, George Lockhart, 1849–1917," in *Dictionary of American Biography*, 20 vols. (New York: Scribner's, 1928–36), 15:634–35. For Rives's remarks at the 1911 alumni dinner, see NMB Papers, box 1, Rare Book and Manuscript Library, Columbia University.

30. Quoted in Upton Sinclair, *The Goose-step: A Study of American Education* (Pasadena: self-published, 1924), 30.

31. James Kip Finch, "Parsons, William Barclay, 1859–1932," *Dictionary of American Biography*, 14:276–78; William Barclay Parsons Papers, Columbia University Archives–Columbiana Library.

32. John W. Burgess to trustees, December 31, 1908, Burgess Papers, Columbia University Archives–Columbiana Library.

33. Jean Strouse, *Morgan: American Financier* (New York: Random House, 1999); Saul Engelbourg and Leonard Bushkoff, *The Man Who Found the Money: John Stewart Kennedy and the Financing of the Western Railroads* (East Lansing: Michigan State University Press, 1996); Horace W. Carpentier Papers, Columbia University Archives–Columbiana Library.

34. NMB to George L. Rives, April 30, 1903, Rives Papers.

35. NMB to Francis S. Bangs, April 20, 1903, Bangs Papers, Columbia University Archives–Columbiana Library.

36. On the absence of early Rockefeller benefactions, see Frederick P. Keppel, *Columbia* (New York: Oxford University Press, 1914), x–xi.

37. William Bayard Cutting to Seth Low, January 28, 1895, William Bayard Cutting Papers, Columbia University Archives–Columbiana Library. Also see there NMB to Cutting, April 28, 1905.

38. NMB to Marcellus Hartley Dodge, September 28, 1915; Dodge to NMB, October 7, 1915, Marcellus Hartley Dodge Papers, Columbia University Archives–Columbiana Library.

39. Horace W. Carpentier to NMB, March 6, 1906, Carpentier Papers, Columbia University Archives–Columbiana Library.

40. George Santayana, quoted in Elizabeth Hardwick, ed., *The Selected Letters of William James* (New York: Farrar, Straus and Cudahy, 1961), xiv. See Carpentier to NMB, January 25, 1907, Carpentier Papers.

41. Francis S. Bangs to NMB, February 14, 1906, Bangs Papers; Carpentier to NMB, January 25, 1907, Carpentier Papers; NMB to Trustee Edward Mitchell, February 7, 1907, Edward Mitchell Folder, Columbia University Archives–Columbiana Library.

42. Horace W. Carpentier to Seth Low, July 20, 1901, Carpentier Papers. See William Theodore de Bary, "East Asian Studies at Columbia: The Early Years," *Columbia Magazine*, spring 2002, 10–19.

43. Francis S. Bangs to NMB, February 14, 1906, Francis S. Bangs Papers, Columbia University Archives–Columbiana Library. See Bangs to Trustee Edward B. Coe, August 31, 1910, Bangs Papers.

44. Francis S. Bangs to NMB, October 29, 1909, Francis S. Bangs Papers.

45. Columbia Trustees Minutes, March 4, 1907, February 3, 1908, November 2, 1908.

46. George L. Rives to NMB, October 9, 1907, Rives Papers.

47. For trustees during the Butler era, see appendix A.

48. Timothy M. Cheesman to NMB, September 18, 1916, Cheesman Folder, Columbia University Archives–Columbiana Library.

49. Columbia University Trustees Minutes, March 1, 1909.

50. NMB to Francis S. Bangs, February 10, 1908, Bangs Papers.

51. Francis S. Bangs to NMB, January 11, 1907, Bangs Papers. Butler's later insistence that all board members be men "whose interest, and whose only interest, is Columbia University" could well have stemmed from this encounter.

52. Edward Mitchell to NMB, January 15, 1907, Mitchell Folder, Columbia University Archives–Columbiana Library; NMB to Francis S. Bangs, February 10, 1908, Bangs Papers.

53. See chap. 1.

54. See chap. 2.

55. See chap. 3 and appendix B for comparative enrollments of mid-nineteenth-century colleges.

56. See chap. 5.

57. See chaps. 5 and 6.

58. The term "on the make" was applied to Michigan State University in the early 1960s. See Warren Hinckle, "MSU: University On the Make," *Ramparts* 4 (April, 1966): 11–23.

59. On the Cooper Union merger, see Columbia University Trustees Minutes, June 1, 1903. On the mergers with the New York College of Pharmacy and the New York School of Optometry, see College of Pharmacy, Trustees Minutes, March 7, 1904. On Cooper Union merger possibility, see Columbia University Trustees Minutes, June 1, 1903. On NYU merger discussions, see G. Allen Conway, "Columbia and NYU Consolidation: A Study in Urban Social Consciousness" (Ph.D. diss., New York University, 1974). On Newark annex as feeder to Columbia Law School, see NMB to Francis S. Bangs, April 14, 1910, Bangs Papers. See also John A. Burrell, *A History of Adult Education at Columbia University* (New York: Columbia University Press, 1954), 46–47.

60. NMB to George L. Rives, November 20, 1914, Rives Papers. See also Columbia University Trustees Minutes, May 3, 1915.

61. For undergraduate enrollments at Columbia's peers in the Early Butler era, see appendix B.

62. Trustee Rives's son went to Yale, but his daughter attended Barnard.

63. This pattern was visible among the sons of trustees, who, while going elsewhere to college, went to Columbia's Law School or the Medical School. See chap. 9.

64. See appendix B for Ph.D.s.

65. *A Century of Doctorates* (Washington, D.C.: National Academy of Sciences, 1978).

66. Bangs to NMB, February 11, 1908, Bangs Papers. See Carpentier to NMB, November 25, 1902, Carpentier Papers.

67. NMB to Francis S. Bangs, April 14, 1910, Bangs Papers.

68. Columbia University Trustees Minutes, November 7, 1910; "Toastmaster Remarks," Alumni Dinner, October 7, 1911, NMB Papers, box 1.

69. See appendix C.

70. William J. McGill, Oral History interview, June 26, 1979.

71. NMB to Frederick P. Keppel, June 7, 1905, Keppel Papers, Columbia University Archives–Columbiana Library. See also Keppel, *Columbia*, chap. 2.

72. Thorstein Veblen, *The Higher Learning in America: A Memorandum of the Governing of Universities by Businessmen* (1918; reprint, Palo Alto: Stanford Reprints, 1956), 85.

73. Rudolph Tombo Jr., "University Registration Statistics, *Science*, December 8, 1905, 729–40.

74. Rudolph Tombo to Jerome D. Greene, October 25, 1905, Eliot Papers, Harvard University Archives, Harvard University; NMB, President's Annual Report, October 5, 1914. On Eliot's acknowledging the existence of a "friendly rivalry," see Columbia librarian James H. Canfield to Charles W. Eliot, December 23, 1905, Eliot Papers, Harvard University Archives, Harvard University.

75. For 1913–14 enrollments, see Keppel, *Columbia*, appendix D; for 1915 enrollments, see appendix B.

76. I have found no usable rankings of professional schools before the 1920s. What I claim here, however, is consistent with the 1909 survey of fourteen major universities in Edwin D. Slosson, *Great American Universities* (New York: 1910).

77. R. Gordon Hoxie, ed., *A History of the Faculty of Political Science, Columbia University* (New York: Columbia University Press, 1954); John Herman Randall Jr., ed. *A History of the Faculty of Philosophy, Columbia University* (New York: Columbia university Press, 1957. No history of the Faculty of Pure Science was published as part of the Bicentennial Series in which both the Hoxie and Randall volumes appeared.

78. Charles Camic and Yu Xie, "The Statistical Turn in American Social Science: Columbia University, 1890–1915," *American Sociological Review* 59 (1994): 773–805; Stephen P. Turner, "The World of Academic Quantifiers: The Columbia University Family and Its Connections," in Martin Blumer, Kevin Bales, and Kathryn Kish Sklar, eds., *The Social Survey in Historical Perspective, 1880–1940* (Cambridge: Cambridge University Press, 1991), 269–90; George J. Stigler, "Henry L. Moore and Statistical Economics," in *Essays in the History of Economics* (Chicago: University of Chicago Press, 1965); Robert Novick, *That Noble Dream: The "Objectivity Question" and the American Historical Profession* (Cambridge: Cambridge University Press, 1988), 89.

79. William James to Henry James, February 14, 1907, in Ignas K. Skrupskelis and Elizabeth M. Berkeley, eds., *William and Henry James: Selected Letters* (Charlottesville: University of Virginia Press, 1997), 481–82. See Randall, *Faculty of Philosophy*; de Bary, "East Asian Studies at Columbia"; Robert A. McCaughey, *International Studies and Academic Enterprise: A Chapter in the Enclosure of American Learning* (New York: Columbia University Press, 1984), 30, 35.

80. Charles E. Rosenberg, "The Social Environment of Scientific Innovation: Factors in the Development of Genetics in the United States," in *No Other Gods: On Science and Social Thought* (Baltimore: Johns Hopkins University Press, 1976), 196–209; Eric R. Kan-

dell, "Thomas Hunt Morgan at Columbia University: Genes, Chromosomes, and the Origins of Modern Biology," *Columbia Magazine*, fall 1999, 29–35.

81. Slosson, *Great American Universities*, 8, 479, 71–72, 402–3, 76, 446.

82. For a timeline of Butler's presidential contemporaries, see Lawrence R. Veysey, *The Emergence of the American University* (Chicago: University of Chicago Press, 1965), 447.

8. 1917: TWILIGHT OF IDOLS

1. Edward Mitchell to Nicholas Murray Butler (hereafter NMB), February 13, 1906, Mitchell Folder, Columbia University Archives–Columbiana Library.

2. NMB, *Across the Busy Years: Recollections and Reflections* (New York: Scribner's, 1939), 1:161. See chap. 7.

3. Ibid., chap. 7.

4. NMB to Charles A. Beard, March 5, 1908, Charles A. Beard Papers, Columbia University Archives–Columbiana Library.

5. NMB to George L. Rives, December 10, 1914, George L. Rives Papers, Columbia University Archives–Columbiana Library.

6. This number includes Barnard College and Teachers College, which had their own deans, chosen by the schools' trustees, and small administrative staffs of their own. See appendix B.

7. Frederick P. Keppel, *Columbia* (New York: Oxford University Press, 1914), 42–43.

8. William Summerscales, *Affirmation and Dissent: Columbia's Response to the Crisis of World War One* (New York: Teachers College Press, 1970), chap. 2.

9. William H. Carpenter Papers and Adam Leroy Jones Papers, Columbia University Archives–Columbiana Library.

10. Ellen C. Lagemann, "Keppel, Frederick P., 1875–1943," in *American National Biography* (New York: Oxford University Press, 1999), 12:617–19; Frederick P. Keppel Papers, Columbia University Archives–Columbiana Library.

11. NMB to Frederick P. Keppel, October 6, 1910; Frederick P. Keppel to NMB, September 24, 1910, Keppel Papers.

12. For the McCulloch case, see chap. 5.

13. For Chandler, see chap. 4. For Osgood, see Dixon Ryan Fox, *Herbert Levi Osgood: An American Scholar* (New York: Columbia University Press, 1924).

14. Seth Low to Trustee Edward B. Coe, December 15, 1900, Edward B. Coe folder, Columbia University Archives–Columbiana Library.

15. Vincent Freimarck, "Woodberry, George E., 1855–1930," in *American National Biography*, 23:785–87; R. B. Hovet, "George Edward Woodberry: Genteel Exile," *New England Quarterly* 23 (December 1950): 504–26.

16. Brander Matthews, *These Many Years: Recollections of a New Yorker* (New York: Scribner's, 1917); Howard Stein, "Brander Matthews and Theater Studies at Columbia," *Columbia Magazine*, spring 2002, 20–27.

17. Oscar James Campbell, "English and Comparative Literature," in John Herman Randall Jr., *A History of the Faculty of Philosophy, Columbia University* (New York: Columbia University Press, 1957), 66–76.

18. Charles W. Eliot to George S. Woodberry, July 28, 1903, Charles William Eliot Papers, Harvard University Archives, Harvard University.

19. NMB to Francis S. Bangs, May 5, 1902, Francis S. Bangs Papers, Columbia University Archives–Columbiana Library; Bangs to NMB, May 2, 1902, Bangs Papers; Eliot quoted in Edmund Clarence Stedman to George S. Woodberry, May 5, 1902, George S. Woodberry, Papers, Harvard University Archives; C. W. Eliot to Woodberry, July 23, 1903, Woodberry Papers; Woodberry to Lewis Einstein, December 26, 1903, Woodberry Papers.

20. Woodberry to Barrett Wendell, September 22, 1905, Woodberry Papers.

21. NMB to George L. Rives, February 6, 1904, Rives Papers.

22. "Prof. MacDowell Follows Prof. Woodberry in Resigning," *New York Times*, February 4, 1904, 16. See NMB to Rives, February 6, 1904; Alan Levy, "MacDowell, Edward, 1861–1908," in *American National Biography*, 14:222–24.

23. Rives to NMB, May 23, 1905, Rives Papers. Shortly after his resignation, MacDowell was run over by a carriage and sustained injuries that curtailed his composing and led to his death at forty-seven.

24. George H. Genzel, "Peck, Harry Thurston, 1856–1914," in *Dictionary of American Biography*, 20 vols. (New York: Scribner's, 1928–36), 14:377–79.

25. Columbia University Trustees Minutes, October 3, 1910; NMB to Frederick P. Keppel, October 6, 1910, Keppel Papers.

26. Robert F. Martin, "Spingarn, Joel Elias, 1875–1939," in *American National Biography*, 20:476–78.

27. George L. Rives to NMB, March 5, 1911, Rives Papers. See Columbia University Trustees Minutes, April 4, 1910; *A Question of Academic Freedom, Being the Official Correspondence Between Nicholas Murray Butler . . . and J. E. Spingarn* (New York, 1911).

28. Frederick P. Keppel to NMB, September 24, 1910, Keppel Papers.

29. James McKeen Cattell to Seth Low, December 21, 1895; Cattell to NMB, April 19, 1904, James McKeen Cattell Papers, Columbia University Archives–Columbiana Library. See also Dorothy Ross, "Cattell, James McKeen, 1860–1944," in *Dictionary of American Biography*, 23:148–51.

30. Cattell to NMB, February 3, 1903, Cattell Papers.

31. Cattell to NMB, February 15, 1907, Cattell Papers.

32. James McKeen Cattell, "University Control," *Science* 23 (1906): 475–77, entire series reprinted in A. T. Poffenberger, ed., *James McKeen Cattell: Man of Science* (Lancaster, Pa.: Science Press, 1947), 2:265–304.

33. Cattell to NMB, February 25, 1907; NMB to Cattell, February 27, 1907, Cattell Papers.

34. NMB to Cattell, February 27, 1907; Cattell to NMB, January 8, 1909, Cattell Papers.

35. NMB to Seth Low, March 29, 1909, copy in Cattell Papers. See Cattell to NMB, February 20, 1909, Cattell Papers.

36. Bangs to NMB, February 27, 1909, Bangs Papers.

37. Cattell to NMB, May 15, 1909, Cattell Papers. See Cattell to NMB, January 8, 1909; NMB to Cattell, January 10, 1909, Cattell Papers.

38. Cattell to NMB, November 24, 1909; NMB to Cattell, November 26, 1909; Cattell to NMB, January 4, 1910, Cattell Papers.

39. NMB to Francis S. Bangs, December 1, 1910; Bangs to NMB, December 3, 1910; NMB to Bangs, December 5, 1910, Bangs Papers. See Cattell to NMB, November 21, 1910, Cattell Papers.

40. Francis S. Bangs to NMB, March 14, 1911, Bangs Papers; Cattell to George L. Rives, May 13, 1913, Cattell Papers. See minutes of the Columbia University Trustees Committee on Education, May 1, 1913, copy included in Cattell Papers; Cattell to Members of the Century Association, May 8, 1913.

41. Edward L. Thorndike and Robert S. Woodworth to NMB, May 12, 1913; F. J. E. Woodbridge to NMB, May 13, 1913; E. B. Wilson to NMB, May 20, 1913; George L. Rives to Cattell, May 21, 1913, Cattell Papers.

42. Cattell, memorandum to members of the Columbia University Faculty Club, January 10, 1917, Cattell Papers.

43. Franz Boas to NMB, September 24, 1914, Franz Boas Papers, Columbia University Archives–Columbiana Library; John W. Burgess to NMB, June 28, 1906, April 6, 1910, Burgess Papers. Franz Boas and William H. Carpenter were active in organizing the Columbia chapter of the Germanistic Society of America in 1904. See Boas to Carpenter, November 29, 1904, Boas Papers.

44. E. R. Fuhrman, "Giddings, Franklin H., 1855–1931," in *American National Biography*, 8:943–44. For Giddings and Beard as pro-British, see Carol S. Gruber, *Mars and Minerva: World War One and the Uses of the Higher Learning in America* (Baton Rouge: Louisiana University Press, 1975).

45. Ernest R. May, *The World War and American Isolation, 1914–1917* (Cambridge: Harvard University Press, 1959), 41. See William Summerscales, *Affirmation and Dissent: Columbia's Response to the Crisis of World War One* (New York: Teachers College Press, 1970), 46.

46. Theodore Roosevelt to James Bryce, March 31, 1915, in Elting Morison, ed., *The Letters of Theodore Roosevelt* (Cambridge: Harvard University Press, 1954), 8:915. See John W. Burgess, *The Present Crisis in Europe* (New York: German-American Literary Defense Committee, 1914); idem, *America's Relation to the Great War* (Chicago: A. C. McClurg, 1916).

47. Warren I. Cohen, *The American Revisionists: The Lessons of Intervention in World War I* (Chicago: University of Chicago Press, 1967), 146 passim. See NMB to Marcellus Hartley Dodge, September 28, 1915; Dodge to NMB, October 7, 1915, Marcellus Hartley Dodge Papers, Columbia University Archives–Columbiana Library; May, *The World War and American Isolation*.

48. May, *World War and American Isolation*, part 5.

49. Alan Ryan, *John Dewey and the High Tide of American Liberalism* (New York: Norton, 1995), 156–57; Christopher Lasch, *The New Radicalism in America, 1889–1963: The Intellectual as a Social Type* (New York: Knopf, 1965), chap. 6.

50. *Randolph Bourne: The Radical Will, Selected Writings 1911–1918*, ed. Olaf Hansen (Berkeley: University of California Press, 1977), 307–18, 336–47, 342. See also Casey Blake, *Beloved Community: The Cultural Criticism of Randolph Bourne, Van Wyck Brooks, Waldo Frank, and Lewis Mumford* (Chapel Hill: University of North Carolina Press, 1990).

51. NMB to President Woodrow Wilson, February 13, 1917, cited in Columbia University Trustees Minutes, March 5, 1917.

52. Columbia University Trustees Minutes, March 5, 1917.

53. NMB, speech at the alumni luncheon, June 6, 1917, quoted in Summerscales, *Affirmation and Dissent*, 99–100.

54. Carol S. Gruber, "Academic Freedom at Columbia University, 1917–1918: The Case of James McKeen Cattell," *AAUP Bulletin* 58 (September 1972): 297–305.

55. E. R. A. Seligman to NMB, March 3, 1917, copy in Cattell Papers.

56. Seligman to Cattell, June 18, 1917, Cattell Papers.

57. NMB to William Barclay Parsons, July 2, 1917, William Barclay Parsons Papers, Columbia University Archives–Columbiana Library.

58. Cattell to Columbia Board of Trustees, October 3, 1917, Cattell Papers. See Walter P. Metzger, *Academic Freedom in the Age of the University* (New York: Columbia University Press, 1961), 224–28.

59. University Council Minutes, October 1, 1917, cited in Summerscales, *Affirmation and Dissent*, 91; John Pine to William Barclay Parsons, October 2, 1917, Parsons Papers.

60. Columbia University Trustees Minutes, October 4, 1917. See Summerscales, *Affirmation and Dissent*, 93.

61. Bangs to NMB, December 13, 1917, Bangs Papers.

62. Bangs to NMB, September 20, 1917, Bangs Papers.

63. William Barclay Parsons to NMB, July 2, 1917, Parsons Papers; Columbia University Trustees Minutes, April 21, 1916. See NMB to Charles A. Beard, April 25, 1916, Beard Papers.

64. NMB to Frederick P. Keppel, November 28, 1940, Keppel Papers. See Ellen Nore, *Charles A. Beard: An Intellectual Biography* (Carbondale; Southern Illinois University Press, 1983), 28–37, 72–86; Charles A. Beard to NMB, October 20, 1911, May 24, 1913, March 5, 1915, Beard Papers.

65. John W. Burgess to NMB, March 25, 1912, Burgess Papers. On Beard and the trustees, see Charles A. Beard, "Statement of Facts in the Matter of the Committee of Education of the Board of Trustees of Columbia University and Professor Charles A. Beard," Charles A. Beard Papers, De Pauw University, Greencastle, Indiana.

66. Quoted in Ellen Nore, *Charles A. Beard: An Intellectual Biography* (Carbondale: Southern Illinois Press, 1983), 63.

67. Charles A. Beard to NMB, February 15, 1917, Beard Papers. Beard's own rendering of his 1916 dealings with the trustees is provided in a "Statement of Facts in the Matter of the Committee of Education of the Board of Trustees of Columbia University and Professor Charles A. Beard."

68. Charles A. Beard to Columbia University Trustees, October 8, 1917, included in Columbia University Trustees Minutes, November 5, 1917.

69. "Columbia's Deliverance," *New York Times*, October 10, 1917; Annie Nathan Meyer, letter to *New York Times*, October 13, 1917; Alfred Cruikshank to NMB, October 10, 1917, copy in Beard Papers.

70. Japanese and Chinese students' petition of October 12, 1917, and Peithologian Society protest statement of October 14, 1917, in Beard Papers.

71. William Pepperell Montague, letter to New York *Tribune*, October 12, 1917; Henry R. Mussey to E. R. A Seligman, November 26, 1917, copy in Columbia University Trustees Minutes, December 3, 1917.

72. Francis S. Bangs to NMB, December 13, 1917, Bangs Papers; Nicholas Murray Butler to Frederick P. Keppel, December 28, 1918, Keppel Papers.

73. NMB to George T. Ingraham, October 8, 1917, Ingraham Papers, Columbia University Archives–Columbiana Library; James Harvey Robinson resignation letter, quoted in Columbia University Trustees Minutes, May 5, 1919. See Joan S. Rubin, "Durant, Will, 1885–1981," in *American National Biography*, 7:146–48; James Frigugli-etti, "Robinson, James Harvey, 1863–1936," ibid., 18:658–61; Peter M. Rutkoff and William B. Scott, *New School: A History of the New School for Social Research* (New York: Free, 1986); Alvin Johnson, *Pioneer's Progress: An Autobiography* (New York: Viking, 1952).

74. Francis S. Bangs to NMB, February 14, 1918, Bangs Papers. See Ryan, *John Dewey*, 203–9. On Boas at Barnard in the 1920s, see Rosalind Rosenberg, *Changing the Subject: A History of Women at Columbia* (New York: Columbia University Press, forthcoming).

75. Gruber, *Mars and Minerva*; Lawrence E. Gelfand, *The Inquiry: American Preparations for Peace, 1917–1919* (New Haven: Yale University Press, 1963).

76. Columbia University Trustees Minutes, May 5, 1919. See Columbia University Trustees Minutes, February 6, 1922.

77. Rexford Tugwell, *To the Lesser Heights of Morningside: A Memoir* (Philadelphia; University of Pennsylvania Press, 1982), 151; John Erskine, *The Memory of Certain Persons* (Philadelphia: Lippincott, 1947), 253.

78. [F. J. E. Woodbridge], undated ten-page statement composed in fall of 1917, after the firings of Cattell and Dana, likely Woodbridge's statement to the University Council, copy in Cattell Papers, Columbiana Collection, CU, 10.

9. JEWS AT COLUMBIA

1. Harold Wechsler, *The Qualified Student: A History of Selective College Admission in America, 1870–1970* (New York: Wiley, 1977); Marcia Graham Synnott, *The Half-Opened Door: Discrimination and Admissions at Harvard, Yale, and Princeton, 1900–1970* (Westport, Conn.; Greenwood, 1979); Dan A. Oren, *Joining the Club: A History of Jews and Yale* (New Haven: Yale University Press, 1985).

2. William H. McNeill, *Hutchins' University: A Memoir of the University of Chicago, 1929–1950* (Chicago: University of Chicago, 1991), 52–53.

3. For Jewish enrollment and graduation data, see appendix B.

4. Kenneth M. Ludmerer, *Time to Heal: American Medical Education from the Turn of the Century to the Era of Managed Care* (New York: Oxford University Press, 1999), 64.

5. Synnott, *The Half-Opened Door*; Oren, *Joining The Club*; Morton Keller and Phyllis Keller, *Making Harvard Modern: The Rise of America's University* (New York: Oxford University Press, 2001), 47–51; author interview with Michael I. Sovern, May 5, 1999.

6. *Vanity Fair* quoted in Heywood Broun and George Britt, *Christians Only: A Study in Prejudice* (New York: Vanguard, 1931), 73. See M. G. Torch, "The Spirit of Morningside: Some Notes on Columbia University," *Menorah Journal* 18 (March 1930): 253.

7. Milton Halsey Thomas, Diary, July 12, 1923, New-York Historical Society; "The Spirit of Morningside," 253–61; Torch, "The Spirit of Morningside," 253, 254; see 253–60.

8. Such phrases regularly appear in the correspondence between Butler and his

trustees and Butler and his administrators. Among the trustees, Bangs, Parsons, and Pine are among the most frequent phrasemakers.

9. Frederick P. Keppel to NMB, October 4, 1912, Frederick P. Keppel Papers, Columbia University Archives–Columbiana Library.

10. A prefatory comment about the term "problem." It is used here in part because it was used throughout the Butler era, in a literal sense, as in, "We have a problem." Its use here, however, allows an implied distinction between a real problem and a one that is socially constructed. Finding the money to operate Columbia constitutes a real problem, while what was characterized early in the twentieth century as Columbia's "Jewish Problem" can now be understood as socially constructed. One difference between real and socially constructed problems is the latter, unlike the former, are susceptible to deconstruction. That's the good news.

11. Madison Grant, *The Passing of the Great Race* (New York: Scribner's, 1918). See Ann Douglas, *Terrible Honesty: Mongrel Manhattan in the 1920s* (New York: Farrar, Straus, 1995); Leonard Dinnerstein, *Anti-Semitism in America* (New York: Oxford University Press, 1994), chaps. 4 and 5.

12. Harold S. Wechsler, "The Selective Function of American College Admission Policies, 1870–1970" (Ph.D. diss., Department of History Columbia University, 1974), 208.

13. See chap. 4.

14. Sven Beckert, *The Monied Metropolis: New York City and the Consolidation of the American Bourgeoisie, 1850–1896* (Cambridge; Cambridge University Press, 2002), 239–40.

15. F. A. P. Barnard, President's Annual Report, 1878; Seth Low, President's Annual Report, October 7, 1895, Columbia University Archives–Columbiana Library.

16. Frederick P. Keppel to William B. Parsons, September 25, 1905, William B. Parsons Papers, Columbia University Archives–Columbiana Library; John B. Pine to Nicholas Murray Butler, April 3, 1906, John B. Pine Papers, Columbia University Archives–Columbiana Library. Fish's defection may also have been the result of Columbia's decision in December 1905 to eliminate intercollegiate football. He became an All-American in football at Harvard.

17. The Prettyman report is discussed in Wechsler, *The Qualified Student*, 147–50.

18. Nicholas Murray Butler (hereafter NMB) to Francis S. Bangs, November 2, 1904, Francis S. Bangs Papers, Columbia University Archives–Columbiana Library. See NMB to Bangs, February 15, 1906; Bangs to NMB, May 6, 1907, Bangs Papers.

19. NMB to Bangs, October 4, 1907, Bangs Papers.

20. NMB to Bangs, November 2, 1904, October 4, 1907, Bangs Papers.

21. Harold Wechsler has suggested a useful distinction between what Pine took to be a morally neutral crisis and more indignant trustees regarded as an institution-wrecking catastrophe (conversation with author, fall 2002).

22. Frederick P. Keppel to NMB, July 19, 1910, Frederick P. Keppel Papers, Columbia University Archives–Columbiana Library. My understanding of Keppel has been helped by discussions with and the writings of Bill Whelan, who is preparing an account of Keppel's deanship.

23. Frederick P. Keppel to NMB, September 15, 1910; September 24, 1910, Keppel Papers.

24. Keppel to NMB, October 4, 1912, Keppel Papers. See appendix B.

25. Keppel to William Barclay Parsons, September 25, 1905, William Barclay Parsons Papers, Columbia University Archives–Columbiana Library.

26. Keppel to NMB, May 13, 1913, Keppel Papers.

27. [Francis S. Bangs], Report of the Committee on Education, Columbia University Trustees Minutes, May 5, 1913.

28. Faculty rejection statement of October 13, 1913 in Keppel Papers. Bangs would likely have appreciated the fact that the residential requirement he proposed in 1912 was just what Myles Cooper had implemented at King's College in 1764—and for a similarly exclusionary purpose. See chap. 1.

29. Keppel to NMB, January 27, 1912; Keppel to Trustee Committee on Education, November 25, 1913, Keppel Papers.

30. NMB to Keppel, January 27, 1914, Keppel Papers.

31. Frederick P. Keppel, *Columbia* (New York: Oxford University Press, 1914), 179–80.

32. Ibid., 180.

33. Ibid.

34. NMB to Francis S. Bangs, January 29, 1906, Bangs Papers.

35. NMB to Keppel, January 27, 1914, Keppel Papers; Adam Leroy Jones, *New Plan of Admissions* (New York: Columbia College, 1913), 20, copy in Adam Leroy Jones folder, Columbia University Archives–Columbiana Library.

36. NMB to Keppel, April 22, 1918, Keppel Papers. On the the personal interview requirement, see Harold S. Wechsler, "The Rise and Fall of Jewish Discrimination at Columbia" (talk to the University Seminar on the History of Columbia University, November 19, 1998), http://beatl.barnard.columbia.edu/cuhistory/archives/wechsler-Text.htm.

37. NMB to Keppel, April 21, 1919, May 5, 1919, Keppel Papers. For Keppel's post-Columbia career, see Ellen C. Lagemann, *The Politics of Knowledge: The Carnegie Corporation, Philanthropy, and Public Policy* (Middletown: Wesleyan University Press, 1989).

38. Quoted in William E. Weld and Kathryn W. Sewry, *Herbert E. Hawkes, Dean of Columbia College, 1918–1943* (New York: Columbia University Press, 1958), 48; Herbert Hawkes to Frederick Paul Keppel, October 2, 1919, Keppel Papers. Hawkes had become independently wealthy through the writing of a widely adopted mathematics textbook while on the Yale faculty.

39. Broun and Britt, *Christians Only*, 89.

40. NMB to William B. Parsons, October 2, 1917, Parsons Papers.

41. The table "Percentage of Jewish Students at Thirty Colleges and Universities, 1918–19" (adapted from data included in *American Jewish Yearbook* 22, no. 5681 [September 13, 1920, to October 2, 1921], 381–93), in Synnott, *The Half-Opened Door*, 16, provides the following percentages for New York institutions: College of the City of New York (79 percent); NYU (48 percent); Hunter (39 percent); Fordham (23 percent); Columbia (21 percent). Other colleges: Harvard (10 percent); Cornell (9 percent); Princeton (3 percent).

42. William B. Parsons to George Rives, November 8, 1913, Parsons Papers.

43. Geraldine Joncich, *The Sane Positivist: A Biography of Edward L. Thorndike* (Middletown: Wesleyan University Press, 1968), chap. 16; Nicholas Lemann, *The Big Test: The*

Secret History of the American Meritocracy (New York: Farrar, Straus, 1999), 17–18, 23; Wechsler, *The Qualified Student*, 158–59.

44. Herbert E. Hawkes to E. B. Wilson, June 16, 1922, Herbert E. Hawkes Papers, Columbia University Archives–Columbiana Library.

45. Ben Wood, Faculty Appointment Card, Columbia University Archives–Columbiana Library. For more on Wood, see Lehman, *The Big Test*, 34–39.

46. Wechsler, *The Qualified Student*, 166–68.

47. Albert W. Putnam to NMB, March 22, 1920, Albert W. Putnam Papers, Columbia University Archives–Columbiana Library. See Columbia University Trustees Minutes, April 5, 1920.

48. Quoted in Weld and Sewry, *Herbert E. Hawkes*, 49; Columbia University Trustees Minutes, May 3, 1926; NMB to Trustee Ambrose D. Henry, January 28, 1924, Ambrose D. Henry Papers, Columbia University Archives–Columbiana Library. On the Cutting Travelling Fellowship's proscription against the children of foreign-born parents, see author interview with Eli Ginzberg, September 19, 1997. On the Bangs fellowship, see Columbia University Trustees Minutes, May 3, 1926. On the Pine bequest, see NMB to Trustee Ambrose D. Henry, January 28, 1924, Ambrose D. Henry Papers, Columbia University Archives–Columbiana Library.

49. Columbia University Trustees Minutes, November 7, 1927. On the DeWitt fellowship, see Columbia University Trustees Minutes, November 7, 1927; Goebel, *School of Law*, 290–91.

50. On Seth Low Junior College, see Columbia University Trustees Minutes, February 6, 1928; John Angus Burrell, *A History of Adult Education at Columbia University* (New York: Columbia University Press, 1954), 53–54. See also Blossom R. Carron, "Seth Low Junior College: A Case Study of an Abortive Experiment" (Ed.D. diss., Teachers College, 1979).

51. Columbia University Trustees Minutes, March 5, 1928. See NMB to Trustee Albert W. Putnam, November 8, 1934, Putnam Papers. On Isaac Asimov, see Isaac Asimov, *In Memory Yet Green: The Autobiography of Isaac Asimov, 1920–1954* (Garden City: Doubleday, 1979), 140–61.

52. Francis S. Bangs to NMB, February 15, 1906, Bangs Papers; Columbia University Trustees Minutes, April 2, 1928. For the religious composition of the board, see appendix A.

53. On St. Stephens/Bard in the 1930s, see Columbia University Trustees Minutes, October 2, 1944.

54. The fact that ethnoreligious classifications were regularly published in the *Columbia Alumni Magazine* in the 1920s and 1930s allows the conclusion that Columbia officials wanted to assure older alums that the situation was not as bad as the general press had it.

55. Herbert E. Hawkes to E. B. Wilson, June 16, 1922, Herbert E. Hawkes Papers, Columbia University Archives–Columbiana Library.

56. Frank Bowles to NMB, January 31, 1935, Frank Bowles Papers, Columbia University Archives–Columbiana Library.

57. Ginzberg interview, September 19, 1997.

58. Author interview with Henry Graff, May 3, 2000. Another Columbia historian, John A. Garraty, whose mother was Jewish, similarly attended Brooklyn College before even thinking of applying to Columbia, where he later received his Ph.D.

59. "The Roots of the Tree," *Princeton Alumni Weekly*, November 17, 1933. I wish to acknowledge the help of Bill Whelan, U.S. Department of State, in directing me to this source. For undergraduate demographics, see appendix B. In its ethnic composition, interwar Columbia was much like the University of Pennsylvania, although Penn retained stronger links to "Proper Philadelphia" than Columbia did to "Knickerbocker New York." See E. Digby Baltzell, *Puritan Boston and Quaker Philadelphia: Two Protestant Ethics and the Spirit of Class Authority and Leadership* (New York: Free, 1979), 258–59; Richard A. Farnum, "Prestige at Three Ivy League Universities: Harvard, Columbia, Penn" (Ph.D. diss., Department of Sociology, University of Pennsylvania, 1990).

60. Quoted in Weld and Sewry, *Herbert E. Hawkes*, 114.

61. For religious preferences of students, see appendix B.

62. Frederick P. Keppel to NMB, October 1, 1909, Keppel Papers.

63. Author interviews with Eli Ginzberg, September 17, 1999; Graff interview, May 3, 2000. For the religious affiliations of the trustees, see appendix A.

64. George Barry Ford, *A Degree of Difference* (New York: Farrar, Straus, 1969).

65. Gerald Beekman to NMB, January 28, 1913, Gerald Beekman Papers, Columbia University Archives–Columbiana Library; David Greer to NMB, January 30, 1915, David Greer Papers, Columbia University Archives–Columbiana Library.

66. Francis S. Bangs to NMB, January 26, 1915, Bangs Papers.

67. NMB to George Rives, January 28, 1913, George L. Rives Papers, Columbia University Archives–Columbiana Library. See Ford, *Degree of Difference*, 105; and *New York Times*, May 9, 1938, 6, col. 2.

68. Quoted in Edmund B. O'Callaghan, ed., *The Documentary History of the State of New York* (Albany, 1849–51), 1:186.

69. George M. Marsden, *The Soul of the American University: From Protestant Establishment to Established Nonbelief* (New York: Oxford University Press, 1994), 429–44. See also Julie A. Reuben, *The Making of the Modern University: Intellectual Transformation and the Marginalization of Morality* (Chicago: University of Chicago Press, 1996).

70. Thomas Merton, *The Seven Storey Mountain* (New York: Harcourt, Brace, 1948). On Merton at Columbia, see Michael Mott, *The Seven Mountains of Thomas Merton* (Boston: Houghton Mifflin, 1984), 95–121. See also Thomas Merton, "Learning to Live," in Wesley First, ed., *University on the Heights* (Garden City: Doubleday, 1969), 187–99.

10. THE INVENTION OF COLUMBIA COLLEGE

1. The best source on the history of American intercollegiate athletics is Ronald A. Smith, *Sports and Freedom: The Rise of Big-Time College Athletics* (New York: Oxford University Press, 1988). On Collins, see "The Official Eddie Collins Web Site," www.cmgww.com/baseball/collins. On Gehrig, see Ray Robinson, "Lou Gehrig: Columbia Legend and American Hero," *Columbia Magazine*, fall 2001, 28–33.

2. Columbia win-loss statistics were provided by the Sports Information Office, Columbia University.

3. Smith, *Sports and Freedom*, 46; see 150, 154. There is very little published on Colum-

bia intercollegiate athletics. I have relied principally on J. N. Arbolino, "The Lion Afield," in Dwight C. Miner, ed., *A History of Columbia College on Morningside* (New York: Columbia University Press, 1954), 199–231; and George Ziegenfuss, "Intercollegiate Athletics at Columbia University" (Ed.D. diss., Teachers College, Columbia University, 1950).

4. Nicholas Murray Butler (hereafter NMB), *Across the Busy Years: Recollections and Reflections* (New York: Scribner's, 1939), 1:85–86.

5. Ziegenfuss, "Intercollegiate Athletics at Columbia University," 112–15.

6. Ronald A. Smith, "Camp, Walter C., 1859–1925," in *American National Biography* (New York: Oxford University Press, 1999), 4:263–65; Ronald A. Smith, ed., *Big-Time Football at Harvard, 1905: The Diary of Coach Bill Reid* (Urbana: University of Illinois Press, 1994), 314 n. 93. See also "Columbia's Football Team of the Century," http://www.columbia.edu/cu/athletics/comm/century/.

7. *Columbia Spectator*, October 25, 1902, 1.

8. Francis S. Bangs to Seth Low, February 26, 1900; Bangs to NMB, December 21, 1905, Francis S. Bangs Papers, Columbia University Archives–Columbiana Library.

9. Albert W. Putnam to NMB, December 23, 1905, Albert W. Putnam Papers, Columbia University Archives–Columbiana Library.

10. Henry Beech Needham, "The College Athlete," *McClure's Magazine* 25 (June/July 1905): 115–28, 260–73; Albert W. Putnam to NMB, December 23, 1905, November 13, 1910, Putnam Papers; Horace W. Carpentier to NMB, January 25, 1906, Horace W. Carpentier Papers, Columbia University Archives–Columbiana Library; Smith, *Sports and Freedom*, 198–99.

11. Quoted in Hugh Hawkins, *Between Harvard and America: The Educational Leadership of Charles W. Eliot* (New York: Oxford University Press, 1972), 115. See NMB, Memorandum on Athletic Sports and Intercollegiate Contests, November 8, 1906, Columbia University Archives–Columbiana Library; Hugh Hawkins, *Between Harvard and America: The Educational Leadership of Charles W. Eliot* (New York: Oxford University Press, 1972), 113–15; Ronald A. Smith, "Harvard and Columbia and a Reconsideration of the 1905–06 Football Crisis," *Journal of Sport History* 8 (winter 1981): 5–19. Stanford and the University of California also briefly dropped football.

12. Ziegenfuss, *Columbia Athletics*, 128–35. In point of fact, Columbia did not play Harvard in football between 1905 and 1948.

13. George L. Rives to NMB, October 11, 1915, George L. Rives Papers, Columbia University Archives–Columbiana Library.

14. Andrew S. Dolkart, *Morningside Heights: A History of Its Architecture and Development* (New York: Columbia University Press, 1998), 171–72.

15. Howard Savage, *American College Athletics* (New York: Carnegie Foundation for the Advancement of Teaching, 1928). On Percy Haughton, see Edwin Pope, *Football's Greatest Coaches* (Atlanta: Tupper and Love, 1955), 105–15. Haughton's overall record of eight wins, five losses, and two ties, alas, makes him Columbia's only football coach with a winning overall record. On Walter Koppisch, see "Columbia's Football Team of the Century," http://www.columbia.edu/cu/athletics/comm/century/. In 1930 the trustees assumed full responsibility for football and all intercollegiate sports, placing daily supervision in the hands of an athletic director who reported to the president.

16. On Lou Little, see Pope, *Football's Greatest Coaches*, 164–73.

17. Ray Robinson, "Lou Gehrig: Columbia Legend and American Hero," *Columbia Magazine*, fall 2001, 28–33. On George Gregory, see the obituary in *New York Times*, May 21, 1994, sec. 1, 11, col. 5.

18. William E. Weld and Kathryn W. Sewry, *Herbert E. Hawkes, Dean of Columbia College, 1918–1943* (New York: Columbia University Press, 1958).

19. James L. Shulman and William Bowen, *The Game of Life: College Sports and Educational Values* (Princeton: Princeton University Press, 2001), 50–51.

20. On Reed Harris, see Robert Cohen, *When the Old Left Was Young: Student Radicals and America's First Mass Student Movement* (New York: Oxford University Press, 1993), 53–-68. See also James Wechsler, *The Age of Suspicion* (New York: Random House, 1953), 21–27. On Wechsler as a sports fan, see James A. Wechsler, "Politics and Football," in Wesley First, ed., *University on the Heights* (Garden City: Doubleday, 1969), 149–54.

21. Charley Rosen, *The Wizard of Odds: How Jack Molinas Almost Destroyed the Game of Basketball* (New York: Seven Stories, 2001).

22. Frederick Rudolph, *Curriculum: A History of the American Undergraduate Course of Study Since 1636* (San Francisco: Jossey-Bass, 1977), 1; see also ibid., 236–37, 256–57; and idem, *The American Collage and University: A History* (1962; reprint, Athens: University of Georgia Press, 1990), chaps. 7, 18. On Rudolph, see John R. Thelin, "Introductory Essay," in Rudolph, *The American College*, ix–xxiii.

23. Rudolph, *The American College*, 455–56.

24. Jacques Barzun, *A College Plan in Action: A Review of Working Principles at Columbia College* (New York: Columbia University Press, 1946); Lionel Trilling, "Columbia College in the Van Amringe and Keppel Era," and Justus Buchler, "Reconstruction in the Liberal Arts," in Miner, *A History of Columbia College*, 14–47, 48–135, respectively; Daniel Bell, *The Reforming of General Education: The Columbia College Experience in Its National Setting* (New York: Columbia University Press, 1966; reprint, New York: Anchor, Doubleday, 1968).

25. David Denby, *Great Books: My Adventures with Homer, Rousseau, Woolf, and Other Indestructible Writers of the Western World* (New York: Simon and Schuster, 1996); Timothy P. Cross, *An Oasis of Order: The Core Curriculum at Columbia College* (New York: Columbia College, 1995).

26. Rudolph, *Curriculum*, 245–48.

27. Noah Porter, *The American Colleges and the American Public* (1870; reprint, New York: Arno, 1969), 33. On F. A. P. Barnard and the elective system, see chap. 5.

28. John W. Burgess, *Reminiscences of an American Scholar: The Beginnings of Columbia University* (New York: Columbia University Press, 1934; reprint, New York: Arno, 1966), 166. See Brooks Mather Kelley, *Yale: A History* (New Haven: Yale University Press, 1974), 344.

29. Hawkins, *Between Harvard and America*, 90–96.

30. Ibid., 80–84; Robert A. McCaughey, "The Transformation of American Academic Life: Harvard University, 1821–1892," *Perspectives in American History* 8 (1974): 261–62.

31. For enrollment statistics, see appendix B.

32. John Erskine, *George Edward Woodberry: An Appreciation* (New York: New York Public Library, 1930); Lawrence R. Veysey, *The Emergence of the American University* (Chicago: University of Chicago Press, 1965), 224.

33. John Erskine, *The Memory of Certain Persons* (Philadelphia: Lippincott, 1947), 11. For further autobiographical details, see ibid.; and idem, *My Life as a Teacher* (Philadelphia: Lippincott, 1948).

34. John Erskine, "The College on Forty-Ninth Street," in *The Memory of Certain Persons*, 71, 91. For Erskine's discussions of Van Amringe, MacDowell, and Woodberry, see ibid., 70–71, 72–79, 88–89, respectively.

35. John Erskine, "The Graduate School," in *Memory of Certain Persons*, 114–16.

36. John Erskine, "Amherst College," in *Memory of Certain Persons*, 125.

37. John Erskine, "The New Columbia," in *Memory of Certain Persons*, 193, 216.

38. John Erskine, "The Moral Obligation to be Intelligent," in *Memory of Certain Persons*, 228–34. The text of the essay can be found in John Erskine, *The Moral Obligation to be Intelligent, and Other Essays* (New York: Duffield, 1916), 3–32. The same title is aptly used in a recent collection of essays by Lionel Trilling, *The Moral Obligation to be Intelligent: Selected Essays*, ed. Leon Wieseltier (New York: Farrar, Straus, 2000).

39. Erskine, *Memory of Certain Persons*, 229–32.

40. John Erskine, "Reading in Great Books," in ibid., 341–45.

41. Erskine, *My Life as a Teacher*, 196–97.

42. Erskine, *My Life as a Teacher*, 166, 167.

43. Ibid., 81. See William F. Jones, "Woodbridge, Frederick J. E., 1867–1940," in *American National Biography*, 23: 787–89;

44. Cross, *Oasis of Order*, 11–13.

45. Ibid., 10.

46. Irwin Edman, *Human Traits and Their Social Significance* (New York: Columbia University Press, 1919); Rexford Tugwell, *American Economic Life and the Means of Its Improvement* (New York: Harcourt, Brace, 1925); Carlton J. H. Hayes, *A Political and Social History of Modern Europe* (New York: Macmillan, 1916). On Edman's experiences teaching in the core curriculum, see Irwin Edman, "The College: A Memoir of Forty Years," in Miner, *Columbia College on Morningside Hights*, 3–13.

47. Cross, *Oasis of Order*, 5–23; Rexford Tugwell, *To the Lesser Heights of Morningside: A Memoir* (Philadelphia: University of Pennsylvania Press, 1982).

48. On the decontemporization process, see David J. Lease, "General Education at Columbia, 1890–1940" (Ph.D. diss., Teachers College, 1988), chap. 9.

49. On the cultural broadening of CC, see ibid., chap. 10. See also Cross, *Oasis of Order*, 49–51.

50. Cross, *Oasis of Order*, 24–38; John Erskine, "Great Books," in *My Life as a Teacher*, 341–45.

51. Mortimer Adler, *Philosopher at Large: An Intellectual Autobiography* (New York: Macmillan, 1977); Mark Van Doren, *Autobiography of Mark Van Doren* (New York: Harcourt, Brace, 1958).

52. Irwin Edman, *A Philosopher's Holiday* (New York: Viking, 1938), 144.

53. George Santayana, *Character and Opinion in the United States* (New York: Dou-

bleday, 1956); Henry Seidel Canby, *Alma Mater: The Gothic Age of the American College* (New York: Farrar and Rinehart, 1936).

54. Cross, *Oasis of Order*, 48–51.

55. Adler, *Philosopher at Large*, chap. 8; Gerald Grant and David Riesman, *The Perpetual Dream: Reform and Experiment in the American College* (Chicago: University of Chicago Press, 1978), 40–76.

56. Ernest L. Boyer, *College: The Undergraduate Experience in America* (New York: Harper and Row, 1987), 99–100. I owe this citation to Timothy P. Cross.

57. Van Doren, *Autobiography*, 121. On John J. Coss, see Cross, *Oasis of Order*, 10. On Edman, see Adler, *Philosopher at Large*, 26. On McKeon, see Tim Obermiller, "Will the Real Richard McKeon Stand Up?" *University of Chicago Magazine* (January 1994), uchicago-magazine@uchicago.edu. On Krutch, see John Margolis, "Joseph Wood Krutch: Cultural Critic," *Columbia Magazine*, summer 2000, 37–41; Paul N. Parish, "Krutch, Joseph Wood, 1893–1970," in *American National Biography*, 12:939–41. On Weaver, see Lionel Trilling, "A Recollection of Raymond Weaver," in Wesley First, ed., *University on the Heights* (Garden City: Doubleday, 1969), 5–13. On Jacques Barzun, see author interview, February 5, 1998. On Tugwell, see Tugwell, *To the Lesser Heights of Morningside*. Lionel Trilling also saw himself this way, although his famous "Colloquium on Important Books" was not technically part of the Core.

58. Van Doren, *Autobiography* 211. See Dorothy Van Doren, *The Professor and I* (New York: Appleton-Century-Crofts, 1959).

59. On Weaver, see Trilling, "A Recollection of Raymond Weaver," 5–13.

60. Author interview with Jacques Barzun, February 6, 1998.

61. On Grayson Kirk's experience with CC, see chap. 12.

62. Cross, *Oasis of Order*, 94, 95, quoting Robert L. Belknap and Richard Kuhns, *Tradition and Innovation: General Education and the Reintegration of the University: A Columbia Report* (New York: Columbia University Press, 1977), 53.

63. Cross, *Oasis of Order*, 90, asserts that the Core "is an expensive way to teach" but does not provide data to substantiate the assertion.

64. On alumni support for the Core, see Herman Wouk (CC 1934), "A Doubled Magic," in First, *University on the Heights*, 85–88.

65. It is here that David Denby's *Great Books*, with its personal view from the front row, is especially valuable.

66. Both Cross and Denby provide lists of the required readings of the Core.

67. Erskine, "Great Books," 343.

68. Norman Podhoretz, *Making It* (New York: Random House, 1967), 1. See also ibid., 49–54.

69. Erskine, *My Life as a Teacher*, 171; Trilling, "A Recollection of Raymond Weaver," 6; Van Doren, *Autobiography*, 129. For Adler on Coss, see Adler, *Philosopher at Large*, 36. See Rachel Hadas, "The Many Lives of Moses Hadas," *Columbia Magazine*, fall 2001, 22–27; Van Doren, *Autobiography*, 129.

70. Diana Trilling, "Lionel Trilling: A Jew at Columbia," *Commentary* 67, no. 3 (March 1979): 40–46; Carl E. Schorske, *A Life of Learning*, ACLS Occasional Paper, no. 1 (Washington, D.C.: American Council of Learned Societies, 1987). Others were less able

to overcome the effects of these prejudices. See Caroline Heilbrun's account of Clifton Fadiman in *When Men Were the Only Models We Had: My Teachers Barzun, Fadiman, Trilling* (Philadelphia: University of Pennsylvania Press, 2002), 27–50.

11. PROSPERITY LOST

1. Nicholas Murray Butler (hereafter NMB), President's Annual Report, 1926–27, Columbia University Trustees Minutes, November 7, 1927.

2. NMB, President's Annual Report, 1919–1920, Columbia University Trustees Minutes, November 1, 1920.

3. Andrew S. Dolkart, *Morningside Heights: A History of Its Architecture and Development* (New York: Columbia University Press, 1998), appendix, "Building List," 341–56.

4. Willard V. King to NMB, July 19, 1917, Willard V. King Papers, Columbia University Archives–Columbiana Library.

5. *New York Times*, March 17, 1903, 7.

6. Seymour E. Harris, *Economics of Harvard* (New York: McGraw-Hill, 1970); Roger L. Geiger, *To Advance Knowledge: The Growth of American Research Universities, 1900–1940* (New York: Oxford University Press, 1986), 247.

7. William Parsons Barclay to NMB, December 3, 1907, William Parsons Barclay Papers, Columbia University Archives–Columbiana Library.

8. For arguments as to why Columbia did not raise money from alumni, see chap 7.

9. On the "cult" of alumni at Harvard, Yale, and Princeton, see Frederick Rudolph, *The American College and University: A History* (1962), intro. John R. Thelin (Athens: University of Georgia Press, 1990), 428–29.

10. On the board's declining wealth, see Marcellus Hartley Dodge to NMB, November 11, 1927, Marcellus Hartley Dodge Papers, Columbia University Archives–Columbiana Library.

11. This persisted into the 1950s, or so Grayson Kirk discovered upon becoming president in 1953; see Grayson Kirk, Oral History interview, July 27, 1987.

12. NMB to trustees, Columbia University Trustees Minutes, January 3, 1921.

13. Ibid.

14. Albert R. Lamb, *The Presbyterian Hospital and the Columbia-Presbyterian Medical Center, 1868–1943* (New York: Columbia University Press, 1955).

15. Columbia University Trustees Minutes, March 2, 1903.

16. Donald Fleming, *William H. Welch and the Rise of Modern Medicine* (Boston: Little, Brown, 1954); Kenneth M. Ludmerer, *Learning to Heal: The Development of American Medical Education* (New York: Basic, 1985).

17. For the requirement of two years of college for admission to Physicians & Surgeons, see Columbia University Trustees Minutes, March 2, 1908. For the 1904 affiliation with New York College of Pharmacy, see Columbia University Trustees Minutes, March 7, 1904.

18. Lamb, *Presbyterian Hospital*, 74.

19. Steven C. Wheatley, *The Politics of Philanthropy: Abraham Flexner and Medical Education* (Madison: University of Wisconsin Press, 1988), 90–91.

20. Ibid., 91–92. See Daniel M. Fox and Marcia L. Meldrum, "Edward S. Harkness,

1879–1940," in *American National Biography* (New York: Oxford University Press, 1999), 10:86–88.

21. Lamb, *Presbyterian Hospital*, 75–80.

22. Abraham Flexner, *Medical Education in the United States and Canada*, Bulletin No. 4 (New York: Carnegie Foundation for the Advancement of Teaching, 1910); idem, *Abraham Flexner: An Autobiography* (New York: Simon and Schuster, 1960); Wheatley, *Politics of Philanthropy*, 46–54. See also Thomas N. Bonner, *Iconoclast: Abraham Flexner and a Life in Learning* (Baltimore: Johns Hopkins University Press, 2002), 156–59.

23. Donald Fleming, "The Full-Time Controversy," *Journal of Medical Education* 30, no. 7 (July 1955): 398–406; Lamb, *Presbyterian Hospital*, 156–60.

24. Wheatley, *Politics of Philanthropy*, 94–98.

25. Ibid., 95–96.

26. William Darrach, "Memorandum on the School of Medicine," December 13, 1919, cited in Wheatley, *Politics of Philanthropy*, 97, and excerpted in Lamb, *Presbyterian Hospital*, 155–56.

27. Lamb, *Presbyterian Hospital*, 160–62.

28. Quoted in Wheatley, *Politics of Philanthropy*, 145; William Barclay Parsons to NMB, June 2, 1924, William Barclay Parsons Papers, Columbia University Archives–Columbiana Library. Flexner's antipathy to Butler and Columbia comes through clearly in Abraham Flexner, *Universities: American English German* (New York, Oxford University Press, 1930), 130–45.

29. Lamb, *Presbyterian Hospital*, 185–87, 228–29, 232–33.

30. Ibid., 249–53. For health sciences annual expenditures, see appendix C. In 2002 the health science's budget of $1.115 billion represents more than half the university's budget.

31. For Butler on administering the Columbia-Presbyterian Medical Center, see Bonner, *Iconoclast*, 158–59.

32. Harry Atkins, *The Dean: Willard C. Rappleye and the Evolution of American Medical Education* (New York: Josiah Macy Foundation, 1975), 64.

33. Columbia University Trustees Minutes, May 2, 1927; see also the minutes for February 7, 1927.

34. NMB to Willard V. King, November 26, 1928, King Papers; Marcellus Hartley Dodge to Nicholas Murray Butler, November 14, 1927, Marcellus Hartley Dodge Papers, University Archives–Columbiana Library. These seven names are mentioned in Columbia University Trustees Minutes, vol. 49, March 4, 1929. See the earlier listing in NMB to Dodge, December 17, 1928, Dodge Papers.

35. NMB, President's Annual Report, 1927–28, October 1, 1928.

36. O'Brien obituary in *New York Times*, June 17, 1937, sec. 1, 23, col. 1; NMB to Willard V. King, November 26, 1928. On O'Brien, see obituary in *New York Times*. On Bouvier, see John H. Davis, *The Bouviers: Portrait of an American Family* (New York: Farrar, Strauss, 1969). Bouvier was the father of "Black Jack" Bouvier and the grandfather of Jacqueline Kennedy Onassis.

37. Bernard M. Baruch, *Baruch: My Own Story* (New York: Holt, Rinehart, 1957).

38. NMB to Stephen G. Williams, November 1, 1927, Stephen G. Williams Papers, Columbia University Archives–Columbiana Library.

39. Andrew L. Kaufman, *Cardozo* (Cambridge: Harvard University Press, 1998). Among the Jews mentioned as possible trustees were Jesse Seligman, Jacob Schiff, James Speyer, and Irving Lehman.

40. John B. Pine to NMB, December 15, 1913, John B. Pine Papers, Columbia University Archives–Columbiana Library; Kaufman, *Cardozo*, 23–25. See also Stephen Birmingham, *Our Crowd: The Great Jewish Families of New York* (New York: Harper and Row, 1967).

41. NMB to William Barclay Parsons, January 12, 1928, Parsons Papers.

42. Stephen G. Williams to NMB, October 31, 1927, Williams Papers.

43. Willard V. King to NMB, November 26, 1928; Columbia University Trustees Minutes, November 7, 1927.

44. Paul Ritterband and Harold S. Wechsler, *Jewish Learning in American Universities* (Bloomington: Indiana University Press, 1994), chap. 7. Also see Laurence E. Balfus, "Jewish Studies at Columbia University," master's thesis, Columbia University, 2000.

45. Columbia University Trustees Minutes, February 7, 1927.

46. NMB to William Barclay Parsons, May 12, 1931, Parsons Papers; President's Annual Report, 1931–32, Columbia University Trustees Minutes, November 7, 1932.

47. Columbia University Trustees Minutes, vol. 49, November 4, 1929. On the Rockefeller Center lease, see Philip M. Hayden, Secretary, Columbia University, to H. Bronson Cowan, December 29, 1948, William Bloor Papers, Columbia University Archives–Columbiana Library.

48. Columbia University Trustees Minutes, vol. 51, October 6, 1930.

49. William J. McGill, Oral History interview, July 5, 1979.

50. NMB to Marcellus Hartley Dodge, June 10, 1930, Dodge Papers.

51. For annual giving, see appendix C.

52. For drops in enrollments during the Depression, see appendixes B and C.

53. A word here about Columbia's interwar "endowment." The term had not acquired the precise meaning now generally accepted: the value of a university's marketable assets other than its academic plant. Instead, it was variously reported to refer to the university's total assets, the total assets commanded by the Columbia trustees, Columbia assets excluding the physical plant, Columbia assets available for all specific and unspecified university purposes, and that part of the so-called unrestricted endowment available for immediate expenses (i.e., not tied up in real estate). Another wrinkle was that real estate assets, as opposed to securities that had a readily determinable market value, were carried throughout the Butler era at book value, that is, either their last assessed evaluation or as a multiple of current annual rents. In good times when land values were increasing, this meant that the actual value was understated, while in bad times, overstated. For budgets and deficits in the 1930s, see appendix C.

54. Geiger, *To Advance Knowledge*, 276–77.

55. NMB to Albert W. Putnam, April 2, 1940, Putnam Papers.

56. Columbia University Trustees Minutes, January 3, 1921; NMB to Archibald Douglas, October 3, 1936; Archibald Douglas to NMB, January 7, 1931, Archibald Douglas Papers, Columbia University Archives–Columbiana Library.

57. Albert W. Putnam to NMB, November 8, 1934, Albert W. Putnam Papers, Columbia University Archives–Columbiana Library.

58. On faculty size in the 1930s, see appendix B.

59. Author interview with Jacques Barzun, February 5, 1998.

60. Diana Trilling, *The Beginning of the Journey: The Marriage of Diana and Lionel Trilling* (New York: Harcourt, Brace, 1993), 170.

61. See, for example, Arthur Joseph Hughes, "Carlton J. H. Hayes: Teacher and Historian" (Ph.D. diss., Columbia University, 1970).

62. Stephen Sargent Visher, *Scientists Starred 1903–1943 in "American Men of Science"* (Baltimore: Johns Hopkins University Press, 1947; reprint, New York: Arno, 1975), 312. For more on Columbia and university rankings, see appendix B.

63. Hans Zinsser to Columbia University Board of Trustees, Columbia University Trustees Minutes, February 5, 1923. See Philip K. Wilson, "Zinsser, Hans, 1878–1940," in *American National Biography*, 24:247–49.

64. W. W. Cook to Columbia Board of Trustees, May 17, 1922, quoted in Columbia University Trustees Minutes, October 2, 1922; NMB, President's Annual Report, 1921–22, November 6, 1922. See Julius Goebel Jr., *A History of the School of Law, Columbia University* (New York: Columbia University Press, 1955), 273. See also ibid., 272–74; Morton Horowitz, *The Transformation of American Law, 1870–1960: The Crisis of Legal Orthodoxy* (New York: Oxford University Press, 1992), chap. 6; Alpheus T. Mason, *Harlan Fiske Stone: Pillar of the Law* (New York: Viking, 1956).

65. William O. Douglas, *Go East, Young Man: The Early Years* (New York: Random House, 1974), chap. 11; Goebel, *School of Law*, 297–305; William Twining, *Karl Llewellyn and the Realist Movement* (London: Weidenfeld and Nicolson, 1973).

66. Toby E. Huff, "Ogburn, William Fielding, 1886-1959," in *American National Biography*, 16:631–32.

67. Morton and Phyllis Keller, *Making Harvard Modern: The Rise of America's University* (New York: Oxford University Press, 2001), chap. 4; Geiger, *To Advance Knowledge*, 193–97.

68. William H. McNeill, *Hutchins' University: A Memoir of the University of Chicago, 1929–1950* (Chicago: University of Chicago Press, 1991); Geiger, *To Advance Knowledge*, 196–200, 211–14; John R. Thelin, "Robert Gordon Sproul, 1891–1975," in *American National Biography*, 20:510–12.

69. William B. Dinsmoor, "The Department of Fine Arts and Archeology," in John Herman Randall Jr., ed. *A History of the Faculty of Philosophy, Columbia University* (New York: Columbia university Press, 1957), 252–69. For rankings of Columbia departments in the 1930s, see appendix B.

70. William T. de Bary, "East Asian Studies at Columbia: The Early Years," *Columbia Magazine*, spring 2002, 10–19; Robert A. McCaughey, *International Studies and Academic Enterprise: A Chapter in the Enclosure of American Learning* (New York: Columbia University Press, 1984), chaps. 3 and 4.

71. De Bary, "East Asian Studies," 12; McCaughey, *International Studies*, 99–100.

72. Laura Fermi, *Illustrious Immigrants: The Intellectual Migration from Europe, 1930–41* (Chicago: University of Chicago Press, 1968); Donald Fleming and Bernard Bailyn, eds. *The Intellectual Migration: Europe and America, 1930–1960* (Cambridge: Harvard University Press, 1969). For European émigrés who did find a place at Columbia in the 1930s, see appendix A. They include the sociologist Paul Lazarsfeld, who came to the United States from Austria in 1933 and joined the Columbia faculty in 1939; the German-

born art historian Margarite Beiber, who came to Barnard in 1934 via England; the Austrian-born biochemist Erwin Chargaff, who became a faculty member at P & S in 1935; the Polish-born political scientist Franz Neuman, who came to the United States and Columbia in 1936; the German-born Julius Held, who came to Barnard in 1937; the physicist Enrico Fermi, who left Italy for the United States and Columbia in 1939; the Hungarian-born physicist Leo Szilard, who came to the United States in 1937 and Columbia in 1939; the historian of philosophy Paul O. Kristeller, a German who came from Italy to the United States and Columbia in 1939; and the Russian-born linguist Roman Jacobson, who came to the United States in 1942 and Columbia in 1943.

73. Alfred Kazin, *Starting Out in the Thirties* (Boston: Little, Brown, 1965), 49.

74. Milton Halsey Thomas, Diary, February 1, 1937, New-York Historical Society.

75. Frank Fackenthal to Marcellus Hartley Dodge, October 21, 1942, Dodge Papers. See *New York Times*, September 6, 1968, sec. 1, 43, col. 1.

76. On Jessup as a prospect, see Thomas, Diary, April 30, 1935. On Fox, see Wendell Tripp, "Dixon Ryan Fox, 1887–1944," in *American National Biography*, 8:336–37.

77. NMB to William Barclay Parsons, May 26, 1931, Parsons Papers.

78. On William S. Paley, see Albert Auster, "Paley, William S., 1910-1990," in *American National Biography*, 16:931–32.

79. Kaufman, *Cardozo*, 470.

80. The first favorable mention of Ochs by Dodge is in Marcellus Hartley Dodge to NMB, December 3, 1924, Dodge Papers.

81. On Marcellus Hartley Dodge, see *New York Times*, December 26, 1963, sec. 1, 27, col. 2.

82. Dodge to NMB, September 22, 1932, Dodge Papers. See Iphigene Ochs Sulzberger, as told to her granddaughter Susan W. Dryfoos, *Iphigene: Memoirs of Iphigene Ochs Sulzberger of The New York Times Family* (New York: Dodd, Mead, 1981).

83. Dodge to NMB, September 22, 1932, Dodge Papers.

84. Ibid.

85. NMB to Dodge, September 23, 1932, Dodge Papers.

86. NMB to Dodge, September 21, 1932; NMB to Dodge, September 23, Dodge Papers.

87. NMB to Dodge, September 24, 1932, Dodge Papers. Ochs died in 1934.

88. NMB to Dodge, November 22, 1932, Dodge Papers. See also Dodge to Frank Fackenthal, November 9, 1935, Dodge Papers; Edwin Black, *IBM and the Holocaust: The Strategic Alliance Between Nazi Germany and America's Most Powerful Corporation* (New York: Crown, 2002).

89. Archibald Douglas to NMB, January 7, 1931, Archibald Douglas Papers, Columbia University Archives–Columbiana Library.

90. For list of chairmen of the board of trustees, see appendix A.

91. Dodge on Coykendall, Columbia University Trustees Minutes, January 9, 1933.

92. Ibid.

93. Ibid.; *New York Times*, April 2, 1937, sec. 1, 25, col. 6.

94. James T. Shotwell, Oral History interview, 1952; *New York Times*, March 27, 1942, 25, col. 8. For Diana Trilling's comments on Butler's drinking, see her "Lionel Trilling: A Jew at Columbia," *Commentary* 67, no. 3 (March 1979): 44.

95. This is conjecture, awaiting a more definitive account of Butler's complicated relationship with national politics by Michael Rosenthal.

96. Albert Marrin, *Nicholas Murray Butler* (Boston: Twayne, 1976). On Butler's internationalism in the 1930s, see NMB, *Across the Busy Years: Recollections and Reflections* (New York: Scribner's, 1940), 2:86–227.

97. On the dysfunctional family, dearth of friends, and end of travel, see Edward Le Comte, "Dinner with Butler and Eisenhower: A Columbia Memoir," *Commentary* 81, no. 1 (January 1986): 56–63.

98. *New York Times*, June 11, 1939, sec. 1, 26, col. 1.

99. On Butler's failing health, see Thomas, Diary, June 3, 1940.

100. NMB to Frederick R. Coudert, September 29, 1944, Coudert Papers, Columbia University Archives–Columbiana Library.

12. COLUMBIA IN THE AMERICAN CENTURY

1. Much of my understanding of the postwar American academic research scene is derived from Roger L. Geiger, *Research and Relevant Knowledge: American Research Universities Since World War II* (New York: Oxford University Press, 1993). For contemporary concerns, see I. L. Kandell, *The Impact of the War Upon American Education* (Chapel Hill: University of North Carolina Press, 1948).

2. Luce coined the term in 1941 in a *Fortune* editorial opposing American isolationism.

3. Nathan Pusey, *The Age of the Scholar: Observations on Education in a Troubled Decade* (Cambridge: Harvard University Press, 1963); Richard M. Freeland, *Academia's Golden Age: Universities in Massachusetts, 1945–1970* (New York: Oxford University Press, 1992); Stuart W. Leslie, *The Cold War and American Science: The Military-Industrial-Academic Complex at MIT and Stanford* (New York: Columbia University Press, 1993).

4. Geiger, *Research and Relevant Knowledge*, 31.

5. For the endowment, see appendix C; Andrew S. Dolkart, *Morningside Heights: A History of Its Architecture and Development* (New York: Columbia University Press, 1998), 199–201. For the buildings, see appendix D.

6. For enrollment data, see appendix B.

7. Keith W. Olson, *The G.I. Bill, the Veterans, and the Colleges* (Lexington; University of Kentucky Press, 1974), 69–70.

8. Geiger, *Research and Relevant Knowledge*, chap. 2; Alice M. Rivlin, *The Role of the Federal Government in Financing Higher Education* (Washington, D.C.: Brookings Institution, 1961).

9. Olson, *The G.I. Bill*, 71–72.

10. Frank D. Fackenthal, Oral History interview, December 1952.

11. On Butler's superannuated administrators, see Grayson Kirk, Oral History interview, November 11, 1985.

12. For biographical data on Columbia presidents, see appendix A.

13. Grayson Kirk, Oral History interview, January 14, 1987. On Fackenthal, see Fackenthal interview, December 1952. See also Frank D. Fackenthal, *The Greater Power and Other Addresses* (Freeport, N.Y.: Books for Libraries, 1949).

14. NMB to Frederick Coykendall, June 25, 1947, Coykendall Papers, Columbia University Archives–Columbiana Library. See Travis B. Jacobs, *Eisenhower at Columbia* (New Brunswick, N.J.: Transaction, 2001), 27. I have relied extensively on Jacobs's thorough account of this period in Columbia's history.

15. Jacobs, *Eisenhower at Columbia*, 23–25.

16. Ibid., 21; Jacques Barzun, "Reminiscences of the Columbia History Department, 1923–1975," *Columbia Magazine*, winter 2000.

17. Jacobs, *Eisenhower at Columbia*, 13, 15, 32, 34. Albert C. Jacobs was the author's father.

A note on the Columbia-Trinity relationship: Jacobs's last qualification raises a question: was the unofficial requirement that the president of Columbia be Episcopalian still in force in 1945 when the search for Butler's successor began? It is important to recall that no such requirement was included in any of the three charters under which Columbia has been governed since the original one written for King's College in 1754. The 1784 and 1787 charters specifically prohibited the regents/trustees from favoring one religion over another, as did the 1810 charter, which remains in force. Columbia was thus legally free to elect a non-Episcopalian president. But the vestrymen of Trinity Church were also presumably free to reclaim ownership of the Lower Estate, the original Trinity endowment, rents from which had accrued to the College since the land had been provided in 1755 as the site for the original College. In 1945 the Lower Estates property carried a book value of $2.4 million and generated annual rents of $150,000. (For Columbia University's income from real estate, see appendix C.)

Thus the practice of limiting presidential eligibility to Episcopalians, like the use of either Episcopal (or generic Christian) liturgy in religious services and reserving a seat on the board for the rector of Trinity Church, did have a historical and economic rationale, if not a legal basis. Accordingly, in 1945 both the current rector of Trinity Church, Frederick Fleming, and one of his predecessors at Trinity, long since the Episcopal bishop of New York, the Right Reverend Dr. Clarence Manning, were trustees. Among the other twenty members of the board, at least eight were Episcopalians, and four served as Trinity vestrymen. (For the religious affiliations of the Butler trustees, see appendix A.)

The trustees might still have felt constrained by the prospect that the Lower Estate's revenues would be jeopardized if they selected a non-Episcopalian president, but the fact that the eventual selection of a non-Episcopalian—Eisenhower—in 1947 did not result in the vestrymen exercising their retaliatory rights suggests that some prior understanding had been reached allowing them to elect the particular non-Episcopalian they did. In 1950 the vestrymen of Trinity Church permanently gave over the ownership of the Lower Estates to Columbia in exchange for one dollar. In 1960 the rector of Trinity Church, John Heuss, for ten years a largely absentee member of the board of trustees, submitted his resignation from the board, thereby ending a tradition of ex officio membership that went back 214 years. (For the 1950 transfer, see Columbia University Trustees Minutes, April 3, 1950. On Rector John Heuss giving up the Trinity Church seat, see unpublished paper by Trinity Church historian Arthur Ben Chitty, "King's College, Late Columbia University, New York, New York, 1754–," 14–16, copy provided author by Professor Kenneth T. Jackson.)

H. Moran Weston, the next Episcopal minister to serve on the board, elected in 1969, was an African American and rector of the predominately black St. Phillip's Church, located in Harlem. In recent years, Episcopalian board members have seldom numbered more than three or four at any one time and may not even be known to each other as such. In 1994, the phrase "in the year of our Lord," used in the dating of trustee meetings in the official minutes, was quietly dropped. Since then, the king's crown, one of the images carried forward from the 1750s into the twentieth century, regularly had its crosses removed for official uses. Columbia's de-Christianization is virtually complete (author interview with Marion Jemmott, December 2, 1997).

18. Jacobs, *Eisenhower at Columbia*, 20.

19. Harry J. Carman, Oral History interview, 1962, in Elizabeth B. Mason and Louis M. Starr, eds., *The Oral History Collection of Columbia University* (New York: Oral History Research Office, Columbia University, 1979), 46; Jacobs, *Eisenhower at Columbia*, 21; author interview with Jacques Barzun, February 5, 1998.

20. Jacobs, *Eisenhower at Columbia*, 22–24, 27, 28.

21. Ibid., 23.

22. Ibid., 30, 31.

23. Ibid., 31, 32, 39.

24. Ibid., 19, 32, 43–44.

25. Ibid., 43–44.

26. Ibid., 33.

27. Dwight D. Eisenhower, *At Ease: Stories I Tell to Friends* (New York: Doubleday, 1967), 336.

28. Douglas M. Black, Oral History interview, 1967.

29. The Eisenhower portrait was commissioned by Marcellus Hartley Dodge and painted by Thomas E. Stephens. It hangs on the main southwest stairway of Butler Library.

30. Donald Davidson, *Lee in the Mountains—and Other Poems* (New York: Scribner's, 1949), 3–7; Eisenhower, *At Ease*, 346–47; Grayson Kirk, Oral History interview, "The Eisenhower Administration [at Columbia]," May 12, 1975, Dwight D. Eisenhower Library, Abilene, Kansas.

31. Dwight D. Eisenhower to Thomas I. Parkinson, June 23, 1947, in Louis Galambos, ed., *Papers of Dwight David Eisenhower* (Baltimore: Johns Hopkins University Press, 1978), 8:1775–76. See Jacobs, *Eisenhower at Columbia*, 45–47.

32. Eisenhower to Parkinson, June 23, 1947.

33. Ibid., 57–58.

34. Ibid., 87. Ike also hinted as much earlier in Eisenhower to Frederick Coykendall, November 12, 1947, *Papers of DDE*, 9:2055–56.

35. On presidential tenures, see appendix A. On the *Spectator*'s take on Ike, see Max Frankel, *The Times of My Life and My Life with The Times* (New York: Random House, 1999), 95–111.

36. Author interview with Eli Ginzberg, September 19, 1997; Travis Jacobs, "Eisenhower's Columbia Presidency" (paper presented at the Columbia University Seminar on the History of Columbia University, January 27, 1997); Grayson Kirk, Oral History interview, May 21, 1985.

37. Grayson Kirk, Oral History interview, May 10, 1985.

38. Ibid. See Jacobs, *Eisenhower at Columbia*, 172–75.

39. Kirk interview, May 10, 1985.

40. Barzun interview, February 5, 1998.

41. Jacobs, *Eisenhower at Columbia*, 195–96; Kirk interview, May 10, 1985.

42. Ginzberg interview, September 19, 1997.

43. On Ike's views on federal aid to education, see Jacobs, *Eisenhower at Columbia*, 153, 183–84. On Columbia faculty politics, see Paul Lazarsfeld, *The Academic Mind: Social Scientists in a Time of Crisis* (Glencoe, Ill.: Free, 1958).

44. Jacobs, *Eisenhower at Columbia*, 290–98.

45. Frankel, *The Times of My Life*, 103–7.

46. Jacobs, *Eisenhower at Columbia*, 250–62.

47. Columbia University Trustees Minutes, December 5, 1952.

48. Kirk interview, May 10, 1985.

49. William J. McGill, Oral History interview, June 29, 1979; remarks at Memorial Service for Grayson Kirk, St. Paul's Chapel, 1998.

50. Benjamin Buttenweiser, Oral History interview, 1981; Millicent McIntosh, Oral History interview, 1966; Douglas M. Knight, *Street of Dreams: The Nature and Legacy of the 1960s* (Durham, N.C.: Duke University Press, 1989), 132.

51. Knight, *Street of Dreams*, 133. For Kirk on Butler, see Kirk interview, May 10, 1985.

52. Jacques Barzun, *The House of Intellect* (New York: Harper, 1959), 85; Barzun interview, February 5, 1998.

53. Jemmott interview, December 2, 1997; author interview with Carl Hovde, August 21, 1997.

54. On the age of Columbia University presidents at installation, see appendix A.

55. Kirk interview, May 10, 1985.

56. Ibid.

57. On Conant and Rabi's concurrence, see Grayson Kirk, Oral History interview, October 16, 1987.

58. Grayson Kirk, Oral History interview, July 22, 1987.

59. Ginzberg interview, September 19, 1997.

60. Ellen W. Schrecker, *No Ivory Tower: McCarthyism and the Universities* (New York: Oxford University Press, 1986), 255–58; Sigmund Diamond, *Compromised Campus: The Collaboration of Universities with the Intelligence Community, 1945–1955* (New York: Oxford University Press, 1992).

61. Schrecker, *No Ivory Tower*, 91.

62. Grayson Kirk, Oral History interview, September 3, 1987. See Schrecker, *No Ivory Tower*, 179–80. On the treatment of Chinese scholars elsewhere, see John K. Fairbank, *Chinabound: A Fifty-Year Memoir* (New York: Harper and Row, 1982).

63. Schrecker, *No Ivory Tower*, 255–57; Grayson Kirk, Oral History interview, September 23, 1987.

64. Columbia University Trustees Minutes, October 6, 1952.

65. Kirk interview, October 16, 1987.

66. Schrecker, *No Ivory Tower*, 255; Diamond, *Compromised Campus*.

67. Grayson Kirk, Oral History interview, September 23, 1987.

68. Grayson Kirk, *The Study of International Relations in American Colleges and Universities* (New York: Council on Foreign Relations, 1947).

69. Kirk interview, January 14, 1987.

70. Kirk interview, May 10, 1985.

71. Ibid.

72. Grayson Kirk, Oral History interview, May 17, 1985.

73. Ibid.

74. Kirk interview, November 11, 1985.

75. Ernest R. May, *"Lessons" of the Past: The Use and Misuse of History in American Foreign Policy* (New York: Oxford University Press, 1973); Robert A. McCaughey, *International Studies and Academic Enterprise: A Chapter in the Enclosure of American Learning* (New York: Columbia University Press, 1984), 135–40.

76. Kirk interview, October 16, 1987.

77. Charles H. Behre, Charles Frankel, Maxwell Gensamer, Arthur W. MacMahon [chair], Ernest J. Simmons, and Howard R. Williams, *Report on the Future of the University* (New York: Columbia University Press, 1958).

78. Alistair Cooke, ed., *The Vintage Mencken* (New York: Vintage, 1955), 223.

79. Grayson Kirk, Oral History interview, April 26, 1988.

80. On Columbia's two-book bookkeeping, see William J. McGill, Oral History interview, July 3, 1980.

81. Kirk interview, April 26, 1988.

82. Kirk interview, October 16, 1987. See Jemmott interview, December 2, 1997.

83. McGill interview, July 3, 1980.

84. [William S. Paley], *The Role of the Trustees of Columbia University* (New York: Special Trustees Committee, 1957), 9. See Kirk interview, October 16, 1987. For Kirk's trustees, see appendix A.

85. Columbia University Trustees Minutes, April 3, 1905. On Dwight and Chandler, see chap. 6. For tenures of various deans of the professional schools, see appendix A.

86. On Rappleye, see chap. 11

87. On Rappleye's departure, see Columbia University Trustees Minutes, April 4, 1959.

88. Courtney Brown, *The Dean Meant Business* (New York: Graduate School of Business, Columbia University, 1983), part 1. Brown may be unique among Columbia autobiographers since Samuel Johnson to see fit to provide his readers with a genealogy, which traces his American lineage to Newbury, Massachusetts, 1635.

89. Ibid., chap. 9.

90. Ibid., 144; see 142–45.

91. Ibid., chap. 9; author interview with Peter Buchanan, August 29, 2002.

92. Brown, *The Dean Meant Business*, 148–53.

93. On the rising fortunes of the Business School, see chap. 20.

94. Brown, *The Dean Meant Business*, 165–73.

95. McGill interview, July 3, 1980; Brown, *The Dean Meant Business*, 171; author interview with Michael I. Sovern, May 5, 1999.

96. Brown, *The Dean Meant Business*, 171–74.

97. Grayson Kirk, Oral History interview, June 26, 1985. For Kirk's reaction to *The Dean Meant Business*, I relied on a 1999 conversation with Chauncey Olinger, who was editor of Brown's autobiography and conducted Kirk's Oral History interviews in 1985–86.

98. Grayson Kirk, Oral History interview, May 26, 1986. See author interview with Seymour Melman, November 5, 1997.

99. Kirk interview, May 26, 1986.

100. Kirk interview, September 23, 1987; McIntosh interview, 1966.

13. A SECOND FLOWERING

1. Travis B. Jacobs, *Eisenhower at Columbia* (New Brunswick, N.J.: Transaction, 2001), 21–22.

2. Author interview with Henry Graff, May 3, 2000. See author interview with Marion E. (Betty) Jemmott, December 2, 1997.

3. Clark Kerr, "The Realities of the Federal Grant University," *The Uses of the University* (Cambridge: Harvard University Press, 1964), 46–84.

4. Alice M. Rivlin, *The Role of the Federal Government in Financing Higher Education* (Washington, D.C.: Brookings Institution, 1961); Harold Orlans, *The Effects of Federal Programs on Higher Education* (Washington, D.C.: Brookings Institution, 1962).

5. Fon W. Boardman Jr., *Columbia: An American University in Peace and War* (New York: Columbia University Press, 1944), 51–83; Roger L. Geiger, *Research and Relevant Knowledge: American Research Universities Since WW II* (New York: Oxford University Press, 1993), chap. 1.

6. Vannevar Bush, *Science: The Endless Frontier* (Washington, D.C.: U.S. Government Printing Office, 1945); Geiger, *Research and Relevant Knowledge*, chap. 1.

7. Geiger, *Research and Relevant Knowledge*, 16–18.

8. Grayson Kirk, Oral History interview, January 14, 1987.

9. Orlans, *The Effects of Federal Programs on Higher Education*, 9. See Kirk remarks on the IDA, Columbia University Trustees Minutes, March 7, 1960.

10. Grayson Kirk to Trustees, Columbia University Trustees Minutes, May 6, 1963. See William G. Bowen, *The Federal Government and Princeton University* (Princeton: Princeton University Press, 1962).

11. Don K. Price, *The Scientific Estate* (Cambridge: Harvard University Press, 1965), 33.

12. John S. Rigden, *Rabi: Scientist and Citizen* (New York: Basic, 1987); see also Samuel Devons, "I. I. Rabi: Physics and Science at Columbia, in America, and Worldwide," *Columbia Magazine*, summer 2001, 36–49.

13. Nicholas Murray Butler (hereafter NMB) to Trustees [confidential], appended to Columbia University Trustees Minutes, May 3, 1926.

14. Daniel Kevles, *The Physicists: The History of a Scientific Community in Modern America* (New York: Knopf, 1977).

15. Rigden, *Rabi*, chap. 2; Albert B. Costa, "Urey, Harold C., 1893–1981," *American National Biography* (New York: Oxford University Press, 1999), 22:123–26.

16. Rigden, *Rabi*, 30–38.

17. Ibid., 30; see 38–45.

18. Ibid., 46–67.

19. Ibid., 66.

20. Ibid., 90.

21. Ibid., 101.

22. Ibid., 124; see 124–67.

23. Stephane Groueff, *Manhattan Project: The Untold Story of the Making of the Atomic Bomb* (Boston: Little, Brown, 1967), 19–23, 180–84.

24. Rigden, *Rabi*, 238–39; author interview with Jonathan Cole, July 2, 2001.

25. Rigden, *Rabi*, 185–90.

26. Devons, "I. I. Rabi."

27. Rigden, *Rabi*, 181–83; 96; Polykarp Kusch, Oral History interview, May 17, 1968.

28. For Columbia Nobel laureates, see appendix A. See also Charles H. Townes, "A Life in Physics: Bell Telephone and WW II, Columbia University and the Laser, MIT and Government Service, California and Research in Astrophysics," Regional Oral History Office, Bancroft Library, University of California, 1994.

29. Rigden, *Rabi*, 71, 116; see 68–72. On Hayner, see Rosalind Rosenberg, *Changing the Subject: A History of Women at Columbia* (New York: Columbia University Press, forthcoming).

30. Ibid., 191. See Robert K. Merton, "The Matthew Effect in Science," *Science* 159 (January 1968): 55–63. On the "Rabi Tree," see Rigden, *Rabi*, 9–16.

31. Robert J. Birgeneau, Ralph J. Cicerone, Arnold Levine, Jeremiah P. Ostriker, and Richard N. Zare, "The Future of the Natural Sciences at Columbia: Report of the Academic Review Committee, Faculty of Arts and Sciences, March 6, 2002," Office of Vice President of Arts and Sciences, Columbia University.

32. Stuart W. Leslie, *The Cold War and American Science: The Military-Industrial-Academic Complex at MIT and Stanford* (New York: Columbia University Press, 1993), 45; Grayson Kirk to Trustees, Columbia University Trustees Minutes, February 4, 1963.

33. Francis X. Sutton, "The Ford Foundation and Columbia" (talk at the University Seminar on the History of Columbia University, November 16, 1999), 1–13, http://beatl.barnard.columbia.edu/cuhistory.

34. Merle Curti and Roderick Nash, *Philanthropy in the Shaping of American Higher Education* (New Brunswick, N.J.: Rutgers University Press, 1965); Howard J. Savage, *Fruit of an Impulse: Forty-Five Years of the Carnegie Foundation, 1905–1950* (New York: Carnegie Foundation, 1953).

35. Francis X. Sutton, "The Ford Foundation: The Early Years," *Daedalus* 116 (winter 1987): 41–91. The next three richest universities in 1950 were Yale ($125 million), Texas ($102 million), and Columbia ($82 million).

36. Robert A. McCaughey, *International Studies and Academic Enterprise: A Chapter in the Enclosure of American Learning* (New York: Columbia University Press, 1984), 144–45; see chap. 6. See C. Rowan Gaither, *Report of the Study for the Ford Foundation on Policy and Program* (Detroit: Ford Foundation, 1949).

37. Ibid., 154–55.

38. Sutton, "The Ford Foundation and Columbia," 1.

39. Quoted in McCaughey, *International Studies*, 182; see 168, 182–95. See Sutton, "The Ford Foundation and Columbia," 3–6.

40. Sutton, "The Ford Foundation and Columbia," 5–6.

41. McCaughey, *International Studies*, 102–9.

42. Robert B. Hall, *Area Studies in American Universities* (New York: Social Science Research Council, 1947); John Shelton Curtiss, "Geroid Tanguary Robinson," in idem, ed., *Essays in Russian and Soviet History in Honor of Geroid T. Robinson* (New York: Columbia University Press, 1963), xi–xx; Philip E. Mosely, obituary, *New York Times*, January 14, 1972, sec. 1, 36, col. 1.

43. L. Carrington Goodrich, "The Department of Chinese and Japanese," in Herman

Randall, ed., *A History of the Faculty of Philosophy, Columbia University* (New York: Columbia University Press, 1957), 245–51; Wm. Theodore de Bary, "East Asian Studies at Columbia: The Early Years," *Columbia Magazine*, spring 2002, 10–19.

44. Sutton, "The Ford Foundation and Columbia," 5; L. Gray Cowan, *A History of the School of International Affairs* (New York: Columbia University Press, 1954).

45. McCaughey, *International Studies*, 145; Dorothy Soderlund, ed., *Directory, Foreign Area Fellows, 1952–1972* (New York: Social Science Research Council, 1973).

46. McCaughey, *International Studies*, 186.

47. Sutton, "The Ford Foundation and Columbia," 5–6.

48. Dwight Macdonald, *The Ford Foundation: The Men and the Millions* (New York: Reynal and Hitchcock, 1956); Waldemar A. Nielson, *The Big Foundations* (New York: Columbia University Press, 1972).

49. McCaughey, *International Studies*, 116.

50. Sutton, "The Ford Foundation and Columbia," 7.

51. Ibid, 2–3. See also Herbert Kramer and Barbara Morris, "Money in Search of a Mission," Project Evaluation Report No. 001988, June 1970, Ford Foundation Archives, New York City.

52. McCaughey, *International Studies*, 241–42.

53. Sutton, "The Ford Foundation and Columbia University," 6.

54. McGeorge Bundy, *Annual Report of the Ford Foundation, 1966–1967* (New York: Ford Foundation, 1967), 6–7; [Elinor Barber], "A Closeout Review of ITR and Columbia University," Elinor Barber to Francis X. Sutton, June 1, 1973, Columbia folder, International Training and Research Program files, Ford Foundation Archives, Ford Foundation, New York City. Sutton noted that a quarter-century later, in 1999, Columbia remained the second most favored of all the university beneficiaries of Ford Foundation largesse, having received in all some $150.5 million (including grants to Barnard and Teachers College), as compared to Harvard's $152.9 million. Chicago was third, but way back, at $107.7 million.

55. McCaughey, *International Studies*, 192–93.

56. Ibid., 211–18.

57. Robert A. McCaughey, "American University Teachers and Opposition to the Vietnam War: A Reconsideration," *Minerva* 14 (autumn 1976): 307–29; Edward Said, *Orientalism* (New York: Pantheon, 1978); Gayatri C. Spivak, *The Spivak Reader: Selected Works* (New York: Routledge, 1996).

58. Courtney Brown, *The Dean Meant Business* (New York: Graduate School of Business, Columbia University, 1983), chap. 9.

59. Jean M. Converse, "The Bureau of Applied Social Research: The First Wave," in *Survey Research in the United States: Roots and Emergence, 1890–1960* (Berkeley: University of California Press, 1987), 267–304; Allen H. Barton, "Paul Lazarsfeld and the Invention of the University Institute for Applied Social Research," in Burkhardt Holtzer and Jiri Nehnevajsa, eds., *Organizing for Social Research* (Cambridge: Schenkman, 1982), 17–83.

60. Paul Lazarsfeld, "An Episode in the History of Social Research: A Memoir," *Perspectives in American History* 2 (1968): 270–337, 272–74.

61. Ibid., 274–76, 293–334.

62. Robert K. Merton, *A Life of Learning*, ACLS Occasional Paper No. 25 (New York: American Council of Learned Societies, 1994), 15–17.

63. Converse, "The Bureau," 274–75. See Lazarsfeld, "An Episode in the History of Social Research," 331–33. See also Barton, "Paul Lazarsfeld," 17–83.

64. Converse, "The Bureau," 277.

65. Ibid., 270–72.

66. Ibid.

67. Ibid., 272–75, 507–8; Jacques Barzun, *The American University: How It Runs— Where It Is Going* (New York: Harper and Row, 1968), 144–45; C. Wright Mills, *The Sociological Imagination* (New York: Oxford University Press, 1959), 65–67.

68. Remarks of Gillian Lindt at the Lazarsfeld centennial, Columbia University, September 29, 2001, notes taken by author.

69. Robert K. Merton, *The Student-Physician: Introductory Studies in the Sociology of Medical Education* (Cambridge: Harvard University Press, 1957); William J. McGill, Oral History interview, June 26, 1979.

70. On the Lazarsfeld-Merton era and its progeny, see Lewis A. Coser, ed., *The Idea of Social Structure: Papers in Honor of Robert K. Merton* (New York: Harcourt, Brace, 1975); Patricia L. Kendall, ed., *The Varied Sociology of Paul F. Lazarsfeld* (New York: Columbia University Press, 1982).

71. Edward Shils, "Tradition, Ecology, and Institution in the History of Sociology," in Gerald Holton, ed., *The Twentieth-Century Sciences: Studies in the Biographies of Ideas* (New York: Norton, 1972), 33–99.

72. Lionel Trilling, quoted in Mark Krupnick, *Lionel Trilling and the Fate of Cultural Criticism* (Evanston: Northwestern University Press, 1986), 9. While this is admittedly a somewhat arbitrary selection, there is some statistical basis for it. Of the five core Columbia intellectuals designated here, all but Barzun (whose exclusion I attribute to his politics and choice of publishing outlets more than to any relative absence of prominence or prestige) are included among the "Seventy Most Prestigious Contemporary American Intellectuals" in 1970 as per Charles Kadushin, *The American Intellectual Elite* (Boston: Little, Brown, 1974), 30. Bell and Trilling number among the top ten, Hofstadter in the top twenty.

73. Diana Trilling, *The Beginning of the Journey: The Marriage of Diana and Lionel Trilling* (New York: Harcourt, Brace, 1993), 23–44.

74. McGill interview, June 26, 1979. See Mark Van Doren, "Jewish Students I Have Known," *Menorah Journal* 13 (June 1927): 266–69.

75. Trilling, *Beginning of the Journey*, 88–93.

76. Diana Trilling, "Lionel Trilling: A Jew at Columbia," *Commentary* 67, no. 3 (March 1979): 46; see 43–46.

77. Lionel Trilling, "A Personal Memoir," in Dora B. Weiner and William R. Keylor, eds., *From Parnasus: Essays in Honor of Jacques Barzun* (New York: Harper and Row, 1976), xv–xxii.

78. Author interview with Jacques Barzun, February 5, 6, 1998.

79. Merton, *A Life of Learning*, 9.

80. Ibid., 11–20; Morton Hunt, " 'How Does It Come to Be?': A Profile of Robert K. Merton," *New Yorker*, January 28, 1961, 39–63. See Robert K. Merton, *Science, Technology and Society in Seventeenth-Century England* (1938; reprint, New York: Fertig, 1970).

81. Stanley Elkins and Eric McKitrick, "Richard Hofstadter: A Progress," in idem, eds., *The Hofstadter Aegis: A Memorial* (New York: Knopf, 1974), 300–367.

82. A bibliography of Hofstadter's writings, provided by one of his students, Paula Fass, appears in Elkins and McKitrick, *The Hofstadter Aegis*, 368–81.

83. Malcolm Waters, *Daniel Bell* (London: Routledge, 1996), 13–16; Irving Kristol, *Reflections of a Neoconservative* (New York: Basic, 1983), 8–13.

84. Waters, *Bell*, 15–16; Peter Steinfels, *The Neoconservatives* (New York: Simon and Schuster, 1979), chap. 7.

85. Both Hofstadter and Barzun moved to the East Side in the mid-1960s. On Mills, see Kathryn and Damek Mills, eds., *C. Wright Mills: Letters and Autobiographical Writings* (Berkeley: University of California Press, 2000).

86. Bell's *Reforming General Education* is dedicated to Trilling; Trilling's *The Liberal Imagination* is dedicated to Jacques Barzun. On the book clubs, see Arthur Krystal, ed., *A Company of Readers* (New York: Free, 2001); see also the review by Louis Menard, "Culture Club," *New Yorker*, October 15, 2002, 202–5.

87. Elkins and McKitrick, "Richard Hofstadter," 335. On Columbia intellectuals as stylists, see Jacques Barzun, *Clio and the Doctors: Psycho-History, Quanto-History, and History* (Chicago: University of Chicago Press, 1974).

88. Lionel Trilling, 1974 foreword to *The Liberal Imagination* (1950; reprint, New York: Harcourt Brace Jovanovich, 1979), iv. See Elkins and McKitrick, "Richard Hofstadter," 335.

89. Jacques Barzun, *God's Country and Mine* (Boston: Little, Brown and Company, 1954), 159.

90. Kazin, *New York Jew*, 193–94.

91. Lionel Trilling to Dwight Miner, July 26, 1952, Dwight Miner Papers, box 1, Rare Book and Manuscript Library, Columbia University. See Lionel Trilling, "Columbia College in the Van Amringe and Keppel Era," in Dwight Miner, ed., *A History of Columbia College on Morningside* (New York: Columbia University Press, 1954), 14–47.

92. On Hofstadter's talents as a lecturer, see Elkins and McKitrick, "Richard Hofstadter," 351–52.

93. Daniel Bell, *The Reforming of General Education: The Columbia College Experience in Its National Setting* (New York: Columbia University Press, 1966; reprint, New York: Anchor, Doubleday, 1968). See Richard Hofstadter and Walter Metzger, *The Rise of Academic Freedom in the United States* (New York: Columbia University Press, 1955); Richard Hofstadter and Wilson Smith, eds., *American Higher Education: A Documentary History*, 2 vols. (Chicago: University Press, 1961; Richard Hofstadter, "The Revolution in Higher Education," in Arthur M. Schlesinger and Morton White, eds., *Paths of American Thought* (Boston: Houghton Mifflin, 1963), 269–90.

94. On Hofstadter specifically, author interview with Eric L. McKitrick, October 4, 2001.

95. Lionel Trilling, Oral History interview, May 23, 1968; Richard Hofstadter and Walter P. Metzger, *The Development of Academic Freedom in the United States* (New York: Columbia University Press, 1955), 274; Richard Hofstadter, "The 214th Columbia University Commencement Address," *American Scholar* 37 (autumn 1968): 589; Bell, *The Reforming of General Education*, 308.

96. Kathryn Mills and Damek Mills, eds., *C. Wright Mills: Letters and Autobiograph-*

ical Writings (Berkeley: University of California Press, 2000), 10; David A. Hollinger, "Academic Culture at Michigan, 1938–1988: The Apotheosis of Pluralism," *Rackham Reports* 37 (1988–1989): 63.

97. Ibid., 73.

98. Ibid., 76.

99. Quoted in Krupnick, *Lionel Trilling*, 31–32. See Susanne Klingenstein, "Lionel Trilling (1905–1975): Representative Man," in *Jews in the American Academy, 1900–1940* (New Haven: Yale University Press, 1991); Alfred Kazin, *New York Jew* (New York: Knopf, 1978), 42–44, 191–92; Richard Hofstadter, *The Age of Reform: From Bryan to FDR* (New York: Knopf, 1955).

100. Quoted in Elkins and McKitrick, "Richard Hofstadter," 319; William Barrett, *The Truants: Adventures Among the Intellectuals* (New York: Anchor, 1982), 184.

101. C. Vann Woodward, *Mississippi Valley Historical Review* 35 (March 1949): 682.

102. Lionel Trilling, *The Liberal Imagination: Essays on Literature and Society* (New York: Viking, 1950), 10; Richard Hofstadter, *The Progressive Historians: Turner, Beard, Parrington* (New York: Knopf, 1968), iv; Robert K. Merton, "On Sociological Theories of the Middle Range," *Social Theory and Social Structure*, enl. ed. (New York: Free, 1968), 39–72; Craig Calhoun, ed., *Dictionary of the Social Sciences* (New York: Oxford University Press, 2002), 308. See Lionel Trilling, *The Middle of the Journey* (New York: Scribner's, 1947); Daniel Bell, *The End of Ideology: On the Exhaustion of Political Ideas in the Fifties* (New York: New, 1952). Richard Hofstadter, upon being apprised by a junior colleague that there was a tenure opening at some institution outside New York, commented, "I don't know anyone there. In fact, I doubt think I know anyone who knows anyone there" (McKitrick interview, October 4, 2001).

103. Hofstadter, "214th Columbia University Commencement Address," 589. For critics of the Columbia intellectuals, see, e.g., John Rodden, ed., *Lionel Trilling and the Critics* (Lincoln: University of Nebraska Press, 1999).

104. Max Frankel, *The Times of My Life and My Life with The Times* (New York: Random House, 1999), 96; see 94–102. See Roy Cohn, *The Autobiography of Roy Cohn* (New York: Lyle Stuart, 1988).

105. Dan Wakefield, *New York in the Fifties* (Boston: Houghton Mifflin, 1992), 31; see also 29–30.

106. Gerald Nicosia, *Memory Babe: A Critical Biography of Jack Kerouac* (Berkeley: University of California Press, 1983), chaps. 2 and 3.

107. Wakefield, *New York in the Fifties*, 42, 46.

108. Author interview with Michael I. Sovern, August 8, 2001.

109. Author interview with Carl Hovde, August 21, 1997.

110. Mark D. Naison, remarks at 30th reunion of Columbia '68 participants, May 1968, Columbia University. See also idem, *White Boy: A Memoir* (Philadelphia: Temple University Press, 2002), 33–36.

111. Norman Podhoretz, *Making It* (New York: Random House, 1967), 51–52, 3; see 3–56.

112. Carolyn G. Heilbrun, *When Men Were the Only Models We Had: My Teachers Barzun, Fadiman, Trilling* (Philadelphia: University of Pennsylvania Press, 2002); Barbara Aronstein Black, "Something to Remember, Something to Celebrate: Women at

Columbia Law School," *Columbia Law Review* 102 (October 2002): 1451–68. Black students did not begin to be recruited to Columbia College or Barnard until 1963.

113. Robert H. Knapp and Joseph J. Greenbaum, *The Younger American Scholar: His Collegiate Origins* (Chicago: University of Chicago Press, 1953); Robert H. Knapp, *The Origins of American Humanistic Scholars* (Englewood Cliffs, N.J.: Prentice-Hall, 1964). For Barnard and Columbia graduates subsequently receiving Ph.D.s, see appendix B.

114. Author interview with Michael I. Sovern, May 5, 1999; author interview with Eli Ginzberg, September 19, 1997.

115. M. Elizabeth Tidball and Vera Kistiakowsky, "Baccalaureate Origins of American Scientists and Scholars," *Science* 193 (August 20, 1976): 646–52. See also Robert A. McCaughey, *Scholars and Teachers: The Faculties of Select Liberal Arts Colleges and Their Place in American Higher Learning* (New York: Barnard College and the Andrew W. Mellon Foundation, 1994).

116. James A. Davis, *Great Aspirations: The Graduate School Plans of America's College Seniors* (Chicago: Aldine, 1964), 42. See Truman remarks, Columbia University Trustees Minutes, May 6, 1963. John Updike's 1971 short story "When Everyone was Pregnant" is included in his collection *Museums and Women* (New York: Knopf, 1972).

117. Hans Rosenhaupt, *Graduate Students: Experience at Columbia University, 1940–1956* (New York: Columbia University Press, 1958), 93. See Allan M. Cartter, *Ph.D.'s and the Academic Labor Market* (New York: McGraw-Hill, 1976), 103.

118. Cole interview, July 2, 2001. See Nicholas Lemann, *The Big Test: The Secret History of the American Meritocracy* (New York: Farrar, Straus, 1999), 149.

119. Author interview with Fritz Stern, December 19, 2002.

14. AFTERNOON ON THE HUDSON

1. An extensive oral history of the Lamont-Doherty Earth Observatory (as it was renamed in 1968) was conducted in the late 1990s under the auspices of the Oral History Research Office of Columbia University. As all the interviews from this project become available to researchers, some of the judgments offered here will undoubtedly require modification.

2. Author interview with T. William de Bary, August 26, 1997; T. William de Bary Oral History interview, May 27, 1997, Lamont-Doherty Project.

3. Columbia University Trustees Minutes, October 5, 1953.

4. William J. McGill, Oral History interview, September 12, 1997.

5. Kirk Polking, "Maurice Ewing, 1906–1974," in *Oceanographers and Explorers of the Sea* (New York: Enslow, 1999), 11–21. See also John Ewing and Betty Ewing, Oral History interview, May 26, 1996, June 3, 1998, and June 28, 1998, Lamont-Doherty Project.

6. Frank Press, Oral History interview, May 8, 1997. See Wallace S. Broecker, Oral History interview, June 6, 1997, Lamont-Doherty Project.

7. On the Vetleson Prize, see Columbia University Trustees Minutes, October 5, 1959. On Ewing's driven nature, see Broecker interview, June 6, 1997.

8. Press interview, May 8, 1997.

9. Ibid.

10. De Bary interview, May 27, 1997; William J. McGill, Oral History interview, September 15, 1997, Lamont-Doherty Project.

11. William Aspray, "Was Early Entry a Competitive Advantage? US Universities That Entered Computing in the 1940s," *IEEE Annals of the History of Computing*, July–September 2000, 42–87. I wish to acknowledge the contributions of Frank da Cruz, a longtime member of the Columbia computing staff, who is constructing a Web-based chronological history of computing at Columbia. See http://www.columbia.edu/acis/history. Also useful is an unpublished paper provided me by its author, Bruce Gilchrist, "Computing at Columbia University: A Brief Historical Overview," December 1979, 1–9.

12. Aspray, "Was Early Entry a Competitive Advantage?" 66–72. On Hollerwith, see da Cruz, http://www.columbia.edu/acis/history. See also Edwin Black, *IBM and the Holocaust* (New York: Crown, 2001), 24–40. In 1911 Hollerwith sold part of his interest in the technology to what would eventually become International Business Machines (IBM]) though the tabulators themselves continued to be called "Hollerwith Machines."

13. See Frank da Cruz, http://www.columbia.edu/acis/history.

14. Ibid.

15. Quoted in Frank da Cruz, entry for December 20, 1944, "Computing at Columbia Timeline," http://www.columbia.edu/acis/history. See Aspray, "Was Early Entry a Competitive Advantage?" 66–67.

16. Ibid., 67–70.

17. Ibid., 71.

18. Jacques Barzun, *Clio and the Doctors: Pyscho-History, Quanto-History, and History* (Chicago: University of Chicago Press, 1974).

19. Attributed to Joseph Traub, in Aspray, "Was Early Entry a Competitive Advantage?" 71.

20. Aspray, "Was Early Entry a Competitive Advantage?" 71–72.

21. William J. McGill, Oral History interview, June 26, 1979.

22. C. P. Snow, *The Two Cultures and the Scientific Revolution* (Cambridge: Cambridge University Press, 1959), 2, 15–16, 23.

23. Lionel Trilling, "The Leavis-Snow Controversy," in *The Works of Lionel Trilling: Beyond Culture* (New York: Harcourt Brace Jovanovich, 1965), 143; see 126–54. See F. R. Leavis, "The Significance of C. P. Snow," *Spectator* (London), March 9, 1962, 297–303.

24. John S. Rigden, *Rabi: Scientist and Citizen* (New York: Basic, 1987), 258n.

25. Barzun's remark appears in his comments on the education budget, Columbia University Trustees Minutes, February 20, 1959.

26. For comparative statistics on science faculty, see appendix B.

27. For the "pound for pound" qualification, see author interview with Jonathan Cole, July 2, 2001. For Columbia science in the early twentieth century, see chap. 7.

28. On the academic interests of Columbia presidents, see appendix A.

29. For Columbia's principal administrative officers, see appendix A.

30. Jacques Barzun, *Science: The Glorious Entertainment* (New York: Harper and Row, 1964).

31. For the locations of the science facilities, see appendix D.

32. Author interview with George Fraenkel, May 10, 1999.

33. McGill interview, June 26, 1979. Consistent with this putative antiurban bias is the otherwise strange fact that Columbia's scientists have been—and are—more likely to reside in the suburbs than their nonscience colleagues.

34. On the science faculty not teaching undergraduates, see Jacques Barzun, *The American University: How It Runs, Where It Is Going* (New York: Harper and Row, 1968), 54–56.

35. Daniel Bell, *The Reforming of General Education: The Columbia College Experience in Its National Setting* (New York: Columbia University Press, 1966; reprint, New York: Anchor, Doubleday, 1968), 271–72. This is not to minimize the number of Columbia undergraduates in the era of the core curriculum who have gone on to important careers in science, including the Nobel biologist Joshua Lederberg (CC 1944), the geneticist Paul Marks (CC 1945), the Nobel chemist Roald Hoffman (CC 1958), the biologist Robert Pollack (CC 1961), and the astrophysicist Stephen M. Kahn (CC 1976). It is to aver that the list of writers, poets, novelists, and humanistic scholars is substantially longer.

36. *Columbia Spectator*, November 26, 1968, 3.

37. Hannelore Minna Adamson, "The Columbia Crisis of 1968: The Role of the Faculty" (Ph.D. diss., Department of Sociology, Columbia University, 1975).

38. Andrew S. Dolkart, *Morningside Heights: A History of Its Architecture and Development* (New York: Columbia University Press, 1998), 354.

39. Ibid., 419 n. 153, 334, 450 n. 21.

40. Ibid., 427 n. 84, 356.

41. William J. McGill, Oral History interview, July 5, 1979; "Barnard Master Plan Revealed," *Columbia Spectator*, January 23, 2003, 1, 7.

42. Dolkart, afterword to *Morningside Heights*, 325–40.

43. Author interview with Jacques Barzun, February 6, 1998; Barry Bergdoll, *Mastering McKim's Plan: Columbia's First Century on Morningside Heights* (New York: Miriam and Ira D. Wallach Art Gallery, Columbia University, 1997); Grayson Kirk, Oral History interview, October 16, 1987.

44. For space comparisons among universities, see appendix D.

45. Kirk interview, October 16, 1987.

46. Nicholas Murray Butler, *Across the Busy Years: Recollections and Reflections* (New York: Scribner's, 1939), 166–67; McGill interview, July 5, 1979.

47. Dolkart, *Morningside Heights*, 275–86.

48. Ibid., 286–92.

49. Ibid., 325–40.

50. Robert A. M. Stern, Thomas Mellins, and David Fishman, *New York, 1960: Architecture and Urbanism Between the Second World War and the Bicentennial* (New York: Monacelli, 1995).

51. Dolkart, *Morningside Heights*, 329–31; Morningside Heights, Inc., "The Chronology of Morningside Heights Inc, 1947–1972" (New York, 1972, mimeograph), Columbia University Archives–Columbiana Library.

52. MHI, "Chronology," 2–14; Grayson Kirk, Oral History interview, September 23, 1987.

53. Lewis Yablonsky, *The Violent Gang* (New York: Macmillan, 1962).

54. Dolkart, *Morningside Heights*, 330–32.

55. Kirk interview, September 23, 1987.

56. Ibid.

57. Dolkart, *Morningside Heights*, 334, 336.

58. MHI, "Chronology," 14–19.

59. Dolkart, *Morningside Heights*, 336.

60. Grayson Kirk, Oral History interview, June 26, 1988; Barzun quoted in *Columbia Spectator*, March 15, 1965, 1. Barzun had this to say about Salmen: "If any future historian of the university should choose to linger over my own name, I would wish it recorded that my chief contribution is that I persuaded Stanley Salmen to join the central administration at a critical time" (Barzun, *The American University*, 193n).

61. Vincent J. Cannato, *Ungovernable City: John Lindsay and the Struggle to Save New York* (New York: Basic, 2001).

62. Columbia University Trustees Minutes, January 3, 1966; Kirk interview, October 16, 1987.

63. McGill interview, June 26, 1979.

64. Ibid. See Barzun, *The American University*, 45.

65. On Columbia as a raider, see chaps. 6 and 7.

66. McGill interview, June 26, 1979.

67. Ibid.

68. For changes in faculty size among leading postwar universities, see appendix B.

69. On Yale's strategy in the postwar era, see Brooks Mather Kelley, *Yale: A History* (New Haven: Yale University Press, 1974), chap. 20; see also the forthcoming history of Yale in the twentieth century by Gaddis Smith.

70. Author interview with Jacques Barzun, February 5, 1998.

71. Author interview with David J. Rothman, October 28, 1997.

72. Barzun, *The American University*, 49–51; [Archibald Cox], *Crisis at Columbia: Report of the Fact-Finding Commission Appointed to Investigate the Disturbances at Columbia University in April and May 1968* (New York: Random House, Vintage, 1968), 42; author interview with Henry Graff, May 3, 2000.

73. On the general subject of ranking, see David S. Webster, *Academic Quality Ratings of American Colleges and Universities* (Springfield, Ill.: Thomas, 1986); Roger L. Geiger, *Research and Relevant Knowledge: American Research Universities Since World War II* (New York: Oxford University Press, 1993), 211–17. The three rankings appeared in Hayward B. Keniston, *Graduate Study and Research in the Arts and Sciences at the University of Pennsylvania* (Philadelphia: University of Pennsylvania Press, 1959); Allan M. Cartter, *An Assessment of Quality in Graduate Education* (Washington, D.C.: American Council on Education, 1966); Kenneth D. Roose and Charles Andersen, *A Rating of Graduate Programs* (Washington, D.C.: American Council of Education, 1970).

74. [Arthur MacMahon, exec. dir.], *The Report of the President's Committee on the Educational Future of Columbia University* (New York: Trustees of Columbia University, November 1957), 13–14. The survey results were later included in Keniston, *Graduate Study and Research*.

75. Keniston, *Graduate Study and Research*, 119, 120–146; Cartter, *Assessment of Quality*, 100, 107 (general assessments), 68 (physics), 34 (economics), 56 (pyschology). Meanwhile, the opposite was happening to Stanford, which improved its standings between

1962 and 1969 by doubling (from eight to sixteen) the number of its departments among the top five. See Geiger, *Research and Relevant Knowledge*, 129–32.

76. Columbia University Trustees Minutes, February 20, 1959.

77. William J. McGill, Oral History interview, July 3, 1980. See appendix C.

78. Grayson Kirk, Oral History interview, July 5, 1979.

79. Barzun interview, February 6, 1998.

80. Author interview with Marion E. (Betty) Jemmott, December 2, 1997.

81. Ibid.

82. McGill interview, June 26, 1979.

83. Bruce L. R. Smith, *American Science Policy Since World War II* (Washington, D.C.: Brookings Institution, 1990), chap. 4; Geiger, *Research and Relevant Knowledge*, chap. 8; [Louis Henkin, chair], *Report on External Funding Activities at Columbia University* (New York: Columbia University, 1968), 7–8.

84. Statistics from which these conclusions are drawn appear in [Andrew Cordier], *Report of the President for the Year 1968–1969* (New York: Columbia University, fall 1969), Columbia University Archives–Columbiana Library.

85. Abraham Flexner, *Universities: American English German* (New York: Oxford University Press), 133; see 54–58, 136.

86. On Columbia College antipathy to General Studies, see [MacMahon], *The Educational Future of the University*, 79–84. On GS misgivings about the level at which some of its courses were pitched, see John B. Burrell, *A History of Adult Education at Columbia University* (New York: Columbia University Press, 1954), 67–68.

87. Polykarp Kusch, Report to President Cordier, February 1970, Polykarp Kusch folder, Columbia University Archives–Columbiana Library.

88. An anecdote: When John A. Garraty, later a distinguished member of the Columbia history department, defended his dissertation in 1948, his dissertation sponsor, Professor John Krout, introduced himself and warmly congratulated Garraty for the successful defense, assuring Garraty that "I read the entire dissertation" (author interview with John A. Garraty, January 15, 2003).

89. Graff interview, May 3, 2000; Cordier, *Report of the President*.

90. Cordier, *Report of the President*, 37–50, esp. 43.

91. William Bloor to Grayson Kirk, January 2, 1958, William Bloor Papers, Columbia University Archives–Columbiana Library; McGill interview, July 5, 1979. In 1960 Texas ranked first, with an endowment of $357 million; Harvard followed, with $322 million; then came Yale, with $205 million. The University of Chicago ranked fifth, with an endowment of $133 million. See Harry Hansen, ed., *World Almanac and Book of Facts* (New York: New York World Telegram, 1961), 502. For endowment data and rankings, see also appendix C. On the annual return on the Rockefeller property in the 1960s, see McGill interview, July 5, 1979.

92. Grayson Kirk, Oral History interview, June 29, 1989.

93. Kirk interview, October 16, 1987. On Columbia fund-raising, see chap. 11. On the Paley offer, see Benjamin Buttenweiser, Oral History interview, 1981.

94. On indifference of Graduate Faculties to fund-raising, see Kirk interview, June 26, 1988; Courtney C. Brown, *The Dean Meant Business* (New York: Graduate School of Business, Columbia University, 1983), 168.

95. Barzun's view is inferred from his remarks on the general topic of fund-raising in *The American University*, 200–203, passim. On Ford's front-loading of the Campaign for Columbia, see Francis X. Sutton, "The Ford Foundation and Columbia University" (talk to the Columbia University Seminar on the History of Columbia University, November 16, 1999); "$200 Million Campaign Launched," *New York Times*, November 1, 1966, 1:1.

96. Columbia University Trustees Minutes, June 5, October 2, 1967.

97. On the Kirk-Truman relationship, see Grayson Kirk, Oral History interview, March 19, 1991; David B. Truman, "Reflections on the Columbia Disorders of 1968" (1992, rev. 1995), Oral History Research Office, Columbia University.

98. For Columbia College deans by their tenure, see appendix A.

99. On Truman's deanship, see author interview with Carl Hovde, August 21, 1997; Rothman interview, October 28, 1997.

100. Charles W. Everett, "'Most Glad to Teach . . . ,'" in Dwight Miner, ed., *Columbia College on Morningside* (New York: Columbia University Press, 1954), 136–62.

101. Author interview with George K. Fraenkel, May 17, 1999; author's review of Columbia College catalogs in the 1960s; Robert Belknap, testimony to the Cox commission, May 29, 1968, transcript in Rare Book and Manuscript Library, Columbia University.

102. Graff interview, May 3, 2000.

103. John A. Burrell, *A History of Adult Education at Columbia University* (New York: Columbia University Press, 1954); Fraenkel interview, May 3, 1999.

104. Author's direct experience as a Barnard College faculty member since 1969; see also Robert A. McCaughey, *A Statistical Profile of the Barnard College Faculty, 1900–1974* (New York: Barnard College, 1974).

105. For the basis of some of the tension, see Henry Johnson, *The Other Side of Main Street: A History Teaching from Sauk Centre* (New York: Columbia University Press, 1942), 200–201. See Lawrence A. Cremin, David A. Shannon, and Mary Evelyn Townshend, *A History of Teachers College, Columbia University* (New York: Columbia University Press, 1954), 244–56.

106. Hovde interview, August 21, 1997. See [MacMahon], *The Educational Future of the University*, 57–84; author interview with Arlene Jacobs, June 11, 1999; Ann Matthews, "Rage in a Tenured Position," *New York Times*, November 8, 1992, sec. 6, 47, col. 1.

107. Hovde interview, August 21, 1997; author interview with C. Lowell Harriss, September 5, 1997; Barzun interview, February 5, 1998; Graff interview, May 3, 2000.

108. Grayson Kirk, Oral History interview, March 22, 1987.

109. Barzun, *The American University*, 207; see 207–39.

110. De Bary interview, August 26, 1997; author interview with Fritz Stern, December 19, 2002.

15. RIDING THE WHIRLWIND: COLUMBIA '68

1. For historical perspectives on student rowdiness, see Stephen J. Novak, *Rites of Youth: American Colleges and Student Revolt, 1798–1815* (Cambridge: Harvard University Press, 1977); Helen Lefkowitz Horowitz, *Campus Life: Undergraduate Cultures from the End of the Eighteenth Century to the Present* (New York: Knopf, 1987).

2. Sam Tanenhaus, *Whittaker Chambers: A Biography* (New York: Random House, 1987). On the apolitical character of Columbia undergraduate life in the 1920s, see David Cort, "The Army That Never Ran Away," in Wesley First, *University in the Heights* (Garden City: Doubleday, 1969), 19–23, 19.

3. Robert Cohen, *When the Old Left Was Young: Student Radicals and America's First Mass Student Movement* (New York: Oxford University Press, 1993); James A. Wechsler (CC 1935), as quoted in Arthur Schlesinger Jr., *The Age of Roosevelt: The Politics of Upheaval* (Boston: Houghton Mifflin, 1960), 174.

4. James Wechsler, "Politics and Football," in First, *University on the Heights*, 149–54.

5. Grayson Kirk, Oral History interview, May 26, 1989; author interview with Seymour Melman, November 5, 1997.

6. Mike Wallace, Oral History interview, December 15, 1983, Student Movement Project, Oral History Research Office, Columbia University.

7. George Keller, "Negroes and the College," *Columbia College Today*, fall 1964, 15–19; author interview with Roger Lehecka, October 30, 1997. Of the forty-one black students interviewed following their April 30 arrest for occupying Hamilton Hall, 85 percent received financial aid, 72 percent were the first in their family to go to college, and 55 percent were from working-class backgrounds. See Robert Liebert, *Radical and Militant Youth: A Psychoanalytic Study* (New York: Praeger, 1971).

8. On black social life at Columbia, see Ruth Louie (BC 1971), correspondence with author, January 28, 2003.

9. William Sales, remarks at 30th reunion of Columbia '68 participants, May 12, 1998, notes taken by author.

10. Ray Brown and Bill Sales, in Stephen Donadio, "Seven Interviews," *Partisan Review* 35 (summer 1968): 376–81; Dean Alexander B. Platt, Oral History interview, May 17, 1968.

11. Irwin Unger, *The Movement: A History of the American New Left, 1959–1972* (New York: Harper and Row, 1974), chap. 3; Tom Hayden, *Reunion: A Memoir* (New York: Random House, 1988).

12. Author interview with Lewis Cole, October 14, 1997.

13. Jerry Avorn and Robert Friedman, *Up Against the Ivy Wall: A History of the Columbia Crisis* ((New York: Atheneum, 1969), 31–32; Mark Rudd, "Columbia: Notes on the Student Rebellion," in Carl Oglesby, ed., *New Left Reader* (New York: Grove, 1968), 290–312.

14. On the CCC, see Cathleen Cook, secretary to Columbia Citizenship Council, Oral History interview, May 15, 1968.

15. Herbert A. Deane, testimony to the Cox commission, May 16, 1968; A. Bruce Goldman, testimony to the Cox commission, May 27, 1968, transcript in Rare Book and Manuscript Library, Columbia University.

16. Grayson Kirk, Oral History interview, August 24, 1988.

17. This conclusion is supported by the arrest statistics. See appendix B.

18. Cole interview, October 14, 1997. The radical contingent also included at least one Barnard student, Josephine Drexel Duke, who came from wealthy and socially privileged circumstances. Another woman, the GSAS student Randi Eisenberg, did manage to secure a significant place in SDS deliberations. See Randi Eisenberg, "The Strike: A

Critical Reappraisal," *Ripsaw—The Journal of the Graduate Student Union* 1 (December 1968): 37–45.

19. Cole interview, October 14, 1997. The substantial presence of Jews in the ranks of the Columbia student left was not peculiar to Columbia but reflective of the student left nationally. See Kenneth J. Heineman, *Campus Wars: The Peace Movement at American State Universities in the Vietnam Era* (New York: New York University Press, 1993), 98–99, 105–6.

20. Grayson Kirk, Oral History interview, September 26, 1989. Full disclosure: the author went to college on an NROTC scholarship, spent four years as a naval officer, and remains convinced that he was not militarized by the process.

21. On police on campus after NROTC disruptions, see Kirk interview, September 26, 1989.

22. Paul Vilardi, testimony to the Cox commission, May 14, 1968.

23. *Columbia Spectator*, April 27, 1967, 1.

24. Grayson Kirk, Oral History interview, March 19, 1991; Platt interview, May 17, 1968.

25. Grayson Kirk, Oral History interview, December 11, 1989.

26. Kirk interview, September 26, 1989.

27. Platt interview, May 17, 1968.

28. Ibid.

29. Grayson Kirk, "Memorandum to the University Community," *Columbia Daily Spectator*, September 25, 1967, 1; Jeffrey Fowley et al., "Statement of Class Officers Supporting Open Recruiting," n.d. (probably early January 1968); *Columbia Daily Spectator*, November 1, 1967, 1, 5; [Gerald Feinberg, David Rothman, Warner R. Schilling, Howard W. Schless, and Allan Silver (chair)], "Report of the Committee on Recruitment by Outside Agencies to the Faculty of Columbia College," November 8, 1967, Columbia University Archives–Columbiana Library; "Report of the President's Advisory Committee on Student Life," including "President's Advisory Committee on Student Life: Minority Report of Four Student Members," fall 1967, copy in Cox commission Files, Rare Book and Manuscript Library, Columbia University. Three of the four "student members" were Eric Foner, David Ment, and Peter Bierstedt.

30. "Real Radicalism," *Columbia Daily Spectator*, October 30, 1967, 2.

31. Columbia University Trustees Minutes, October 2, 1967.

32. Kirk interview, March 19, 1991. See Columbia University Trustees Minutes, January 8, 1968.

33. The best contemporary treatment of the Morningside Gym project is Roger Starr, "The Case of the Columbia Gym," *Public Interest*, no. 13 (fall 1968), 102–21. See also the testimony of Harold McGuire to the Cox commission, May 20, 1968, and the contrary testimony from Basil Patterson, July 2, 1968.

34. On the administration's lack of enthusiasm for the gym, see McGuire's testimony to the Cox commission. See also David B. Truman, "Reflections on the Columbia Disorders of 1968" (1992, rev. 1995), Oral History Research Office, Columbia University.

35. On Moses as the source of the idea of building the gym in Morningside Park, see Courtney C. Brown, *The Dean Meant Business* (New York: Graduate School of Business, Columbia University, 1983), 168.

36. On early community support, see McGuire's testimony to the Cox commission.

37. Starr, "The Case of the Columbia Gym," 103.

38. For the cost escalations, see McGuire's testimony to the Cox commission.

39. Starr, "The Case of the Columbia Gym, 111–13.

40. For additional features, see the testimony of McGuire and Patterson to the Cox commission.

41. Vincent J. Cannato, *Ungovernable City: John Lindsay and His Struggle to Save New York* (New York: Basic, 2001), 233–34. Hoving continued to oppose the gym in Morningside throughout his term as parks commissioner. Ironically, when he resigned in 1970 to become director of the Metropolitan Museum, one of his first projects was to provide the museum with additional space by extending it deeper into Central Park.

42. Author interview with Eli Ginzberg, September 19, 1997.

43. Lack of support for the gym among students was confirmed by a survey taken by the Ted Kremer Society on April 25, 1968. Of 6,426 students polled, 4,093 (64 percent) favored ending gym construction, while only 24 percent supported the demonstration tactics of SDS and SAS. See Referendum Committee to Professor Alan Westin, April 28, 1968, *Columbia Spectator*, April 29, 1968, 1. Stopping construction of the gym had a 65 percent approval rating among the 769 faculty polled in the week following the police action, according to the Bureau of Applied Social Research, "Student and Faculty Response to the Columbia Crisis: A Preliminary Report Based on Partial Returns" (May 20, 1968, mimeograph), 6, Columbia University Archives–Columbiana Library.

44. Reported in *Columbia Spectator*, December 4, 1967, 1.

45. On the gym as a defining issue for black students, see Platt interview, May 17, 1968; Mark D. Naison, *White Boy: A Memoir* (Philadelphia: Temple University Press, 2002), 89; Brown and Sales, in Donadio, "Seven Interviews."

46. Bob Feldman and Mark Rudd, "How to Get SDS Moving Again and Screw the University All in One Fell Swoop," n.d. (probably mid-February 1968), mimeograph in author's possession.

47. Author interview with Lewis Cole, October 14, 1997; Hayden, *Reunion*, 275; Nancy Bieberman, remarks at 30th reunion of Columbia '68 participants, May 12, 1998, notes taken by author.

48. David Rothman, Oral History interview, May 13, 1968; Bruce Smith, Oral History interview, May 10, 1968; Immanuel Wallerstein, Oral History interview with *Spectator* reporters Robert Friedman and Andrew Crane, mid-June 1968; Orest Ranum, Oral History interview, May 13, 1968. See Seymour Melman, Oral History interview, May 22, 1968; Marvin Harris, Oral History interview, May 13, 1968; Anika Bodroghkozy, "After the Revolution: A Talk with Mark Rudd," *Broadway*, November 25, 1986, 4–7.

49. Avorn and Friedman, *Up Against the Ivy Wall*, 30–31; Platt interview, May 17, 1968.

50. Columbia University Trustees Minutes, November 6, 1967.

51. On the administration's mishandling of questions about IDA, see Avorn and Friedman, *Up Against the Ivy Wall*, 15–18.

52. Seymour Melman, *The Permanent War Economy: American Capitalism in Decline* (New York: Simon and Schuster, 1974); Columbia University Trustees Minutes, January 8, 1968.

53. Peter Schneider, "Surprise Sit-In Blocks Dow," *Junior Paper Tiger* (journal of the Columbia University Students for Democratic Society), February 26, 1968, 1; Platt, interview, May 17, 1968.

54. Truman, "Reflections on the Columbia Disorders."

55. Platt interview, May 17, 1968. The six undergraduates identified were Mark Rudd, Nick Freudenberg, Ted Gold, John Jacobs, Ed Hyman (CC 1969), and Morris Grossner.

56. As later stated in SDS, "Six Demands," press release, April 23, 1968, Student Protest Collection, Columbia University Archives–Columbiana Library.

57. On the presidential shakeup and SDS concerns about the efforts to engage students in the presidential campaigns of Eugene McCarthy and Robert Kennedy, see Jay Facciola, testimony to the Cox commission, May 21, 1968.

58. James Baldwin, *The Fire Next Time* (New York: Dial Press, 1963). See *Columbia Spectator*, April 5, 1968, 1. On Lindsay's efforts to contain the situation, see Cannato, *The Ungovernable City*, 210–15.

59. Rev. John D. Cannon, Oral History interview, May 9, 1968.

60. Michael Stern, "Walkout Disrupts Memorial to King," *Columbia Daily Spectator*, April 10, 1968, 1. On the reaction to Cannon's seeming endorsement of Rudd's disruption of the services, see Herbert A. Deane, Oral History interview, May 16, 1968.

61. On Fritz Stern's encounter with Rudd, see Mark Flanigan, Oral History interview, May 16, 1968. Richard Hofstadter made the same Weimar analogy in a WKCR interview on April 25, during which he characterized SDS as representative of "the fascism of the left." See Wallace interview, December 15, 1983.

62. For SDS activities on eve of the April 23 demonstration, Avorn, *Up Against the Ivy Wall*, 38–39.

63. Mark Rudd, "Letter to Uncle Grayson," reprinted in Avorn and Friedman, *Up Against the Ivy Wall*, 25–27. The phrase was said to be used by police on the street when stopping blacks for questioning.

64. Jay Facciola (CC 1974; CU Law 1983), Oral History interview, May 21, 1968.

65. On SDS plans for the sun dial demonstration, see Avorn and Friedman, *Up Against the Ivy Wall*, 34; on the administration's countermeasures, see Flanigan interview, May 16, 1968; Thomas S. Colahan, Oral History interview, May 17, 1968.

66. Avorn and Friedman, *Up Against the Ivy Wall*, 38–40

67. On the fears of a Harlem invasion, see Walter Metzger, Oral History interview, May 15, 1968. See also Diana Trilling, "On the Steps of Low Library," in *We Must March My Darlings* (New York: Harcourt Brace Jovanovich, 1975), 85–88.

68. On the sun dial maneuverings, see Flanigan interview, May 16, 1968.

69. Michael Stern, "1 Arrested in Park in Violent Protest," *Columbia Daily Spectator*, April 24, 1968, 1.

70. On the sequestering of Dean Coleman, see Avorn and Friedman, *Up Against the Ivy Wall*, 54–58; *Columbia Spectator*, April 24, 1968, 1; Henry Coleman, conversation with author, January 28, 2003. Suggestive of the as-yet-not-serious character of the proceedings, the *Spectator* referred to the student action in Hamilton as a "sleep-in."

71. Michael Stern, "Outsiders Influence SDS Action," *Columbia Daily Spectator*, April 25, 1968, 1. On black-white relations that evening, see Ruth Louie (BC 1971), correspondence with author, January 28, 2003.

72. On the spontaneous character of these early actions, Lewis Cole interview, October 14, 1997.

73. Facciola interview, May 21, 1968; Flanigan interview, May 16, 1968. According to Flanigan, the person recommending the seizure of another building was an unidentified faculty member.

74. Some reports have students being provided a key to Low by a disgruntled member of the staff. On the early departure of most of the occupiers, see Robert Stamberg, communication with author, November 15, 2002. For those students who stayed on in Low, see Frank da Cruz, "Columbia University 1968," http://www.columbia.edu/acis/ history/1968.html.

75. For the SDS vote against further building occupations, see Avorn and Friedman, *Up Against the Ivy Wall*, 80. On the Avery takeover, see Richard Rosenkranz, *Across the Barricades* (New York: Lippincott, 1971).

76. Flanigan interview, May 16, 1968. The principal members of the Majority Coalition included Paul Vilardi (CC 1968), Kenneth Tomecki (CC 1968), Anthony Ciccone (CC 1970), Robert Wolfe (CC 1968), Frank Dann (CC 1968), and Bruce Bono (CC 1968). See Vilardi and other members of the Majority Coalition, testimony to the Cox commission, July 12, 1968.

77. Melman interview, May 22, 1968. See Mark Jaffe, "Coalition Challenges Low Strikers," *Columbia Daily Spectator*, April 29, 1968, 1.

78. Grayson Kirk, Oral History interview, October 3, 1968; David Truman, Oral History interview, October 4, 1968; author interview with Arlene Jacobs, June 11, 1999.

79. Barry Gottehrer, *The Mayor's Man* (Garden City: Doubleday, 1975), chap. 7.

80. On the administration's dealings with the police, see Truman interview, October 4, 1968; Truman, "Reflections on the Columbia Disorders."

81. Kirk interview, October 3, 1968. See Jacobs interview, June 11, 1999.

82. Author interview with Eugene Galanter, September 24, 1997.

83. Minutes of Special Meeting, Faculty of Columbia College, April 24, 1968, Student Protest Collection, Columbia University Archives–Columbiana Library. See Smith interview, May 10, 1968; *Columbia Spectator*, April 25, 1968, 1.

84. Minutes of Special Meeting, April 24, 1968. On the administration's disappointment with the outcome of the meeting, see Truman, "Reflections on the Columbia Disorders."

85. Rothman interview, May 13, 1968.

86. Ibid. See Truman, "Reflections on the Columbia Disorders."

87. On birth of the AHFG, see Metzger interview, May 15, 1968.

88. Metzger interview, May 15, 1968. On the AHFG talking teams sent to the buildings, see Avorn and Friedman, *Up Against the Ivy Wall*, 93–95; author interview with Allan Silver, January 5, 1998; Rothman interview, May 13, 1968.

89. Avorn and Friedman, *Up Against the Ivy Wall*, 162. See ibid., 95; Facciola interview, May 21, 1968; Joel Frader, Oral History interview, May 15, 1968.

90. Schilling quoted in Paul Vilardi, Oral History interview, May 17, 1968; Metzger interview, May 15, 1968. See author interview with C. Lowell Harriss, September 5, 1997; author interview with T. William de Bary, August 26, 1997. On the size of the Wollman gathering, see Flanigan interview, May 16, 1968.

91. Kenneth Barry, "Plainclothes Police Club CU Faculty," *Columbia Daily Spectator*, April 26, 1968, 1. Some conservative faculty critical of what they took to be the AHFG's power grab contended that Greeman's wound had been self-inflicted. See Eugene Galanter, testimony to the Cox commission, June 26, 1968. Truman later acknowledged that his announcement was "more abrupt and peremptory than it should have been" ("Reflections on the Columbia Disorders," 121; see 117–31).

92. Kirk interview, October 3, 1968; Truman quoted in Oren Root Jr., "Use of Police Postponed as Negotiations Continue," *Columbia Daily Spectator*, April 26, 1968, 1–2. See Patterson, testimony to the Cox commission, July 2, 1968.

93. On the visit by Carmichael and Brown to Hamilton, see Arthur Kokot, "Two Black Leaders Support Strikers," *Columbia Daily Spectator*, April 27, 1968. On the AHFG moving closer to supporting full amnesty, see Smith interview, May 10, 1968.

94. Among the several accounts of Rudd's blowoff of the AHFG for not endorsing amnesty, see Marvin Harris, testimony to the Cox commission, June 15, 1968; Orest Ranum, "To Members of the Ad Hoc Faculty," April 27, 1968, copy in author's possession.

95. Smith interview, May 10, 1968.

96. Bettina Berch, Oral History interview, December 15, 1983.

97. Kenneth Clark, testimony before the Cox commission, July 2, 1968; Hayden, *Reunion*, 275–79; Avorn and Friedman, *Up Against the Ivy Wall*, 172–73.

98. On SDS intentions as of Friday, see Galanter interview, September 24, 1997. On the Sunday picnickers, see Smith interview, May 10, 1968. The judgment that the SDS/Strike leadership sought a confrontation with the police, though shared at the time by many observer participants not sympathetic to Rudd, is my own.

99. On the AHFG "bitter pill" resolution team, see Rothman interview, May 13, 1968; Robert Fogelson, Oral History interview, May 9, 1968; author interview with David Rothman, October 28, 1997.

100. Rothman interview, May 13, 1968. The text of of the "bitter pill" resolutions is reprinted in Avorn and Friedman, *Up Against the Ivy Wall*, 157.

101. For the idea of collective punishment as de facto amnesty, see Marvin Harris, testimony to the Cox commission, June 15, 1968.

102. Text of the AHFG summary resolution 4 reads:
These proposals being in our judgment a just solution to the crisis our University is presently undergoing, we pledge that:
a. If the president will not adopt these proposals, we shall take all measures within our several consciences to prevent the use of force to vacate these buildings.
b. If the President does accept our proposals but the students in the buildings refuse to evacuate these buildings, we shall refuse further to interpose ourselves between the Administration and the students.
("Resolution of the Ad Hoc Faculty Group" [April 28, 1968],
Columbia Spectator, April 24, 1968, 7)

103. On Truman's distress with the "bitter pill" resolutions, see Truman, "Reflections on the Columbia Disorders." On Westin's agreement not to bring them forward for a vote, see his testimony before the Cox commission, June 5, 1968.

104. De Bary interview, August 26, 1997.

105. Author interview with Sigmund Diamond, August 29, 1997; Kirk interview, December 11, 1989.

106. On the Sunday joint faculties meeting, see Peter Kenen, Oral History interview, May 16, 1968; Kenen, "Notes on '68," written later in 1968, in possession of Fritz Stern; Marion E. (Betty) Jemmott, Oral History interview, September 16, 1999.

107. Diamond interview, August 29, 1997; Deane interview, May 16, 1968.

108. Author interview with Michael I. Sovern, May 12, 1999.

109. Robert B. Stulberg, "Majority Coalition Blockades Low," *Columbia Daily Spectator*, April 29, 1968, 1. For pictures of the Low confrontation, see "A Great University Under Siege," *Life Magazine*, May 10, 1968, 36–47.

110. Rothman interview, May 13, 1968. See Fogelson interview, May 9, 1968.

111. On the Strike Coordinating Committee's efforts to keep occupiers in the buildings, see Platt interview, May 17, 1968. On the struggles around Low, see da Cruz, "Columbia University 1968." On the coverage by the *Times*, see Harrison Salisbury, *A Time of Change: A Reporter's Tale of Our Time* (New York: Harper and Row, 1988), 173–75; Robert Friedman, Oral History interview, February 1992.

112. *New York Times*, April 30, 1968, sec. 1, 49, col. 1.

113. On the Linda LeClair affair, see Rosalind Rosenberg, *Changing the Subject: A History of Women at Columbia* (New York: Columbia University Press, forthcoming). The estimate of Barnard participants in the Columbia occupations is based on subsequent arrest statistics and author interview with Barbara Schmitter, September 15, 1997.

114. "Statement by President Grayson Kirk," April 29, 1968, Office of Public Information, Columbia University. Truman believed Kirk "went a considerable distance towards accepting the terms of the ultimatum" ("Reflections on the Columbia Disorders," 135). See Avorn and Friedman, *Up Against the Ivy Wall*, 169–71.

115. On the Strike Coordinating Committee's rejection of the "bitter pill" resolutions, see Avorn and Friedman, *Up Against the Ivy Wall*, 174–75. On the Majority Coalition's acceptance of them, see Vilardi interview, May 17, 1968.

116. On the AHFG efforts to get Lindsay or Rockefeller to intervene, see Gottehrer, *The Mayor's Man*, 167–69; Fogelson interview, May 9, 1968.

117. George K. Fraenkel, testimony to the Cox commission, July 25, 1968; author interview with George K. Fraenkel, August 27, 1997.

118. Gottehrer, *The Mayor's Man*, 137, 169; see 133–37.

119. David Truman, testimony to the Cox commission, May 21, 1968; Fraenkel, Testimony to the Cox commission, July 25, 1968.

120. On the *New York Times*'s persistent underestimating the numbers of students in the buildings, see Lawrence Berger, testimony to the Cox commission, May 21, 1968.

121. Kirk interview, October 3, 1968. That many of the students occupying the buildings did not fit this economically privileged image did nothing to mitigate the perceived class character of the confrontation.

122. Avorn and Friedman, *Up Against the Ivy Wall*, 186–87.

123. Ibid., 188–90; Peter Stamberg, interview with Emily Moscowitz, April 2002, in author's possession; Frank da Cruz, correspondence with author, November 15, 2002. See also da Cruz, "Columbia University 1968."

124. Rosenkranz, *Across the Barricades*, 216–31.

125. Avorn and Friedman, *Up Against the Ivy Wall*, 191–92; Berch interview, December 15, 1983; Wallace interview, December 15, 1983.

126. Hayden, *Reunion*, 280–82.

127. Interim Report Prepared by the First Deputy Commissioner of Police to the Commissioner of Police, May 4, 1968, cited in Avorn and Friedman, *Up Against the Ivy Wall*, 181. Reported injuries included ninety-two student occupiers and bystanders and seventeen policemen.

128. Author interview with Carl Hovde, August 21, 1997.

129. Ibid.

130. Fogelson interview, May 9, 1968; Kenen interview, May 16, 1968. A subsequent inquiry by the Police Civilian Review Board did determine that the police deployed excessive force police in clearing South Field. See Michael A. Baker, *Police on Campus: The Mass Police Action at Columbia University, Spring 1968* (New York: New York Civil Liberties Union, 1969).

131. Allan H. Barton, "The Columbia Crisis: Campus, Vietnam, and the Ghetto," *Public Opinion Quarterly* 32, no. 3 (fall 1968): 333–51.

132. SDS flyer in Student Protest Collection, Columbia University Archives–Columbiana Library. See *Columbia Spectator*, April 30, 1968, 1; May 1, 1968, 1; May 2, 1968, 1.

133. See Fraenkel, testimony to the Cox commission, July 25, 1968; Truman, "Reflections on the Columbia Disorders." The Abe Rosenthal story in the May 1, 1968, *New York Times* was widely cited as evidence of the *Times*'s proadministration coverage.

134. Sovern interview, May 12, 1999; Avorn and Friedman, *Up Against the Ivy Wall*, 211. See Smith interview, May 10, 1968; author interview with Bruce Smith, June 19, 2002.

135. Sovern interview, May 12, 1999.

136. For the text of the Rosenberg Resolutions, see Avorn and Friedman, *Up Against the Ivy Wall*, 213.

137. Sovern interview with author, May 12, 1999.

138. Ibid.; Ginzberg interview, September 19, 1997.

16. IT'S ABOUT COLUMBIA

1. Author interview with Henry Graff, May 3, 2000.

2. On the Independent Faculty Group, see Charles Parsons, in Stephen Donadio, "Seven Interviews," *Partisan Review* 35, no. 3 (summer 1968): 381–86. See also Hannelore Minna Adamson, "The Columbia Crisis of 1968: The Role of the Faculty" (Ph.D. diss., Department of Sociology, Columbia University, 1975); author interview with Carl Hovde, August 21, 1997. See also appendix A.

3. Polykarp Kusch, Oral History interview, May 17, 1968.

4. Grayson Kirk cited these efforts in his Oral History interview, September 26, 1989. See also author interview with Fritz Stern, December 19, 2002.

5. Warner Schilling, Oral History interview, June 17, 1968; Herbert A. Deane, Oral History interview, May 16, 1968.

6. William J. McGill, Oral History interview, July 3, 1980.

7. Lionel Trilling, Oral History interview, May 23, 1968; Donadio, "Seven Interviews," 392.

8. Lionel Trilling, *Sincerity and Authenticity* (Cambridge: Harvard University Press, 1972), 171–172.

9. Ibid.

10. Jacques Barzun, *The American University: How It Runs—Where It Is Going* (New York: Harper and Row, 1968), xii. See Daniel Bell, "Columbia and the New Left," *The Public Interest*, no. 13 (fall 1968): 61–101. On Bell's departure, see author interview with George Fraenkel, May 10, 1999.

11. Richard Hofstadter, "214th Commencement Address, Columbia University," *American Scholar* 37 (autumn 1968): 583; idem, Oral History interview, May 15, 1968. On Hofstadter at this time as viewed by one of his favorite graduate students, see Mike Wallace, Oral History interview, December 15, 1983, Student Protest Project, Oral History Research Office, Columbia University.

12. For the following reconstruction of the history of the Executive Committee of the Faculty, I have relied primarily on the recollections of three of its members, Eli Ginzberg, Michael I. Sovern, and William T. de Bary, as well as the extensive coverage of its activities by the *Columbia Spectator*. Thomas Mathewson, the executive director of the University Senate, was also helpful in providing materials on the senate's creation. See Executive Committee of the Faculty, "Preliminary Proposals for the Creation of a University Senate and a Student Assembly," September 10, 1968, and "Proposal for a University Senate," March 20, 1969, Office of the University Senate, Low Library, Columbia University.

13. *Columbia Spectator*, May 1, 1968, 1; author interview with Eli Ginzberg, September 19, 1997.

14. Ginzberg interview, September 19, 1997.

15. Author interview with William T. de Bary, August 26, 1997; Ginzberg interview, September 19, 1997.

16. Bruce Smith, Oral History interview, May 10, 1968. See author interview with Bruce Smith, June 19, 2002; Stern interview December 19, 2002.

17. Hovde interview, August 21, 1997.

18. David J. Rothman, Oral History interview, May 13, 1968; Marvin Harris, Oral History interview, May 13, 1968. See Harold McGuire, testimony to the Cox commission, May 15, 1968, transcript in Rare Book and Manuscript Library, Columbia University; Columbia University Trustees Minutes, May 9, 1968'.

19. Columbia University Trustees Minutes, November 18, 1968.

20. Ginzberg interview, September 19, 1997; Columbia University Trustees Minutes, May 6, 1968.

21. Columbia University Trustees Minutes, May 6, 1968.

22. Ginzberg interview, September 19, 1997; author interview with Michael I. Sovern, May 5, 1999.

23. Columbia University Trustees Minutes, May 6, 1968. The Association of Alumni of Columbia College was even less open to compromise, having three days earlier called for the immediate expulsion of all demonstrating students.

24. Sovern interview, May 5, 1999. On Hogan's cooperativeness, see Ginzberg interview, September 19, 1997; Hovde interview, August 21, 1997; Sovern interview, May 5, 1999.

25. On the post-1968 turnover on the board, see appendix A.

26. The recognizable Jewish members included Arthur Ochs Sulzberger, William Paley, Abram Abeloff, Benjamin Buttenweiser, Percy Uris, Lawrence Wien, and Arthur Krim.

27. Columbia University Trustees Minutes, October 7, 1968. For the changing composition of the board, see appendix A.

28. Author interview with Lewis Cole, October 14, 1997. On the ECOF strategy for dealing with students, see Ginzberg interview, September 19, 1997; Sovern interview, May 5, 1999.

29. Mark Rudd and Lewis Cole, in Donadio, "Seven Interviews," 373. For material relating to Students for a Restructured University, see SRU folder, Student Protest and Action Collection, Columbia University Archives–Columbiana Library. See also SRU members Xandra Kayden, John Thoms, and Nigel Paneth, testimony to the Cox commission, July 16, 1968.

30. Trilling interview, May 23, 1968.

31. On black demands, see Ray Brown and Bill Sales, in Donadio, "Seven Interviews."

32. On continued efforts to recruit black students in Columbia College, see Hovde interview, August 9, 1999.

33. Trilling interview, May 23, 1968. On winning over black students, see Ginzberg interview, September 19, 1997.

34. Kayden, Thoms, and Paneth, testimony to the Cox commission, July 16, 1968.

35. Thoms statement, SRU folder.

36. For SRU's response to the 114th Street action, see John Thoms statement of May 16, 1968, in SRU folder.

37. On Hamilton II, see Dean Alexander Platt, testimony to the Cox commission, July 15, 1968; Frank da Cruz, correspondence with author, November 15, 2002.

38. SRU statement, May 22, 1968, SRU folder. On the faculty reaction to Hamilton II, see [Archibald Cox], *Crisis at Columbia: Report of the Fact-Finding Commission Appointed to Investigate the Disturbances at Columbia University in April and May 1968* (New York: Random House, Vintage, 1968), 179–86. On the reactions of the ECOF and student groups, see [Cox], *Crisis at Columbia*, 182–86.

39. On the Law School disruption, see Jonah Raskin, *Out of the Whale: Growing Up in the American Left* (New York: Links, 1974).

40. Paul Berman, *A Tale of Two Utopias* (New York: Norton, 1996), 89. See Raskin, *Out of the Whale*, chap. 8.

41. Berman, *Two Utopias*, 89. On Gilbert, see *New York Times*, October 23, 1981, sec. 1, 1, col. 3; October 24, 1981, sec. 1, 1, col. 3; November 18, 1981, sec. 2, 2, col. 6.

42. On conservatives' responses to restructuring efforts, see Louis Orans and Michael Kogan, testimony to the Cox commission, May 15, 1968.

43. On the politics and workings of the *Columbia Spectator* from 1968 to 1970, see author interview with Michael Rothfeld, May 14, 2002. See also Robert Friedman, Oral History Interview, December 15, 1983.

44. Sovern interview, May 5, 1999.

45. Murray Kempton, "Thoughts on Columbia," *New York Post*, April 30, 1968, 47. See James Wechsler, "Columbia Fumbles," *New York Post*, May 10, 1968, 49.

46. On *New York Times* coverage, see Salisbury, *A Time of Change*, 173–75, 297. For other coverage, see the following articles in *Newsweek*: "Columbia at Bay," May 6, 1968, 40–53; "The End of a Siege—and an Era," May 13, 1968, 59–62; "To the Barricades," June 3, 1968, 3; "Columbia: The Next Act," July 29, 1968, 55; "A Matter of Basics," August 12, 1968, 48–50; "Tough Talk at Columbia," August 26, 1968, 55; "Why Columbia Happened," October 14, 1968, 96. See also Friedman interview, December 15, 1983.

47. "Mutiny at a Great University," *Life*, May 10, 1968, 36–49.

48. Tom Hayden, "Two, Three, Many Columbias," *Ramparts* 6, no. 11 (June 15, 1968): 40; Mailer quoted in Roger Kahn, *The Battle for Morningside Heights* (New York: Morrow, 1970), 37. See Dotson Rader and Craig Anderson, "Report from the Barricades: Rebellion at Columbia," *New Republic*, May 11, 1968, 9–11.

49. William F. Buckley, "In Defense of the Police," *New York Post*, May 9, 1968, 49.

50. Daniel Bell, "Columbia and the New Left," *Public Interest*, no. 13 (fall 1968), 61–101; Zbigniew Brzezinski, "Revolution and Counterrevolution (But Not Necessarily About Columbia!)," *New Republic*, June 1, 1968, 23–25; Danwart Rustow, "Days of Crisis," *New Leader*, May 20, 1968, 5–12.

51. Truman's statement reported in *Newsweek*, May 13, 1968, 60; [Cox], *Crisis at Columbia*, 37 (see also for an assessment of "Partners in the Park"). See Grayson Kirk, "Letter to Friends of Columbia," May 1968, Columbia University Archives– Columbiana Library; "Partners in the Park" (New York: Trustees of Columbia University, summer 1968), available in Cox Commission alpha file, Rare Book and Manuscript Library.

52. On the genesis of the fact-finding commission and administration opposition, see author interview with Michael Sovern, May 12, 1999.

53. A transcript and several boxes of supporting documents of the Cox commission hearings are on deposit in Rare Book and Manuscript Library. The commission's costs were underwritten by a grant from the Ford Foundation.

54. Columbia University Trustees Minutes, August 15, 1968.

55. Marvin Harris, testimony to the Cox commission, June 5, 1968.

56. Courtney C. Brown, *The Dean Meant Business* (New York: Graduate School of Business, Columbia University, 1983), 203. On Truman's secretary's doings, see author interview with Arlene Jacobs, June 11, 1999.

57. On the search committee interview of Truman, see author interview with Giulio Pontecorvo, September 25, 1997. In his "Reflections on the Columbia Disorders of 1968" (1992, rev. 1995, Oral History Research Office), Truman acknowledged that he suffered from "acute depression" in the months after May 1968.

58. There is both a transcript of the minutes and an audio tape of the September 12, 1968, meeting of joint faculties on deposit at the Columbia University Archives– Columbiana Library.

59. Author interview with Sigmund Diamond, August 29, 1997.

60. Minutes of joint faculties meeting, September 12, 1968.

61. Ibid.

62. Ibid. The audiotape is in the author's possession.

63. Minutes of joint faculties meeting, September 12, 1968.

64. Cox Commission Papers, Rare Book and Manuscript Library.

65. Bruce Goldman, testimony to the Cox commission, May 27, 1968; Mark Kessel-

man, testimony to the Cox commission, May 22, 1968. The feet-on-table incident occurred during the testimony of Reverend E. Kendall Smith, on June 25, 1968.

66. [Cox], *Crisis at Columbia.*, 187–99.

67. Columbia University Trustees Minutes, October 7, 1968.

68. George Keller, "Six Weeks That Shook Morningside," *Columbia College Today*, spring 1968 (though it did not appear until late 1968), 9. See de Bary interview, August 26, 1997; George Keller, correspondence with author, summer 2001.

69. *The Owl* 10, no. 10 (December 4, 1968): 3–5; author interview with Carl Hovde, August 9, 1999; Carl Hovde, "A Statement on *Columbia College Today*," February 13, 1969, Columbia University Archives–Columbiana Library; de Bary interview, August 26, 1997. After leaving Columbia, Keller went on to become chair of Higher Education Studies at the University of Pennsylvania's Graduate School of Education.

70. Jerry Avorn and Robert Friedman, *Up Against the Ivy Wall: A History of the Columbia Crisis* (New York: Atheneum, 1969); James Kunen, *The Strawberry Statement: Notes of a College Revolutionary* (New York: Random House, 1969).

71. Roger Kahn, *The Battle for Morningside Heights: Why Students Rebel* (New York: Morrow, 1970).

72. [Cox], *Crisis at Columbia*, 195.

73. George J. Lankevich, "Cordier, Andrew Wellington, 1901–1975," in *Dictionary of American Biography* (New York: Scribner's, 1994), supp. 9, 191–93; Jacobs interview, June 11, 1999.

74. Lankevich, "Cordier."

75. "Trustees Announce Dean Cordier Will Serve as Acting President," *New York Times*, August 24, 1968, sec. 1, 21, col. 5.

76. Carl Hovde interview, August 9, 1999.

77. Friendly's comment on Cordier is reported in author interview with William T. de Bary, May 27, 1999; Hovde interview, August 9, 1999.

78. William G. McGill, Oral History interview, July 5, 1979.

79. Remark attributed to Polykarp Kusch in Fraenkel interview, May 10, 1999. On the difficulties of attracting faculty into the administration, see de Bary interview, August 26, 1997.

80. Fraenkel interview, May 10, 1984; Hovde interview, August 9, 1999.

81. Mark Rudd interview, *Boston Globe*, October 1, 1968, quoted in Diana Trilling, "On the Steps of Low Library," in *We Must March My Darlings* (New York: Harcourt Brace Jovanovich, 1975), 97.

82. [Louis Henkin], *Report of the Columbia University Committee on Relations with Outside Agencies* (June 1968), copy of report in files of the Cox Commission, Rare Book and Manuscript Library. Other committee members included Charles Walling, William T. de Bary, and Charles Wagley.

83. Ibid., 19–21. See Columbia University Trustees Minutes, August 6, 1968.

84. Columbia University Trustees Minutes, May 15, 1969.

85. Columbia University Trustees Minutes, March 3, 1969. On McGuire, see obituary in *New York Times*, December 3, 1981, sec. 1, 25, col. 1.

86. Minutes of the joint faculties meeting, September 12, 1968, copy in possession of Michael I. Sovern. Criminal charges were not dropped for students arrested on both

April 30 and May 22. At least some students were charged with two counts of criminal trespass (a felony), plus criminal mischief and resisting arrest. And at least one student was in court for three years before accepting a misdemeanor conviction. See Frank da Cruz, correspondence with author, November 15, 2002.

87. Transcript of the joint faculties meeting, September 12, 1968. A still earlier proposal for a university senate was contained in the minority report accompanying the "Report of the President's Advisory Committee on Student Life" (copy made available to author by Michael I. Sovern), which President Kirk left unread in 1967–68.

88. Executive Committee of the Faculty to Faculty of Columbia University, Preliminary Proposals for the Creation of a University Senate and a Student Assembly, September 10, 1968, copy in Office of the University Senate, Low Library.

89. On the competing plans for the senate and the debates, see *Columbia Daily Spectator*, October 10, 1968, 1, 3; [Lawrence E. Walsh], Alumni Recommendations for the Future Governance and Operation of Columbia University, August 12, 1968, Columbia University Archives–Columbiana Library.

90. On SRU's warming to the concept of a university senate, see SRU folder in Student Protest and Action Collection.

91. Executive Committee of the Faculty, Proposal for a University Senate, March 20, 1969, copy in Office of the University Senate, Low Library.

92. Referendum outcomes as reported in Columbia University Trustees Minutes, May 1, 1968.

93. On SRU's repudiation of SDS, see SRU folder in Student Protest and Action Collection.

94. "Report on the First Term of the Columbia University Senate, 1969–71," *Columbia University Senate Bulletin*, no. 1971–1, summer 1971; Sovern interview, May 5, 1999.

17. A TOUGH PLACE

1. Author interview with Eli Ginzberg, September 19, 1997.

2. William J. McGill, Oral History interview, June 26, 1979. See Ginzberg interview, September 19, 1997.

3. William J. McGill, Oral History interview, July 5, 1979, September 12, 1997.

4. McGill interview, July 5, 1979.

5. Ibid.

6. Ibid.; McGill interview, June 26, 1979.

7. McGill interview, July 5, 1979.

8. Ibid.

9. Kenneth Lamott, "From La Jolla to Harlem: Bill McGill Takes Over Columbia's Hot Campus," *New York Times Sunday Magazine*, August 23, 1970, 14–19; McGill interview, June 26, 1979. See McGill interview, July 5, 1979.

10. William J. McGill, *The Year of the Monkey: Revolt on Campus, 1968–69* (New York: McGraw-Hill, 1982).

11. Ibid., 4–5, 34.

12. McGill interview, June 26, 1979.

13. Ibid. See *New York Times*, February 4, 1970, sec. 1, 40, col. 3.

14. McGill interview, June 26, 1979; idem, Oral History interview, July 2, 1980; William J. McGill, "The Best and Worst of Living," *San Diego Evening Tribune*, January 21, 1982, copy provided to author by George K. Fraenkel.

15. McGill, *The Year of the Monkey*, 5; idem, "The Value of New York," *New York Times*, December 18, 1977, sec. 1, 199.

16. "McGill Visits Campus," *New York Times*, April 10, 1970, sec. 1, 26, col. 1; McGill, *The Year of the Monkey*, 26; author interview with George K. Fraenkel, August 2, 1997.

17. McGill interview, July 2, 1980. See author interview with William T. de Bary, May 27, 1999.

18. McGill, *The Year of the Monkey*, 2.

19. De Bary interview, May 27, 1999. McGill's own description of his actions at the April disturbance was sufficiently damning that the trustees felt it necessary to include in the minutes of their meeting two weeks later that "it was unanimously agreed that the president had done a magnificent job under very trying circumstance. There was a unanimous vote of confidence in the President" (Columbia University Trustees Minutes, April 26, 1972).

20. McGill interview, July 5, 1979. Both then dean of Columbia College Carl Hovde and Associate Dean Henry Coleman have indicated that there was no conscious change in admissions policies but that Catholic schools had become more cooperative in assisting Columbia recruitment efforts (Henry Coleman, discussion with author, January 24, 2003).

21. McGill was especially admiring of Nelson Rockefeller, declaring him "the most glamorous politician" he had ever met (McGill interview, July 2, 1979).

22. McGill interview, July 5, 1979; "Ford to City: Drop Dead," *New York Daily News*, October 30, 1975, 1. On New York's problems, see Martin Shefter, *Political Crisis, Fiscal Crisis: The Collapse and Revival of New York City* (New York: Columbia University Press, 1992).

23. William J. McGill, Oral History interview, May 23, 1980.

24. Ibid. See Columbia University Trustees Minutes, October 5, 1970; "A Summary of Resolutions and Discussions in the University Senate, May 1969–April 2001," Office of the University Senate, Low Library, Columbia University.

25. In September 1997, in preparation for his interviews in connection with the oral history of Lamont-Doherty Earth Observatory, McGill prepared a memo "Problems Confronting WMG as He Began His Duties at CU in the Fall of 1970," September 1997, Lamont-Doherty Oral History Project. I have drawn on it here extensively. See appendix C for financial data.

26. McGill, "Problems"; McGill interview, July 5, 1979; author interview with George K. Fraenkel, May 24, 1999.

27. On Cordier's spending, see McGill interview, July 5, 1979; author interview with Carl Hovde, August 9, 1999; Fraenkel interview, May 24, 1999.

28. Andrew S. Dolkart, *Morningside: A History of Its Architecture and Development* (New York: Columbia University Press, 1998), 336.

29. Columbia University Trustees Minutes, June 4, 1970; McGill interview, May 23, 1980.

30. McGill interview, June 26, 1979. See author interview with Marion Jemmott, December 2, 1997.

31. McGill, "Problems."

32. McGill interview, July 5, 1979.

33. Columbia University Trustees Minutes, December 2, 1968; Krim quoted in McGill interview, July 5, 1979.

34. Columbia University Trustees Minutes, September 14, October 5, 1970.

35. McGill interview, July 5, 1979. See McGill, "Problems."

36. Columbia University Trustees Minutes, April 6, 1970.

37. Columbia University Trustees Minutes, January 4, 1971; McGill interview, July 5, 1979.

38. Author interview with Michael Sovern, May 5, 1999.

39. The principal sources for this episode are the interviews of President McGill and then Provost de Bary, conducted as part of the oral history of the Lamont-Doherty Earth Observatory and taped in 1997 by the Oral History Research Office at Columbia University.

40. McGill interview, September 12, 1997; William J. McGill, Oral History interview, September 15, 1997; de Bary interview, May 27, 1997. See also Wallace Broecker, Oral History interview, May 8, 1997.

41. McGill interview, September 15, 1997.

42. McGill interview, July 5, 1979; William J. McGill, Oral History interview, July 3, 1980.

43. Columbia University Trustees Minutes, October 4, 1971, October 1, 1973.

44. McGill interview, July 5, 1979.

45. Ibid. For another view of the evolving budgetary process in the 1970s, see William T. de Bary, *Report of the Provost, 1971–1978* (New York: Columbia University, August 1978), 25–26.

46. De Bary, *Report of the Provost*, 21–23; author interview with George K. Fraenkel, May 17, 1997.

47. On the School of Library Service, see de Bary, *Report of the Provost*, 14. On the disaffiliation of the Pharmacy School, see Columbia University Trustees Minutes, November 1, 1971, June 4, 1973. On Barnard-Columbia financial relations, see chap. 18.

48. Columbia University Trustees Minutes, June 5, 1978, March 5, 1979, May 7, 1979; McGill interview, May 23, 1980. See appendix C.

49. Fraenkel interview, May 17, 1999. My principal sources here, besides Fraenkel, are William T. de Bary, Carl Hovde, Marion Jemmott, and Arlene Jacobs, all 1970s denizens of Low Library. McGill later put the Columbia administrative style into a comparative perspective when he characterized Roger Rosenblatt's account of Harvard in the early 1970s in *Coming Apart: A Memoir of the Harvard Wars of 1969* (Boston: Little, Brown, 1997) "as a subject of amusement to people who went to Columbia because of his intensity of reaction to things that we would brush off." Columbia, he went on, "is a far more hardened community than Harvard" (McGill interview, September15, 1997).

50. Polykarp Kusch, Oral History interview, April 1962. On Kusch, see McGill interview, July 5, 1997; de Bary interview, May 27, 1999; 1975 exchange of letters between McGill and Kusch, Kusch folder, McGill folder, Columbia University Archives–Columbiana Library. See also Polykarp Kusch, Oral History interview, April 1972.

51. McGill interview, July 5, 1979. See William T. de Bary, "Remarks at McGill Memorial Service," December 2, 1997, St. Paul's Chapel, Columbia University, provided to author by William T. de Bary.

52. De Bary interview, May 27, 1999. See McGill interview, July 2, 1980.

53. McGill interview, July 2, 1980.

54. Author interviews with George K. Fraenkel, spring 1999.

55. Ibid.

56. McGill interview, July 5, 1979.

57. Ibid.; McGill, *Year of the Monkey*, 211–12.

58. McGill interview, July 5, 1979.

59. Author interview with Roger Hackett, October 16, 2001. See McGill interview, September 12, 1997.

60. George K. Fraenkel, Oral History interview, June 1, 1999.

61. McGill interview, September 12, 1997; William J. McGill, "Remarks at the New York Police Department 60th Communion Breakfast," March 12, 1978, William J. McGill press folder, Columbia University Archives–Columbiana Library.

62. Monsignor Christopher Maloney, correspondence with author, October 20, 2002.

63. "Columbia University Names Michigan's Lee C. Bollinger President," *Columbia News*, October 8, 2001, 1; author interview with Roger Hackett, October 17, 2001; author interview with Roger Lehecka, November 14, 2001. The absence of any discussion as to Bollinger's religion was confirmed by the chair of the presidential search committee; see author interview with Henry L. King, May 13, 2002.

64. Columbia University Trustees Minutes, April 4, 1977.

65. Author interview with Thomas Q. Morris, September 4, 2002. See Yale Enson and Mary Dickinson Chamberlin, "Cournand and Richards and the Bellevue Cardiopulmonary Laboratory," *Columbia Magazine*, fall 2001, 34–44. This section on Columbia health sciences, as well as the one in chap. 20, benefited greatly from the author's discussions with Drs. Allen Formicola, Herbert Pardes, Thomas Q. Morris, and Robert L. Goldberger. Special thanks also to Mr. Michael Meyer for sharing his detailed knowledge of the history of the Columbia-Presbyterian Medical Center.

66. Harry Atkins, *The Dean: Willard C. Rappleye and the Evolution of American Medical Education* (New York: Josiah Macy Foundation, 1975)

67. [Arthur MacMahon, exec. dir.], *The Report of the President's Committee on the Educational Future of Columbia University* (New York: Trustees of Columbia University, November 1957), 155–56. In general, see ibid., 155–73.

68. Leonidas Stefanis and Lewis P. Rowland, "H. Houston Merritt and Neurosyphilis, Then and Now," *P&S Medical Review* 2, no. 2 (April 15, 1995): 28–35.

69. McGill interview, July 5, 1979. See Columbia University Trustees Minutes, January 20, 1969.

70. McGill, interview, July 5, 1979; author interviews with Morris, September 4, 2002, and January 7, 2003; Allen Formicola, September 24, 2002; Herbert Pardes, October 25, 2002.

71. Kenneth M. Ludmerer, *Time to Heal: American Medical Education from the Turn of the Century to the Era of Managed Care* (New York: Oxford University Press, 1999), chap. 12; [Louis Henkin], *Report on External Agencies* (New York: Columbia University,

May 31, 1968), copy in Cox Commission Papers, Rare Book and Manuscript Library, Columbia University.

72. Morris interview, September 4, 2002.

73. Ibid.; Ludmerer, *Time to Heal*, 219. For criticism of the present arrangements, see Arnold S. Relman, "Why Johnny Can't Operate: The Crisis in Medical Training in America," *New Republic*, October 2, 2000, 37–43.

74. McGill interview, July 2, 1980; Columbia Trustees Minutes, May 4, 1970.

75. Peter Wortsman, "Profile: Paul Marks '49," *P&S Journal* 15, no. 3 (fall 1995): 36–38.

76. McGill interview, July 2, 1980; Morris interview, September 4, 2002.

77. Tapley's appointment had been questioned by some trustees who remembered his involvement in the Strickman fiasco, but their doubts were overcome by strong endorsements from Marks and McGill. See Columbia University Trustees Minutes, June 4, 1973.

78. Morris interview, September 4, 2002.

79. McGill interview, July 5, 1979. See Morris interview, September 4, 2002.

80. For the more recent history of the health sciences, see chap. 20.

18. BOTTOMING OUT

1. For Columbia-Barnard relations in the twentieth century from the Barnard perspective, see Marian Churchill White, *A History of Barnard College* (New York: Columbia University Press, 1954); [Marian Churchill White and Marjorie H. Dobkin], *A History of Barnard College: Published in Honor of the Seventy-Fifth Anniversary of the College* (New York: Barnard College, 1964); Virginia C. Gildersleeve, *Many a Good Crusade: Memoirs* (New York: Macmillan, 1954); Millicent C. McIntosh, "Reminiscences," Oral History interview, 1966, Oral History Research Office, Columbia University (hereafter OHRO).

2. See appendix B.

3. Calculated from a review of faculty listings in the 1940–41 catalogs of Columbia's professional schools and faculties. See Rosalind Rosenberg, *Changing the Subject: A History of Women at Columbia* (New York: Columbia University Press, forthcoming).

4. Laurel Furumoto, "Ladd-Franklin, Christine, 1847–1930," *American National Biography* (New York: Oxford University Press, 1999), 13:26–28; Margaret M. Caffrey, "Benedict, Ruth Fulton, 1887–1948," ibid., 2:556–58; Virginia Yans-McLaughlin, "Mead, Margaret, 1901–1978," ibid., 15:209–12.

5. On Hayner, see Margaret W. Rossiter, *Women Scientists in America: Struggles and Strategies to 1940* (Baltimore: Johns Hopkins University Press, 1982), 257. On Nicholson, see Oscar James Campbell, "The Department of English and Comparative Literature," in John Herman Randall Jr., ed., *A History of the Faculty of Philosophy, Columbia University* (New York: Columbia University Press, 1957), 77, 95. See also Andrea Walton, "Woman at Columbia: A Study of Power and Empowerment in the Lives of Six Scholars" (Ph.D. diss., Teachers College, 1997).

6. See appendix A. The seven Columbia arts and science appointments included Chien-Shiung "Madame" Wu, a physicist, who came to Columbia as an assistant professor in 1944 with a Berkeley Ph.D., after teaching at Smith and Princeton; she was made

an associate professor in 1952, a full professor in 1959; Jeanne Mahle Pleasants, an associate professor of linguistics, who first came to Barnard from Europe in the 1930s, before moving over to Columbia in 1938; Margarite Bieber, a professor of art history and another European émigré who had started out on Morningside Heights at Barnard; Jane Gaston-Mahler, a linguist; Susanne Nobbe, a junior faculty in English in 1930s; and Mary Caldwell, a junior faculty in chemistry in the 1930s.

7. Marion E. Jemmott, Oral History interviews, March 29, April 9, July 21, November 9, 2000; author interview, December 2, 1997.

8. Nancy Bieberman, remarks at 30th reunion of 1968 participants, Columbia University, May 12, 1998.

9. Kate Millett was a member of the Barnard philosophy department, Catherine Stimpson a member of the Barnard English department; Heilbrun a member of the Columbia English department. See Carolyn Heilbrun, *When Men Were the Only Models We Had: My Teachers Barzun, Fadiman, Trilling* (Philadelphia: University of Pennsylvania Press, 2002), 2.

10. On the history of CWL, see Rachel Du Plessis, "Columbia Women's Liberation," *Barnard Alumnae* 59 (spring 1970): 12–18. See also Rosenberg's forthcoming *Changing the Subject*, and idem, "The 'Woman Question' at Columbia: From John W. Burgess to Judith Shapiro" (talk to the University Seminar on the History of Columbia University, Columbia University, February 17, 1999).

11. Columbia Women's Liberation, *Report of Committee on Discrimination Against Women Faculty* (mimeographed report, December 1969); Linda Greenhouse, "Columbia Accused of Bias Against Women," *New York Times*, January 11, 1970, sec. 1, 35, col. 1.

12. Du Plessis, "Columbia Women's Liberation," 12–18.

13. For Washington action on the CWL *Report*, see Rosenberg, "Calling in the Feds," in *Changing the Subject*.

14. William J. McGill, Oral History interview, July 5, 1979. See also "Part One: Officers of Instruction," in Ivan Berg, Barbara Filner, Nina G. Garsoian, Frances Hoffman, Leonard Leavy, John Patterson, Mary Payer, and Francine Sobey, eds., *Commission on the Status of Women/Columbia University* (New York: Columbia University Senate, March 1975), chap. 1.

15. *Commission on Status of Women*, 1–16.

16. Ibid. On Pottinger's rejection of Columbia's affirmative action statement, see Columbia University Trustees Minutes, December 6, 1971.

17. Columbia University Trustees Minutes, March 6, 1972; Columbia University Affirmative Action Plan, April 10, 1972, Columbia University Archives–Columbiana Library.

18. Rosenberg, "Calling in the Feds."

19. Insofar as the same 1972 legislation that extended antidiscriminatory protections to all educational institutions also extended the coverage of the 1963 Equal Pay Act, Columbia, like all universities, could now expect to have their compensation policies critically examined by those who suspected they discriminated against women. See ibid.

20. Jemmott interview, December 2, 1997.

21. Author interview with George K. Fraenkel, June 1, 1999.

22. McGill interview, June 26, 1979. In one of his last communications before his

death, on October 20, 1997, McGill apologized to Marian Jemmott for having delayed her deserved promotion so long (Jemmott interview, December 2, 1997).

23. Frances Hoffman, interview with Rosalind Rosenberg, 1999, discussed in Rosenberg, *Changing the Subject.*

24. Ibid.; McGill interview, July 5, 1979.

25. *Commission on the Status of Women/Columbia University* (New York: Columbia University Senate, March 1975), epigraph.

26. McGill interview, June 26, 1979; William J. McGill, Oral History interview, September 12, 1997.

27. *Commission on Status of Women,* 20.

28. Author's personal knowledge.

29. Between 1971 and 1990 the number of women increased from 67 to 131, while the number of men declined from 494 to 425, a net swing of 133 members. See appendix B.

30. Virginia Gildersleeve, *Many a Good Crusade: Memoirs* (New York: Macmillan, 1954), 62–64, 101–2.

31. Rosalind Rosenberg, "Virginia Gildersleeve: Opening the Doors," *Columbia Magazine,* summer 2001, 24–34; author interview with Eli Ginzberg, September 19, 1997.

32. On Trilling's dismissiveness of women academics, see Heilbrun, *When Men Were the Only Models,* 86–99; James Trilling, "My Father and the Weak-Eyed Devils," *American Scholar* 68 (spring 1999): 17–44, 27–28.

33. McIntosh, "Reminiscences"; Robert A. McCaughey, *A Statistical Profile of the Barnard College Faculty, 1900–1974* (New York: Barnard College, 1974).

34. McCaughey, *Statistical Profile,* 48.

35. Ibid., 49–57; Janet Alperstein, "The Influence of Boards of Trustees, Senior Administrators, and Faculty in the Decision of Woman's Colleges to Remain Single Sex in the 1980s" (Ed.D. diss., Teachers College, Columbia University 2001).

36. McCaughey, *Statistical Profile,* 49–50.

37. Author interviews with George K. Fraenkel, May 10, 12, 1999; Columbia University Trustees Minutes, December 7, 1970.

38. President William J. McGill to Trustees, December 7, 1970. In 2002–3, about 60 percent of Barnard's total income is from tuition.

39. Grayson Kirk, Oral History interview, May 26, 1989

40. Ibid.

41. Author interview with Bruce Bassett, December 2, 1998.

42. Author interview with George K. Fraenkel, May 24, 1999.

43. McCaughey, *Statistical Profile of the Barnard Faculty,* 43–57.

44. White, *A History of Barnard College,* 191–98.

45. Marjorie H. Dobkin, "The McIntosh Era," in [White and Dobkin], *A History of Barnard College,* 96–113; McCaughey, *Statistical Profile,* passim; George K. Fraenkel to William J. McGill, memorandum on Columbia-Barnard Relationship, January 29, 1976, in author's possession.

46. Fraenkel to McGill, January 29, 1976; Fraenkel interview, May 24, 1999; Eugene F. Rice, chairman, "Report of the Arts and Sciences Policy Advisory Committee," October 18, 1977, Columbia University Archives–Columbiana Library.

47. On Columbia's tenure process as developed in the 1950s, see Jacques Barzun, *The American University: How It Runs—Where It Is Going* (New York: Harper and Row, 1968), 37–42.

48. Allan M. Cartter, *Ph.D.'s and the Academic Labor Market* (New York: McGraw-Hill, 1976), chaps. 6 and 9; Robert A. McCaughey, *Scholars and Teachers: The Faculties of Select Liberal Arts Colleges and Their Place in American Higher Learning* (New York: Barnard College and the Andrew W. Mellon Foundation, 1994), 31–47.

49. Of the sixty-five tenured faculty at Barnard in 2002–3, all but five have been tenured under the 1973 ad hoc provisions. See McCaughey, *Scholars and Teachers*, chap. 3.

50. Author interview with Carl Hovde, August 9, 1999.

51. Ibid.

52. Author interview with Gerald Sherwin (CC 1955), June 8, 2002.

53. Author interviews with Jonathan Cole (CC 1964), July 2, 2001, and with Carl Hovde, August 8, 1999.

54. Hovde interview, August 8, 1999; Henry Coleman, communication with author, January 20, 2003.

55. Thomas Kelly, "Professor Michael Rosenthal Recalls 41 years at CU," *Columbia Daily Spectator*, January 25, 2000, 1, 6.

56. Author interview with William T. de Bary, May 27, 1999.

57. First remark in 1989, second in 1978, both confirmed in Peter R. Pouncey to author, April 30, 2002. See Fred Schneider, "McGill Announces Selection of Pouncey as College Dean," *Columbia Daily Spectator*, March 27, 1972, 1; de Bary interview, May 27, 1999; Hovde interview, August 9, 1999.

58. De Bary interview, May 27, 1999; McGill interview, July 5, 1979; Pouncey to author, April 30, 2002.

59. *New York Times*, November 25, 1975, sec. 1, 27, col. 3; November 30, 1975, sec. 1, 61, col. 1; McGill interview, July 5, 1979; author interview with George K. Fraenkel, May 17, 1999. See also Jamie Katz, "The Pounce and the State of the College," *Columbia College Today*, summer 1975, 2–3; and Dan Fastenberg, "The Columbia College Deanship of Peter R. Pouncey" (paper submitted for course "Social History of Columbia University," April 22, 2002). Pouncey has since returned to New York from Amherst and regularly teaches a section of literature humanities.

60. De Bary interview, May 27, 1999; McGill interview, July 5, 1980.

61. [Steven Marcus], *Report on the Presidential Commission on Academic Priorities in the Arts and Sciences* (New York: Columbia University, 1979), 1. The author was a member of the Marcus commission.

62. *Report of the Presidential Commission*, 194, 222, 206. In general, see ibid., 182–232.

63. Ibid., 23–130, 61, 67, 75, 112, 46.

64. Ibid., 131. In general, see ibid., 131–175. See also Kenneth D. Roose and Charles J. Anderson, *A Rating of Graduate Programs* (Washington, D.C.: American Council of Education, 1970); Malcolm G. Scully, "The Well-Known Universities Lead in Ratings of Faculty Reputations," *Chronicle of Higher Education* 19 (January 15, 1979): 6–7.

65. *Report of the Presidential Commission*, 132–33.

66. Ibid., 17–18.

67. Author interview with Michael I. Sovern, May 5, 1999.

68. *New York Times*, August 22, 1971, sec. 1, 37, col. 1; McGill interview, July 5, 1979; *New York Times*, May 10, 1975, sec. 1, 31, col. 6.

69. William J. McGill, Oral History interview, July 2, 1980; author interview with Henry Graff, May 3, 2000. See also William J. McGill, "Problems Confronting WMG as He Began His Duties at CU in the Fall of 1970," September 1997, Lamont-Doherty Oral History Project, OHRO.

70. McGill interview, July 5, 1980. On Butler's entertaining, see Diana Trilling, "Lionel Trilling: A Jew at Columbia," *Commentary* 67, no. 3 (March 1979), 40; see 46.

71. Author interview with Michael I. Sovern, May 5, 1999. See author interview with Roger Lehecka, October 31, 2001.

72. McGill interview, September 12, 1997; July 5, 1979.

73. McGill obituary, *New York Times*, October 21, 1997, sec. D, 23.

19. COLUMBIA RECOVERED

1. Author interview with Michael I. Sovern, August 2, 2001.

2. Ibid.

3. Ibid.

4. Golden Anniversary Committee, *Michael Sovern's 50 Years at Columbia* (New York: Columbia Law School, 1999). For Sovern in 1968, see chap. 16.

5. William McGill, Oral History interview, July 3, 1980; author interview with Eli Ginzberg, September 19, 1997. On Polshek, see Susan M. Straus, "History VII: 1968–1981," in Richard Oliver, ed., *The Making of an Architect, 1881–1981: Columbia University in the City of New York* (New York: Rizzoli, 1981), 243–63. On Yavitz, see Lalla R. Grimes, *Portrait of a Leader: Dean Boris Yavitz* (New York: privately printed, 1998), copy provided by Grimes.

6. Michael I. Sovern, correspondence with author, December 15, 2002. See author interview with Robert E. Pollack, July 16, 2002.

7. See chap. 18.

8. *New York Times*, December 14, 1975, sec. 1, 67, col. 3. For the text of the Breslow report, see *Columbia University Record* 6 (April 24, 1981): 1, 3.

9. For the Barnard perspective, see Janet Alperstein, "The Influence of Boards of Trustees, Senior Administrators, and Faculty on the Decision of Woman's Colleges to Remain Single-Sex in the 1980s" (Ed.D. diss., Teachers College, Columbia University, 2001), chap. 5.

10. Author interview with George K. Fraenkel, May 17, 1999.

11. On Mattfeld's appointment, see *New York Times*, November 13, 1975, sec. 1, 82, col. 6. On the salary disparity, see author interview with George K. Fraenkel, May 24, 1999.

12. Author's direct experience as a member of the Barnard College faculty.

13. "Barnard College and Columbia on Collision Course," *New York Times*, May 30, 1976, sec. 1, 1, col. 4; William J. McGill, Oral History interview, July 5, 1980.

14. "Barnard President Resigns After 4 Years," *New York Times*, May 29, 1980, sec. 1, 1, col. 2. On Futter's appointment, see *New York Times*, July 8, 1980, sec. 2, 1, col. 5.

15. Author's direct experience as a Barnard faculty member. On Barnard's negotiating position, see Alperstein, "The Decision of Woman's Colleges to Remain Single-Sex

in the 1980s," chap. 5. See also Rosalind Rosenberg, *Changing the Subject: A History of Women at Columbia* (New York: Columbia University Press, forthcoming).

16. Columbia University Trustees Minutes, May 4, 1981.

17. Columbia University Trustees Minutes, December 7, 1980.

18. Michael I. Sovern, interview with Leslie Banner, December 4, 1997, for a proposed book on university presidential experiences (transcript, dated May 4, 2001, provided author by the interviewee). See author interview with Michael I. Sovern, August 8, 2001. On the Columbia College faculty view, see author interviews with Carl Hovde, August 9, 1999; with Don Hood, April 17, 2000; with Robert Pollack, June 28, 2002.

19. On Barnard's subsequent struggles, see chap. 20.

20. Columbia University Trustees Minutes, May 3, 1982. For admissions data, see *Columbia University Record* 12 (July 6, 1986): 1.

21. *Columbia University Record* 12 (July 6, 1986): 3.

22. The Columbia College class entering in the fall of 1987 had a minority representation of 28 percent%. See *Columbia University Record* 12 (May 22, 1987): 1.

23. On the Columbia-Barnard Athletic Consortium, see *Columbia University Record* 9 (March 4, 1983): 1.

24. *Columbia University Record* 10 (May 22, 1987): 1; Pollack interview, June 28, 2002.

25. Author interview with Peter Buchanan, August 29, 2002.

26. Author interview with Robert L. Goldberger, July 31, 2002. On Richard Axel, see *Columbia University Record* 24 (April 9, 1999): 1.

27. Goldberger interview, July 31, 2002; Sovern correspondence, December 15, 2002.

28. See chaps. 12 and 14 on the history of the Rockefeller lease.

29. Krim quoted in McGill interview, July 5, 1979. See author interview with Michael I. Sovern, May 5, 1999; Sovern interview, December 4, 1997, 9.

30. Sovern interview, December 4, 1997, 9; Sovern interview, May 5, 1999. See Maureen Dowd, "Columbia Is to Get $400 Million in Rockefeller Center Land Sale," *The New York Times*, February 66, 1985, sec. A, 1. Part of the reason the Rockefellers were willing to pay an above-market price was that they had Japanese customers waiting in the wings, ready to buy Rockefeller Center, land and all.

31. Sovern interview, December 4, 1997, 10. See Columbia University Trustees Minutes, February 4, 1985.

32. Buchanan interview, August 29, 2002.

33. William J. McGill, Oral History interview, July 2, 1980. On Columbia fund-raising into the 1970s, see Report of Peter E. Buchanan to Trustees, Columbia University Trustees Minutes, January 5, 1976.

34. Buchanan interview, August 29, 2002

35. *New York Times*, November 9, 1982, sec. 2, 1, col. 1.

36. On the success of the 1982–87 campaign, see Buchanan interview, August 29, 2002; *New York Times*, May 12, 1987, sec. 2, 5, col. 6.

37. Morris Dickstein, *Gates of Eden* (1977; reprint, Basic, 1989), 259; idem, "Columbia Recovered," *New York Times Sunday Magazine*, 32–35, 64–68.

38. Letter from President William McGill to Students, May 3, 1978, copy in Columbia University Trustees Minutes, June 5, 1978.

39. Columbia University Senate Resolutions, Summer 1970 Actions, no. 3; October 13,

1978. no. 3, "The University Senate: Substantive Resolutions and Main Topics of Discussion, May 1969–April 2001," May 29, 2001, University Senate Office, Low Library, Columbia University; Columbia University Trustees Minutes, May 7, 1984.

40. Columbia University Trustees Minutes, October 7, 1985 (the minutes refer to a July 17, 1985 statement rejecting total divestment); Sovern interviews, December 4, 1997, 15–16; May 5, 1999.

41. *Columbia University Record* 13 (August 3, 1987): 1.

42. Sovern interview, December 4, 1997, 17; see 15–17.

43. Author interview with Carl Hovde, August 21, 1997.

44. Data from Abeles, Schwartz, Haeckel, and Solverblatt, "Notebook of Analyses and Project Outlines, Long Range Planning Committee, Columbia-Presbyterian Medical Center," 1982, Archives and Special Collections, Augustus C. Long Health Sciences Library.

45. Walter Bourne, survey of Columbia Presbyterian Medical Center personnel, 1986, summary in Archives and Special Collections, Augustus C. Long Health Sciences Library.

46. Abeles, Schwartz, Haeckel, and Solverblatt, "Notebook of Analyses," 61.

47. Goldberger interview, July 31, 2002; author interview with Thomas Q. Morris, September 4, 2002.

48. Remarks made at a Morningside Heights Inc. meeting on December 4, 1992, included in Columbia University Trustees Minutes, December 5, 1992. The *New York Times* provided extensive and sympathetic coverage, as well as editorial support, for Columbia's development of the Audubon site. See May 10, 1991, sec. B, 1, col. 1, June 28, sec. B, 1, col. 2; July 30, sec. A, 14, col. 1; August 4, sec. 1, 25, col. 5; August 9, sec. B, 3, col. 6, August 22, sec. B, 1, col. 5; August 27, sec. A, 16, col. 1.

49. Sovern interview, December 4, 1997, 15–16; Columbia University Trustees Minutes, March 6, 1993.

50. *New York Times*, March 23, 1987, sec. 2, 2, col. 3; April 8, sec. 2, 5, col. 1; April 23, sec. 2, 2, col. 3.

51. *New York Times*, August 5, 1987, sec. 2, 2, col. 5.

52. Report quoted in Sovern interview, December 4, 1997, 6. On Sovern's honeymoon, see Sovern interviews, December 4, 1997, 14–15; May 5, 1999; August 8, 2001; author interview with Robert F. Goldberger, July 31, 2002. It is likely that at this time the trustees also began authorizing the substantial raises in his salary that pushed him to the top of the list of most highly paid university presidents, a fact first publicized in 1989.

53. Sovern interviews, December 4, 1997, 15; May 5, 1999.

54. See author interviews with Lionel Pincus, May 10, 2001; with Jerry Speyer, July 17, 2001; with Edward N. Costikyan, May 28, 2002; with Henry L. King, May 13, 2002; with Corinne H. Rieder, January 4, 2001.

55. "Sovern Announces 3-Provost Plan," *University Record* 5 (April 22, 1980): 1; Columbia University Trustees Minutes, May 5, 1980.

56. Goldberger interview, July 31, 2002.

57. Hood interview, April 17, 2000; Goldberger interview, July 31, 2002; author interview with George K. Fraenkel, May 5, 1999.

58. Pollack interview, July 16, 2002.

59. Author interviews with Don C. Hood, Robert E. Pollack, and Jonathan Cole, July

2, 2001; William Theodore de Bary to Robert E. Pollack, October 6, 1987, copy provided author by the recipient.

60. Pollack interview, July 16, 2002; Cole interview, July 2, 2002; Michael I. Sovern, correspondence with author, fall 2002.

61. Goldberger interview, July 31, 2002; Hood interview, July 2, 2001; Pollack interviews, July 2, 2001, July 16, 2002; Rieder interview, January 4, 2001.

62. Numbers calculated by author from *American Doctoral Dissertations, 1970–71* (Ann Arbor, Mich.: Dissertation Abstracts International, 1972); *American Doctoral Dissertations, 1999–2000* (Ann Arbor, Mich.: ProQuest Information, 2002). On the declining place of arts and sciences within universities nationally in the 1980s, see William G. Bowen and Julie Ann Sosa, *Prospects for Faculty in the Arts and Sciences* (Princeton: Princeton University Press, 1989), 43.

63. Author interviews with Herbert Pardes, October 25, 2002; with Allan J. Formicola, September 24, 2002; with Barbara A. Black, September 26, 2002.

64. Hood interview, April 17, 2000; author interview with Norman Mintz, May 8, 2002; Pardes interview, October 25, 2002.

65. Columbia University Trustees Minutes, June 3, 1991. See [Robert F. Goldberger], *Strategies of Renewal: Report of the Presidential Commission on the Future of the University* (New York: Columbia University, May 1987); Hovde interview, August 9, 1999.

66. Remarks by art historian David Rosand, quoted in Minutes of the Columbia College Faculty Meeting, October 19, 1987, Columbia College; Sovern interview, May 5, 1999. See author interview with William T. de Bary, May 27, 1999.

67. On the financial problems of the late 1980s and early 1990s, see Sovern interviews, August 8, 2001, May 5, 1999; Cole interview, July 2, 2001; Hood interviews, July 2, 2001, April 17, 2000; Buchanan interview, August 29, 2002; Pincus interview, May 10, 2001; Speyer interview, July 17, 2001; King interview, May 13, 2002; Costikyan interview, May 28, 2002; author interview with John Masten, September 9, 2002.

68. Columbia University Trustees Minutes, October 7, 1991.

69. On changes in federal and state government funding, policies, see Columbia University Trustees Minutes, February 4, 1991, March 7, 1992. For the Barnard payments, I drew on my personal experience as Barnard dean of the faculty.

70. Sovern interview, December 4, 1997, 21.

71. *New York Times*, April 11, 1992, sec. 1, 29, col. 5; *New York Times*, November 27, 1991, sec. A, 1, col. 1; Hood, interview, April 17, 2000; author interview with David J. Helfand, October 29, 2002.

72. *New York Times*, April 11, 1992, sec. 1, 1, col. 1; May 25, 1992, sec. 1, 1, col. 1; King interview, May 13, 2002.

73. Sovern interview, December 4, 1997, 25.

74. Sovern interview, August 8, 2001; author interview with Jonathan Cole, July 16, 2001.

75. The "rap on Mike" was derived from interviews with his supporters and critics, all cited above.

76. On senior administrators staying on, see author interview with Lionel Pincus, May 16, 2001.

77. Columbia University Trustees Minutes, June 4, 1993.

20. THE WAY WE ARE

1. Author interview with Henry L. King, May 13, 2002. Professor of history Kenneth T. Jackson was the faculty member on the committee.

2. Author interviews with George Rupp, May 22 and July 18, 2001.

3. Ibid.; King interview, May 13, 2002.

4. King interview, May 13, 2002; Rupp interviews, May 22 and July 18, 2001.

5. Rupp interview, May 22, 2001.

6. Ibid. The other ordained presidents were Samuel Johnson (1754–62); Myles Cooper (1763–75); Benjamin Moore (1801–10); and William Harris (1811–29).

7. Rupp interview, July 18, 2001; *New York Times*, February 2, 1993, B, 2, col. 5.

8. *Columbia Summer Spectator*, June 9, 1993, 4. See *New York Times*, June 4, 1993, sec. B, 1, col. 3; Rupp interview, July 18, 2001; author interview with Roger Bagnall, June 13, 2002.

9. Author interview with Carolyn Bynum, August 7, 2002.

10. Ibid.; author interview with Corrine H. Rieder, January 4, 2001; author interview with Lionel I. Pincus, May 10, 2001; King interview, May 13, 2002; Bynum interview, August 7, 2002.

11. Author interviews with John Masten, September 9, 2002; with Pincus, May 16, 2000.

12. Author interviews with Jonathan R. Cole, July 2, 2001; Allan J. Formicola, September 24, 2002; and Meyer Feldberg, October 8, 2002.

13. *New York Times*, July 3, 1997, sec. B, 4, col. 1; July 28,1997, sec. B, 1, col. 5; author interview with David H. Cohen, September 11, 2002.

14. Author interviews with Thomas Q. Morris, September 4, 2002; with Meyer Feldberg, October 8, 2002. The Giuliani renaissance, in point of fact, has its origins in the earlier Koch and Dinkins administrations.

15. Pincus interview, May 16, 2001; author interview with Jerry Speyer, July 17, 2001; King interview, May 13, 2002; Masten interview, September 9, 2002. See also [John Masten], *Columbia University: Repositioning Columbia's Endowment for the 21st Century* (New York: Office of the Vice President for Finance, Columbia University, 2001).

16. Pincus interview, May 10, 2001; Masten interview, September 9, 2002. Nearly two-thirds (64 percent) of the endowment growth between 1991 and 2000 was attributable to capital appreciation. See [Masten], *Columbia University*, 11.

17. Author interview with Carl Hovde, August 9, 1999; Pincus interview, May 10, 2002; Rupp interview, July 18, 2001. Board Chairman Stephen Friedman compared Rupp's executive skills with those of Jack Welch, head of General Electric. For an informed and appreciative student perspective on the Rupp presidency, see Ben Casselman, "The Rupp Years in Perspective," *Columbia Daily Spectator*, April 25, 2002, 1, 5; April 26, 2002, 1–7; April 29, 2002, 1–7; May 1, 2002, 1–5; May 3, 2002, 1–9.

18. Author interview with Thomas Q. Morris, August 29, 2002; Formicola interview, September 24, 2002; author interview with Herbert Pardes, October 25, 2002. The assistance of Stephen E. Novak, archivist, Augustus C. Long Health Sciences Library, and Michael Meyer in matters relating to the history of Columbia health sciences is gratefully acknowledged.

19. Author interview with Robert F. Goldberger, July 31, 2002.

20. Ibid.; Morris interview, August 29, 2002.

21. Author interview with Michael I. Sovern, August 8, 2001; Morris interview, August 29, 2002; Formicola interview, September 24, 2002. The count of Medical School deans begins with the remerger of P & S with Columbia in 1891. See appendix A.

22. Pardes interview, October 25, 2002; Morris interviews September 4, 2002; author interview with Thomas Q. Morris, January 7, 2003.

23. Pardes interview, October 25, 2002.

24. The university provost retained control over the bulk of the patent and royalties income produced, although upwards of 90 percent was attributable to discoveries and inventions by faculty in the health sciences. It was this income, which by the late 1990s came to represent more than 10 percent of the university's overall income, that underwrote the many intended-for-profit enterprises (e.g., Fathom, a distance-learning portal) and interdisciplinary undertakings (e.g., Biosphere II, the Earth Institute) that were spearheaded by Vice Provost Michael Crow.

25. Pardes interview, October 25, 2002.

26. Ibid.

27. Formicola interview, September 24, 2002. On the Mailman gift, see "School of Public Health to be named for the Mailman Family," *The Reporter (Columbia University Health Sciences Division)* 9, no. 4 (September 1998): 1.

28. Morris interview, August 29, 2002.

29. Author interview with Barbara A. Black, September 26, 2002. See Feldberg interview, October 8, 2002.

30. Feldberg interview, October 8, 2002.

31. Ibid. Two of these collaborative appointments brought the economists Jeffrey Sachs from Harvard and Joseph Stiglitz from Chicago to Columbia.

32. Masten interview, September 9, 2002; Cohen interview, September 11, 2002.

33. Rupp interview, July 18, 2001. See Masten interview, September 9, 2002. For presidential fund-raising tallies, see appendix C.

34. Feldberg interview, October 8, 2002; Morris interview, August 29, 2002; Black interview, September 26, 2002. On the Business School, see Della Bradshaw, "Business Education," see *Financial Times*, January 20, 2003, 1; and Cecily J. Fluke, "Ranking the B-Schools," *Forbes*, October 15, 2001, 16.

35. Formicola interview, September 24, 2002.

36. Ibid.; Cohen interview, September 11, 2002. On the School of Journalism, see James Boylan, *Pulitzer School: Columbia University School of Journalism, 1903–2003* (New York: Columbia University Press, forthcoming).

37. Schuyler Chapin, Peter Smith, and Bruce W. Ferguson, conversations with author, April 30, 2002; [Robert F. Goldberger], *Strategies of Renewal: Report of the Presidential Commission on the Future of the University* (New York: Columbia University, May 1987), 110–12.

38. Bruce W. Ferguson, *Press ON: Columbia University School of the Arts: A Premier Arts Institution in New York City* (New York: Columbia University School of the Arts Development and Alumni Relations, December 2001); George L. Rives to Nicholas Murray Butler, May 23, 1905, George L. Rives Papers, Columbia University Archives–

Columbiana Library. See *School of the Arts News* (New York: Columbia University School of the Arts Development and Alumni Relations, fall 2002).

39. Hugh Davis Graham and Nancy Diamond, *The Rise of American Research Universities* (Washington, D.C.: Johns Hopkins University Press, 1997). See appendix B. for changes in rankings.

40. Cohen interview, September 11, 2002.

41. Robert J. Birgeneau, Ralph J. Cicerone, Arnold Levine, Jeremiah P. Ostriker, and Richard N. Zare, "The Future of the Natural Sciences at Columbia: Report of the Academic Review Committee, Faculty of Arts and Sciences, March 6, 2002," Office of Vice President of Arts and Sciences, Columbia University. The nine departments reviewed were astronomy, biological sciences, chemistry, ecology, evolution and environmental biology, earth and environmental sciences, mathematics, physics, psychology, and statistics.

42. "Reseeding Ivy: Columbia in Comeback from Troubles," *New York Times*, November 1, 1999, sec. 1, 2, col. 1. See [Goldberger], *Strategies of Renewal*; Jonathan Cole, "The Future of Columbia's Excellence: Longer Term Perspectives," a presentation to the Columbia University Trustees, Columbia University Trustees Minutes, June 5, 1999.

43. The author's direct experience as dean of the faculty, Barnard College, in the first year of the Rupp administration. I have also benefited from important insights into recent Barnard history provided by Rosalind Rosenberg and Judith Shapiro, president of Barnard College. Financial matters have been much clarified through discussions with Lewis Wyman, VP of planning and research.

44. *New York Times*, April 9, 1982, sec. 2, 3, col. 1.

45. Author's direct experience as Barnard dean of the faculty and confirmed by interview with Lewis Wyman, October 28, 2002.

46. *New York Times*, August 8, sec. 2, 1, col. 6; Pollack interview, July 16, 2002. See Robert A. McCaughey, *Scholars and Teachers: The Faculties of Select Liberal Arts Colleges and Their Place in American Higher Learning* (New York: Barnard College/Andrew W. Mellon Foundation, 1994), 34–36, 96–99.

47. Boswell quoting Johnson in 1777, as William Dodd's execution for forgery approached (he was eventually hanged), as printed in *Boswell's Life of Johnson*, ed. George Birkbeck Hill, rev. L. F. Powell (Oxford: Oxford University Press, Clarendon, 1934–1964), 3:167. My thanks to the eminent Johnsonian James Basker. Financial aid expenses continued to grow through the 1980s, until they came to represent 22 percent of Barnard's operating budget in 1995; they thereafter dropped back to 16 percent (author interview with Lewis Wyman, October 30, 2002).

48. On curricular reform, see Dorothy U. Denburg, "Curricular Change: A Case Study in Successful Innovation" (Ed.D. diss., Teachers College, 1986).

49. Author's direct experience.

50. Denburg, "Curricular Change," 215–16; author's direct experience.

51. On Barnard benefiting from the demise of so many women's colleges, see Francine Prose, "Seven Sisters, Minus One," *New York Times*, April 24, 1999, sec. A, 19.

52. Helene L. Kaplan, remarks at dinner honoring Ellen V. Futter, Barnard College, February 12, 2003; author interview with Lewis Wyman, October 10, 2002. For Barnard admission statistics, see appendix B.

53. On the Sulzberger gift, see *New York Times*, October 18, 1991, section B, 2:4. On increased applications, see Judith Shapiro, "President's Page," *Barnard*, winter 2000, 3, 9.

54. College counsel Kathryn J. Rodgers was named acting president in 1993–94.

55. *New York Times*, March 22, 1994, sec. A, 1, col. 6; October 24, 1994, B, 10: 4. This strategy is espoused by author.

56. [Judith R. Shapiro], *The 2000 Barnard College Self-Study* (New York: Barnard College, September 2000).

57. Patricia A. Graham, "Cremin, Lawrence A., 1925–1990," in *American National Biography* (New York: Oxford University Press, 1999), 5:722–23.

58. Author interview with David Ment and Bette Winick, October 17, 2002.

59. *Best Graduate Schools —2003 Edition* (Washington: U.S. News and World Report, 2003), 46.

60. George Rupp, Remarks, in Columbia University Trustees Minutes, December 7, 1996.

61. John Henry Van Amringe to Seth Low, July 31, 1897, Van Amringe Papers, Columbia University Archives—Columbiana Library.

62. Quoted in Gene R. Hawes, "The Men from Morningside," in Dwight Miner, ed., *A History of Columbia College on Morningside* (New York: Columbia University Press, 1954), 260–62.

63. William J. McGill, Oral History interview, July 5, 1979, Oral History Research Office, Columbia University. See Pollack interview, July 16, 2002.

64. Jonathan Cole, remarks on Columbia College, Columbia University Trustees Minutes, June 3, 1991.

65. *Columbia Spectator*, April 25, 2002, 1. See Hovde interview, August 9, 1999. For Rupp on the need for a state-of-the-art student center, see author interview with Roger Lehecka, October 30, 1997.

66. On new buildings in the Rupp era, see appendix D.

67. *Columbia Spectator*, April 25, 2002, 1, 5. On the culture shock often attending arrival at Columbia, see Bynum interview, August 7, 2002.

68. On the recent demographic character of the Columbia College student body, see appendix B.

69. Bagnall interview, June 13, 2002; Henry C. Pinkham, communication with author, February 17, 2003. For the beginnings of the process, see George K. Fraenkel, Memorandum to Members of the Faculty of the Graduate School of Arts and Sciences, August 31, 1983, copy in author's possession.

70. Cohen interview, September 11, 2002; author interview with Alan Brinkley, October 2, 2002. The fact that President Bollinger indicated plans to teach a section of the Core regularly may have the same positive effect on faculty volunteering to do likewise as President McGill's attendance at Sunday mass prompted a rise in communicants.

71. For applications-admits-matriculate data, see appendix B.

72. On Columbia College's demographic diversity, see Institutional Research, Office of the Provost. The figures for the Columbia College class entering fall 2001: Asian (12 percent), black (9 percent), Hispanic (8 percent), other (4 percent), unknown (11 percent), white (57 percent).

73. Pollack interview, July 16, 2002; author interview with Gerald Sherwin, June 18,

2002; [Austin E. Quigley], *Columbia College: A Time of Transition* (New York: Columbia College, February 2002)}, chart 12.

74. A secondary effect of an improvement in alumni giving would be its positive impact on Columbia's rankings in *U.S. News and World Report*, which puts much weight on alumni giving in calculating student satisfaction. See Judith Shapiro, "On *US News and World Report* Rankings," *Barnard Magazine*, winter 1998, 3, 7. Annual giving rates at some of Columbia's peers in 2001: Princeton, 66 percent; Harvard, 46 percent; Yale, 46 percent ([Quigley], *Columbia College*, 24).

75. Lee C. Bollinger, "Inaugural Address," October 3, 2002, http://www.columbia.edu/cu/president/inaugural.html.

EPILOGUE: WORTH THE CANDLE?

1. Morton Keller and Phyllis Keller, *Making Harvard Modern: The Rise of America's University* (New York: Oxford University Press, 2001), xiii.

2. These are the author's estimates, although those of students/graduates draw on recent data provided by the Office of University Development and Alumni Affairs and from *Columbia University's Contribution to the New York City Economy* (New York: Office of the Vice President for Administration, Columbia University, 1996). See also [George Rupp], *President's Report 2000: Columbia University and New York City* (New York: Columbia University, 2001).

3. For an estimate of total expenditures, see appendix C. For the use of space, see appendix D.

4. Roger Hackett, "Columbians in Public Life" (talk to the University Seminar on the History of Columbia University, November 21, 2000), and subsequent communications with the author.

5. For Columbia-related Nobel Prize winners, see appendix A. The most recent Nobelers include the economists William Vickery (1996), Robert Mondell (1999), and Joseph Stiglitz (2001), the physicist Horst Stormer (1998), and the physiologist Eric Kandell (2001). Stiglitz and Stormer received their Nobels for work performed before they joined the Columbia faculty. See also data on scholarly honors provided by Erikson Biographical Institute, Inc., of Providence, Rhode Island, in appendixes A and B and Karen W. Arenson, "Reseeding Ivy: Columbia on Comeback Trail From Troubles," *New York Times*, November 1, 1999, sec. B, 1.

6. For listings of Columbia graduates prominently engaged in the arts, see appendix A.

7. [Rupp], *President's Report 2000*, 8–23, 40–47.

8. *Columbia University's Contribution*, 52–59.

9. [Rupp], *President's Report 2000*, 48–52.

10 For the demographic composition of the Columbia trustees, see appendix A.

11. For the recent demographic composition of the faculty, see "Full-Time Faculty Distribution by Minority Status, Citizenship, and Tenure Status, Fall 2001" (New York: Office of the Vice Provost for Academic Administration, Columbia University, 2001). See also appendix B.

12. On student demographics, see "Total Student Percentage Enrollment by Ethnic-

ity and Program, 2001," in *Statistical Abstract, 2002* (New York: Office of Planning and Research, 2003), http://www.columbia.edu/cu/opir/2002enrol.htm.

13. Thomas Jefferson, "A Bill for the More General Diffusion of Knowledge," in Julian P. Boyd, ed., *The Papers of Thomas Jefferson* (Princeton, N.J.: Princeton University Press, 1950), 2:527.

14. Frederick A. P. Barnard, *President's Annual Report* (New York: Columbia College, 1881), 60.

The most distinctive feature about Columbia's recorded history is its unevenness in quantity and quality. This applies equally to primary sources and secondary accounts, official and otherwise, as well as to its physical artifacts.

First, the good news. No nineteenth-century college left behind better direct access to its undergraduate life or trustee doings than did Columbia in the diaries of George Templeton Strong. Similarly, the oral histories compiled by the Oral History Research Office within days of the tumultuous events of April 1968, along with the transcripts of the Cox commission and the journalistic efforts of the staff of the *Columbia Daily Spectator*, constitute an unparalleled source for observing a great university in the act of unraveling.

As for secondary accounts of parts of Columbia's history, David C. Humphrey's *From King's College to Columbia, 1746–1800* (New York: Columbia University Press, 1976) is as good a telling of a colonial college's founding and first half-century as we have. Nor has any twentieth-century university been better served by its architectural historians than has Columbia by Andrew S. Dolkart's *Morningside Heights: A History of Its Architecture and Development* (New York: Columbia University Press, 1998) and Barry Bergdoll's *Mastering McKim's Plan: Columbia's First Century on Morningside Heights* (New York: Miriam and Ira D. Wallach Art Gallery, Columbia University, 1997). Travis B. Jacobs's *Eisenhower at Columbia* (New Brunswick, N.J.: Transaction, 2001) is a solid and unflinching account of a single presidency, while Harold Wechsler's *The Qualified Student: A History of Selective College Admission in America, 1870–1970* (New York: Wiley, 1977) is a sensitive and discerning treatment of Columbia's not-so-distant history of anti-Semitism. Rosalind Rosenberg's *Changing the Subject: A History of Women at Columbia* (Columbia University Press, forthcoming) should immediately supersede the treatment accorded her subject here, as should Michael Rosenthal's forthcoming biography of Nicholas Murray Butler.

It is also Columbia's good fortune that the accounts of the Columbia Core by Jacques Barzun (*A College Plan in Action: A Review of Working Principles at Columbia College* [New York: Columbia University Press, 1946]), Daniel Bell (*The Reforming of General Education: The Columbia College Experience in Its National Setting* ([New York: Columbia University Press, 1966; reprint, New York: Anchor, Doubleday, 1968]), Timothy P. Cross (*An Oasis of Order: The Core Curriculum at Columbia College* [New York: Columbia College, 1995]), and David Denby (*Great Books: My Adventures with Homer, Rousseau, Woolf, and Other Indestructible Writers of the Western World* [New York: Simon and Schuster, 1996]), however they differ in approach, all succeed in infusing Columbia's curricular history with life, sparkle, and intellectual import. Would that Columbia's still largely enshrouded financial history had received comparable attention.

Columbia's official histories constitute a mixed bag. The earliest of these histories, that by Clement Clark Moore (*The Early History of Columbia College* [1825; reprint, New York: Columbia University Press, 1940]), is little more than an anecdotal sketch appropriate to its first presentation, as a talk to the alumni. That of his nephew, Nathaniel F.

Moore, *An Historical Sketch of Columbia College, in the City of New York* (New York: Columbia College, 1846), has a similar character. Subsequent efforts by John Henry Van Amringe, first in 1876 and later in 1898, which together make up most of Brander Matthews edited volume *A History of Columbia University, 1754–1904* (New York: Columbia University Press, 1904), are more substantive but no less filiopietistic. Frederick P. Keppel's *Columbia* (New York: Oxford University Press, 1914), while engagingly written and not without critical bite, is of more value for its comments on Keppel's own Columbia than for its historical narrative.

It is in the outpouring of historical commentary attending the university's bicentennial in 1954 where the unevenness of Columbia's historiography is most in evidence. Of the commissioned histories, that of Julius Goebel Jr., *A History of the School of Law, Columbia University* (New York: Columbia University Press, 1955), is a substantial and reliable account. Though shorter and less documented, so is Marian Churchill White's *History of Barnard College* (New York: Columbia University Press, 1954). Other single-authored histories, such as James Kip Finch's *History of the School of Engineering, Columbia University* (New York: Columbia University Press, 1954) and John A. Burrell's *History of Adult Education at Columbia University* (New York: Columbia University Press, 1954), are more factually reliable than interpretively adventurous.

Three multiauthored volumes were also published as part of the bicentennial history. That edited by Gordon Hoxie, *A History of the Faculty of Political Science, Columbia University* (New York: Columbia University Press, 1954), is still a useful accounting of the rise of the social sciences at Columbia, as well as of the origins of the graduate program more generally. That edited by Dwight Miner, *A History of Columbia College on Morningside* (New York: Columbia University Press, 1954), is alone among the commissioned histories in occasionally escaping the classroom and libraries with accounts of extracurricular and alumni doings. That edited by John Herman Randall Jr., *A History of the Faculty of Philosophy, Columbia University* (New York: Columbia University Press, 1957), appeared three years after the bicentennial and several of the departmental essays have a forcibly extracted quality about them.

Perhaps as important as what was included in the bicentennial histories was what was left out. Neither a history of the Faculty of Pure Science or of the Medical School was published. This fact, when combined with the thinness of Finch's *History of the Engineering School*, resulted in a serious underrepresentation of the sciences in the telling of Columbia's first two centuries. The other missing piece was the comprehensive history of Columbia, which the general editor, Dwight Miner, labored over but never published. The combined effect of these gaps was to make Columbia's history, largely told in the discrete histories of individual schools and, in the case of the arts and sciences, as the history of individual departments, tilt in the direction of the social sciences and humanities, ending up as less than the sum of its many parts. Nor is the relative neglect of the sciences rectified by the autobiographies of John W. Burgess (*Reminiscences of an American Scholar: The Beginnings of Columbia University* [New York: Columbia University Press, 1934; reprint, New York: Arno, 1966]) and Nicholas Murray Butler (*Across the Busy Years: Recollections and Reflections*, 2 vols.

[New York: Scribner's, 1939, 1940]), the former wholly caught up in the fortunes of the social sciences and the later increasingly given over to matters at some remove from Morningside.

It needs also to be said that Columbia has been relatively cavalier about preserving its historical record. It was not until 1961 that the University Archives–Columbiana Collection was officially created, as distinct from the files maintained by the Office of the Secretary of the University. The Columbia College Papers, which constitute the early documentary history of Columbia, are for some considerable patches of that history imperiously silent. To be sure, many important personal papers of faculty have been preserved in the university's Rare Book and Manuscript Library, but the fact remains that Columbia has not been as aggressive in archiving the papers of its graduates, faculty, and officers as have other universities. Nor until recently has it provided the resources for the proper processing of the official records it has preserved.

Other manuscript depositories that contain substantial material relating to Columbia include the New-York Historical Society, where the complete diaries of George Templeton Strong are located; the Rockefeller Foundation Archives; the Ford Foundation Archives; and the Harvard University Archives, where the Charles William Eliot Papers are located and exquisitely organized.

Among other historians of Columbia, I should like to point to the efforts of two who are relatively neglected, Milton Halsey Thomas and Roger Howson, both of whom labored during the last years of the Butler presidency under circumstances not conducive to the critical institutional analysis both were committed to publishing. Among Howson's work is *His Excellency a Trustee and Some Other Columbia Pieces* (New York: Columbia University Bookstore, 1945). With Allan Nevins, Thomas coedited the four volumes of *The Diary of George Templeton Strong* (New York: Macmillan Company, 1952); his master's thesis, "The Gibbs Affair at Columbia in 1854" (History, 1942) is another useful contribution. His diary, on deposit at the New-York Historical Society, is also a valuable insiders's rendering of Columbia from the 1920s to 1959. A third historian worthy of more attention is Dwight C. Miner, who, like Howson, generously left the research materials for his unfinished history of Columbia University in the capable hands of the Rare Books and Manuscript Library for others to benefit from his labors.

Where Columbia's history has been best and singularly served has been by its collections in oral history, which date back to 1948 and the founding efforts of Allan Nevins. Interviewing, transcribing, and making transcripts available to researchers have since been carried on by successive directors of the Oral History Research Office, including Louis M. Starr, Elizabeth B. Mason, Ronald J. Grele, and Mary Marshall Clark. It was in recognition of the value of this collection for me that I have recorded, roughly transcribed, and deposited at the OHRO, located in the Butler Library at Columbia University, as many of my sixty interviews as circumstances allowed. May they serve the next historian who takes up Columbia's ongoing story.

Interviews Conducted by the Author, 1997–2003

INTERVIEWEE	TIMING	PRINCIPAL TOPIC/S
Roger Bagnall	June 2002	administration, 1990s
Jacques Barzun	February 1998	CU, 1920s–70s
Barbara A. Black	September 2002	Law School
Peter Buchanan	August 2002	CU fund-raising, 1970s–80s
Carolyn Bynum	August 2002	administration, 1990s
Schuyler Chapin	April 2002	CU Arts, 1970s–80s
David H. Cohen	September 2002	administration, 1990s
Jonathan Cole	July 2001	Columbia, 1960s–2001
Edward N. Costikyan	May 2002	trustee affairs, 1980s–90s
Frank Da Cruz	June 2001	CU '68; computing at CU
Lewis Cole	October 1997	CU '68
Theodore W. de Bary	August 1997, May 1999	CU, 1930s–80s
Sigmund Diamond	August 1997	CU, 1950s–60s; CU '68
Meyer Feldberg	October 2002	Business School, 1990s–2002
Bruce W. Ferguson	January 2003	CU Arts, 1998–2003
Allen Formicola	September 2002	School of Dentistry
George K. Fraenkel	August 1997, summer 1999	CU '68; administration, 1970s, early 1980s
Julian Franklin	August 1997	CU '68
Eugene Galanter	September 1997	CU '68
Eli Ginzberg	September 1997	CU, 1920s–80s
Robert F. Goldberger	July 2002	Medical School; CU administration, 1980s
Henry Graff	May 2000	CU, 1940s–80s
C. Lowell Harriss	September 1997	CU '68
Louis Henkin	October 1997	CU '68
Don C. Hood	April 2000	administration, 1980s
Carl Hovde	August 1997, August 1999	CU '68; administration, 1970s; CU, 1940s–90s
Arlene Jacobs	June 1999	Low Library, 1960s-70s
Marian Jemmott	December 1997	Low Library, 1950s–80s
Henry L. King	May 2002	trustee affairs, 1980s–90s
Fred Knubel	December 1997	press relations, 1960s–80s
Roger Lehecka	October 2001	CC, 1970s–80s
John Masten	September 2002	CU finances, 1990s–2002
Seymour Melman	November 1997, January 2002	CU '68; Engineering School
Norman Mintz	May 2002	administration, 1980s

Thomas Q. Morris	September 2002, January 2003	CU Health Sciences
John Mundy	April 2000	CU '68
Richard Naum	April 1999	CU fund-raising, 1990s
Herbert Pardes	October 2002	CU Health Sciences
Lionel Pincus	May 2001	trustee affairs, 1980s–90s
Robert E. Pollack	June 2002	CC, 1980s
Giulio Pontecorvo	September 1997	CU '68; Business School
Eugene Rice	April 2000	CU '68; CU-BC relations
Corinne Rieder	January 2001	administration, 1980s–90s
Michael Rothfeld	May 2002	CU '68
David J. Rothman	October 1997	CU '68
George Rupp	summer 2001	administration, 1993–2001
Judith Shapiro	summer 2002	Barnard College, 1994–2002
Gerald Sherwin	June 2002	CC alumni affairs; athletics
Shlomo Shinnar	May 2002	CU' 68; Jewish activities
Bruce L. R. Smith	August 2002	CU '68
Michael I. Sovern	May 1999, August 2001	CU '68; administration, 1969–93
Jerry Speyer	July 2001	trustee affairs, 1980s–90s
Fritz Stern	September 1997, December 2002	CU, 1940s–90s